Ordnance Survey

# STREET ATLAS Berkshire

## Contents

| | |
|---|---|
| III | Key to map symbols |
| IV | Key to map pages |
| VI | Route planning |
| VIII | Administrative and Postcode boundaries |
| 1 | Street maps |
| 154 | Index of hospitals, industrial estates, railway stations, schools, shopping centres, street names and universities |

PHILIP'S

First edition published 1990
First colour edition published 1996
Second colour edition published 2000 by

George Philip Ltd, a division of
Octopus Publishing Group Ltd
2-4 Heron Quays London E14 4JP

ISBN 0-540-07676-7 (hardback)
ISBN 0-540-07677-5 (spiral)



To the best of the Publishers' knowledge, the information in this atlas was correct at the time of going to press. No responsibility can be accepted for any errors or their consequences.

The representation in this atlas of a road, track or path is no evidence of the existence of a right of way.

**The mapping between pages 1 and 153 (inclusive) in this atlas is derived from Ordnance Survey® OSCAR® and Land-Line® data, and Landranger® mapping.**

Ordnance Survey, OSCAR, Land-line and Landranger are registered trade marks of Ordnance Survey, the national mapping agency of Great Britain.

Printed and bound in Spain by Cayfosa

## Digital Data

The exceptionally high-quality mapping found in this book is available as digital data in TIFF format, which is easily convertible to other bit-mapped (raster) image formats. The data can be provided as pages or, in some regions, as larger extracts can also be supplied on paper.

The index is also available in digital form as a standard database table. It contains all the details found in the printed index together with the National Grid reference for the map square in which each entry is named.

For further information and to discuss your requirements, please contact Philip's on 020 7531 8440 or george.philip@philips-maps.co.uk

| | |
|---|---|
| 22a | **Motorway** with junction number |
| | **Primary route** - dual carriageway and single |
| | **A road** - dual carriageway and single |
| | **B road** - dual carriageway and single |
| | **Minor road** - dual carriageway and single |
| | **Other minor road** - dual carriageway and single |
| | **Road under construction** |
| | **Pedestrianised area** |
| DY7 | **Postcode boundaries** |
| | **County and Unitary Authority boundaries** |
| | **Railway** |
| | **Tramway, miniature railway** |
| | **Rural track, private road or narrow road in urban area** |
| | **Gate or obstruction to traffic** (restrictions may not apply at all times or to all vehicles) |
| | **Path, bridleway, byway open to all traffic, road used as a public path** |

The representation in this atlas of a road, track or path is no evidence of the existence of way

| | |
|---|---|
| 126, 94 | **Adjoining page indicators** |

| | | | |
|---|---|---|---|
| Allot Gdns | **Allotments** | Meml | **Memorial** |
| Acad | **Academy** | Mon | **Monument** |
| Cemy | **Cemetery** | Mus | **Museum** |
| C Ctr | **Civic Centre** | Obsy | **Observatory** |
| CH | **Club House** | Pal | **Royal Palace** |
| Coll | **College** | PH | **Public House** |
| Crem | **Crematorium** | Recn Gd | **Recreation Ground** |
| Ent | **Enterprise** | Resr | **Reservoir** |
| Ex H | **Exhibition Hall** | Ret Pk | **Retail Park** |
| Ind Est | **Industrial Estate** | Sch | **School** |
| Inst | **Institute** | Sh Ctr | **Shopping Centre** |
| Ct | **Law Court** | TH | **Town Hall/House** |
| L Ctr | **Leisure Centre** | Trad Est | **Trading Estate** |
| LC | **Level Crossing** | Univ | **University** |
| Liby | **Library** | Wks | **Works** |
| Mkt | **Market** | YH | **Youth Hostel** |

| | |
|---|---|
| Walsall | **Railway station** |
| | **London Underground station** |
| | **Private railway station** |
| | **Bus, coach station** |
| | **Ambulance station** |
| | **Coastguard station** |
| | **Fire station** |
| | **Police station** |
| | **Accident and Emergency entrance to hospital** |
| H | **Hospital** |
| + | **Places of worship** |
| i | **Information Centre** (open all year) |
| P | **Parking** |
| P&R | **Park and Ride** |
| PO | **Post Office** |
| | **Camping site** |
| | **Caravan site** |
| | **Golf course** |
| | **Picnic site** |
| Prim Sch | **Important buildings, schools, colleges, universities and hospitals** |
| River Medway | **Water name** |
| | **Stream** |
| | **River or canal** - minor and major |
| | **Water** |
| | **Tidal water** |
| | **Woods** |
| | **Houses** |
| House | **Non-Roman antiquity** |
| VILLA | **Roman antiquity** |

■ The dark grey border on the inside edge of some pages indicates that the mapping does not continue onto the adjacent page

■ The small numbers around the edges of the maps identify the 1 kilometre National Grid lines

**The scale of the maps is 5.52 cm to 1 km**
**3½ inches to 1 mile 1: 18103**

0 — ¼ — ½ — ¾ — 1 mile
0 — 250 m — 500 m — 750 m — 1 kilometre

# Key to map pages

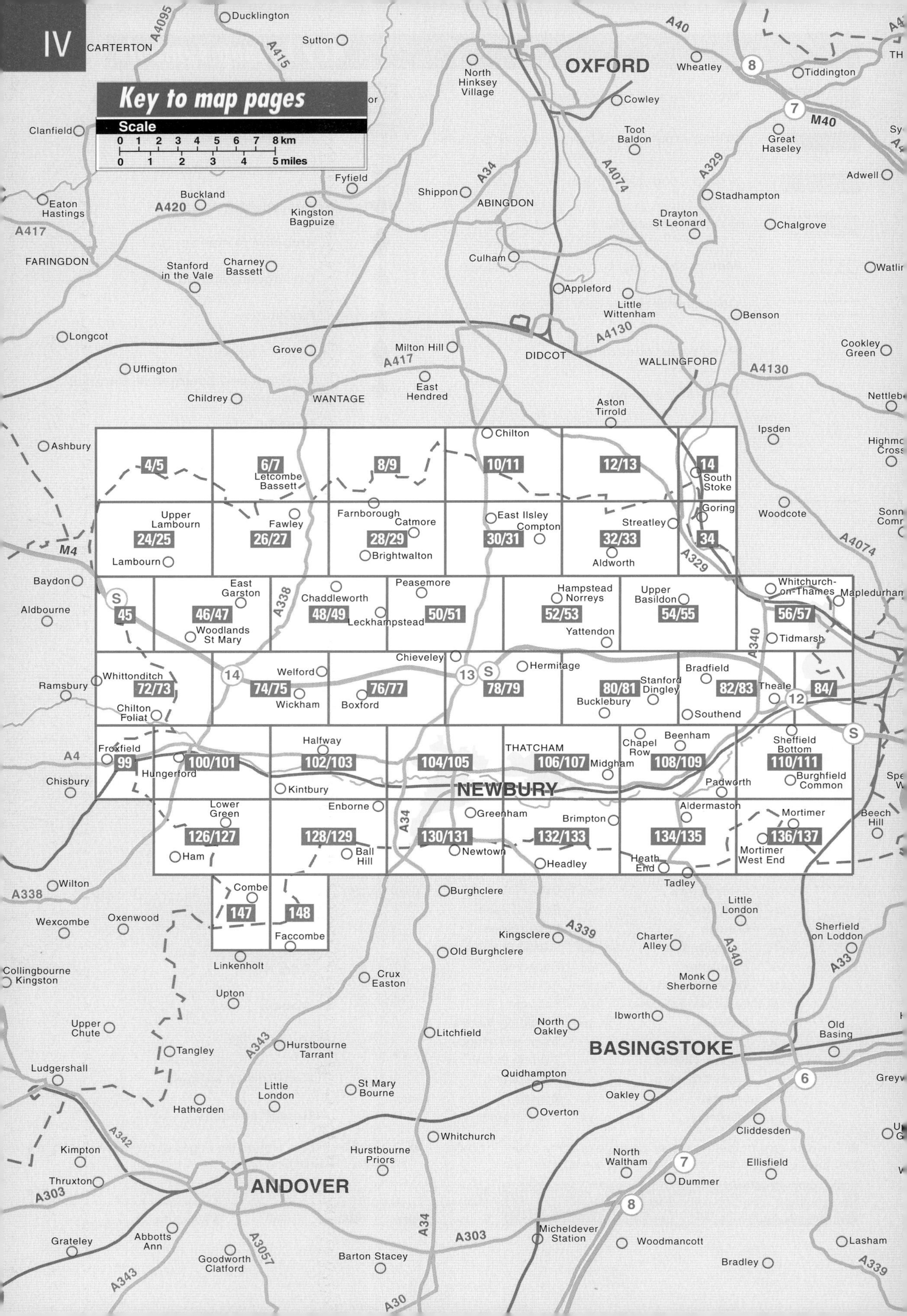

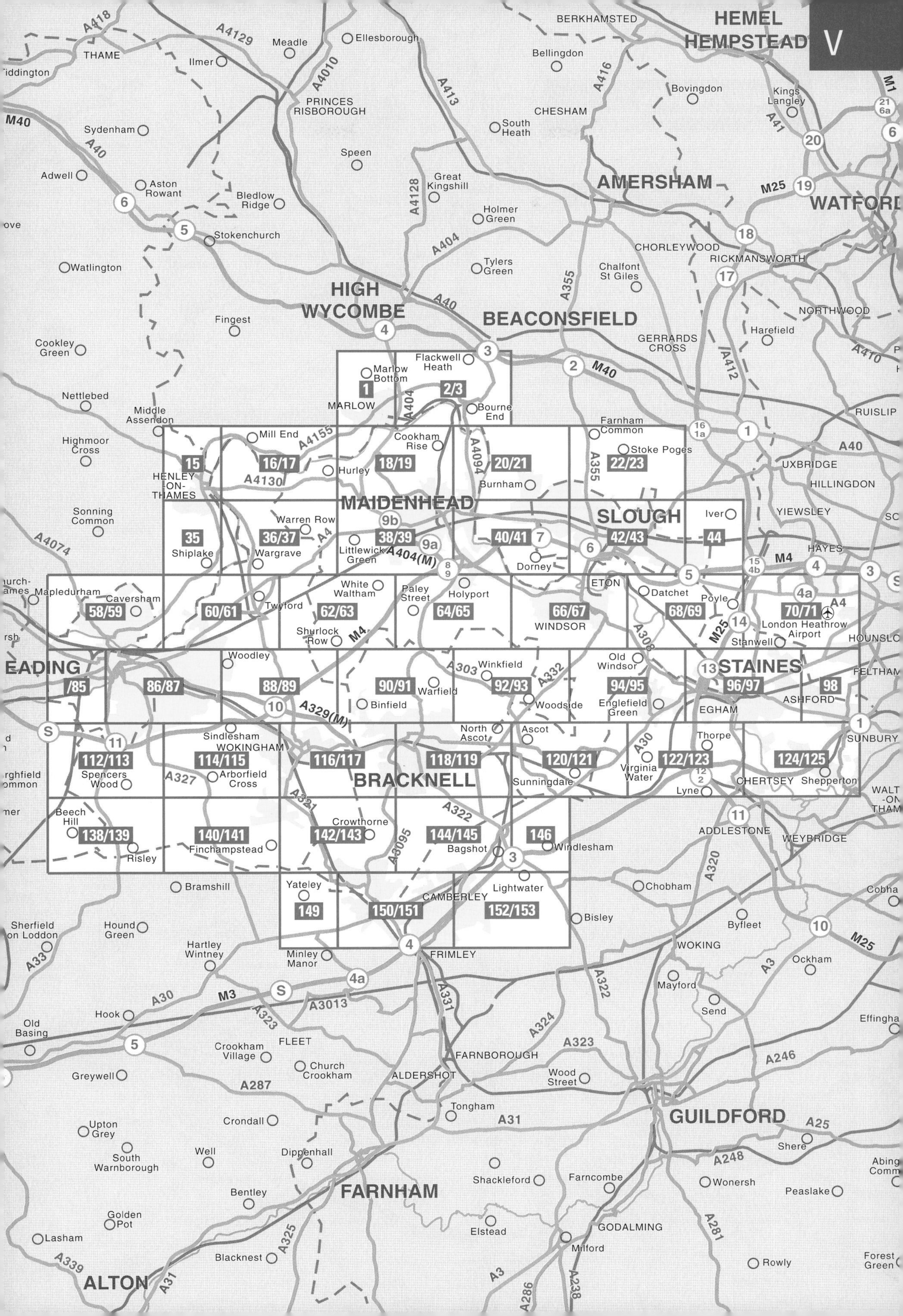

HEMEL HEMPSTEAD
BERKHAMSTED
THAME
A418
A4129
Meadle
Ellesborough
Ilmer
A4010
PRINCES RISBOROUGH
A413
Bellingdon
A416
Bovingdon
Kings Langley
M1
CHESHAM
M40
Sydenham
A40
South Heath
Speen
A41
20
Adwell
Aston Rowant
Great Kingshill
AMERSHAM
M25
19
WATFORD
6
Bledlow Ridge
A4128
Holmer Green
5
Stokenchurch
A404
18
CHORLEYWOOD
RICKMANSWORTH
Watlington
Tylers Green
Chalfont St Giles
A355
17
HIGH WYCOMBE
A40
BEACONSFIELD
NORTHWOOD
4
Fingest
Cookley Green
GERRARDS CROSS
Harefield
3
Flackwell Heath
2
M40
A412
A410
Marlow Bottom
1
2/3
MARLOW
Nettlebed
Middle Assendon
Bourne End
Farnham Common
RUISLIP
Highmoor Cross
Mill End
A4155
Cookham Rise
A4094
16 1a
1
A40
15
16/17
Hurley
18/19
20/21
Stoke Poges
22/23
UXBRIDGE
HENLEY-ON-THAMES
A4130
Burnham
HILLINGDON
MAIDENHEAD
SLOUGH
Sonning Common
Warren Row
9b
Iver
YIEWSLEY
35
36/37
A4
38/39
40/41
7
42/43
44
Shiplake
Wargrave
Littlewick Green
A404(M)
9a
6
Dorney
HAYES
A4074
8 9
M4
15 4b
4
3
ETON
5
Mapledurham
Caversham
White Waltham
Paley Street
Holyport
Datchet
4a
Poyle
A4
58/59
60/61
Twyford
62/63
64/65
66/67
68/69
70/71
WINDSOR
A308
M25
14
London Heathrow Airport
Shurlock Row
M4
Stanwell
HOUNSLOW
Woodley
A303
Winkfield
A332
Old Windsor
13
STAINES
FELTHAM
READING
/85
86/87
88/89
90/91
Warfield
92/93
94/95
96/97
98
10
A329(M)
Binfield
Woodside
Englefield Green
EGHAM
ASHFORD
S
11
Sindlesham
WOKINGHAM
North Ascot
Ascot
A30
Thorpe
1
SUNBURY
112/113
114/115
116/117
118/119
120/121
122/123
124/125
Spencers Wood
A327
Arborfield Cross
BRACKNELL
Sunningdale
Virginia Water
12 2
Lyne
CHERTSEY
Shepperton
Beech Hill
A321
A322
138/139
140/141
142/143
Crowthorne
144/145
146
Windlesham
11
ADDLESTONE
WEYBRIDGE
Risley
Finchampstead
A3095
Bagshot
3
A320
Bramshill
Yateley
Lightwater
Chobham
CAMBERLEY
149
150/151
152/153
Bisley
Byfleet
Sherfield on Loddon
Hound Green
4
FRIMLEY
10
Hartley Wintney
Minley Manor
WOKING
M25
A33
4a
A331
A322
A3
Ockham
A30
M3
S
Mayford
Hook
A3013
A323
Send
Old Basing
5
A324
Effingham
FLEET
Crookham Village
A323
Church Crookham
FARNBOROUGH
A246
Greywell
ALDERSHOT
Wood Street
A287
Tongham
A31
GUILDFORD
A25
Crondall
Upton Grey
Shere
South Warnborough
Well
Dippenhall
A248
Shackleford
Farncombe
Wonersh
Bentley
FARNHAM
Peaslake
Golden Pot
Elstead
A281
GODALMING
Lasham
Milford
A325
Blacknest
Rowly
A339
ALTON
A31
A3
A286
A238
Forest Green

Route planning
Scale
0 1 2 3 4 5 6 7 8 km
0 1 2 3 4 5 miles
OXFORD
ABINGDON
DIDCOT
WANTAGE
WALLINGFORD
FARINGDON
READING
NEWBURY
THATCHAM
HUNGERFORD
BASINGSTOKE
ANDOVER
Whitchurch
Kingsclere
Tadley
Pangbourne
Theale
Goring
Harwell
Lambourn
Wheatley
Kidlington
Membury Services
Sutton Scotney Services
Wheatley Services
M4
M3
M40
A34
A4
A338
A339
A303
A417
A420
A415
A329
A4074
A4130
WHITE HORSE
CHILTERN
NORTH

Shabbington
THAME
Aston Sandford
Kingsey
Owlswick
Kimble Wick
Little Kimble
WENDOVER
BERKHAMSTED
Cholesbury
Bourne End
HEMEL HEMPSTEAD
Towersey
Ilmer
Meadle
Ellesborough
Askett
St Leonards
Buckland Common
Moreton
Longwick
Monks Risborough
Pitch Green
Dunsmore
Wendover Dean
Asheridge
Bellingdon
Ashley Green
Whelpley Hill
Felden
Bedmond
Emmington
Tetsworth
Sydenham
PRINCES RISBOROUGH
Great Hampden
Little Hampden
The Lee
Lee Clump
Chartridge
Lye Green
Rucklers Lane
Kings Langley
Ballinger Common
Bovingdon
Bledlow
Saunderton
Loosley Row
Lacey Green
South Heath
Botley
CHESHAM
Chipperfield
Abbots Langley
Chinnor
Great Missenden
Hyde Heath
Flaunden
Adwell
Postcombe
Kingston Blount
Speen
Prestwood
Little Kingshill
Chesham Bois
Belsize
Bucks Hill
Sarratt
South Weston
Aston Rowant
Crowell Hill
Bledlow Ridge
Upper North Dean
Great Kingshill
Little Missenden
AMERSHAM
Latimer
Chenies
Chandler's Cross
Lewknor
Radnage
Saunderton Sta
Walter's Ash
Holmer Green
Little Chalfont
WATFORD
Pyrton
Shirburn
The City
Stokenchurch
Bradenham
Naphill
Hughenden Valley
Penn Street
CHORLEYWOOD
Croxley Green
Cuxham
Watlington
Beacon's Bottom
West Wycombe
Downley
Hazlemere
Tylers Green
Coleshill
Chalfont St Giles
RICKMANSWORTH
Christmas Common
HIGH WYCOMBE
Winchmore Hill
Britwell Salome
Ibstone
Totteridge
Penn
Heronsgate
Horn Hill
South Oxhey
Eastbury
Northend
Cadmore End
Wycombe Marsh
Knotty Green
Seer Green
Chalfont Common
Jordans
Maple Cross
NORTHWOOD
Turville Heath
Greenfield
Turville
Fingest
Lane End
Booker
Loudwater
West Hyde
Chalfont St Peter
Cookley Green
Pishill
Skirmett
Frieth
Flackwell Heath
BEACONSFIELD
Harefield
Russell's Water
Park Corner
Stonor
Marlow Bottom
Little Marlow
Wooburn Green
GERRARDS CROSS
Ruislip Common
Rockwell End
Wooburn
Eastcote
Nettlebed
Fawley
Lower Woodend
Hambleden
Bourne End
Hedsor
Hedgerley
RUISLIP
Highmoor Cross
Bix
MARLOW
Mill End
Medmenham
Cookham Dean
Cookham
Burnham Beeches
Fulmer
Denham
Ickenham
Stoke Row
Lower Assendon
HENLEY-ON-THAMES
Aston
Remenham Hill
Hurley
Cookham Rise
Farnham Common
Stoke Poges
Iver Heath
UXBRIDGE
HILLINGDON
Shepherd's Green
Checkendon
Cockpole Green
Burchett's Green
Taplow
Burnham
Farnham Royal
Iver
Cowley
YIEWSLEY
Yeading
Sonning Common
Rotherfield Greys
Rotherfield Peppard
Warren Row
MAIDENHEAD
SLOUGH
HAYES
Harpsden
Knowl Hill
Littlewick Green
Woodlands Park
Bray
Dorney
Upton
Langley
WEST DRAYTON
Kidmore End
Lower Shiplake
Wargrave
Hare Hatch
White Waltham
Binfield Heath
Tokers Green
Shiplake
Dunsden Green
Waltham St Lawrence
Boveney
ETON
Colnbrook
Sipson
Mapledurham
Emmer Green
Twyford
Ruscombe
Holyport
Oakley Green
Datchet
Poyle
Longford
Cranford
Purley on Thames
Play Hatch
Fifield
WINDSOR
Horton
London Heathrow Airport
Paley Street
Caversham
Whistley Green
Shurlock Row
Hawthorn Hill
Old Windsor
Wraysbury
Stanwell
Hatton
Tilehurst
Woodley
Windsor Forest
Hythe End
East Bedfont
Hurst
Winkfield
GREAT PARK
Cranbourne
STAINES
FELTHAM
Calcot
READING
Whitley
Warfield
Winkfield Row
Woodside
Englefield Green
EGHAM
ASHFORD
Winnersh
Binfield
Newell Green
North Ascot
SUNBURY
Laleham
Sindlesham
BRACKNELL
Ascot
Sunningdale
Virginia Water
Thorpe
Littleton
Burghfield
Three Mile Cross
Arborfield
Easthampstead
Grazeley
Shinfield
Barkham
WOKINGHAM
Sunninghill
Lyne
Shepperton
WALTON-ON-THAMES
Spencers Wood
Farley Hill
Arborfield Garrison
Windlesham
Chobham Common
ADDLESTONE
CHERTSEY
Swallowfield
Wick Hill
Caesar's Camp
Surrey Hill
Bagshot
Ottershaw
WEYBRIDGE
Beech Hill
Finchampstead
Crowthorne
Burrowhill
Hersham
Riseley
Eversley
CAMBERLEY
Royal Military Academy
Lightwater
Chobham
Woodham
Whiteley Village
Stratfield Saye
Yateley
Sandhurst
Bagshot Heath
West End
Stratfield Turgis
Bramshill
Eversley Cross
Frogmore
Horsell
Byfleet
Cobham
Turgis Green
Heckfield
Hazeley
Blackwater
Donkey Town
Chobham Ridges
Bisley
Pyrford
Wisley
Stoke D'Abernon
Hound Green
Mattingley
Hartfordbridge
Hawley
Fox Lane
FRIMLEY
Deepcut
Brookwood
Knaphill
WOKING
Hartley Wespall
West Green
Hartley Wintney
Minley Manor
West Heath
Cove
Mayford
Ripley
Ockham
Effingham Junc Sta
Church End
Rotherwick
Phoenix Green
Mytchett
Pirbright
Send
Hook
FLEET
FARNBOROUGH
Winchfield
Henley Park
Worplesdon
Fairlands
Pitch Place
West Horsley
East Horsley
Newnham
Old Basing
Dogmersfield
North Warnborough
Church Crookham
Crookham Village
Normandy
Wood Street
Stoughton
Burpham
West Clandon
Up Nately
Greywell
Odiham
ALDERSHOT
Long Valley
East Clandon
Mill Lane
Ewshot
Heath End
Ash
Flexford
Onslow Village
GUILDFORD
Upton Grey
Crondall
Hale
Tongham
Hog's Back
Puttenham
Gomshall
Long Sutton
FARNHAM
Seale
Compton
Shalford
Albury
Shere
Abinger Hammer
Wotton
South Warnborough
Well
Runfold
Chilworth
Sutton Abinger
Weston Patrick
Dippenhall
Farncombe
Blackheath
Wonersh
Farley Green
Peaslake
Southrope
Bentley
Shackleford
Bramley
Shamley Green
Hurt Wood
Golden Pot
Rowledge
Waverley Abbey
Peper Harow
GODALMING
Upper Froyle
Millbridge
Tilford
Elstead
Thorncombe Street
Lasham
Shalden
Holybourne
Bucks Horn Oak
Blacknest
Spreakley
Milford
Busbridge
Frensham
Wheelerstreet
Hydestile
Rowly
Bentworth
Binsted
Wheatley
Rushmoor
Forest Green
Ewhurst
ALTON
Wyck
East Worldham
Kingsley
Thursley
Witley
Hascombe
Hambledon
Cranleigh
Walliswood
CHILTERN HILLS
HUNDREDS OF AYLESBURY
CHILTERN HUNDREDS
NORTH DOWNS

# Major administrative and Postcode boundaries

County and unitary authority boundaries

Postcode boundaries

Area covered by this atlas

Scale

0 5 10 15 km

0 5 10 miles

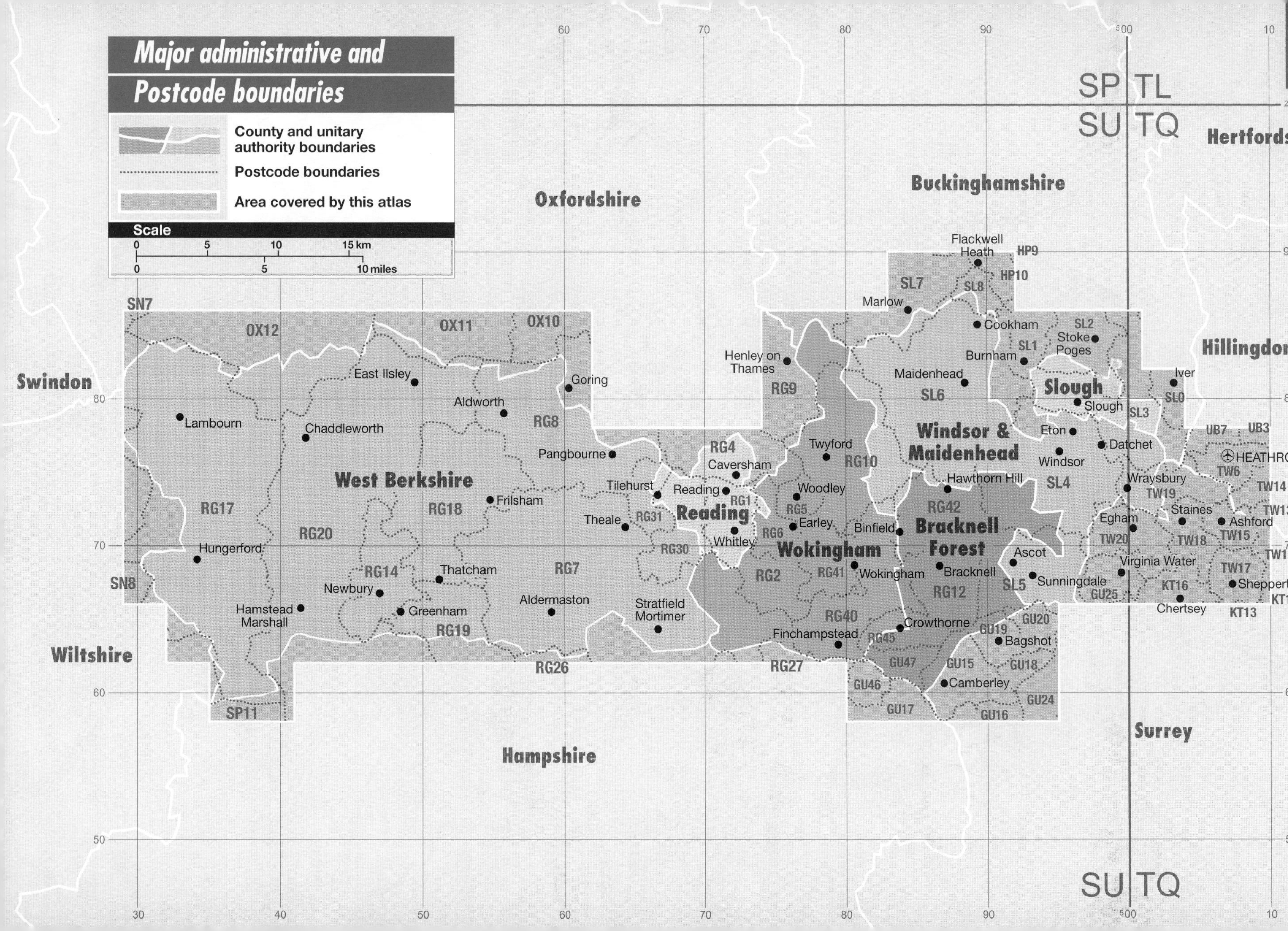

2

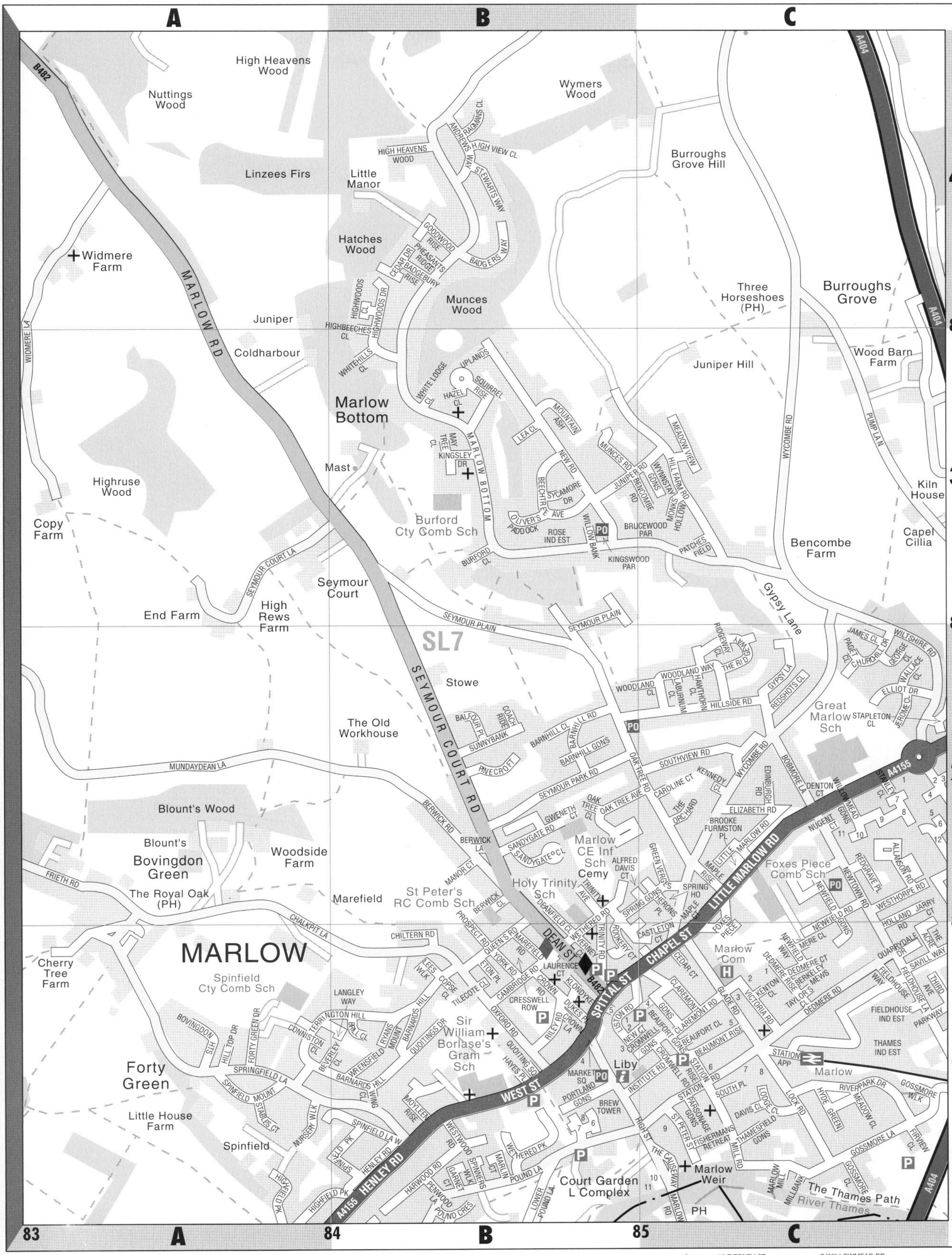


B1
1 BRAEMAR CT
2 CHISWICK LODGE
3 LISTON CT
4 LIME BARN
5 MORRIS PL
6 BARLEY WAY
7 MALTHOUSE WAY
8 PORTLANDS MEWS

18

C1
1 BEECH CT
2 VICTORIA CT
3 GLADE HO
4 ST JAMES CTYD
5 LEIGHTON HO
6 MONKSWOOD CT
7 LITTLE BOLTONS
8 PENN CT
9 TEMPLARS PL

2

10 TIERNEY CT
11 DUNSTABLE HO
C2
1 EASTWOOD CT
2 WILTSHIRE RD
3 MILE ELM
4 BEECHINGSTOKE
5 BUTLER CT
6 BYRON CL
7 MEAD CL
8 WILLOWMEAD RD
9 WILLOWMEAD SQ
10 WILLOWMEAD CL
11 ROMNEY CT
12 SHELLEY RD

1

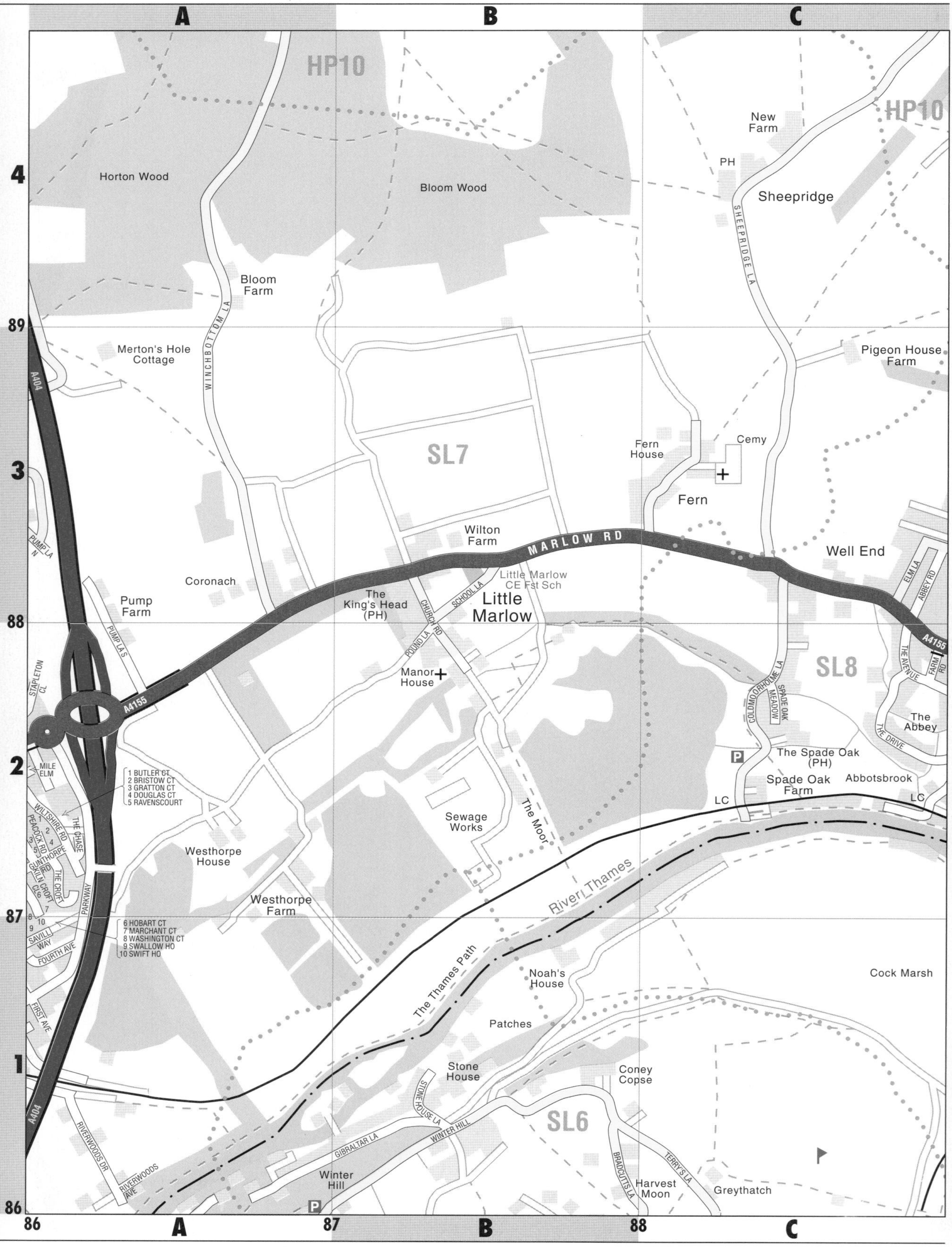
A
B
C
HP10
Horton Wood
Bloom Wood
New Farm
PH
Sheepridge
SHEEPRIDGE LA
Bloom Farm
WINCHBOTTOM LA
Merton's Hole Cottage
Pigeon House Farm
A404
SL7
Fern House
Cemy
Fern
Wilton Farm
MARLOW RD
Well End
PUMP LA N
Coronach
Little Marlow CE Fst Sch
SCHOOL LA
Little Marlow
The King's Head (PH)
CHURCH RD
Pump Farm
PUMP LA S
ELM LA
ABBEY RD
A4155
STAPLETON CL
POUND LA
Manor House
SL8
THE AVENUE
FARM RD
COLDMOORHOLME LA
SPADE OAK MEADOW
The Abbey
THE DRIVE
MILE ELM
1 BUTLER CT
2 BRISTOW CT
3 GRATTON CT
4 DOUGLAS CT
5 RAVENSCOURT
P
The Spade Oak (PH)
Spade Oak Farm
Abbotsbrook
LC
WILTSHIRE RD
PEACOCK RD
THE CHASE
GUNTHORPE RD
KILN CROFT CL
THE CROFT
Sewage Works
The Moor
Westhorpe House
Westhorpe Farm
River Thames
PARKWAY
SAVILL WAY
FOURTH AVE
6 HOBART CT
7 MARCHANT CT
8 WASHINGTON CT
9 SWALLOW HO
10 SWIFT HO
The Thames Path
Noah's House
Cock Marsh
FIRST AVE
Patches
Stone House
Coney Copse
STONE HOUSE LA
SL6
WINTER HILL
GIBRALTAR LA
RIVERWOODS DR
RIVERWOODS AVE
Winter Hill
BRADCUTTS LA
TERRY'S LA
Harvest Moon
Greythatch
4
3
2
1
89
88
87
86
86
87
88

1

19

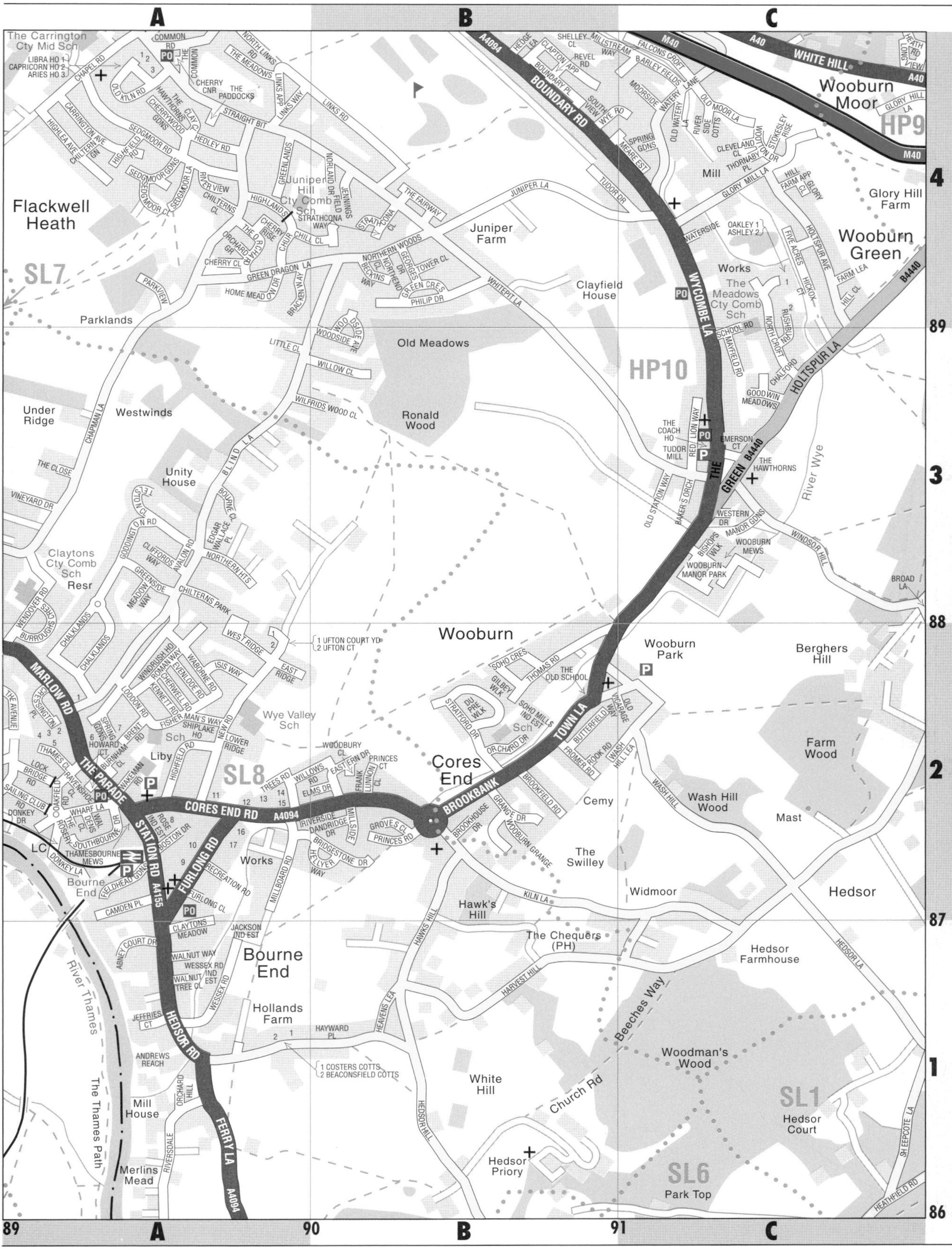


20

A2
1 ROWAN HO
2 COKERS CT
3 RUSSELL HO
4 RAY HO
5 GRANT HO
6 ORCHARD HO
7 BAILEY HO
8 BOURNE END BSNS CTR
9 EGHAMS CT
10 HYLAND HO
11 FARRIER CT
12 MOUNT PLEASANT COTTS
13 SYCAMORE CL
14 THE WILLOWS
15 THE MAPLES
16 MEADOW BANK
17 THE COURTYARD

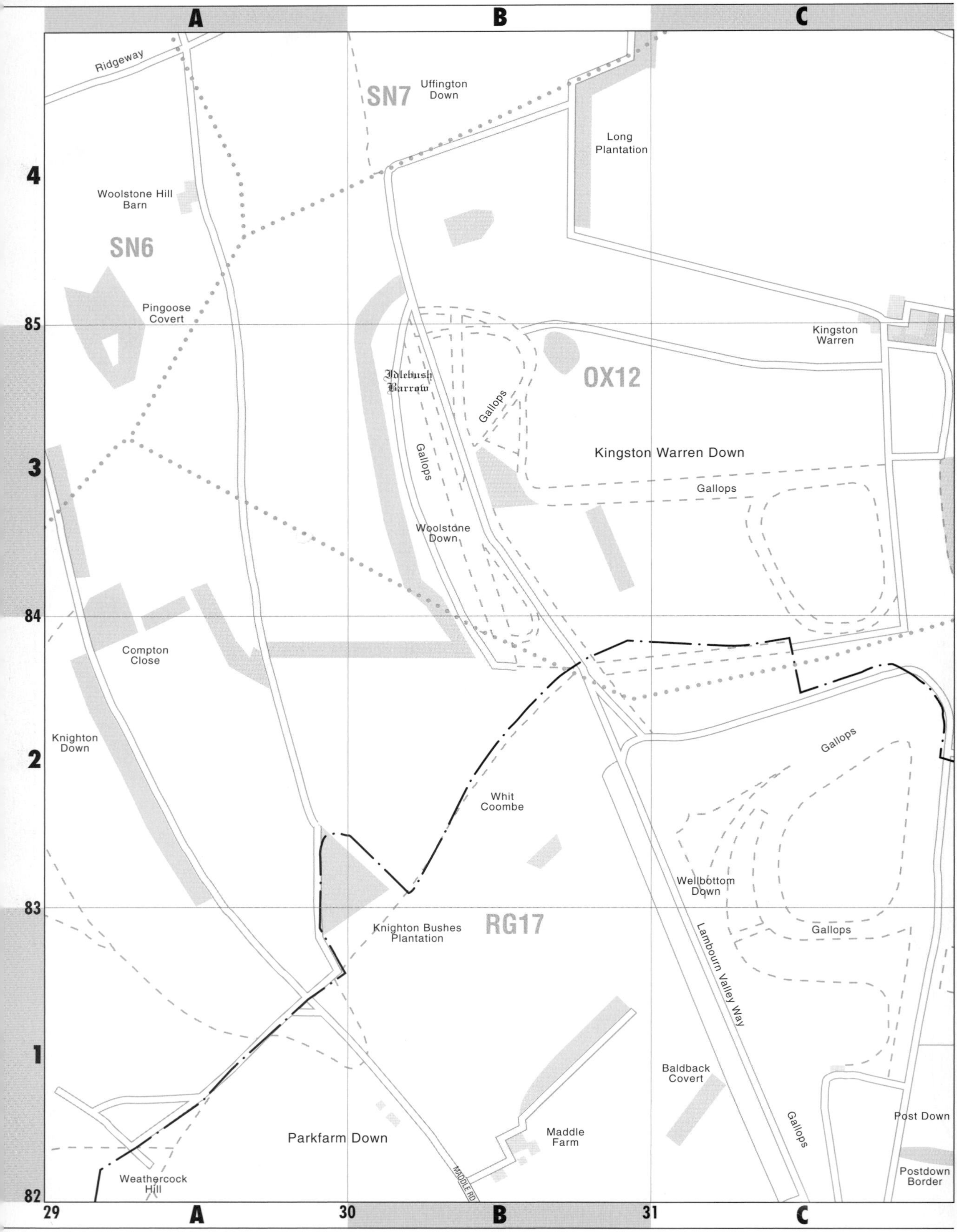
A
B
C
Ridgeway
SN7
Uffington Down
Long Plantation
Woolstone Hill Barn
SN6
Pingoose Covert
Kingston Warren
Idlebush Barrow
OX12
Gallops
Gallops
Kingston Warren Down
Gallops
Woolstone Down
Compton Close
Knighton Down
Gallops
Whit Coombe
Wellbottom Down
Knighton Bushes Plantation
RG17
Gallops
Lambourn Valley Way
Baldback Covert
Gallops
Post Down
Maddle Farm
Parkfarm Down
MADDLE RD
Weathercock Hill
Postdown Border
4
85
3
84
2
83
1
82
29
30
31

24

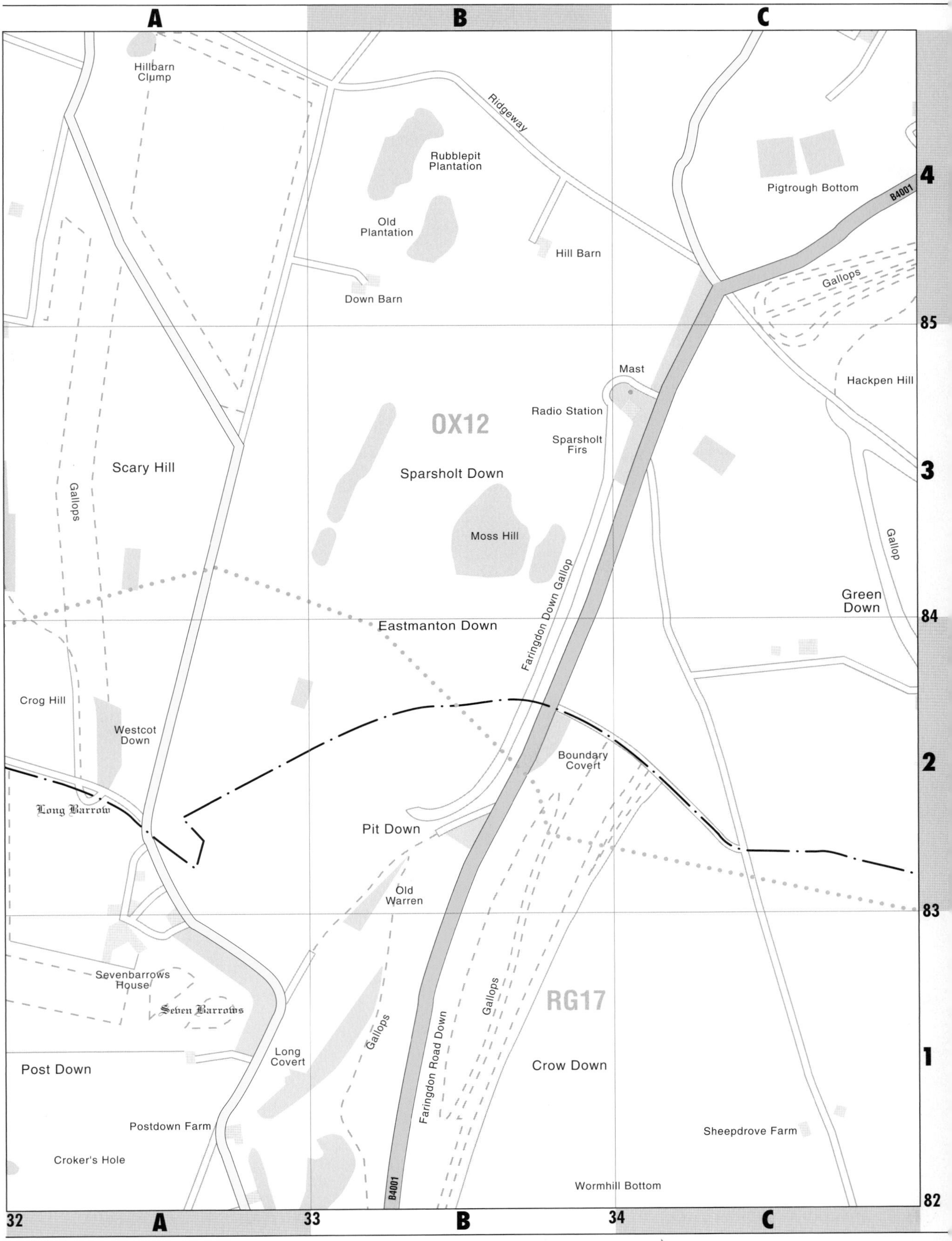
A
B
C
Hillbarn Clump
Ridgeway
Rubblepit Plantation
Old Plantation
Down Barn
Hill Barn
Pigtrough Bottom
B4001
4
Gallops
85
Mast
Hackpen Hill
Radio Station
OX12
Sparsholt Firs
Scary Hill
Gallops
Sparsholt Down
3
Moss Hill
Gallop
Faringdon Down Gallop
Green Down
Eastmanton Down
84
Crog Hill
Westcot Down
Boundary Covert
2
Long Barrow
Pit Down
Old Warren
83
Sevenbarrows House
Seven Barrows
RG17
Gallops
Faringdon Road Down
Gallops
Long Covert
Post Down
Crow Down
1
Postdown Farm
Sheepdrove Farm
Croker's Hole
Wormhill Bottom
B4001
82
32
A
33
B
34
C

5

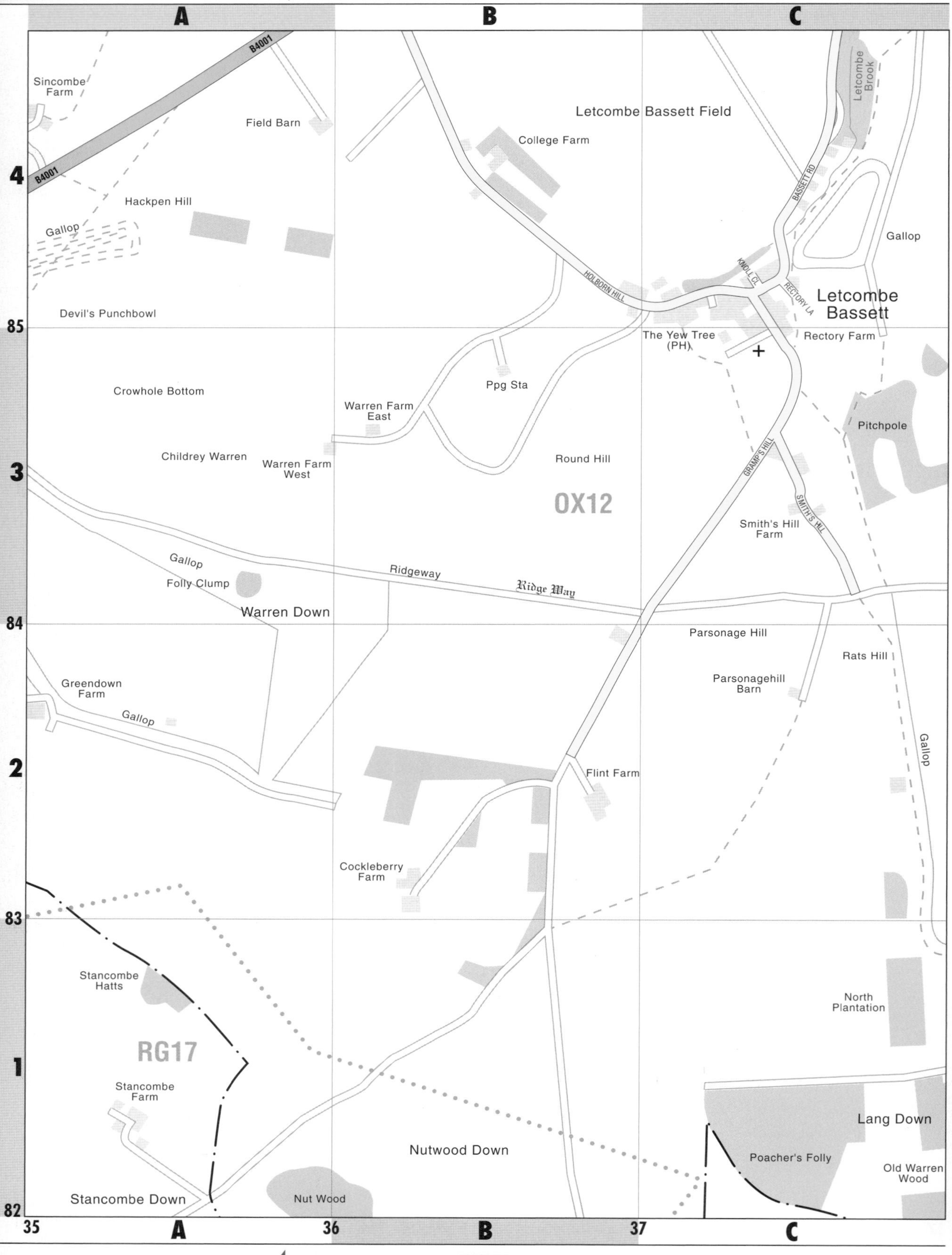

A
B
C
4
85
3
84
2
83
1
82
35
36
37
B4001
Sincombe Farm
Field Barn
Hackpen Hill
Gallop
Devil's Punchbowl
Crowhole Bottom
Childrey Warren
Warren Farm West
Warren Farm East
Ppg Sta
College Farm
Letcombe Bassett Field
Letcombe Brook
BASSETT RD
KNOLL CL
RECTORY LA
HOLBORN HILL
Letcombe Bassett
The Yew Tree (PH)
Rectory Farm
Gallop
Pitchpole
Round Hill
GRAMP'S HILL
SMITH'S HILL
OX12
Smith's Hill Farm
Gallop
Folly Clump
Warren Down
Ridgeway
Ridge Way
Parsonage Hill
Rats Hill
Parsonagehill Barn
Greendown Farm
Gallop
Gallop
Flint Farm
Cockleberry Farm
Stancombe Hatts
RG17
North Plantation
Stancombe Farm
Lang Down
Nutwood Down
Poacher's Folly
Old Warren Wood
Stancombe Down
Nut Wood


5

26

8

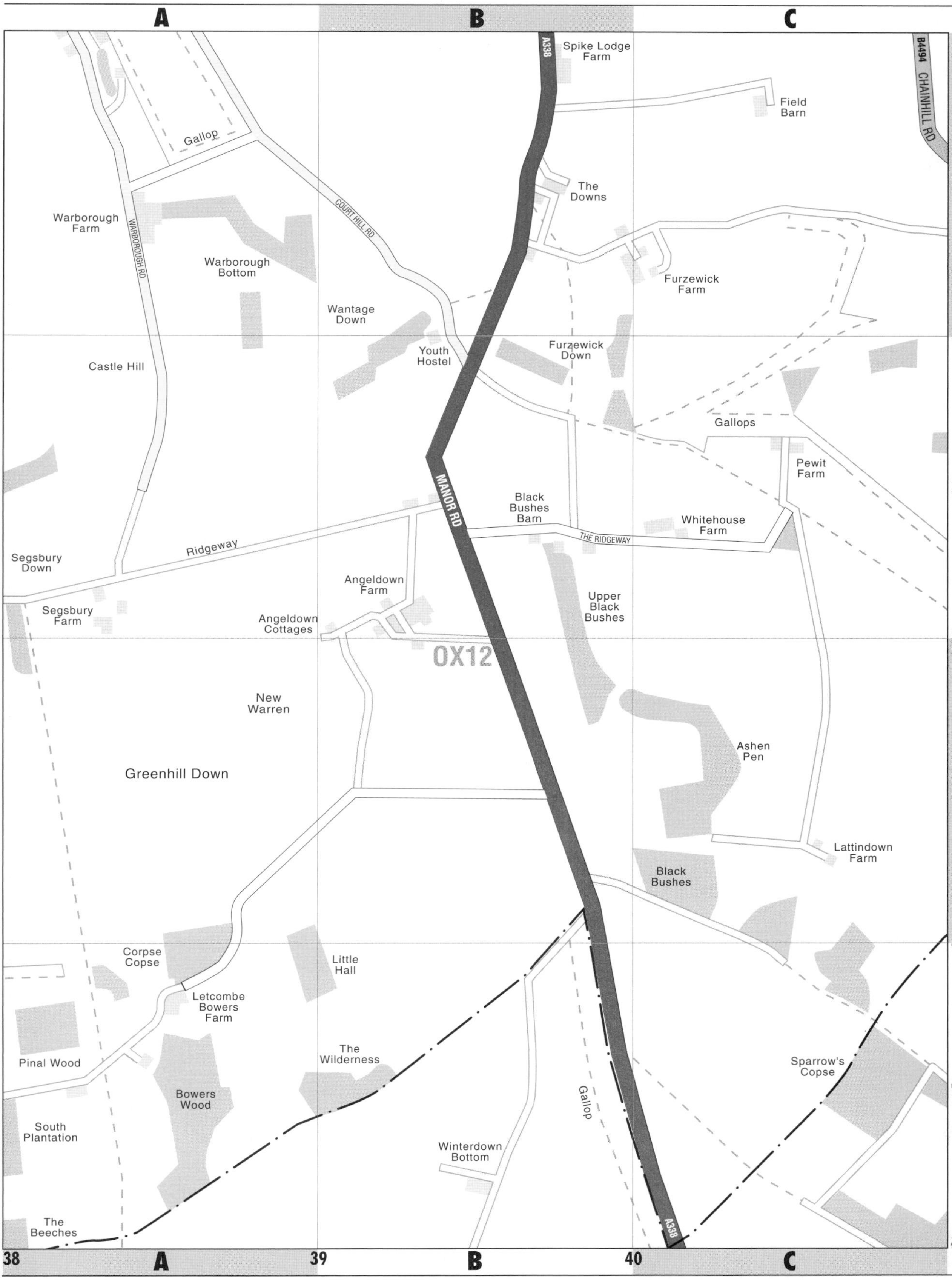
A
B
C
A338
Spike Lodge Farm
B4494 CHAINHILL RD
Field Barn
Gallop
The Downs
Warborough Farm
WARBOROUGH RD
COURT HILL RD
Warborough Bottom
Furzewick Farm
Wantage Down
Youth Hostel
Furzewick Down
Castle Hill
Gallops
Pewit Farm
MANOR RD
Black Bushes Barn
Whitehouse Farm
THE RIDGEWAY
Ridgeway
Segsbury Down
Segsbury Farm
Angeldown Farm
Angeldown Cottages
Upper Black Bushes
OX12
New Warren
Ashen Pen
Greenhill Down
Lattindown Farm
Black Bushes
Corpse Copse
Little Hall
Letcombe Bowers Farm
The Wilderness
Pinal Wood
Sparrow's Copse
Bowers Wood
Gallop
South Plantation
Winterdown Bottom
The Beeches
A338
4
85
3
84
2
83
1
82
38
39
40

27

8

7

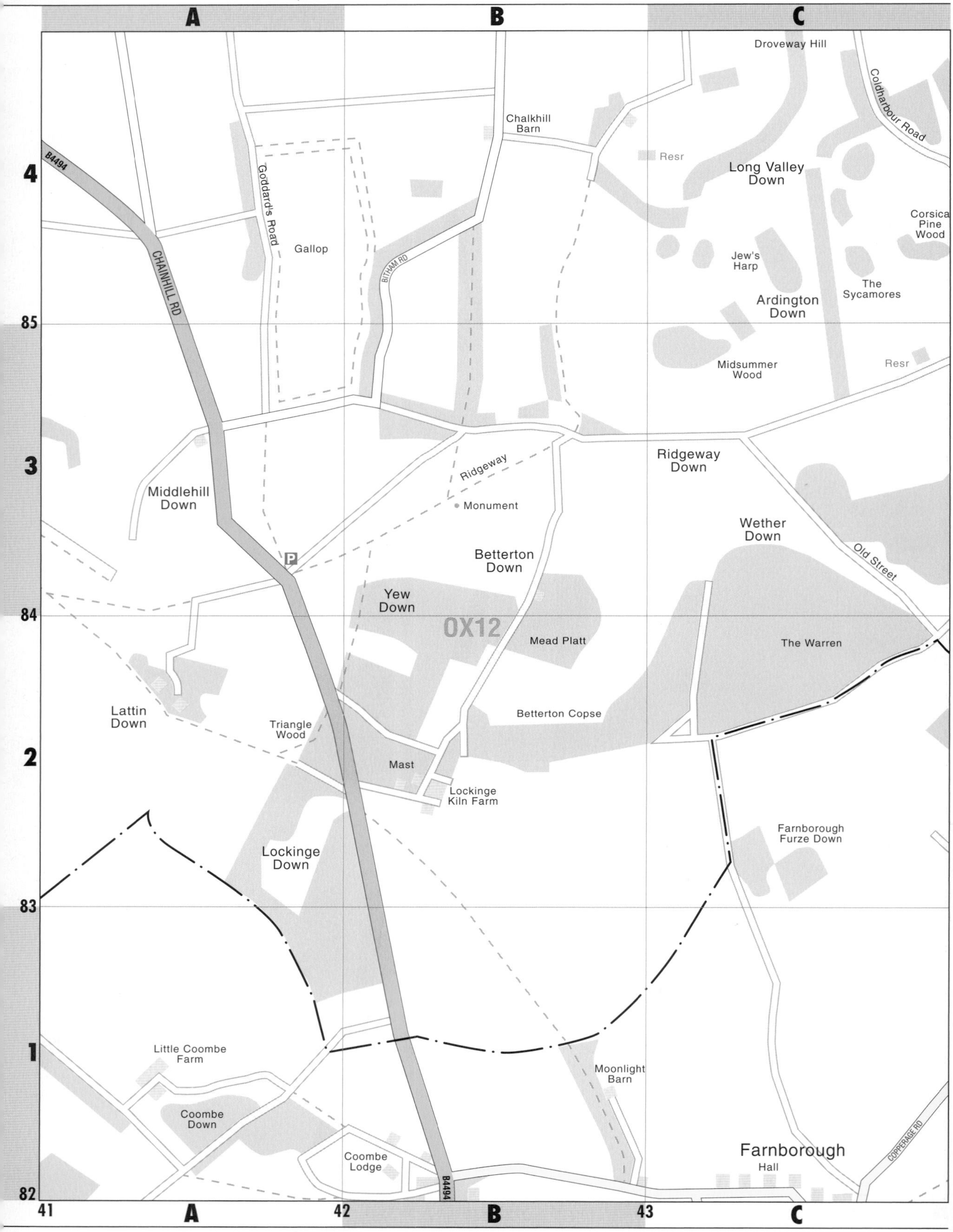
A
B
C
Droveway Hill
Coldharbour Road
Chalkhill Barn
Resr
Long Valley Down
B4494
Goddard's Road
Gallop
BITHAM RD
CHAINHILL RD
Jew's Harp
Corsica Pine Wood
The Sycamores
Ardington Down
Midsummer Wood
Resr
Ridgeway
Ridgeway Down
Middlehill Down
Monument
Wether Down
Betterton Down
Old Street
Yew Down
OX12
Mead Platt
The Warren
Betterton Copse
Lattin Down
Triangle Wood
Mast
Lockinge Kiln Farm
Farnborough Furze Down
Lockinge Down
Little Coombe Farm
Moonlight Barn
Coombe Down
Coombe Lodge
Farnborough
Hall
COPPERAGE RD
B4494
4
85
3
84
2
83
1
82
41
42
43

7

28

10

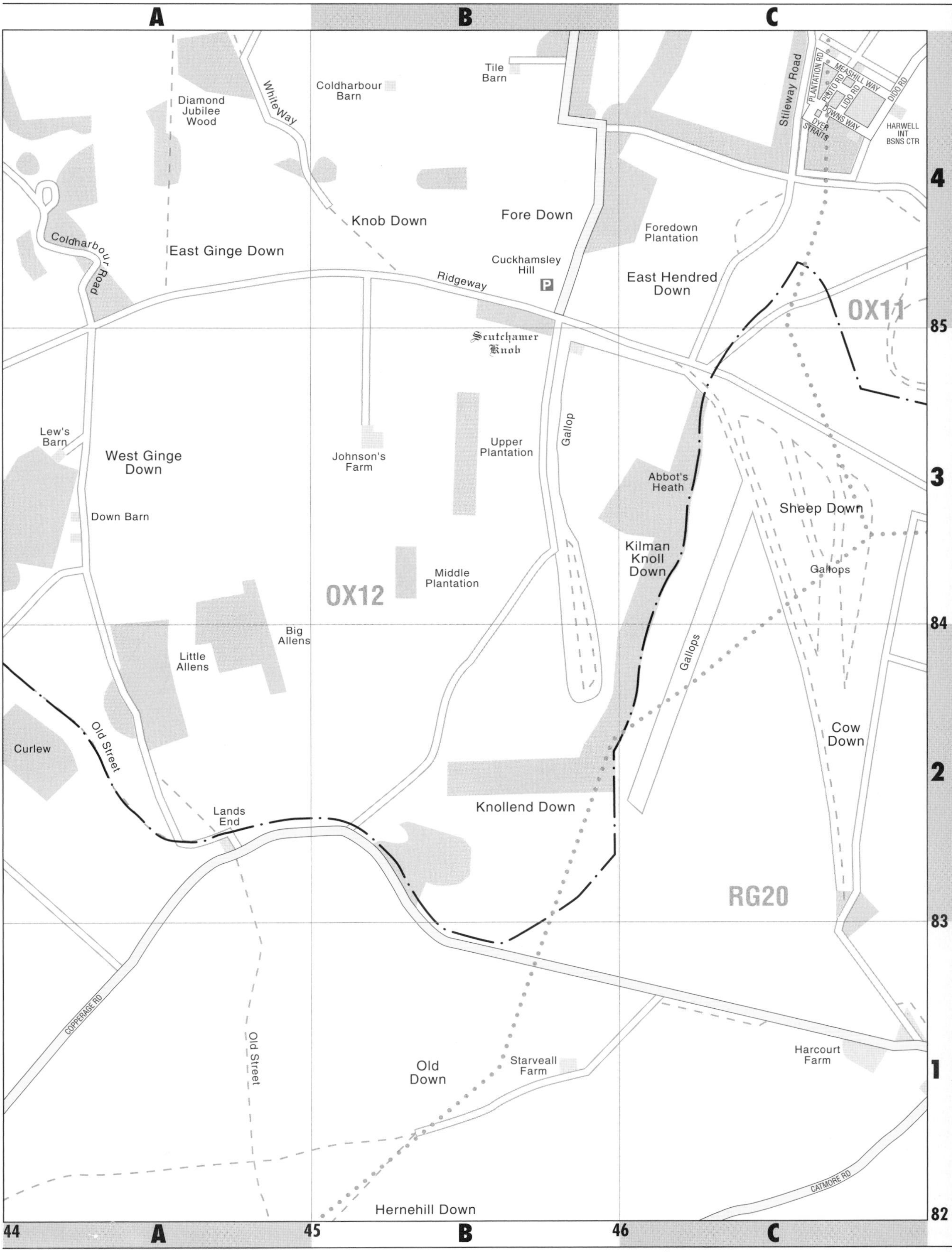

A
B
C
Tile Barn
Coldharbour Barn
Diamond Jubilee Wood
WhiteWay
Stileway Road
PLANTATION RD
PLUTO RD
MEASHILL WAY
LIDO RD
DIDO RD
DOWNS WAY
DYER STRAITS
HARWELL INT BSNS CTR
4
Knob Down
Fore Down
Foredown Plantation
Coldharbour Road
East Ginge Down
Cuckhamsley Hill
Ridgeway
East Hendred Down
OX11
85
Scutchamer Knob
Gallop
Lew's Barn
West Ginge Down
Johnson's Farm
Upper Plantation
Abbot's Heath
3
Down Barn
Sheep Down
Kilman Knoll Down
Middle Plantation
Gallops
OX12
Big Allens
84
Little Allens
Gallops
Old Street
Cow Down
Curlew
2
Lands End
Knollend Down
RG20
83
COPPERAGE RD
Old Street
Harcourt Farm
Old Down
Starveall Farm
1
CATMORE RD
Hernehill Down
82
44
45
46
A
B
C


29

10

9

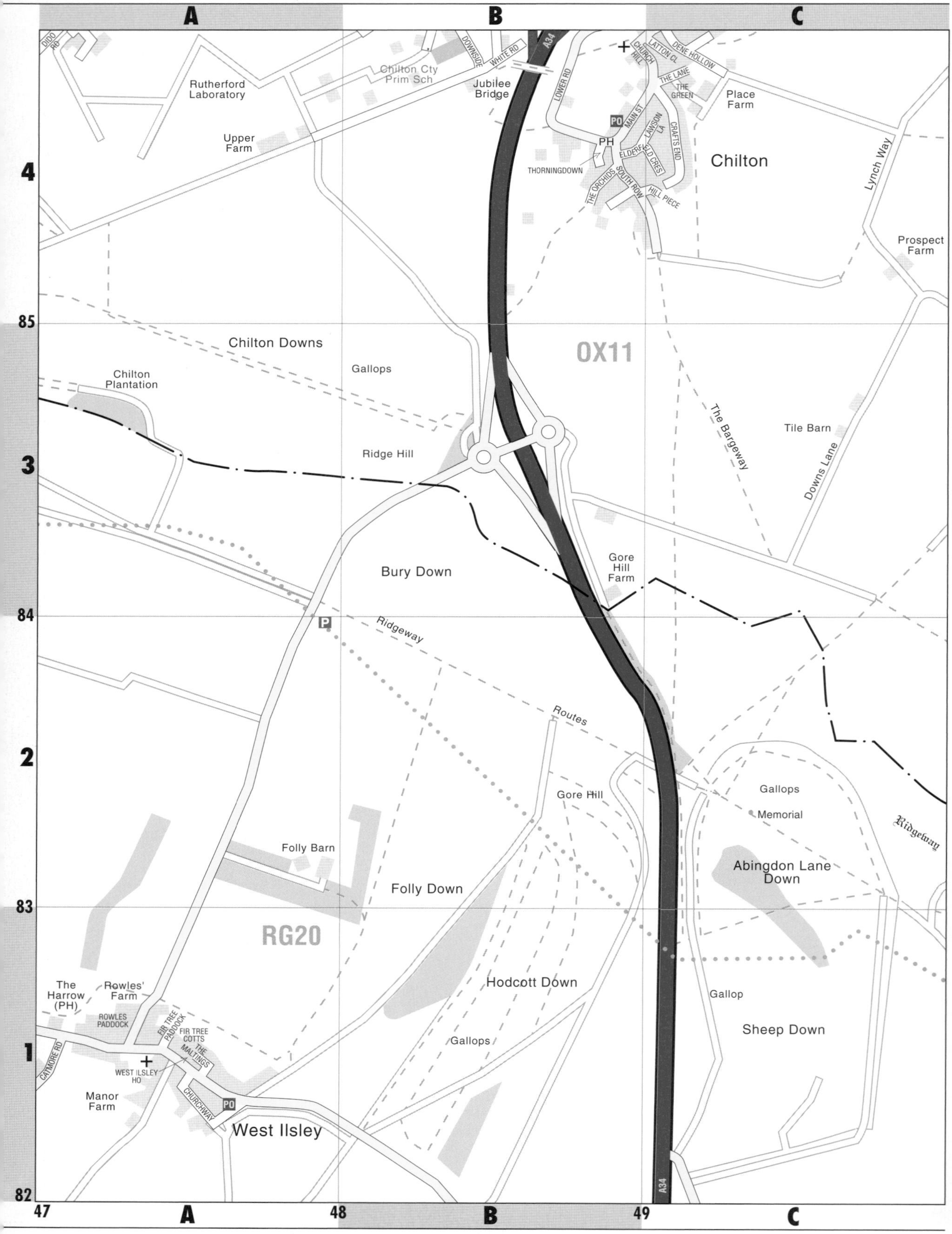
A
B
C
4
85
3
84
2
83
1
82
47
48
49
DIDO RD
Rutherford Laboratory
Upper Farm
Chilton Cty Prim Sch
DOWNSIDE
WHITE RD
Jubilee Bridge
A34
LOWER RD
CHURCH HILL
LATTON CL
DENE HOLLOW
THE LANE
THE GREEN
Place Farm
PO
MAIN ST
LAWSON LA
CRAFTS END
PH
THORNINGDOWN
ELDERFIELD CRES
THE ORCHIDS
SOUTH ROW
HILL PIECE
Chilton
Lynch Way
Prospect Farm
Chilton Downs
Gallops
OX11
Chilton Plantation
The Bargeway
Tile Barn
Ridge Hill
Downs Lane
Bury Down
Gore Hill Farm
P
Ridgeway
Routes
Gore Hill
Gallops
Memorial
Ridgeway
Folly Barn
Abingdon Lane Down
Folly Down
RG20
Hodcott Down
The Harrow (PH)
Rowles' Farm
ROWLES PADDOCK
FIR TREE PADDOCK
FIR TREE COTTS
THE MALTINGS
Gallop
Gallops
Sheep Down
CATMORE RD
WEST ILSLEY HO
Manor Farm
CHURCHWAY
PO
West Ilsley
A34

9
30

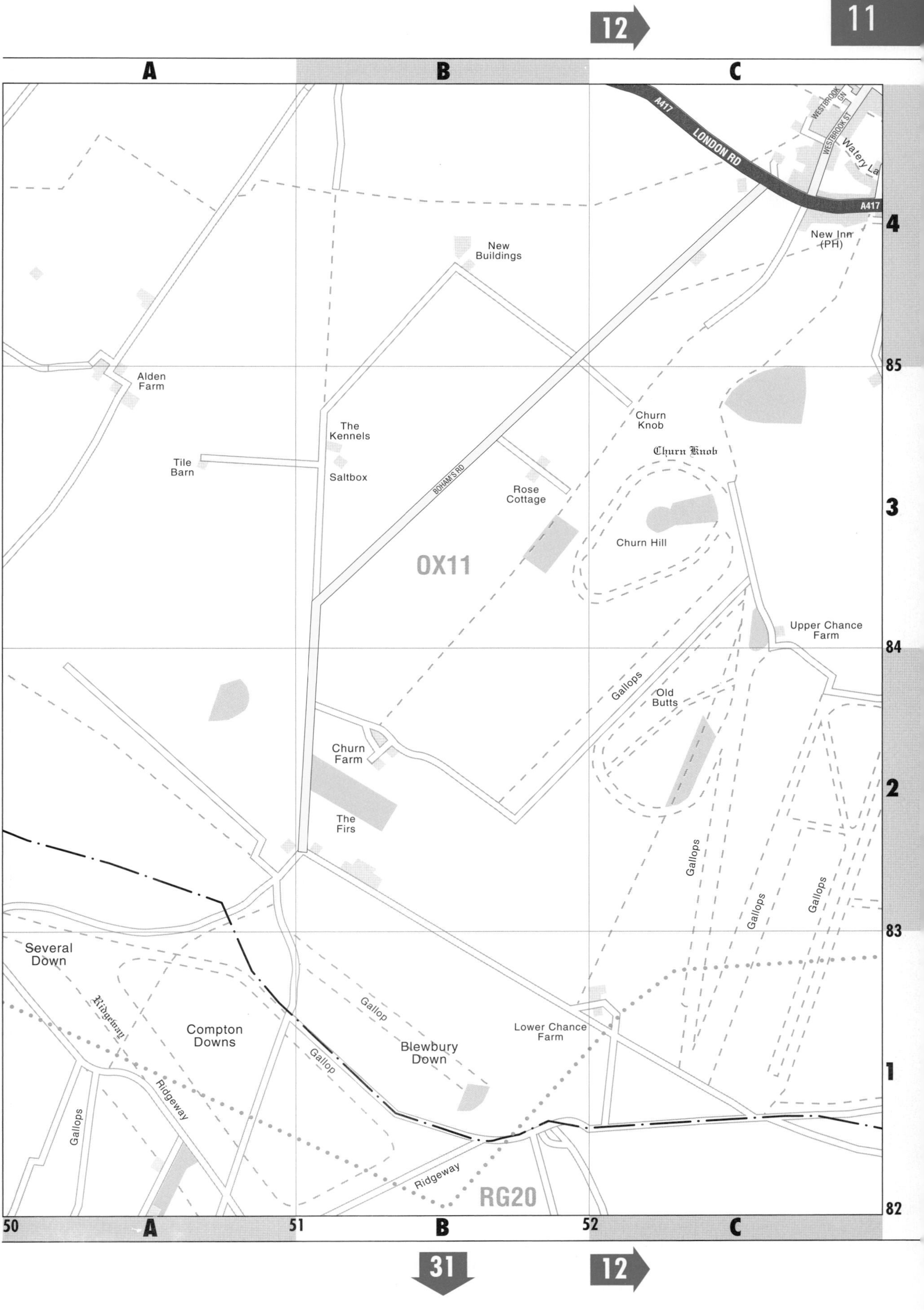
12
A
B
C
A417
LONDON RD
WESTBROOK GN
WESTBROOK ST
Watery La
A417
4
New Inn (PH)
New Buildings
85
Alden Farm
The Kennels
Churn Knob
Churn Knob
Tile Barn
Saltbox
BOHAM'S RD
Rose Cottage
3
Churn Hill
OX11
Upper Chance Farm
84
Gallops
Old Butts
Churn Farm
2
The Firs
Gallops
Gallops
Gallops
83
Several Down
Gallop
Ridgeway
Compton Downs
Lower Chance Farm
Blewbury Down
Gallop
1
Ridgeway
Gallops
Ridgeway
RG20
82
50
A
51
B
52
C
31
12

11

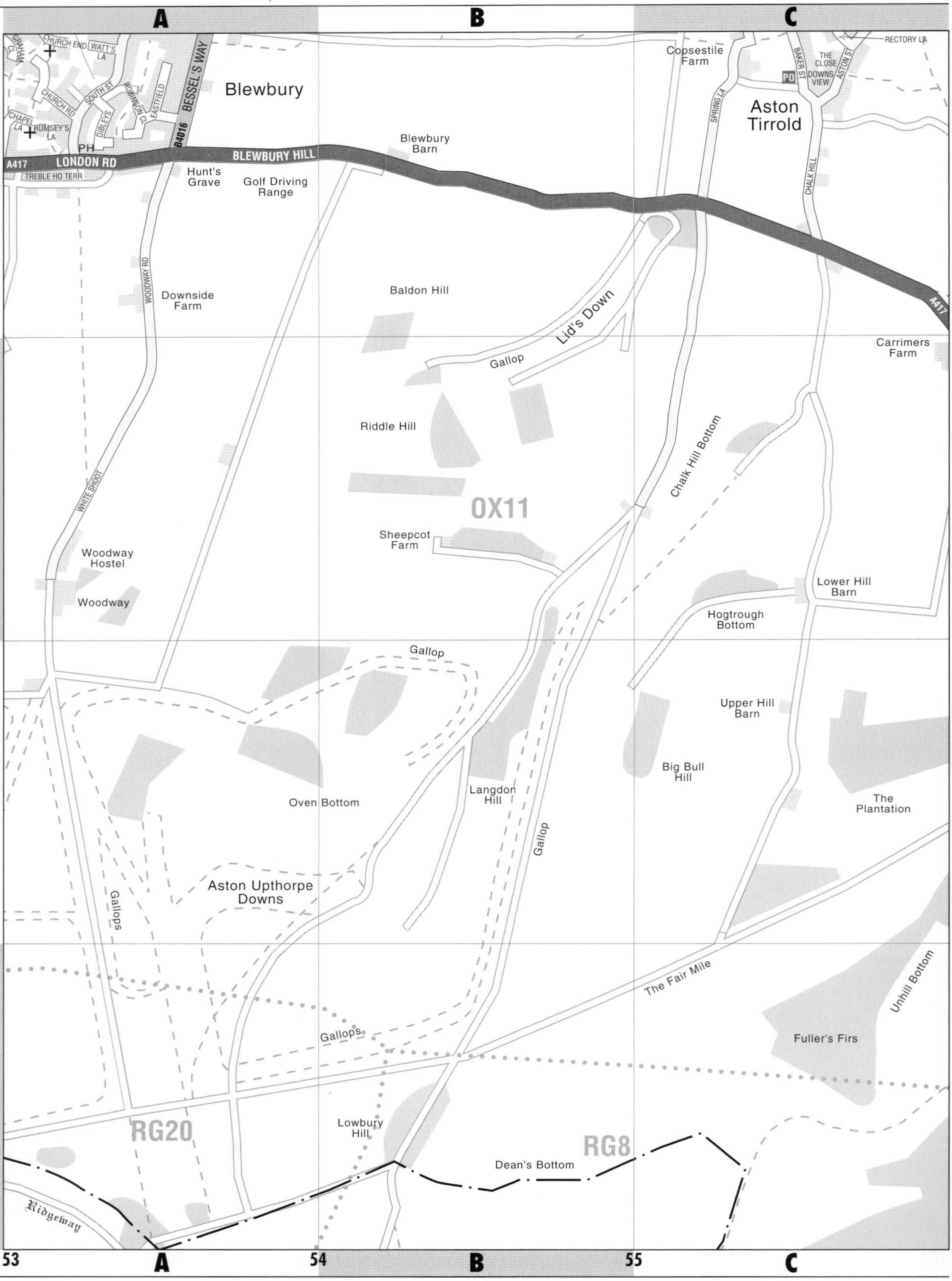
A
B
C
Blewbury
Copsestile Farm
RECTORY LA
BAKER ST
THE CLOSE
DOWNS VIEW
ASTON ST
PO
Aston Tirrold
SPRING LA
CHURCH END
WATT'S LA
GRAHAM CL
CHURCH RD
SOUTH ST
ROBINSON CL
EASTFIELD
BESSEL'S WAY
B4016
CHAPEL LA
RUMSEY'S LA
DIBLEYS
PH
A417
LONDON RD
BLEWBURY HILL
TREBLE HO TERR
Hunt's Grave
Golf Driving Range
Blewbury Barn
CHALK HILL
WOODWAY RD
Downside Farm
Baldon Hill
Lid's Down
Gallop
Carrimers Farm
Riddle Hill
Chalk Hill Bottom
WHITE SHOOT
OX11
Sheepcot Farm
Woodway Hostel
Woodway
Lower Hill Barn
Hogtrough Bottom
Upper Hill Barn
Big Bull Hill
Langdon Hill
Oven Bottom
The Plantation
Aston Upthorpe Downs
Gallops
The Fair Mile
Unhill Bottom
Fuller's Firs
RG20
Lowbury Hill
RG8
Dean's Bottom
Ridgeway
4
85
3
84
2
83
1
82
53
54
55

11
32

14

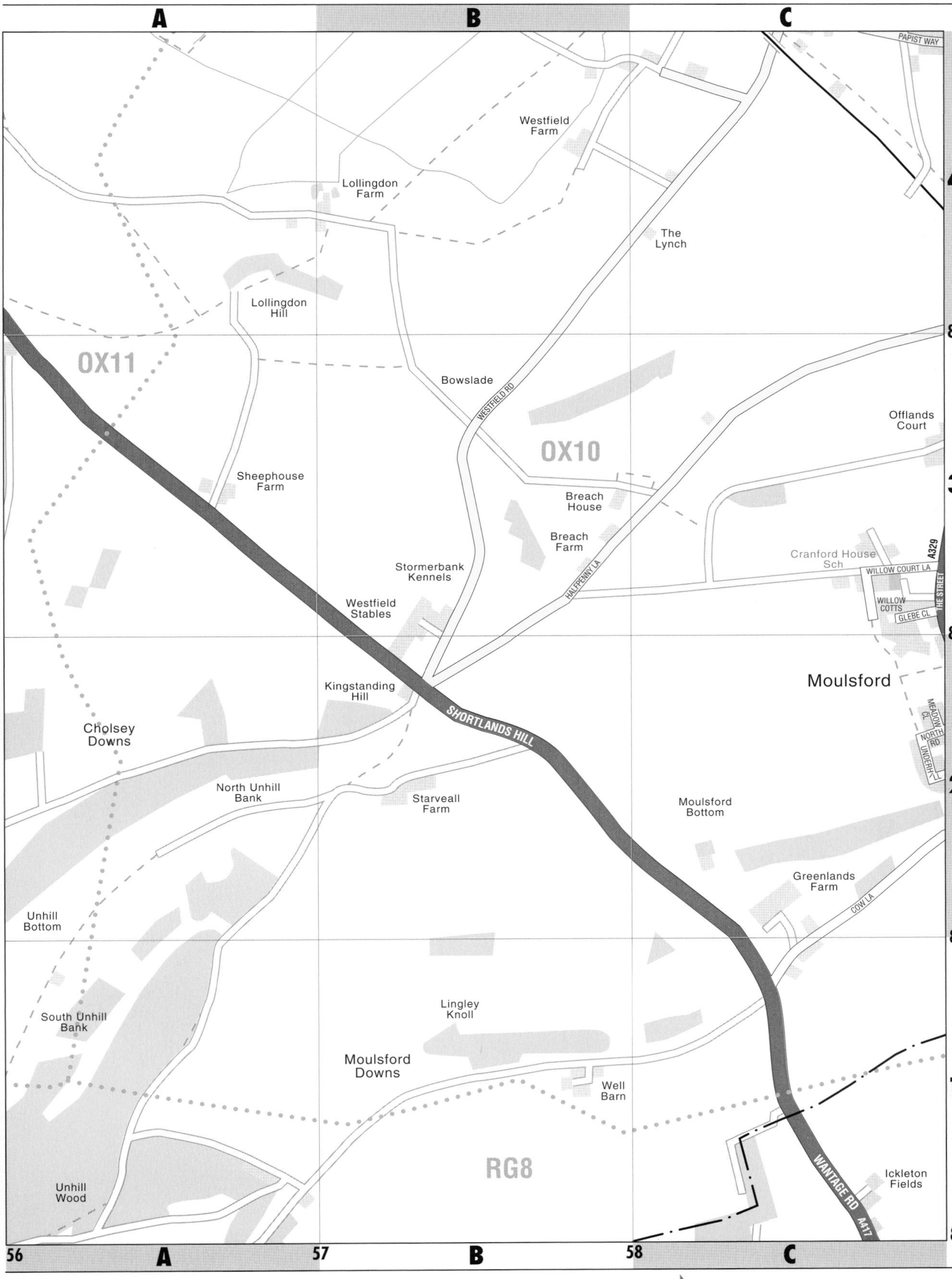
A
B
C
PAPIST WAY
Westfield Farm
Lollingdon Farm
The Lynch
4
Lollingdon Hill
85
OX11
Bowslade
WESTFIELD RD
Offlands Court
OX10
Sheephouse Farm
3
Breach House
Breach Farm
Cranford House Sch
A329
WILLOW COURT LA
Stormerbank Kennels
HALFPENNY LA
WILLOW COTTS
THE STREET
GLEBE CL
Westfield Stables
84
Kingstanding Hill
Moulsford
Cholsey Downs
SHORTLANDS HILL
MEADOW CL
NORTH RD
UNDERHILL
North Unhill Bank
Starveall Farm
2
Moulsford Bottom
Greenlands Farm
COW LA
Unhill Bottom
83
Lingley Knoll
South Unhill Bank
Moulsford Downs
1
Well Barn
RG8
WANTAGE RD
A417
Ickleton Fields
Unhill Wood
82
56
57
58
A
B
C

33

14

13

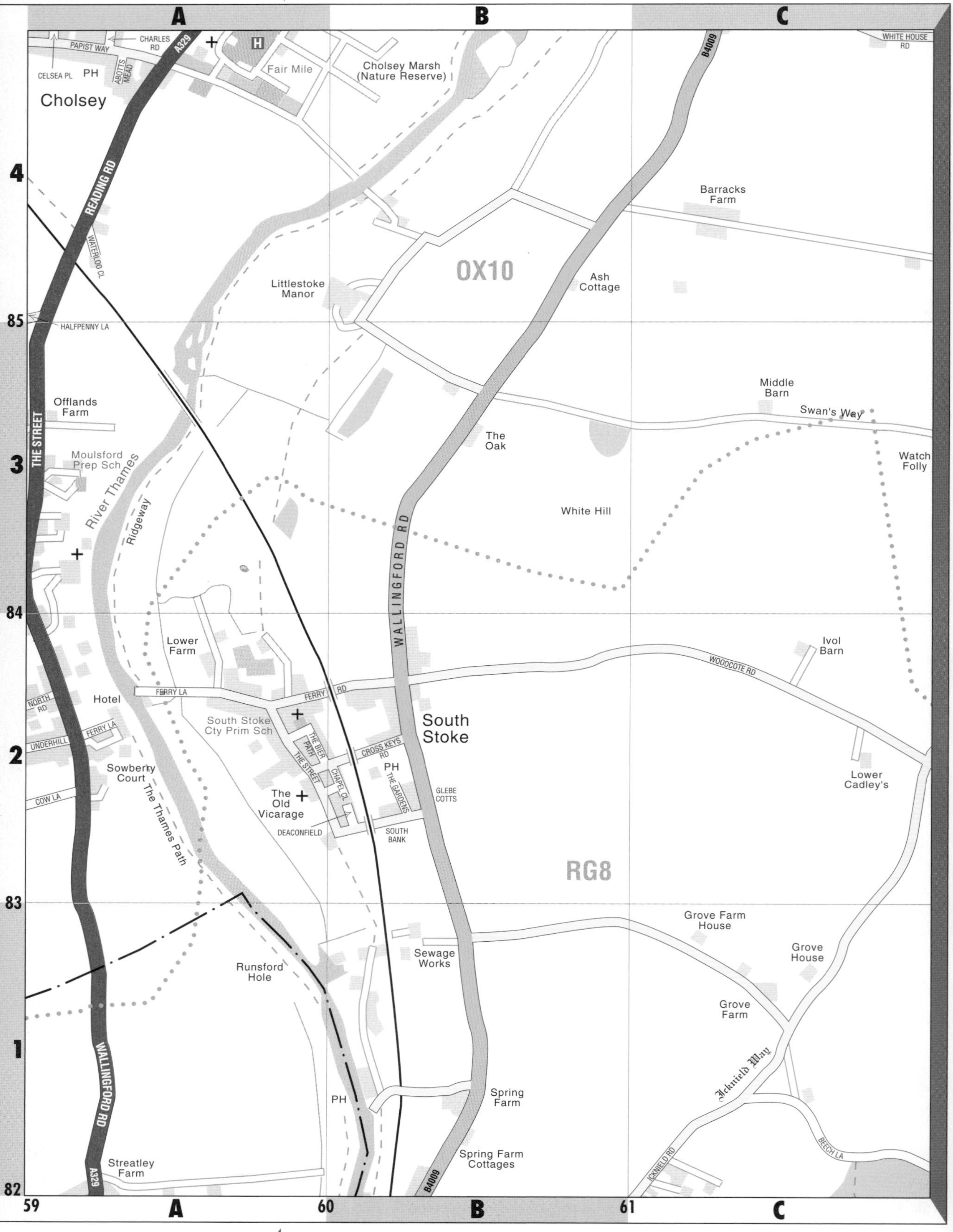
A
B
C
PAPIST WAY
CHARLES RD
A329
CELSEA PL
PH
ABOTTS MEAD
Cholsey
Fair Mile
Cholsey Marsh (Nature Reserve)
B4009
WHITE HOUSE RD
4
READING RD
WATERLOO CL
Barracks Farm
OX10
Littlestoke Manor
Ash Cottage
85
HALFPENNY LA
Offlands Farm
Middle Barn
Swan's Way
THE STREET
Moulsford Prep Sch
River Thames
The Oak
Watch Folly
3
Ridgeway
White Hill
WALLINGFORD RD
84
Lower Farm
Ivol Barn
WOODCOTE RD
FERRY LA
FERRY RD
NORTH RD
Hotel
South Stoke Cty Prim Sch
South Stoke
FERRY LA
UNDERHILL
THE BIER PATH
CROSS KEYS RD
2
Sowberry Court
THE STREET
CHAPEL CL
PH
Lower Cadley's
COW LA
The Thames Path
The Old Vicarage
THE GARDENS
GLEBE COTTS
DEACONFIELD
SOUTH BANK
RG8
83
Grove Farm House
Sewage Works
Grove House
Runsford Hole
Grove Farm
1
WALLINGFORD RD
Icknield Way
PH
Spring Farm
BEECH LA
Streatley Farm
Spring Farm Cottages
ICKNIELD RD
A329
B4009
82
59
A
60
B
61
C

13
34

16

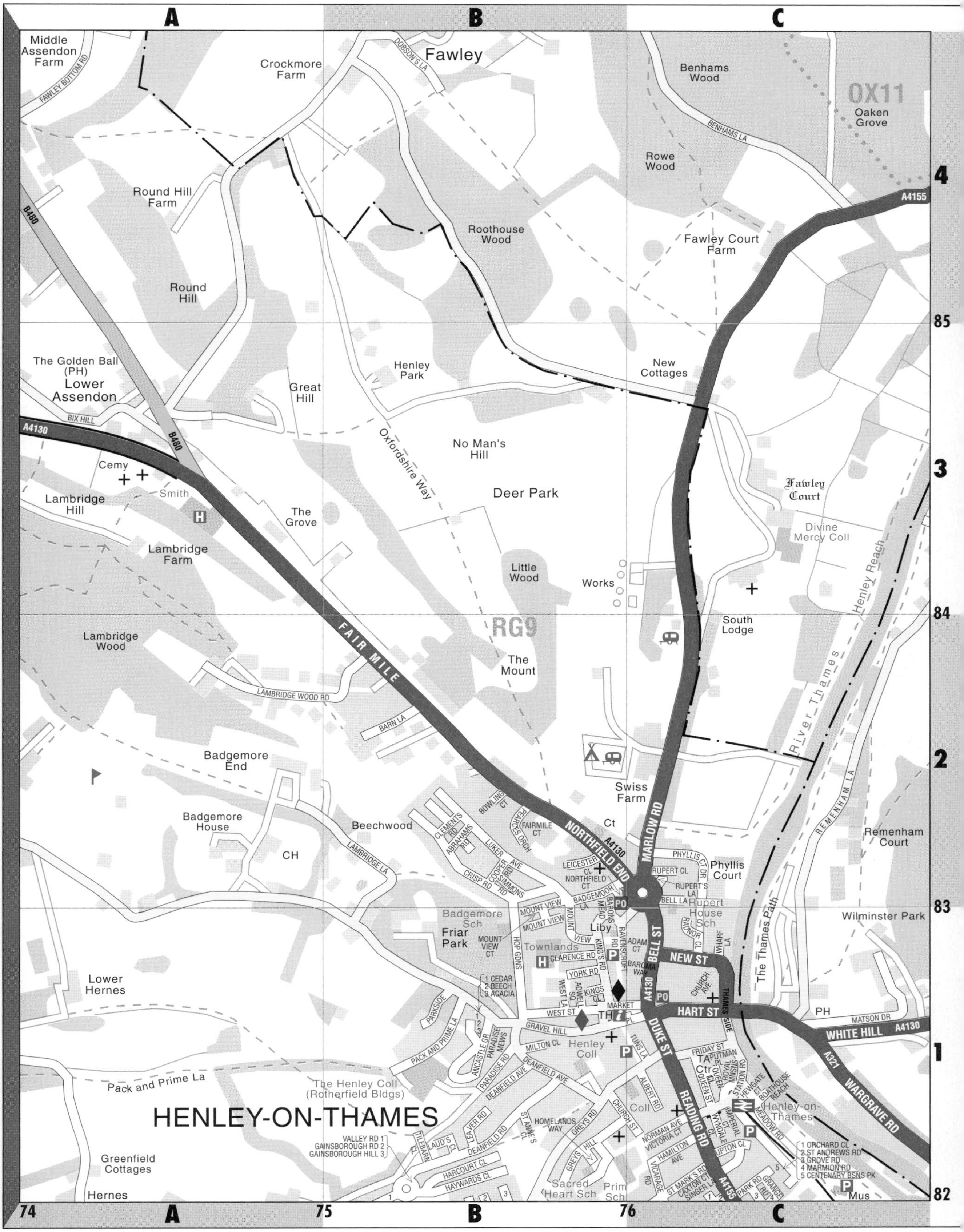

A
B
C
Middle Assendon Farm
FAWLEY BOTTOM RD
Crockmore Farm
DOBSON'S LA
Fawley
Benhams Wood
OX11
Oaken Grove
BENHAMS LA
Rowe Wood
4
A4155
B480
Round Hill Farm
Roothouse Wood
Fawley Court Farm
Round Hill
85
The Golden Ball (PH)
Lower Assendon
Great Hill
Henley Park
New Cottages
BIX HILL
A4130
B480
Oxfordshire Way
No Man's Hill
3
Cemy
Smith
Lambridge Hill
Deer Park
Fawley Court
The Grove
Divine Mercy Coll
Lambridge Farm
Little Wood
Works
Henley Reach
84
Lambridge Wood
FAIR MILE
RG9
South Lodge
The Mount
LAMBRIDGE WOOD RD
River Thames
BARN LA
2
Badgemore End
Swiss Farm
REMENHAM LA
BOWLING CT
PEARCES ORCH
NORTHFIELD END
MARLOW RD
Badgemore House
Beechwood
CLEMENTS RD
ABRAHAMS RD
FAIRMILE CT
Ct
Remenham Court
CH
LAMBRIDGE LA
LUKER AVE
A4130
PHYLLIS CT DR
Phyllis Court
LEICESTER CL
RUPERT CL
CRISP RD
COOPER RD
SIMMONS RD
NORTHFIELD CT
RUPERT'S LA
BADGEMOOR LA
PO
BELL LA
Rupert House Sch
83
Badgemore Sch
MOUNT VIEW
MOUNT VIEW
Wilminster Park
Friar Park
MOUNT VIEW CT
MOUNT VIEW
BARONS MEAD
KING'S RD
RAVENSCROFT RD
Liby
ADAM CT
BELL ST
RAYNOR CL
WHARF LA
The Thames Path
HOP GDNS
Townlands
CLARENCE RD
NEW ST
BAROMA WAY
Lower Hernes
YORK RD
1 CEDAR
2 BEECH
3 ACACIA
WEST LA
ADWELL SQ
KINGS CL
CHURCH AVE
MARKET PL
A4130
PO
THAMES SIDE
PH
MATSON DR
WEST ST
TH
HART ST
GRAVEL HILL
PARKSIDE
PACK AND PRIME LA
WHITE HILL
A4130
1
ANCASTLE GR
PARADISE MEWS
MILTON CL
Henley Coll
TUNS LA
DUKE ST
FRIARY ST
TA Ctr
PUTMAN PL
ROYAL ANDREW
QUEEN ST
STATION RD
A321
PARADISE RD
DEANFIELD AVE
DEANFIELD AVE
HEWGATE CT
BOATHOUSE REACH
WARGRAVE RD
Pack and Prime La
The Henley Coll (Rotherfield Bldgs)
DEANFIELD AVE
ALBERT RD
READING RD
HENLEY-ON-THAMES
CHURCH ST
Coll
Henley-on-Thames
MEADOW RD
LEA VER RD
DEANFIELD RD
ST ANNE'S CL
HOMELANDS WAY
GREYS RD
NORMAN AVE
VICTORIA CT
IMPERIAL CT
WYNDALE CL
VALLEY RD 1
GAINSBOROUGH RD 2
GAINSBOROUGH HILL 3
TILEBARN CL
LAUD'S CL
GREYS HILL
HAMILTON AVE
UPTON CL
1 ORCHARD CL
2 ST ANDREWS RD
3 GROVE RD
4 MARMION RD
5 CENTENARY BSNS PK
Greenfield Cottages
HARCOURT CL
HAYWARDS CL
VICARAGE RD
ST MARK'S RD
CAYTON CT
SINGER LA
A4155
PARK RD
GRANGE RD
Sacred Heart Sch
Prim Sch
Hernes
Mus
82
74
75
76


35

16

15

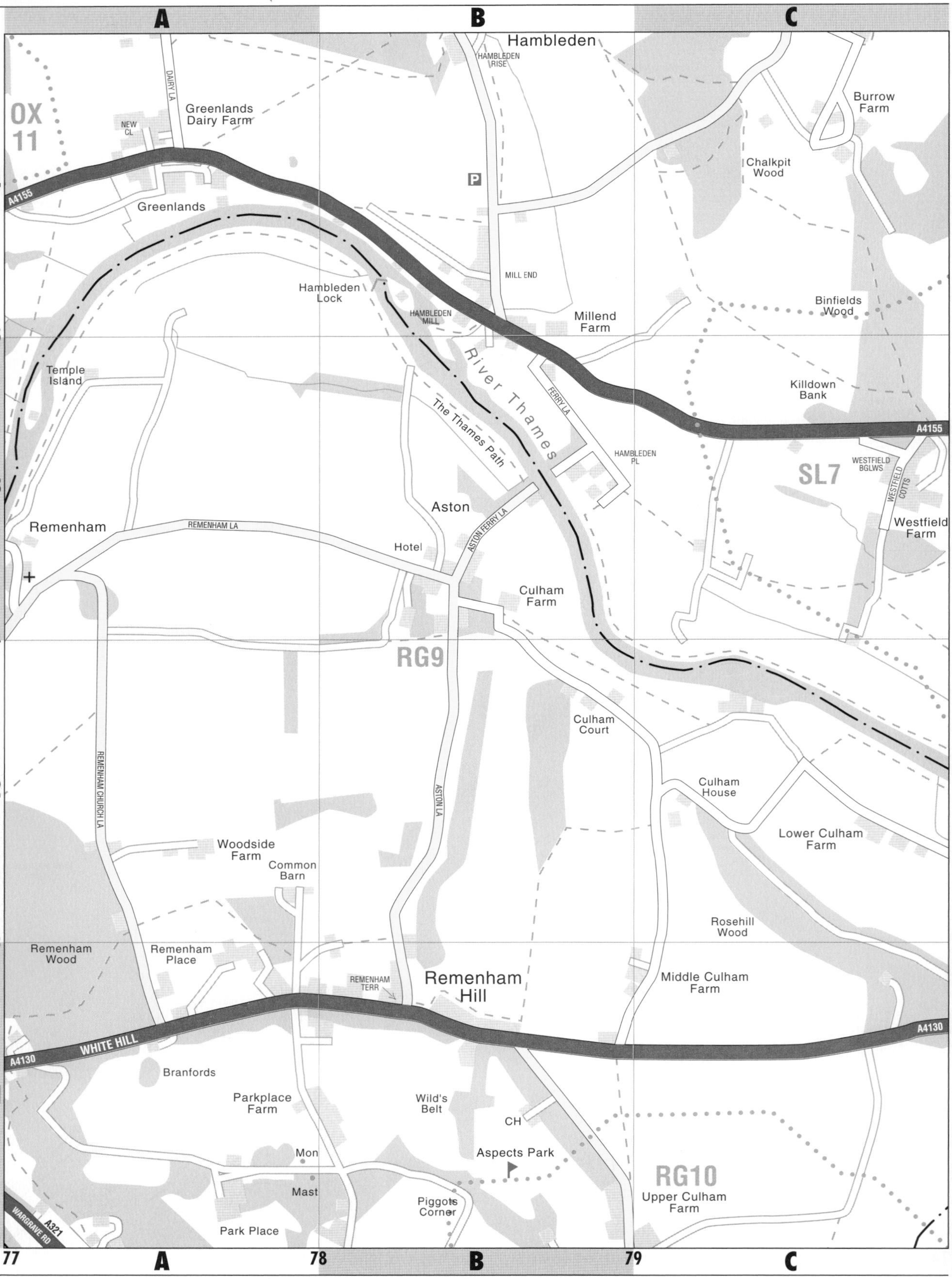

A
B
C
Hambleden
HAMBLEDEN RISE
DAIRY LA
Greenlands Dairy Farm
NEW CL
OX 11
Burrow Farm
Chalkpit Wood
4
A4155
Greenlands
MILL END
Hambleden Lock
HAMBLEDEN MILL
Millend Farm
Binfields Wood
85
Temple Island
River Thames
The Thames Path
FERRY LA
Killdown Bank
A4155
HAMBLEDEN PL
WESTFIELD BGLWS
WESTFIELD COTTS
SL7
3
Aston
Remenham
REMENHAM LA
ASTON FERRY LA
Hotel
Westfield Farm
Culham Farm
84
RG9
Culham Court
2
REMENHAM CHURCH LA
ASTON LA
Culham House
Lower Culham Farm
Woodside Farm
Common Barn
Rosehill Wood
83
Remenham Wood
Remenham Place
REMENHAM TERR
Remenham Hill
Middle Culham Farm
A4130
WHITE HILL
A4130
Branfords
1
Parkplace Farm
Wild's Belt
CH
Mon
Aspects Park
RG10
Mast
Piggotts Corner
Upper Culham Farm
WARGRAVE RD
A321
Park Place
82
77
78
79


15

36

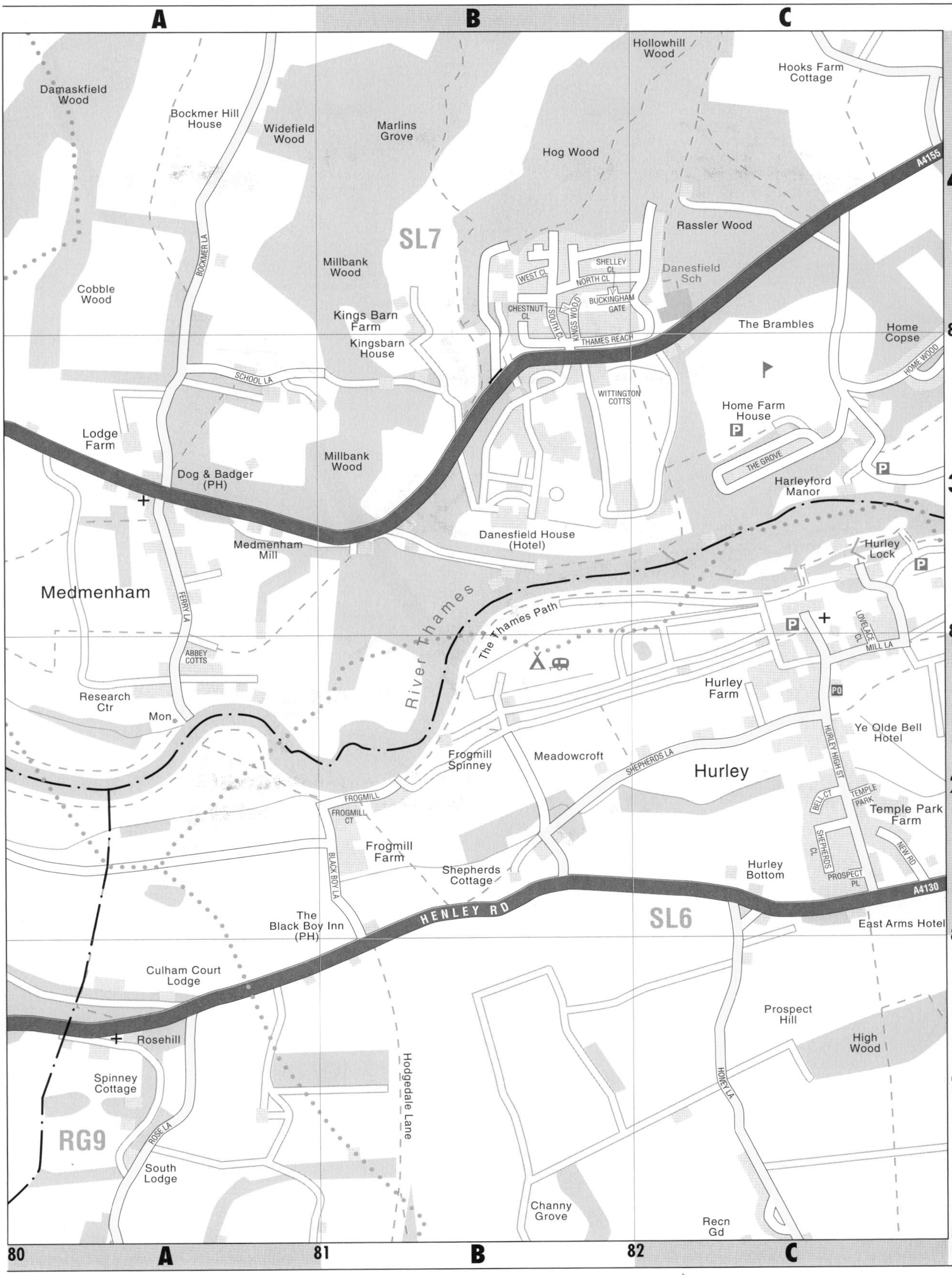
A
B
C
Damaskfield Wood
Bockmer Hill House
Widefield Wood
Marlins Grove
Hollowhill Wood
Hooks Farm Cottage
Hog Wood
A4155
4
SL7
Rassler Wood
Millbank Wood
Cobble Wood
BOCKMER LA
SHELLEY CL
WEST CL
NORTH CL
Danesfield Sch
CHESTNUT CL
SOUTH CL
KINGS WOOD
BUCKINGHAM GATE
THAMES REACH
Kings Barn Farm
Kingsbarn House
The Brambles
Home Copse
85
HOME WOOD
SCHOOL LA
WITTINGTON COTTS
Home Farm House
Lodge Farm
THE GROVE
Millbank Wood
Dog & Badger (PH)
Harleyford Manor
3
Danesfield House (Hotel)
Medmenham Mill
Hurley Lock
Medmenham
FERRY LA
River Thames
The Thames Path
LOVELACE CL
84
MILL LA
ABBEY COTTS
Research Ctr
Hurley Farm
Mon
Ye Olde Bell Hotel
Frogmill Spinney
Meadowcroft
SHEPHERDS LA
Hurley
HURLEY HIGH ST
2
FROGMILL
FROGMILL CT
BELL CT
TEMPLE PARK
Temple Park Farm
Frogmill Farm
SHEPHERDS CL
BLACK BOY LA
Shepherds Cottage
Hurley Bottom
PROSPECT PL
NEW RD
A4130
HENLEY RD
The Black Boy Inn (PH)
SL6
East Arms Hotel
83
Culham Court Lodge
Prospect Hill
Rosehill
High Wood
Spinney Cottage
Hodgedale Lane
HONEY LA
1
RG9
ROSE LA
South Lodge
Channy Grove
Recn Gd
82
80
81
82

17
1

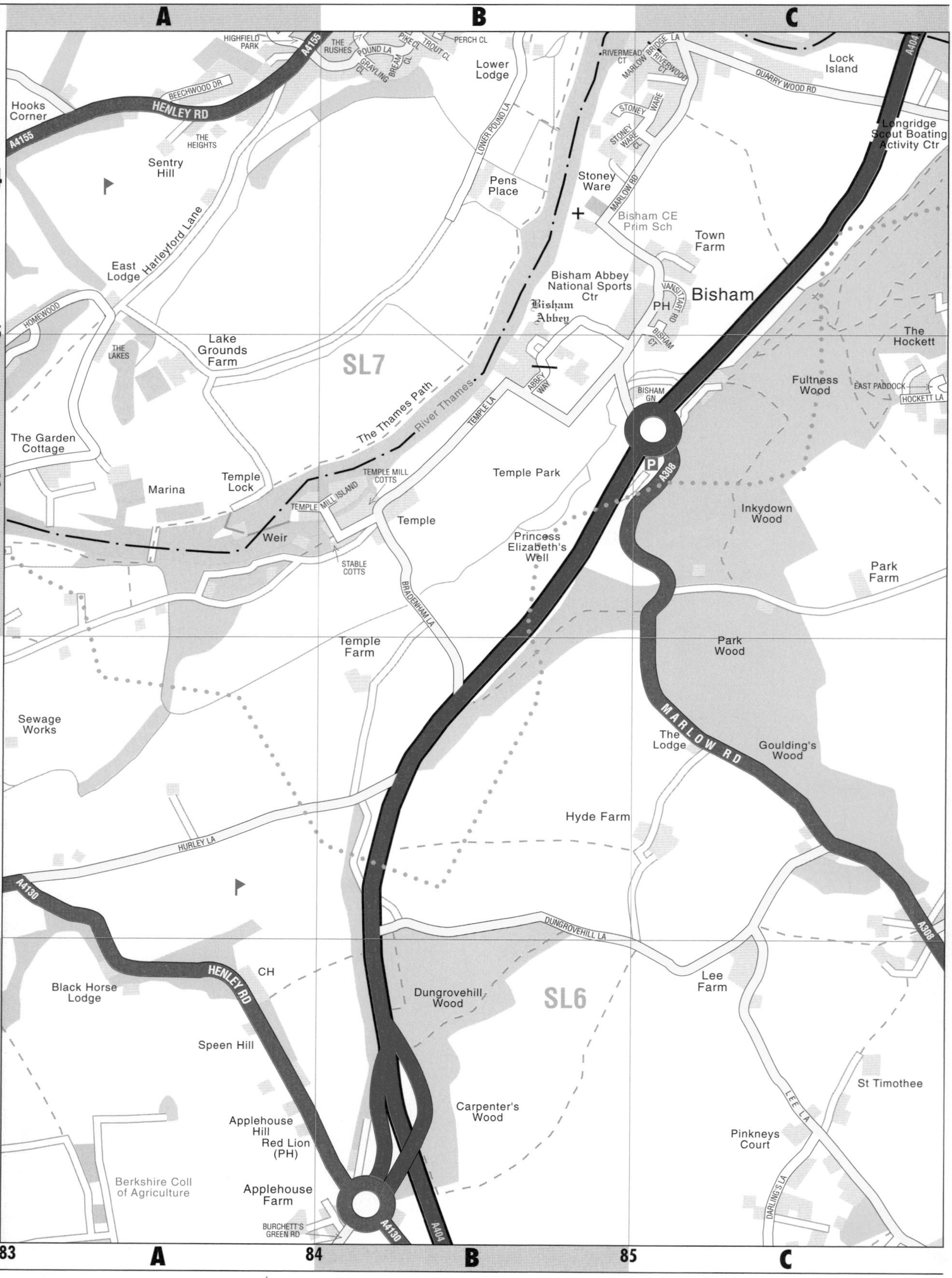
A
B
C
HIGHFIELD PARK
THE RUSHES
POUND LA
GRAYLING
BREAM CL
PIKE CL
TROUT CL
PERCH CL
Lower Lodge
RIVERMEAD CT
MARLOW BRIDGE LA
RIVERWOOD CT
Lock Island
A404
QUARRY WOOD RD
A4155
BEECHWOOD DR
HENLEY RD
Hooks Corner
THE HEIGHTS
Sentry Hill
LOWER POUND LA
STONEY WARE
STONEY WARE CL
Longridge Scout Boating Activity Ctr
Pens Place
Stoney Ware
MARLOW RD
Bisham CE Prim Sch
Town Farm
Harleyford Lane
East Lodge
Bisham Abbey National Sports Ctr
Bisham Abbey
VANSITTART RD
PH
Bisham
HOMEWOOD
BISHAM CT
The Hockett
THE LAKES
Lake Grounds Farm
SL7
ABBEY WAY
BISHAM GN
Fultness Wood
EAST PADDOCK
HOCKETT LA
The Thames Path
River Thames
TEMPLE LA
The Garden Cottage
P
A308
Temple Park
Marina
Temple Lock
TEMPLE MILL COTTS
TEMPLE MILL ISLAND
Inkydown Wood
Temple
Weir
Princess Elizabeth's Well
STABLE COTTS
Park Farm
BRADENHAM LA
Temple Farm
Park Wood
Sewage Works
The Lodge
MARLOW RD
Goulding's Wood
Hyde Farm
HURLEY LA
A4130
DUNGROVEHILL LA
A308
HENLEY RD
CH
Lee Farm
Black Horse Lodge
Dungrovehill Wood
SL6
Speen Hill
St Timothee
LEE LA
Carpenter's Wood
Applehouse Hill
Red Lion (PH)
Pinkneys Court
Berkshire Coll of Agriculture
Applehouse Farm
DARLING'S LA
BURCHETT'S GREEN RD
A4130
A404
4
85
3
84
2
83
1
82
83
84
85

17
38

2
20

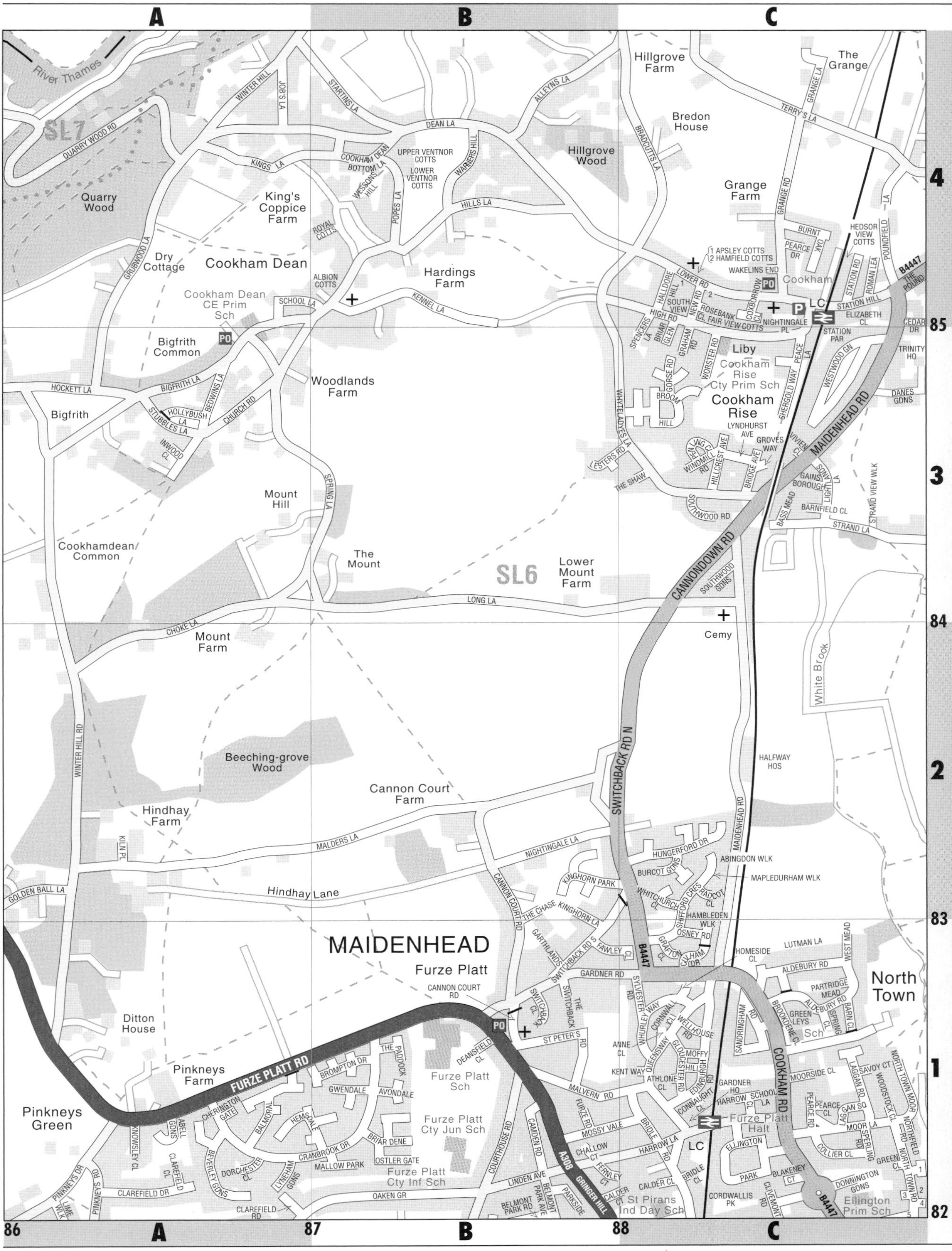


39
20

C1
1 NORTH TOWN CL
2 ALYSON CT
3 NORTH GN
4 NORTH TOWN MEAD
5 NORTHDEAN

19
3

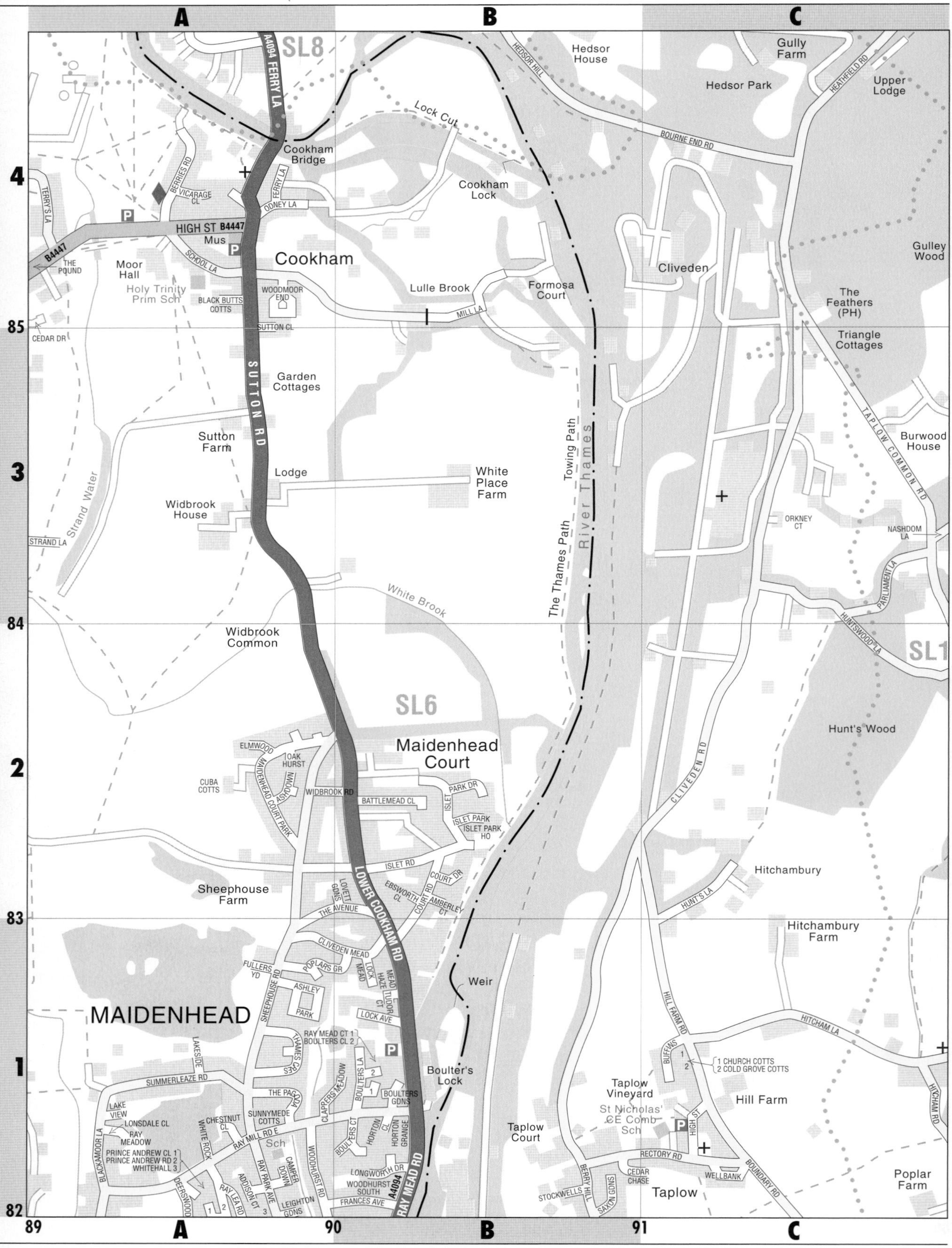
A
B
C
SL8
A4094 FERRY LA
Hedsor House
Gully Farm
Hedsor Park
Upper Lodge
HEDSOR HILL
HEATHFIELD RD
Lock Cut
BOURNE END RD
Cookham Bridge
Cookham Lock
4
TERRY'S LA
BERRIES RD
VICARAGE CL
FERRY LA
ODNEY LA
HIGH ST B4447
Mus
B4447
THE POUND
Moor Hall
SCHOOL LA
Cookham
Cliveden
Gulley Wood
Holy Trinity Prim Sch
WOODMOOR END
BLACK BUTTS COTTS
Lulle Brook
Formosa Court
MILL LA
The Feathers (PH)
85
CEDAR DR
SUTTON CL
Triangle Cottages
SUTTON RD
Garden Cottages
Sutton Farm
Towing Path
River Thames
TAPLOW COMMON RD
Burwood House
3
Strand Water
Lodge
White Place Farm
Widbrook House
ORKNEY CT
NASHDOM LA
STRAND LA
The Thames Path
PARLIAMENT LA
White Brook
84
Widbrook Common
HUNTSWOOD LA
SL1
SL6
Hunt's Wood
ELMWOOD
OAK HURST
Maidenhead Court
2
CUBA COTTS
MAIDENHEAD COURT PARK
ASHDOWN
WIDBROOK RD
BATTLEMEAD CL
PARK DR
ISLET PARK
ISLET PARK HO
ISLET
CLIVEDEN RD
ISLET RD
COURT DR
LOWER COOKHAM RD
Sheephouse Farm
LOVETT GDNS
EBSWORTH CL
COURT RD
AMBERLEY CT
Hitchambury
HUNT'S LA
83
THE AVENUE
Hitchambury Farm
CLIVEDEN MEAD
FULLERS YD
POPLARS GR
MEAD
LOCK MEAD
HAZE
MEAD TUDOR CT
Weir
SHEEPHOUSE RD
ASHLEY PARK
MAIDENHEAD
LOCK AVE
HILL FARM RD
HITCHAM LA
LAKESIDE
THAMES CRES
RAY MEAD CT 1
BOULTERS CL 2
BUFFINS
1 CHURCH COTTS
2 COLD GROVE COTTS
1
CLAPPERS MEADOW
BOULTERS LA
Boulter's Lock
SUMMERLEAZE RD
Taplow Vineyard
Hill Farm
THE PAGODA
BOULTERS GDNS
LAKE VIEW
SUNNYMEDE COTTS
LONSDALE CL
CHESTNUT CL
St Nicholas' CE Comb Sch
HIGH ST
HITCHAM RD
RAY MEADOW
Taplow Court
RAY MILL RD E
Sch
HORTON CL
HORTON GRANGE
BOULTERS CT
BLACKAMOOR LA
PRINCE ANDREW CL 1
PRINCE ANDREW RD 2
WHITEHALL 3
WHITE ROCK
RAY PARK AVE
CAMPER DOWN
WOODHURST RD
RECTORY RD
LONGWORTH DR
CEDAR CHASE
WELLBANK
BOUNDARY RD
Poplar Farm
DEERSWOOD
RAY LEA RD
ADDISON CT
LEIGHTON GDNS
WOODHURST SOUTH
FRANCES AVE
A4094
RAY MEAD RD
STOCKWELLS
BERRY HILL
SAXON GDNS
Taplow
82
89
90
91

19
40

22

A
B
C
Abbey Wood
Root Mound
Brook End Farm
Lower Brook End
Littleworth Corner
Kilnwood
Beeches Way
Dorney Wood
Whitespark Wood
SL2
HORSESHOE HILL
PARK LA
Cabrook
Little Barns Wood
CURRIERS LA
Tower Wood
Towerwood
Burnham Beeches
CH
Lambournes Wood
Dorney Wood
Victoria Drive
Lord Mayors Drive
Juniper Grove
PUMPKIN HILL
Wymers Wood
DROPMORE RD
DORNEY WOOD RD
Pumpkin Hill Cottage
NASHDOM LA
Fox Den
Pumpkin Hill
PH
NIGHTINGALE PARK
HAWTHORN LA
THOMPKINS LA
Longmead
LONGMEAD LA
ROSE HILL
Rose Hill House
Snowball Farm
Poyle Cottages
Hunts Wood Farm
Rose Hill
CHALK PIT
SL1
GROVE RD
HUNTSWOOD LA
Rose Hill Farm
BRICKFIELD LA
Westalls
Hotel
High Meadow
GREEN LA
CH
CROW PIECE LA
ALLERDS RD
TAPLOW COMMON RD
BOWMANS CL
REDWOOD
WYMERS WOOD RD
Burnham
Cant's Hill
Burnham Grove
ASHCROFT CT
POYLE LA
CHEVELEY GDNS
HAZELHURST RD
BENTLEY PARK
Bottom Waltons
Grovefield Hotel
PINK LA
WYMERS
GRENVILLE CL
LINKSWOOD RD
Grove Wood
NORTH BURNHAM CL
NORTHLA DR
NDS
BOTTOM WALTONS CARAVAN SITE
OXFORD AVE
CAMBRIDGE AVE
WYNDHAM CRES
THE FAIRWAY
WALTON LA
SL2
WILLOW WOOD CL
HALL MEADOW
PIPERS CL
AMBERS DR
Hitcham Park
TOCKLEY WAY
BALDWIN RD
FARNHAM LA
SAMPSONS GN
NEVILLE CT
Court Farm
CLONMEL WAY
ALMOND RD
BAY TREE CT
FAIRFIELD RD
LONG DR
PIPERS CT
FARNHAM LA
ROKESBY RD
LILAC CT
THE GORE
BREDWARD CL
COURT LA
MASCOLL PATH
WAVELL GDNS
ALMA CT
DOVE HOUSE CRES
GORE RD
MINNIECROFT RD
BRITWELL RD
Grenville Court
HETHERINGTON CL
ROKESBY RD
HITCHAM LA
Hitcham House Farm
HAMILTON GDNS
OLD FIVES CT
PO
1 THE GRANGE
2 GREEN LANE CT
PERRYMAN WAY
TRAVIC RD
MARUNDEN GN
Sch
WILMOT RD
P
GAVESTON RD
CALBROKE RD
CLEARES PASTURE
BURN WLK
MIDDLE WLK
P
HIGH ST
JENNERY LA
LYNCH HILL LA
SLOUGH
UMBERVILLE WAY
GOODWIN RD
CHILWICK RD
SUMMERS RD
DAWES EAST RD
HATCHGATE GDNS
Sch
SKYDMORE PATH
Lent
EIGHT ACRES
LENT GREEN LA
CHURCH ST
LINCOLN HATCH LA
HOGFAIR LA
THE POUND
Burnham Gram Sch
LOWER BRITWELL RD
STRATFORD CL
NEWPORT RD
GARRARD RD
CECIL WAY
HITCHAM HOUSE
New Cut
LENT RISE RD
LENT GN
THE PRECINCTS
PARKGATE
SANDS FARM DR
DOWNING PATH
WINTOUN PATH
LONG FURLONG DR
BASSETT WAY
ALICE LA
ST PETER'S CL
WINDSOR LA
SHENSTONE DR
ST MICHAEL'S CT
HAYMILL RD
WORDSWORTH RD
BARTELOTTS RD
COVERDALE WAY
EGERTON RD
MAGPIE WAY
FAIRVIEW RD
Britwell
Orchardville
PERRYFIELDS WAY
STOMP RD
Liby
SHOREHAM RISE
RAMSEY CT
TENNYSON WAY
VAUGHAN WAY
KESTREL PATH
PEMBERTON RD
TOMLIN RD
VERMONT RD
FOSTERS PATH
ORCHARDVILLE
PERRY HO
The Priory
WINDSOR CL
BURNHAM LA
PORTLAND CL
KINGSLEY PATH
BLUMFIELD CT
WHITTAKER RD
NORTHMEAD RD
LOVEGROVE DR
NEWCHURCH RD
HITCHAM RD
BURLINGTON RD
THE GREEN
Sch
PRIORY RD
BLUMFIELD CRES
LITTLE BROOK AVE
MARESCROFT RD
SCAFELL RD
TEESDALE RD
4
85
3
84
2
83
1
82
92
93
94
A
B
C

41

22

21

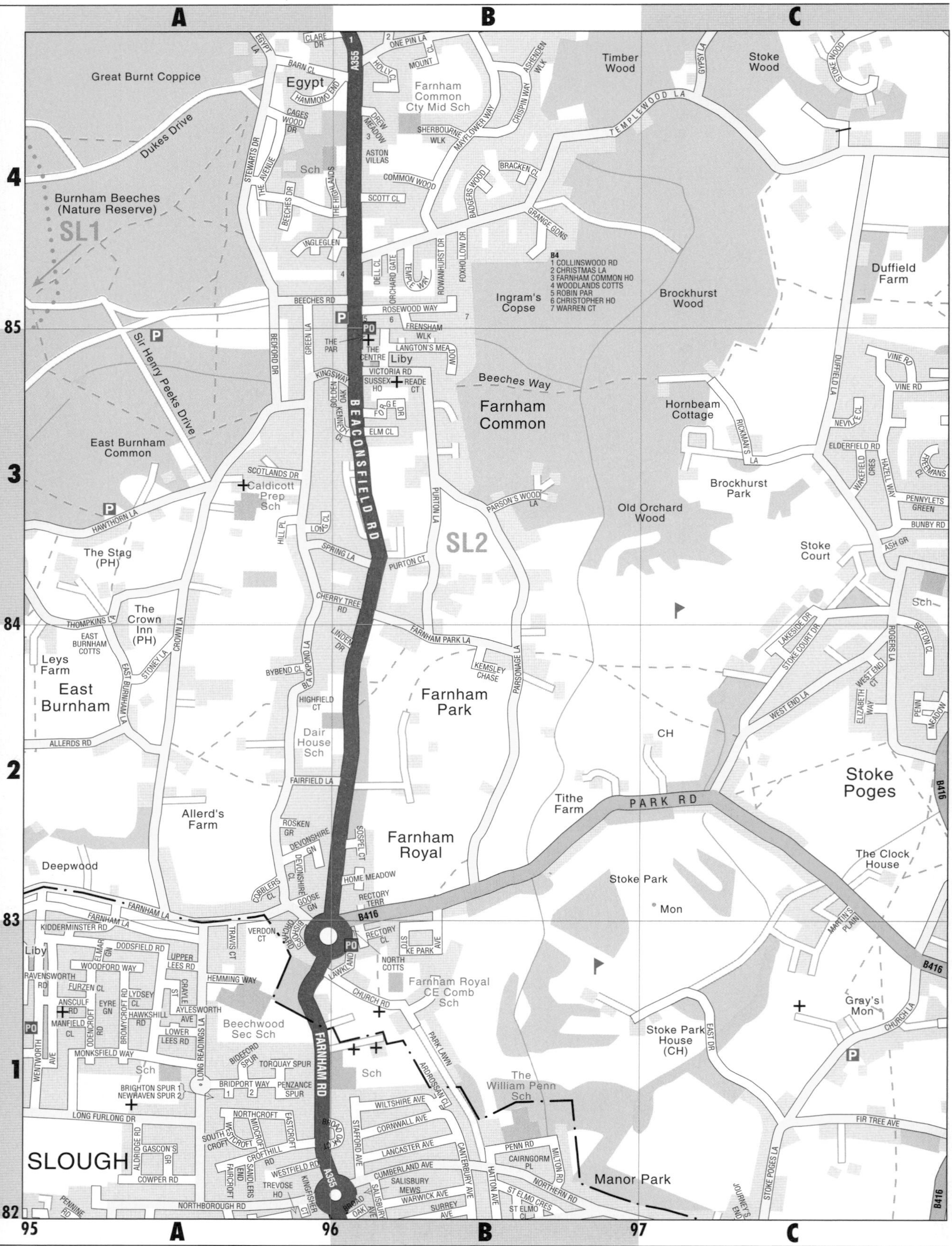
A
B
C
4
85
3
84
2
83
1
82
95
96
97
Great Burnt Coppice
Egypt
Dukes Drive
Burnham Beeches
(Nature Reserve)
SL1
Sir Henry Peeks Drive
East Burnham
Common
HAWTHORN LA
The Stag
(PH)
THOMPKINS LA
The
Crown
Inn
(PH)
EAST
BURNHAM
COTTS
Leys
Farm
East
Burnham
EAST BURNHAM LA
STONEY LA
CROWN LA
ALLERDS RD
Allerd's
Farm
Deepwood
FARNHAM LA
KIDDERMINSTER RD
Liby
DODSFIELD RD
WOODFORD WAY
RAVENSWORTH RD
FURZEN CL
ANSCULF RD
MANFIELD CL
ODENCROFT RD
EYRE GN
BROMYCROFT RD
LYDSEY CL
HAWKSHILL RD
UPPER LEES RD
CRAYLE ST
AYLESWORTH AVE
LOWER LEES RD
MONKSFIELD WAY
WENTWORTH AVE
Sch
BRIGHTON SPUR
NEWHAVEN SPUR
LONG FURLONG DR
SLOUGH
ALDRIDGE RD
GASCON'S GR
COWPER RD
NORTHBOROUGH RD
PENNINE RD
HEMMING WAY
TRAVIS CT
VERDON CT
Beechwood
Sec Sch
LONG READINGS LA
BIDEFORD SPUR
TORQUAY SPUR
BRIDPORT WAY
PENZANCE SPUR
NORTHCROFT
MIDCROFT
EASTCROFT
SOUTHCROFT
WESTCROFT
CROFTHILL
FAIRCROFT
END
SANDLERS
TREVOSE HO
WESTFIELD RD
KINGFISHER CT
FARNHAM RD
A355
BROAD OAK
CLARE DR
EGYPT LA
BARN CL
HAMMOND END
CAGES WOOD DR
STEWARTS DR
THE AVENUE
BEECHES DR
Sch
THE HIGHLANDS
INGLEGLEN
BEECHES RD
BEDFORD DR
GREEN LA
SCOTLANDS DR
Caldicott
Prep
Sch
HILL PL
KINGSWAY
BEACONSFIELD RD
ONE PIN LA
HOLLY CL
MOUNT
Farnham
Common
Cty Mid Sch
DREW MEADOW
ASTON VILLAS
SHERBOURNE WLK
MAYFLOWER WAY
CRISPIN WAY
ASHENDEN WLK
COMMON WOOD
SCOTT CL
BRACKEN CL
BADGERS WOOD
GRANGE GDNS
DELL CL
ORCHARD GATE
TEMPLE WAY
ROWANHURST DR
FOXHOLLOW DR
ROSEWOOD WAY
FRENSHAM WLK
LANGTON'S MEADOW
THE PAR
THE CENTRE
Liby
VICTORIA RD
SUSSEX HO
READE CT
GOLDEN OAK
KENNEDY CL
FORGE DR
ELM CL
PURTON LA
LONG CL
SPRING LA
PURTON CT
CHERRY TREE RD
LINDEN DR
FARNHAM PARK LA
KEMSLEY CHASE
PARSONAGE LA
BYBEND CL
BLACKPOND LA
HIGHFIELD CT
Dair
House
Sch
FAIRFIELD LA
ROSKEN GR
DEVONSHIRE GN
DEVONSHIRE CL
COBBLERS CL
GOOSE GN
HOME MEADOW
SOSPEL CT
RECTORY TERR
B416
RECTORY CL
STOKE PARK AVE
NORTH COTTS
LAWKLAND
CHURCH RD
Farnham Royal
CE Comb
Sch
PARK LAWN
ARDROSSAN CL
Sch
WILTSHIRE AVE
CORNWALL AVE
LANCASTER AVE
CUMBERLAND AVE
SALISBURY MEWS
WARWICK AVE
SURREY AVE
STAFFORD AVE
SALISBURY AVE
CANTERBURY AVE
HATTON AVE
PENN RD
CAIRNGORM PL
MILTON RD
NORTHERN RD
ST ELMO CRES
ST ELMO CL
The
William Penn
Sch
Manor Park
Farnham
Park
Farnham
Royal
Farnham
Common
SL2
Beeches Way
PARSON'S WOOD LA
Ingram's
Copse
B4
1 COLLINSWOOD RD
2 CHRISTMAS LA
3 FARNHAM COMMON HO
4 WOODLANDS COTTS
5 ROBIN PAR
6 CHRISTOPHER HO
7 WARREN CT
Timber
Wood
TEMPLEWOOD LA
GYPSY LA
Stoke
Wood
STOKE WOOD
Brockhurst
Wood
Hornbeam
Cottage
RICKMAN'S LA
Brockhurst
Park
Old Orchard
Wood
Tithe
Farm
PARK RD
CH
Stoke Park
Mon
Stoke Park
House
(CH)
EAST DR
Duffield
Farm
DUFFIELD LA
VINE RD
VINE RD
NEVILLE CL
ELDERFIELD RD
WAKEFIELD CRES
HAZELL WAY
FREEMANS CL
PENNYLETS GREEN
BUNBY RD
ASH GR
Stoke
Court
Sch
LAKESIDE DR
STOKE COURT DR
ROGERS LA
SEFTON CL
WEST END LA
WEST END CT
ELIZABETH WAY
PENN MEADOW
Stoke
Poges
B416
The Clock
House
MARTIN'S PLAIN
Gray's
Mon
CHURCH LA
FIR TREE AVE
STOKE POGES LA
JOURNEY'S END

21

42

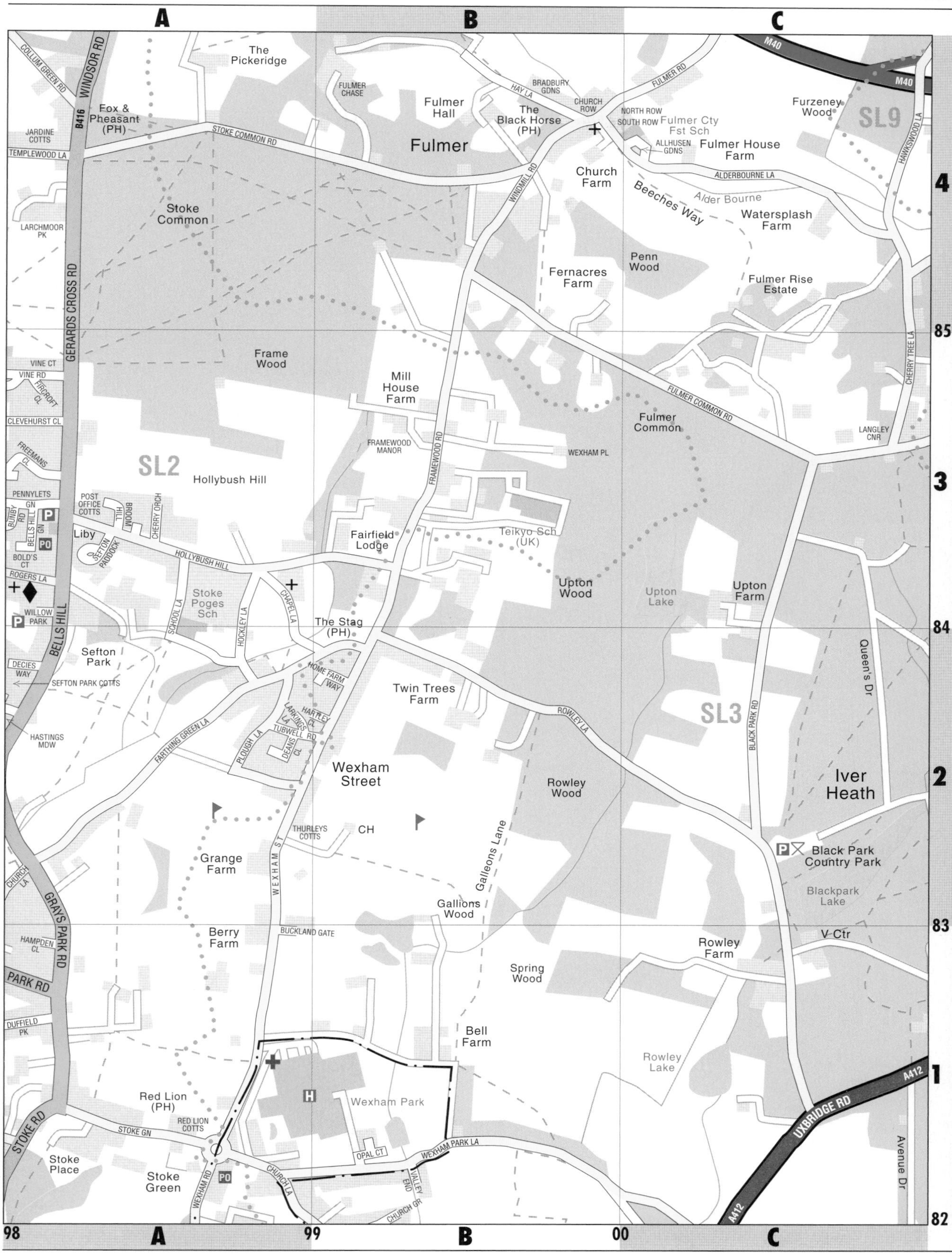
A
B
C
M40
COLLUM GREEN RD
WINDSOR RD
The Pickeridge
FULMER CHASE
Fulmer Hall
HAY LA
BRADBURY GDNS
The Black Horse (PH)
CHURCH ROW
FULMER RD
NORTH ROW
SOUTH ROW
Fulmer Cty Fst Sch
ALLHUSEN GDNS
Fulmer House Farm
Furzeney Wood
SL9
HAWKSWOOD LA
Fox & Pheasant (PH)
B416
JARDINE COTTS
TEMPLEWOOD LA
STOKE COMMON RD
Fulmer
WINDMILL RD
Church Farm
ALDERBOURNE LA
Alder Bourne
Beeches Way
Watersplash Farm
4
Stoke Common
LARCHMOOR PK
GERARDS CROSS RD
Penn Wood
Fernacres Farm
Fulmer Rise Estate
85
Frame Wood
VINE CT
VINE RD
FIRCROFT CL
CHERRY TREE LA
Mill House Farm
FULMER COMMON RD
CLEVEHURST CL
FREEMANS CL
Fulmer Common
LANGLEY CNR
FRAMEWOOD MANOR
FRAMEWOOD RD
WEXHAM PL
SL2
Hollybush Hill
3
PENNYLETS GN
POST OFFICE COTTS
BROOM HILL
CHERRY ORCH
BUNBY RD
BELLS HILL GN
P
PO
Liby
SEFTON PADDOCK
Fairfield Lodge
Teikyo Sch (UK)
BOLD'S CT
HOLLYBUSH HILL
ROGERS LA
Stoke Poges Sch
CHAPEL LA
Upton Wood
Upton Lake
Upton Farm
WILLOW PARK
SCHOOL LA
HOCKLEY LA
The Stag (PH)
84
BELLS HILL
Sefton Park
Queen's Dr
DECIES WAY
SEFTON PARK COTTS
HOME FARM WAY
Twin Trees Farm
HARTLEY CL
LARKINGS LA
TUBWELL RD
ROWLEY LA
SL3
BLACK PARK RD
HASTINGS MDW
FARTHING GREEN LA
PLOUGH LA
DEANS CL
Wexham Street
Rowley Wood
2
Iver Heath
THURLEYS COTTS
CH
WEXHAM ST
Galleons Lane
Black Park Country Park
Grange Farm
CHURCH LA
GRAYS PARK RD
Blackpark Lake
Gallions Wood
Berry Farm
BUCKLAND GATE
V Ctr
83
HAMPDEN CL
Rowley Farm
Spring Wood
PARK RD
DUFFIELD PK
Bell Farm
Rowley Lake
1
A412
Red Lion (PH)
H
Wexham Park
UXBRIDGE RD
RED LION COTTS
STOKE GN
STOKE RD
WEXHAM PARK LA
Avenue Dr
Stoke Place
OPAL CT
Stoke Green
CHURCH LA
VALLEY END
WEXHAM RD
CHURCH GR
82
98
99
00

4

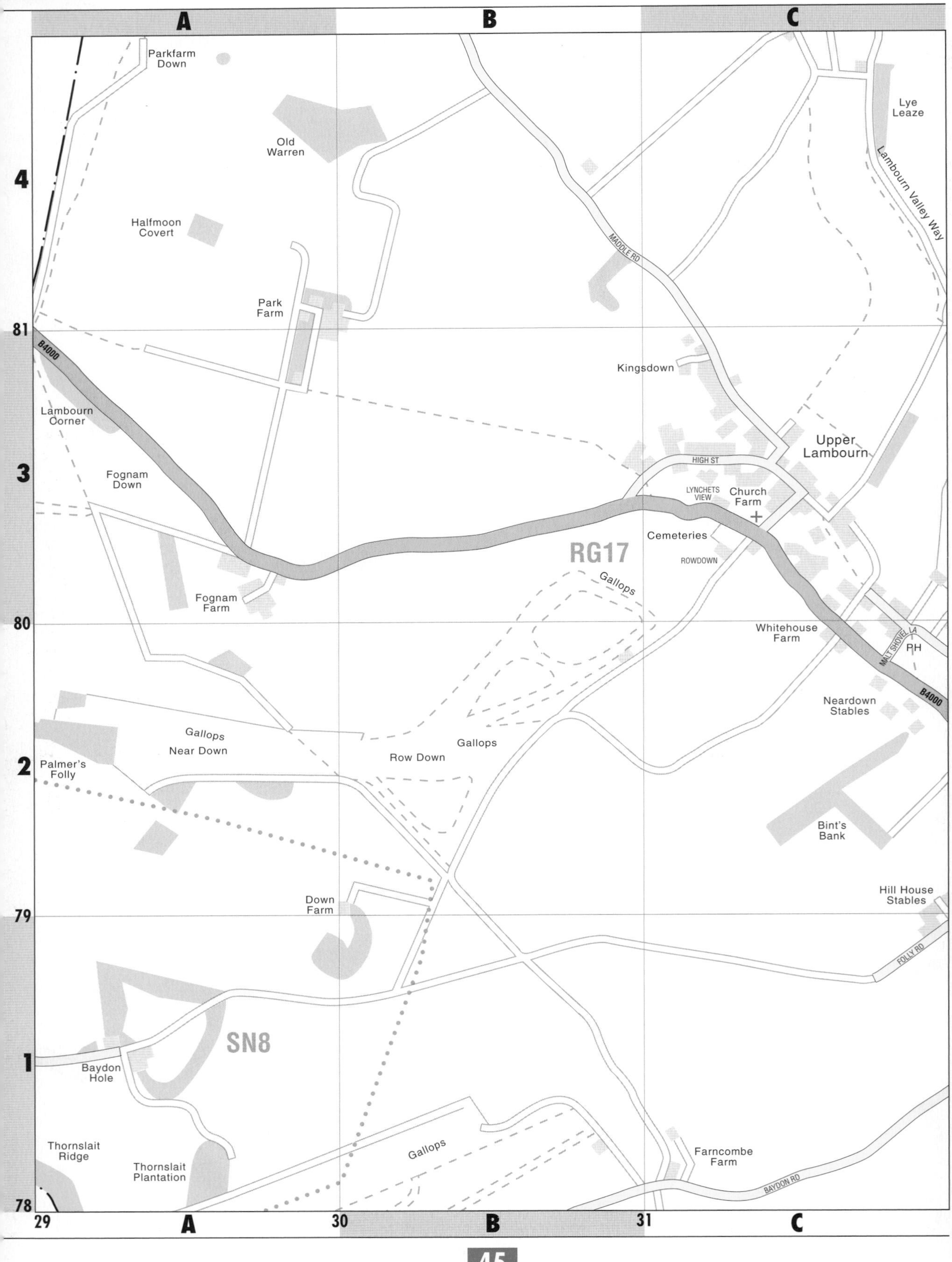
A
B
C
Parkfarm Down
Old Warren
Halfmoon Covert
Park Farm
B4000
Lambourn Corner
Fognam Down
Fognam Farm
Lye Leaze
Lambourn Valley Way
MADDLE RD
Kingsdown
Upper Lambourn
HIGH ST
LYNCHETS VIEW
Church Farm
Cemeteries
ROWDOWN
RG17
Gallops
Whitehouse Farm
MALT SHOVEL LA
PH
Neardown Stables
Gallops
Near Down
Row Down
Gallops
Palmer's Folly
Bint's Bank
Down Farm
Hill House Stables
FOLLY RD
SN8
Baydon Hole
Thornslait Ridge
Thornslait Plantation
Gallops
Farncombe Farm
BAYDON RD
4
81
3
80
2
79
1
78
29
30
31

45

5
26

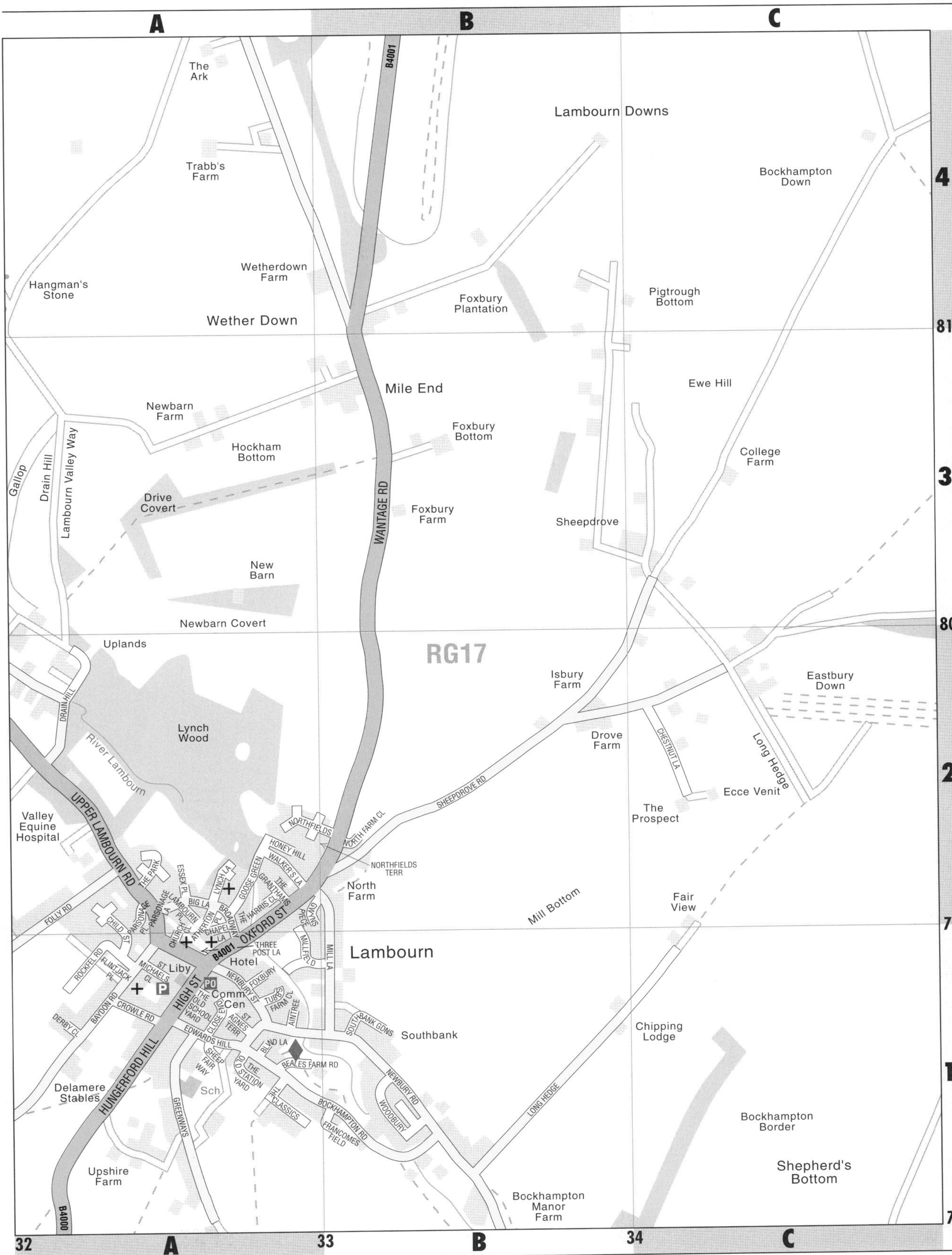
A
B
C
B4001
The Ark
Lambourn Downs
Trabb's Farm
Bockhampton Down
4
Wetherdown Farm
Hangman's Stone
Wether Down
Foxbury Plantation
Pigtrough Bottom
81
Mile End
Ewe Hill
Newbarn Farm
Foxbury Bottom
Hockham Bottom
College Farm
Gallop
Drain Hill
Lambourn Valley Way
3
Drive Covert
WANTAGE RD
Foxbury Farm
Sheepdrove
New Barn
Newbarn Covert
80
Uplands
RG17
Isbury Farm
Eastbury Down
DRAIN HILL
Lynch Wood
Drove Farm
CHESTNUT LA
River Lambourn
Long Hedge
2
UPPER LAMBOURN RD
SHEEPDROVE RD
Ecce Venit
The Prospect
Valley Equine Hospital
NORTHFIELDS
NORTH FARM CL
HONEY HILL
NORTHFIELDS TERR
WALKER'S LA
THE PARK
ESSEX PL
LYNCH LA
GOOSE GREEN
THE GRANTHAMS
North Farm
Mill Bottom
Fair View
FOLLY RD
PARSONAGE LA
LAMBOURN PL
BIG LA
BROADWAY
THE HARRIS CL
OXFORD ST
PARSONAGE PL
CHILD ST
CHURCH LA
ATHERTON CL
CHAPEL LA
LYNCH LA
PIECE
79
B4001
THREE POST LA
MILLFIELD
MILL LA
Lambourn
ST MICHAELS CL
Liby
Hotel
ROCKFEL RD
FLINTJACK PL
PO
NEWBURY ST
FOXBURY
P
HIGH ST
Comm Cen
TUBBS FARM CL
AINTREE
BAYDON RD
CROWLE RD
THE OLD SCHOOL YARD
CLOSE END
ST AGNES TERR
SOUTHBANK GDNS
Southbank
DERBY CL
EDWARDS HILL
Chipping Lodge
BLIND LA
BEALES FARM RD
SHEEP FAIR WAY
THE OLD STATION YARD
1
NEWBURY RD
HUNGERFORD HILL
Delamere Stables
Sch
THE CLASSICS
BOCKHAMPTON RD
WOODBURY
LONG HEDGE
Bockhampton Border
GREENWAYS
FRANCOMES FIELD
Upshire Farm
Shepherd's Bottom
Bockhampton Manor Farm
B4000
78
32
A
33
B
34
C

46
26

25
6

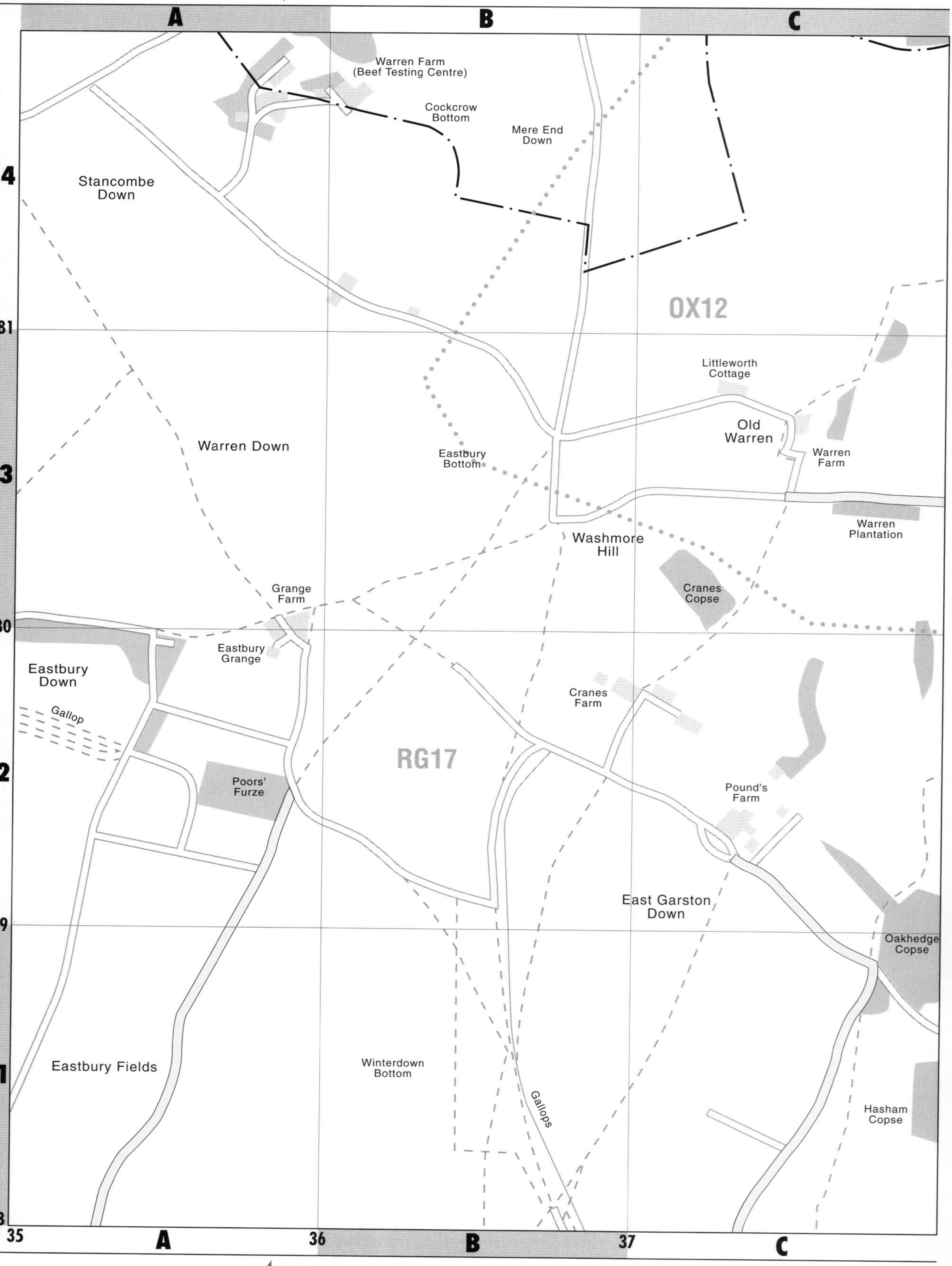
A
B
C
Warren Farm
(Beef Testing Centre)
Cockcrow
Bottom
Mere End
Down
Stancombe
Down
4
OX12
81
Littleworth
Cottage
Old
Warren
Warren
Farm
Warren Down
Eastbury
Bottom
3
Warren
Plantation
Washmore
Hill
Cranes
Copse
Grange
Farm
80
Eastbury
Grange
Eastbury
Down
Gallop
Cranes
Farm
RG17
2
Poors'
Furze
Pound's
Farm
East Garston
Down
79
Oakhedge
Copse
1
Eastbury Fields
Winterdown
Bottom
Gallops
Hasham
Copse
78
35
36
37
A
B
C

25
47

7
28

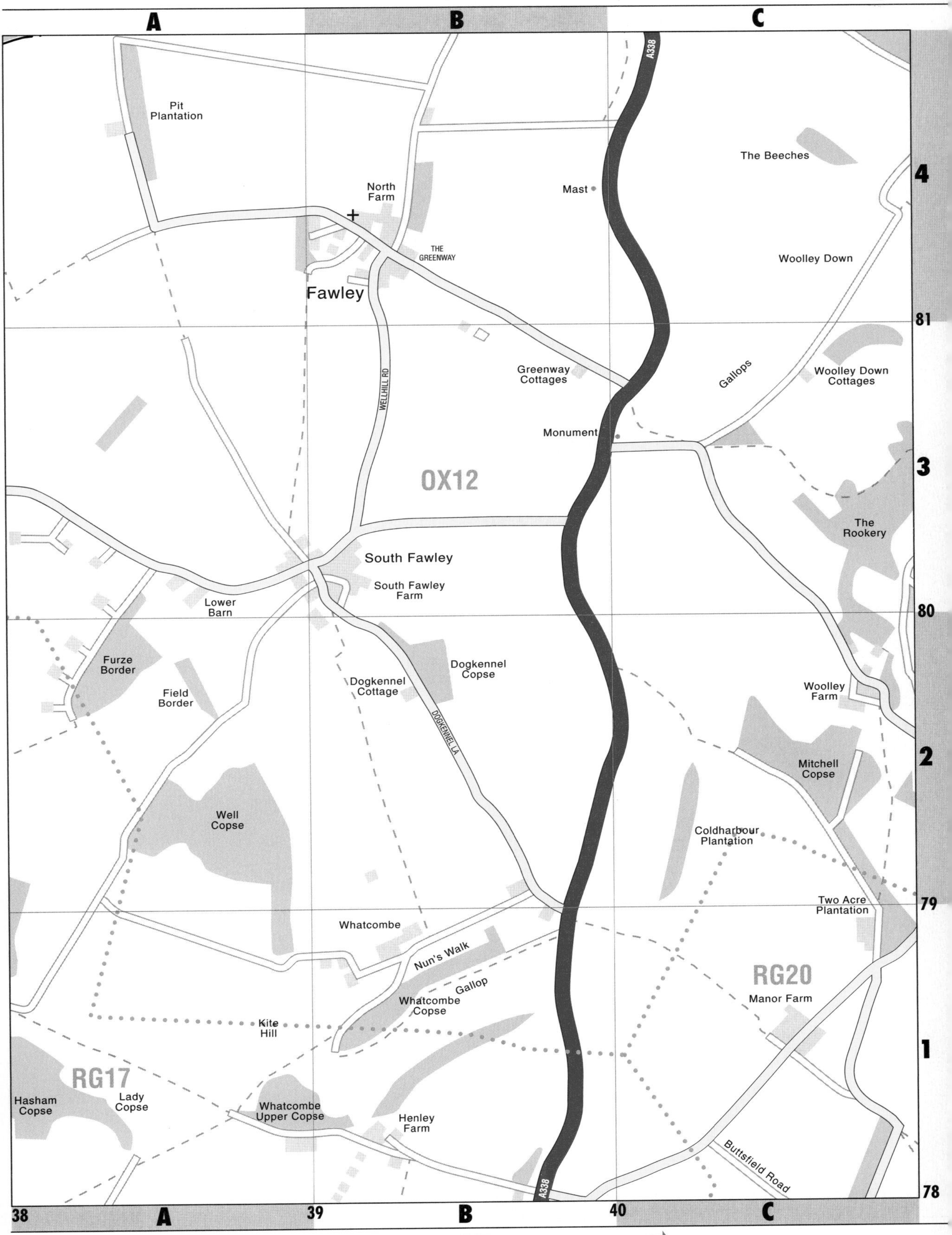
A
B
C
Pit Plantation
North Farm
THE GREENWAY
Fawley
Mast
The Beeches
Woolley Down
A338
WELLHILL RD
Greenway Cottages
Gallops
Woolley Down Cottages
Monument
OX12
The Rookery
South Fawley
South Fawley Farm
Lower Barn
Furze Border
Field Border
Dogkennel Cottage
Dogkennel Copse
DOGKENNEL LA
Woolley Farm
Mitchell Copse
Well Copse
Coldharbour Plantation
Two Acre Plantation
Whatcombe
Nun's Walk
Gallop
Whatcombe Copse
RG20
Manor Farm
Kite Hill
RG17
Hasham Copse
Lady Copse
Whatcombe Upper Copse
Henley Farm
Buttsfield Road
4
81
3
80
2
79
1
78
38
39
40

48
28

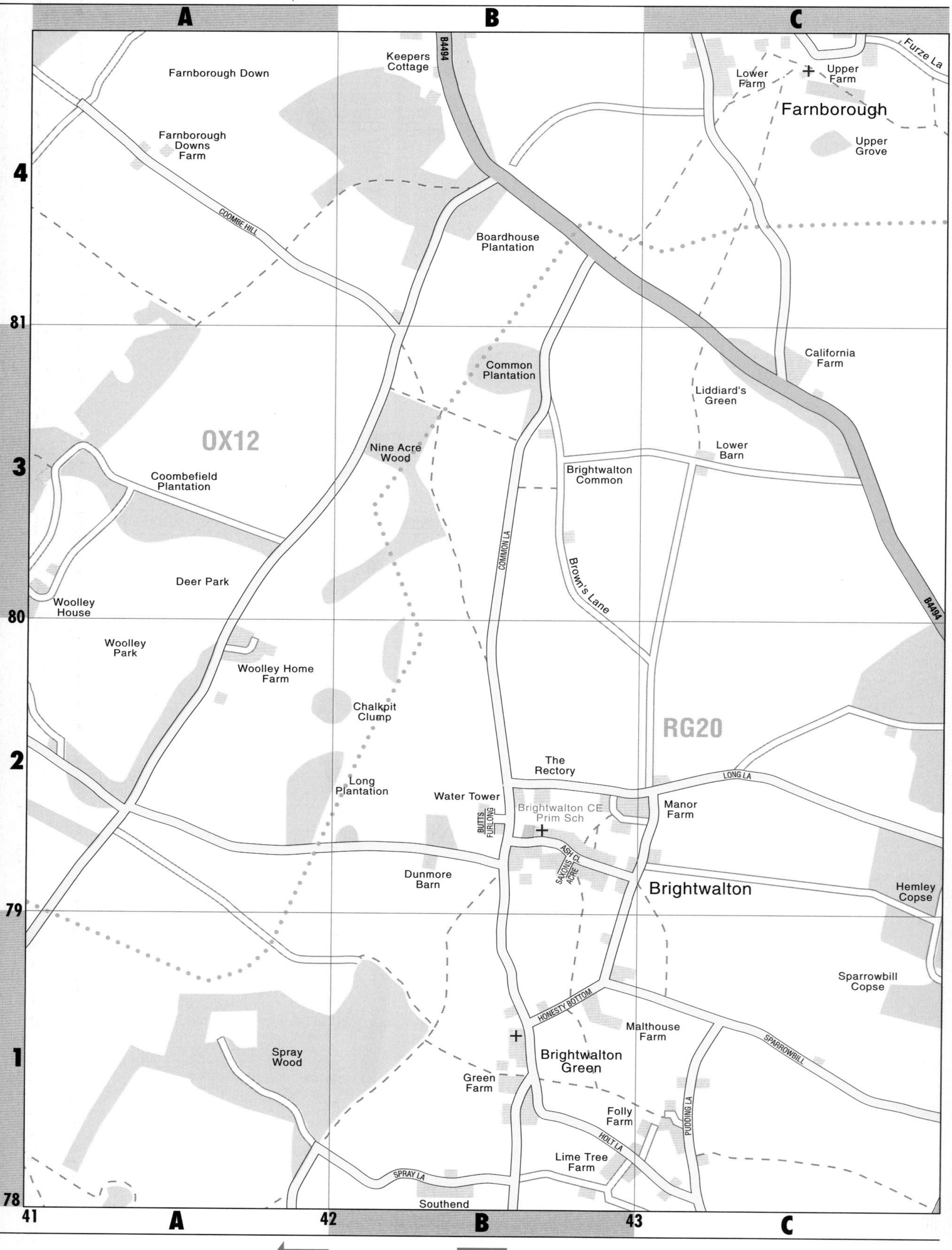
A
B
C
4
81
3
80
2
79
1
78
41
42
43
Farnborough Down
Keepers Cottage
B4494
Furze La
Lower Farm
Upper Farm
Farnborough
Upper Grove
Farnborough Downs Farm
COOMBE HILL
Boardhouse Plantation
Common Plantation
California Farm
Liddiard's Green
OX12
Lower Barn
Nine Acre Wood
Coombefield Plantation
Brightwalton Common
COMMON LA
Brown's Lane
Deer Park
Woolley House
Woolley Park
Woolley Home Farm
Chalkpit Clump
RG20
The Rectory
LONG LA
Long Plantation
Water Tower
Brightwalton CE Prim Sch
Manor Farm
BUTTS FURLONG
ASH CL
SAXONS ACRE
Dunmore Barn
Brightwalton
Hemley Copse
Sparrowbill Copse
HONESTY BOTTOM
Malthouse Farm
Spray Wood
Brightwalton Green
SPARROWBILL
Green Farm
Folly Farm
PUDDING LA
HOLT LA
Lime Tree Farm
SPRAY LA
Southend

9
30

A
B
C
Furze Lane
OX12
Whiteshute Row
Parkwood
Old Street
Old Down Row
The Barracks
4
Heath Copse
Hodcott Copse
81
Hodcott Buildings
CATMORE RD
Wickslett Copse
Wickslett Row North
3
Woolvers Borders
High Robins
Woolvers Barn
Catmore
Old Street
Catmore Farm
Dark Lane
80
RG20
Parson's Row
Round Copse
Lilley
Warren Row
Redlane Barn
Fox & Cubs (PH)
Witnam's Copse
Wilkins Barne
Redlane Road
2
Lilley Copse
Hunham Copse
Redlane Wood
Green Lane
LONG LA
The Broadway
Witnam's Barn
79
Earl's Grove
Larches
SHEEP LEAZE LA
Barrow Hill
Heath Barn
Old Street Lane
1
Whitelands
FIELD RD
HAILEY LA
SPARROWBILL
Rowdown Farm
Hailey Copse
B4494
PEASEMORE HILL
78
44
45
46

50
30

29
10

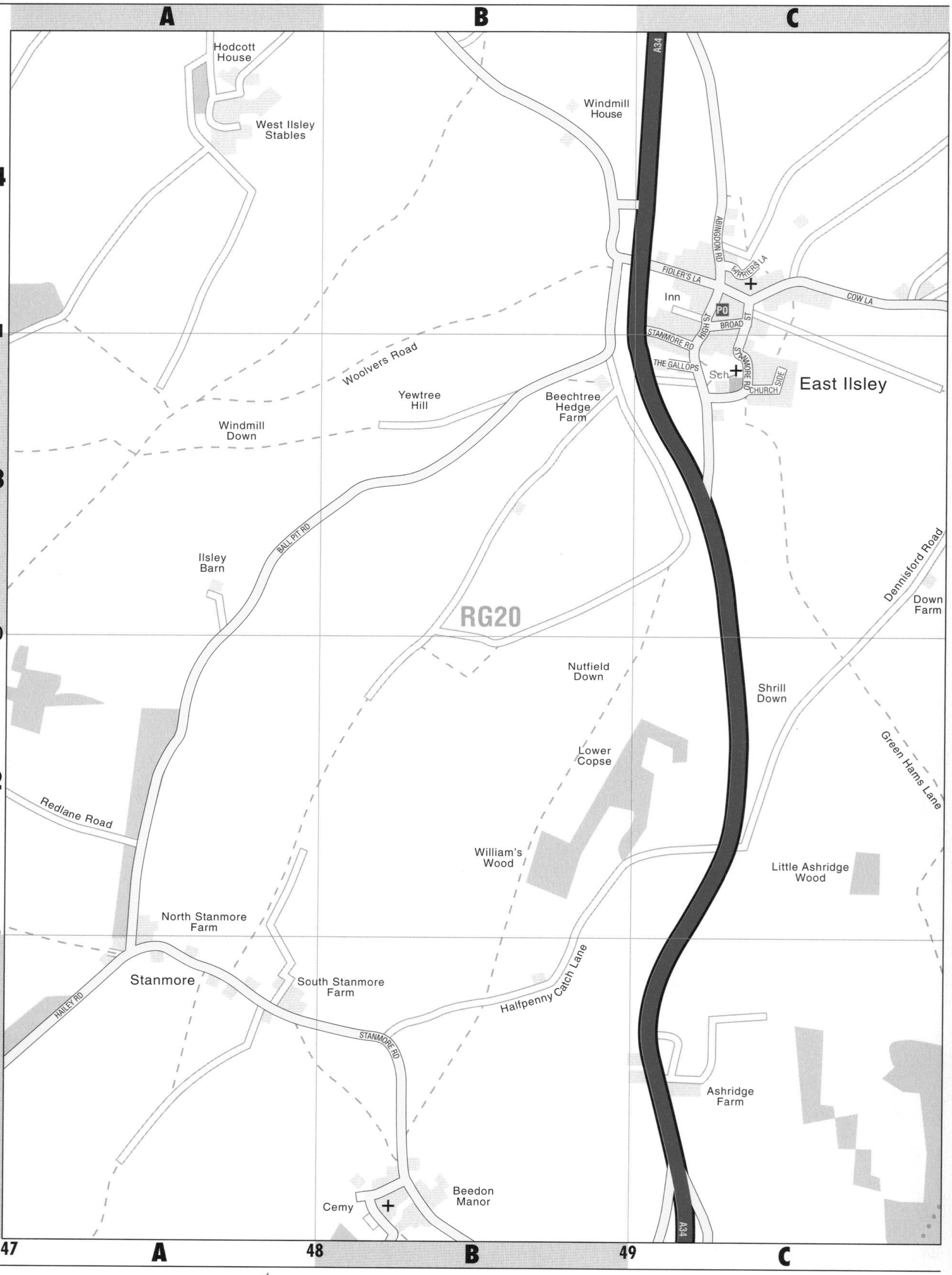
A
B
C
4
3
2
1
81
80
79
78
47
48
49
Hodcott House
West Ilsley Stables
Windmill House
A34
ABINGDON RD
FARRIERS LA
FIDLER'S LA
COW LA
Inn
PO
HIGH ST
BROAD ST
STANMORE RD
THE GALLOPS
Sch
STANMORE RD
CHURCH SIDE
East Ilsley
Woolvers Road
Yewtree Hill
Beechtree Hedge Farm
Windmill Down
BALL PIT RD
Ilsley Barn
RG20
Dennisford Road
Down Farm
Nutfield Down
Shrill Down
Green Hams Lane
Lower Copse
Redlane Road
William's Wood
Little Ashridge Wood
North Stanmore Farm
Stanmore
South Stanmore Farm
Halfpenny Catch Lane
HAILEY RD
STANMORE RD
Ashridge Farm
Beedon Manor
Cemy

29
51

11
32

A
B
C
A
B
C
4
3
2
1
81
80
79
78
50
51
52
Ilsley Barn Farm
Ridgeway
East Ilsley Down
Roden Farm
Ilsley Arch
Compton Downs
Superity Farm
Stocks Farm
Agricultural Research Station
RG20
CHURN RD
Thorndown Folly
WHITEWALLS CL
WALLINGFORD RD
HOCKHAM RD
MEADOW CL
CHEAP ST
HORN ST
YEW TREE STABLES
Hostel
COMPTON MANOR
Inn
Compton
HIGH ST
PO
OLD STATION BSNS PK
ILSLEY RD
MANOR BGLWS
Church Farm
FAIRFIELD
NEWBURY LA
WESTFIELDS
MANOR CRES
GORDON CRES
SCHOOL RD
WILSON CL
Compton CE Prim Sch
Mayfield Farm
MAYFIELD COTTS
BURRELL RD
SHEPHERDS RISE
ALDWORTH RD
CHESERIDGE RD
The Downs Sch
Recn Ctr
SHEPHERDS MOUNT
SHEPHERDS HILL
Warnham's Cottages
Cradlicote Coppice
Hawk Croft Copse
Hill Barn
Ash Close
Warnham Lane
Woodview
New Farm
COOMBE RD
Cheseridge Farm
Green Hams Lane
River Pang
Compton Crossing
Compton Wood
Cheseridge Wood
Ashridge Wood
Cow Down
Woodend Farm
RG18

52
32

31 12

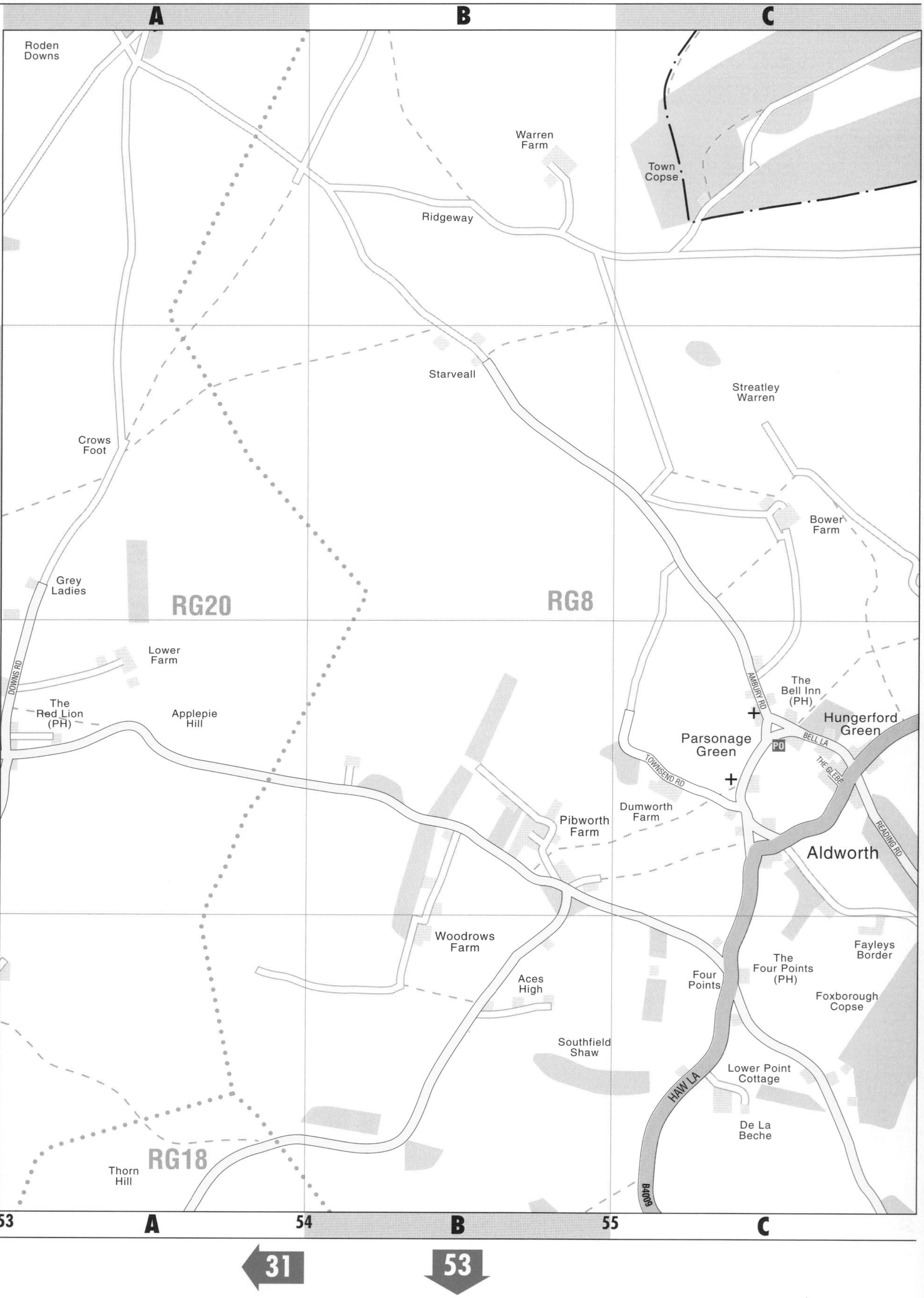
A
B
C
Roden Downs
Warren Farm
Town Copse
Ridgeway
4
81
Starveall
Streatley Warren
Crows Foot
3
Bower Farm
Grey Ladies
RG20
RG8
80
DOWNS RD
Lower Farm
The Red Lion (PH)
Applepie Hill
AMBURY RD
The Bell Inn (PH)
Hungerford Green
Parsonage Green
BELL LA
PO
2
TOWNSEND RD
THE GLEBE
Dumworth Farm
Pibworth Farm
READING RD
Aldworth
79
Woodrows Farm
Fayleys Border
The Four Points (PH)
Four Points
Aces High
Foxborough Copse
Southfield Shaw
1
HAW LA
Lower Point Cottage
De La Beche
RG18
Thorn Hill
B4009
78
53
54
55
A
B
C

31 53

13
34

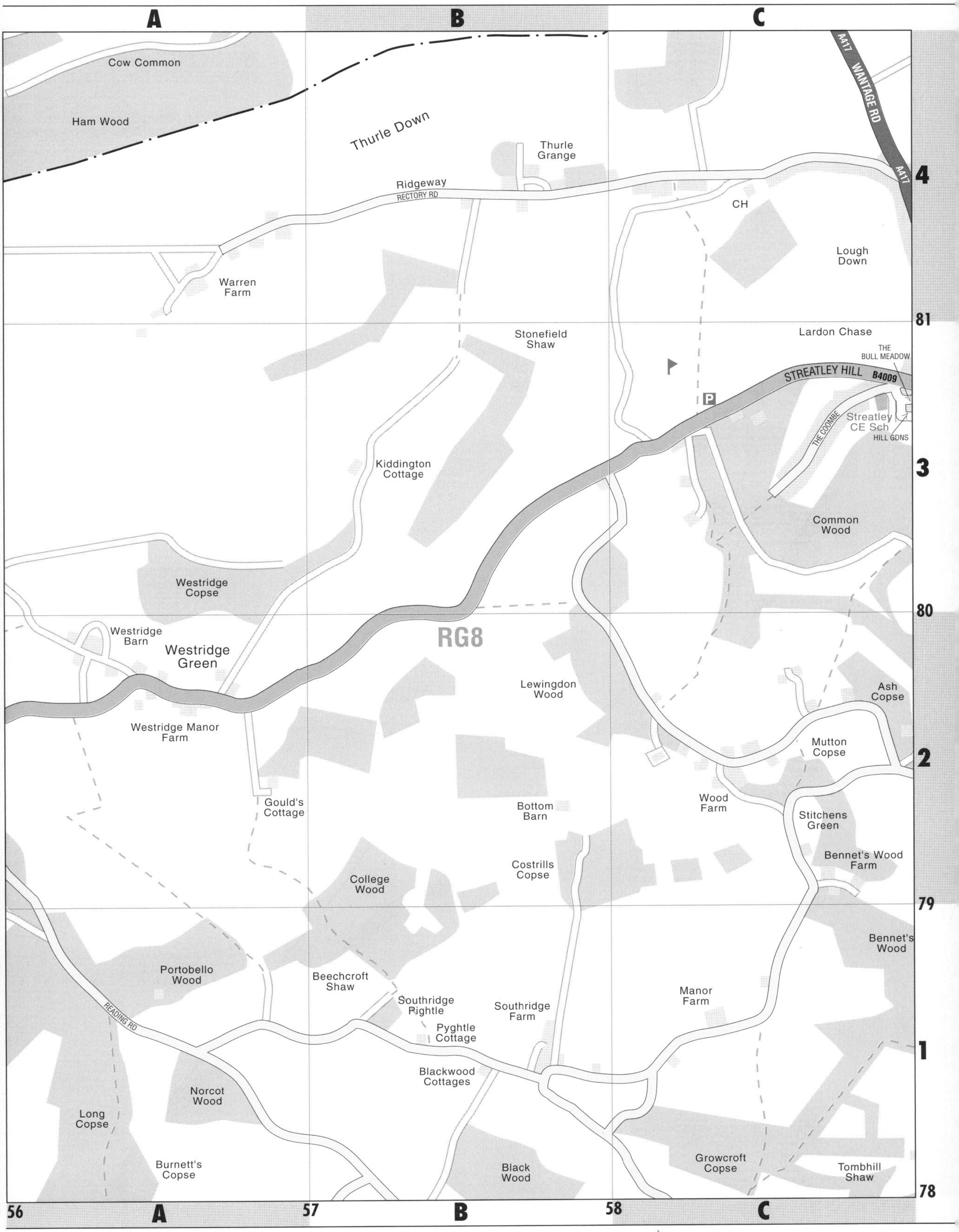
A
B
C
Cow Common
Ham Wood
Thurle Down
Thurle Grange
Ridgeway
RECTORY RD
A417
WANTAGE RD
CH
Lough Down
Warren Farm
Stonefield Shaw
Lardon Chase
THE BULL MEADOW
STREATLEY HILL
B4009
P
Streatley CE Sch
THE COOMBE
HILL GDNS
Kiddington Cottage
Common Wood
Westridge Copse
Westridge Barn
Westridge Green
RG8
Lewingdon Wood
Ash Copse
Westridge Manor Farm
Mutton Copse
Gould's Cottage
Bottom Barn
Wood Farm
Stitchens Green
Bennet's Wood Farm
Costrills Copse
College Wood
Bennet's Wood
Portobello Wood
Beechcroft Shaw
Southridge Pightle
Southridge Farm
Manor Farm
READING RD
Pyghtle Cottage
Blackwood Cottages
Norcot Wood
Long Copse
Burnett's Copse
Black Wood
Growcroft Copse
Tombhill Shaw
4
81
3
80
2
79
1
78
56
57
58

54
34

33
14

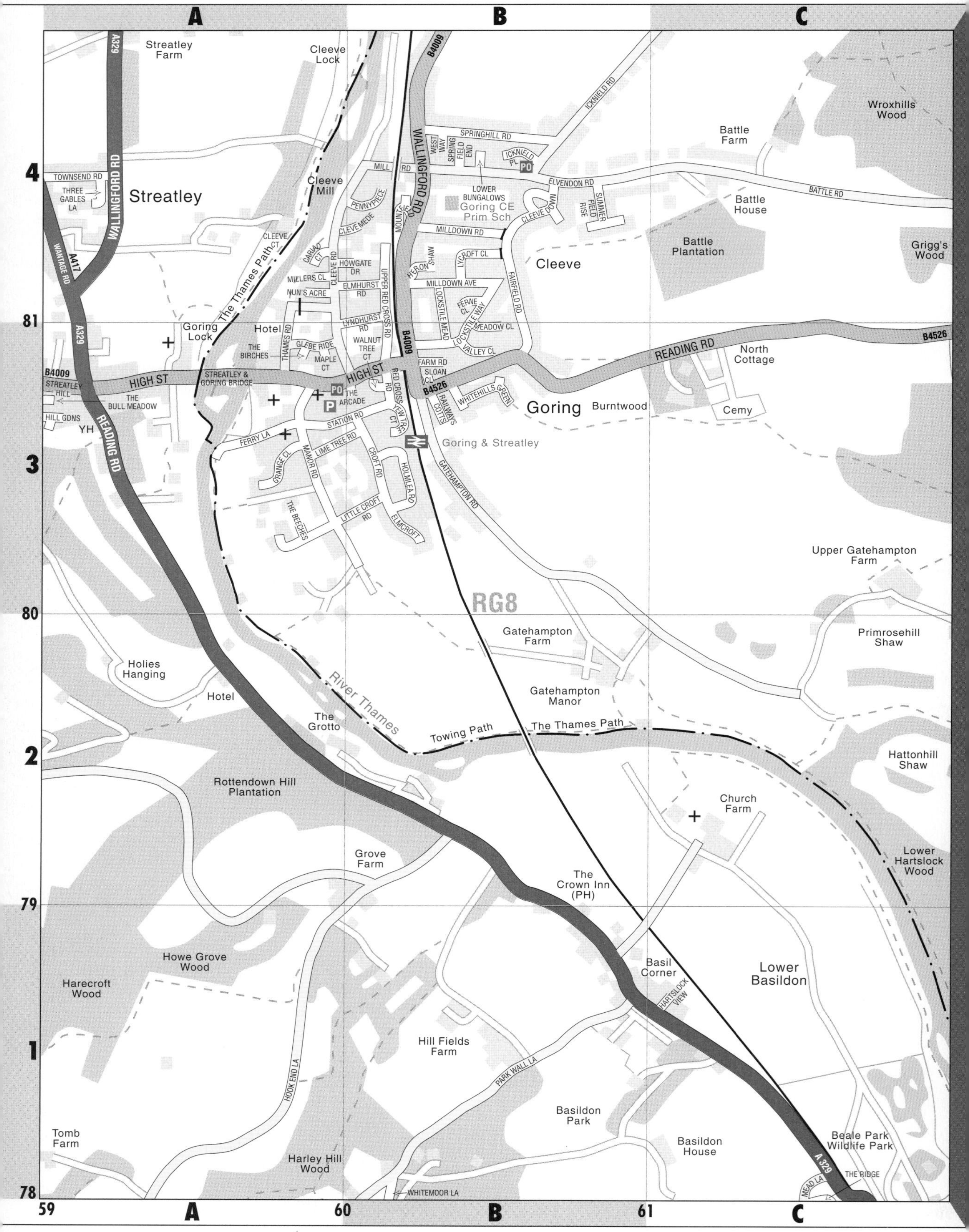
A
B
C
4
81
3
80
2
79
1
78
59
60
61
Streatley Farm
Cleeve Lock
A329
B4009
Wroxhills Wood
Battle Farm
SPRINGHILL RD
ICKNIELD RD
WEST WAY
SPRING FIELD END
ICKNIELD PL
PO
MILL RD
WALLINGFORD RD
TOWNSEND RD
THREE GABLES LA
Streatley
Cleeve Mill
LOWER BUNGALOWS
Goring CE Prim Sch
ELVENDON RD
BATTLE RD
Battle House
PENNYPIECE
CLEEVE MEDE
MOUNTFIELD
CLEEVE DOWN
FIELD RISE
SUMMER
MILLDOWN RD
Battle Plantation
Grigg's Wood
CLEEVE CT
A417
WANTAGE RD
CABIAD CT
HOWGATE DR
HERON SHAW
LYCROFT CL
Cleeve
The Thames Path
MILLERS CL
CLEEVE RD
ELMHURST RD
UPPER RED CROSS RD
MILLDOWN AVE
NUN'S ACRE
LOCKSTILE MEAD
FERNE CL
FAIRFIELD RD
LOCKSTILE WAY
LYNDHURST RD
MEADOW CL
B4526
Goring Lock
Hotel
THAMES RD
GLEBE RIDE
WALNUT TREE CT
VALLEY CL
READING RD
North Cottage
THE BIRCHES
MAPLE CT
FARM RD
SLOAN CL
STREATLEY HILL
HIGH ST
STREATLEY & GORING BRIDGE
HIGH ST
PO
THE ARCADE
RED CROSS RD
YEW TREE CT
RAILWAY COTTS
WHITEHILLS GREEN
Goring
Burntwood
Cemy
THE BULL MEADOW
P
HILL GDNS
YH
STATION RD
FERRY LA
LIME TREE RD
Goring & Streatley
GRANGE CL
MANOR RD
CROFT RD
HOLMLEA RD
GATEHAMPTON RD
THE BEECHES
LITTLE CROFT RD
ELMCROFT
Upper Gatehampton Farm
RG8
Gatehampton Farm
Primrosehill Shaw
Holies Hanging
River Thames
Gatehampton Manor
Hotel
The Grotto
Towing Path
The Thames Path
Hattonhill Shaw
Rottendown Hill Plantation
Church Farm
Grove Farm
Lower Hartslock Wood
The Crown Inn (PH)
Howe Grove Wood
Basil Corner
Lower Basildon
Harecroft Wood
HARTSLOCK VIEW
Hill Fields Farm
PARK WALL LA
HOOK END LA
Basildon Park
Tomb Farm
Basildon House
Beale Park Wildlife Park
Harley Hill Wood
A329
THE RIDGE
MEAD LA
WHITEMOOR LA

33
55

15
36

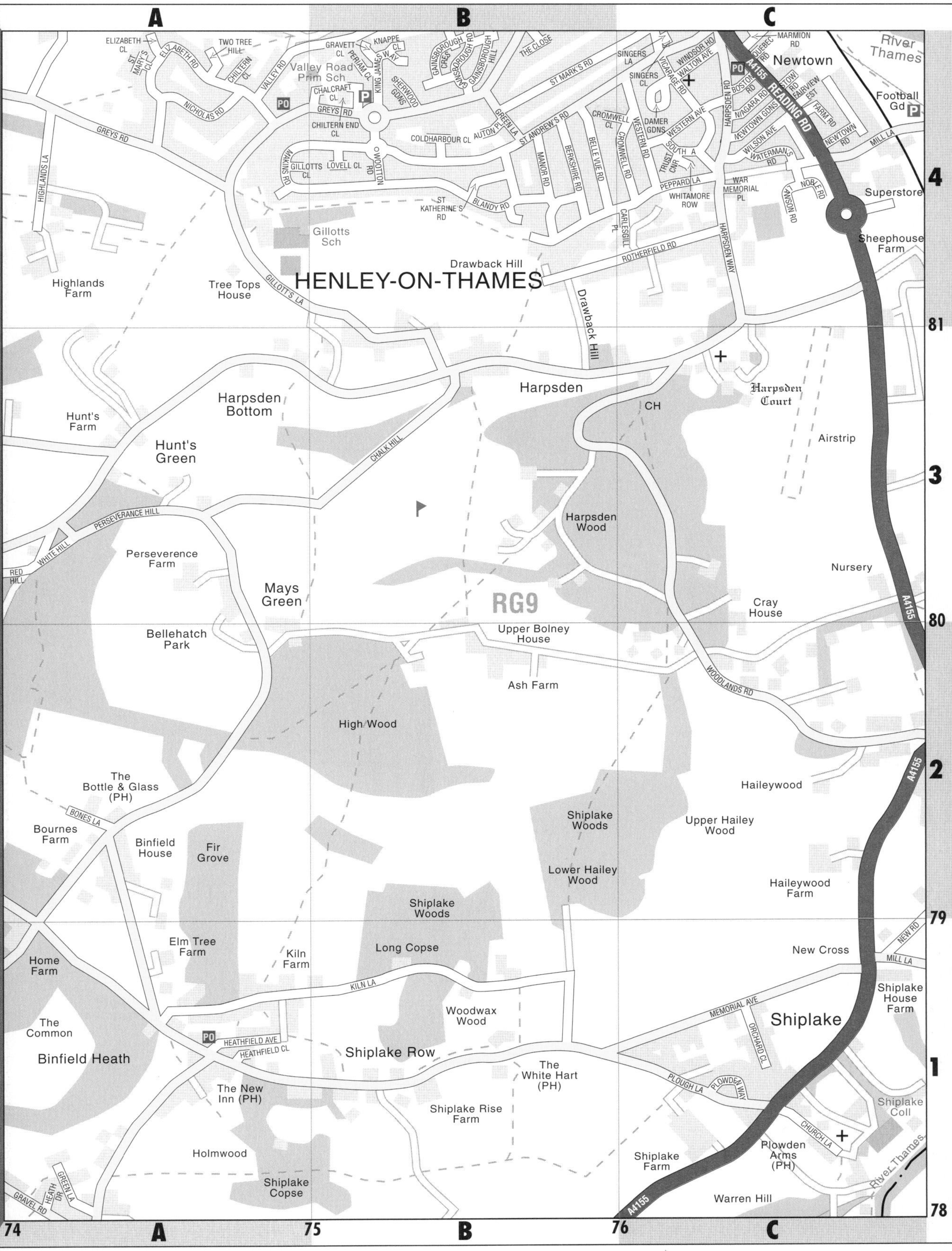
A
B
C
HENLEY-ON-THAMES
Newtown
River Thames
Football Gd
Valley Road Prim Sch
Gillotts Sch
Highlands Farm
Tree Tops House
Drawback Hill
Superstore
Sheephouse Farm
Harpsden
Harpsden Court
CH
Airstrip
Harpsden Bottom
Hunt's Farm
Hunt's Green
Harpsden Wood
Perseverence Farm
Mays Green
Nursery
RG9
Cray House
Bellehatch Park
Upper Bolney House
Ash Farm
High Wood
The Bottle & Glass (PH)
Haileywood
Bournes Farm
Binfield House
Fir Grove
Shiplake Woods
Upper Hailey Wood
Lower Hailey Wood
Haileywood Farm
Elm Tree Farm
Kiln Farm
Long Copse
New Cross
Home Farm
Shiplake House Farm
Woodwax Wood
Shiplake
The Common
Binfield Heath
Shiplake Row
The White Hart (PH)
The New Inn (PH)
Shiplake Rise Farm
Shiplake Coll
Holmwood
Shiplake Farm
Plowden Arms (PH)
Shiplake Copse
Warren Hill
ELIZABETH CL
ST MARY'S CL
ELIZABETH RD
TWO TREE HILL
CHILTERN CL
VALLEY RD
NICHOLAS RD
GRAVETT CL
KNAPPE CL
KING JAMES WAY
PERIAM CL
GAINSBOROUGH CRES
GAINSBOROUGH RD
GAINSBOROUGH HILL
THE CLOSE
ST MARK'S RD
SINGERS LA
SINGERS CL
WINDSOR HO
WALTON AVE
VICARAGE RD
MARMION RD
QUEBEC RD
A4155 READING RD
CHALCRAFT CL
GREYS RD
SHERWOOD GDNS
CHILTERN END CL
GREEN LA
AUTON PL
COLDHARBOUR CL
ST ANDREW'S RD
CROMWELL CL
DAMER GDNS
WESTERN AVE
HARPSDEN RD
BOSTON RD
NIAGARA RD
NEWTOWN GDNS
FAIRVIEW EST
FARM RD
NEWTOWN RD
MILL LA
WILSON AVE
WATERMAN'S RD
MAKINS RD
GILLOTTS CL
LOVELL CL
WOOTTON RD
MANOR RD
BERKSHIRE RD
BELLE VUE RD
CROMWELL RD
WESTERN RD
TRUST CNR
SOUTH AVE
PEPPARD LA
WHITAMORE ROW
WAR MEMORIAL PL
NOBLE RD
LAWSON RD
HIGHLANDS LA
ST KATHERINE'S RD
BLANDY RD
CARLESGILL PL
HARPSDEN WAY
ROTHERFIELD RD
GILLOTT'S LA
CHALK HILL
PERSEVERANCE HILL
WHITE HILL
RED HILL
WOODLANDS RD
A4155
BONES LA
NEW RD
MILL LA
KILN LA
MEMORIAL AVE
ORCHARD CL
HEATHFIELD AVE
HEATHFIELD CL
PLOUGH LA
PLOWDEN WAY
CHURCH LA
GRAVEL RD
HEATH DR
GREEN LA
PO
P
74
75
76
78
79
80
81
1
2
3
4

60
36

35
16

A B C

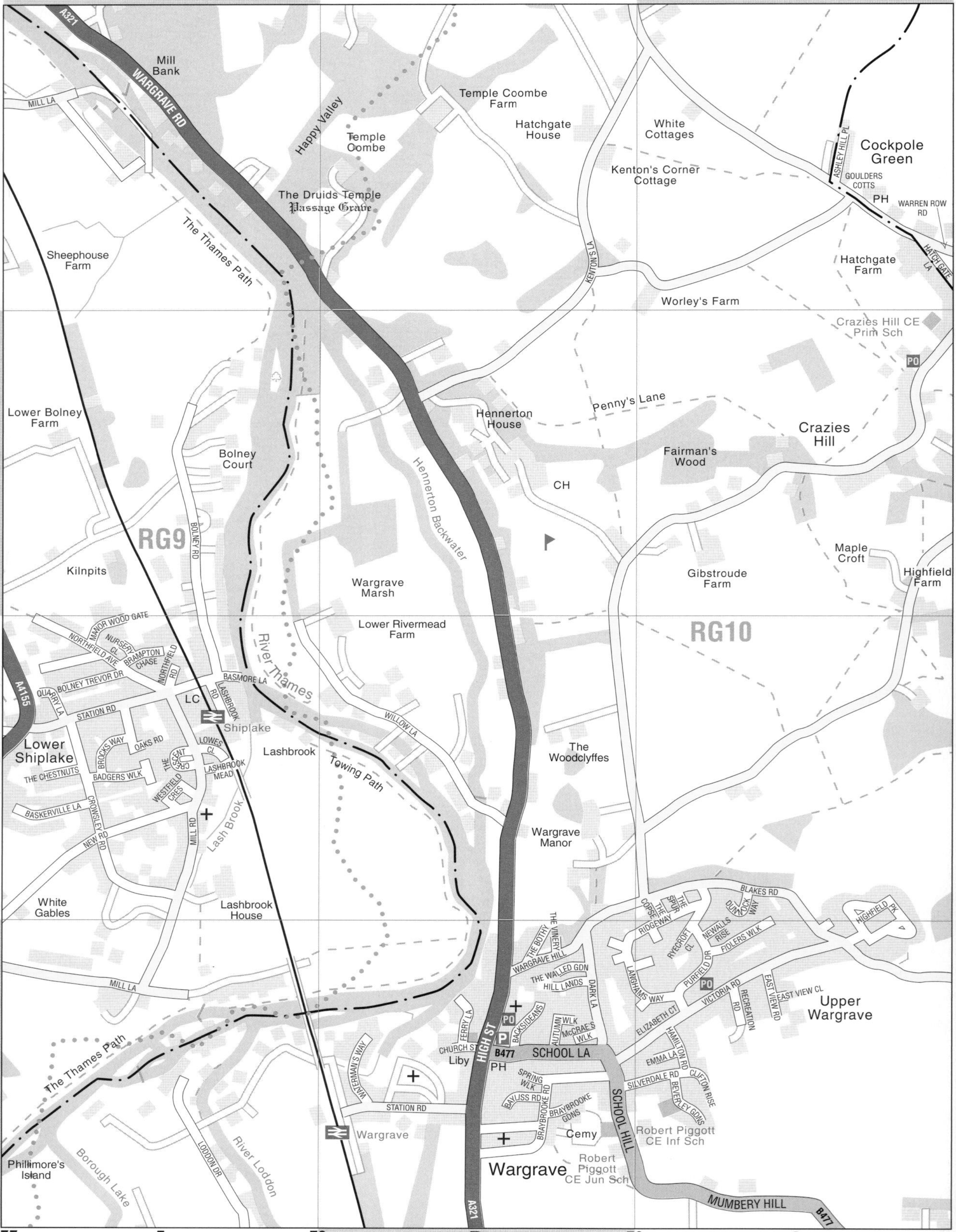


4
81
3
80
2
79
1
78

77 A 78 B 79 C

35
61

17
38

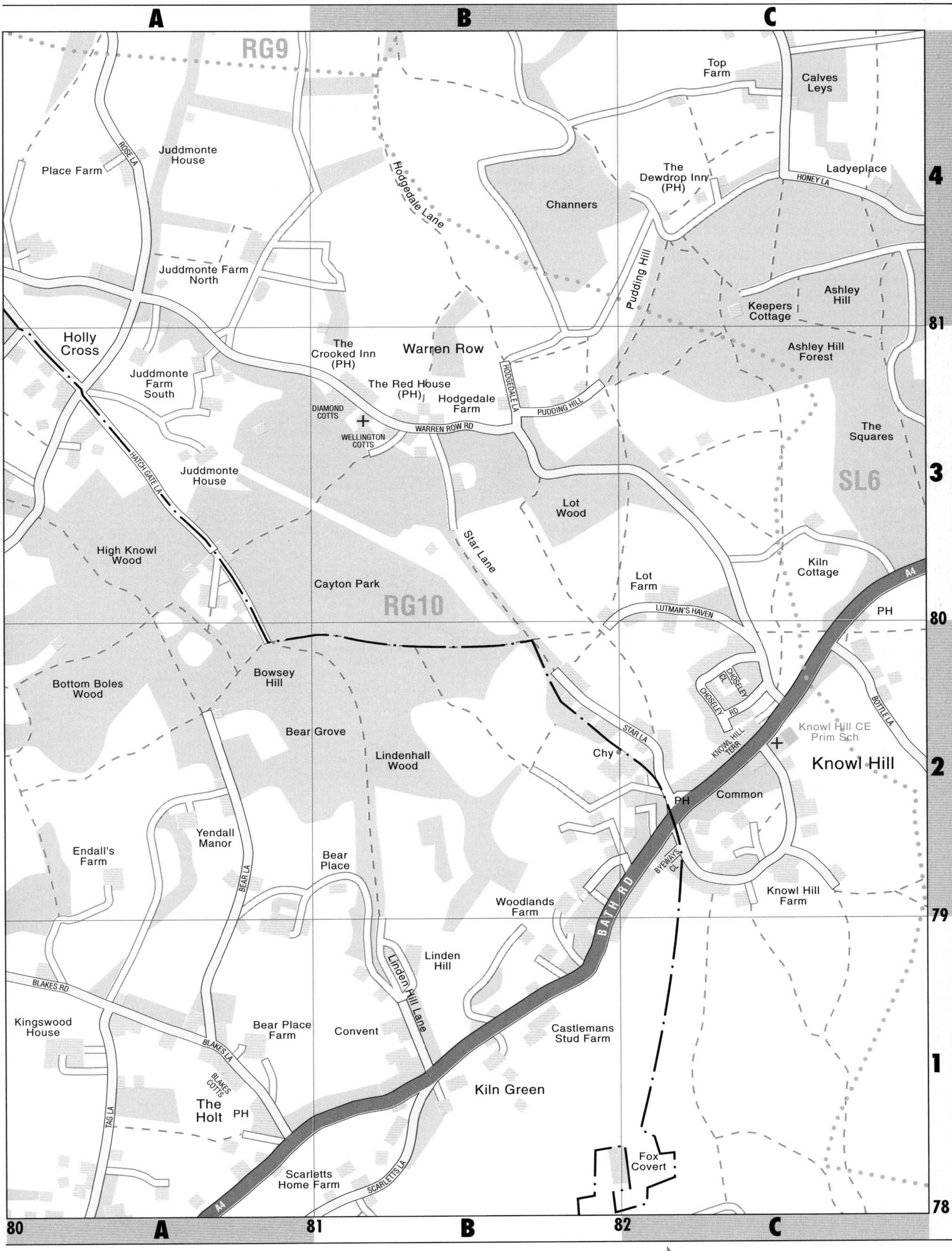
A
B
C
RG9
RG10
SL6
Place Farm
Juddmonte House
Rose La
Juddmonte Farm North
Holly Cross
Juddmonte Farm South
Juddmonte House
Hatch Gate La
High Knowl Wood
Bottom Boles Wood
Bowsey Hill
Bear Grove
Endall's Farm
Yendall Manor
Bear La
Bear Place
Kingswood House
Blakes Rd
Blakes La
Blakes Cotts
Tag La
The Holt
PH
Bear Place Farm
Convent
Scarletts Home Farm
Scarletts La
A4
Hodgedale Lane
The Crooked Inn (PH)
Warren Row
The Red House (PH)
Diamond Cotts
Wellington Cotts
Warren Row Rd
Hodgedale Farm
Hodgedale La
Pudding Hill
Star Lane
Cayton Park
Lindenhall Wood
Linden Hill
Linden Hill Lane
Woodlands Farm
Bath Rd
Kiln Green
Castlemans Stud Farm
Fox Covert
Channers
The Dewdrop Inn (PH)
Top Farm
Calves Leys
Ladyeplace
Honey La
Keepers Cottage
Ashley Hill
Ashley Hill Forest
The Squares
Lot Wood
Lot Farm
Lutman's Haven
Kiln Cottage
Choseley Cl
Choseley Rd
Knowl Hill Terr
Star La
Chy
PH
Common
Byeways Cl
Knowl Hill CE Prim Sch
Knowl Hill
Bottle La
Knowl Hill Farm
4
81
3
80
2
79
1
78
80
81
82

62
38

37
18

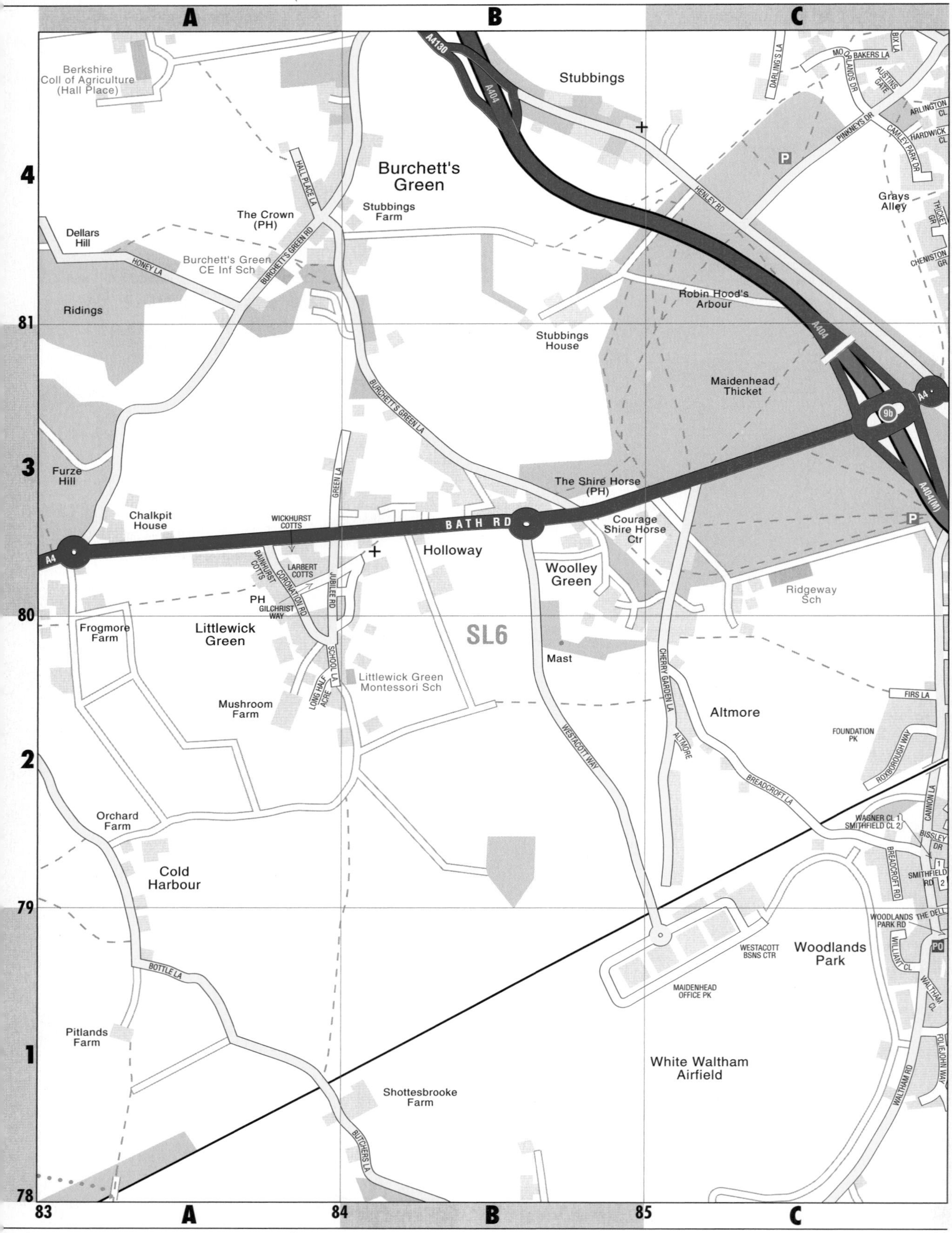
A
B
C
4
3
2
1
81
80
79
78
83
84
85
Berkshire Coll of Agriculture (Hall Place)
Stubbings
A4130
A404
Burchett's Green
HALL PLACE LA
The Crown (PH)
Stubbings Farm
Dellars Hill
HONEY LA
Burchett's Green CE Inf Sch
BURCHETT'S GREEN RD
Ridings
HENLEY RD
Robin Hood's Arbour
Stubbings House
Maidenhead Thicket
DARLING'S LA
MOORLANDS DR
BAKERS LA
BIX LA
AUSTINS GATE
PINKNEYS DR
ARLINGTON CL
CAMLEY PARK DR
HARDWICK CL
Grays Alley
THICKET GR
CHENISTON GR
P
9b
A4
A404(M)
BURCHETT'S GREEN LA
Furze Hill
GREEN LA
The Shire Horse (PH)
Chalkpit House
WICKHURST COTTS
BATH RD
Courage Shire Horse Ctr
Holloway
Woolley Green
BARNHURST COTTS
LARBERT COTTS
CORONATION RD
JUBILEE RD
PH
GILCHRIST WAY
Ridgeway Sch
Frogmore Farm
Littlewick Green
SL6
SCHOOL LA
Mast
LONG HALF ACRE
Littlewick Green Montessori Sch
CHERRY GARDEN LA
FIRS LA
Mushroom Farm
Altmore
ALTMORE
FOUNDATION PK
ROXBOROUGH WAY
WESTACOTT WAY
BREADCROFT LA
CANNON LA
Orchard Farm
WAGNER CL 1
SMITHFIELD CL 2
BISSLEY DR
BREADCROFT RD
SMITHFIELD RD
Cold Harbour
WOODLANDS PARK RD
THE DELL
WESTACOTT BSNS CTR
Woodlands Park
PO
WILLIANT CL
MAIDENHEAD OFFICE PK
WALTHAM CL
BOTTLE LA
Pitlands Farm
FOLIEJOHN WAY
White Waltham Airfield
WALTHAM RD
Shottesbrooke Farm
BUTCHERS LA

37
63

19

40

C4
1 HIGH ST MALL
2 WHITE HART RD
3 QUEENS WLK MALL
4 KINGS WLK
5 NICHOLSONS CTR
6 BROADWAY MALL
7 BROCK LA MALL
8 QUEEN'S LA
9 REGENT CT
10 OLD POST OFFICE LA

64

40

39
20

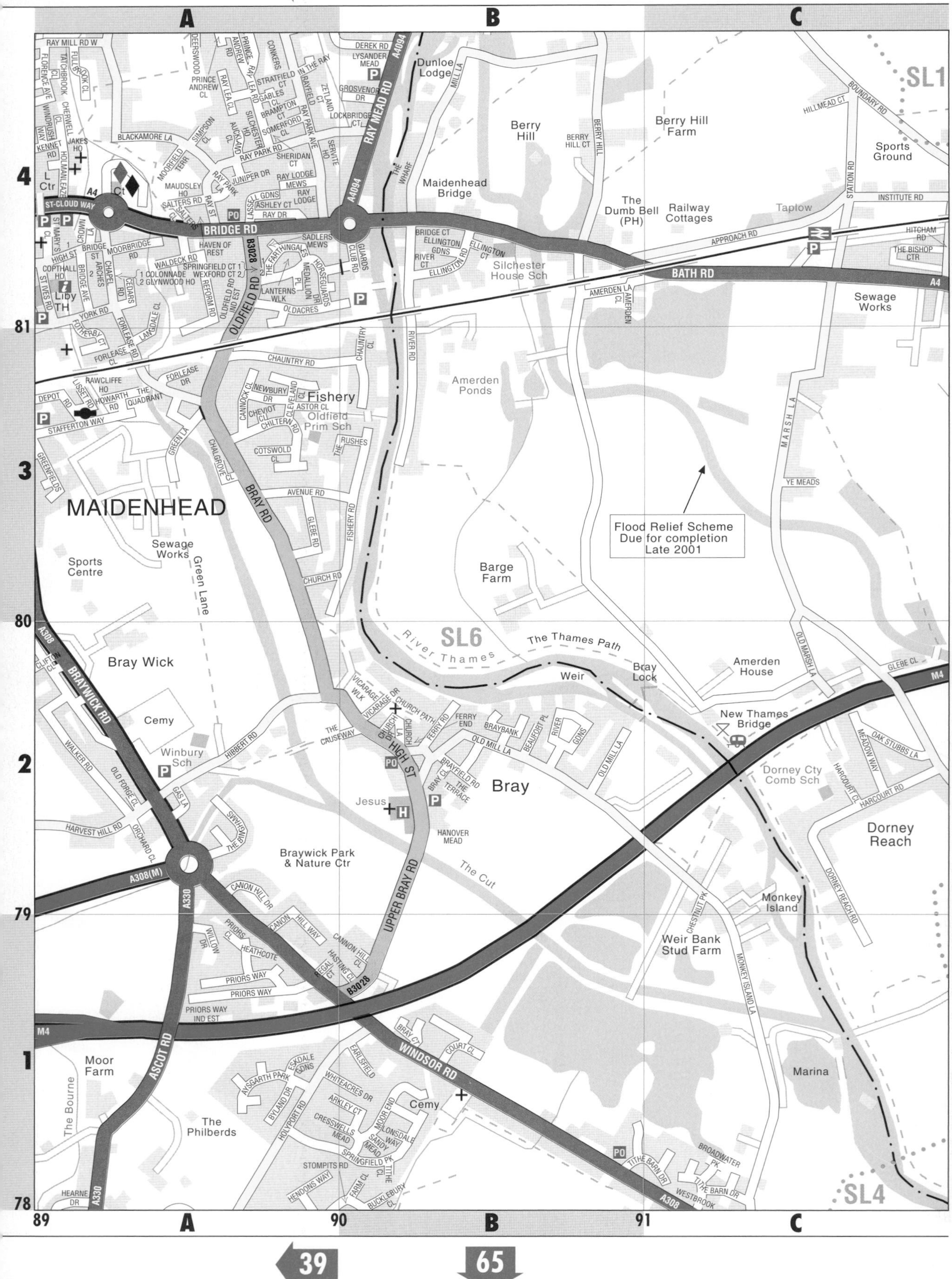
A
B
C
4
3
2
1
81
80
79
78
89
90
91
MAIDENHEAD
SL1
SL6
SL4
Berry Hill
Berry Hill Farm
Sports Ground
Maidenhead Bridge
The Dumb Bell (PH)
Railway Cottages
Taplow
Dunloe Lodge
BRIDGE RD
BATH RD
RAY MEAD RD
A4094
A4
B3028
ST-CLOUD WAY
BLACKAMORE LA
OLDFIELD RD
BRAY RD
Silchester House Sch
Sewage Works
Amerden Ponds
Fishery
Oldfield Prim Sch
Flood Relief Scheme
Due for completion
Late 2001
Barge Farm
Sports Centre
Green Lane
River Thames
The Thames Path
Weir
Bray Lock
Amerden House
New Thames Bridge
Bray Wick
BRAYWICK RD
A308
Cemy
Winbury Sch
HIGH ST
Bray
Jesus
Dorney Cty Comb Sch
Dorney Reach
Braywick Park & Nature Ctr
The Cut
UPPER BRAY RD
A308(M)
A330
Monkey Island
Weir Bank Stud Farm
MONKEY ISLAND LA
M4
Moor Farm
ASCOT RD
WINDSOR RD
The Bourne
The Philberds
Marina
Liby
TH
L Ctr

39
65

C3
1 SHERIDAN CT
2 SELWYN PL
3 BOWER CT
4 LEWINS FARM CT
5 WATERMAN CT
6 BIDDLES CL
7 MOLYNS MEWS

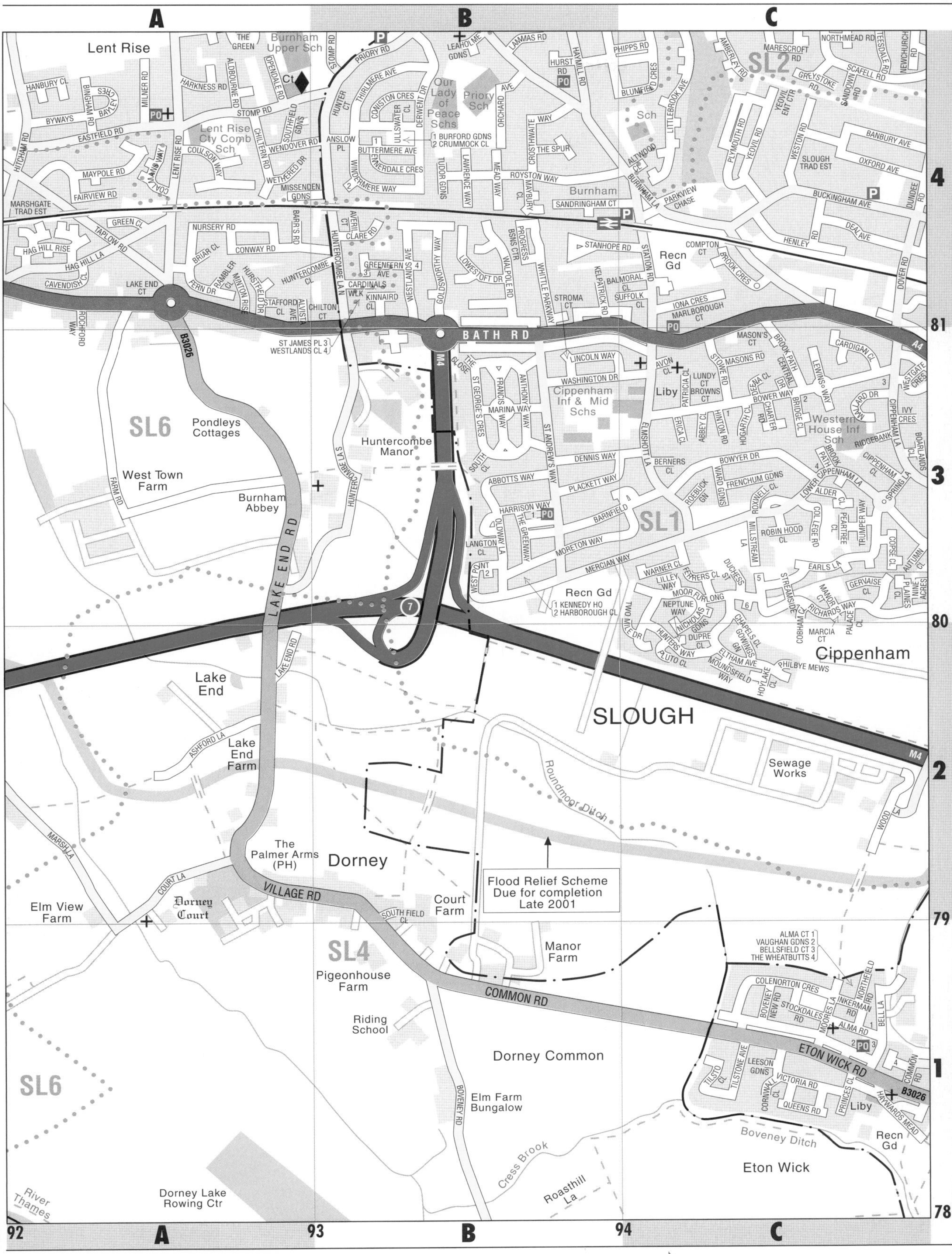

41
22

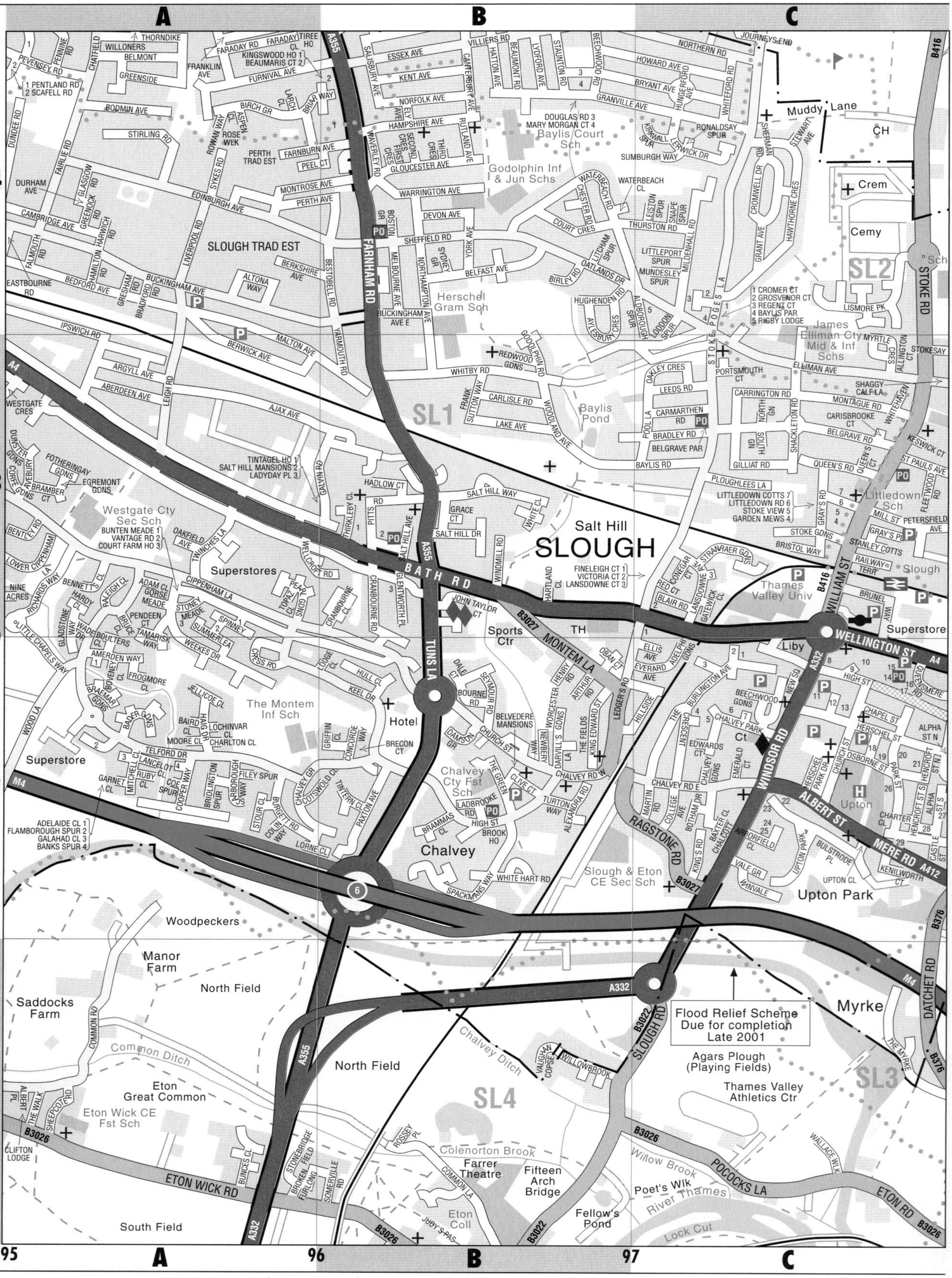


C2
1 BURLINGTON CT
2 BURLINGTON RD
3 HILPERTON RD
4 TOWER HO
5 ASHBOURNE HO
6 SHAFTESBURY CT
7 MOORSTOWN CT
8 PRUDENTIAL BLDGS
9 MACKENZIE ST
10 MACKENZIE MALL
11 OLD CROWN
12 BUCKINGHAM GDNS
13 THE VILLAGE SH CTR
14 LEOPOLD MALL
15 CURZON MALL
16 CHANDOS MALL
17 TOWN SQ
18 VICTORIA ST
19 BISHAM CT
20 BEMBRIDGE CT
21 STEPHENSON CT
22 ETON WLK
23 ST ANDREWS CT
24 LINCOLN CT
25 LOCKSLEY CT
26 SPRUCE CT
27 DARTMOUTH CT
28 ALBERT CL
29 MANOR CT

41
67

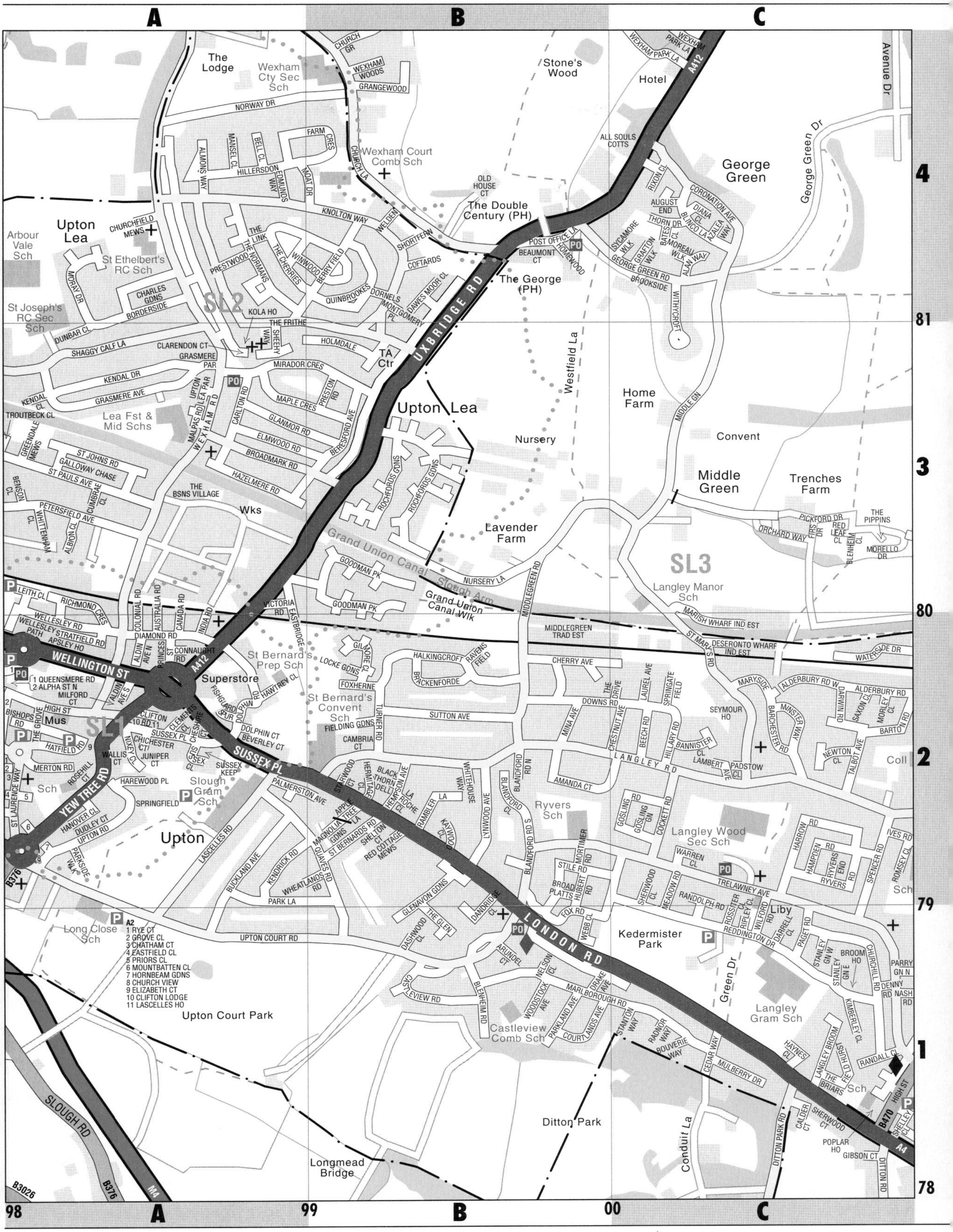
A
B
C
The Lodge
Wexham Cty Sec Sch
Stone's Wood
Hotel
NORWAY DR
Wexham Court Comb Sch
George Green
Upton Lea
Arbour Vale Sch
St Ethelbert's RC Sch
St Joseph's RC Sec Sch
The Double Century (PH)
The George (PH)
UXBRIDGE RD
A412
SL2
Westfield La
Home Farm
Convent
Middle Green
Trenches Farm
Lea Fst & Mid Schs
Nursery
Lavender Farm
THE BSNS VILLAGE
Wks
Grand Union Canal
Slough Arm
Grand Union Canal Wlk
SL3
Langley Manor Sch
MIDDLEGREEN TRAD EST
WELLINGTON ST
Superstore
St Bernard's Prep Sch
St Bernard's Convent Sch
Mus
SL1
SUSSEX PL
Slough Gram Sch
YEW TREE RD
Upton
Ryvers Sch
Langley Wood Sec Sch
LANGLEY RD
LONDON RD
Kedermister Park
Liby
Long Close Sch
A2
1 RYE CT
2 GROVE CL
3 CHATHAM CT
4 EASTFIELD CL
5 PRIORS CL
6 MOUNTBATTEN CL
7 HORNBEAM GDNS
8 CHURCH VIEW
9 ELIZABETH CT
10 CLIFTON LODGE
11 LASCELLES HO
Upton Court Park
Castleview Comb Sch
Langley Gram Sch
Green Dr
Ditton Park
Conduit La
Longmead Bridge
SLOUGH RD
B3026
B376
M4
B470
A4
Coll
4
81
3
80
2
79
1
78
98
99
00

43

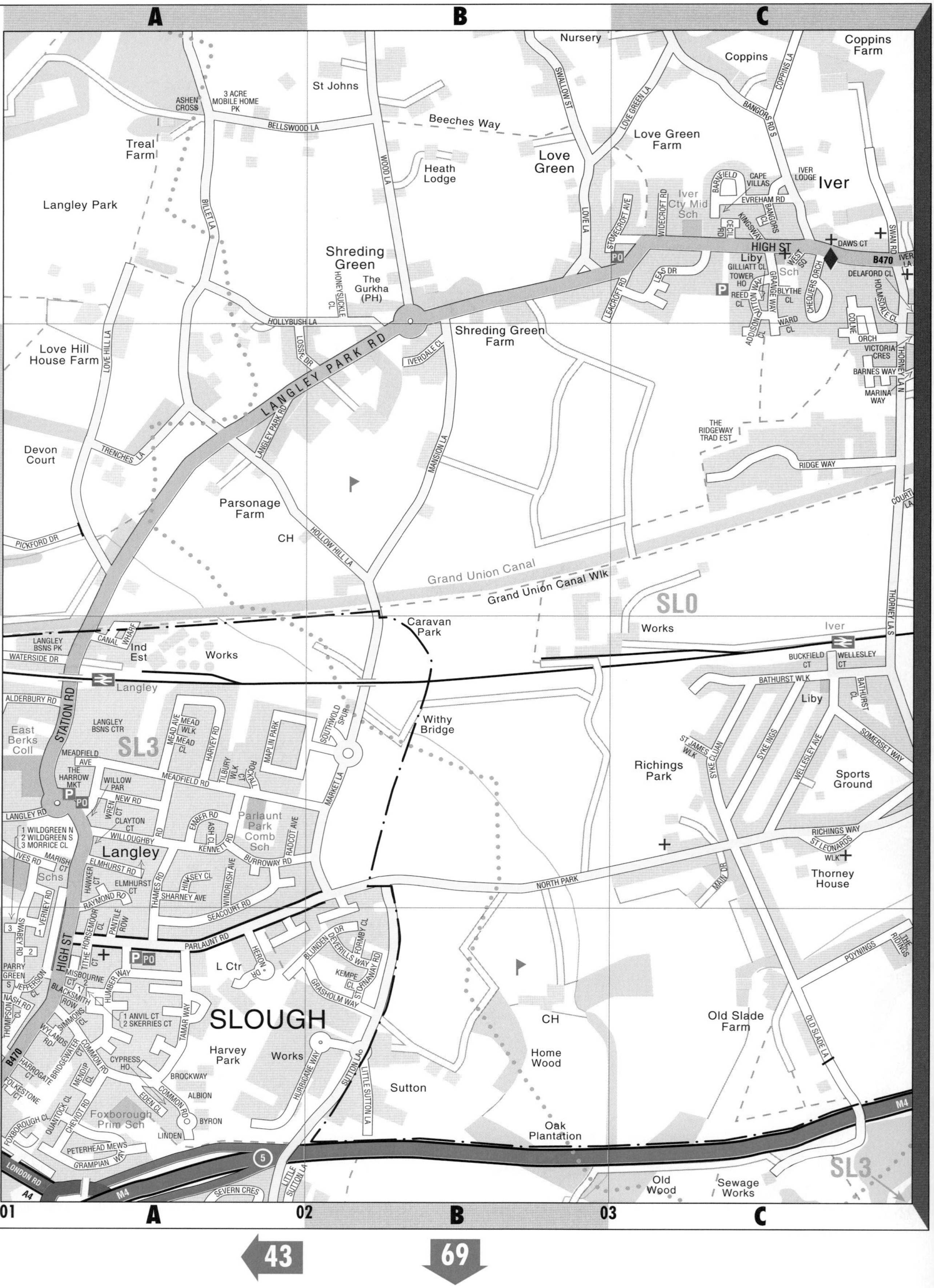
A
B
C
4
3
2
1
81
80
79
78
01
02
03
Nursery
Coppins
Coppins Farm
COPPINS LA
St Johns
ASHEN CROSS
3 ACRE MOBILE HOME PK
BELLSWOOD LA
Beeches Way
SWALLOW ST
LOVE GREEN LA
BANGORS RD S
Love Green Farm
Treal Farm
WOOD LA
Heath Lodge
Love Green
Iver
IVER LODGE
CAPE VILLAS
BARNFIELD
EVREHAM RD
Iver Cty Mid Sch
Langley Park
BILLET LA
STONECROFT AVE
WIDECROFT RD
LOVE LA
KINGSWAY
BANGORS CL
CECIL RD
HIGH ST
DAWS CT
SWAN RD
B470
IVER LA
Shreding Green
The Gurkha (PH)
HONEYSUCKLE CL
LEAS DR
LEACROFT RD
Liby
GILLIATT CL
TOWER HO
WEST SQ
Sch
DELAFORD CL
HOLMSDALE CL
REED CL
GRANGE WAY
BLYTHE CL
CHEQUERS ORCH
LUTTON WAY
ADDISON CL
WARD CL
COLNE ORCH
VICTORIA CRES
BARNES WAY
MARINA WAY
THORNEY LA N
HOLLYBUSH LA
Love Hill House Farm
LOVE HILL LANE
LANGLEY PARK RD
LOSSIE DR
IVERDALE CL
Shreding Green Farm
Devon Court
TRENCHES LA
LANGLEY PARK RD
MANSION LA
THE RIDGEWAY TRAD EST
RIDGE WAY
COURT LA
Parsonage Farm
CH
HOLLOW HILL LA
PICKFORD DR
Grand Union Canal
Grand Union Canal Wlk
SL0
THORNEY LA S
Caravan Park
Works
Iver
LANGLEY BSNS PK
CANAL WHARF
Ind Est
WATERSIDE DR
Works
BUCKFIELD CT
WELLESLEY CT
BATHURST WLK
BATHURST CL
Langley
ALDERBURY RD
STATION RD
Withy Bridge
Liby
SOMERSET WAY
East Berks Coll
LANGLEY BSNS CTR
SL3
MEAD AVE
MEAD WLK
MEAD CL
HARVEY RD
MAPLIN PARK
SOUTHWOLD SPUR
ST JAMES WLK
SYKE CLUAN
SYKE INGS
WELLESLEY AVE
MEADFIELD AVE
THE HARROW MKT
WILLOW PAR
MEADFIELD RD
TILBURY WLK
ROCKALL CT
MARKET LA
Richings Park
Sports Ground
NEW RD
WREN CT
CLAYTON CT
LANGLEY RD
EMBER RD
ASH CL
Parlaunt Park Comb Sch
RADCOT AVE
1 WILDGREEN N
2 WILDGREEN S
3 MORRICE CL
WILLOUGHBY RD
KENNETT RD
RICHINGS WAY
ST LEONARDS WLK
Langley
IVES RD
MARISH CT
ELMHURST RD
BURROWAY RD
Schs
HAWKER CT
ELMHURST CT
HINSEY CL
SHARNEY AVE
WINDRUSH AVE
NORTH PARK
MAIN DR
Thorney House
VERNEY RD
RAYMOND RD
THAMES RD
SEACOURT RD
HORSEMOOR CL
PANTILE ROW
SWABEY RD
HIGH ST
PARLAUNT RD
BLUNDEN DR
DEVERILLS WAY
FORMBY CL
THE RIDINGS
POYNINGS
PARRY GREEN S
TITHE CT
JEFFERSON CL
MISBOURNE CT
HUMBER WAY
L Ctr
HERON DR
KEMPE CL
STOPHAM WAY
NASH RD
BLACKSMITH ROW
GRASHOLM WAY
THOMPSON CL
SIMMONDS CL
1 ANVIL CT
2 SKERRIES CT
TAMAR WAY
SLOUGH
CH
Old Slade Farm
OLD SLADE LA
WYLANDS RD
BRIDGEWATER CT
COMMON RD
B470
HARROGATE CT
Harvey Park
Works
HURRICANE WAY
SUTTON LA
LITTLE SUTTON LA
Home Wood
CYPRESS HO
BROCKWAY
Sutton
MENDIP CL
FOLKESTONE CT
EDEN CL
ALBION
COMMON RD
QUANTOCK CL
CHEVIOT RD
Foxborough Prim Sch
BYRON
Oak Plantation
M4
FOXBOROUGH CL
LINDEN
PETERHEAD MEWS
GRAMPIAN WAY
5
SL3
LONDON RD
A4
M4
SEVERN CRES
LITTLE SUTTON LA
Old Wood
Sewage Works

43

69

24
46

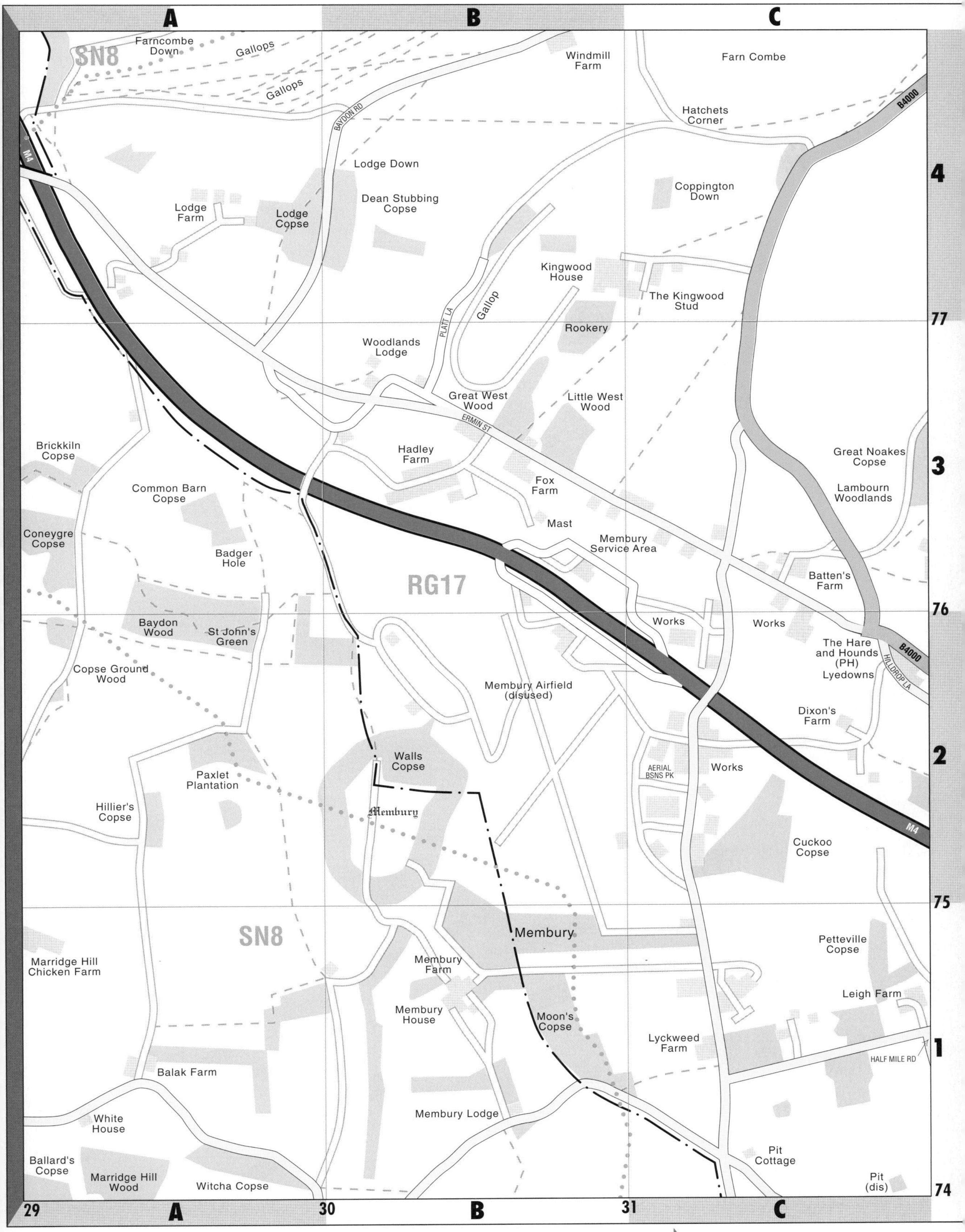
A
B
C
SN8
Farncombe Down
Gallops
Gallops
Windmill Farm
Farn Combe
Hatchets Corner
B4000
M4
BAYDON RD
Lodge Down
Dean Stubbing Copse
Coppington Down
Lodge Farm
Lodge Copse
Kingwood House
The Kingwood Stud
Gallop
PLATT LA
Rookery
Woodlands Lodge
Great West Wood
Little West Wood
ERMIN ST
Brickkiln Copse
Hadley Farm
Fox Farm
Great Noakes Copse
Common Barn Copse
Lambourn Woodlands
Mast
Coneygre Copse
Membury Service Area
Badger Hole
RG17
Batten's Farm
Baydon Wood
St John's Green
Works
Works
The Hare and Hounds (PH)
Lyedowns
B4000
HILLDROP LA
Copse Ground Wood
Membury Airfield (disused)
Dixon's Farm
Walls Copse
AERIAL BSNS PK
Works
Paxlet Plantation
Hillier's Copse
Membury
Cuckoo Copse
M4
SN8
Membury
Petteville Copse
Marridge Hill Chicken Farm
Membury Farm
Leigh Farm
Membury House
Moon's Copse
Lyckweed Farm
HALF MILE RD
Balak Farm
White House
Membury Lodge
Ballard's Copse
Marridge Hill Wood
Witcha Copse
Pit Cottage
Pit (dis)
4
77
3
76
2
75
1
74
29
A
30
B
31
C

72
46

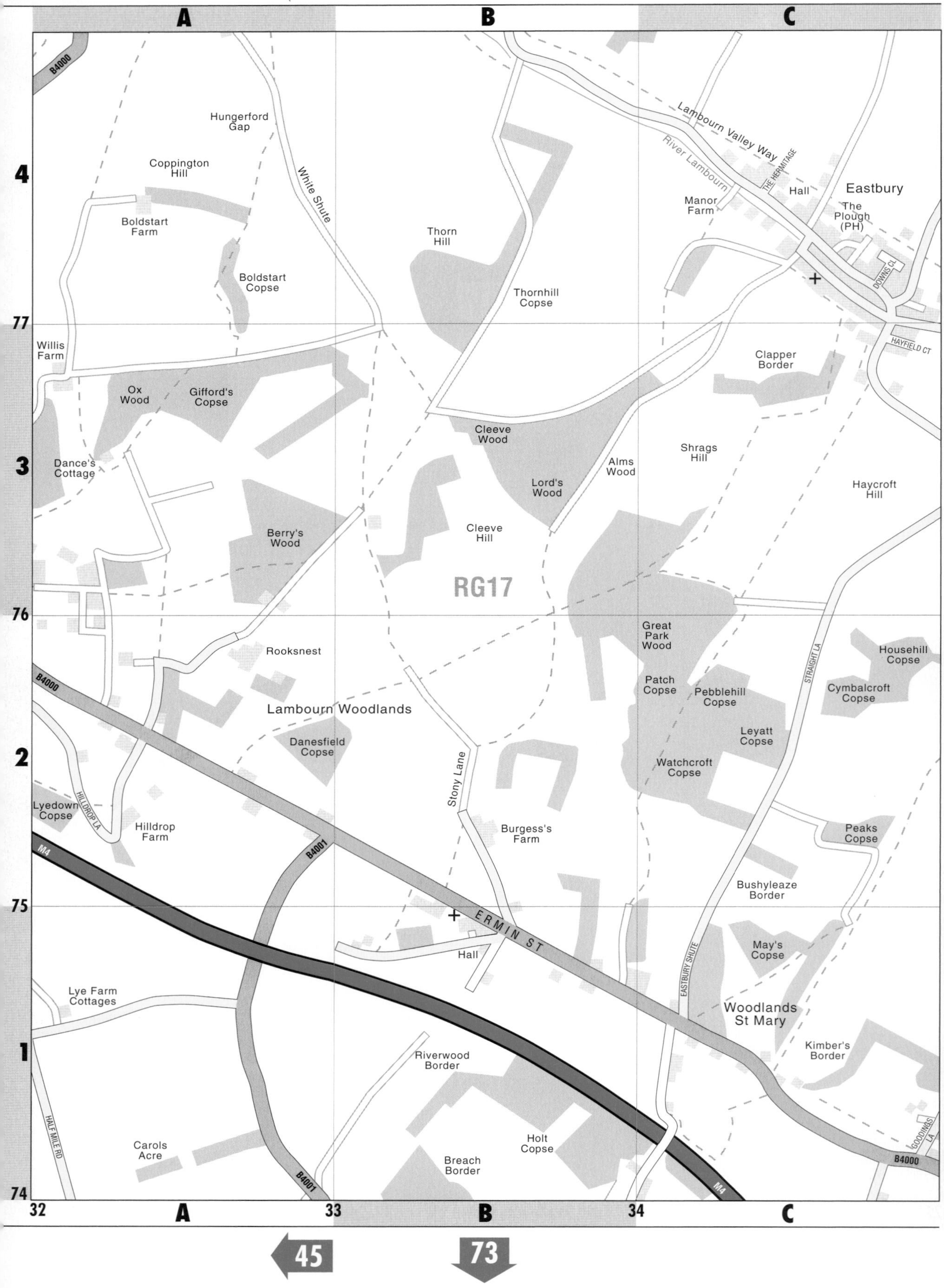
A
B
C
4
77
3
76
2
75
1
74
32
33
34
B4000
Hungerford Gap
Coppington Hill
White Shute
Boldstart Farm
Boldstart Copse
Thorn Hill
Thornhill Copse
Lambourn Valley Way
River Lambourn
THE HERMITAGE
Hall
Eastbury
Manor Farm
The Plough (PH)
DOWNS CL
HAYFIELD CT
Willis Farm
Ox Wood
Gifford's Copse
Clapper Border
Cleeve Wood
Dance's Cottage
Shrags Hill
Alms Wood
Lord's Wood
Haycroft Hill
Berry's Wood
Cleeve Hill
RG17
Great Park Wood
Rooksnest
Househill Copse
Patch Copse
Pebblehill Copse
Cymbalcroft Copse
STRAIGHT LA
Lambourn Woodlands
Danesfield Copse
Leyatt Copse
Stony Lane
Watchcroft Copse
HILLDROP LA
Lyedown Copse
Hilldrop Farm
Burgess's Farm
Peaks Copse
M4
B4001
Bushyleaze Border
ERMIN ST
May's Copse
Hall
EASTBURY SHUTE
Lye Farm Cottages
Woodlands St Mary
Kimber's Border
Riverwood Border
HALF MILE RD
GOODINGS LA
Holt Copse
Carols Acre
Breach Border

26
48

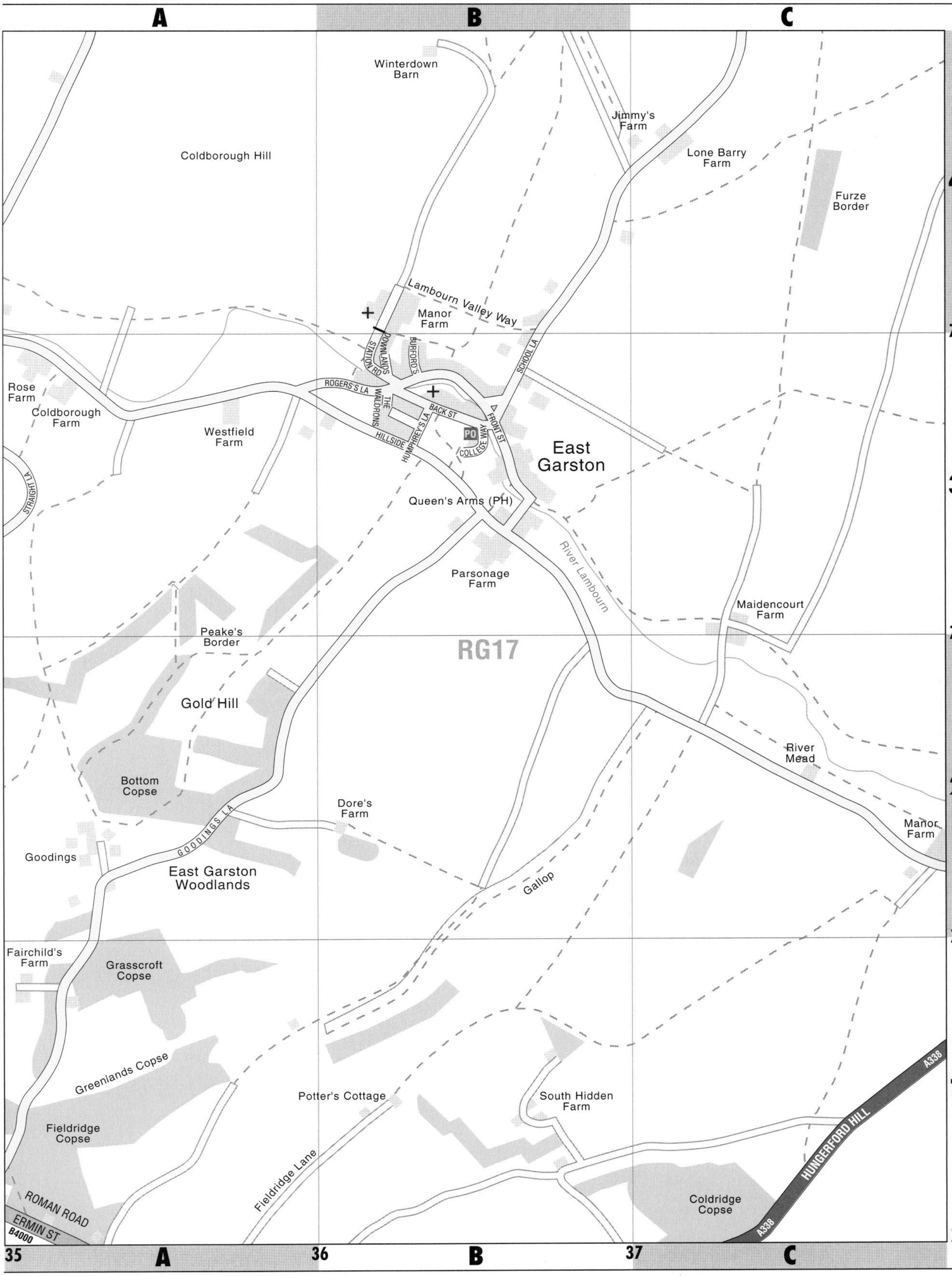
A
B
C
Winterdown Barn
Coldborough Hill
Jimmy's Farm
Lone Barry Farm
Furze Border
4
Lambourn Valley Way
Manor Farm
77
DOWNLANDS
STATION RD
BURFORD'S
SCHOOL LA
Rose Farm
Coldborough Farm
ROGERS'S LA
THE WALDRONS
BACK ST
FRONT ST
Westfield Farm
HILLSIDE
HUMPHREY'S LA
PO
COLLEGE WAY
East Garston
STRAIGHT LA
3
Queen's Arms (PH)
River Lambourn
Parsonage Farm
Maidencourt Farm
Peake's Border
76
RG17
Gold Hill
River Mead
Bottom Copse
2
Dore's Farm
Manor Farm
GOODINGS LA
Goodings
East Garston Woodlands
Gallop
Fairchild's Farm
Grasscroft Copse
75
A338
Greenlands Copse
1
Potter's Cottage
South Hidden Farm
Fieldridge Copse
HUNGERFORD HILL
Fieldridge Lane
Coldridge Copse
ROMAN ROAD
ERMIN ST
B4000
A338
74
35
36
37

74
48

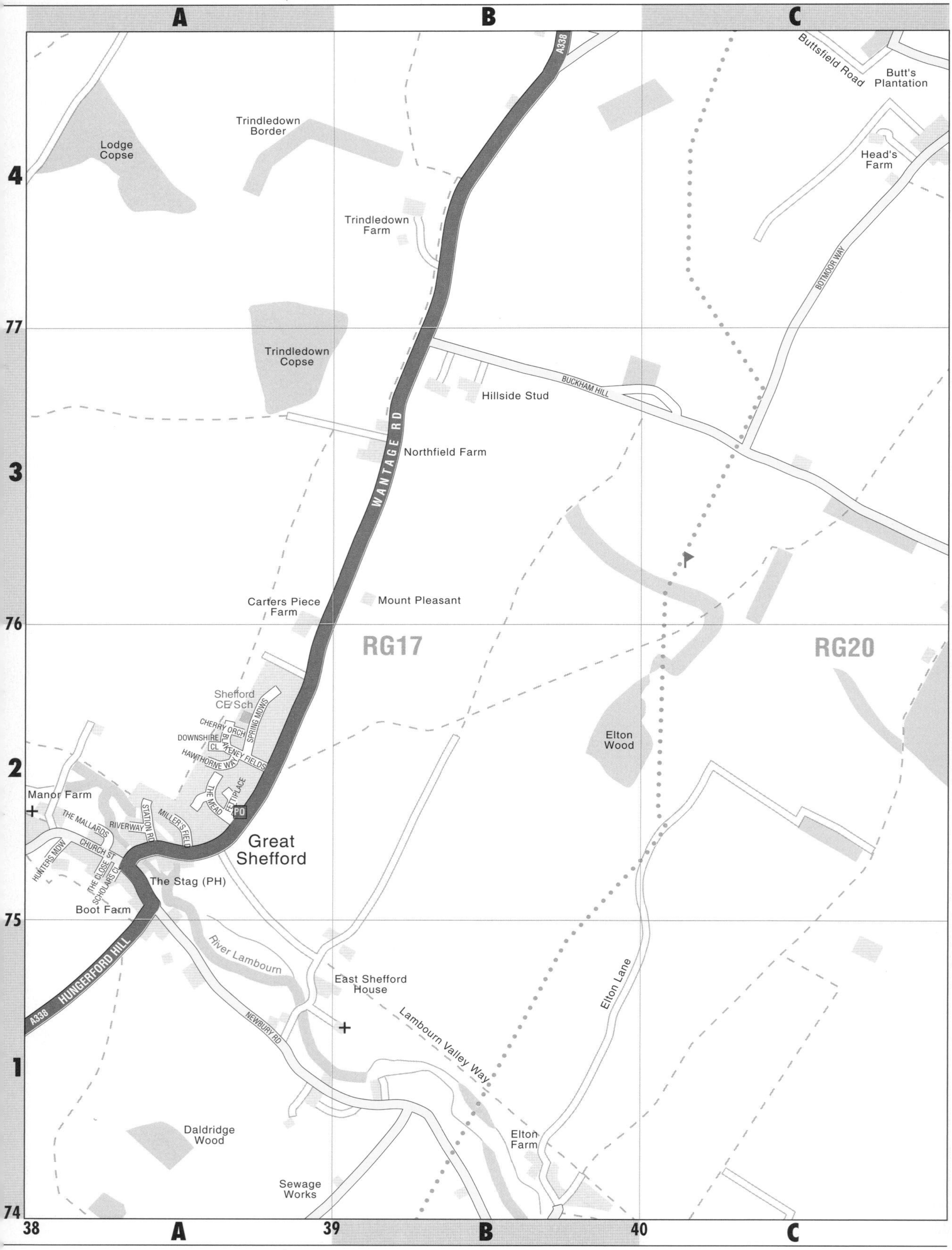
A
B
C
4
77
3
76
2
75
1
74
38
39
40
A338
Buttsfield Road
Butt's Plantation
Trindledown Border
Lodge Copse
Head's Farm
Trindledown Farm
BOTMOOR WAY
Trindledown Copse
BUCKHAM HILL
Hillside Stud
WANTAGE RD
Northfield Farm
Carters Piece Farm
Mount Pleasant
RG17
RG20
Shefford CE Sch
CHERRY ORCH
SPRING MDWS
DOWNSHIRE CL
BLAKENEY FIELDS
HAWTHORNE WAY
FETTIPLACE
THE MEAD
Elton Wood
Manor Farm
PO
THE MALLARDS
RIVERWAY
STATION RD
MILLER'S FIELD
CHURCH ST
HUNTERS MDW
THE CLOSE
SCHOLARS CL
Great Shefford
The Stag (PH)
Boot Farm
River Lambourn
HUNGERFORD HILL
A338
East Shefford House
Elton Lane
Lambourn Valley Way
NEWBURY RD
Daldridge Wood
Elton Farm
Sewage Works
A
B
C

A B C

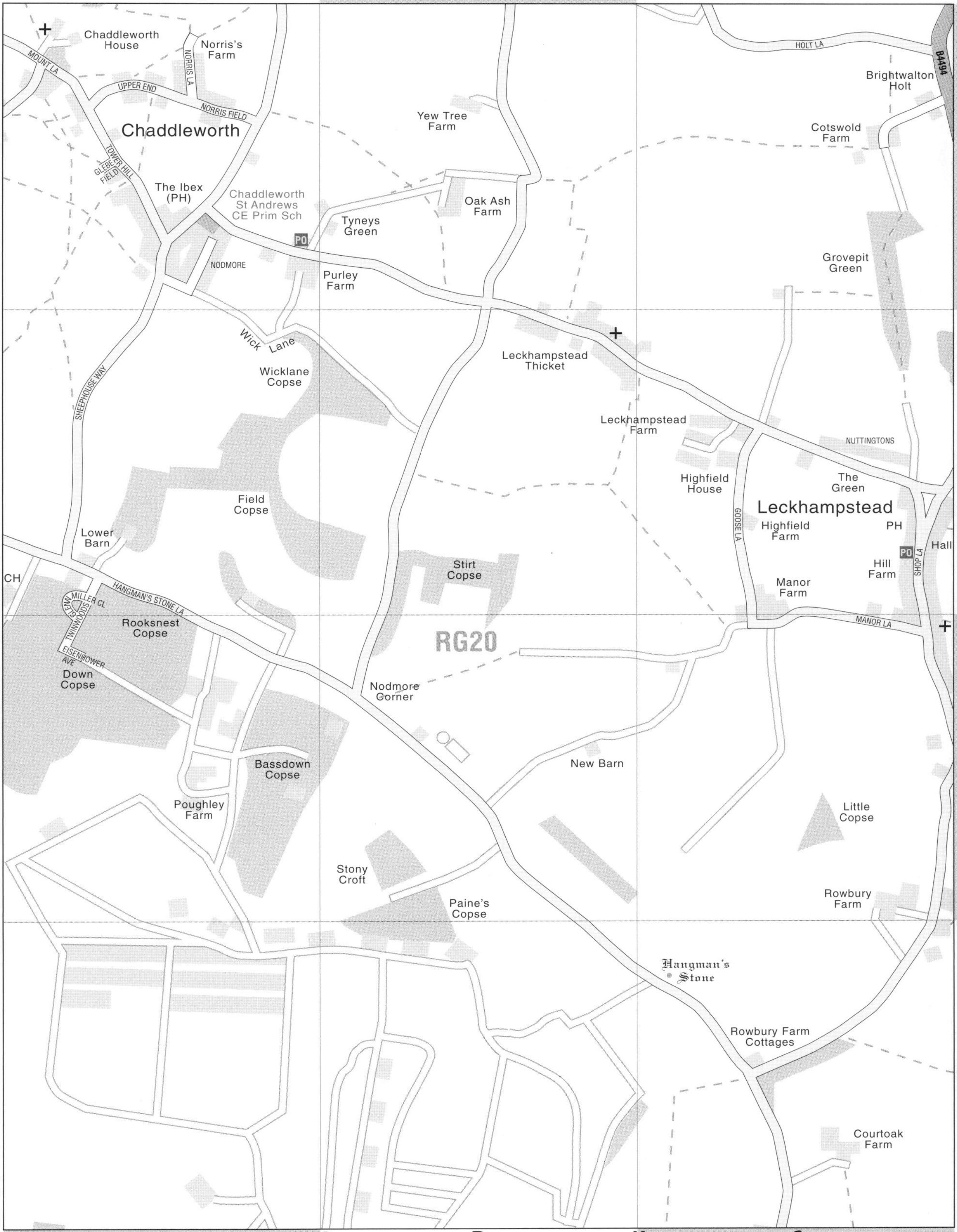


41 A 42 B 43 C

49
29

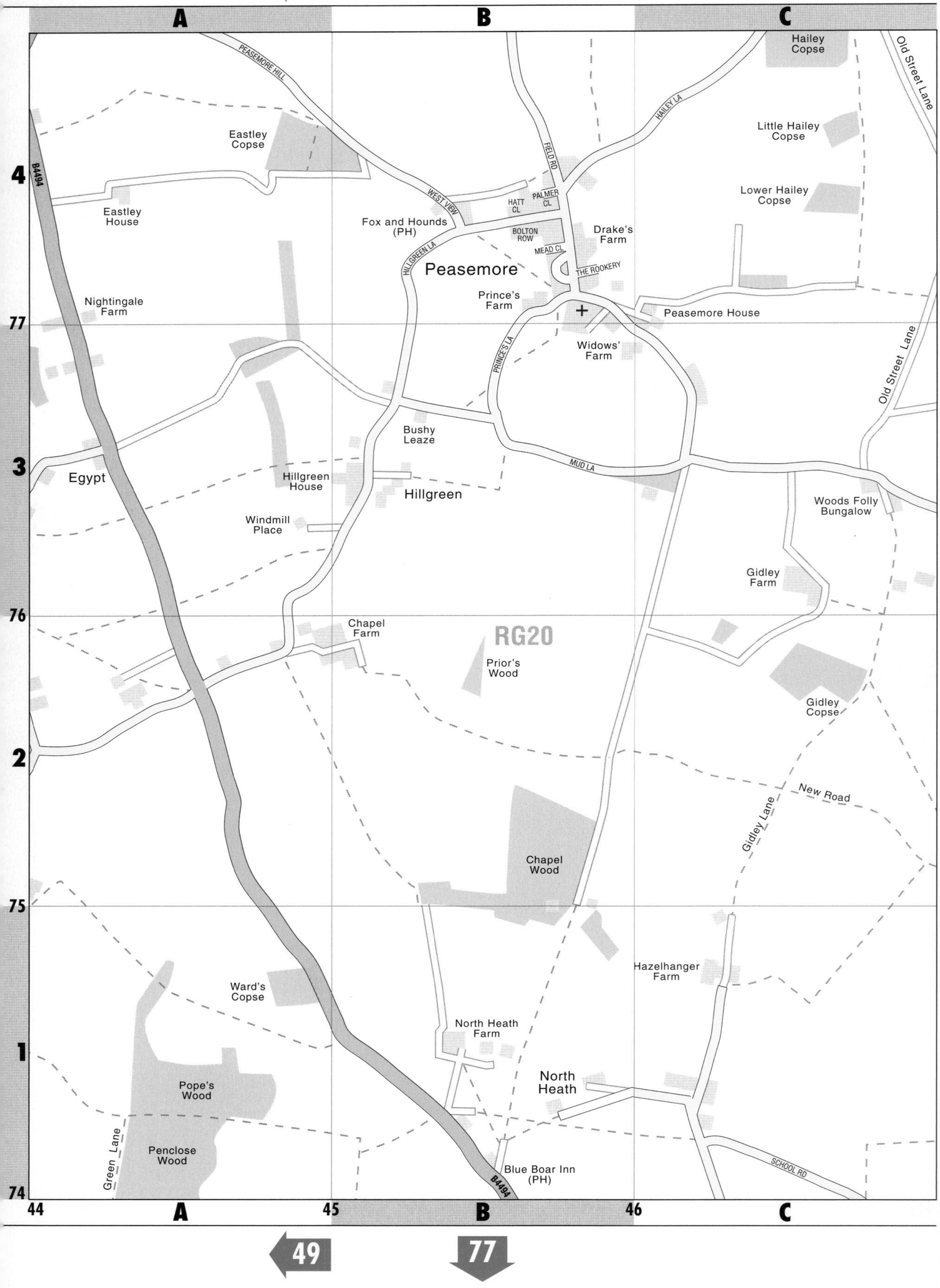
A
B
C
4
77
3
76
2
75
1
74
44
45
46
PEASEMORE HILL
Eastley Copse
Eastley House
B4494
Nightingale Farm
Egypt
Hillgreen House
Windmill Place
Hillgreen
Bushy Leaze
Fox and Hounds (PH)
WEST VIEW
HILLGREEN LA
Peasemore
FIELD RD
HATT CL
PALMER CL
BOLTON ROW
MEAD CL
THE ROOKERY
Drake's Farm
Prince's Farm
PRINCE'S LA
Widows' Farm
HAILEY LA
Hailey Copse
Old Street Lane
Little Hailey Copse
Lower Hailey Copse
Peasemore House
MUD LA
Woods Folly Bungalow
Gidley Farm
Chapel Farm
RG20
Prior's Wood
Gidley Copse
New Road
Gidley Lane
Chapel Wood
Hazelhanger Farm
Ward's Copse
North Heath Farm
North Heath
Pope's Wood
Penclose Wood
Green Lane
Blue Boar Inn (PH)
SCHOOL RD

49
77

30
52

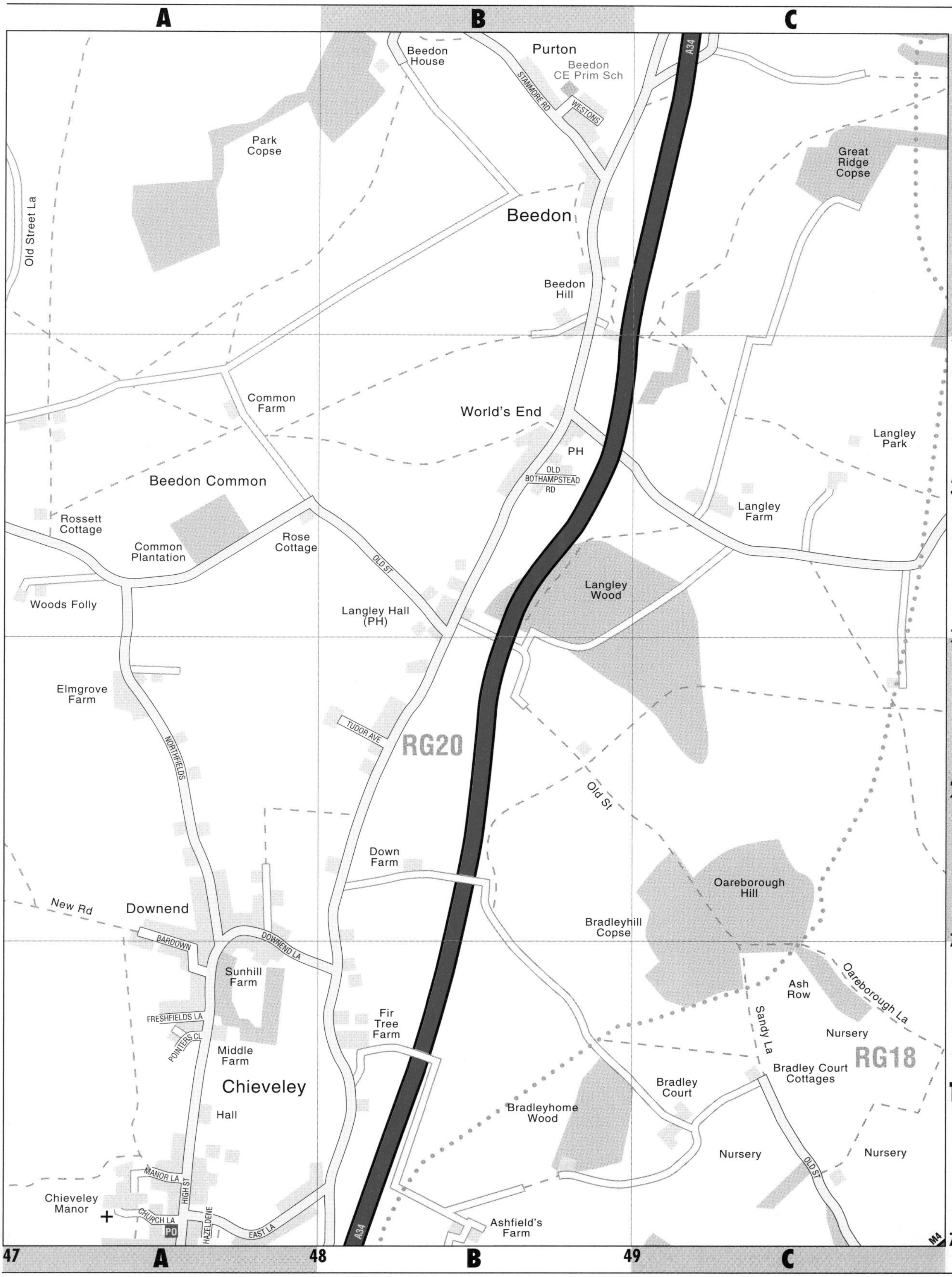
A
B
C
Beedon House
Purton
Beedon CE Prim Sch
STANMORE RD
WESTONS
A34
Park Copse
Old Street La
Great Ridge Copse
Beedon
4
Beedon Hill
77
Common Farm
World's End
PH
OLD BOTHAMPSTEAD RD
Langley Park
Beedon Common
3
Rossett Cottage
Common Plantation
Rose Cottage
Langley Farm
OLD ST
Langley Wood
Woods Folly
Langley Hall (PH)
76
Elmgrove Farm
TUDOR AVE
RG20
NORTHFIELDS
Old St
2
Down Farm
New Rd
Downend
Oareborough Hill
Bradleyhill Copse
BARDOWN
DOWNEND LA
75
Sunhill Farm
Ash Row
Oareborough La
Sandy La
FRESHFIELDS LA
Fir Tree Farm
POINTERS CL
Nursery
Middle Farm
Bradley Court Cottages
RG18
Chieveley
Bradley Court
1
Hall
Bradleyhome Wood
Nursery
Nursery
MANOR LA
HIGH ST
OLD ST
Chieveley Manor
CHURCH LA
PO
HAZELDENE
EAST LA
Ashfield's Farm
M4
74
47
48
49

78
52

51
31

A
B
C
4
3
2
1
77
76
75
74
50
51
52
Perborough Castle
RG20
Floodcross Cottage
Banterwick Farm
Northfield Row
Little Ridge Copse
Ramsworth Cottages
Milkhill Farm
Uplands
Green Hams La
Allen's Row
River Pang
Five Ways
New Copse
Middle Barn
THE OLD SCHOOL
STATION HILL
WATER ST
WEST VIEW COTTS
HILLCREST
Hampstead Norreys
THE CLOSE
SCOTTALLS LA
Oakhouse Farm
Laycroft Wood
THE CUTTINGS
PENDALS CL
B4009
NEWBURY HILL
CHURCH ST
Bothampstead Farm
Oakhouse Cottages
Hampstead Norreys CE Prim Sch
Hollingsworth
RG18
Westbrook Copse
Park Wood
Bothampstead
Trumpletts Farm
Malthouse
Down Wood
New Cottages
Hatchgate Cottages
The Thatched Cottage
Eling
Elingpark Copse
Eling Farm
Four Elms
Oareborough La
Pimbus Shaw
EVERINGTON LA
Sand Pit
Common Barn Cottages
Heather Piece
Spring Plantation
Everington Hill
Newhouse Farm
Furze Hill
M4
B4009

51
79

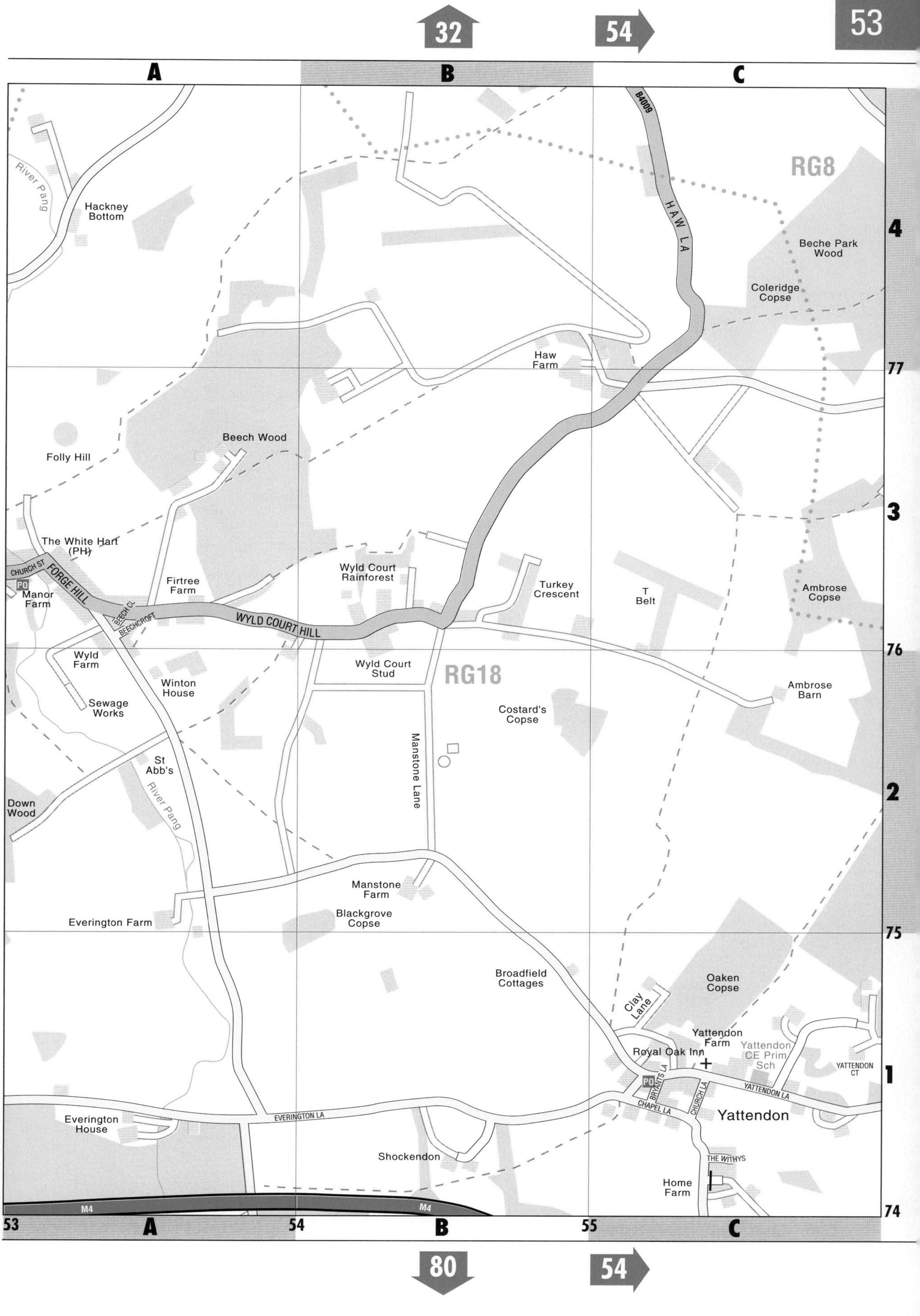
32
54
A
B
C
RG8
B4009
HAW LA
Hackney Bottom
River Pang
Beche Park Wood
Coleridge Copse
Haw Farm
Beech Wood
Folly Hill
The White Hart (PH)
CHURCH ST
FORGE HILL
PO
Manor Farm
Firtree Farm
BEECH CL
BEECHCROFT
WYLD COURT HILL
Wyld Court Rainforest
Turkey Crescent
T Belt
Ambrose Copse
Wyld Farm
Wyld Court Stud
RG18
Winton House
Sewage Works
Ambrose Barn
Costard's Copse
St Abb's
Manstone Lane
Down Wood
Manstone Farm
Everington Farm
Blackgrove Copse
Broadfield Cottages
Oaken Copse
Clay Lane
Yattendon Farm
Royal Oak Inn
Yattendon CE Prim Sch
YATTENDON CT
BRYANTS LA
CHURCH LA
YATTENDON LA
CHAPEL LA
Yattendon
Everington House
EVERINGTON LA
Shockendon
THE WITHYS
Home Farm
M4
4
77
3
76
2
75
1
74
53
54
55
80
54

53
33

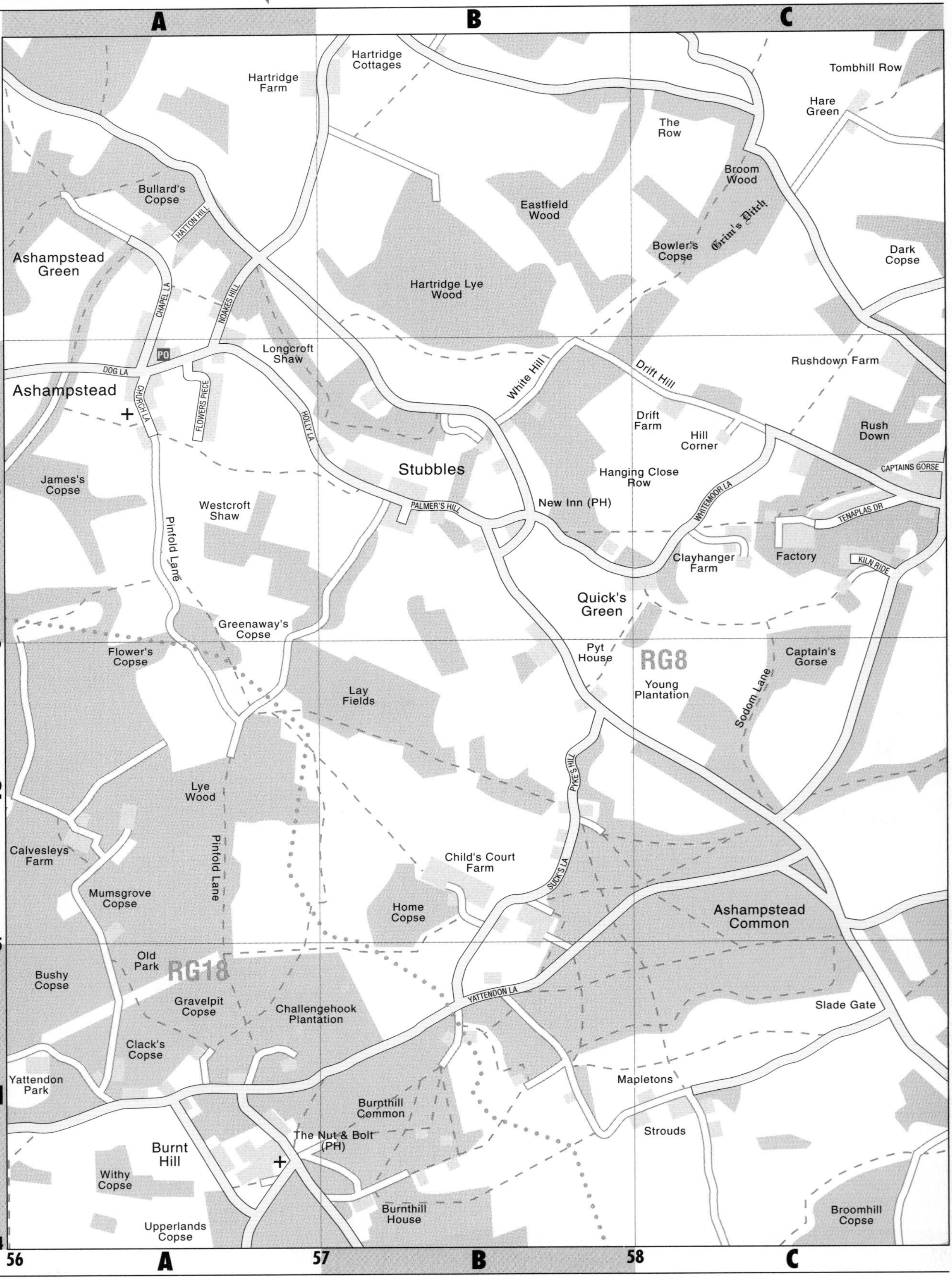
A
B
C
Hartridge Cottages
Hartridge Farm
Tombhill Row
Hare Green
The Row
Broom Wood
Bullard's Copse
HATTON HILL
Eastfield Wood
Grim's Ditch
Bowler's Copse
Dark Copse
Ashampstead Green
CHAPEL LA
NOAKES HILL
Hartridge Lye Wood
PO
Longcroft Shaw
DOG LA
Ashampstead
CHURCH LA
FLOWERS PIECE
HOLLY LA
White Hill
Drift Hill
Rushdown Farm
Drift Farm
Hill Corner
Rush Down
CAPTAINS GORSE
James's Copse
Stubbles
Hanging Close Row
Westcroft Shaw
PALMER'S HILL
New Inn (PH)
WHITEMOOR LA
TENAPLAS DR
Pinfold Lane
Clayhanger Farm
Factory
KILN RIDE
Quick's Green
Greenaway's Copse
Flower's Copse
Pyt House
RG8
Captain's Gorse
Lay Fields
Young Plantation
Sodom Lane
Lye Wood
PYKE'S HILL
Calvesleys Farm
Child's Court Farm
SUCK'S LA
Mumsgrove Copse
Home Copse
Ashampstead Common
Bushy Copse
Old Park
RG18
Gravelpit Copse
YATTENDON LA
Challengehook Plantation
Slade Gate
Clack's Copse
Yattendon Park
Mapletons
Burnthill Common
Burnt Hill
The Nut & Bolt (PH)
Strouds
Withy Copse
Burnthill House
Broomhill Copse
Upperlands Copse
4
77
3
76
2
75
1
74
56
57
58

53
81

34
56

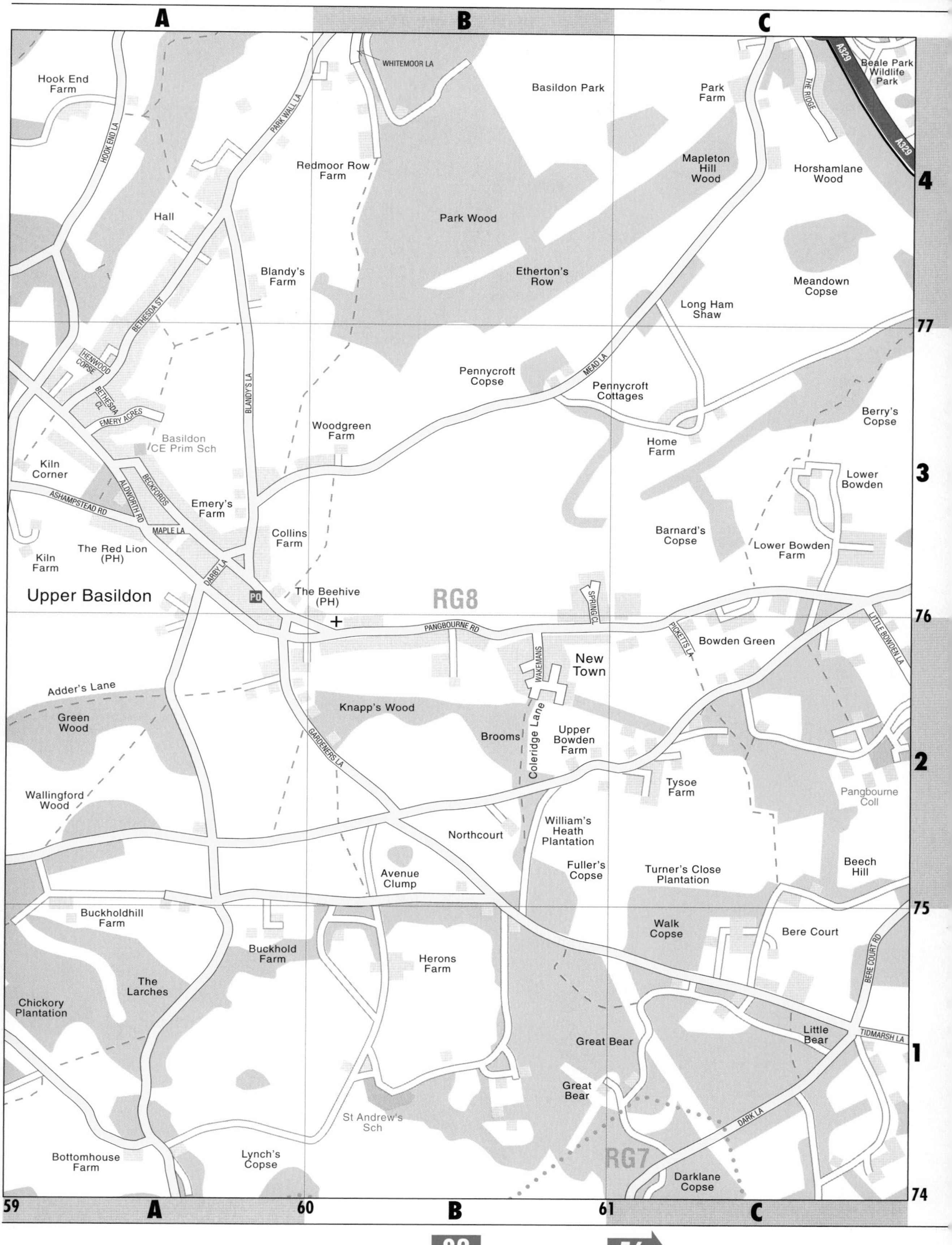
A
B
C
Hook End Farm
WHITEMOOR LA
Basildon Park
Park Farm
THE RIDGE
A329
Beale Park Wildlife Park
HOOK END LA
PARK WALL LA
Redmoor Row Farm
Mapleton Hill Wood
Horshamlane Wood
4
Hall
Park Wood
Blandy's Farm
Etherton's Row
Meandown Copse
BETHESDA ST
Long Ham Shaw
77
HENWOOD COPSE
BETHESDA CL
EMERY ACRES
BLANDY'S LA
Pennycroft Copse
MEAD LA
Pennycroft Cottages
Berry's Copse
Basildon CE Prim Sch
Woodgreen Farm
Home Farm
Kiln Corner
Lower Bowden
3
ASHAMPSTEAD RD
ALDWORTH RD
BECKFORDS
Emery's Farm
MAPLE LA
Collins Farm
Barnard's Copse
Kiln Farm
The Red Lion (PH)
Lower Bowden Farm
DARBY LA
Upper Basildon
PO
The Beehive (PH)
RG8
SPRING CL
76
PANGBOURNE RD
PICKETTS LA
Bowden Green
LITTLE BOWDEN LA
WAKEMANS
New Town
Adder's Lane
Knapp's Wood
Green Wood
Brooms
Coleridge Lane
Upper Bowden Farm
GARDENERS LA
2
Tysoe Farm
Wallingford Wood
Pangbourne Coll
William's Heath Plantation
Northcourt
Fuller's Copse
Beech Hill
Avenue Clump
Turner's Close Plantation
75
Buckholdhill Farm
Walk Copse
Bere Court
BERE COURT RD
Buckhold Farm
Herons Farm
The Larches
Chickory Plantation
Little Bear
TIDMARSH LA
Great Bear
1
Great Bear
St Andrew's Sch
DARK LA
Bottomhouse Farm
Lynch's Copse
RG7
Darklane Copse
74
59
60
61
A
B
C

82
56

55

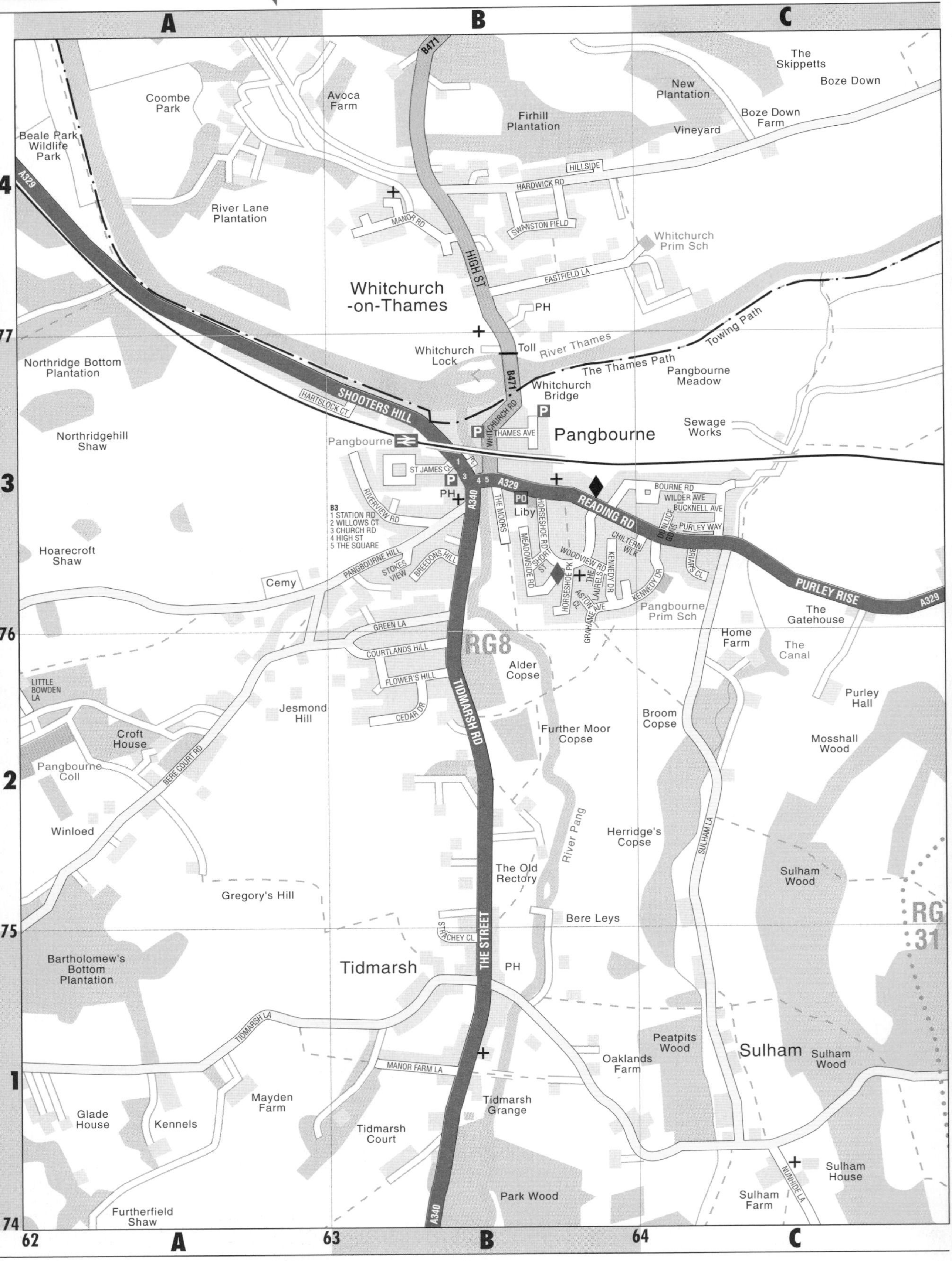
A
B
C
The Skippetts
Boze Down
New Plantation
Coombe Park
Avoca Farm
Firhill Plantation
Boze Down Farm
Vineyard
Beale Park Wildlife Park
B471
HILLSIDE
HARDWICK RD
A329
River Lane Plantation
MANOR RD
SWANSTON FIELD
Whitchurch Prim Sch
HIGH ST
EASTFIELD LA
Whitchurch -on-Thames
PH
Towing Path
Whitchurch Lock
Toll
River Thames
Northridge Bottom Plantation
The Thames Path
Pangbourne Meadow
Whitchurch Bridge
HARTSLOCK CT
SHOOTERS HILL
WHITCHURCH RD
THAMES AVE
Pangbourne
Sewage Works
Northridgehill Shaw
Pangbourne
ST JAMES CL
BOURNE RD
WILDER AVE
BUCKNELL AVE
PURLEY WAY
READING RD
A340
PH
Liby
THE MOORS
HORSESHOE RD
RIVERVIEW RD
B3
1 STATION RD
2 WILLOWS CT
3 CHURCH RD
4 HIGH ST
5 THE SQUARE
Hoarecroft Shaw
PANGBOURNE HILL
STOKES VIEW
BREEDONS HILL
MEADOWSIDE RD
SHORT ST
WOODVIEW RD
CHILTERN WLK
DUNLUCE GDNS
BRIARS CL
KENNEDY DR
THE LAURELS
HORSESHOE PK
ASTON CL
GRAHAME AVE
PURLEY RISE
Cemy
Pangbourne Prim Sch
The Gatehouse
GREEN LA
RG8
Home Farm
The Canal
COURTLANDS HILL
Alder Copse
LITTLE BOWDEN LA
FLOWER'S HILL
Purley Hall
Jesmond Hill
CEDAR DR
TIDMARSH RD
Broom Copse
Croft House
Further Moor Copse
Mosshall Wood
BERE COURT RD
Pangbourne Coll
River Pang
Winloed
Herridge's Copse
SULHAM LA
The Old Rectory
Sulham Wood
Gregory's Hill
Bere Leys
RG 31
STRACHEY CL
Bartholomew's Bottom Plantation
THE STREET
Tidmarsh
PH
TIDMARSH LA
Peatpits Wood
Oaklands Farm
Sulham
Sulham Wood
MANOR FARM LA
Mayden Farm
Tidmarsh Grange
Glade House
Kennels
Tidmarsh Court
Sulham House
NUNHIDE LA
Sulham Farm
Park Wood
Furtherfield Shaw
77
76
75
74
4
3
2
1
62
63
64

55
83

58

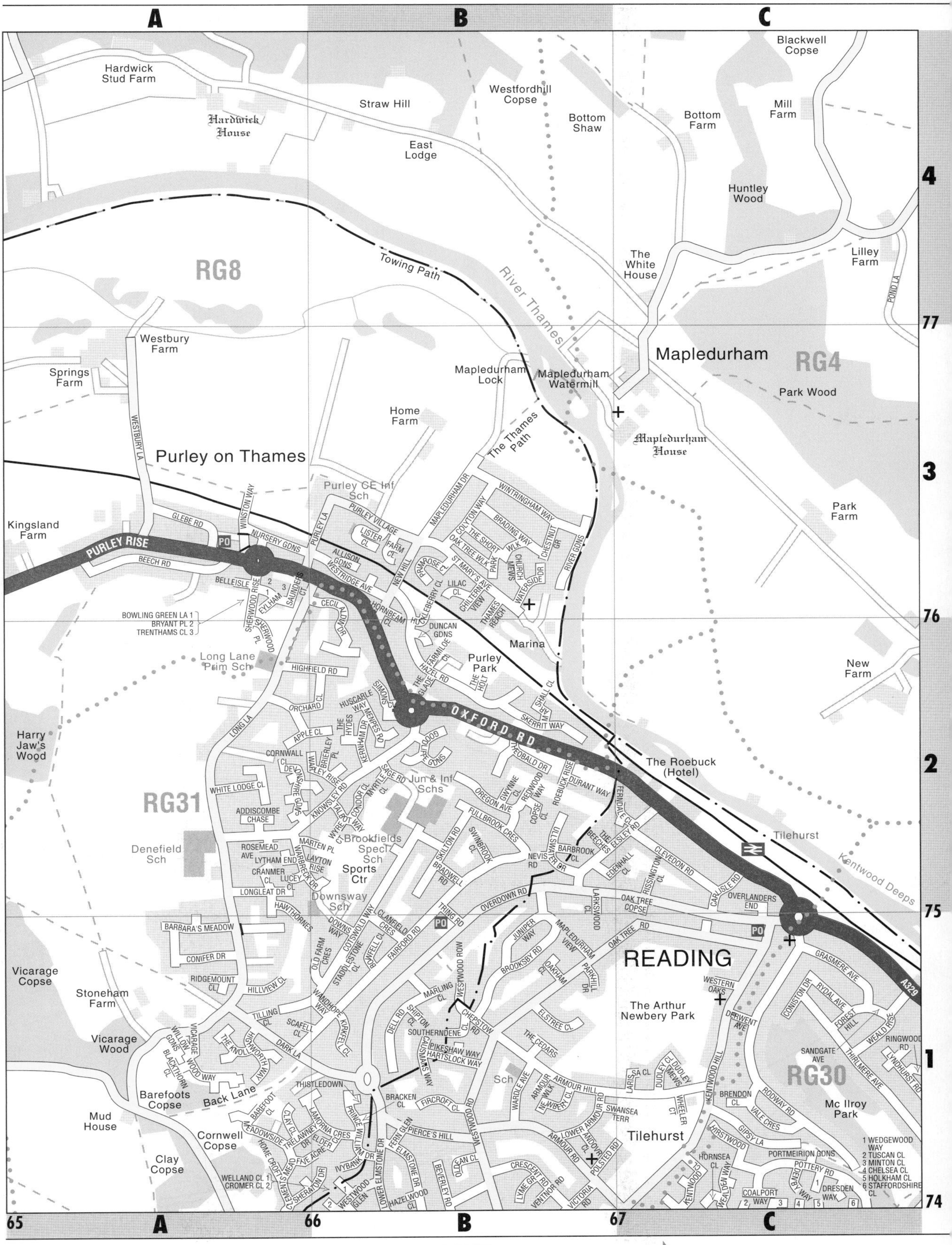
A
B
C
4
3
2
1
77
76
75
74
65
66
67
Hardwick Stud Farm
Hardwick House
Straw Hill
Westfordhill Copse
East Lodge
Bottom Shaw
Bottom Farm
Blackwell Copse
Mill Farm
Huntley Wood
RG8
Towing Path
River Thames
The White House
Lilley Farm
POND LA
Westbury Farm
Springs Farm
Mapledurham Lock
Mapledurham Watermill
Mapledurham
RG4
Park Wood
Mapledurham House
Home Farm
WESTBURY LA
Purley on Thames
The Thames Path
Purley CE Inf Sch
Park Farm
Kingsland Farm
PURLEY RISE
GLEBE RD
WINSTON WAY
NURSERY GDNS
PURLEY LA
PURLEY VILLAGE
LISTER CL
FARM CT
MAPLEDURHAM DR
COLYTON WAY
WINTRINGHAM WAY
BRADING WAY
THE SHORT
OAK TREE WLK
CHESTNUT GR
RIVER GDNS
BEECH RD
PO
ALLISON GDNS
WESTRIDGE AVE
NEW HILL
PRIMROSE CL
ST MARY'S AVE
CHURCH MEWS
WATERSIDE DR
BELLEISLE
SHERWOOD RISE
EYLHAM
SAUNDERS CT
CECIL ALDRIDGE
HORNBEAM CL
HUCKLEBERRY CL
LILAC CL
CHILTERN VIEW
THAMES REACH
BOWLING GREEN LA 1
BRYANT PL 2
TRENTHAMS CL 3
DUNCAN GDNS
Marina
New Farm
Long Lane Prim Sch
HIGHFIELD RD
FARMILOE CL
Purley Park
THE GLADE
THE HOLT
SHALL CL
ORCHARD CL
HUSCARLE WAY
SIMONS CL
OXFORD RD
SKERRIT WAY
Harry Jaw's Wood
LONG LA
APPLE CL
THE HYDES
KENHAM DR
MEMPES RD
GOODLIFFE GDNS
CORNWALL CL
DEVONSHIRE GDNS
BRIERLEY PL
WARLEY RISE
SAGE RD
MYRTLE CL
Jun & Inf Schs
TIBBALD DR
REDWOOD WAY
ROEBUCK RISE
DURANT WAY
The Roebuck (Hotel)
RG31
WHITE LODGE CL
KNOWSLEY RD
CONDOR CL
OREGON AVE
GWYNNE CL
COPSE WAY
FERNDALE CL
ELSLEY RD
ADDISCOMBE CHASE
WYRE CT
TALBOT WAY
FULLBROOK CRES
Tilehurst
Kentwood Deeps
Denefield Sch
ROSEMEAD AVE
MARTEN PL
Brookfields Specl Sch
SKILTON RD
SWINBROOK CL
NEVIS RD
BARBROOK CL
THE BEECHES
CLEVEDON RD
LYTHAM END
LAYTON RISE
CRANMER CL
LUCEY CL
WARBRECK DR
Sports Ctr
BRADWELL RD
ULLSWATER DR
EDENHALL CL
RISSINGTON CL
CARLISLE RD
LONGLEAT DR
HAWTHORNES
Downsway Sch
OVERDOWN RD
LARKSWOOD CL
OAK TREE COPSE
OVERLANDERS END
DOWNS WAY
CLANFIELD CRES
TRING RD
BARBARA'S MEADOW
COTSWOLD WAY
FAIRFORD RD
JUNIPER WAY
MAPLEDURHAM VIEW
OAK TREE RD
CONIFER DR
OLD FARM CRES
STADDLESTONE CL
ROWELL CL
BROOKSBY RD
OAKHAM CL
PARKHILL DR
READING
GRASMERE AVE
Vicarage Copse
RIDGEMOUNT CL
HILLVIEW CL
WESTWOOD ROW
WESTERN OAKS
CONISTON DR
RYDAL AVE
A329
Stoneham Farm
MARLING CL
The Arthur Newbery Park
FOREST HILL
WEALD RISE
TILLING CL
WANDHOPE WAY
SCAFELL CL
DELL RD
SHIPTON CL
CHEPSTOW CL
ELSTREE CL
DERWENT AVE
RINGWOOD RD
LYNDHURST RD
Vicarage Wood
WILLOW GDNS
VICARAGE WOOD WAY
THE KNOLL
HIGHWORTH WAY
DARK LA
KIRKFELL CL
SOUTHERNDENE CL
PIKESHAW WAY
HARTSLOCK WAY
CAUSMANS WAY
THE CEDARS
SANDGATE AVE
THIRLMERE AVE
BLACKTHORN CL
Sch
WARDLE AVE
ARMOUR WLK
ARMOUR HILL
LARISSA CL
DUDLEY CL
DUDLEY MEWS
KENTWOOD HILL
RG30
Barefoots Copse
Back Lane
THISTLEDOWN
BABBFOOT
BRACKEN CL
FIRCROFT CL
NEWBERY CL
SWANSEA TERR
WHEELER CT
BRENDON CL
RODWAY RD
Mc Ilroy Park
Mud House
MEADOWSIDE
CLAY CL
TRELAWNEY DR
LAMORNA CRES
ELDER CL
PRINCE WILLIAM DR
FERN GLEN
PIERCE'S HILL
WESTWOOD RD
LOWER ARMOUR RD
ANDOVER CL
Tilehurst
VALE CRES
GIPSY LA
Cornwell Copse
HOME CROFT
YEW ACRE
IVYBANK
LOWER ELMSTONE DR
ELMSTONE DR
BEVERLEY RD
OLDEAN CL
ARMOUR RD
POLSTED RD
HIRSTWOOD
HORNSEA CL
WEALDEN WAY
PORTMEIRION GDNS
POTTERY RD
1 WEDGEWOOD WAY
2 TUSCAN CL
3 MINTON CL
4 CHELSEA CL
5 HOLKHAM CL
6 STAFFORDSHIRE CL
Clay Copse
WELLAND CL 1
CROMER CL 2
CLEMENTS MEAD
SHERATON DR
WESTWOOD GLEN
HAZELWOOD CL
CRESCENT RD
LYME GR
VENTNOR RD
VICTORIA RD
KENTWOOD CL
COALPORT WAY
DENBY WAY
DRESDEN WAY

84
58

57

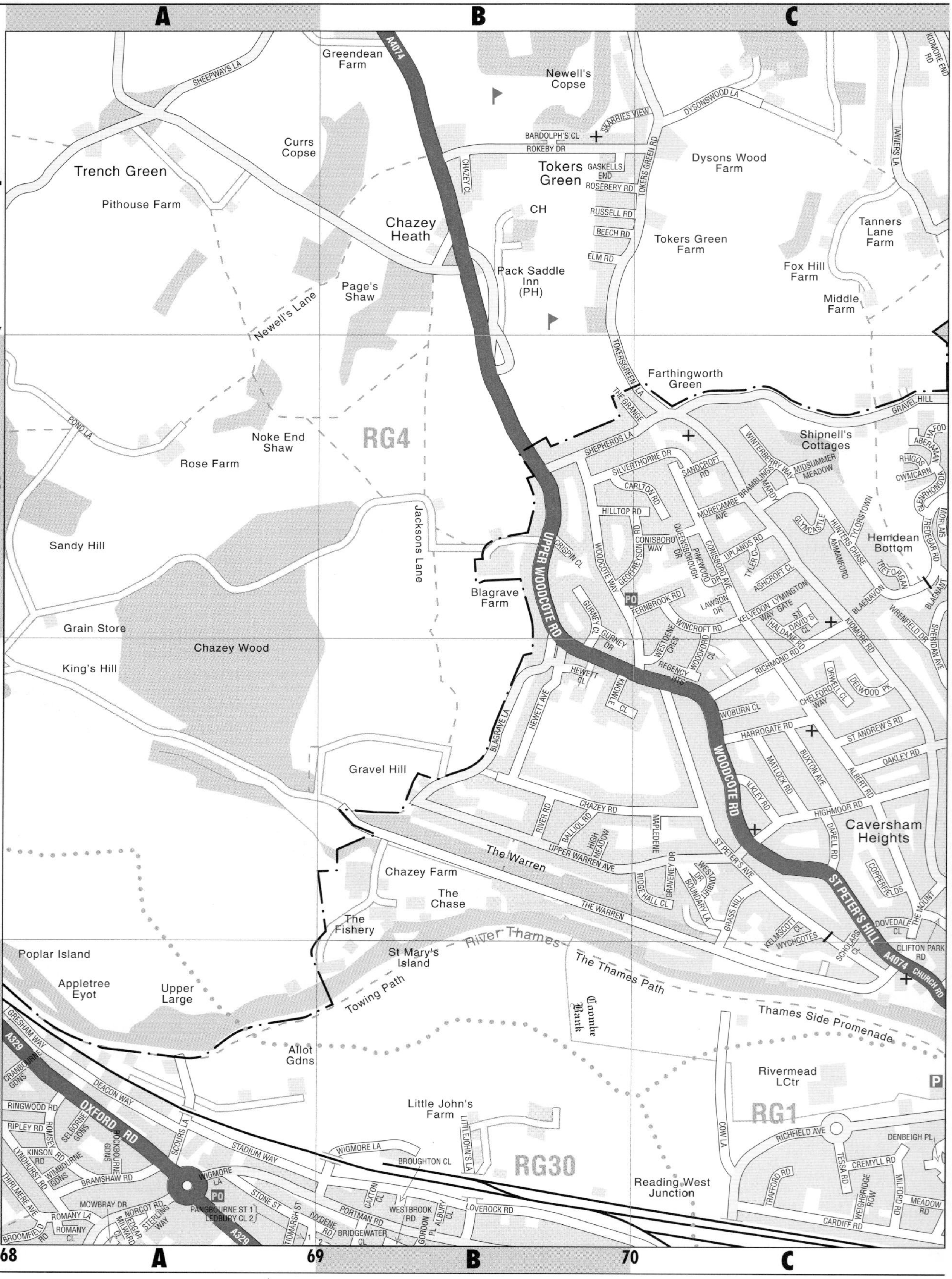
A
B
C
4
3
2
1
77
76
75
74
68
69
70
A4074
Greendean Farm
Newell's Copse
SHEEPWAYS LA
DYSONSWOOD LA
SKARRIES VIEW
BARDOLPH'S CL
ROKEBY DR
Curr's Copse
Trench Green
Pithouse Farm
CHAZEY CL
Tokers Green
GASKELLS END
ROSEBERY RD
TOKERS GREEN RD
Dysons Wood Farm
CH
RUSSELL RD
BEECH RD
ELM RD
Tokers Green Farm
Chazey Heath
Pack Saddle Inn (PH)
Page's Shaw
Newell's Lane
Fox Hill Farm
Middle Farm
Tanners Lane Farm
TANNERS LA
KIDMORE END RD
TOKERSGREEN LA
Farthingworth Green
THE GRANGE
GRAVEL HILL
POND LA
Noke End Shaw
RG4
Rose Farm
SHEPHERDS LA
Shipnell's Cottages
SILVERTHORNE DR
SANDCROFT RD
WINTERBERRY WAY
BRAMBLINGS
MIDSUMMER MEADOW
CARLTON RD
HILLTOP RD
MORECAMBE AVE
GLYNCASTLE
HUNTERS CHASE
TYLORSTOWN
Hemdean Bottom
Jacksons Lane
Sandy Hill
CRISPIN CL
UPPER WOODCOTE RD
CONISBORO WAY
GEOFFREYSON RD
QUEENSBOROUGH DR
PINEWOOD DR
CONISBORO AVE
UPLANDS RD
TYLER CL
ASHCROFT CL
AMMANFORD
BLAENAVON
TREFOREGAN
BLAENANT
WOODCOTE WAY
PO
FERNBROOK RD
LAWSON DR
KELVEDON WAY
LYMINGTON GATE
ST DAVID'S CL
HALDANE RD
KIDMORE RD
WRENFIELD DR
SHERIDAN AVE
Blagrave Farm
Grain Store
GURNEY CL
GURNEY DR
WESTDENE CRES
WINCROFT RD
WOODFORD CL
REGENCY HTS
RICHMOND RD
Chazey Wood
King's Hill
HEWETT CL
HEWETT AVE
KNOWLE CL
WOBURN CL
ORWELL CL
CHELFORD WAY
DELWOOD PK
ST ANDREW'S RD
HARROGATE RD
OAKLEY RD
BLAGRAVE LA
WOODCOTE RD
MATLOCK RD
BUXTON AVE
ALBERT RD
Gravel Hill
ILKLEY RD
HIGHMOOR RD
DARELL RD
Caversham Heights
RIVER RD
CHAZEY RD
BALLIOL RD
HIGH MEADOW
MAPLEDENE
UPPER WARREN AVE
The Warren
ST PETER'S AVE
ST PETER'S HILL
Chazey Farm
The Chase
RIDGE HALL CL
GRAVENEY DR
WESTONBIRT DR
BOUNDARY LA
GRASS HILL
COPPERFIELDS
THE MOUNT
THE WARREN
The Fishery
River Thames
KELMSCOTT CL
WYCHCOTES
SCHOLARS CL
DOVEDALE CL
CLIFTON PARK RD
A4074 CHURCH RD
Poplar Island
St Mary's Island
The Thames Path
Appletree Eyot
Upper Large
Towing Path
Coombe Bank
Thames Side Promenade
GRESHAM WAY
A329
Allot Gdns
Rivermead LCtr
P
CRANBOURNE GDNS
DEACON WAY
RINGWOOD RD
OXFORD RD
RIPLEY RD
ROMSEY RD
SELBORNE GDNS
ROCKBOURNE GDNS
Little John's Farm
RG1
KINSON RD
WIMBOURNE GDNS
SCOURS LA
STADIUM WAY
WIGMORE LA
LITTLEJOHN'S LA
RICHFIELD AVE
DENBEIGH PL
COW LA
LYNDHURST RD
BRAMSHAW RD
BROUGHTON CL
RG30
TESSA RD
CREMYLL RD
THIRLMERE AVE
WIGMORE LA
Reading West Junction
TRAFFORD RD
MOWBRAY DR
STONE ST
CAXTON CL
WEIGHBRIDGE ROW
MILFORD RD
MEADOW RD
NORCOT RD
PANGBOURNE ST
LEDBURY CL
PORTMAN RD
WESTBROOK RD
ALBURY CL
LOVEROCK RD
ROMANY LA
MEDWAR
STERLING WAY
IVYDENE RD
GORDON PL
ROMANY CL
TIDMARSH ST
BRIDGEWATER CL
CARDIFF RD
BROOMFIELD RD
A329

57

85

60

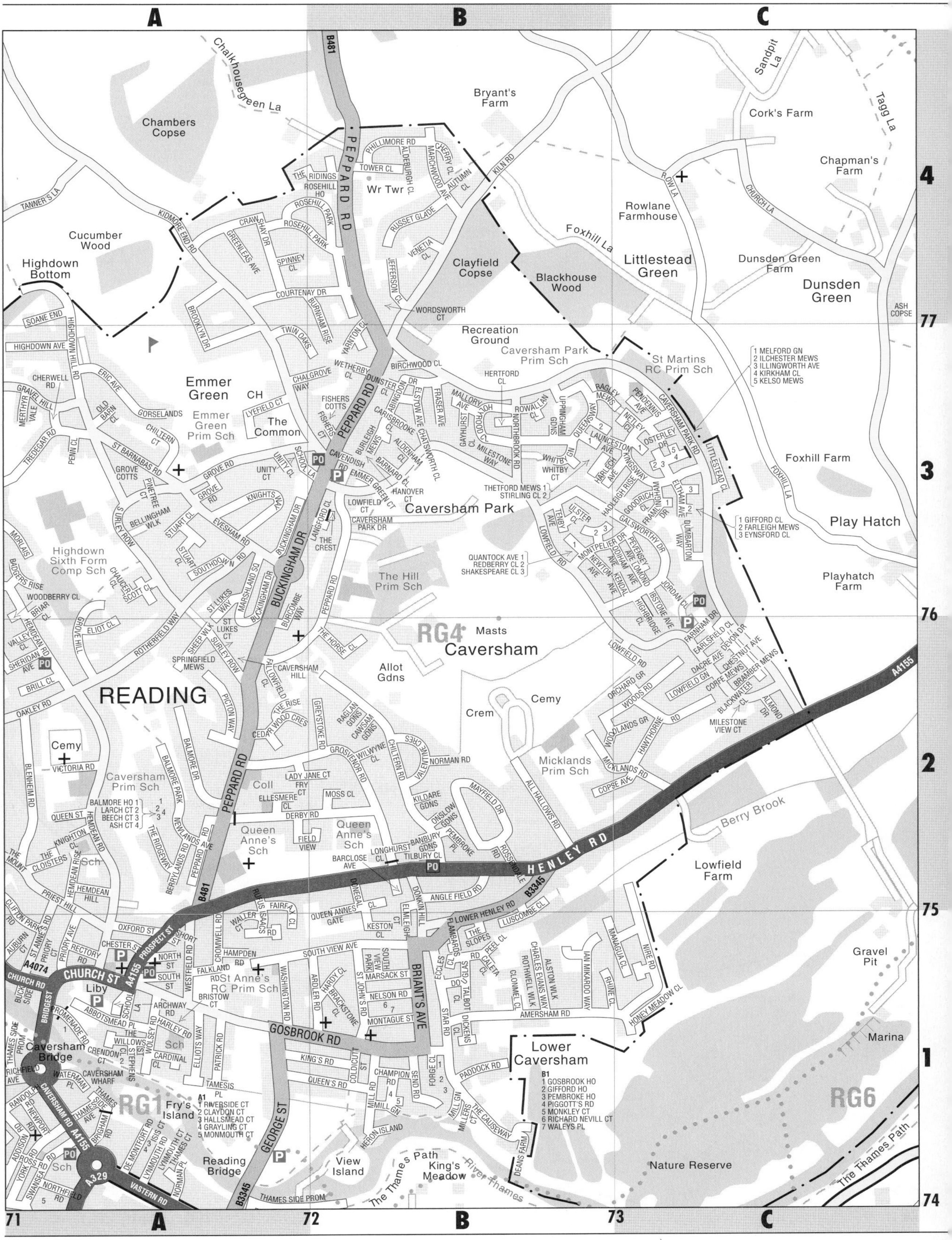
A
B
C
4
3
2
1
77
76
75
74
71
72
73
B481
Chalkhousegreen La
Chambers Copse
Bryant's Farm
Sandpit La
Tagg La
Cork's Farm
Chapman's Farm
Row La
Church La
Rowlane Farmhouse
Foxhill La
Littlestead Green
Dunsden Green Farm
Dunsden Green
Ash Copse
Tanner's La
Kidmore End Rd
Cucumber Wood
Highdown Bottom
Soane End
Highdown Hill Rd
Highdown Ave
Peppard Rd
Phillimore Rd
Tower Cl
The Ridings
Rosehill Ho
Aldeburgh Cl
Marchwood Ave
Cherry Cl
Autumn Cl
Wr Twr
Kiln Rd
Russet Glade
Rosehill Park
Crawshay Dr
Greenleas Ave
Spinney Cl
Venetia Cl
Jefferson Cl
Clayfield Copse
Blackhouse Wood
Courtenay Dr
Burnham Rise
Brooklyn Dr
Twin Oaks
Yarnton Cl
Wordsworth Ct
Recreation Ground
Caversham Park Prim Sch
St Martins RC Prim Sch
1 Melford Gn
2 Ilchester Mews
3 Illingworth Ave
4 Kirkham Cl
5 Kelso Mews
Cherwell Rd
Eric Ave
Gravel Hill
Merthyr Vale
Old Barn Cl
Gorselands
Emmer Green
CH
Lyefield Ct
The Common
Emmer Green Prim Sch
Chalgrove Way
Wetherby Ct
Birchwood Cl
Dunster Cl
Abingdon Dr
Elstow Ave
Fraser Ave
Mallory Ave
Hertford Cl
Rowallan Cl
Uppingham Gdns
Ragley Mews
Pendennis Ave
Caversham Park Rd
Littlestead Cl
Fishers Cotts
Fishers Ct
Carisbrooke Cl
Chatsworth Cl
Gayhurst Cl
Milestone Way
Northbrook Rd
Queensway
Launceston Ave
Netley Cl
Osterley Dr
Tredegar Rd
Penn Cl
Chiltern Ct
St Barnabas Rd
Grove Cotts
Grove Rd
Unity Ct
Unity Cl
School La
Burleigh Mews
Cavendish Ct
Aldenham Cl
Barnard Cl
Emmer Green Ct
Hanover Ct
Whitby Dr
Whitby Ct
Harlech Ave
Kingsway
Foxhill Farm
Pinetree Ct
Bellingham Wlk
Knights Way
Lowfield Ct
Caversham Park Dr
Caversham Park
Thetford Mews 1
Stirling Cl 2
Hadleigh Rise
Goodrich Cl
Framlingham Dr
Eltham Ave
Dumbarton Way
Play Hatch
1 Gifford Cl
2 Farleigh Mews
3 Eynsford Cl
Surley Row
Stuart Cl
Evesham Rd
Buckingham Dr
Langford Cl
The Crest
Tenby Ave
Ulster Cl
Galsworthy Dr
Highdown Sixth Form Comp Sch
Chaucer Cl
Scott Cl
Southdown Rd
Marshland Sq
Burcombe Way
The Hill Prim Sch
Quantock Ave 1
Redberry Cl 2
Shakespeare Cl 3
Lowfield Rd
Montpelier Dr
Newton Ave
Odiham Ave
Pevensey Ave
Lomond Ave
Kendal Ave
Playhatch Farm
Morlais
Badgers Rise
Woodberry Cl
Briar Cl
Hemdean Rd
Grove Hill
Eliot Cl
Rotherfield Way
St Lukes Way
St Lukes Ct
The Horse Cl
RG4
Masts
Caversham
Jordan Cl
Ibstone Ave
Highbridge Cl
Farnham Dr
Earlsfield Cl
Devon Dr
Dacre Ave
Chestnut Ave
Valley Cl
Sheridan Ave
Brill Cl
Sheep Wlk
Springfield Mews
Fallowfield Cl
Caversham Hill
Allot Gdns
Orchard Gr
Woods Rd
Lowfield Gn
Corfe Mews
Bramber Mews
Blackwater Cl
Almond Dr
Milestone View Ct
A4155
READING
Picton Way
The Rise
Cedar Wood Cres
Greystoke Rd
Raglan Gdns
Cawsam Gdns
Cemy
Crem
Woodlands Gr
Hawthorne Rd
Oakley Rd
Blenheim Rd
Victoria Rd
Balmore Dr
Grosvenor Rd
Wilwyne Cl
Chiltern Rd
Valentine Cres
Norman Rd
Micklands Prim Sch
Micklands Rd
Copse Ave
All Hallows Rd
Caversham Prim Sch
Balmore Park
Coll
Lady Jane Ct
Fry Ct
Ellesmere Cl
Moss Cl
Kildare Gdns
Onslow Gdns
Mayfield Dr
Berry Brook
Balmore Ho 1
Larch Ct 2
Beech Ct 3
Ash Ct 4
Queen St
Knighton Cl
The Ridgeway
Newlands Ave
Derby Rd
Field View
Queen Anne's Sch
Banbury Gdns
Pembroke Pl
Henley Rd
The Mount
The Cloisters
Hemdean Rise
Sch
Berrylands Rd
Longhurst Cl
Barclose Ave
Tilbury Cl
Rossendale Rd
Lowfield Farm
Priest Hill
Hemdean Hill
Rufus Isaacs Rd
Fairfax Cl
Donegal Cl
Angle Field Rd
B3345
Clifton Park Rd
Auburn Ct
St Anne's Rd
Priory Ct
Priory Ave
Oxford St
Short St
Chester St
Rectory Rd
Waller Ct
Cromwell Rd
Queen Annes Gate
Keston Cl
Elmleigh Ct
Donkin Hill
Lower Henley Rd
Flambards
The Slopes
Luscombe Cl
Manaqua Cl
Nire Rd
Gravel Pit
A4074
Church Rd
Church St
A4155
Prospect St
North St
South St
Westfield Rd
Hampden Rd
Falkland Rd
St Anne's RC Prim Sch
South View Ave
Washington Rd
South View Park
Marsack St
Briant's Ave
Eccles Cl
Caleta Cl
Peel Cl
Charles Evans Way
Alston Wlk
Ian Mikardo Way
Rhine Cl
Honey Meadow Cl
Liby
Buckside
Bridge St
Abbotsmead Pl
Archway Rd
Harley Rd
Bristow Ct
Ardler Rd
Hardy Cl
Brackstone Cl
St John's Rd
Nelson Rd
Montague St
Rothwell Wlk
Clonmell Cl
Talbot Cl
Star Rd
Dickens Cl
Amersham Rd
Marina
Thames Side Prom
Caversham Bridge
Promenade Rd
The Willows
Crendon Ct
Wolsey Rd
St Stephens Cl
Cardinal Cl
Elliots Way
Patrick Rd
Gosbrook Rd
King's Rd
Coldicutt St
Forge Cl
Paddock Rd
Lower Caversham
Richfield Ave
Waterman Pl
Caversham Wharf
Thames Ave
Tamesis Pl
Queen's Rd
Champion Rd
Send Rd
Randolph Rd
Newport Rd
Caversham Rd
Thameside
RG1
Fry's Island
Brigham Rd
A1
1 Riverside Ct
2 Claydon Ct
3 Hallsmead Ct
4 Grayling Ct
5 Monmouth Ct
Mill Rd
Mill Gn
Millers Ct
The Causeway
B1
1 Gosbrook Ho
2 Gifford Ho
3 Pembroke Ho
4 Piggott's Rd
5 Monkley Ct
6 Richard Nevill Ct
7 Waleys Pl
RG6
Addison Rd
York Rd
Ross Rd
Swansea Rd
Northfield Rd
De Montfort Rd
Isis Ct
Lynmouth Rd
Lynmouth Ct
Thames Ct
Norman Pl
George St
Reading Bridge
Heron Island
View Island
The Thames Path
King's Meadow
River Thames
Deans Farm
Nature Reserve
A329
Vastern Rd

86

60

59
35

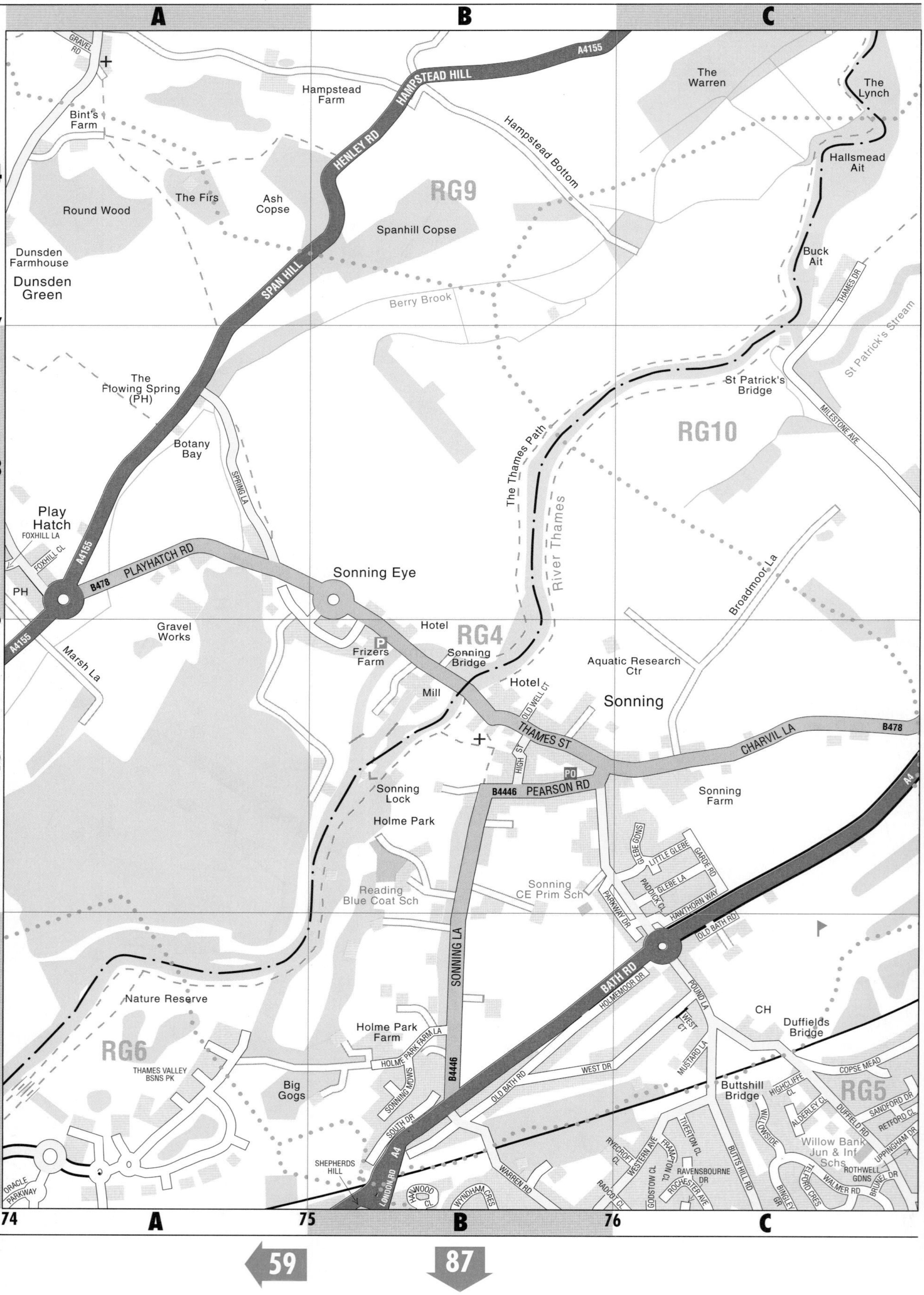
A
B
C
4
3
2
1
77
76
75
74
74
75
76
A4155
HAMPSTEAD HILL
HENLEY RD
SPAN HILL
Hampstead Farm
Hampstead Bottom
The Warren
The Lynch
Hallsmead Ait
Buck Ait
Bint's Farm
Round Wood
The Firs
Ash Copse
Spanhill Copse
RG9
Dunsden Farmhouse
Dunsden Green
Berry Brook
THAMES DR
St Patrick's Stream
St Patrick's Bridge
MILESTONE AVE
RG10
The Flowing Spring (PH)
Botany Bay
SPRING LA
The Thames Path
River Thames
Play Hatch
FOXHILL LA
FOXHILL CL
PH
B478
PLAYHATCH RD
Sonning Eye
Broadmoor La
Gravel Works
Marsh La
Hotel
RG4
Frizers Farm
Sonning Bridge
Aquatic Research Ctr
Hotel
Mill
OLD WELL CT
Sonning
THAMES ST
HIGH ST
CHARVIL LA
B478
A4
PO
B4446
PEARSON RD
Sonning Lock
Sonning Farm
Holme Park
GLEBE GDNS
LITTLE GLEBE
GARDE RD
PADDICK CL
GLEBE LA
HAWTHORN WAY
Reading Blue Coat Sch
Sonning CE Prim Sch
PARKWAY DR
OLD BATH RD
SONNING LA
BATH RD
HOLMEMOOR DR
POUND LA
WEST CT
Nature Reserve
CH
Duffields Bridge
Holme Park Farm
HOLME PARK FARM LA
MUSTARD LA
WEST DR
RG6
THAMES VALLEY BSNS PK
SONNING MDWS
B4446
OLD BATH RD
Buttshill Bridge
HIGHCLIFFE CL
COPSE MEAD
RG5
Big Gogs
SOUTH DR
ALDERLEY CL
DUFFIELD RD
SANDFORD DR
RETFORD CL
TIVERTON CL
RYECROFT CL
WESTERN AVE
FRAMPTON CL
WILLOWSIDE
Willow Bank Jun & Inf Schs
UPPINGHAM DR
SHEPHERDS HILL
A4
LONDON RD
HARWOOD CL
WYNDHAM CRES
WARREN RD
RADCOT CL
GODSTOW CL
RAVENSBOURNE DR
ROCHESTER AVE
BUTTS HILL RD
BINGLEY GR
TELFORD CRES
ROTHWELL GDNS
WALMER RD
BRUNEL DR
ORACLE PARKWAY
A
B
C

59
87

A B C

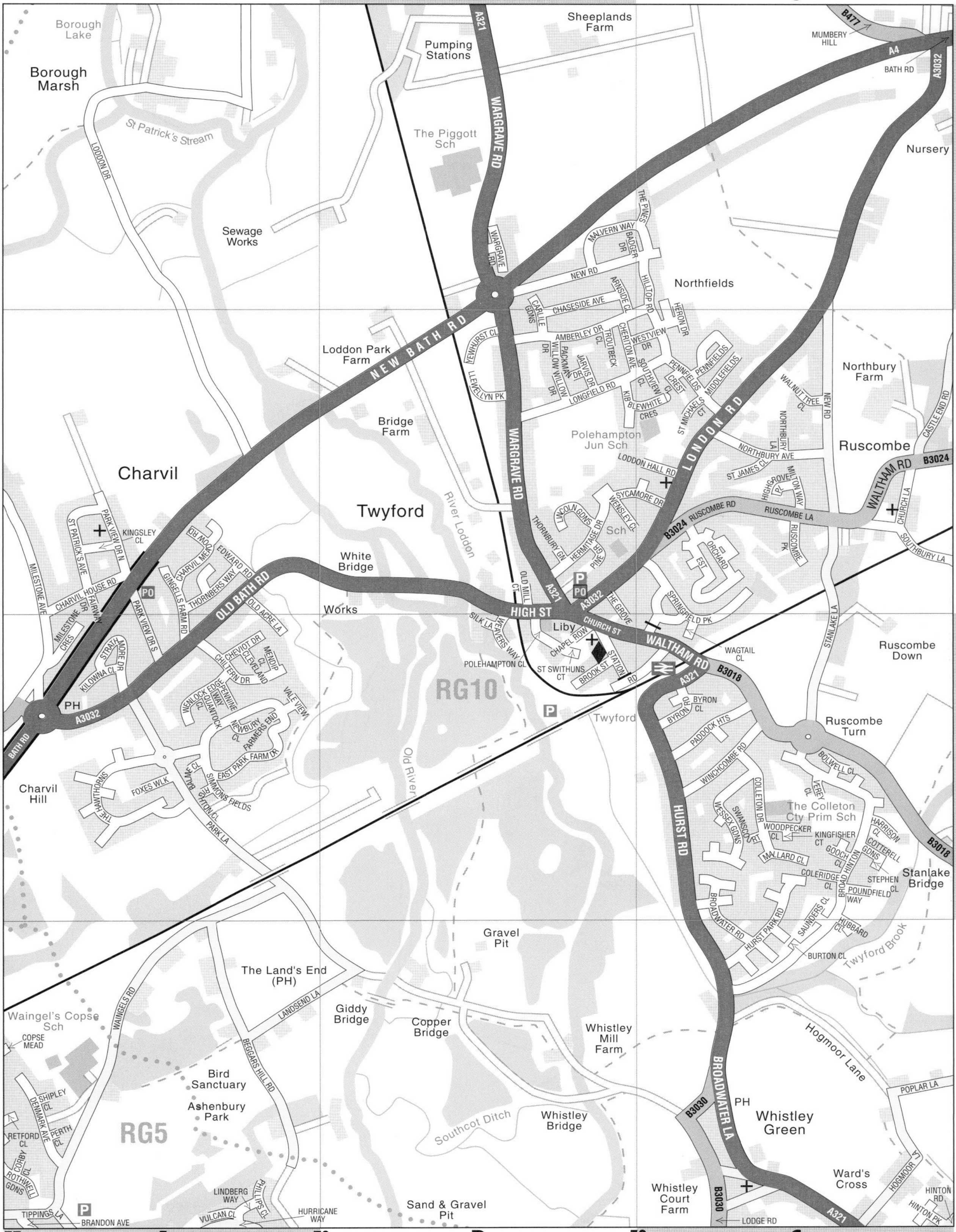


77 78 79
4 3 2 1

61
37
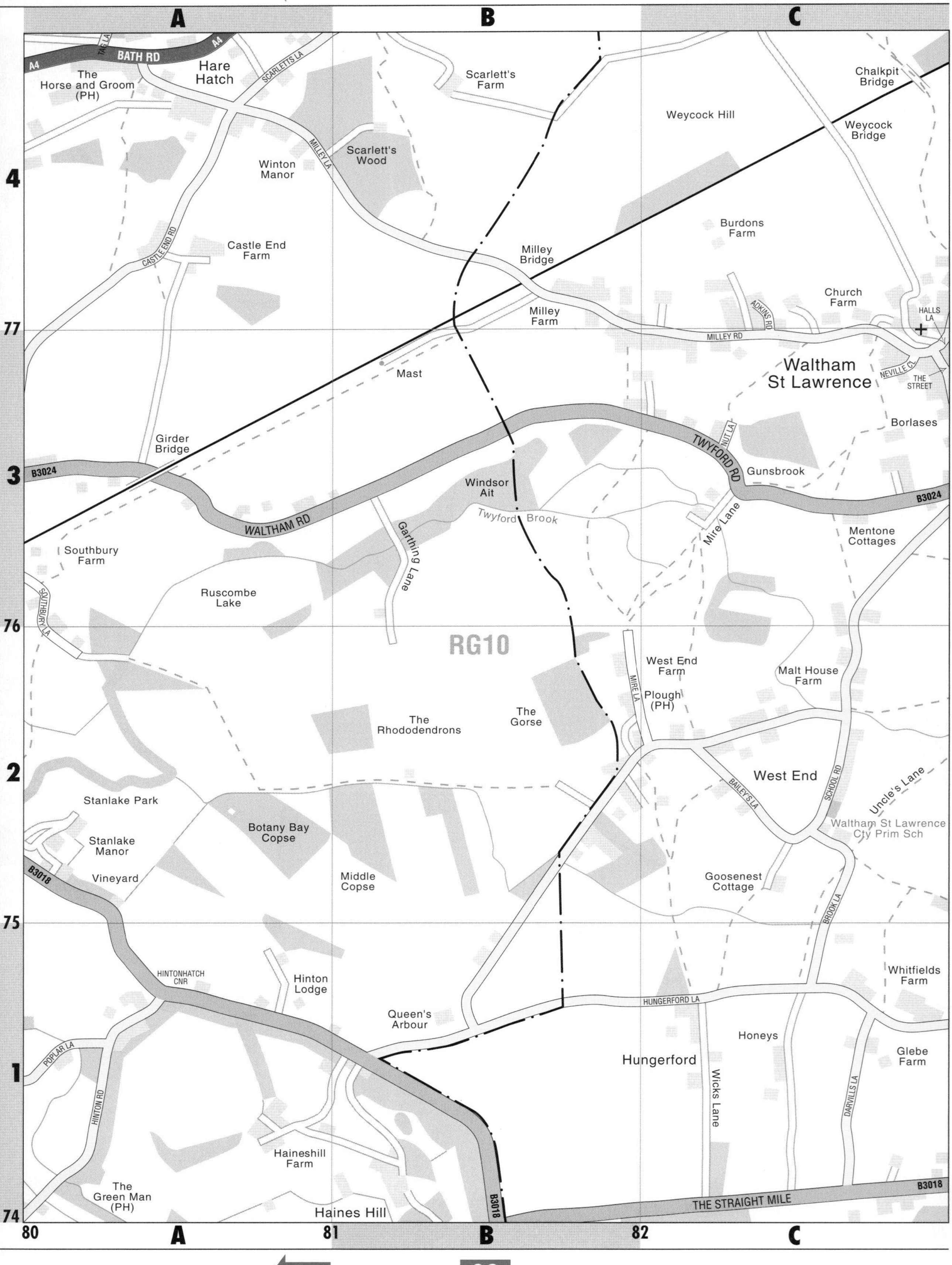
A
B
C
4
77
3
76
2
75
1
74
80
81
82
BATH RD
A4
TAG LA
Hare Hatch
The Horse and Groom (PH)
SCARLETTS LA
Scarlett's Farm
Chalkpit Bridge
Weycock Hill
Weycock Bridge
MILLEY LA
Scarlett's Wood
Winton Manor
Burdons Farm
CASTLE END RD
Castle End Farm
Milley Bridge
Church Farm
ADKINS RD
HALLS LA
Milley Farm
MILLEY RD
Waltham St Lawrence
NEVILLE CL
THE STREET
Mast
Borlases
NUT LA
Girder Bridge
TWYFORD RD
B3024
Gunsbrook
Windsor Ait
WALTHAM RD
Twyford Brook
Mire Lane
Mentone Cottages
Southbury Farm
Garthing Lane
Ruscombe Lake
SOUTHBURY LA
RG10
West End Farm
Malt House Farm
MIRE LA
Plough (PH)
The Rhododendrons
The Gorse
West End
BAILEY'S LA
SCHOOL RD
Uncle's Lane
Stanlake Park
Waltham St Lawrence Cty Prim Sch
Botany Bay Copse
Stanlake Manor
B3018
Vineyard
Middle Copse
Goosenest Cottage
BROOK LA
Whitfields Farm
HINTONHATCH CNR
Hinton Lodge
HUNGERFORD LA
Queen's Arbour
Honeys
POPLAR LA
Hungerford
Glebe Farm
Wicks Lane
DARVILLS LA
HINTON RD
Haineshill Farm
The Green Man (PH)
THE STRAIGHT MILE
Haines Hill
61
89

38
64

A
B
C
Airfield
Sewage Works
GROVE PK
CHURCH VIEW
VICARAGE GDNS
WALTHAM RD
BUTCHERS LA
CHERRYGARDEN LA
Refuse Tip
White Waltham CE Prim Sch
Shottesbrooke Park
White Waltham
Waltham Place
The Beehive (PH)
INNINGS LA
Shottesbrooke Park
BRAEMAR
WALGROVE GDNS
Halls Farm
HALLS LA
Burringham Wood
South Wood
BROADMOOR LA
PUNDLES LA
LITTLEFIELD GREEN
SL6
THE STREET
PO
PH
POOL LA
Marsh Down
Littlefield Green
B3024
Refuse Tip
DOWNFIELD LA
Great Wood
M4
Smewins Farm
DOWNFIELD RD
RG10
Crockford's Bridge
Pondwood Farm
Pond Wood
Uncle's La
Twyford Brook
Crockford's Copse
Long Wood
The Cut
Beenham's Farm
CALLIN'S LA
MARE LA
Old Malt House (Hill Farm)
Beenham's Heath
Little Hazes
Pope's Farm
The Royal Oak (PH)
Great Martins
HUNGERFORD LA
Great Hazes
RG42
HOWE LA
Buck Farm
The Manor
Furze Ground
Shurlock Row
The Plantation
Yate's Farm
The White Hart (PH)
PO
Mare La
Mast
Benhams Copse
Foxley PNEU Sch
Spinningwheel La
Jolly Farmer (PH)
THE STRAIGHT MILE
B3018
M4
WESTLEY MILL
4
77
3
76
2
75
1
74
83
84
85
A
B
C

90
64

63
39
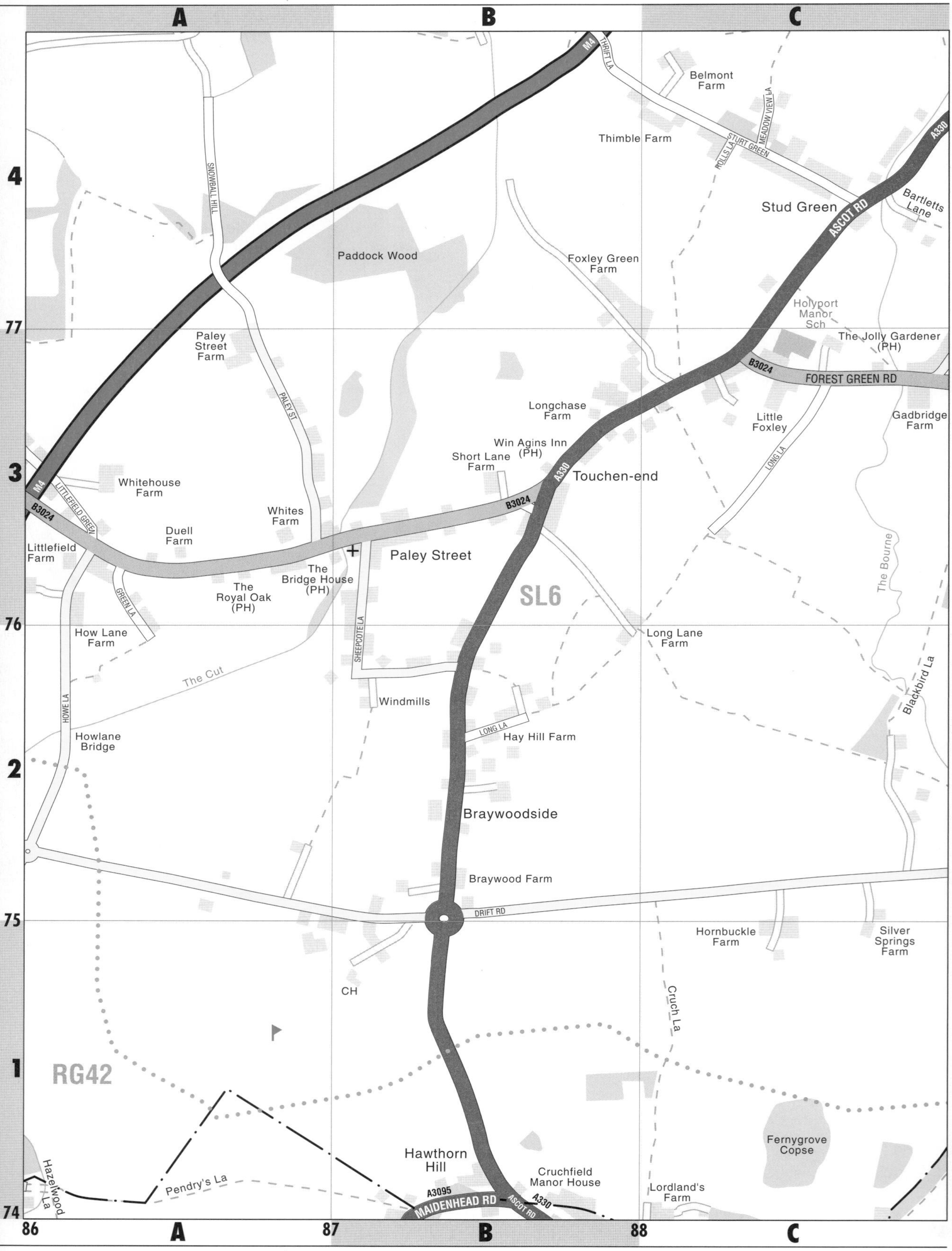
A
B
C
4
77
3
76
2
75
1
74
86
87
88
M4
THRIFT LA
Belmont Farm
MEADOW VIEW LA
Thimble Farm
STURT GREEN
ROLLS LA
A330
SNOWBALL HILL
Stud Green
ASCOT RD
Bartletts Lane
Paddock Wood
Foxley Green Farm
Holyport Manor Sch
The Jolly Gardener (PH)
Paley Street Farm
B3024
FOREST GREEN RD
PALEY ST
Longchase Farm
Little Foxley
Gadbridge Farm
Win Agins Inn (PH)
Short Lane Farm
LONG LA
Touchen-end
Whitehouse Farm
LITTLEFIELD GREEN
Whites Farm
Duell Farm
Littlefield Farm
Paley Street
The Bridge House (PH)
The Royal Oak (PH)
GREEN LA
SL6
The Bourne
How Lane Farm
Long Lane Farm
SHEEPCOTE LA
The Cut
Windmills
Blackbird La
HOWE LA
Howlane Bridge
Hay Hill Farm
Braywoodside
Braywood Farm
DRIFT RD
Hornbuckle Farm
Silver Springs Farm
CH
Cruch La
RG42
Fernygrove Copse
Hazelwood La
Pendry's La
Hawthorn Hill
Cruchfield Manor House
Lordland's Farm
A3095
MAIDENHEAD RD
ASCOT RD
63
91

40
66

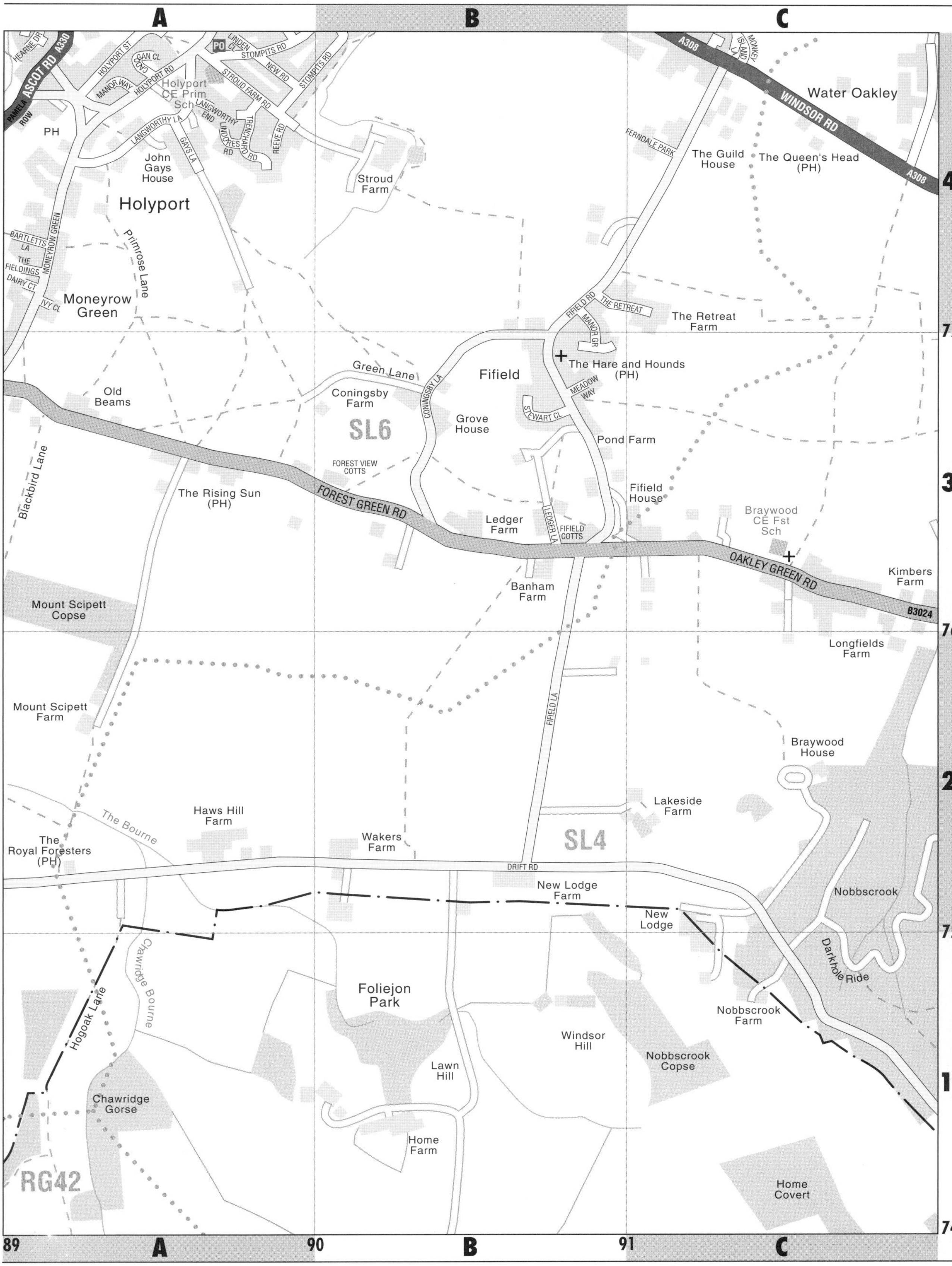
A
B
C
Holyport
Holyport CE Prim Sch
John Gays House
Moneyrow Green
Primrose Lane
Stroud Farm
Water Oakley
WINDSOR RD
A308
The Guild House
The Queen's Head (PH)
The Retreat Farm
The Hare and Hounds (PH)
Fifield
Green Lane
Coningsby Farm
Grove House
Old Beams
SL6
Pond Farm
Fifield House
FOREST GREEN RD
The Rising Sun (PH)
Blackbird Lane
Ledger Farm
Braywood CE Fst Sch
OAKLEY GREEN RD
Kimbers Farm
B3024
Banham Farm
Mount Scipett Copse
Longfields Farm
Mount Scipett Farm
Braywood House
Haws Hill Farm
Lakeside Farm
The Bourne
The Royal Foresters (PH)
Wakers Farm
SL4
DRIFT RD
New Lodge Farm
Nobbscrook
New Lodge
Chawridge Bourne
Foliejon Park
Darkhole Ride
Nobbscrook Farm
Hogoak Lane
Windsor Hill
Lawn Hill
Nobbscrook Copse
Chawridge Gorse
Home Farm
Home Covert
RG42
4
3
2
1
77
76
75
74
89
90
91

92
66

65
41

A B C

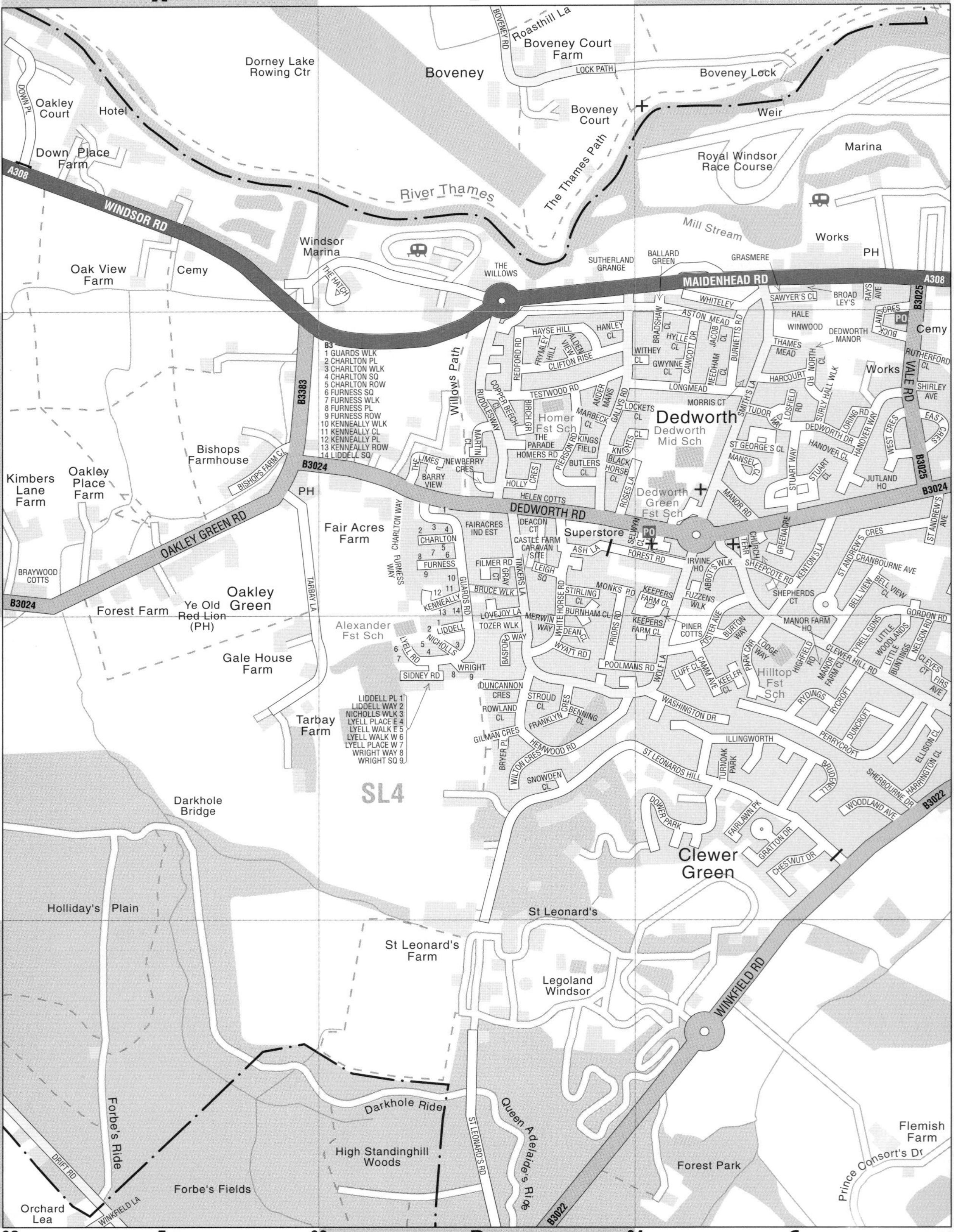


4
77
3
76
2
75
1
74

92 A 93 B 94 C

65
93

42

68

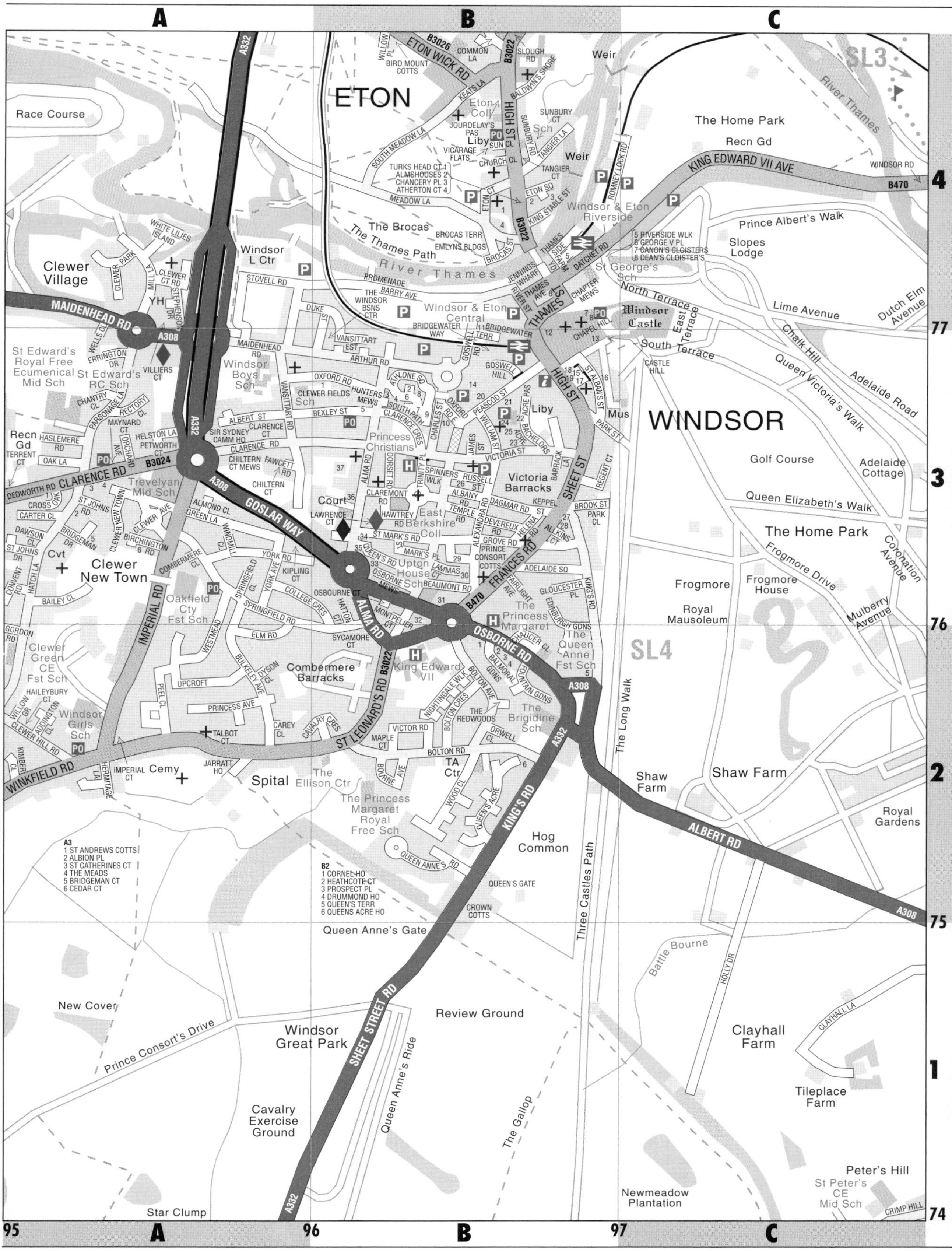


B3
1 BEAUMONT COTTS
2 CAMBRIDGE HO
3 WARD ROYAL PAR
4 CHRISTIAN SQ
5 CRESCENT VILLAS
6 WARD ROYAL
7 BOWES-LYON CL
8 MOUNTBATTEN SQ
9 CHARLES HO
10 QUEEN ANNE'S CT
11 CASTLEVIEW HO
12 HORSESHOE CLOISTERS
13 LODGINGS OF THE MILITARY KNIGHTS
14 KING EDWARD CT
15 CHURCH ST
16 ST ALBANS CL
17 CHURCH LA
18 MARKET ST
19 QUEEN CHARLOTTE ST
20 AMBERLEY PL
21 PEASCOD PL
22 ROYAL FREE CT
23 ELLISON HO
24 SUN PAS
25 HIBBERT'S ALLEY
26 GARFIELD PL
27 KING'S ROAD HO
28 COACHMAN'S LODGE
29 ST LEONARD'S AVE
30 LAMMAS AVE
31 CROSSWAYS CT
32 KNIGHTS PL
33 HOUSTON CT
34 WARWICK CT
35 CHELMSFORD CT
36 CAMPERDOWN HO
37 VISCOUNT CT

94

68

67
43

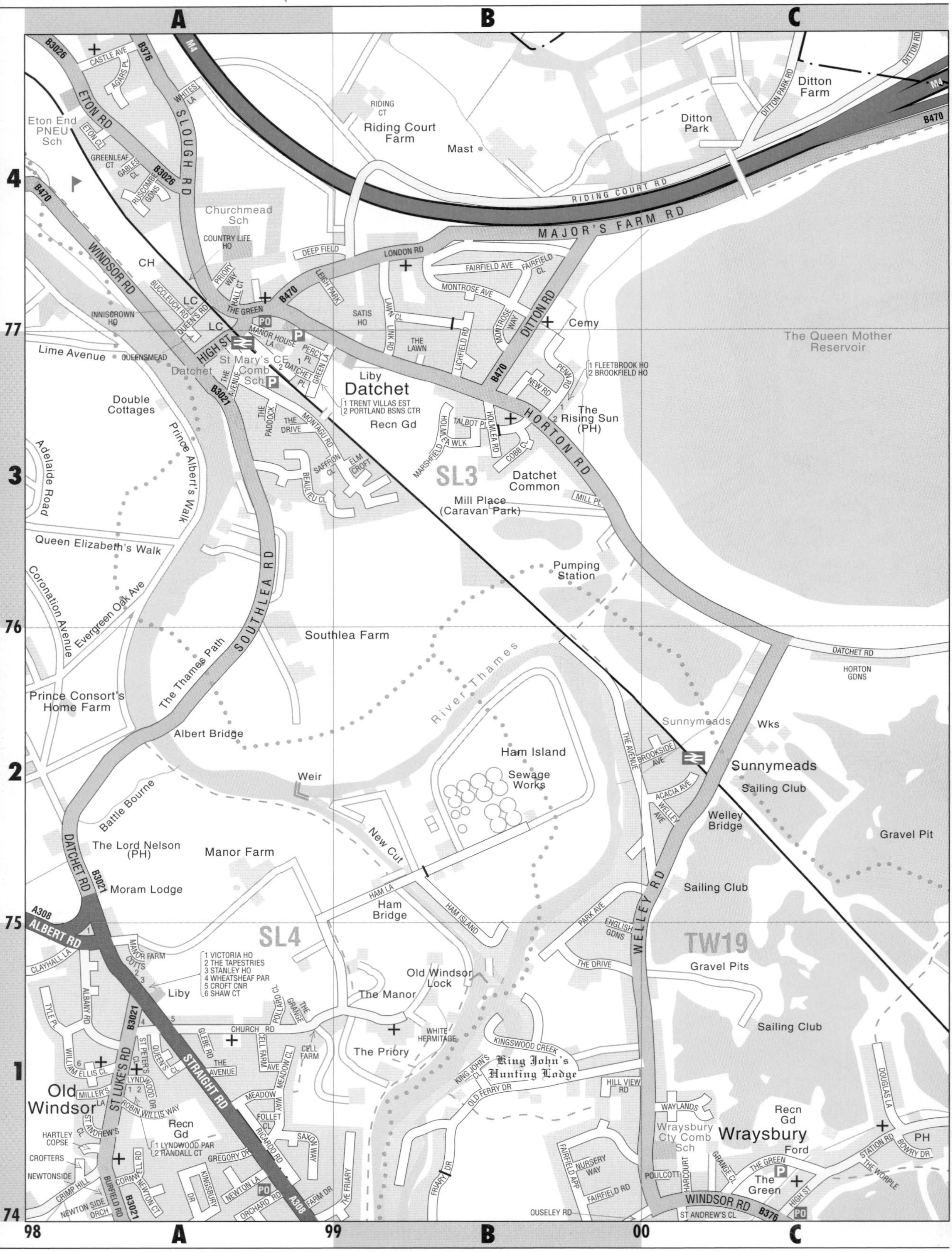
A
B
C
4
77
3
76
2
75
1
74
98
99
00
M4
B3026
B376
CASTLE AVE
AGARS PL
ETON RD
ETON CL
Eton End PNEU Sch
WHITES LA
SLOUGH RD
GREENLEAF CT
GABLES CL
RUSCOMBE GDNS
B470
Churchmead Sch
COUNTRY LIFE HO
WINDSOR RD
CH
PRIORY WAY
HALL CT
BUCCLEUCH RD
QUEEN'S RD
LC
THE GREEN
INNISCROWN HO
PO
HIGH ST
MANOR HOUSE LA
PERCY PL
DATCHET PL
GREEN LA
Lime Avenue
QUEENSMEAD
Datchet
St Mary's CE Comb Sch
THE AVENUE
B3021
Double Cottages
THE PADDOCK
THE DRIVE
MONTAGU RD
SAFFRON CL
ELM CROFT
BEAULIEU CL
Prince Albert's Walk
Adelaide Road
Queen Elizabeth's Walk
Coronation Avenue
Evergreen Oak Ave
SOUTHLEA RD
The Thames Path
Prince Consort's Home Farm
Albert Bridge
Battle Bourne
DATCHET RD
The Lord Nelson (PH)
Manor Farm
Moram Lodge
A308
ALBERT RD
CLAYHALL LA
MANOR FARM COTTS
ALBANY RD
TYLE PL
WILLIAM ELLIS CL
ST LUKE'S RD
ST PETER'S CL
LYNDWOOD DR
QUEEN'S CL
MILLER'S LA
ROBIN WILLIS WAY
Old Windsor
HARTLEY COPSE
ST ANDREW'S CL
CROFTERS
NEWTONSIDE
CRIMP HILL
NEWTON SIDE ORCH
BURFIELD RD
CORNWELL RD
NEWTON CT
Recn Gd
1 LYNDWOOD PAR
2 RANDALL CT
STRAIGHT RD
GREGORY DR
KINGSBURY DR
NEWTON LA
ORCHARD RD
FARM DR
THE FRIARY
Liby
1 VICTORIA HO
2 THE TAPESTRIES
3 STANLEY HO
4 WHEATSHEAF PAR
5 CROFT CNR
6 SHAW CT
GLEBE RD
CHURCH RD
CELL FARM AVE
THE AVENUE
POLLARD CL
THE GRANGE
MEADOW CL
MEADOW WAY
FOLLET CL
RICARDO RD
SAXON WAY
CELL FARM
SL4
The Manor
The Priory
WHITE HERMITAGE
Old Windsor Lock
HAM LA
Ham Bridge
HAM ISLAND
New Cut
Weir
KINGSWOOD CREEK
King John's Hunting Lodge
KING JOHN'S CL
OLD FERRY DR
FRIARY DR
HILL VIEW RD
FAIRFIELD APP
NURSERY WAY
FAIRFIELD RD
OUSELEY RD
RIDING CT
Riding Court Farm
Mast
RIDING COURT RD
MAJOR'S FARM RD
DEEP FIELD
LONDON RD
LEIGH PARK
SATIS HO
LAWN CL
LINK RD
THE LAWN
LICHFIELD RD
FAIRFIELD AVE
FAIRFIELD CL
MONTROSE AVE
MONTROSE WAY
DITTON RD
Cemy
Liby
Datchet
1 TRENT VILLAS EST
2 PORTLAND BSNS CTR
Recn Gd
NEW RD
PENN RD
1 FLEETBROOK HO
2 BROOKFIELD HO
The Rising Sun (PH)
HORTON RD
TALBOT PL
HOLMLEA WLK
HOLMLEA RD
MARSHFIELD
COBB CL
SL3
Datchet Common
Mill Place (Caravan Park)
MILL PL
Pumping Station
Southlea Farm
River Thames
Ham Island
Sewage Works
Ditton Farm
DITTON PARK RD
DITTON RD
Ditton Park
The Queen Mother Reservoir
DATCHET RD
HORTON GDNS
Sunnymeads
Wks
THE AVENUE
BROOKSIDE AVE
Sunnymeads
Sailing Club
ACACIA AVE
WELLEY AVE
Welley Bridge
Gravel Pit
WELLEY RD
Sailing Club
PARK AVE
ENGLISH GDNS
TW19
THE DRIVE
Gravel Pits
Sailing Club
WAYLANDS
Wraysbury Cty Comb Sch
Wraysbury
Recn Gd
DOUGLAS LA
PH
BOWRY DR
STATION RD
THE WORPLE
Ford
GRANGE CL
THE GREEN
The Green
HIGH ST
POULCOTT
HARCOURT
WINDSOR RD
ST ANDREW'S CL
B376

67
95

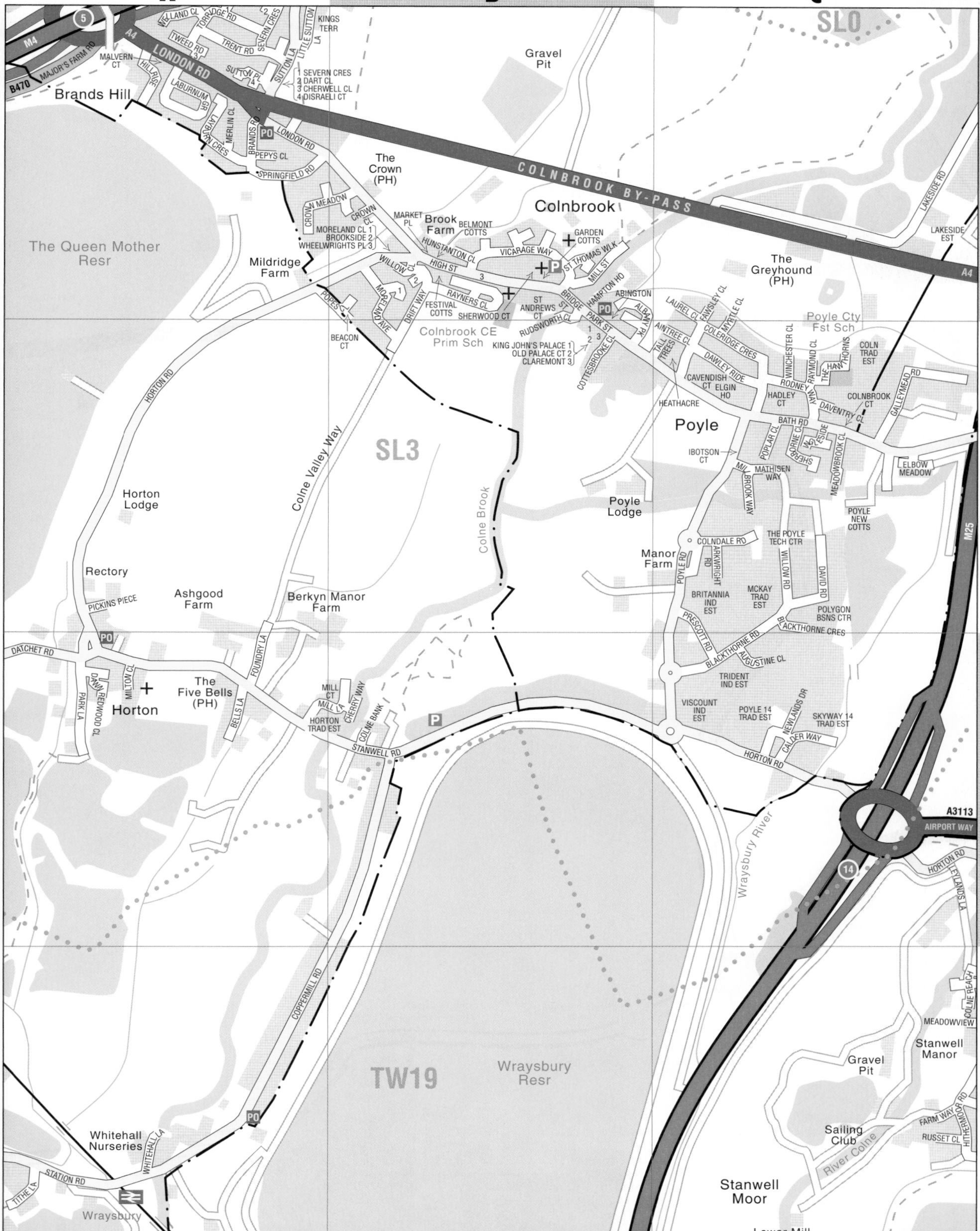
A
B
C
Brands Hill
The Queen Mother Resr
Mildridge Farm
The Crown (PH)
Brook Farm
Colnbrook
Gravel Pit
COLNBROOK BY-PASS
LONDON RD
SL0
SL3
TW19
The Greyhound (PH)
Poyle Cty Fst Sch
Colnbrook CE Prim Sch
Poyle
Poyle Lodge
Manor Farm
Horton Lodge
Colne Valley Way
Colne Brook
Rectory
Ashgood Farm
Berkyn Manor Farm
Horton
The Five Bells (PH)
HORTON RD
DATCHET RD
STANWELL RD
COPPERMILL RD
Wraysbury Resr
Wraysbury River
Whitehall Nurseries
STATION RD
Wraysbury
Stanwell Moor
Gravel Pit
Stanwell Manor
Sailing Club
River Colne
Lower Mill Farm
King George VI Resr
M25
M4
A4
A3113
AIRPORT WAY
B470
4
3
2
1
77
76
75
74
01
02
03

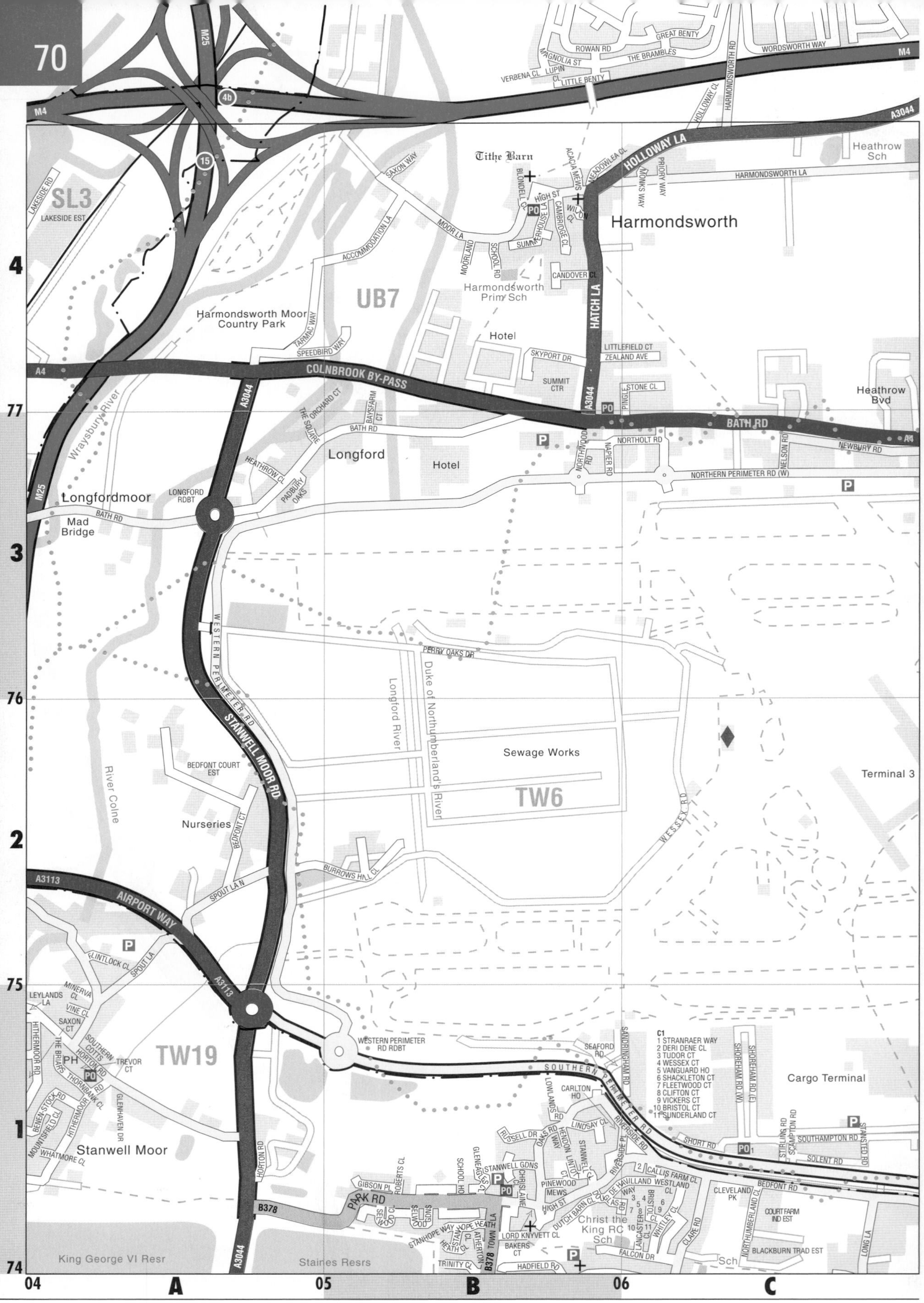
M25
M4
A3044
4b
15
ROWAN RD
GREAT BENTY
WORDSWORTH WAY
THE BRAMBLES
MAGNOLIA ST
VERBENA CL
LUPIN CL
LITTLE BENTY
HARMONDSWORTH RD
HOLLOWAY CL
HOLLOWAY LA
Heathrow Sch
HARMONDSWORTH LA
Tithe Barn
SAXON WAY
BLONDELL CL
HIGH ST
ACACIA MEWS
MEADOWLEA CL
PRIORY WAY
MONKS WAY
CAMBRIDGE CL
WILLOW CL
PO
Harmondsworth
SL3
LAKESIDE RD
LAKESIDE EST
MOOR LA
ACCOMMODATION LA
MOORLAND RD
SCHOOL RD
SUMMERHOUSE LA
CANDOVER CL
Harmondsworth Prim Sch
HATCH LA
UB7
Harmondsworth Moor Country Park
TARMAC WAY
SPEEDBIRD WAY
Hotel
SKYPORT DR
LITTLEFIELD CT
ZEALAND AVE
SUMMIT CTR
A4
COLNBROOK BY-PASS
THE ORCHARD CT
THE SQUARE
BAYSFARM CT
BATH RD
STONE CL
PINGLE
Heathrow Bvd
Wraysbury River
Longford
NORTHWOOD RD
NAPIER RD
NORTHOLT RD
NELSON RD
NEWBURY RD
HEATHROW CL
PADBURY OAKS
NORTHERN PERIMETER RD (W)
P
Longfordmoor
LONGFORD RDBT
Mad Bridge
WESTERN PERIMETER RD
PERRY OAKS DR
Longford River
Duke of Northumberland's River
STANWELL MOOR RD
Sewage Works
TW6
BEDFORD COURT EST
River Colne
Terminal 3
Nurseries
BEDFONT CT
WESSEX RD
A3113
AIRPORT WAY
BURROWS HILL CL
SPOUT LA N
FLINTLOCK CL
SPOUT LA
MINERVA CL
LEYLANDS LA
VINE CL
SAXON CT
HITHERMOOR RD
THE BRIARS
SOUTHERN COTTS
HORTON RD
PH
TREVOR CT
TW19
THORNBANK CL
GLENHAVEN DR
WESTERN PERIMETER RD RDBT
SEAFORD RD
SANDRINGHAM RD
C1
1 STRANRAER WAY
2 DERI DENE CL
3 TUDOR CT
4 WESSEX CT
5 VANGUARD HO
6 SHACKLETON CT
7 FLEETWOOD CT
8 CLIFTON CT
9 VICKERS CT
10 BRISTOL CT
11 SUNDERLAND CT
SHOREHAM RD (W)
SHOREHAM RD (E)
Cargo Terminal
SOUTHERN PERIMETER RD
CARLTON HO
LOWLANDS RD
LINDSAY CL
RIVERSIDE RD
BENEN-STOCK RD
MOUNTSFIELD CL
WHATMORE CL
Stanwell Moor
HORTON RD
RUSSELL DR
OAKS RD
HENDON WAY
STANWELL CT
LINTON CT
RIVERSIDE PL
SHORT RD
STIRLING RD
SCAMPTON RD
SOUTHAMPTON RD
STANSTED RD
SOLENT RD
STANWELL GDNS
CHRISLAINE CL
GLENEAGLES CL
SCHOOL HO
ROBERTS CL
GIBSON PL
PARK RD
B378
PINEWOOD MEWS
CALLIS FARM CL
DE HAVILLAND WAY
WESTLAND CL
BEDFONT RD
CLEVELAND PK
HIGH ST
DUTCH BARN CL
Christ the King RC Sch
LANCASTER CL
BRISTOL CL
WHITLEY CL
CLARE RD
NORTHUMBERLAND CL
COURT FARM IND EST
BLACKBURN TRAD EST
LONG LA
STANHOPE WAY
STANHOPE HEATH
HEATH CL
ATHERTON CL
TOWN LA
LORD KNYVETT CL
BAKERS CT
FALCON DR
HADFIELD RD
TRINITY CL
Sch
King George VI Resr
Staines Resrs
74
75
76
77
04
05
06
A
B
C
1
2
3
4

69
97

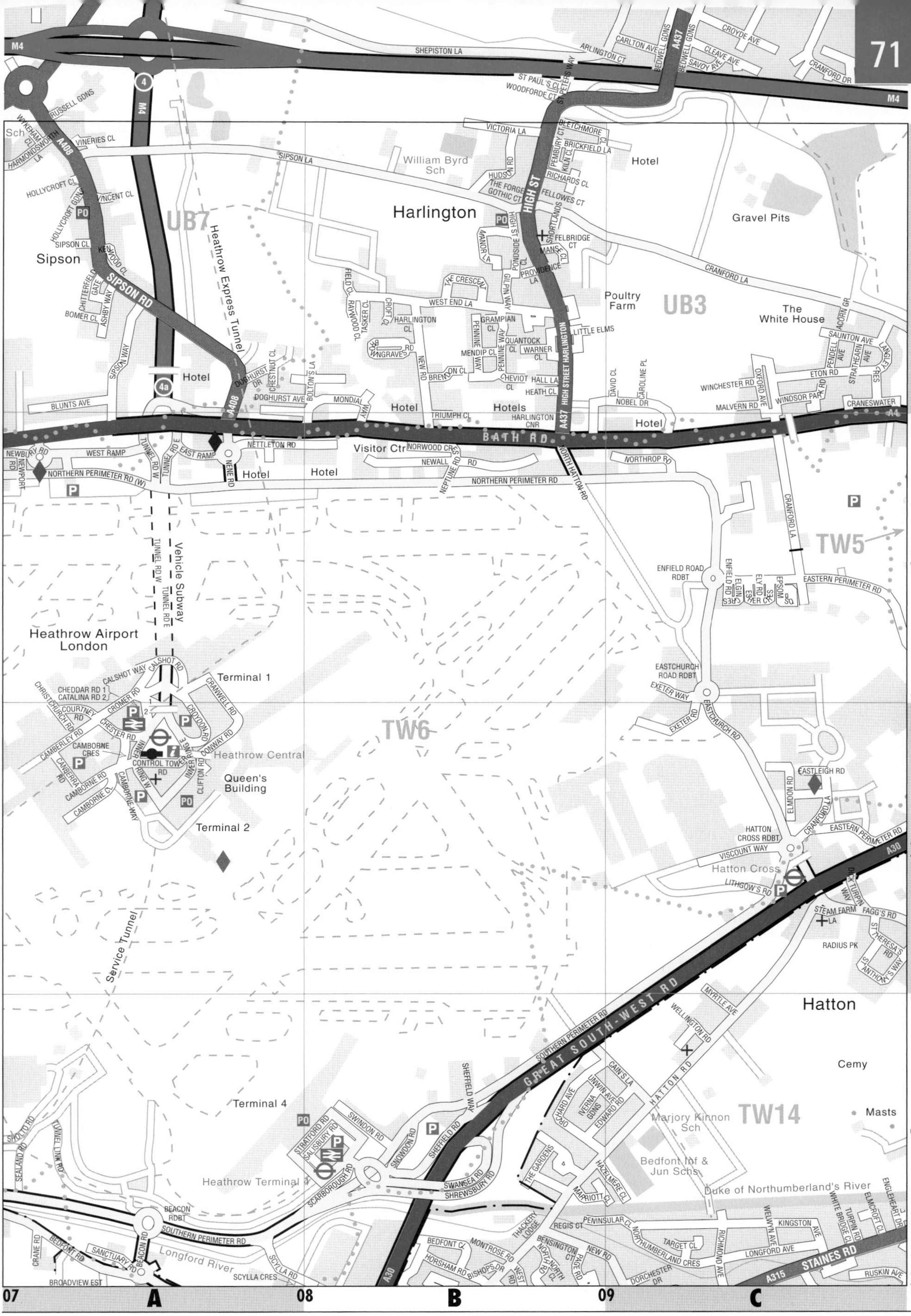
M4
SHEPISTON LA
ARLINGTON CT
CARLTON AVE
BEDWELL GDNS
A437
CROYDE AVE
CLEAVE AVE
SAVOY AVE
CRANFORD DR
ST PAUL'S CL
WOODFORDE CT
ST PETERS WAY
4
RUSSELL GDNS
WYKEHAM CL
HARMONDSWORTH LA
A408
VINERIES CL
Sch
VICTORIA LA
BLETCHMORE CL
PEMBURY CT
BRICKFIELD LA
KILN CL
RICHARDS CL
SIPSON LA
William Byrd Sch
HUDSON RD
THE FORGE
GOTHIC CT
FELLOWES CT
Hotel
Gravel Pits
HOLLYCROFT CL
HOLLYCROFT GDNS
VINCENT CL
PO
UB7
Harlington
HIGH ST
SHORTLANDS
FELBRIDGE CT
MANSE CL
MANOR LA
PONDSIDE CL
HIGH ST CL
PROVIDENCE LA
Heathrow Express Tunnel
SIPSON CL
KEN WOOD CL
Sipson
SIPSON RD
CRANFORD LA
CHITTERFIELD GATE
ASHBY WAY
BOMER CL
FIELD CL
RAYWOOD CL
TASKER CL
CROFT CL
THE CRESCENT
GILPIN WAY
WEST END LA
HARLINGTON CL
GRAMPIAN CL
PENNINE WAY
QUANTOCK CL
WARNER CL
MENDIP CL
BROWNGRAVE RD
NEW RD
BRENDON CL
CHEVIOT CL
HALL LA
HEATH CL
HIGH STREET HARLINGTON
LITTLE ELMS
Poultry Farm
UB3
The White House
ACORN GR
SAUNTON AVE
PENDELL AVE
STRATHEARN AVE
LANGLEY CRES
ETON RD
OXFORD AVE
WINCHESTER RD
WINDSOR PARK RD
MALVERN RD
CRANESWATER
A4
77
DAVID CL
CAROLINE PL
NOBEL DR
SIPSON WAY
4a
Hotel
DOGHURST DR
CHESTNUT CL
BOLTON'S LA
DOGHURST AVE
MONDIAL WAY
BLUNTS AVE
Hotel
Hotels
HARLINGTON CNR
TRIUMPH CL
Hotel
BATH RD
NEWBURY RD
NEWPORT RD
WEST RAMP
TUNNEL RD W
TUNNEL RD E
EAST RAMP
NENE RD
NETTLETON RD
Visitor Ctr
NORWOOD CRES
NEWALL RD
NEPTUNE RD
NORTHROP RD
NORTH HATTON RD
NORTHERN PERIMETER RD (W)
NORTHERN PERIMETER RD
Hotel
Hotel
P
CRANFORD LA
TW5
3
Vehicle Subway
ENFIELD ROAD RDBT
ENFIELD RD
ELGIN CRES
ESHER CL
ELY RD
EPSOM SQ
EASTERN PERIMETER RD
Heathrow Airport London
CALSHOT WAY
CALSHOT RD
Terminal 1
CHEDDAR RD
CATALINA RD
CHRISTCHURCH RD
COURTNEY RD
CROMER RD
CRANWELL RD
CROYDON RD
CHESTER RD
CAMBERLEY RD
CAMBORNE CRES
CANBERRA RD
CAMBORNE RD
CAMBORNE CL
CAMBORNE WAY
INNER RING W
INNER RING E
CONTROL TOWER RD
CONWAY RD
CLIFTON RD
Heathrow Central
Queen's Building
Terminal 2
TW6
EASTCHURCH ROAD RDBT
EXETER WAY
EXETER RD
EASTCHURCH RD
76
EASTLEIGH RD
ELMDON RD
CRANFORD LA
EASTERN PERIMETER RD
HATTON CROSS RDBT
VISCOUNT WAY
Hatton Cross
LITHGOW'S RD
A30
DICK TURPIN WAY
2
STEAM FARM LA
FAGG'S RD
RADIUS PK
ST THERESA'S RD
ST ANTHONY'S WAY
Service Tunnel
GREAT SOUTH-WEST RD
SOUTHERN PERIMETER RD
MYRTLE AVE
WELLINGTON RD
Hatton
75
Cemy
CAIN'S LA
UNWIN AVE
IVERNA GDNS
ORCHARD AVE
EDWARD RD
HATTON RD
SHEFFIELD WAY
Terminal 4
PO
STRATFORD RD
SALISBURY RD
SWINDON RD
SNOWDON RD
SHEFFIELD RD
Marjory Kinnon Sch
TW14
Masts
1
SHOLTO RD
SEALAND RD
TUNNEL LINK RD
Heathrow Terminal 4
SCARBOROUGH RD
SWANSEA RD
SHREWSBURY RD
THE GARDENS
HAZELMERE CL
MARRIOTT CL
Bedfont Inf & Jun Schs
Duke of Northumberland's River
ENGLEHEART DR
ELMCROFT CL
WHITE BRIDGE CL
TURPIN RD
BEACON RDBT
SOUTHERN PERIMETER RD
THACKERY LODGE
REGIS CT
PENINSULAR CL
NORTHUMBERLAND CRES
TARGET CL
RICHMOND AVE
WELWYN AVE
KINGSTON AVE
LONGFORD AVE
CRANE RD
BEDFONT RD
SANCTUARY RD
BEACON RD
Longford River
SCYLLA RD
SCYLLA CRES
BROADVIEW EST
BEDFONT CL
MONTROSE RD
HORSHAM RD
BISHOPS DR
WEST RD
BENSINGTON CT
NORTH CT
PAGE RD
NEW RD
DORCHESTER DR
A315
STAINES RD
RUSKIN AVE
74
07
A
08
B
09
C

98

45

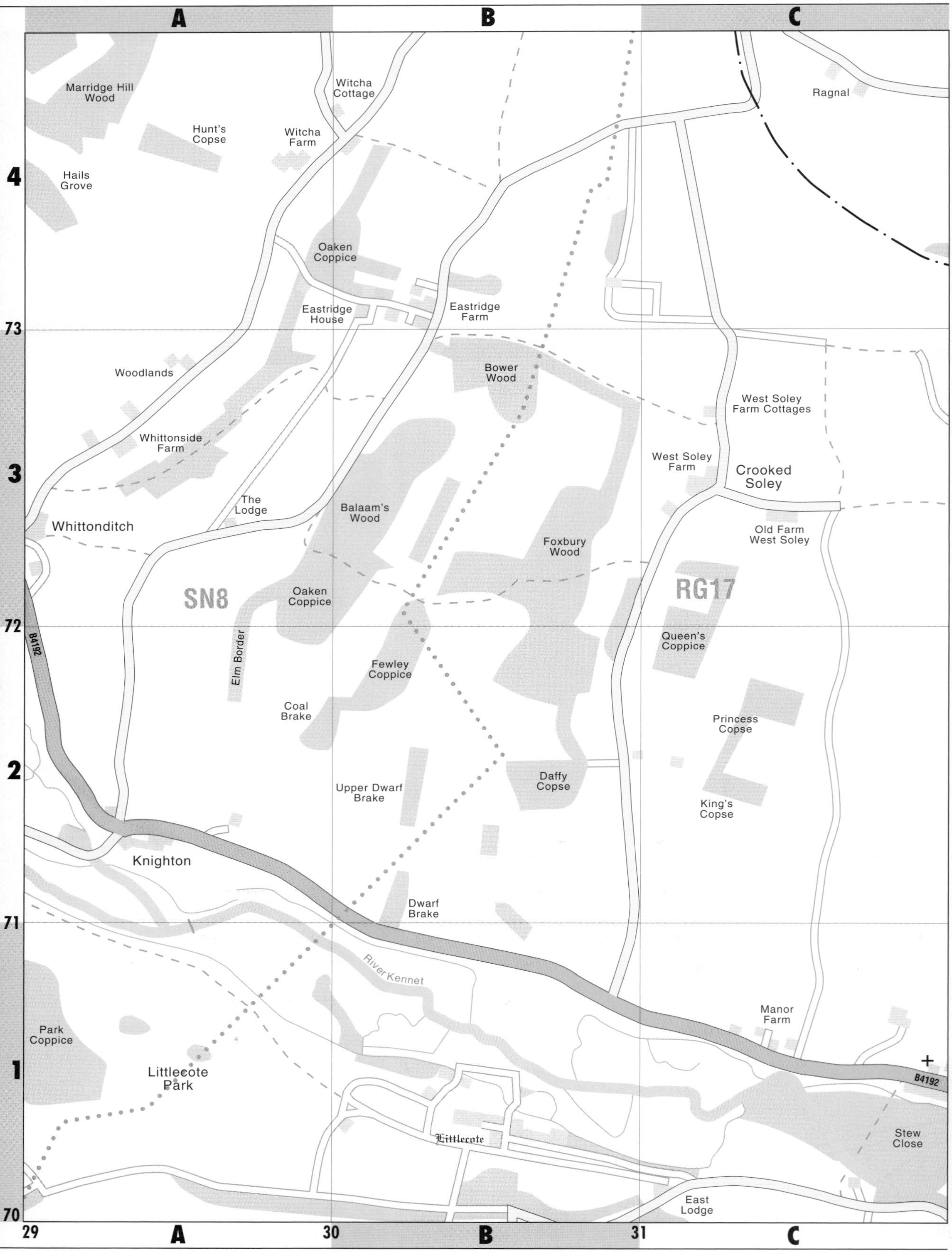
A
B
C
Marridge Hill Wood
Witcha Cottage
Ragnal
Hunt's Copse
Witcha Farm
Hails Grove
Oaken Coppice
Eastridge House
Eastridge Farm
Woodlands
Bower Wood
West Soley Farm Cottages
Whittonside Farm
West Soley Farm
Crooked Soley
The Lodge
Balaam's Wood
Whittonditch
Old Farm West Soley
Foxbury Wood
SN8
Oaken Coppice
RG17
B4192
Queen's Coppice
Elm Border
Fewley Coppice
Coal Brake
Princess Copse
Daffy Copse
Upper Dwarf Brake
King's Copse
Knighton
Dwarf Brake
River Kennet
Manor Farm
Park Coppice
Littlecote Park
B4192
Stew Close
Littlecote
East Lodge
4
73
3
72
2
71
1
70
29
30
31

99

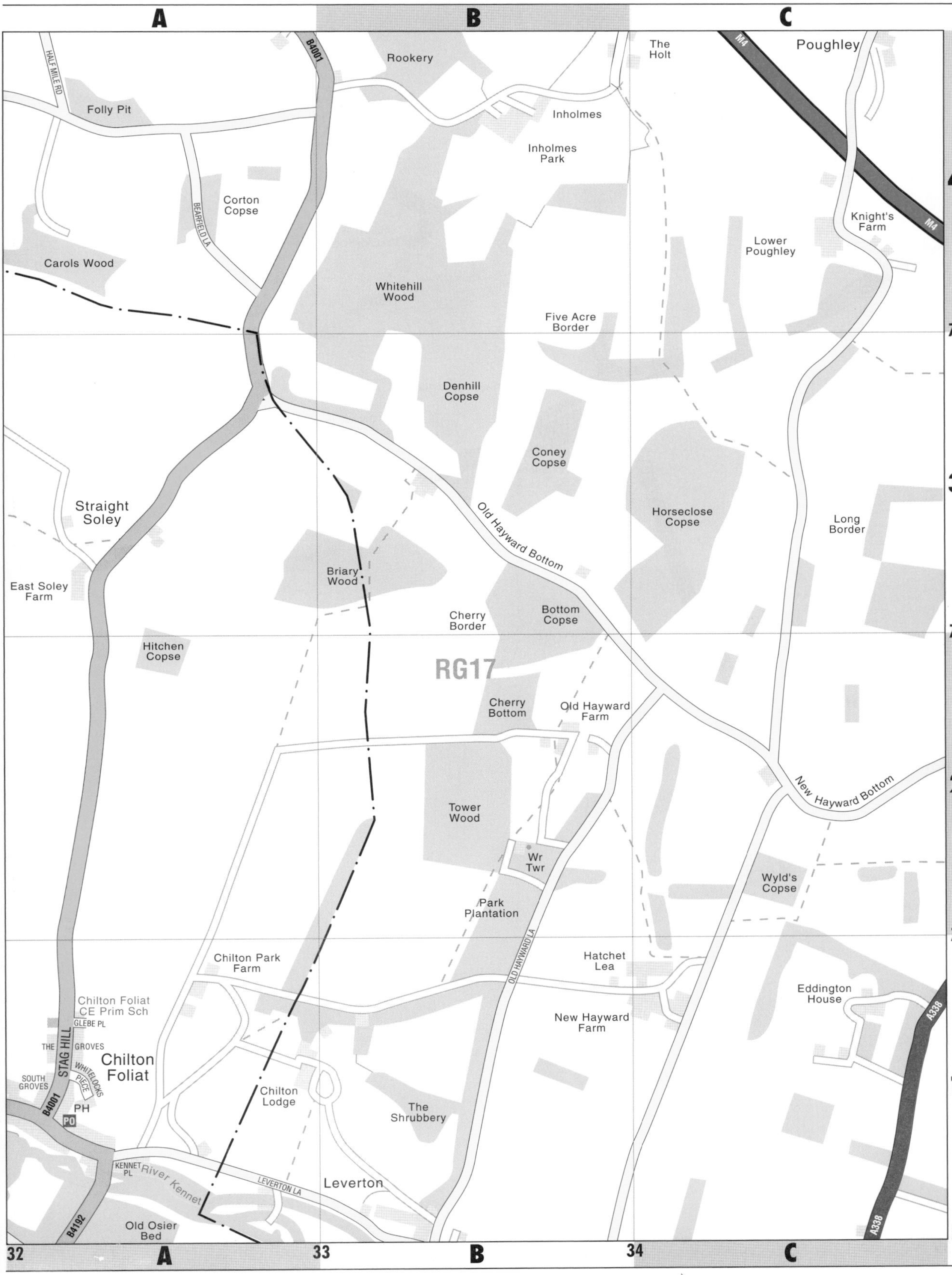
A
B
C
4
3
2
1
73
72
71
70
32
33
34
Poughley
The Holt
Rookery
Folly Pit
HALF MILE RD
B4001
M4
Inholmes
Inholmes Park
Corton Copse
BEARFIELD LA
Knight's Farm
Lower Poughley
Carols Wood
Whitehill Wood
Five Acre Border
Denhill Copse
Coney Copse
Straight Soley
Horsechlose Copse
Long Border
Old Hayward Bottom
East Soley Farm
Briary Wood
Cherry Border
Bottom Copse
Hitchen Copse
RG17
Cherry Bottom
Old Hayward Farm
New Hayward Bottom
Tower Wood
Wr Twr
Wyld's Copse
Park Plantation
OLD HAYWARD LA
Chilton Park Farm
Hatchet Lea
Eddington House
A338
Chilton Foliat CE Prim Sch
New Hayward Farm
GLEBE PL
THE GROVES
STAG HILL
Chilton Foliat
WHITELOCKS PIECE
SOUTH GROVES
PH
PO
Chilton Lodge
The Shrubbery
KENNET PL
River Kennet
LEVERTON LA
Leverton
B4192
Old Osier Bed

73 47

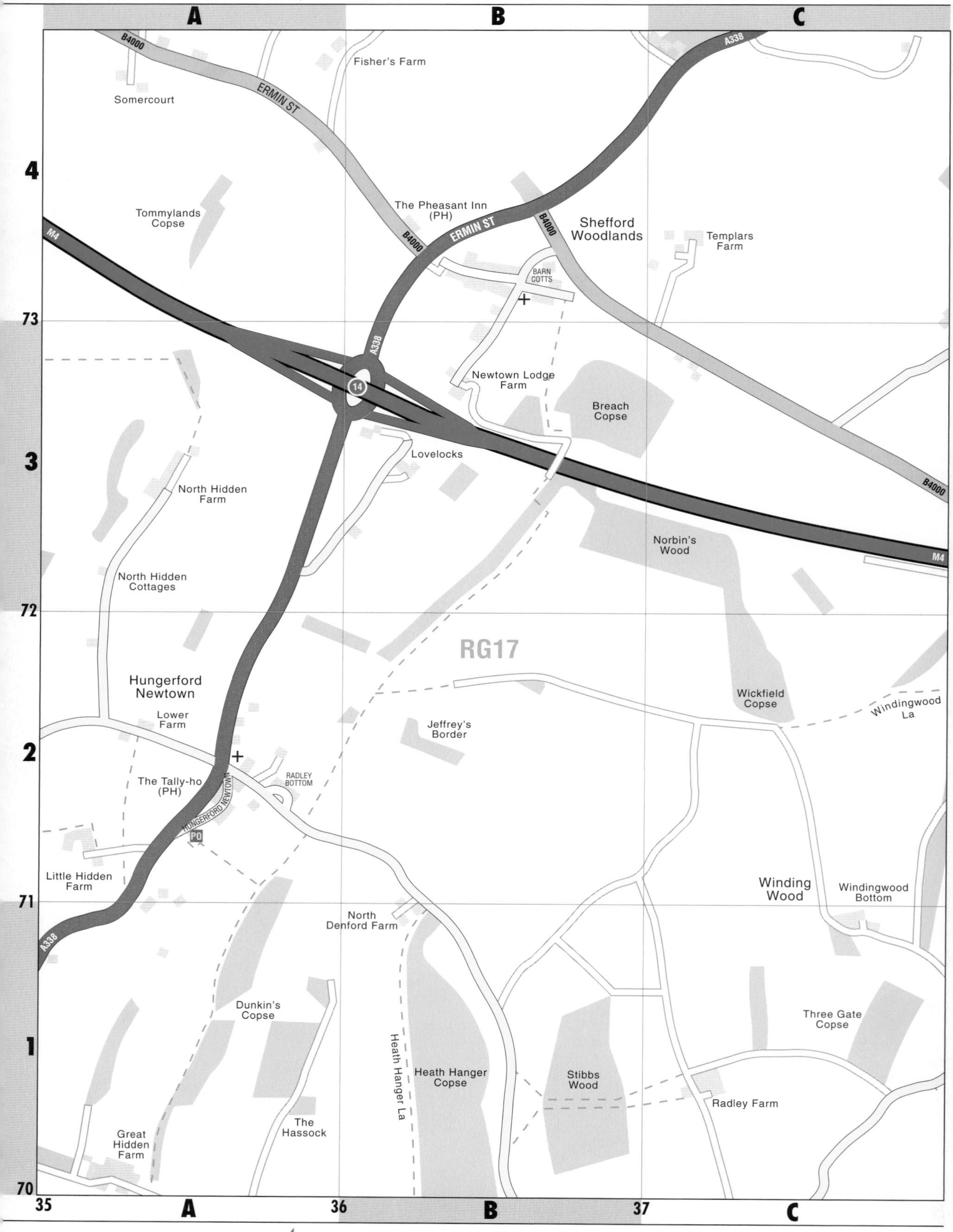
A
B
C
Fisher's Farm
Somercourt
B4000
ERMIN ST
A338
Tommylands Copse
The Pheasant Inn (PH)
Shefford Woodlands
Templars Farm
M4
BARN COTTS
Newtown Lodge Farm
14
Breach Copse
Lovelocks
North Hidden Farm
Norbin's Wood
North Hidden Cottages
RG17
Hungerford Newtown
Lower Farm
Jeffrey's Border
Wickfield Copse
Windingwood La
The Tally-ho (PH)
RADLEY BOTTOM
HUNGERFORD NEWTOWN
PO
Little Hidden Farm
Winding Wood
Windingwood Bottom
North Denford Farm
Dunkin's Copse
Three Gate Copse
Heath Hanger La
Heath Hanger Copse
Stibbs Wood
Radley Farm
The Hassock
Great Hidden Farm
4
73
3
72
2
71
1
70
35
36
37

73 101

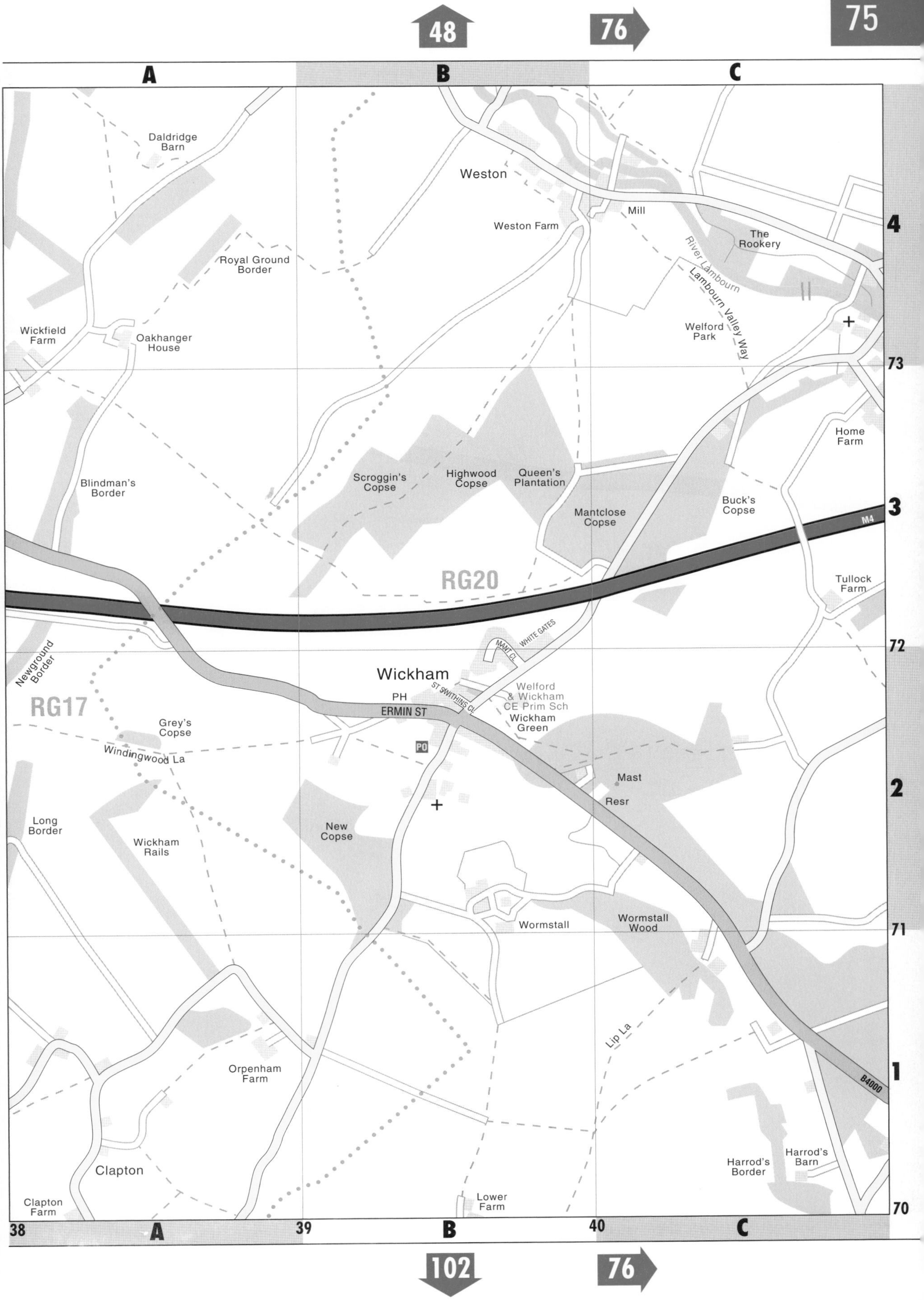
48
76
A
B
C
Daldridge Barn
Weston
Weston Farm
Mill
The Rookery
River Lambourn
Lambourn Valley Way
Royal Ground Border
Wickfield Farm
Oakhanger House
Welford Park
Home Farm
Blindman's Border
Scroggin's Copse
Highwood Copse
Queen's Plantation
Mantclose Copse
Buck's Copse
M4
RG20
Tullock Farm
WHITE GATES
MANT CL
Newground Border
Wickham
PH
ST SWITHINS CL
ERMIN ST
Welford & Wickham CE Prim Sch
Wickham Green
RG17
Grey's Copse
Windingwood La
PO
Mast
Resr
Long Border
Wickham Rails
New Copse
Wormstall
Wormstall Wood
Lip La
Orpenham Farm
B4000
Clapton
Harrod's Border
Harrod's Barn
Clapton Farm
Lower Farm
4
73
3
72
2
71
1
70
38
39
40
102
76

75
49

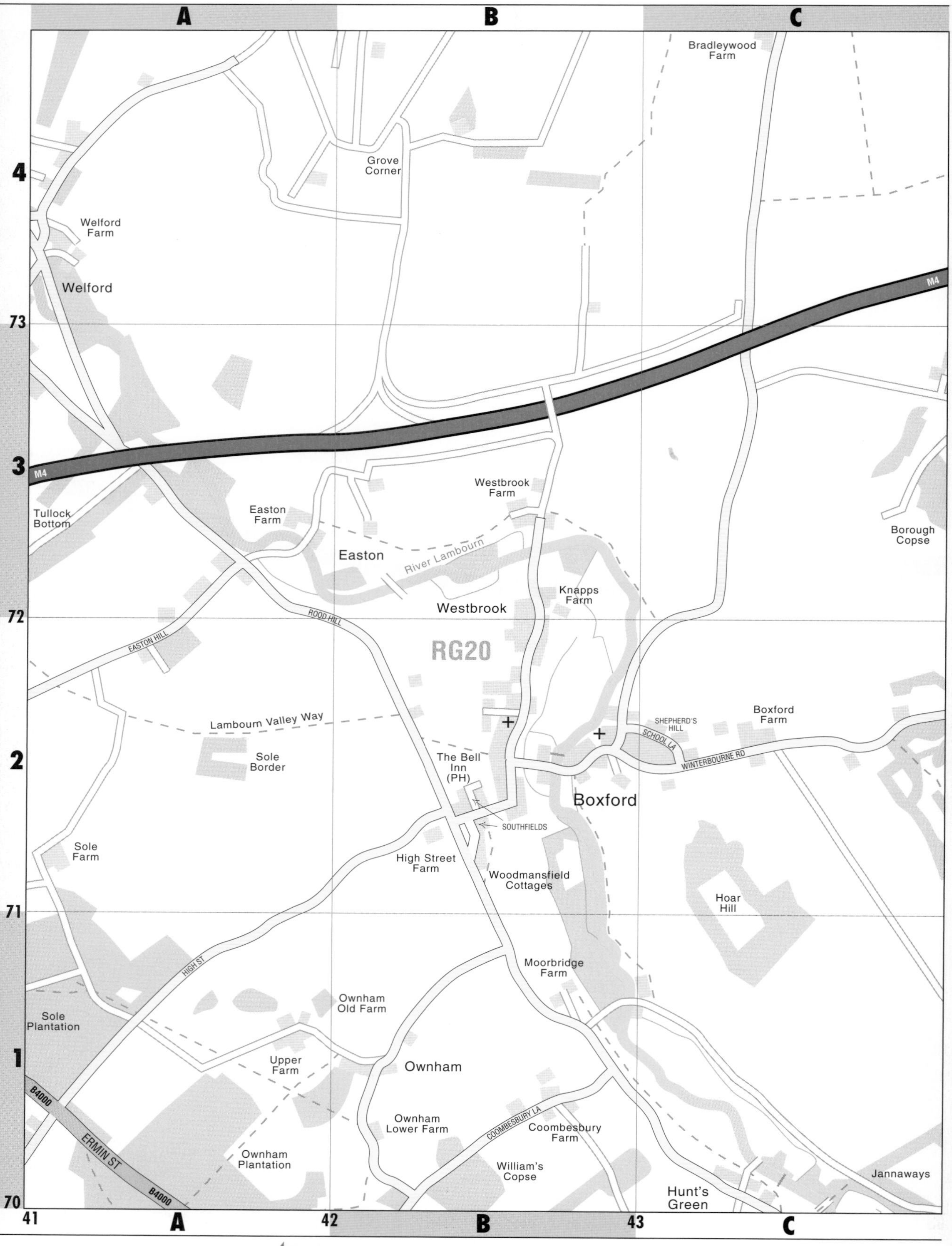
A
B
C
Bradleywood Farm
Grove Corner
Welford Farm
Welford
M4
Tullock Bottom
Easton Farm
Westbrook Farm
Easton
River Lambourn
Borough Copse
Knapps Farm
Westbrook
ROOD HILL
EASTON HILL
RG20
Lambourn Valley Way
SHEPHERD'S HILL
SCHOOL LA
Boxford Farm
WINTERBOURNE RD
Sole Border
The Bell Inn (PH)
Boxford
SOUTHFIELDS
Sole Farm
High Street Farm
Woodmansfield Cottages
Hoar Hill
HIGH ST
Moorbridge Farm
Ownham Old Farm
Sole Plantation
Upper Farm
Ownham
B4000
ERMIN ST
Ownham Lower Farm
COOMBESBURY LA
Coombesbury Farm
Ownham Plantation
William's Copse
Jannaways
Hunt's Green
4
73
3
72
2
71
1
70
41
42
43

75
103

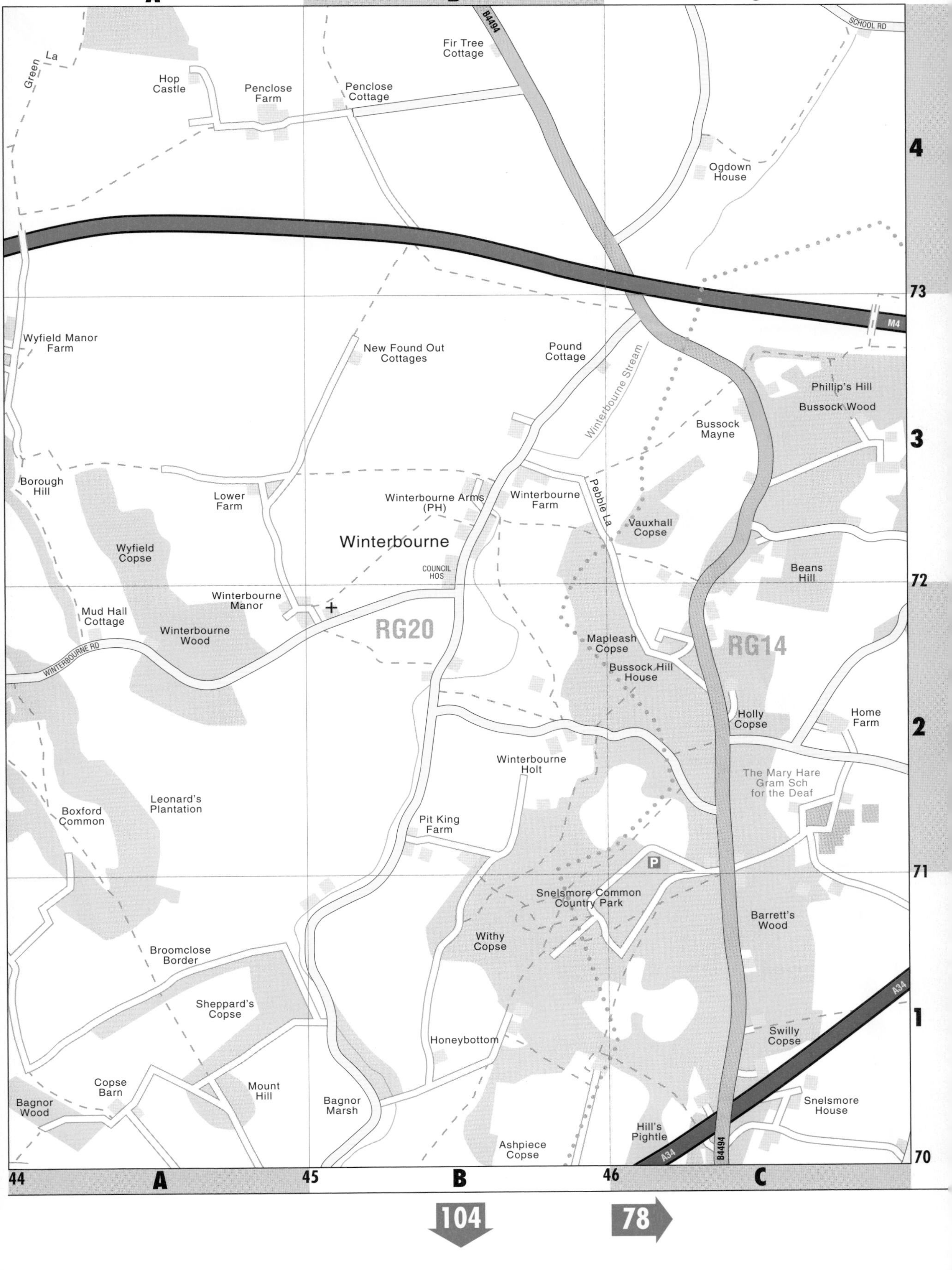
50
78
A
B
C
B4494
Fir Tree Cottage
SCHOOL RD
Green La
Hop Castle
Penclose Farm
Penclose Cottage
4
Ogdown House
73
M4
Wyfield Manor Farm
New Found Out Cottages
Pound Cottage
Winterbourne Stream
Phillip's Hill
Bussock Wood
Bussock Mayne
3
Borough Hill
Lower Farm
Winterbourne Arms (PH)
Winterbourne Farm
Pebble La
Vauxhall Copse
Winterbourne
Wyfield Copse
COUNCIL HOS
Beans Hill
72
Winterbourne Manor
Mud Hall Cottage
Winterbourne Wood
RG20
WINTERBOURNE RD
Mapleash Copse
RG14
Bussock Hill House
Holly Copse
Home Farm
2
Winterbourne Holt
The Mary Hare Gram Sch for the Deaf
Boxford Common
Leonard's Plantation
Pit King Farm
P
71
Snelsmore Common Country Park
Barrett's Wood
Withy Copse
Broomclose Border
A34
Sheppard's Copse
1
Swilly Copse
Honeybottom
Copse Barn
Mount Hill
Bagnor Wood
Bagnor Marsh
Snelsmore House
Hill's Pightle
Ashpiece Copse
A34
B4494
70
44
A
45
B
46
C
104
78

77
51

A
B
C
4
3
2
1
73
72
71
70
47
48
49
Chieveley Prim Sch
HEATHFIELDS
SOWBURY BANK
HIGH ST
SCHOOL RD
Wheatsheaf (PH)
GRACES LA
SOUTHFIELDS
A34
Priorscourt Park
Priorscourt Wood
M4
Priors Court Specl Sch
Church Farm
Horsemoor
Priorscourt Farm
Baker's Row
OLD ST
PRIORS COURT RD
GREEN LA
RG20
Newbury Showground
Radnall Farm
Sch of Military Survey
13
Osmond's Pightle
Hotel
Depot
Copyhold Farm
CRABTREE LA
FAIRCROSS QUARTERS
CLOUGH DR
ROMFORD CL
ROY CL
THOMPSON CL
COLLINS DR
WHITE CL
CRABTREE CL
Kite's Abbey
High Wood
Chieveley Service Area
Faircross Plantation
Marsh La
WOODLANDS CL
Curridge
The Bunk (PH)
KILN DR
KILN TERR
Snelsmore Farm
Park Farm
PLANTATION CL
CURRIDGE PIECE
Breach Copse
Spring Copse
RG18
Lanolee Farm
CHAPEL LA
SANDY CL
SANDY LA
LALEYS GREEN
Chalky La
Grigg's Copse
Curridge Prim Sch
RG14
B4009
Oaklands Farm
The Old Parsonage
Orchard Copse
CURRIDGE GREEN
Rookery Farm
Oaklands
CURRIDGE RD
Arlington Grange Farm
Grange Cottages
Snelsmore East Common
Woodside
LONG LA
Dolman's Row
Grange Farm
Fox and Hounds (PH)
Fisher's Lane Crossing
FISHER'S LA
Ash Plantation
Fisher's Farm
Angel's Hill
A339
Shaw Dene House
Long Lane Poultry Farm
Big Copse

A
B
C
Oare
MANOR LA
B4009
Chalkpit Piece
EVERINGTON LA
Birch Cottage
Rook's Copse
M4
Hermitage Cty Prim Sch
Works
Little Hungerford
Kiln Farm
HAMPSTEAD NORREYS RD
COLYER CL
ORCHARD CL
LEA VIEW
Windmill Farm
CHAPEL LA
Common Firs
4
Box Wood
Roebuck Wood
DEACONS LA
POND LA
YATTENDON RD
Cuckoo Pits
Spring Copse
Hermitage
DINES WAY
KILN CL
RIDGEWAY CL
Parsons Piece
Poundpit Piece
Well La
Box Cottage
PO
73
DOCTORS LA
NEWBURY RD
BRIANTS PIECE
New Plantation
States Hill Wood
Wellhouse Farm
PRIORS COURT RD
PH
LIPSCOMB CL
CRABTREE LA
CHARLOTTE CL
LITTLE SAFFRON
WOODSIDE DR
Pheasant Hill Wood
WELLHOUSE LA
Long Grove
Allen's Allotment
Wellhouse
3
LONG LA
Faircross Farm
Grimsbury Castle
Fifield Farm
MARLSTON RD
Grimsbury Wood
Marlston Cottages
Fairfield Farm
Adams Lane Copse
Round Hill Wood
Grimsbury Bank
72
SANDY CL
RED SHUTE IND EST
Boar's Hole Farm
Brockhurst & Marlston House Prep Schs
SLANTING HILL
RG18
Gravelly Pightles
B4009
SAWMILL RD
The Common
Longlane
RED SHUTE HILL
Fence La
West Wood
2
Money's Allotment
Fence Wood
Hangings Copse
Downe House Sch
Bushnell's Copse
Stonecroft Copse
WILLIS CL
Bucklebury Alley
71
Westrop Green
Nothing Hill
Cold Ash Common
Hunters Hill Wood
Cold Ash Farm
DROVE LA
HERMITAGE RD
Westrop Wood
Sermons Copse
Oaken Copse
Westrop Hill
1
SEWELL CL
FISHER'S LA
GORSE COTTAGE DR
WOODSIDE
ANNADALE
RG7
Malthouse Wood
Westrop Farm
Holly Farm House
Henwicklands Copse
THIRTOVER
Thirtover
ASHMORE GREEN RD
COLD ASH HILL
THE RIDGE
Cold Ash Sch
Salt's Copse
70
50
A
51
B
52
C

79
53

A
B
C
4
3
2
1
73
72
71
70
53
54
55
M4
Frilsham Park
Coombe Wood
Wr Twr
Frilsham Common
Magpie Farm
Manor House
Frilsham Manor Farm
HATCHETS LA
BEECHFIELD
The Pot Kiln (PH)
Stanford Dingley Circular Wlks
Parsonage Farm
The Old Rectory
Frilsham
Thorncuts Cottage
Hawkridge House
High Copse
Whitmoor Copse
Burntbush La
Blackwell Copse
Hawkridge Wood
The Alders
Highwood Copse
Hawkridge Farm
Quavies
RG18
Cray's Copse
Wynalls Copse
Burgess' Copse
Marlston Farm
BROCKS LA
River Pang
Warren Pit
River Barn Farm
Rushdens Farm
Marlston Pightle
New Barn Farm
Withers Farm
Cole's Farm
RG7
Shallow Ford
Holly La
Walnut Tree Cottages
The Old Vicarage
Smithcroft Copse
Bucklebury
Manor House Farm
Hillhouse Farm
Andrew's Copse
TYLER'S LA
FANNY'S LA
BRIFF LA
Bucklebury Farm Park
PEASE HILL
Redhill Copse
Littlefence Wood
The Slade
Picton Farm
Briff View Farm
The Manor

79
107

54
82

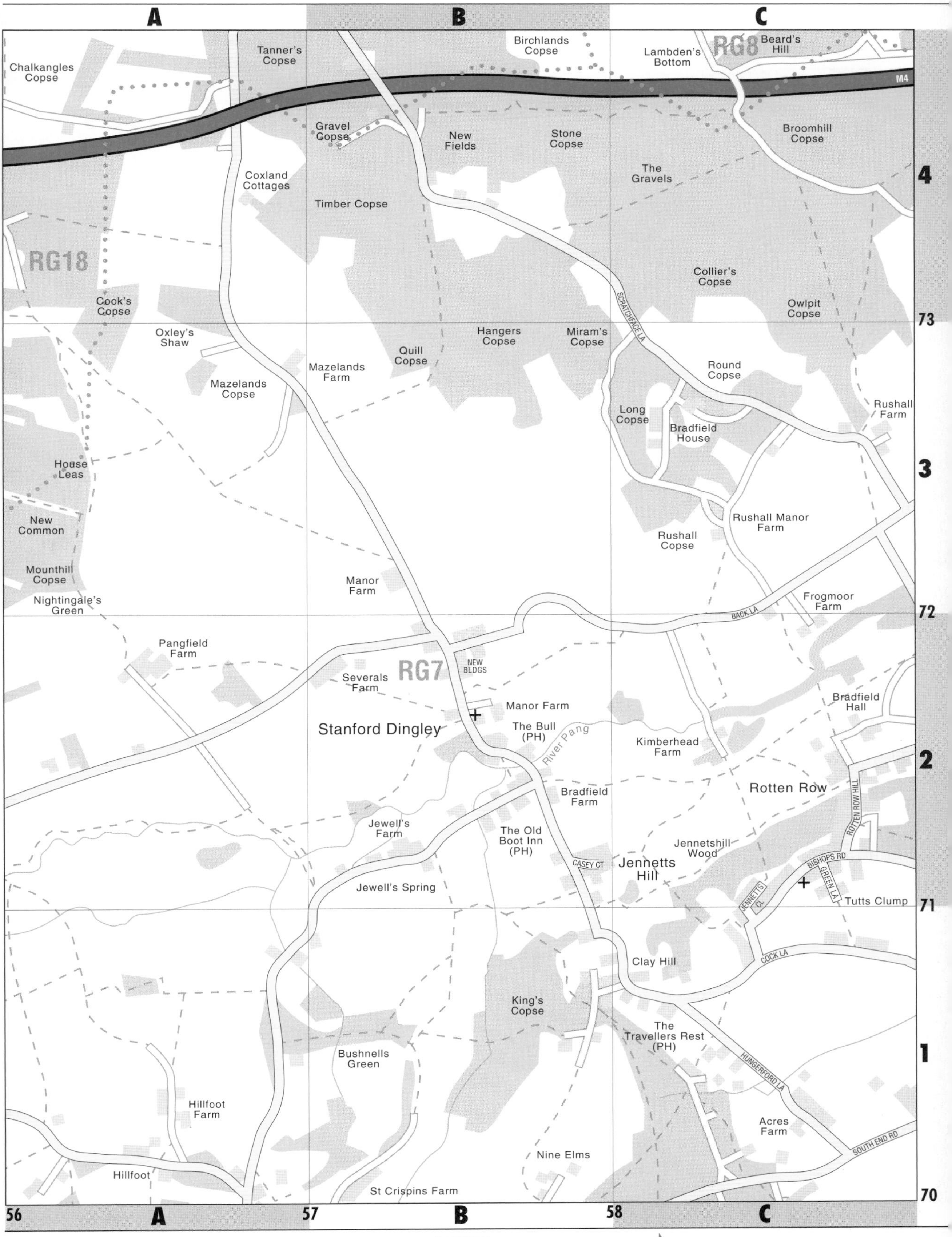
A
B
C
RG8
Beard's Hill
Birchlands Copse
Lambden's Bottom
Tanner's Copse
Chalkangles Copse
M4
Gravel Copse
New Fields
Stone Copse
Broomhill Copse
Coxland Cottages
The Gravels
Timber Copse
4
RG18
Collier's Copse
Cook's Copse
Owlpit Copse
SCRATCHFACE LA
73
Oxley's Shaw
Hangers Copse
Miram's Copse
Quill Copse
Mazelands Farm
Round Copse
Mazelands Copse
Long Copse
Rushall Farm
Bradfield House
House Leas
3
New Common
Rushall Manor Farm
Rushall Copse
Mounthill Copse
Manor Farm
Nightingale's Green
Frogmoor Farm
BACK LA
72
Pangfield Farm
RG7
NEW BLDGS
Severals Farm
Manor Farm
Bradfield Hall
Stanford Dingley
The Bull (PH)
River Pang
Kimberhead Farm
2
Bradfield Farm
Rotten Row
ROTTEN ROW HILL
Jewell's Farm
The Old Boot Inn (PH)
Jennetshill Wood
CASEY CT
Jennetts Hill
BISHOPS RD
GREEN LA
JENNETTS CL
Jewell's Spring
Tutts Clump
71
Clay Hill
COCK LA
King's Copse
The Travellers Rest (PH)
1
Bushnells Green
HUNGERFORD LA
Hillfoot Farm
Acres Farm
SOUTH END RD
Nine Elms
Hillfoot
St Crispins Farm
70
56
57
58

108
82

81 55

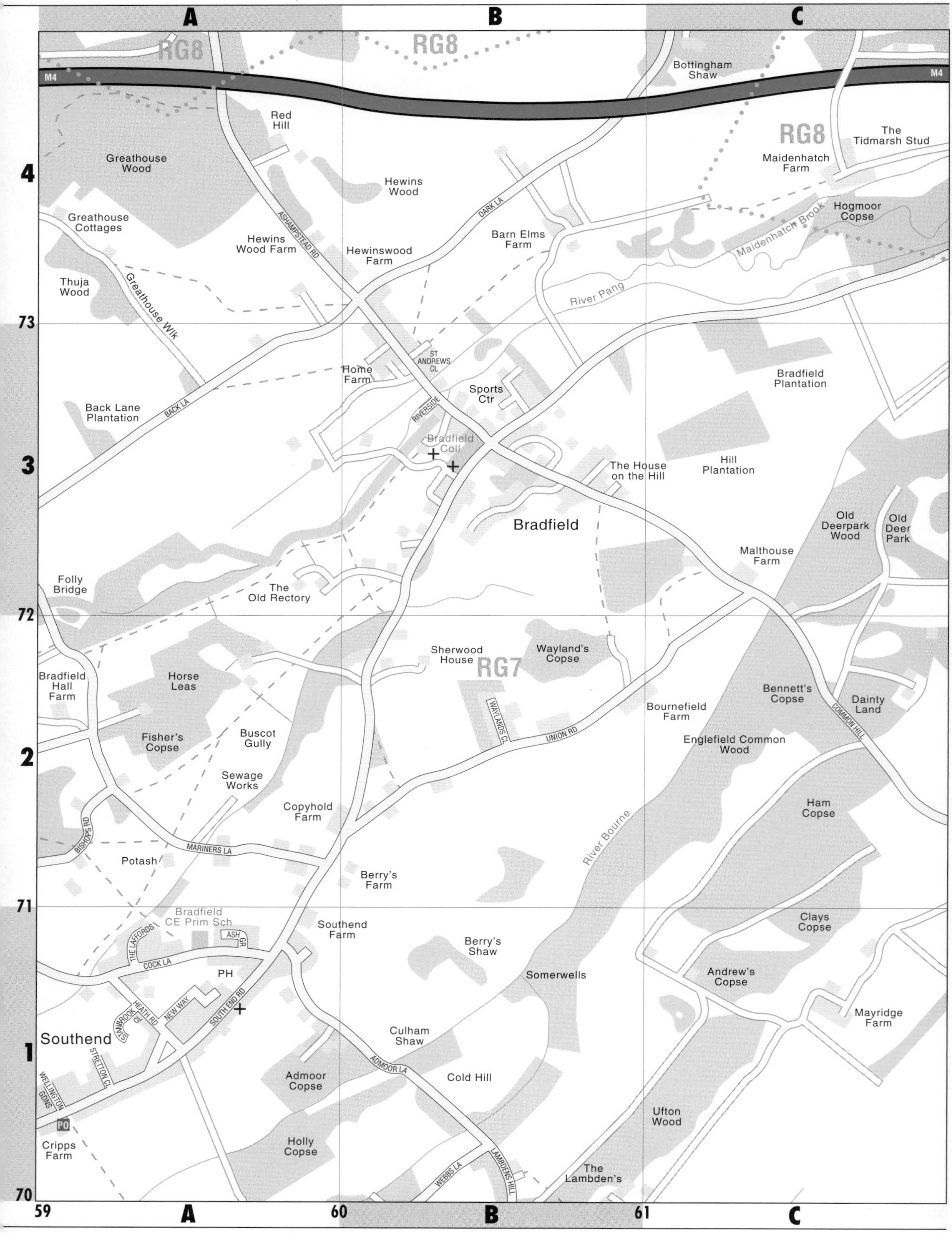
A
B
C
4
3
2
1
73
72
71
70
59
60
61
M4
RG8
RG8
RG8
RG7
Red Hill
Greathouse Wood
Hewins Wood
Greathouse Cottages
Hewins Wood Farm
Hewinswood Farm
Barn Elms Farm
ASHAMPSTEAD RD
DARK LA
Thuja Wood
Greathouse Wlk
Bottingham Shaw
The Tidmarsh Stud
Maidenhatch Farm
Hogmoor Copse
Maidenhatch Brook
River Pang
ST ANDREWS CL
Home Farm
Sports Ctr
RIVERSIDE
Back Lane Plantation
BACK LA
Bradfield Plantation
Bradfield Coll
The House on the Hill
Hill Plantation
Bradfield
Old Deerpark Wood
Old Deer Park
Malthouse Farm
Folly Bridge
The Old Rectory
Sherwood House
Wayland's Copse
Bradfield Hall Farm
Horse Leas
WAYLANDS CL
UNION RD
Bournefield Farm
Bennett's Copse
Dainty Land
COMMON HILL
Englefield Common Wood
Fisher's Copse
Buscot Gully
Sewage Works
Copyhold Farm
Ham Copse
River Bourne
BISHOPS RD
MARINERS LA
Potash
Berry's Farm
Bradfield CE Prim Sch
ASH GR
THE LAFFORDS
Southend Farm
Berry's Shaw
Clays Copse
COCK LA
PH
Somerwells
Andrew's Copse
HEATH RD
NEW WAY
SOUTH END RD
STANBROOK CL
Mayridge Farm
Southend
Culham Shaw
STRETTON CL
ADMOOR LA
Cold Hill
WELLINGTON GDNS
Admoor Copse
PO
Ufton Wood
Cripps Farm
Holly Copse
WEBBS LA
LAMBDENS HILL
The Lambden's

81 109

56
84

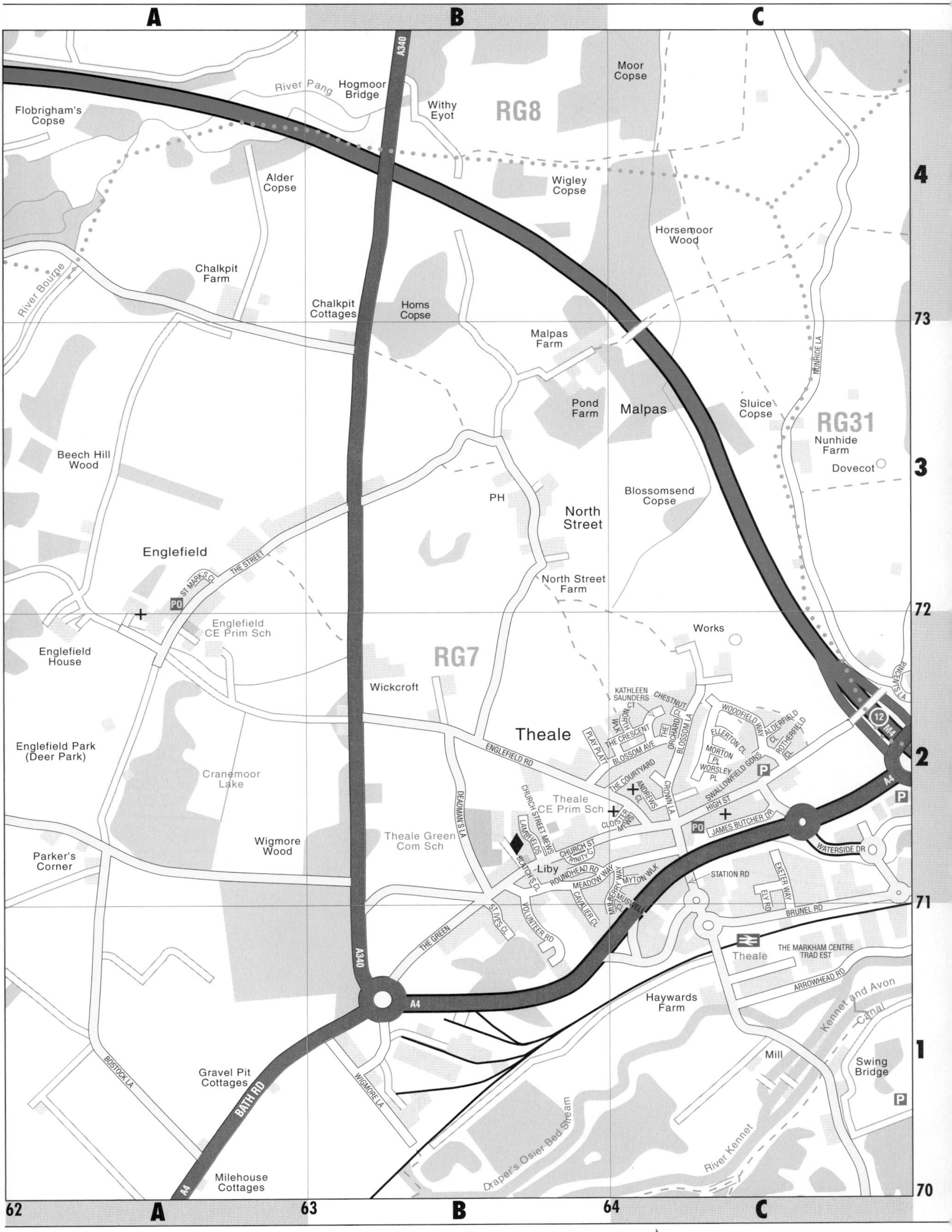
A
B
C
4
73
3
72
2
71
1
70
62
63
64
River Pang
Hogmoor Bridge
Moor Copse
Withy Eyot
RG8
Flobrigham's Copse
A340
Alder Copse
Wigley Copse
Horsemoor Wood
Chalkpit Farm
River Bourne
Chalkpit Cottages
Horns Copse
Malpas Farm
NUNHIDE LA
Pond Farm
Malpas
Sluice Copse
RG31
Nunhide Farm
Dovecot
Beech Hill Wood
PH
North Street
Blossomsend Copse
Englefield
THE STREET
ST MARK'S CL
PO
North Street Farm
Englefield CE Prim Sch
Works
Englefield House
RG7
Wickcroft
KATHLEEN SAUNDERS CT
CHESTNUT CT
NORTH WLK
PLAY PLATT
THE CRESCENT
BLOSSOM AVE
THE ORCHARD
BLOSSOM LA
WOODFIELD WAY
ALDERFIELD CL
ROTHERFIELD CL
ELLERTON CL
MORTON PL
WORSLEY PL
SWALLOWFIELD GDNS
Theale
12
M4
Englefield Park (Deer Park)
ENGLEFIELD RD
Cranemoor Lake
THE COURTYARD
ANDREWS CL
CROWN LA
HIGH ST
A4
P
DEADMAN'S LA
CHURCH STREET MEWS
Theale CE Prim Sch
CLOISTER MEWS
JAMES BUTCHER DR
WATERSIDE DR
Wigmore Wood
Theale Green Com Sch
LAMBFIELDS
CHURCH ST
TRINITY CT
Parker's Corner
BLATCH'S CL
Liby
ROUNDHEAD RD
MEADOW WAY
MULBERRY WAY
MYTON WLK
STATION RD
EXETER WAY
ELY RD
CAVALIER CL
MUSWELL CL
BRUNEL RD
ST IVES CL
VOLUNTEER RD
THE GREEN
Theale
THE MARKHAM CENTRE TRAD EST
ARROWHEAD RD
Kennet and Avon Canal
Haywards Farm
BOSTOCK LA
Mill
Swing Bridge
Gravel Pit Cottages
BATH RD
WIGMORE LA
Draper's Osier Bed Stream
River Kennet
Milehouse Cottages
A4

110
84

83
57

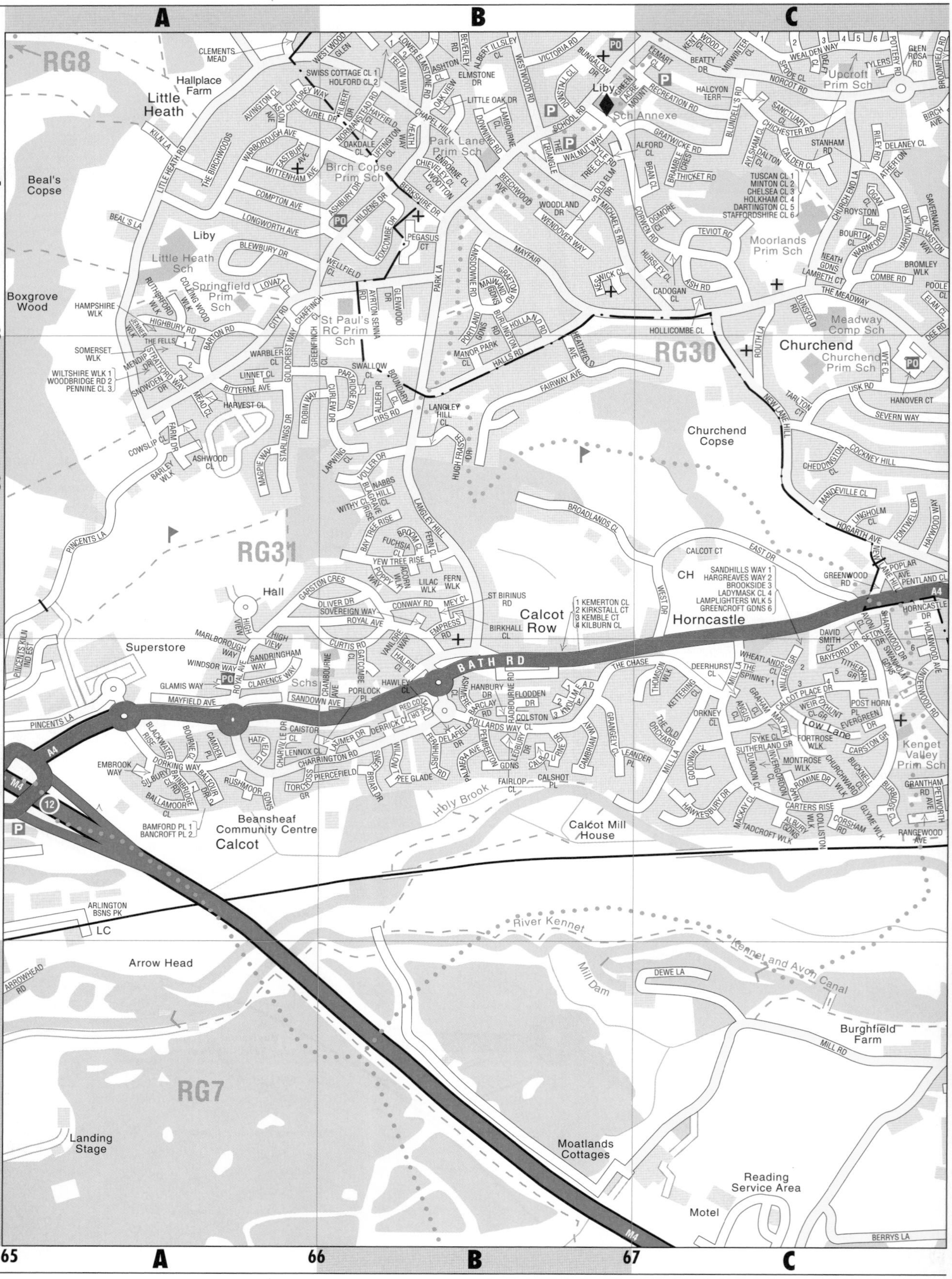
A
B
C
RG8
Little Heath
Hallplace Farm
CLEMENTS MEAD
Beal's Copse
Boxgrove Wood
Little Heath Sch
Springfield Prim Sch
Birch Copse Prim Sch
Park Lane Prim Sch
St Paul's RC Prim Sch
Sch Annexe
Upcroft Prim Sch
Moorlands Prim Sch
Meadway Comp Sch
Churchend
Churchend Prim Sch
RG30
Churchend Copse
RG31
Hall
Superstore
Calcot Row
Horncastle
CH
BATH RD
Schs
Beansheaf Community Centre
Calcot
Calcot Mill House
Holy Brook
Low Lane
Kennet Valley Prim Sch
ARLINGTON BSNS PK
LC
Arrow Head
River Kennet
Kennet and Avon Canal
Mill Dam
DEWE LA
Burghfield Farm
MILL RD
RG7
Landing Stage
Moatlands Cottages
Reading Service Area
Motel
BERRYS LA
M4
A4
12
LITTLE HEATH RD
PINCENTS LA
PARK LA
LANGLEY HILL
FAIRWAY AVE
HOLLICOMBE CL
THE MEADWAY
NEW LANE HILL
BROADLANDS CL
MAYFIELD AVE
4
3
2
1
73
72
71
70
65
66
67

83
111

A B C

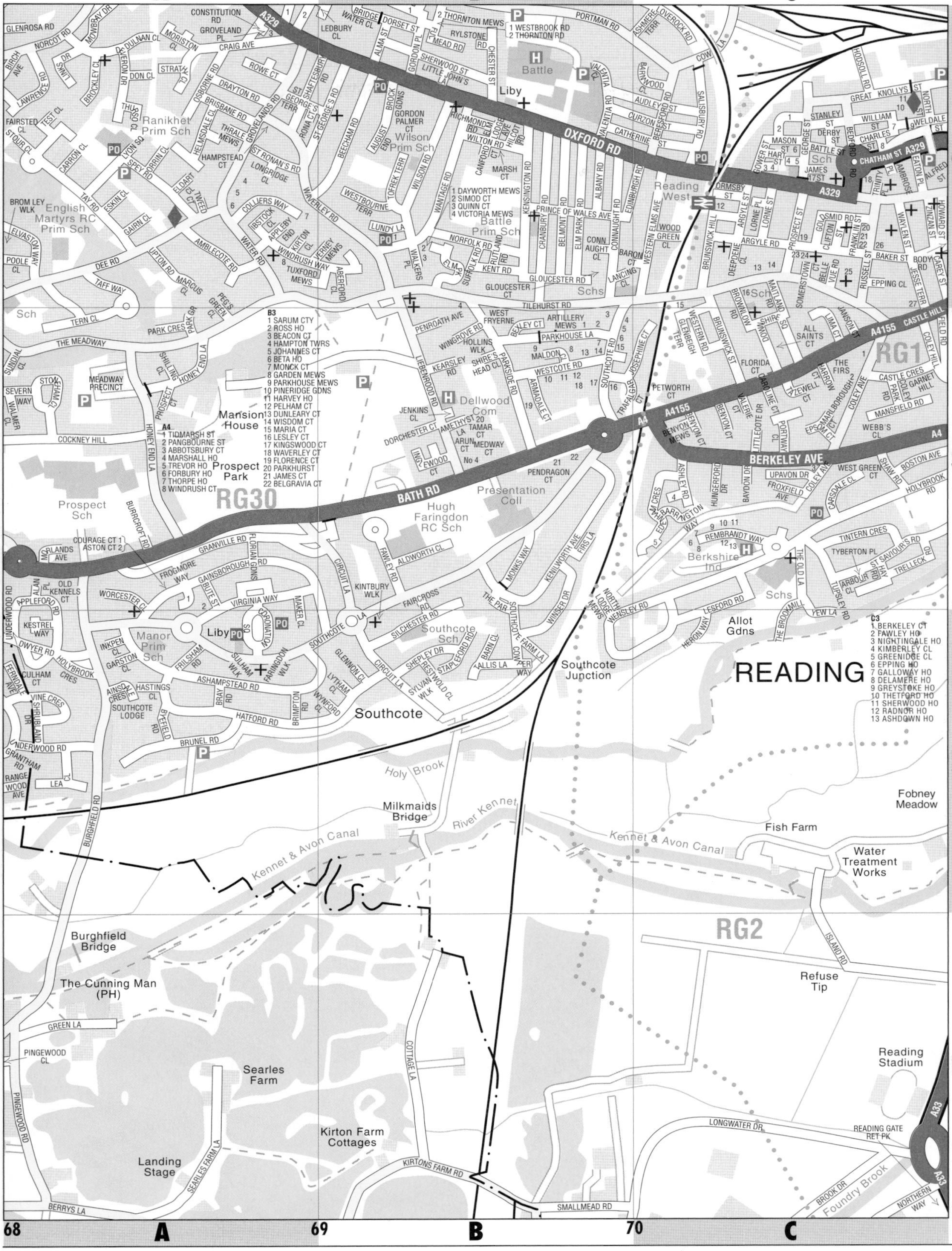

OXFORD RD
A329
BATH RD
A4
A4155
BERKELEY AVE
CASTLE HILL
RG30
RG1
RG2
READING
Reading West
Battle
Liby
Ranikhet Prim Sch
Wilson Prim Sch
Battle Prim Sch
English Martyrs RC Prim Sch
Mansion House
Prospect Park
Prospect Sch
Dellwood Com
Presentation Coll
Hugh Faringdon RC Sch
Manor Prim Sch
Southcote Sch
Southcote
Southcote Junction
Berkshire Ind
Allot Gdns
Holy Brook
River Kennet
Kennet & Avon Canal
Milkmaids Bridge
Fish Farm
Fobney Meadow
Water Treatment Works
Refuse Tip
Reading Stadium
READING GATE RET PK
Burghfield Bridge
The Cunning Man (PH)
Searles Farm
Kirton Farm Cottages
Landing Stage
LONGWATER DR
KIRTONS FARM RD
SMALLMEAD RD
BERRYS LA
PINGEWOOD RD
GREEN LA
COTTAGE LA
SEARLES FARM LA
BURGHFIELD RD
ISLAND RD
Foundry Brook
A33
B3
1 SARUM CTY
2 ROSS HO
3 BEACON CT
4 HAMPTON TWRS
5 JOHANNES CT
6 BETA HO
7 MONCK CT
8 GARDEN MEWS
9 PARKHOUSE MEWS
10 PINERIDGE GDNS
11 HARVEY HO
12 PELHAM CT
13 DUNLEARY CT
14 WISDOM CT
15 MARIA CT
16 LESLEY CT
17 KINGSWOOD CT
18 WAVERLEY CT
19 FLORENCE CT
20 PARKHURST
21 JAMES CT
22 BELGRAVIA CT
A4
1 TIDMARSH ST
2 PANGBOURNE ST
3 ABBOTSBURY CT
4 MARSHALL HO
5 TREVOR HO
6 FORBURY HO
7 THORPE HO
8 WINDRUSH CT
C3
1 BERKELEY CT
2 FAWLEY HO
3 NIGHTINGALE HO
4 KIMBERLEY CT
5 GREENIDGE CL
6 EPPING HO
7 GALLOWAY HO
8 DELAMERE HO
9 GREYSTOKE HO
10 THETFORD HO
11 SHERWOOD HO
12 RADNOR HO
13 ASHDOWN HO
4
73
3
72
2
71
1
70
68
69
70


A B C

A4
1 BELLMAN CT
2 MONTROSE HO
3 FRIARS WLK
4 SHOESMITHS CT
5 HARRIS ARC
6 ANSTEY RD
7 TALBOT CT
8 MALTINGS PL
9 WATERSIDE GDNS
10 SWAN PL
11 YIELD HALL LA
12 THORN LA
13 HIGHBRIDGE WHARF

85

A4
14 CRANE WHARF
15 MARKET WAY
16 MAYFLOWER CT
17 KINGS REACH CT
18 CHAPEL CT
19 SOUTHERN CT

59

A4
20 THE CHAMBERS
21 MARIE DAVIS CT
B4
1 THE PLUMMERY
2 SELBORNE CT
3 GRANTLEY HTS
4 OSPREY CT
5 SIDMOUTH CT
6 GREYS CT
7 PADLEY CT
8 TYRREL CT
9 THE DELL
10 ROYAL CT
11 HARRY TEE CT
12 KENNET SIDE
13 WEIRSIDE CT
14 MORRISS CT
15 MANDELA CT
16 VICTORIA WAY
17 RUPERT WLK
18 ICARUS CT
19 RUPERT SQ
20 KINGSGATE PL
21 HAVEN CT
22 SAXON CT
23 CARNOUSTIE CT
24 HENRY CT
25 EDWARD PL
26 CHARLES PL
27 ALDERNEY CT
28 SHELLEY CT
29 JOHN BALLIOL CT
30 TURNBERRY CT
31 GULLANE CT
32 GLENEAGLES CT
33 TROON CT
34 APPLETON HO
35 ST ANDREWS CT
36 PRESTWICK CT
37 WEAVERS CT

A3
1 BLENHEIM TERR
2 CHERITON CT
3 WILLOW ST
4 AVOCET CT
5 NEW BRIGHT ST
6 FOUNDRY PL
7 GARNET HILL
8 CHURCH TERR
9 ST SAVIOUR'S TERR
10 CRANFORD MEWS
11 RODNEY CT
12 BUNYAN CT
13 BELFORD CT
14 ST GILES CT
15 SOLENT CT
16 HAMBLE CT
17 LETCOMBE CT
18 ELIZABETH MEWS
19 BLENHEIM CT

85

A3
20 DOROTHY ST
21 PRIORS CT
22 NELSON TERR
23 SILVER STREET FLATS
24 WINDSOR SQ
25 JACK PRICE CT
26 AVELEY WLK
27 MELLOR WLK
28 ELIZABETH WLK

113

A3
29 SPRING TERR
30 KINVER WLK
31 BLYTH WLK
32 TAYNTON WLK
33 WESTERHAM WLK

60
88

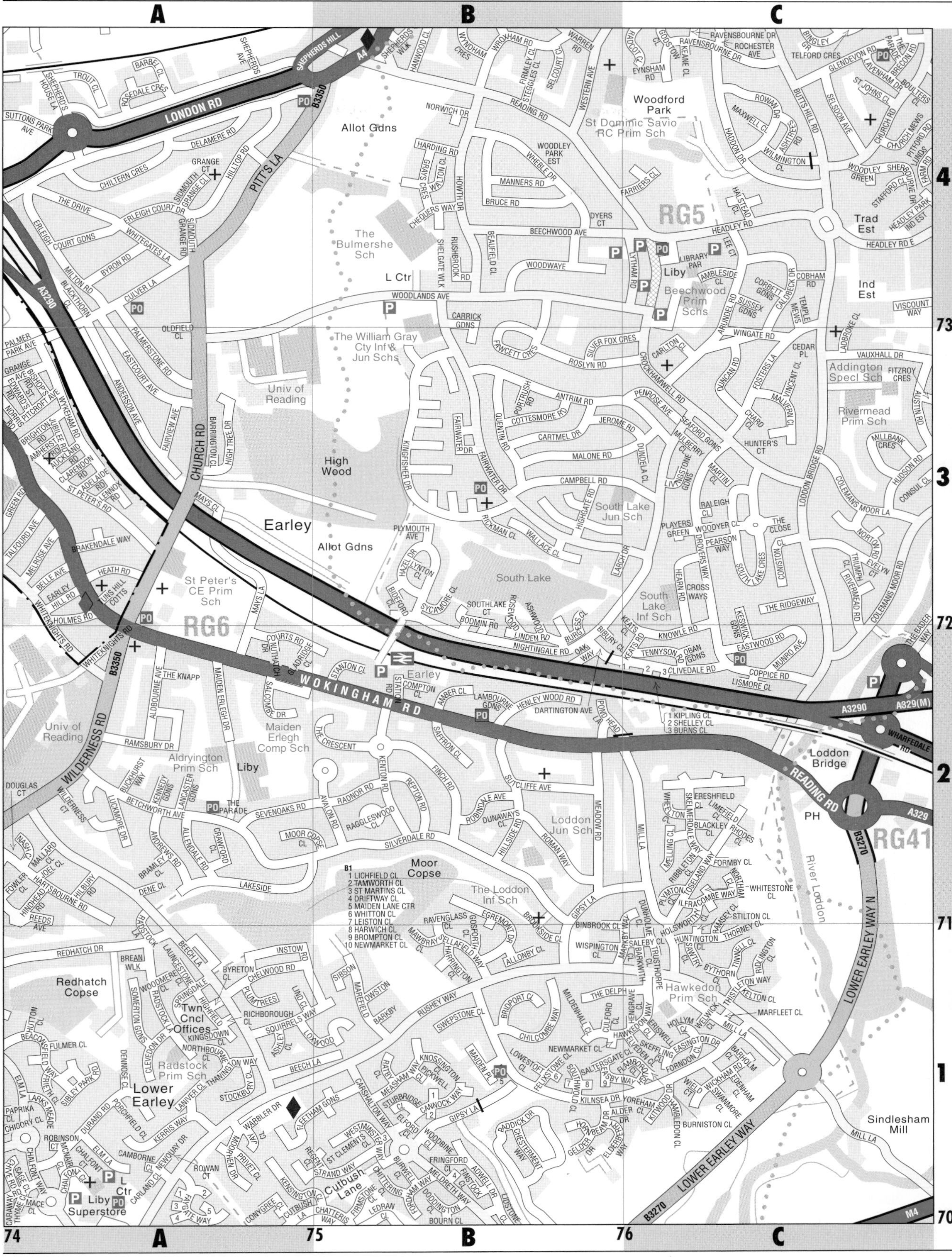


A1
1 WARNSHAM CL
2 SHARPETHORPE CL
3 BERSTEAD CL
4 WATERSFIELD CL
5 RUSTINGTON CL

114
88

87
61

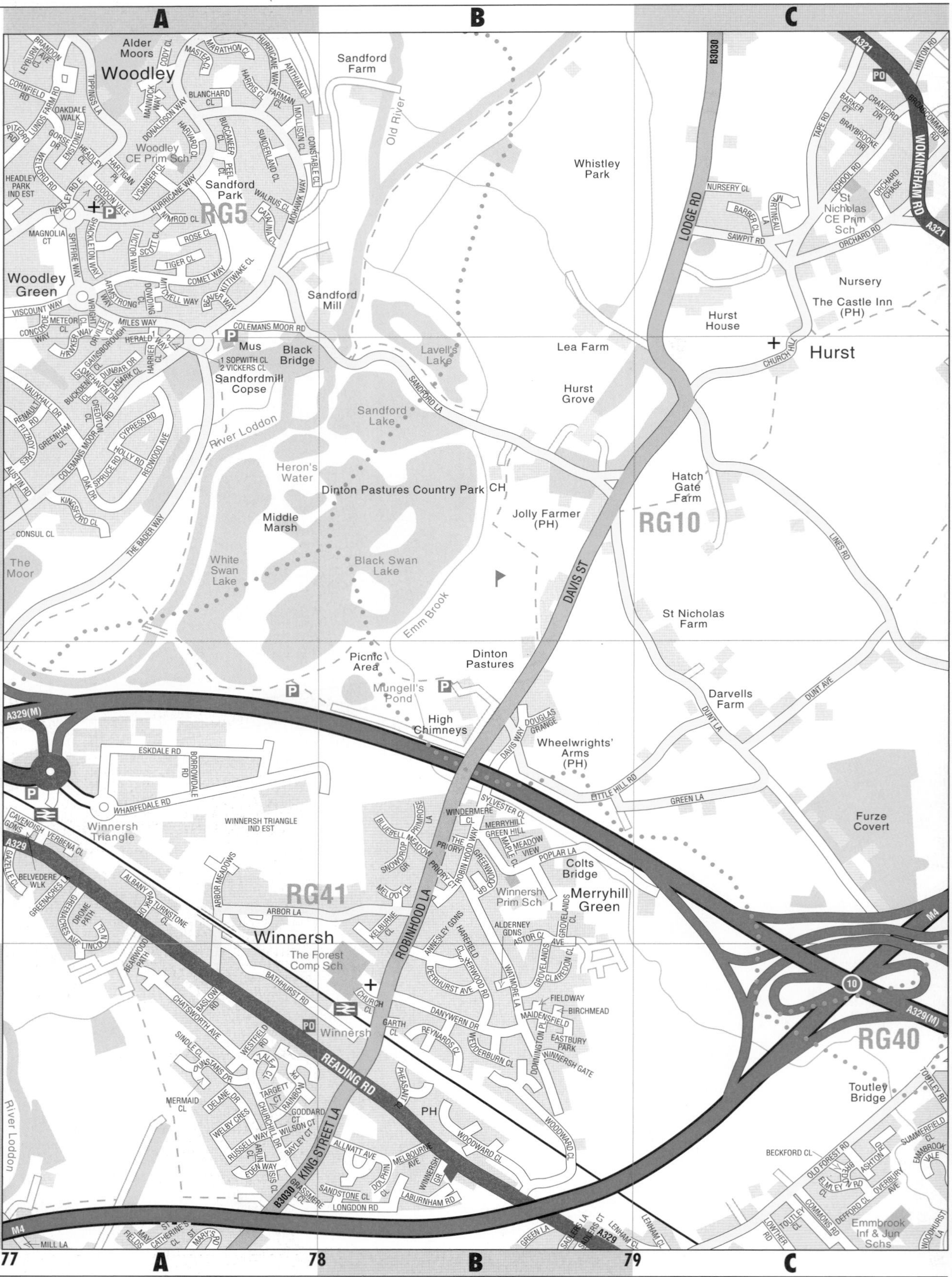
A
B
C
Alder Moors
Woodley
Sandford Farm
Old River
Whistley Park
B3030
A321
PO
HINTON RD
BROADCOMMON RD
WOKINGHAM RD
Woodley CE Prim Sch
Sandford Park
RG5
NURSERY CL
BARBER CL
MARTINEAU LA
SAWPIT RD
ORCHARD RD
St Nicholas CE Prim Sch
SCHOOL RD
ORCHARD CHASE
TAPE RD
BARKER CT
CRANFORD DR
BRAYBROOKE DR
LODGE RD
HEADLEY PARK IND EST
MAGNOLIA CT
Woodley Green
Sandford Mill
Nursery
The Castle Inn (PH)
Hurst House
Lea Farm
Hurst
CHURCH HILL
Hurst Grove
COLEMANS MOOR RD
Mus
Black Bridge
1 SOPWITH CL
2 VICKERS CL
Sandfordmill Copse
Lavell's Lake
SANDFORD LA
Sandford Lake
River Loddon
Heron's Water
Dinton Pastures Country Park
CH
Hatch Gate Farm
Jolly Farmer (PH)
RG10
Middle Marsh
CONSUL CL
THE BADER WAY
KINGSFORD CL
The Moor
White Swan Lake
Black Swan Lake
LINES RD
DAVIS ST
Emm Brook
St Nicholas Farm
Picnic Area
Dinton Pastures
Mungell's Pond
High Chimneys
Darvells Farm
DUNT AVE
DUNT LA
A329(M)
DOUGLAS GRANGE
DAVIS WAY
Wheelwrights' Arms (PH)
ESKDALE RD
BORROWDALE RD
WHARFEDALE RD
LITTLE HILL RD
GREEN LA
Furze Covert
Winnersh Triangle
WINNERSH TRIANGLE IND EST
A329
WINDERMERE CL
SYLVESTER CL
MERRYHILL GREEN HILL
MEADOW VIEW
POPLAR LA
Colts Bridge
RG41
ARBOR LA
ARBOR MEADOWS
TURNSTONE CL
Winnersh Prim Sch
Merryhill Green
M4
Winnersh
The Forest Comp Sch
ROBINHOOD LA
ALDERNEY GDNS
ASTOR CL
GROVELANDS
CLAREDON CL
FIELDWAY
BIRCHMEAD
10
RG40
BATHHURST RD
CHURCH CL
GARTH CL
DANYWERN DR
WEDDERBURN CL
REYNARDS CL
MAIDENSFIELD
EASTBURY PARK
WINNERSH GATE
DONNINGTON PL
READING RD
Toutley Bridge
River Loddon
MERMAID CL
PH
WOODWARD CL
WOODWARD CL
KING STREET LA
B3030
ALLNATT AVE
MELBOURNE AVE
DOLPHIN CL
SANDSTONE CL
LONGDON RD
LABURNHAM RD
BECKFORD CL
OLD FOREST RD
ASHTON CL
SUMMERFIELD CL
EMMBROOK VALE
COMMONS RD
DEFFORD CL
OVERBURY AVE
Emmbrook Inf & Jun Schs
MILL LA
GREEN LA
LENHAM CL
LOWTHER RD
TOUTLEY CL
WOODHURST LA
77
78
79
70
71
72
73
1
2
3
4

87
115

62
90

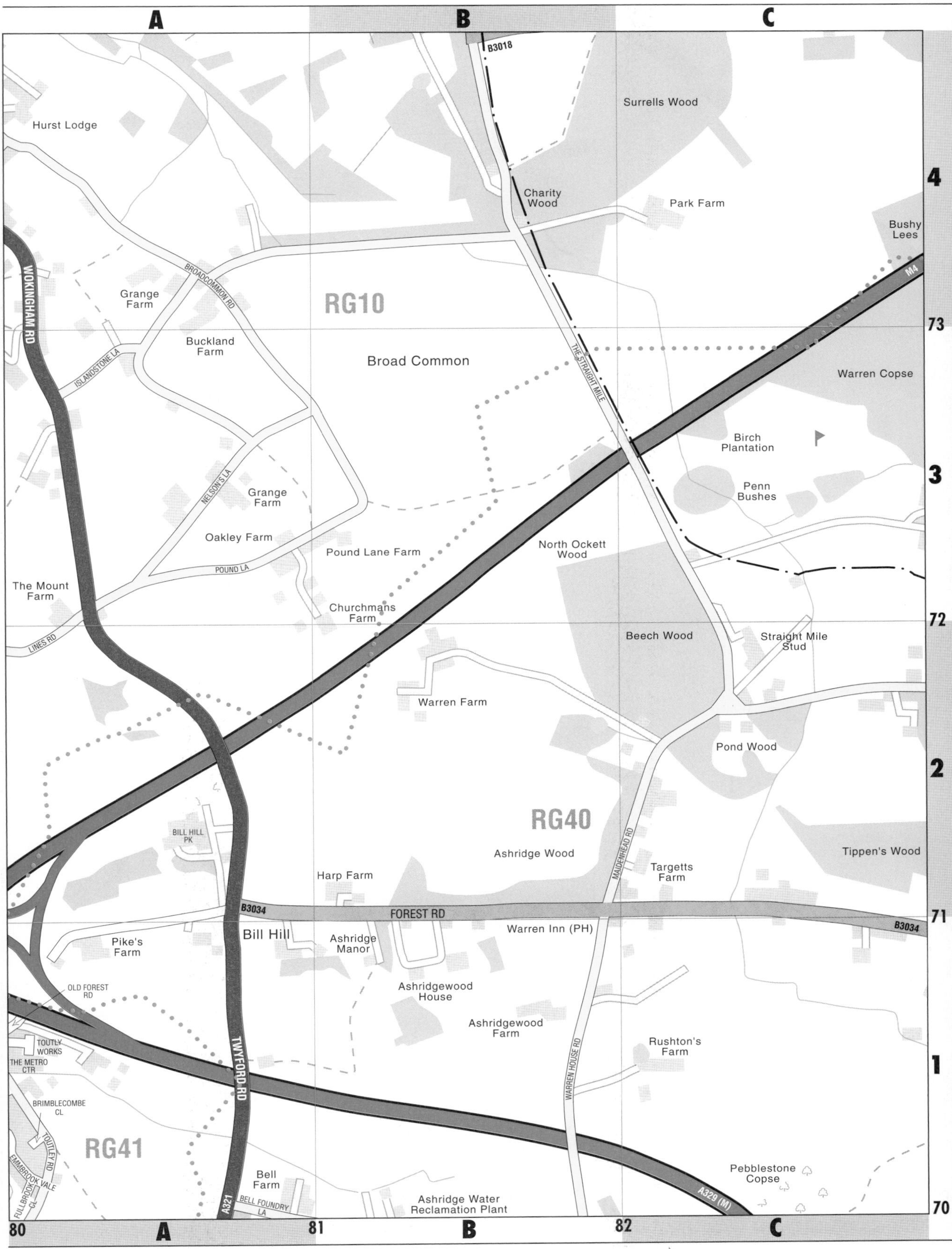
A
B
C
B3018
Surrells Wood
Hurst Lodge
4
Charity Wood
Park Farm
Bushy Lees
M4
WOKINGHAM RD
BROADCOMMON RD
Grange Farm
RG10
73
Buckland Farm
Broad Common
THE STRAIGHT MILE
Warren Copse
ISLANDSTONE LA
Birch Plantation
NELSON'S LA
3
Grange Farm
Penn Bushes
Oakley Farm
Pound Lane Farm
North Ockett Wood
POUND LA
The Mount Farm
Churchmans Farm
72
LINES RD
Beech Wood
Straight Mile Stud
Warren Farm
Pond Wood
2
RG40
BILL HILL PK
MAIDENHEAD RD
Ashridge Wood
Tippen's Wood
Harp Farm
Targetts Farm
B3034
FOREST RD
71
B3034
Warren Inn (PH)
Bill Hill
Pike's Farm
Ashridge Manor
OLD FOREST RD
Ashridgewood House
Ashridgewood Farm
TOUTLY WORKS
THE METRO CTR
Rushton's Farm
TWYFORD RD
1
WARREN HOUSE RD
BRIMBLECOMBE CL
RG41
TOUTLEY RD
EMMBROOK VALE
FULLBROOK CL
Bell Farm
Pebblestone Copse
A321
BELL FOUNDRY LA
Ashridge Water Reclamation Plant
A329 (M)
70
80
A
81
B
82
C

116
90

89
63

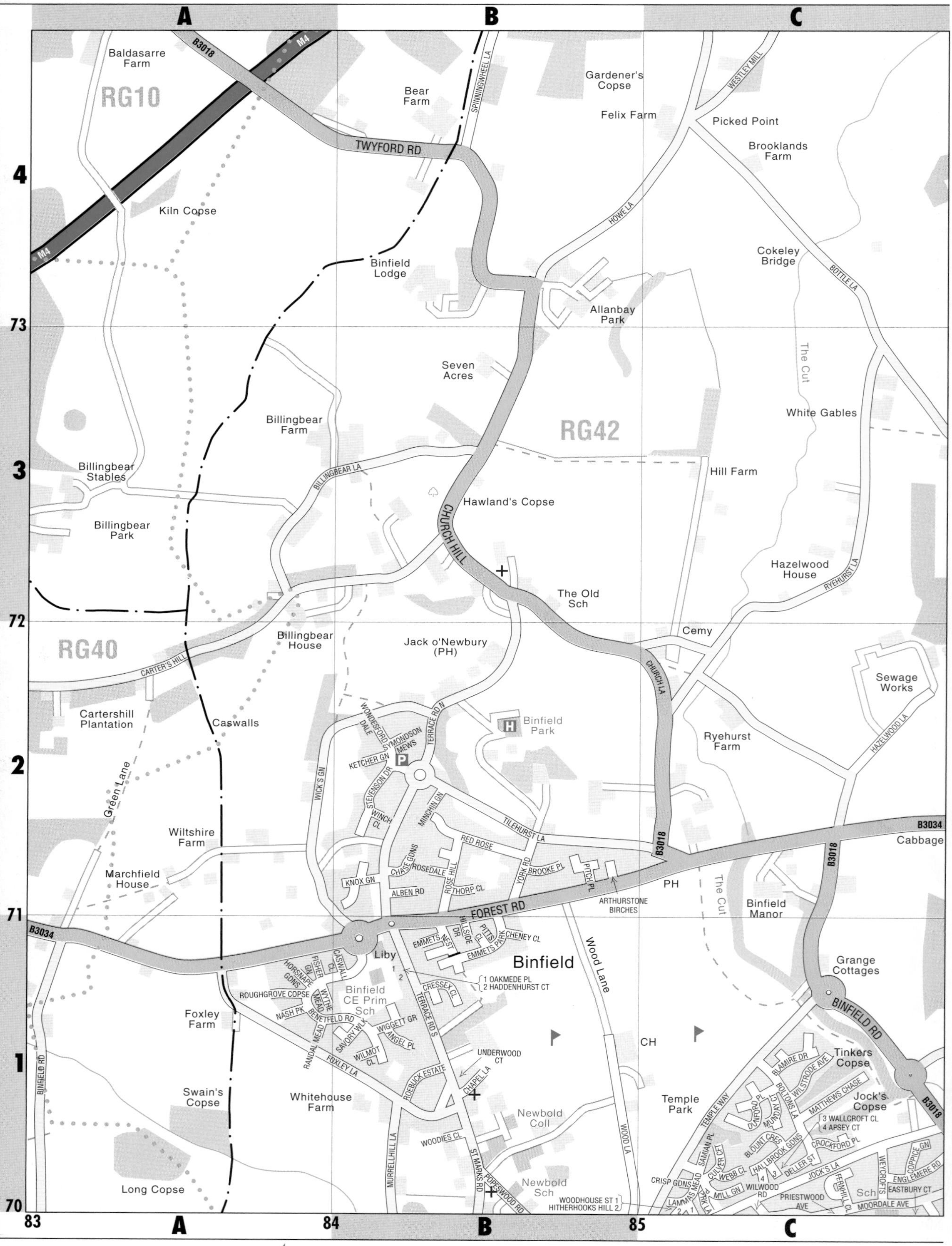
A
B
C
4
73
3
72
2
71
1
70
83
84
85
Baldasarre Farm
RG10
M4
B3018
Bear Farm
SPINNINGWHEEL LA
Gardener's Copse
Felix Farm
WESTLEY MILL
Picked Point
Brooklands Farm
TWYFORD RD
Kiln Copse
HOWE LA
Cokeley Bridge
BOTTLE LA
Binfield Lodge
Allanbay Park
Seven Acres
The Cut
White Gables
Billingbear Farm
RG42
Billingbear Stables
BILLINGBEAR LA
Hill Farm
Hawland's Copse
Billingbear Park
CHURCH HILL
Hazelwood House
RYEHURST LA
The Old Sch
Cemy
RG40
Billingbear House
Jack o'Newbury (PH)
CARTER'S HILL
CHURCH LA
Sewage Works
Cartershill Plantation
Caswalls
WONDESFORD DALE
TERRACE RD N
SYMONDSON MEWS
Binfield Park
Ryehurst Farm
HAZELWOOD LA
KETCHER GN
WICK'S GN
STEVENSON DR
MINCHIN GN
Green Lane
WINCH CL
TILEHURST LA
B3034
Cabbage
Wiltshire Farm
RED ROSE
B3018
Marchfield House
CHASE GDNS
ROSEDALE
ROSE HILL
YORK RD
BROOKE PL
PITCH PL
KNOX GN
ALBEN RD
THORP CL
PH
ARTHURSTONE BIRCHES
Binfield Manor
FOREST RD
HILLSIDE DR
PITTS CL
CHENEY CL
EMMETS NEST
EMMETS PARK
Wood Lane
Grange Cottages
Liby
Binfield
1 OAKMEDE PL
2 HADDENHURST CT
HORSNAPE GDNS
FISHER GN
CASWALL CL
ROUGHGROVE COPSE
WYTHE MEAD
Binfield CE Prim Sch
CRESSEX CL
BINFIELD RD
Foxley Farm
NASH PK
BENETFELD RD
WIGGETT GR
TERRACE RD S
RANDAL MEAD
SAVORY WLK
ANGEL PL
WILMOT CL
CH
Tinkers Copse
FOXLEY LA
UNDERWOOD CT
BLAMIRE DR
WILSTRODE AVE
BINFIELD RD
ROEBUCK ESTATE
CHAPEL LA
MATTHEWS CHASE
Jock's Copse
Swain's Copse
Whitehouse Farm
Temple Park
TEMPLE WAY
DUNFORD PL
MUNDAY CT
BOLTONS LA
Newbold Coll
3 WALLCROFT CL
4 APSEY CT
MURRELLHILL LA
WOODIES CL
WOOD LA
SAMIAN PL
BLOUNT CRES
HALLBROOK GDNS
CROCKFORD PL
ST MARKS RD
CULVER CFT
WEBB CL
DELLER ST
COPPICE GN
JOCK'S LA
CRISP GDNS
WILWOOD RD
FERNHILL CL
WEYCROFTS
ENGLEMERE RD
LAMMAS MEAD
Newbold Sch
POPESWOOD RD
PARK LA
PRIESTWOOD AVE
Sch
EASTBURY CT
Long Copse
WOODHOUSE ST
HITHERHOOKS HILL
MOORDALE AVE

89
117

64 92

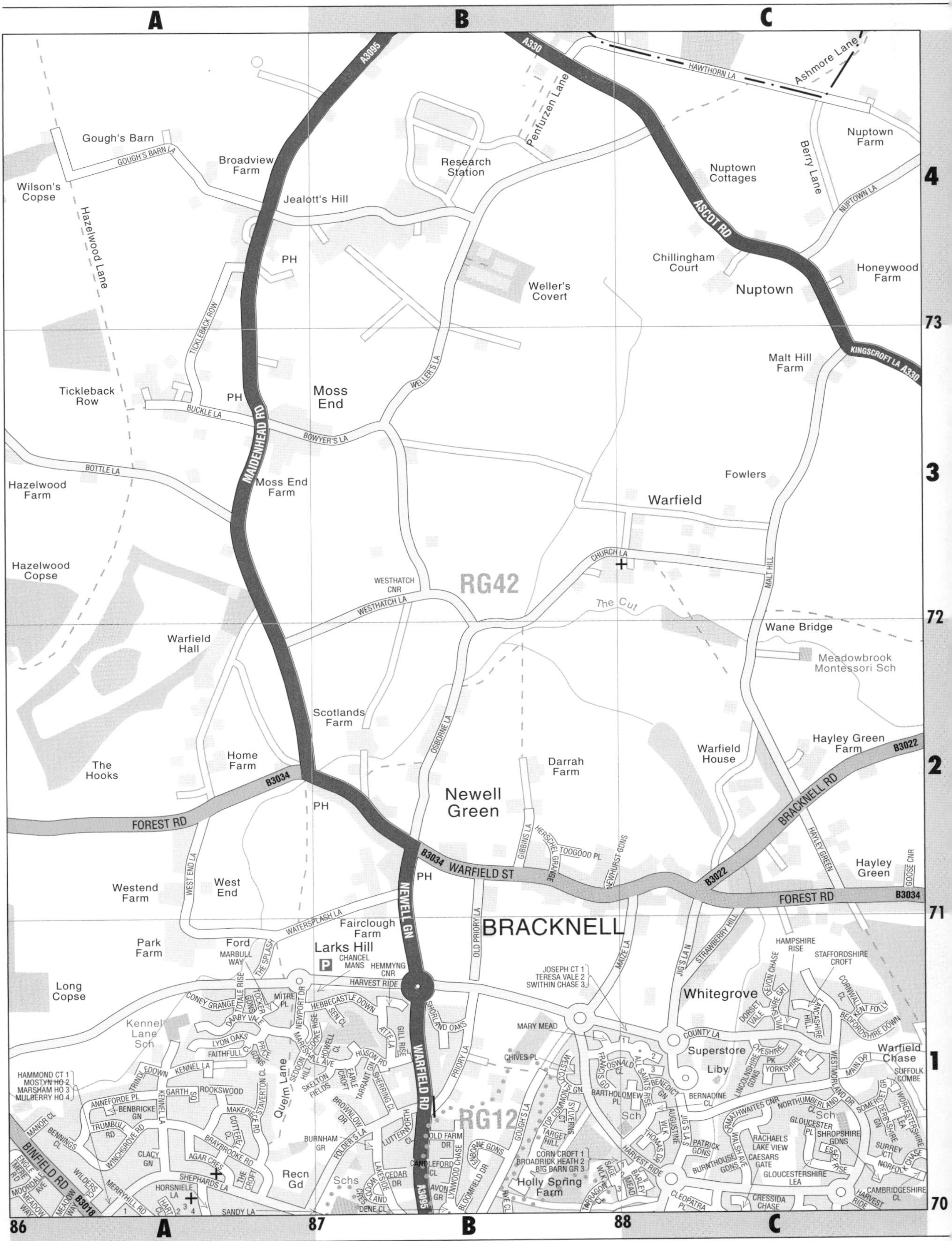
A
B
C
4
3
2
1
73
72
71
70
86
87
88
A3095
A330
HAWTHORN LA
Ashmore Lane
Gough's Barn
GOUGH'S BARN LA
Broadview Farm
Research Station
Penfurzen Lane
Nuptown Farm
Nuptown Cottages
Berry Lane
NUPTOWN LA
Wilson's Copse
Hazelwood Lane
Jealott's Hill
ASCOT RD
PH
Chillingham Court
Nuptown
Honeywood Farm
Weller's Covert
TICKLEBACK ROW
KINGSCROFT LA A330
Malt Hill Farm
Tickleback Row
Moss End
WELLER'S LA
BUCKLE LA
MAIDENHEAD RD
BOWYER'S LA
BOTTLE LA
Hazelwood Farm
Moss End Farm
Fowlers
Warfield
Hazelwood Copse
CHURCH LA
MALT HILL
WESTHATCH CNR
RG42
WESTHATCH LA
The Cut
Wane Bridge
Meadowbrook Montessori Sch
Warfield Hall
Scotlands Farm
OSBORNE LA
Hayley Green Farm
B3022
Warfield House
Darrah Farm
Home Farm
The Hooks
B3034
Newell Green
BRACKNELL RD
FOREST RD
GIBBINS LA
HERSCHEL GRANGE
TOOGOOD PL
NEWHURST GDNS
HAYLEY GREEN
Hayley Green
GOOSE CNR
B3034 WARFIELD ST
WEST END LA
Westend Farm
West End
NEWELL GN
B3034
Fairclough Farm
WATERSPLASH LA
BRACKNELL
OLD PRIORY LA
STRAWBERRY HILL
Park Farm
Ford
MARBULL WAY
THE SPLASH
Larks Hill
CHANCEL MANS
HEMMYNG CNR
HARVEST RIDE
JOSEPH CT 1
TERESA VALE 2
SWITHIN CHASE 3
MAIZE LA
JIG'S LA N
HAMPSHIRE RISE
STAFFORDSHIRE CROFT
Long Copse
Whitegrove
MITRE PL
CONEY GRANGE
TOTALE RISE
TOCKER GDNS
DARBY VALE
HEBBECASTLE DOWN
SHORLAND OAKS
MARY MEAD
CORNWALL CL
KENT FOLLY
BEDFORDSHIRE DOWN
Kennel Lane Sch
LYON OAKS
FAITHFULL CL
MARSHALL AVE
HOWELL CL
ATTE LA
GILL RISE
PRIORY LA
COUNTY LA
Superstore
Liby
Warfield Chase
MAIN DR
SUFFOLK COMBE
HAMMOND CT 1
MOSTYN HO 2
MARSHAM HO 3
MULBERRY HO 4
EDOWN
KENNEL LA
SEDDON HILL
SKELTON FIELDS
EARLE CROFT
HUSON RD
CHIVES PL
OSWALD CL
BENEDICT GN
YORKSHIRE PL
WESTMORLAND DR
ANNEFORDE PL
BENBRICKE GN
GARTH SQ
ROOKSWOOD
MAKEPIECE RD
Quelm Lane
TARRANT GN
SHERRING CL
WARFIELD RD
BARTHOLOMEW PL
ALL SAINTS RISE
BERNADINE CL
LINCOLNSHIRE GDNS
CHESHIRE PK
NORTHUMBERLAND DR
Sch
SOMERSET GR
DERBYSHIRE GN
WORCESTERSHIRE LEA
TRUMBULL RD
WINCHGROVE RD
COTTERELL CL
BROWNLOW DR
HUBBARD CL
RG12
GOUGH'S LA
TOP COMMON
SYLVERNS
TARGET HILL
AUGUSTINE WLK
THOMAS DR
GLOUCESTER PL
SHROPSHIRE GDNS
SURREY CT
ESSEX RISE
NORFOLK CHASE
CLACY GN
BRAYBROOKE RD
BURNHAM GR
FOLDER'S LA
LUTTERNS
OLD FARM DR
CORN CROFT 1
BROADRICK HEATH 2
BIG BARN GR 3
PATRICK GDNS
BURNTHOUSE GDNS
RACHAELS LAKE VIEW
CAESARS GATE
GLOUCESTERSHIRE LEA
BINFIELD RD
MANOR CL
BENNINGS CL
AGAR CRES
SHEPHARDS LA
THE CROFT
Recn Gd
Schs
CANDLEFORD CL
CEDAR DR
AVON GR
LYNWOOD CHASE
BLOOMFIELD DR
ENBORNE GDNS
Holly Spring Farm
TARRAGON CL
SAGE WLK
MEAD
BARLEY
HARVEST RIDE
JIG'S LA S
CLEOPATRA PL
CRESSIDA CHASE
HARVEST RIDE
CAMBRIDGESHIRE CL
ENGLE MERE RD
MOORDALE AVE
MEADOW WAY
WILDERS CL
B3018
MERRYHILL RD
HORSNIELE LA
HART CL
SANDY LA
LAKESIDE
WOOD CRES
DENE CL
A3095

118 92

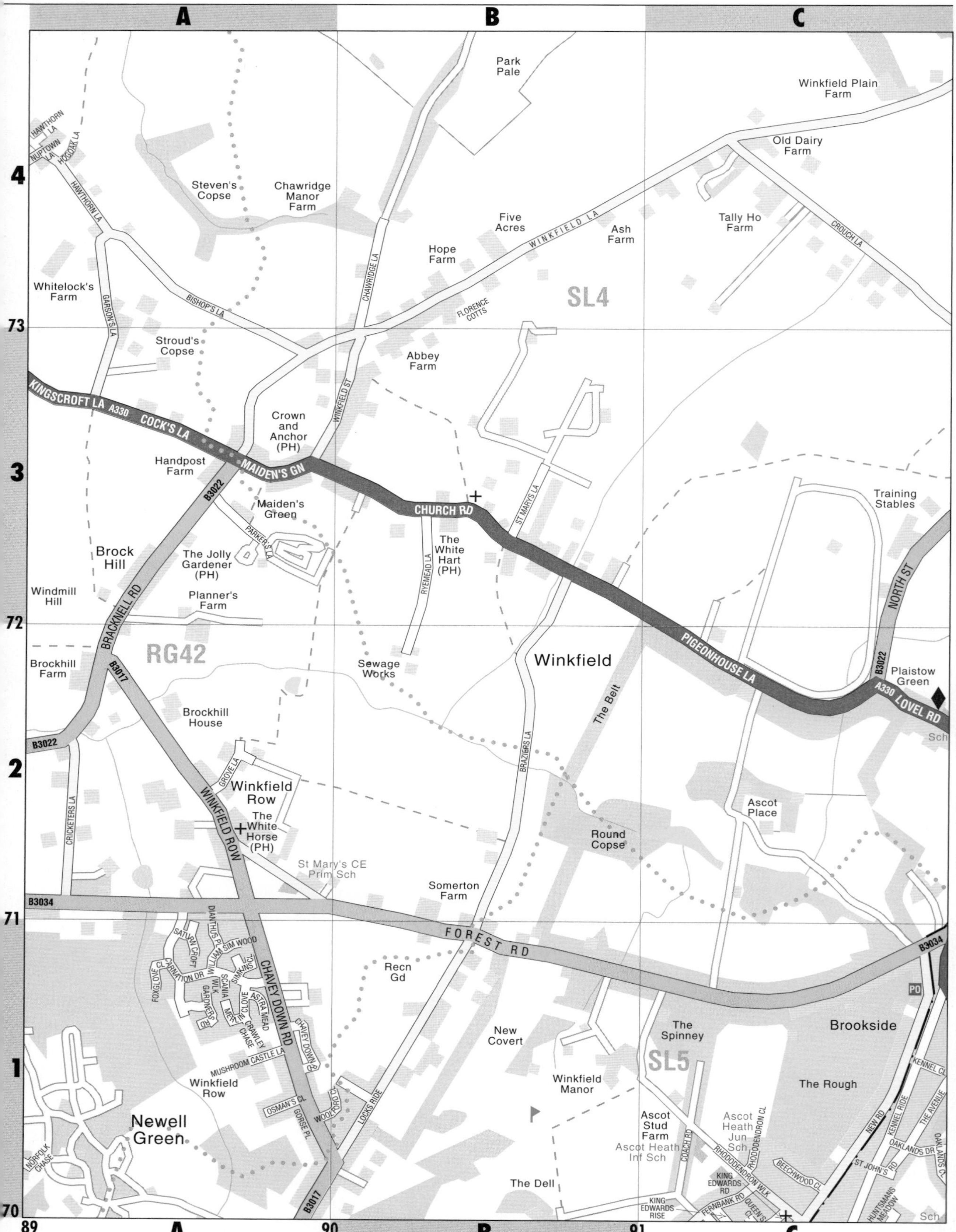
A
B
C
Park Pale
Winkfield Plain Farm
Old Dairy Farm
Steven's Copse
Chawridge Manor Farm
Five Acres
Ash Farm
Tally Ho Farm
Hope Farm
Whitelock's Farm
SL4
Stroud's Copse
Abbey Farm
KINGSCROFT LA A330 COCK'S LA
Crown and Anchor (PH)
Handpost Farm
MAIDEN'S GN
Maiden's Green
CHURCH RD
Training Stables
Brock Hill
The Jolly Gardener (PH)
The White Hart (PH)
Windmill Hill
Planner's Farm
RG42
Winkfield
PIGEONHOUSE LA
Plaistow Green
A330 LOVEL RD
Brockhill Farm
Sewage Works
Brockhill House
The Belt
Winkfield Row
The White Horse (PH)
Ascot Place
Round Copse
St Mary's CE Prim Sch
Somerton Farm
FOREST RD
Recn Gd
New Covert
The Spinney
Brookside
SL5
Winkfield Row
Winkfield Manor
The Rough
Newell Green
Ascot Stud Farm
Ascot Heath Inf Sch
Ascot Heath Jun Sch
The Dell
HAWTHORN LA
NUPTOWN LA
HOGOAK LA
GARSON'S LA
BISHOP'S LA
CHAWRIDGE LA
WINKFIELD LA
CROUCH LA
FLORENCE COTTS
WINKFIELD ST
ST MARYS LA
B3022
BRACKNELL RD
PARKER'S LA
RYEMEAD LA
NORTH ST
B3017
GROVE LA
WINKFIELD ROW
BRAZIERS LA
CRICKETERS LA
B3034
CHAVEY DOWN RD
MUSHROOM CASTLE LA
OSMAN'S CL
GORSE PL
WOODFORD CL
LOCKS RIDE
NORFOLK CHASE
COACH RD
RHODODENDRON WLK
RHODODENDRON CL
KING EDWARDS RD
KING EDWARDS RISE
FERNBANK RD
QUEEN'S CL
BEECHWOOD CL
ST JOHN'S RD
NEW RD
KENNEL RIDE
KENNEL CL
THE AVENUE
OAKLANDS DR
HUNTSMANS MEADOW
Sch
PO
4
73
3
72
2
71
1
70
89
90
91

66
94

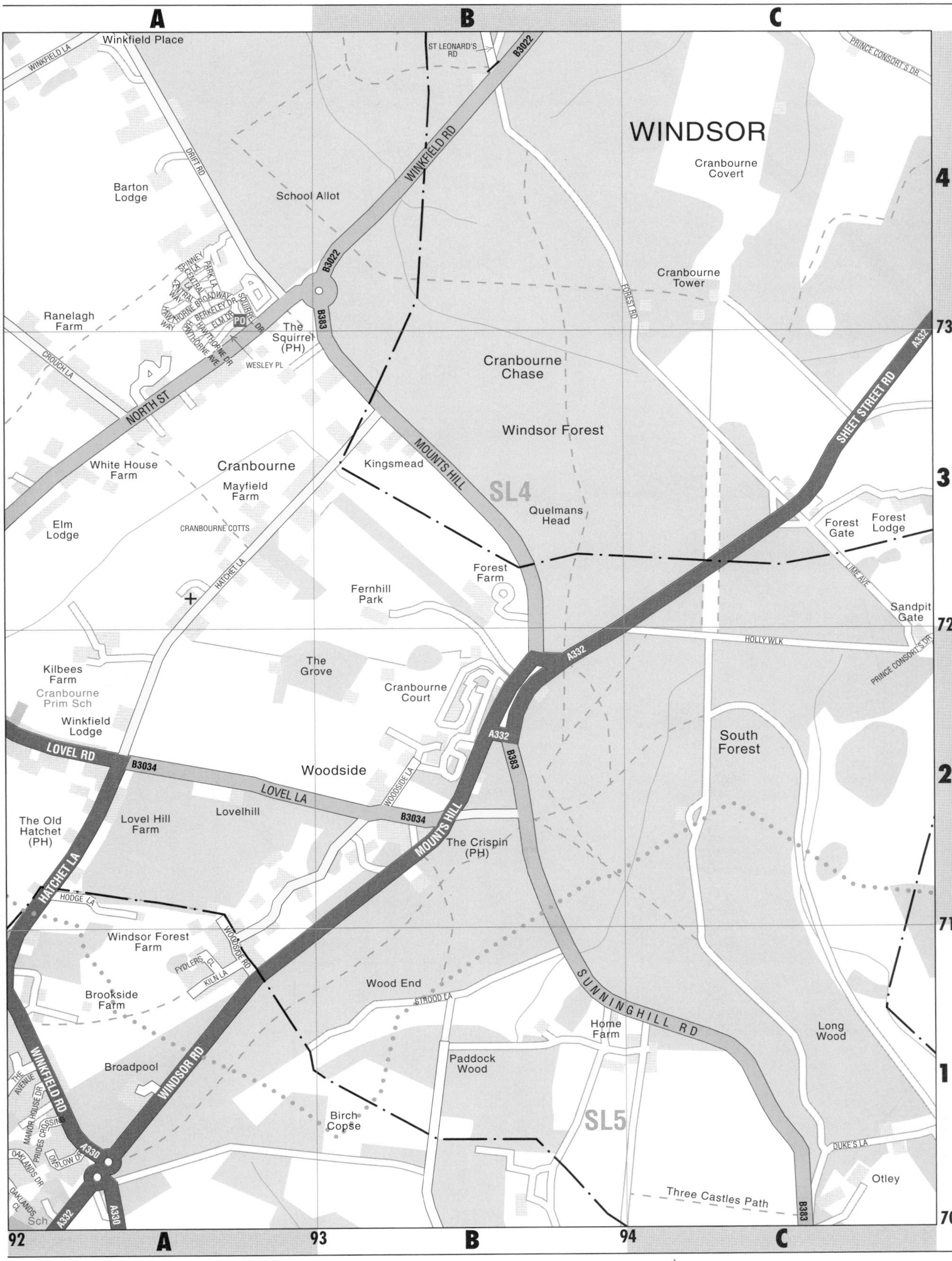
A
B
C
Winkfield Place
WINKFIELD LA
ST LEONARD'S RD
B3022
PRINCE CONSORT'S DR
WINDSOR
Cranbourne Covert
4
DRIFT RD
WINKFIELD RD
Barton Lodge
School Allot
B3022
SPINNEY LA
PARK LA
CENTRAL WAY
BROADWAY
BERKELEY DR
SQUIRREL DR
ELM DR
HAWTHORNE WAY
HAWTHORNE AVE
HAWTHORNE DR
PO
Cranbourne Tower
FOREST RD
Ranelagh Farm
B383
The Squirrel (PH)
73
CROUCH LA
WESLEY PL
A332
Cranbourne Chase
SHEET STREET RD
NORTH ST
Windsor Forest
White House Farm
Cranbourne
Kingsmead
MOUNTS HILL
Mayfield Farm
SL4
3
Quelmans Head
Forest Gate
Forest Lodge
Elm Lodge
CRANBOURNE COTTS
HATCHET LA
Forest Farm
LIME AVE
Fernhill Park
Sandpit Gate
72
HOLLY WLK
A332
PRINCE CONSORT'S DR
The Grove
Kilbees Farm
Cranbourne Prim Sch
Cranbourne Court
Winkfield Lodge
A332
B383
South Forest
LOVEL RD
B3034
Woodside
2
LOVEL LA
WOODSIDE LA
B3034
MOUNTS HILL
The Old Hatchet (PH)
Lovel Hill Farm
Lovelhill
The Crispin (PH)
HATCHET LA
HODGE LA
71
Windsor Forest Farm
WOODSIDE RD
FYDLERS CL
KILN LA
SUNNINGHILL RD
Wood End
STROOD LA
Brookside Farm
Home Farm
Long Wood
Paddock Wood
WINKFIELD RD
Broadpool
WINDSOR RD
1
THE AVENUE
MANOR HOUSE DR
PRIDES CROSSING
Birch Copse
SL5
A330
LOW DR
DUKE'S LA
OAKLANDS DR
OAKLANDS CL
Otley
Three Castles Path
A332
A330
B383
Sch
70
92
93
94

120
94

93
67

A
B
C
4
73
3
72
2
71
1
70
95
96
97
Flemish Farm
A332
SHEET STREET RD
Pickleherring
Pond
Ranger's
Lodge
Beehive
Hill
PRINCE CONSORT'S DR
Russel's
Pond
Fiddle
Covert
Battle Bourne
The Gallop
Seymours
Plantation
Prince of Wales
Pond
THE LONG WLK
Rush
Pond
Bear's
Rails
Bear's Rails
Pond
Cemy
CRIMP HILL
BEARS RAILS
PK
Statue
Snow
Hill
Spring
Hill
Cookes Hill
Richardson's
Lawn
SL4
PO
RICHARDSON'S
LAWN COTTS
THE VILLAGE
QUEEN ANNE'S CL
Isle of
Wight Pond
The
Village
Three Castles Path
Deepstrood
Poets
Lawn
Royal
Lodge
BISHOPSGATE RD
The Fox &
Hounds
(PH)
Queen Anne's Ride
Windsor Great Park
Dark
Wood
The Royal
Prim Sch
Cow
Pond
Bishopsgate
Chapel
Wood
PARK CLOSE
COTTS
MEZEL HILL
COTTS
CUMBERLAND
LODGE
DUKE'S LA
Hilton's
Covert
Mezel
Hill
RHODODENDRON RIDE
The Sun
(PH)
Square
Covert
Wilderness
Park
Close
WICK LA
Slans
Hill
Great
Meadow
Pond
The Savill
Gardens
Parkside
House
Leiper
Hill
Temple
Hill
TW20
P
SL5
Mill
Pond
Norfolk
Farm
Norfolk
Plantation
Statue
Smith's
Lawn
Obelisk
Rosy
Bottom
Obelisk
Pond
Polo Gds

93
121

68
96

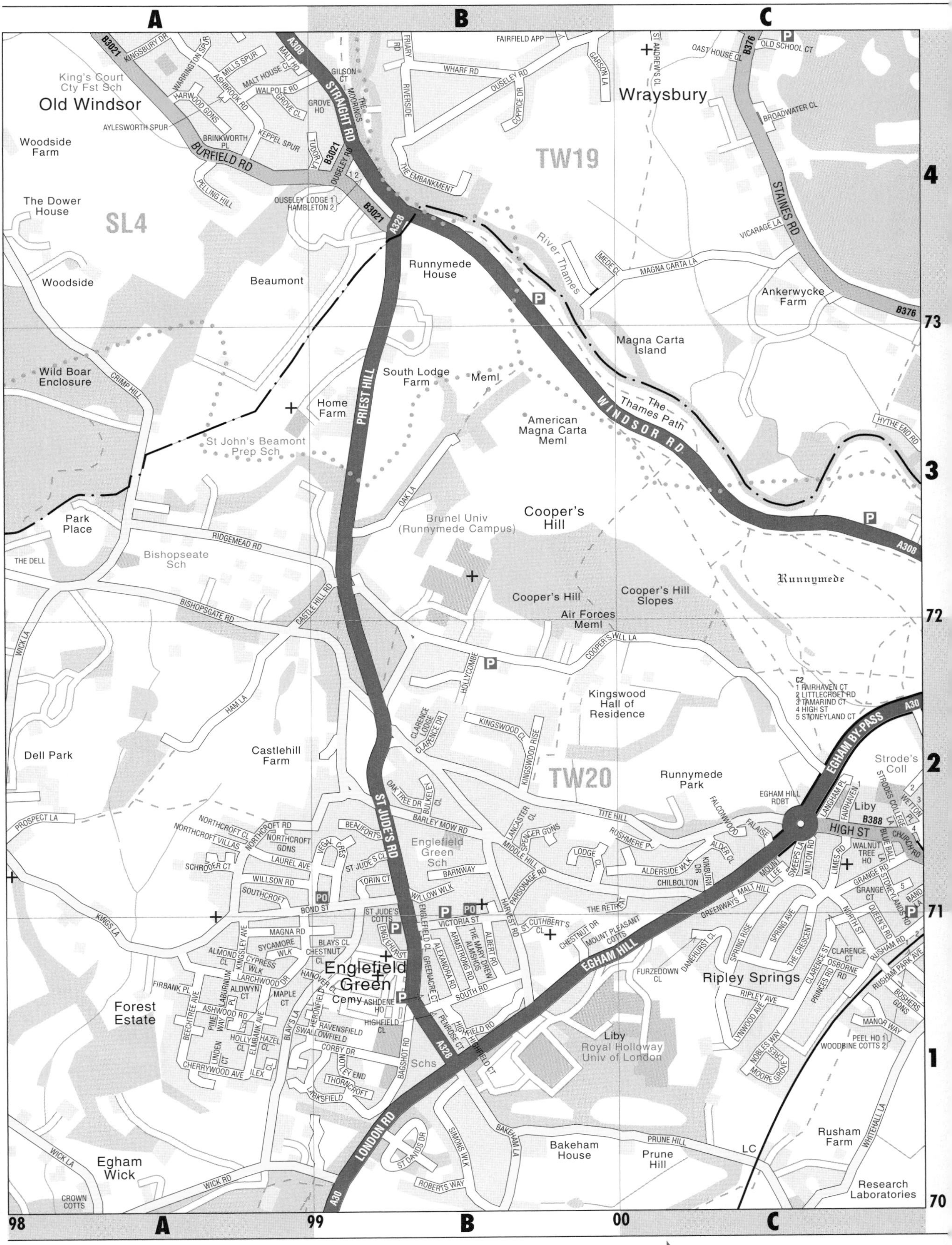
A
B
C
4
3
2
1
73
72
71
70
98
99
00
Old Windsor
King's Court Cty Fst Sch
Woodside Farm
The Dower House
SL4
Woodside
Beaumont
Runnymede House
Wraysbury
TW19
River Thames
Ankerwycke Farm
Magna Carta Island
Wild Boar Enclosure
Home Farm
South Lodge Farm
Meml
American Magna Carta Meml
The Thames Path
WINDSOR RD
St John's Beamont Prep Sch
Park Place
Brunel Univ (Runnymede Campus)
Cooper's Hill
Bishopseate Sch
Runnymede
Cooper's Hill
Cooper's Hill Slopes
Air Forces Meml
Kingswood Hall of Residence
Dell Park
Castlehill Farm
TW20
Runnymede Park
Strode's Coll
Liby
Englefield Green Sch
Englefield Green
Cemy
Forest Estate
Ripley Springs
Liby
Royal Holloway Univ of London
Schs
Egham Wick
Bakeham House
Prune Hill
Rusham Farm
Research Laboratories
CROWN COTTS
LC
STRAIGHT RD
PRIEST HILL
ST JUDE'S RD
EGHAM HILL
EGHAM BY-PASS
LONDON RD
STAINES RD
BURFIELD RD
HIGH ST
RIDGEMEAD RD
BISHOPSGATE RD
CASTLE HILL RD
COOPER'S HILL LA
TITE HILL
WICK LA
WICK RD
PRUNE HILL
BAKEHAM LA
MAGNA CARTA LA
WHARF RD
FAIRFIELD APP
OAST HOUSE CL
OLD SCHOOL CT
BROADWATER CL
VICARAGE LA
HYTHE END RD
KINGSWOOD CL
KINGSWOOD RISE
HOLLYCOMBE
CLARENCE LODGE
CLARENCE DR
OAK TREE DR
BULKELEY CL
BARLEY MOW RD
NORTHCROFT RD
NORTHCROFT CL
NORTHCROFT VILLAS
SCHRODER CT
WILLSON RD
SOUTHCROFT
BOND ST
LAUREL AVE
MAGNA RD
SYCAMORE WLK
ALMOND CL
CYPRESS WLK
LARCHWOOD DR
ALDWYN CT
FIRBANK PL
ASHWOOD RD
HOLLY CL
HAZEL CL
CHERRYWOOD AVE
ILEX CL
MAPLE CT
VICTORIA ST
ALEXANDRA RD
ARMSTRONG RD
ALBERT RD
SOUTH RD
HARVEST RD
PARSONAGE RD
LANCASTER CL
SPENCER GDNS
MIDDLE HILL
LODGE CL
ALDERSIDE WLK
CHILBOLTON
KINBURN DR
FALAISE
FALCONWOOD
ALDER CL
RUSHMERE PL
CHESTNUT DR
MOUNT PLEASANT COTTS
FURZEDOWN CL
DANEHURST CL
SPRING RISE
SPRING AVE
THE CRESCENT
CLARENCE ST
PRINCES RD
OSBORNE RD
RIPLEY AVE
LYNWOOD AVE
NOBLES WAY
MOORE GROVE CRES
MANOR WAY
PEEL HO
WOODBINE COTTS
WHITEHALL LA
RUSHAM RD
RUSHAM PARK AVE
BOSHERS GDNS
SIMONS WLK
ST DAVIDS DR
ROBERTS WAY
CORBY DR
NOTLEY END
THORNCROFT
LARKSFIELD
SWALLOWFIELD
RAVENSFIELD
HERONFIELD
HIGHFIELD RD
PENROSE CT
BAGSHOT RD
PROSPECT LA
KINGS LA
HAM LA
OAK LA
CRIMP HILL
THE DELL
C2
1 FAIRHAVEN CT
2 LITTLECROFT RD
3 TAMARIND CT
4 HIGH ST
5 STONEYLAND CT
EGHAM HILL RDBT
A308
A328
A30
B3021
B376
B388

122
96

95
69

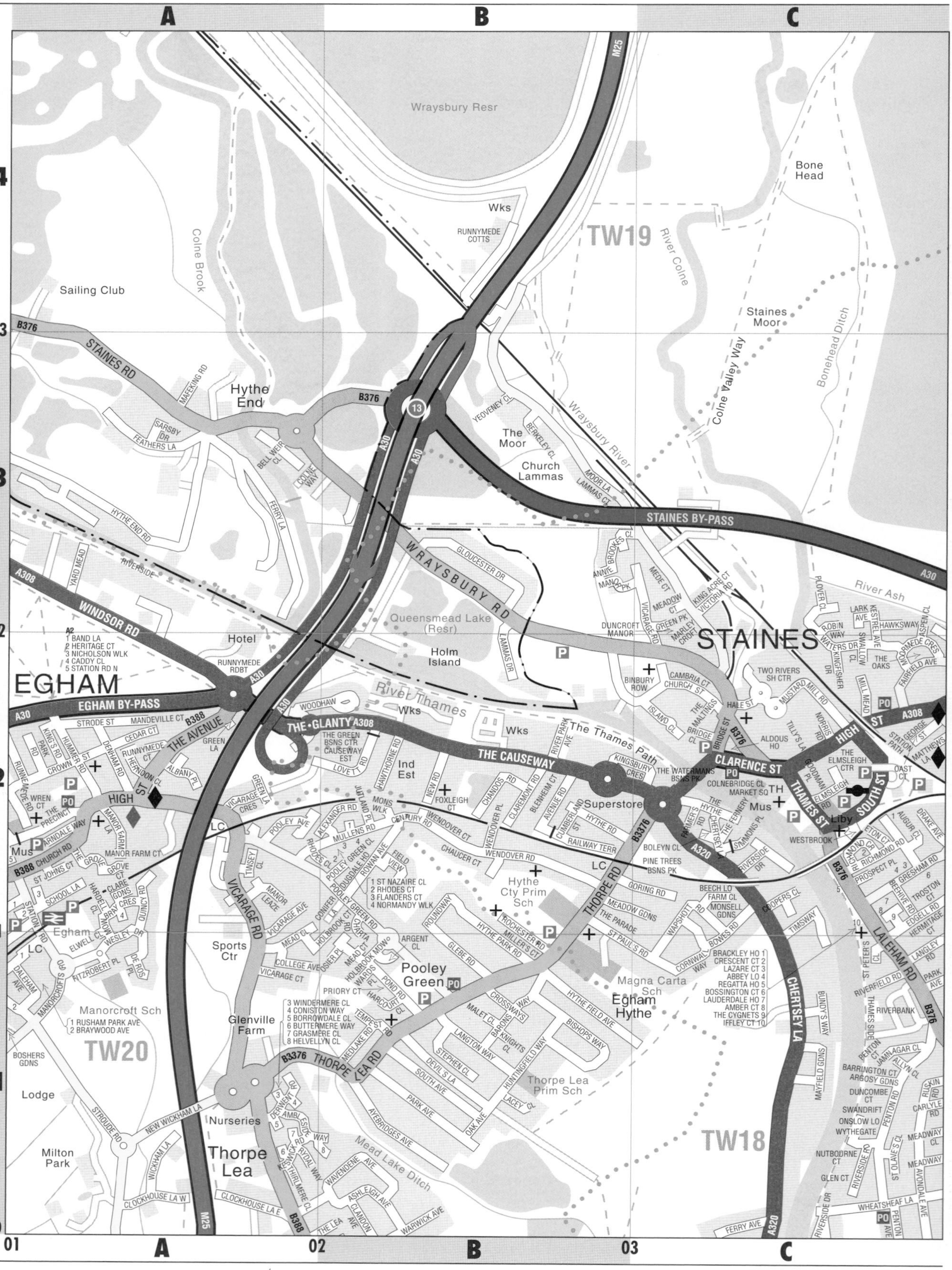
A
B
C
4
73
3
72
2
71
1
70
01
02
03
M25
Wraysbury Resr
Wks
RUNNYMEDE COTTS
TW19
River Colne
Bone Head
Colne Brook
Sailing Club
Staines Moor
Colne Valley Way
Bonehead Ditch
B376
STAINES RD
MAFEKING RD
Hythe End
B376
13
SARSBY DR
FEATHERS LA
BELL WEIR CL
COLNE WAY
A30
YEOVENEY CL
BERKELEY CL
The Moor
Wraysbury River
Church Lammas
MOOR LA
LAMMAS CT
STAINES BY-PASS
HYTHE END RD
FERRY LA
RIVERSIDE
YARD MEAD
A308
WINDSOR RD
GLOUCESTER DR
WRAYSBURY RD
Queensmead Lake (Resr)
Holm Island
LAMMAS DR
BROOKES CL
ANNIE BROOKE
MANOR PK
MEDE CT
MEADOW CT
GREEN PK
MARLEY CROFT
VICARAGE RD
KING ACRE CT
VICTORIA RD
DUNCROFT MANOR
STAINES
PLOVER CL
River Ash
LARK AVE
HAWKSWAY
ROBIN WAY
WATERS DR
KINGFISHER DR
KESTREL AVE
SWALLOW CL
THE OAKS
FAIRFIELD AVE
A2
1 BAND LA
2 HERITAGE CT
3 NICHOLSON WLK
4 CADDY CL
5 STATION RD N
Hotel
RUNNYMEDE RDBT
EGHAM
EGHAM BY-PASS
MANDEVILLE CT
STRODE ST
B388
THE AVENUE
WOODHAW
River Thames
Wks
THE GLANTY
THE GREEN BSNS CTR
CAUSEWAY EST
LOVETT RD
HAWTHORNE RD
Ind Est
NEW RD
Wks
The Thames Path
RIVER PARK AVE
BINBURY ROW
CAMBRIA CT
CHURCH ST
THE MALTINGS
ISLAND CL
BRIDGE CL
BRIDGE ST
HALE ST
TWO RIVERS SH CTR
MUSTARD MILL RD
TILLY'S LA
NORRIS RD
MILL MEAD
HIGH ST
A308
STATION PATH
GEORGE ST
MATTHEWS LA
OAST CT
KING'S RD
PARK
HUMMER RD
CROWN ST
DENHAM RD
CEDAR CT
RUNNYMEDE CT
HERNDON CL
GREEN LA
ALBANY PL
THE CAUSEWAY
CHANDOS RD
CLAREMONT RD
BLENHEIM CT
AVENUE RD
KINGSBURY CRES
THE WATERMANS BSNS PK
CLARENCE ST
COLNEBRIDGE CL
MARKET SQ
TH
Mus
THAMES ST
GOODMAN PL
ELMSLEIGH RD
THE ELMSLEIGH CTR
SOUTH ST
Liby
WESTBROOK
RUNNEMEDE RD
WREN CT
THE PRECINCT
HIGH ST
MANOR FARM LA
ARNDALE WAY
MANOR FARM CT
Mus
B388
CHURCH RD
ST JOHNS CT
THE GROVE
GROVE CT
CLARE GDNS
BRAY CRES
QUINCY RD
SCHOOL LA
HARDELL CL
STATION RD
Egham
ELWELL CL
WESLEY DR
FITZROBERT PL
DE ROS PL
VICARAGE CRES
LC
VICARAGE RD
TIMSEY CL
MANOR LEAZE
VICARAGE AVE
POOLEY AVE
ALEXANDER RD
MULLENS RD
RHODES CL
POOLEY GREEN CL
DUGDALE HO
ROWAN AVE
MONS WLK
CENTURY RD
JUTLAND PL
WENDOVER CT
FOXLEIGH CT
WENDOVER PL
WENDOVER RD
CHAUCER CT
FIELD VIEW
1 ST NAZAIRE CL
2 RHODES CL
3 FLANDERS CT
4 NORMANDY WLK
CUMBERLAND ST
HYTHE RD
RAILWAY TERR
Superstore
B3376
THORPE RD
BOLEYN CL
A320
FARMER'S RD
THE HYTHE
CHERTSEY LA
THE FERNERY
SIMMONS PL
RIVERSIDE DR
PINE TREES BSNS PK
LC
Hythe Cty Prim Sch
GORING RD
BEECH LO
FARM CL
MONSELL GDNS
MEADOW GDNS
THE PARADE
WAPSHOTT RD
ROCHESTER RD
MILLER'S CT
ST PAUL'S RD
BOWES RD
COOPERS CL
TIMSWAY
B376
RICHMOND CT
RICHMOND RD
ETON CL
AUGUR CL
DRAKE AVE
PROSPECT PL
GRESHAM RD
BEEHIVE RD
TROSTON CT
EDGELL RD
HERMITAGE CT
LALEHAM RD
CONIFER LA
HOLBROOK CT
POOLEY GREEN RD
CHARTA RD
ROUNDWAY
ARGENT CL
HOLBROOK MDW
MEAD CT
MEAD CL
Sports Ctr
COLLEGE AVE
OSIER PL
VICARAGE CT
WARDS PL
POND RD
GLEBE RD
HYTHE PARK RD
Pooley Green
PO
PRIORY CT
HARCOURT CL
CROSSWAYS
BARONS WAY
KNIGHTS CL
MALET CL
CORNWALL WAY
BRACKLEY HO 1
CRESCENT CT 2
LAZARE CT 3
ABBEY LO 4
REGATTA HO 5
BOSSINGTON CT 6
LAUDERDALE HO 7
AMBER CT 8
THE CYGNETS 9
IFFLEY CT 10
Magna Carta Sch
Egham Hythe
HYTHE FIELD AVE
BISHOPS WAY
BUNDY'S WAY
ST PETER'S CL
THAMES SIDE
RIVERFIELD RD
RIVERBANK
LANGLEY RD
PARK AVE
B376
Manorcroft Sch
1 RUSHAM PARK AVE
2 BRAYWOOD AVE
TW20
3 WINDERMERE CL
4 CONISTON WAY
5 BORROWDALE CL
6 BUTTERMERE WAY
7 GRASMERE CL
8 HELVELLYN CL
Glenville Farm
TEMPEST RD
MEDLAKE RD
LANGTON WAY
STEPHEN CL
DEVIL'S LA
SOUTH AVE
HUNTINGFIELD WAY
B3376
THORPE LEA RD
Thorpe Lea Prim Sch
LACEY CL
PARK AVE
OAK AVE
MAYFIELD GDNS
PENTON CT
JAMNAGAR CL
ALLYN CL
BARRINGTON CT
ARGOSY GDNS
DUNCOMBE CT
SWANDRIFT
ONSLOW LO
WYTHEGATE
PENTON RD
RUSKIN RD
CARLYLE RD
BOSHERS GDNS
Lodge
STROUDE RD
NEW WICKHAM LA
Nurseries
DERWENT RD
AMBLESIDE
WAY
RYDAL WAY
AVEBRIDGES AVE
Mead Lake Ditch
TW18
MEADWAY CL
MEADWAY
AVONDALE AVE
Milton Park
WICKHAM LA
Thorpe Lea
KESWICK RD
THIRLMERE CL
WAVENDENE AVE
ASHLEIGH AVE
NUTBOURNE CT
RIVERSIDE RD
ST OLAVE'S CL
GLEN CT
CLOCKHOUSE LA W
CLOCKHOUSE LA E
B388
THE LEA
CLANDON AVE
WARWICK AVE
WHEATSHEAF LA
PENTON AVE
FERRY AVE
A320
RIVERSIDE DR
M25

70
98

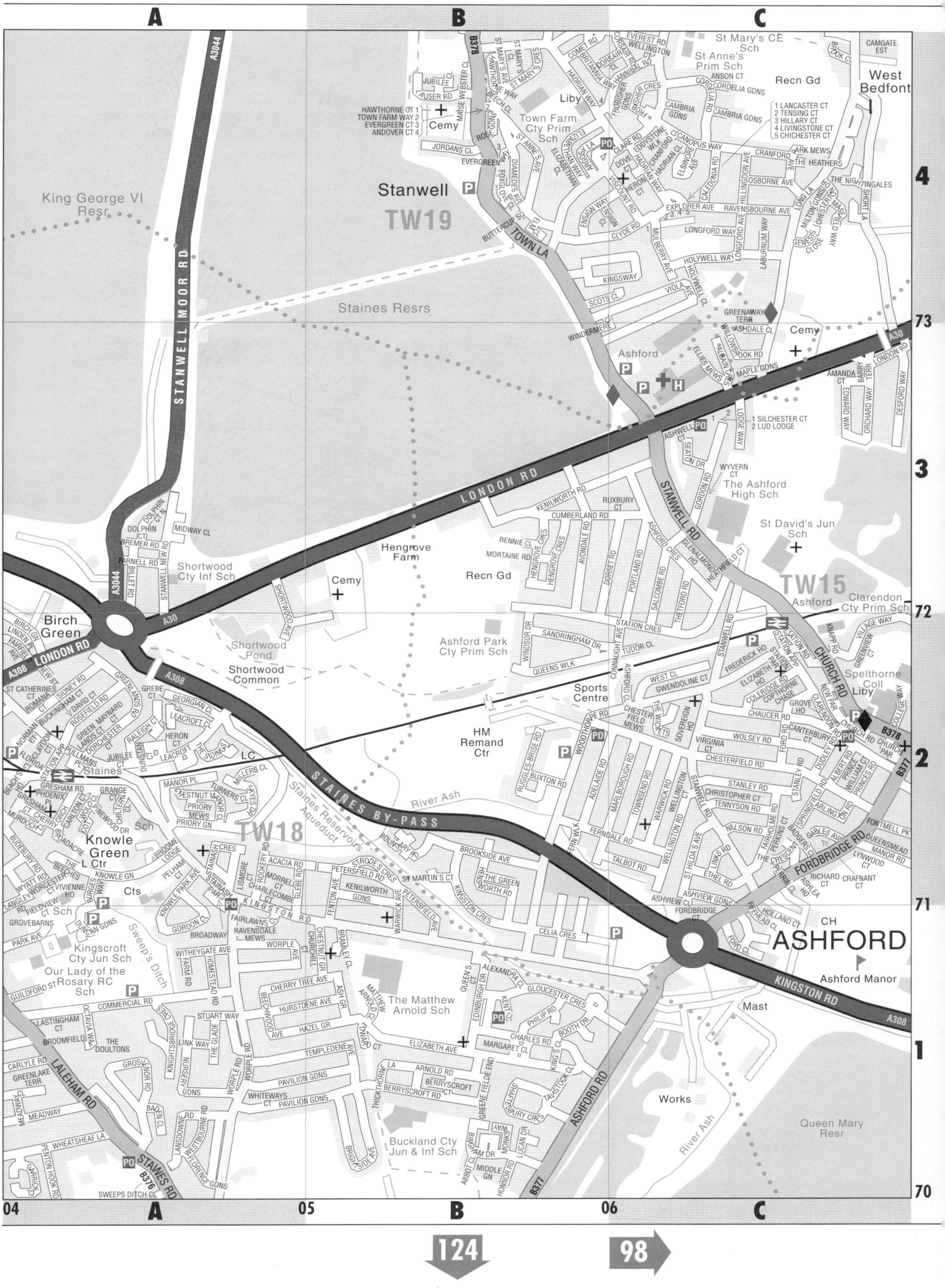
A
B
C
04
05
06
73
72
71
70
4
3
2
1
St Mary's CE Sch
St Anne's Prim Sch
Recn Gd
CAMGATE EST
West Bedfont
1 LANCASTER CT
2 TENSING CT
3 HILLARY CT
4 LIVINGSTONE CT
5 CHICHESTER CT
HAWTHORNE CT 1
TOWN FARM WAY 2
EVERGREEN CT 3
ANDOVER CT 4
Cemy
Liby
Town Farm Cty Prim Sch
PO
King George VI Resr
Stanwell
TW19
Staines Resrs
STANWELL MOOR RD
A3044
B378
TOWN LA
EVEREST RD
WELLINGTON CT
COMET RD
JUBILEE CL
JORDANS CL
EVERGREEN
HADRIAN WAY
CAMBRIA GDNS
CAMBRIA GDNS
CANOPUS WAY
CRANFORD CL
ARK MEWS
THE HEATHERS
THE NIGHTINGALES
OSBORNE AVE
EXPLORER AVE
RAVENSBOURNE AVE
LONGFORD WAY
HOLYWELL WAY
KINGSWAY
SCOTS CL
VIOLA AVE
CLYDE RD
MULBERRY AVE
LABURNUM WAY
GENESIS CLOSE
GREENAWAY TERR
ASHDALE CL
WINDERMERE
Ashford
H
MAPLE GDNS
1 SILCHESTER CT
2 LUD LODGE
ASHWELL CT
SEATON DR
WYVERN CT
The Ashford High Sch
St David's Jun Sch
LONDON RD
A30
KENILWORTH RD
CUMBERLAND RD
RUXBURY CT
DOLPHIN CT
DOLPHIN JCT
MIDWAY CL
BREMER RD
FARNELL RD
BILLET RD
STANWELL NEW RD
Shortwood Cty Inf Sch
Hengrove Farm
Cemy
Recn Gd
RENNIE CL
MORTAINE RD
HENGROVE CRES
AVONDALE RD
DORSET RD
PORTLAND RD
SALCOMBE RD
THETFORD RD
STANWELL RD
GLENALMOND HO
HEATHFIELD CT
TW15
Ashford
Clarendon Cty Prim Sch
Birch Green
LONDON RD
A308
Shortwood Pond
Shortwood Common
Ashford Park Cty Prim Sch
SANDRINGHAM DR
TUDOR CL
QUEENS WLK
STATION CRES
WINDSOR DR
CONNAUGHT AVE
ASHFORD CL
WEST CL
GWENDOLINE CT
Sports Centre
HM Remand Ctr
CHESTERFIELD MEWS
THE WICKETS
SOVEREIGN HO
FREDERICK HO
ELIZABETH HO
STATION APP
CHURCH RD
VILLAGE WAY
Spelthorne Coll
Liby
COLLEGE WAY
CHAUCER RD
CLARENDON RD
WOLSEY RD
CANTERBURY CT
CHURCH PAR
B378
B377
VIRGINIA CT
CHESTERFIELD RD
STANLEY RD
CHRISTOPHER CT
TENNYSON RD
NELSON RD
FONTMELL PK
QUEENSMEAD
MANOR RD
LYNWOOD CT
FORDBRIDGE RD
RICHARD CT
CRAFNANT CT
ST CATHERINES CT
ROMANA CT
GREENLANDS RD
GEORGIAN CL
LEACROFT CL
HERON CT
LEACROFT
JUBILEE
THE SIDINGS
LC
Staines
STAINES BY-PASS
Staines Reservoirs Aqueduct
River Ash
TW18
MANOR PL
CHESTNUT MANOR CL
PRIORY MEWS
PRIORY GN
MILLERS CL
GRESHAM RD
PHOENIX CT
GRANGE CT
Knowle Green L Ctr
Sch
KNOWLE GN
Cts
KNOWLE PARK AVE
GORDON CL
BROADWAY
FAIRLAWNS CL
RAVENSDALE MEWS
WORPLE AVE
KINGSTON RD
ACACIA RD
ROOKERY RD
CHARLECOMBE CT
PETERSFIELD RD
KENILWORTH GDNS
ST MARTIN'S CT
BROOKSIDE AVE
THE GREEN
KINGSTON CRES
CELIA CRES
WARWICK AVE
PETERSFIELD AVE
ADELAIDE RD
MARLBOROUGH RD
TOWNSEND RD
WARWICK RD
WELLINGTON RD
FERNDALE RD
TALBOT RD
ST HILDA'S AVE
LINKS RD
ETHEL RD
ASHVIEW GDNS
ASHVIEW CL
FORDBRIDGE CT
HOLLAND CT
CH
ASHFORD
Ashford Manor
KINGSTON RD
A308
Mast
GROVEBARNS
PARK AVE
DUNCAN GDNS
Kingscroft Cty Jun Sch
Our Lady of the Rosary RC Sch
Sweep's Ditch
WITHEYGATE AVE
HOMESTEAD RD
CHERRY TREE AVE
HURSTDENE AVE
HAZEL GR
BEECHWOOD AVE
The Matthew Arnold Sch
ALEXANDRA CL
GLOUCESTER CRES
KENT CL
PHILIP RD
CHARLES RD
MARGARET CL
BOOTH DR
ELIZABETH AVE
GUILDFORD ST
COMMERCIAL RD
LASTINGHAM CT
BROOMFIELD
THE DOULTONS
STUART WAY
LINK WAY
THE GLADE
NURSERY GDNS
WORPLE RD
TEMPLEDENE AVE
ARNOLD RD
BERRYSCROFT CT
BERRYSCROFT RD
PAVILION GDNS
WHITEWAYS CT
CARLYLE RD
GREENLAKE TERR
MEADWAY
LALEHAM RD
WHEATSHEAF LA
PENTON HOOK RD
GARRICK CL
LANSDOWNE RD
WESTBOURNE RD
FLORENCE GDNS
STAINES RD
B376
SWEEPS DITCH CL
Buckland Cty Jun & Inf Sch
BRIGHTSIDE AVE
BINGHAM DR
MIDDLE GN
ABBOT CL
HONNOR RD
LUCAN DR
SHAFTESBURY CRES
TAVISTOCK GR
KING'S CL
ASHFORD RD
Works
River Ash
Queen Mary Resr

124
98

97
71

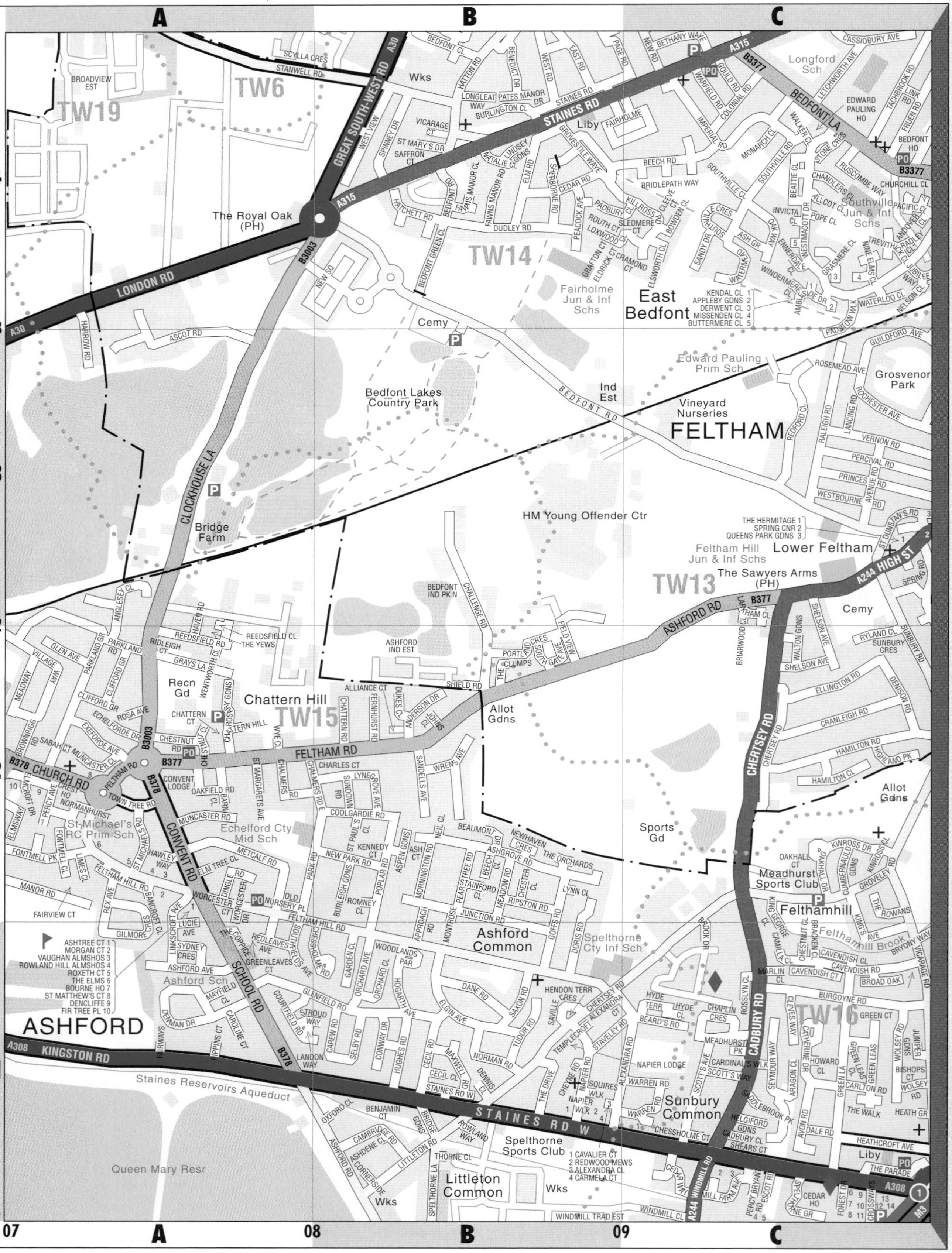


C1
1 TASMAN CT
2 WILLOW CT
3 CATLE CL
4 KILLIGREW HO
5 GRANTHAM HO
6 ASH LODGE
7 LIME LODGE
8 OAK LODGE
9 ELM CT
10 WILLOW LODGE
11 SYCAMORE LODGE
12 ISOBEL HO
13 PRISCILLA HO
14 SUNBURY CROSS CTR

97
125

72
100

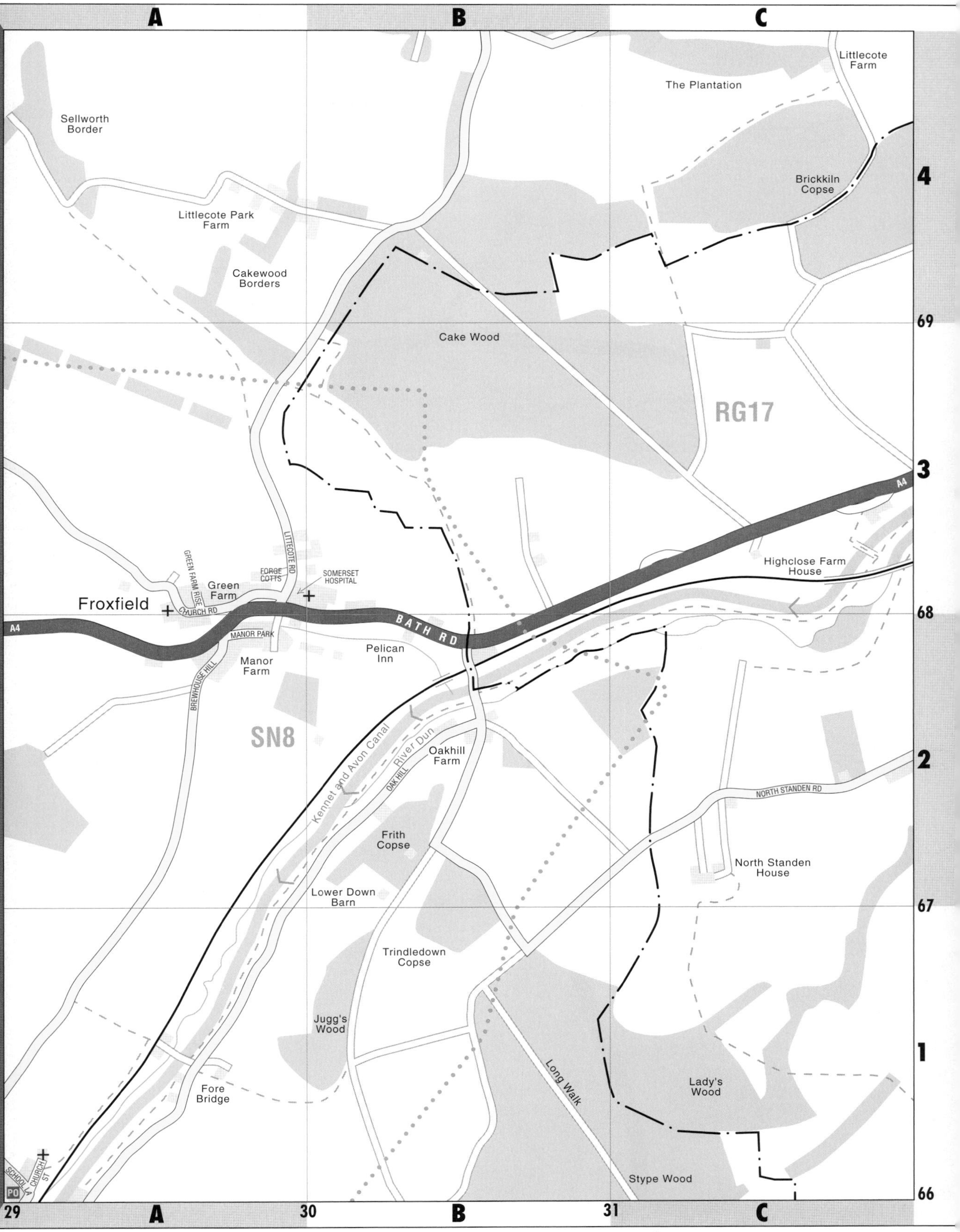
A
B
C
Sellworth Border
Littlecote Park Farm
Cakewood Borders
The Plantation
Littlecote Farm
Brickkiln Copse
Cake Wood
RG17
Froxfield
Green Farm
GREEN FARM RISE
CHURCH RD
FORGE COTTS
LITTLECOTE RD
SOMERSET HOSPITAL
A4
BATH RD
MANOR PARK
BREWHOUSE HILL
Manor Farm
Pelican Inn
Highclose Farm House
SN8
Kennet and Avon Canal
River Dun
OAK HILL
Oakhill Farm
NORTH STANDEN RD
Frith Copse
North Standen House
Lower Down Barn
Trindledown Copse
Jugg's Wood
Long Walk
Fore Bridge
Lady's Wood
Stype Wood
SCHOOL LA
CHURCH ST
PO
4
69
3
68
2
67
1
66
29
30
31

100

99
73

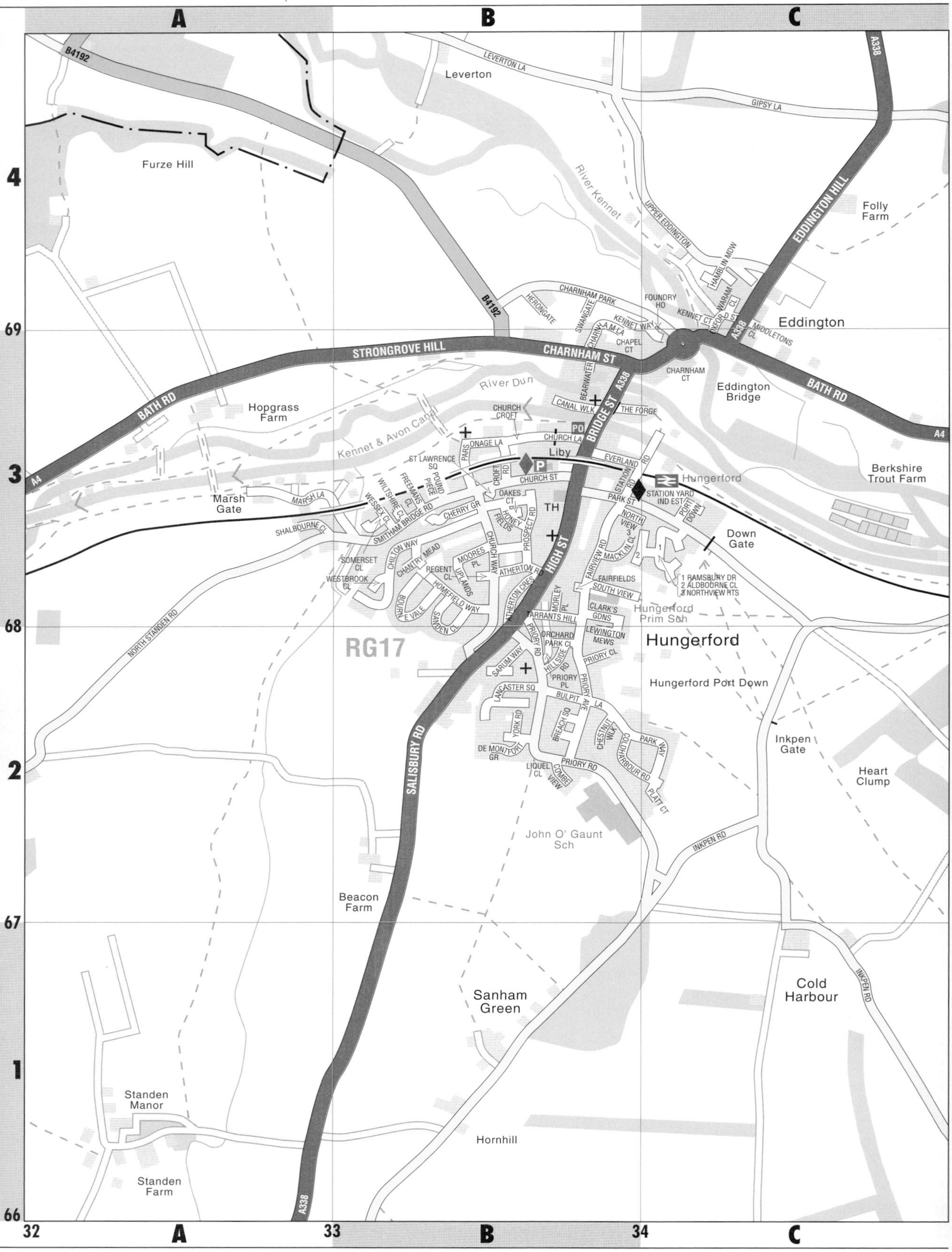
A
B
C
4
69
3
68
2
67
1
66
32
33
34
B4192
LEVERTON LA
Leverton
GIPSY LA
A338
Furze Hill
River Kennet
UPPER EDDINGTON
EDDINGTON HILL
Folly Farm
HAMBLIN MDW
CHARNHAM PARK
HERONGATE
FOUNDRY HO
KENNET CT
WARAM CL
OXFORD ST
Eddington
SWANGATE
KENNET WAY
CHARNHAM LA
CHAPEL CT
MIDDLETONS CL
STRONGROVE HILL
CHARNHAM ST
CHARNHAM CT
Eddington Bridge
BATH RD
River Dun
BEARWATER
BRIDGE ST
Hopgrass Farm
CHURCH CROFT
CANAL WLK
THE FORGE
A4
Kennet & Avon Canal
PO
CHURCH LA
PARSONAGE LA
Liby
EVERLAND RD
Berkshire Trout Farm
ST LAWRENCE SQ
POUND PIECE
CROFT RD
P
CHURCH ST
STATION RD
Hungerford
Marsh Gate
MARSH LA
WESSEX CL
WILTSHIRE CL
FREEMANS CL
OAKES CT
TH
PARK ST
STATION YARD IND EST
PORT DOWN
CHERRY GR
SMITHAM BRIDGE RD
HONEY FIELDS
PROSPECT RD
NORTH VIEW
SHALBOURNE CL
Down Gate
CHILTON WAY
CHANTRY MEAD
CHURCH WAY
HIGH ST
FAIRVIEW RD
MACKLIN CL
SOMERSET CL
MOORES PL
WESTBROOK CL
REGENT CL
UPLANDS
ATHERTON RD
FAIRFIELDS
1 RAMSBURY DR
2 ALDBOURNE CL
3 NORTHVIEW HTS
HOMEFIELD WAY
SOUTH VIEW
BOURNE VALE
SANDEN CL
ATHERTON CRES
MORLEY PL
CLARK'S GDNS
Hungerford Prim Sch
NORTH STANDEN RD
TARRANTS HILL
68
RG17
PRIORY RD
ORCHARD PARK CL
LEWINGTON MEWS
Hungerford
PRIORY CL
SARUM WAY
HILLSIDE RD
PRIORY PL
PRIORY AVE
Hungerford Port Down
LANCASTER SQ
BULPIT LA
YORK RD
BREACH SQ
CHESTNUT WLK
PARK WAY
Inkpen Gate
SALISBURY RD
DE MONTFORT GR
COLDHARBOUR RD
Heart Clump
LIQUEL CL
COMBE VIEW
PLATT CT
John O' Gaunt Sch
INKPEN RD
Beacon Farm
Sanham Green
Cold Harbour
Standen Manor
Hornhill
Standen Farm

99
126

74
102

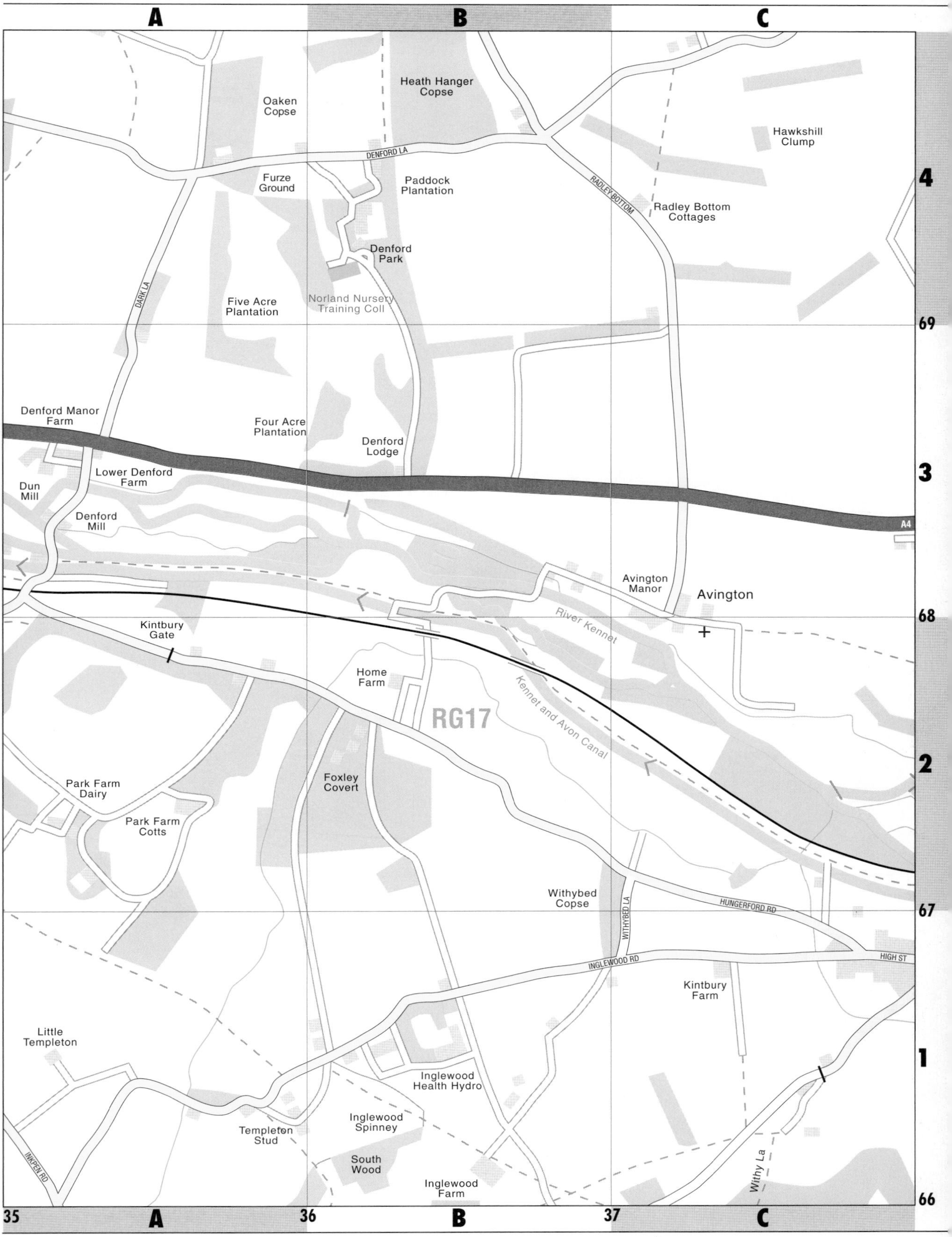


127
102

101
75

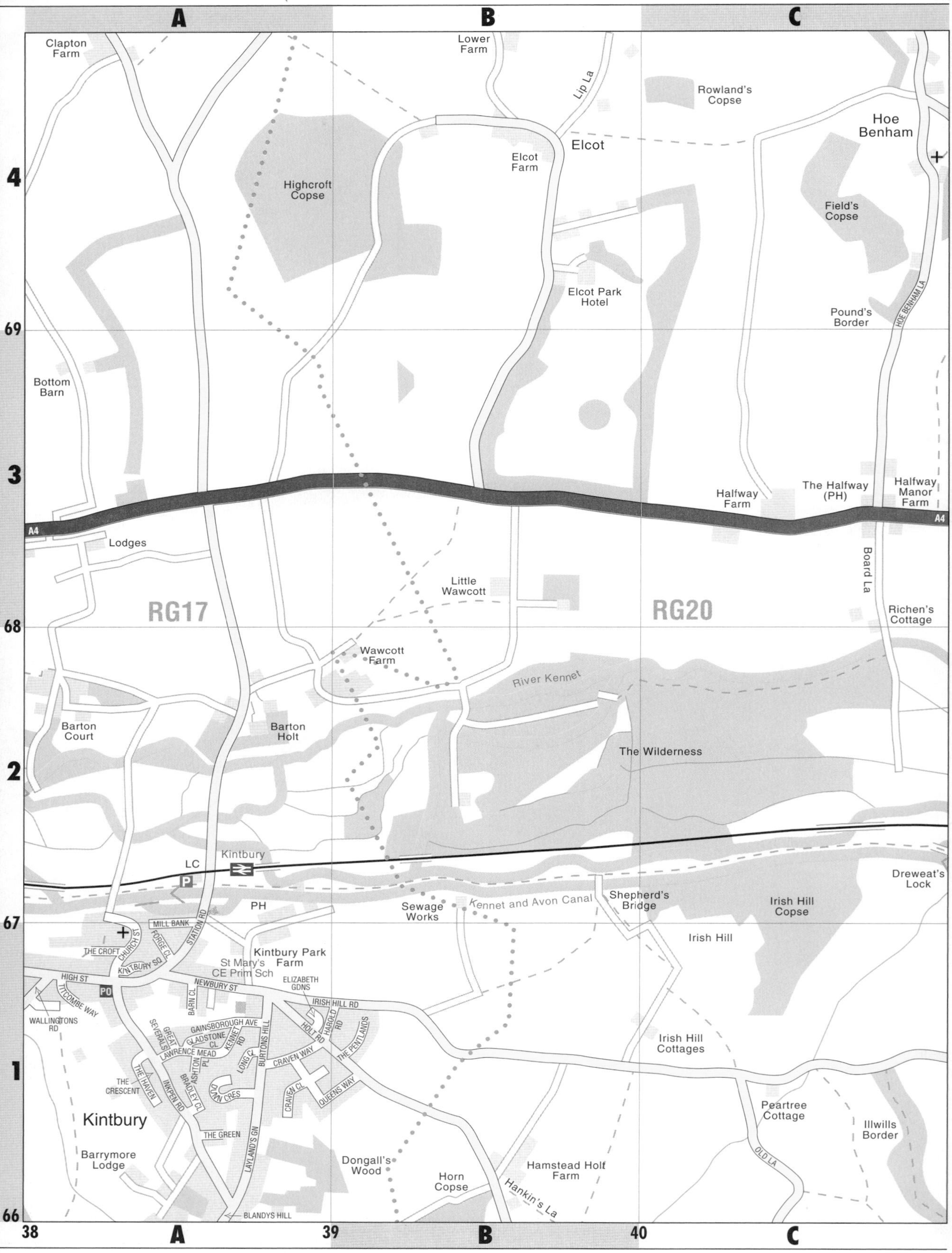


101
128

76
104

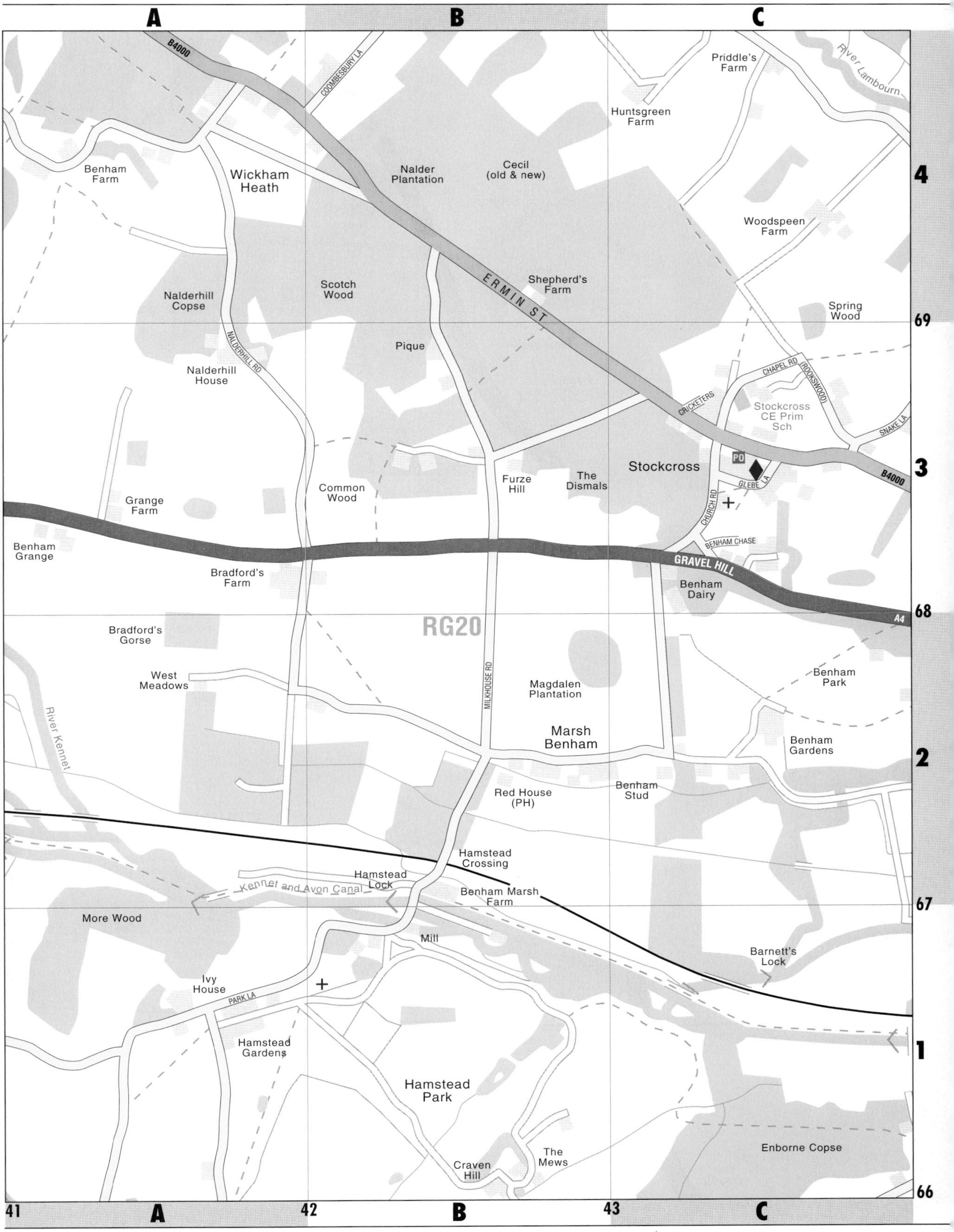


129
104

103
77

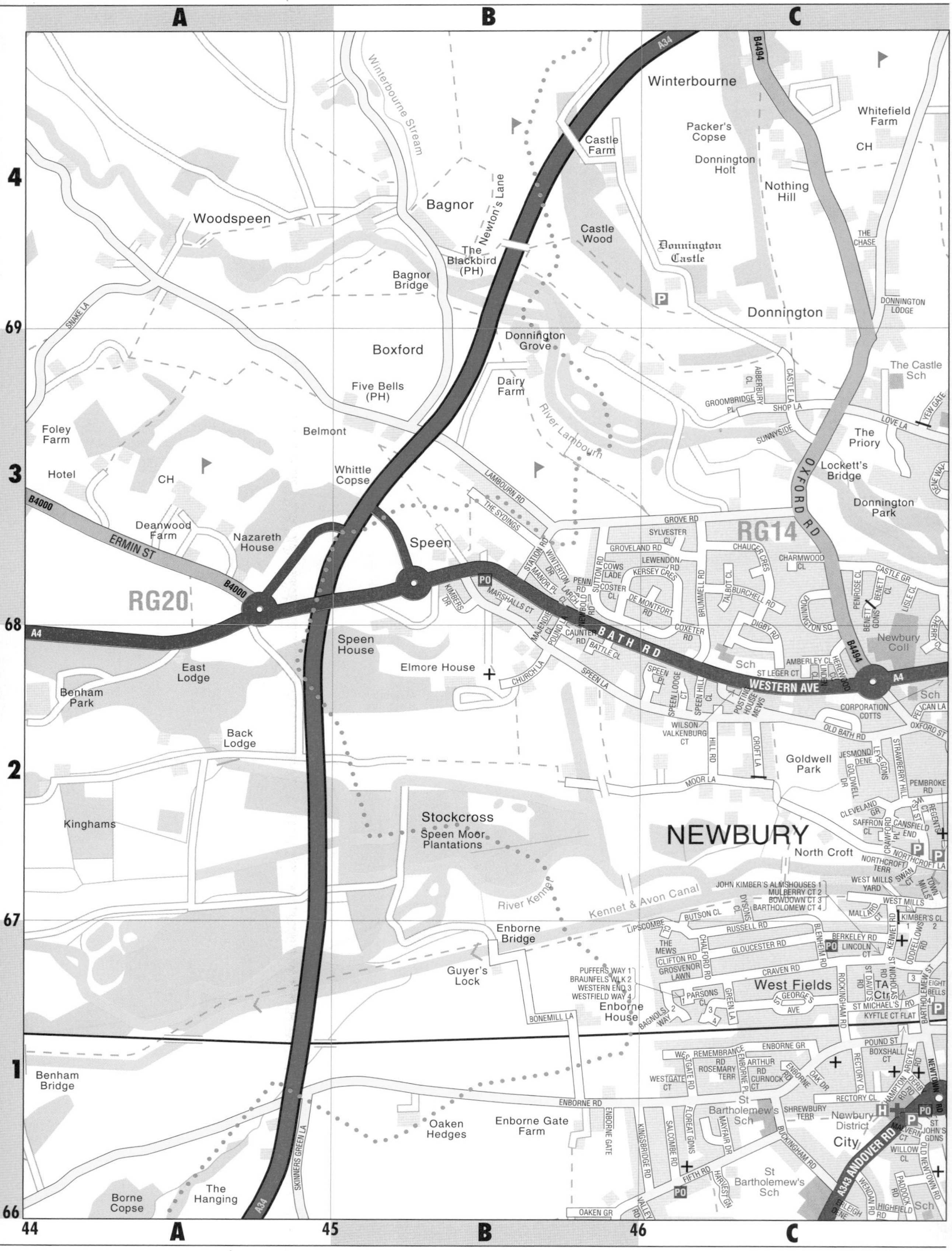


103
130

78 106

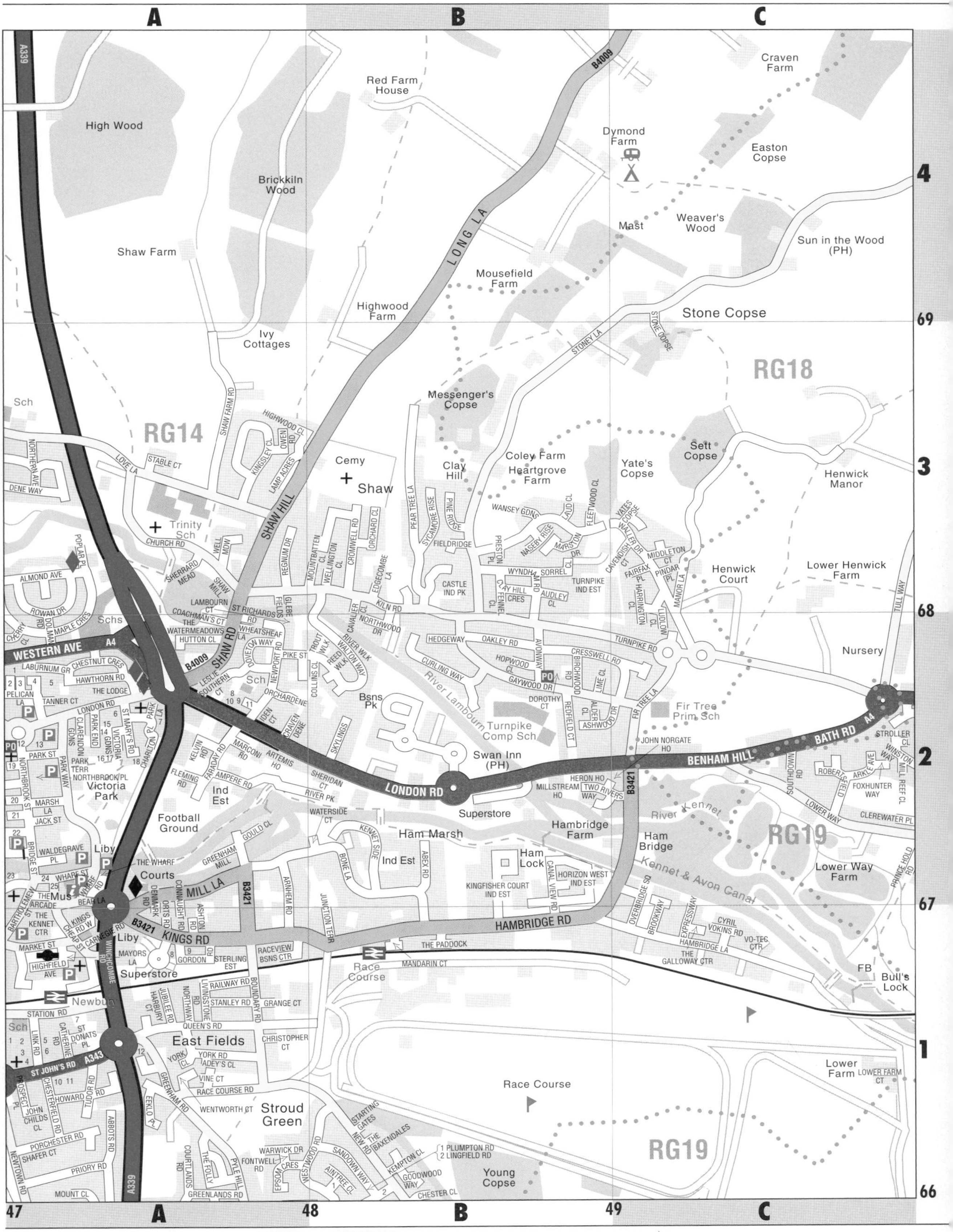


**A1**
1 FAIR CLOSE HO
2 LINK HO
3 MADEIRA PL
4 KENNET CT
5 SHEFFORD LODGE
6 ILCHESTER CT
7 ASHRIDGE CT
8 GORDON CT
9 ROMANO CT
10 HILARY HO
11 QUEENS CT
12 WINCHESTER HO

**A2**
1 CORPORATION COTTS
2 ANGEL CT
3 WESTBOURNE TERR
4 LYNTON CT
5 SPEENHAMLAND CT
6 ST MARY'S CT
7 ST JOSEPH'S CT
8 NORTH VIEW GDNS
9 SOUTH VIEW GDNS
10 KENNET PL
11 NEWPORT CL
12 THE BROADWAY
13 THE PENTANGLE
14 ST MARY'S PL
15 BEECH CT
16 ASH CT
17 CHESTNUT CT
18 CONISTON CT
19 ALBERT RD
20 WEAVER'S WLK
21 CROMWELL PL
22 PEMBROKE RD
23 TOWN MILLS
24 MANSION HOUSE ST
25 MARKET PL

131 106

105
79

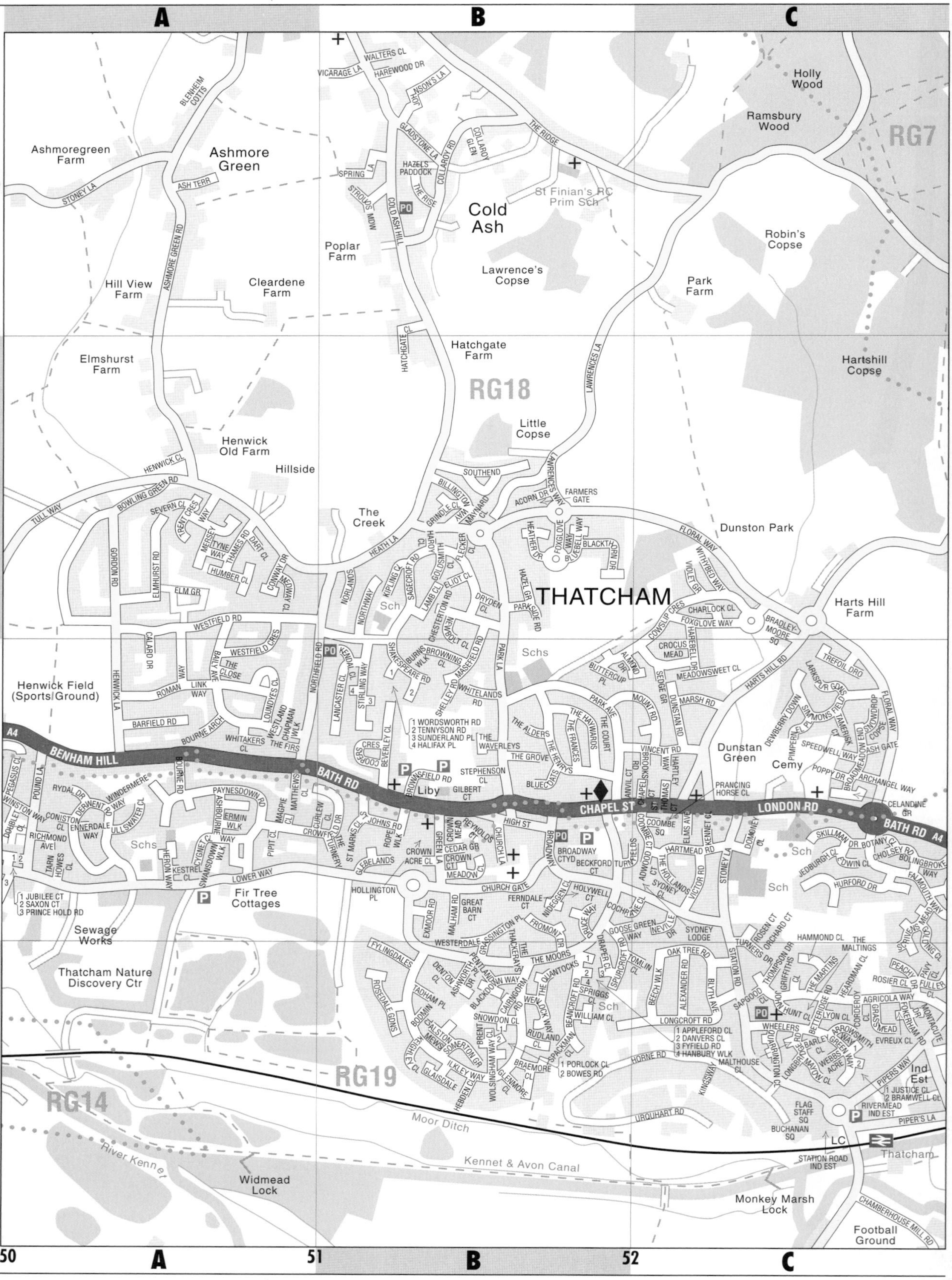


105
132

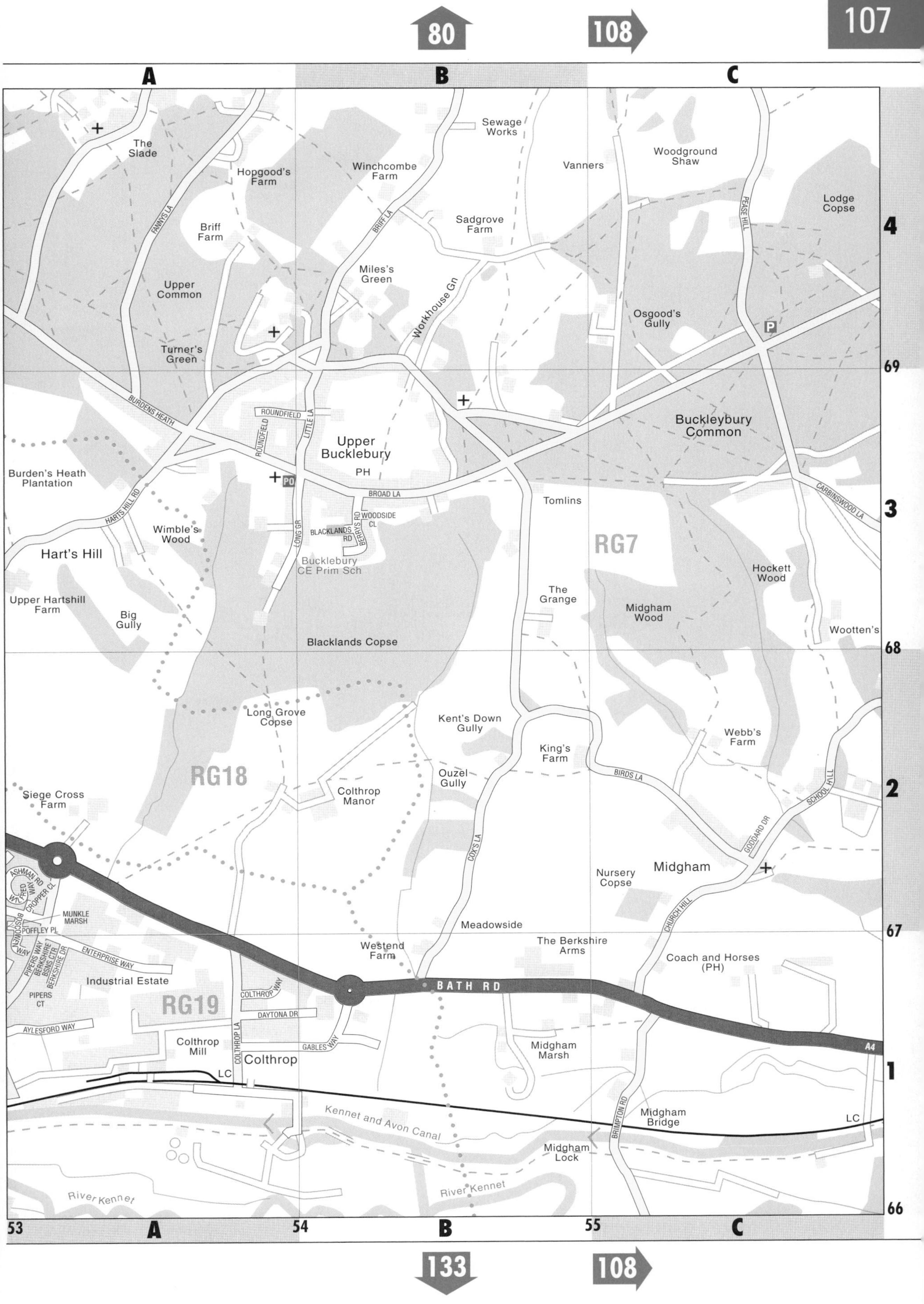
80
108
A
B
C
The Slade
Hopgood's Farm
Winchcombe Farm
Sewage Works
Vanners
Woodground Shaw
Lodge Copse
Briff Farm
Sadgrove Farm
Miles's Green
Upper Common
Workhouse Gn
Osgood's Gully
Turner's Green
Buckleybury Common
Upper Bucklebury
Burden's Heath Plantation
PH
BROAD LA
Tomlins
Wimble's Wood
Hart's Hill
RG7
Bucklebury CE Prim Sch
Hockett Wood
Upper Hartshill Farm
The Grange
Midgham Wood
Big Gully
Blacklands Copse
Wootten's
Long Grove Copse
Kent's Down Gully
Webb's Farm
King's Farm
RG18
Siege Cross Farm
Colthrop Manor
Ouzel Gully
Midgham
Nursery Copse
Meadowside
The Berkshire Arms
Westend Farm
Coach and Horses (PH)
Industrial Estate
BATH RD
RG19
Colthrop Mill
Colthrop
Midgham Marsh
Midgham Bridge
Kennet and Avon Canal
Midgham Lock
River Kennet
LC
A4
4
3
2
1
69
68
67
66
53
54
55
133
108

107 81

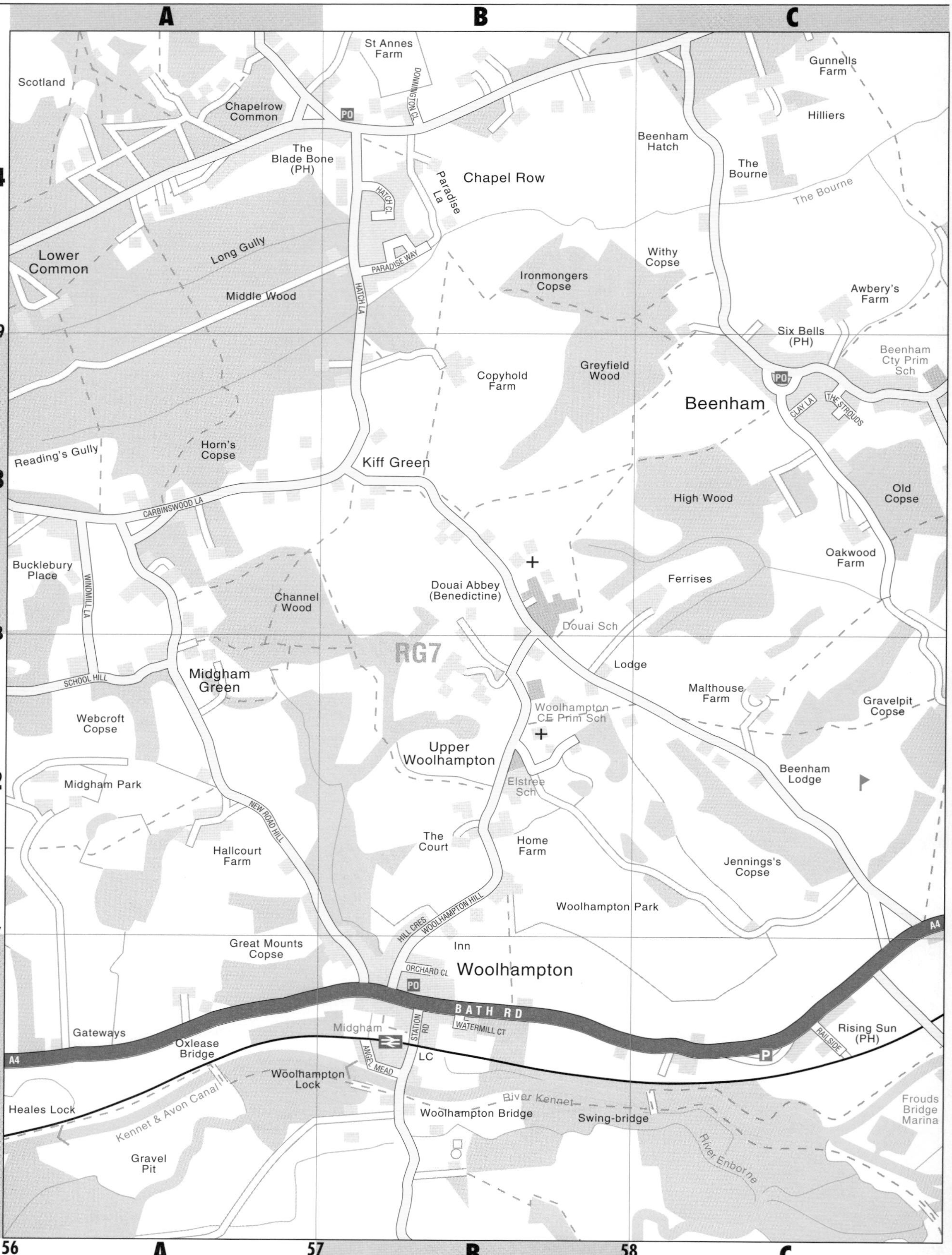


107 134

82
110

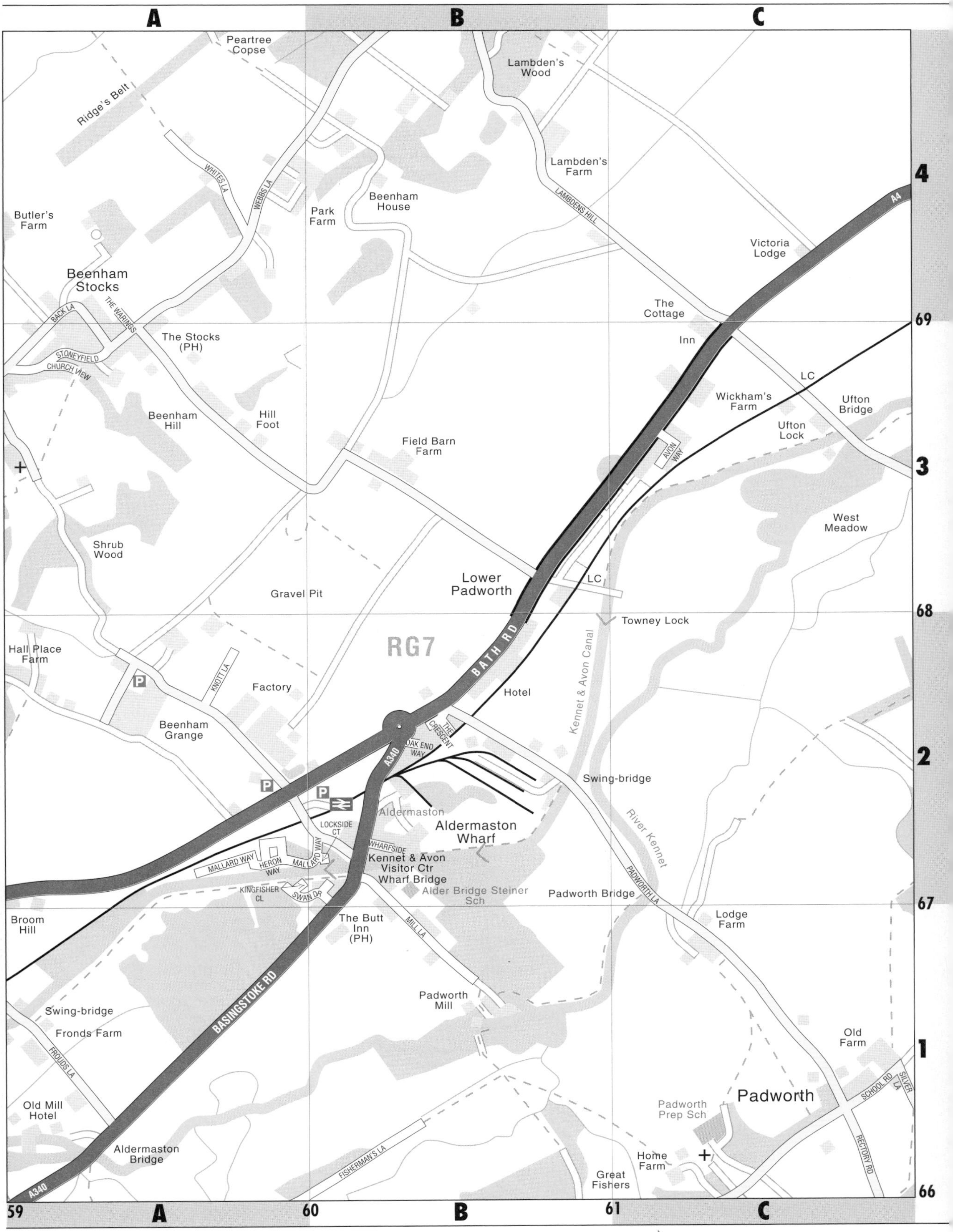


135
110

109
83

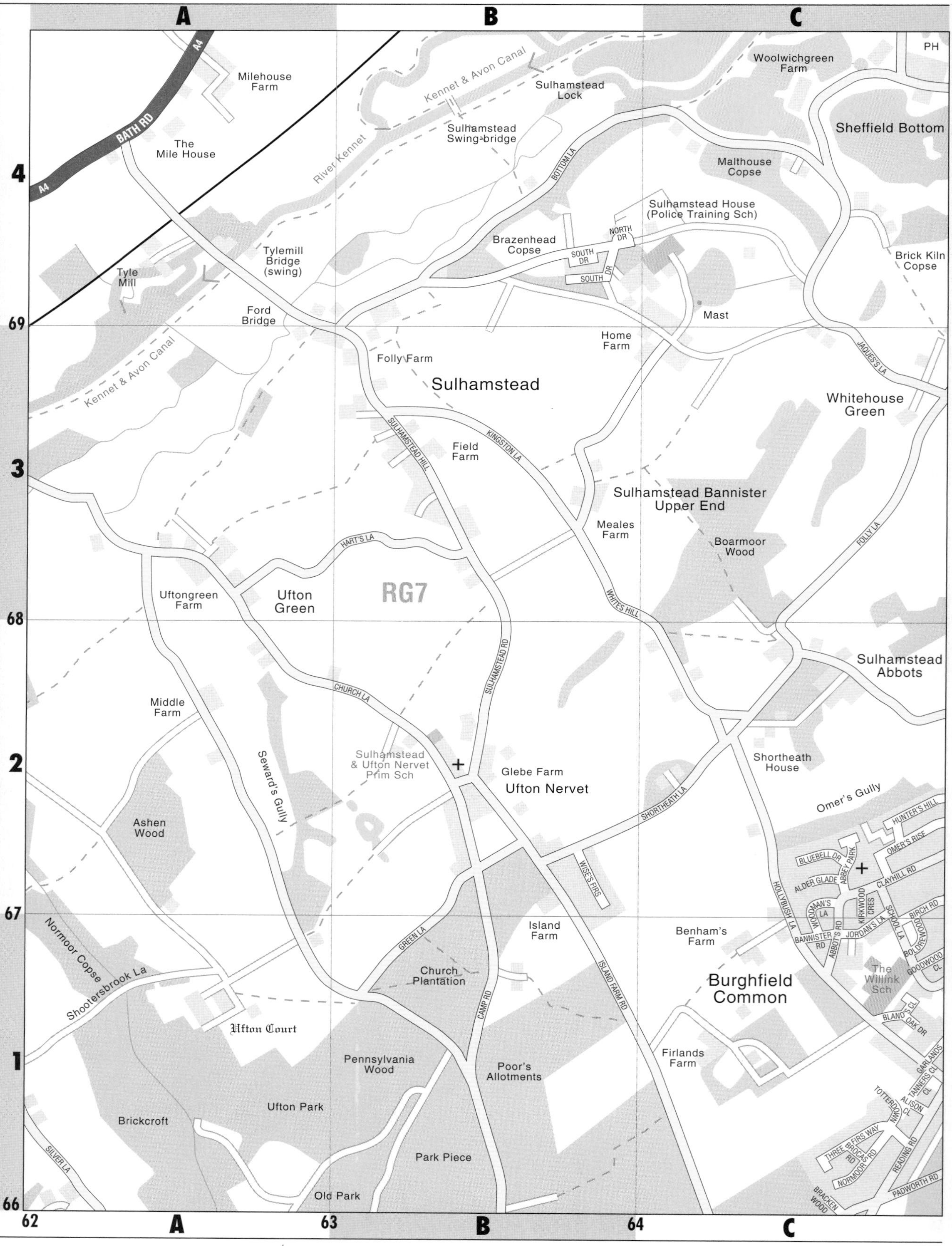


109
136

84
112

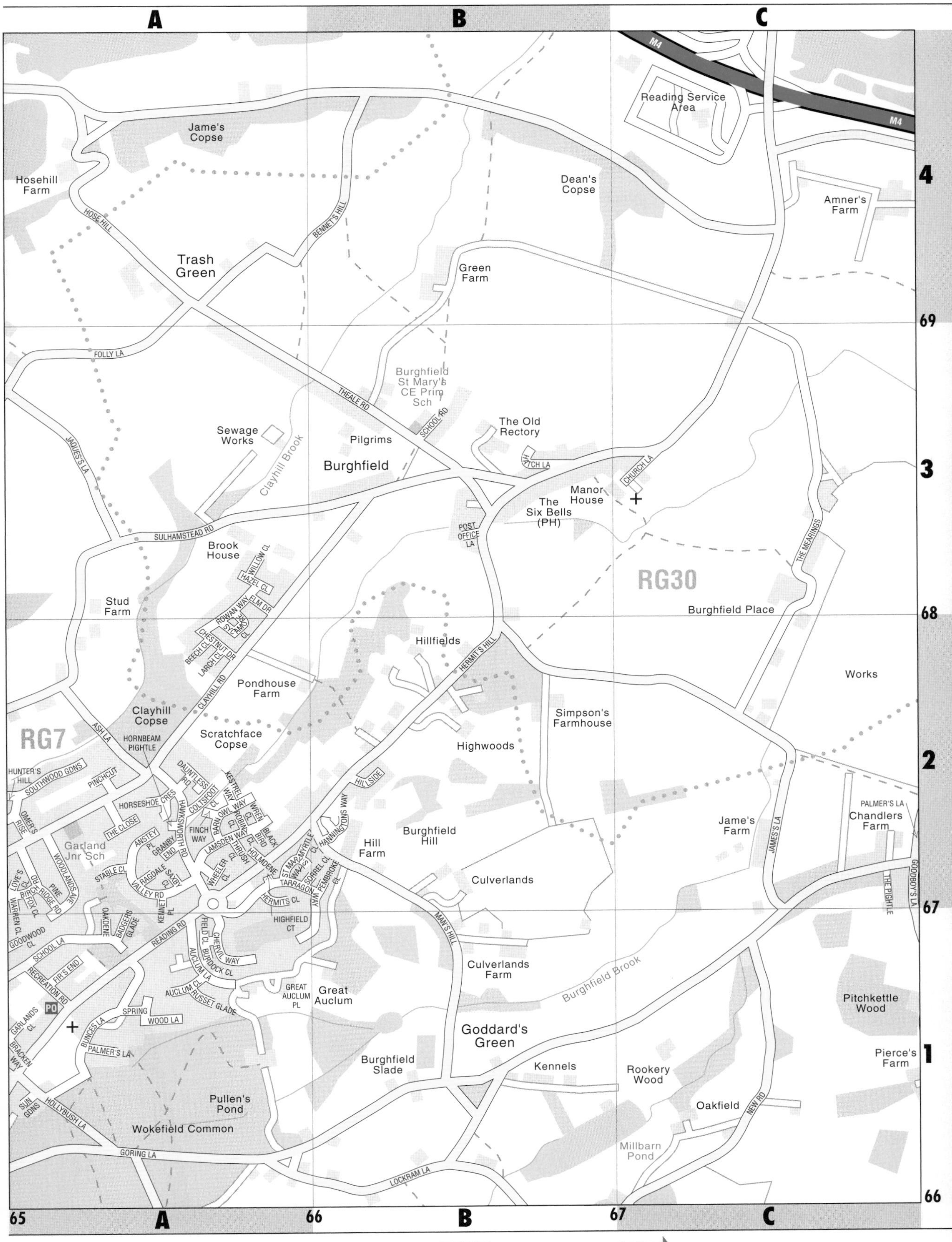


137
112

111 85

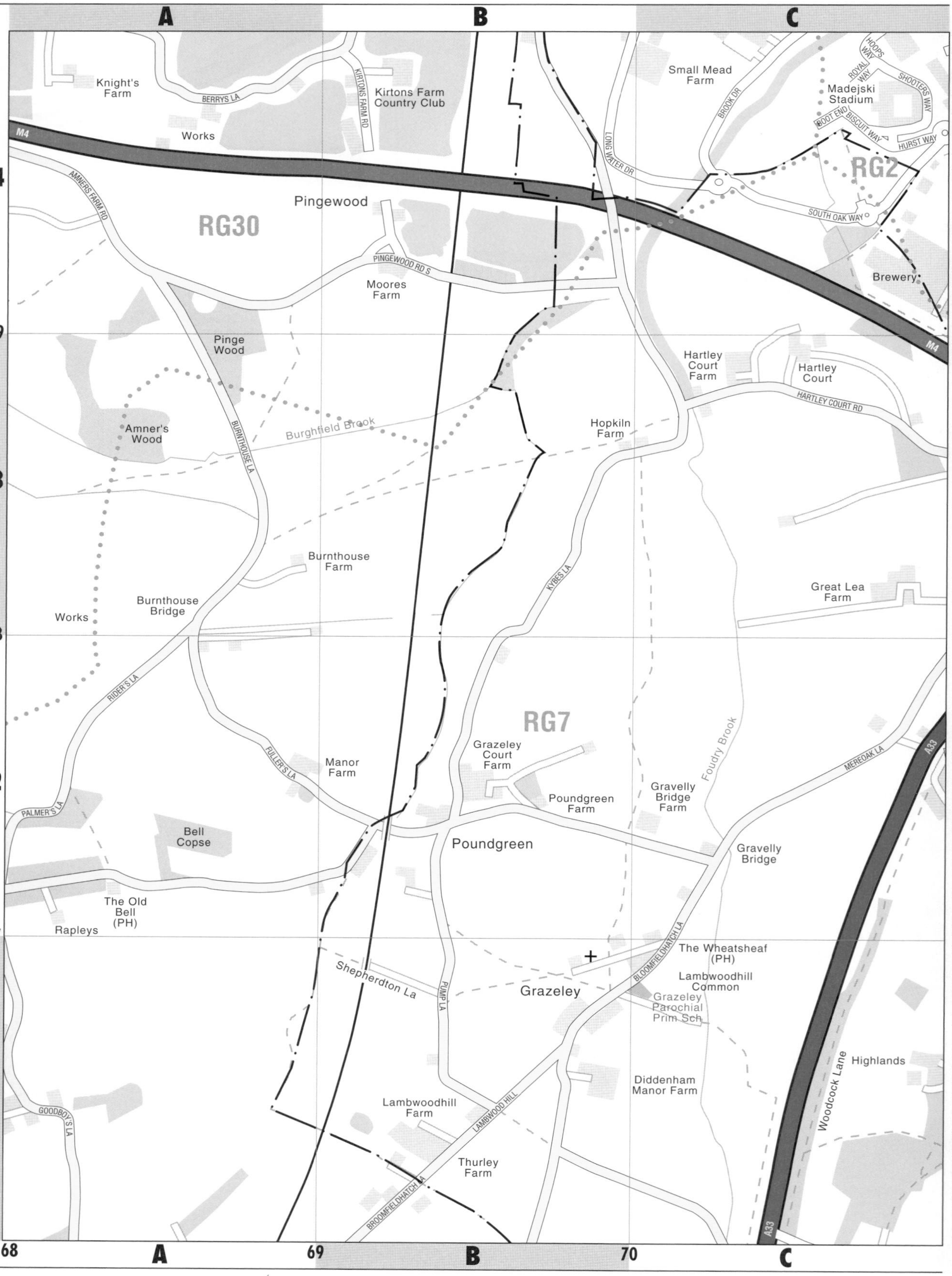


111 138

86
114

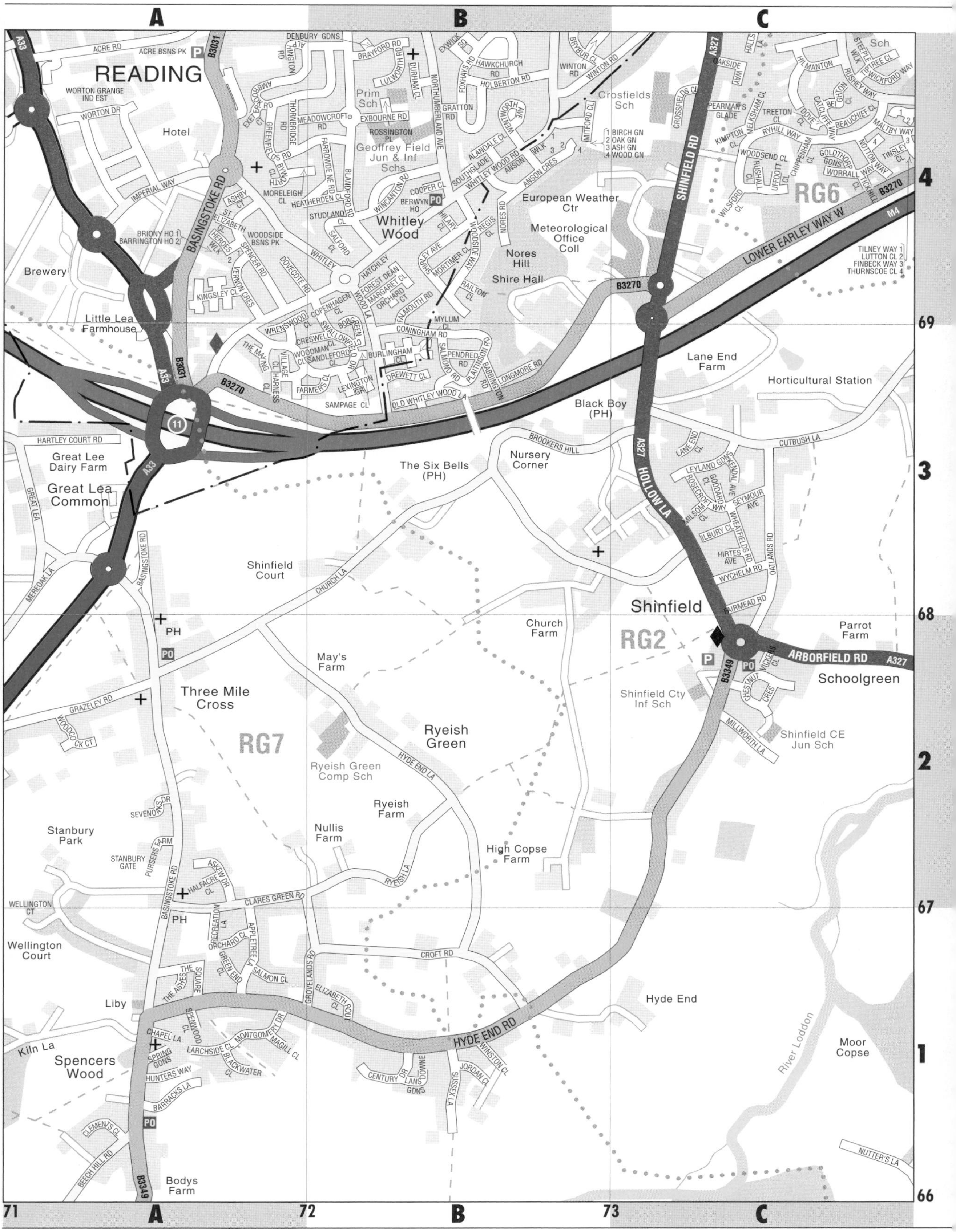


139
114

113 87

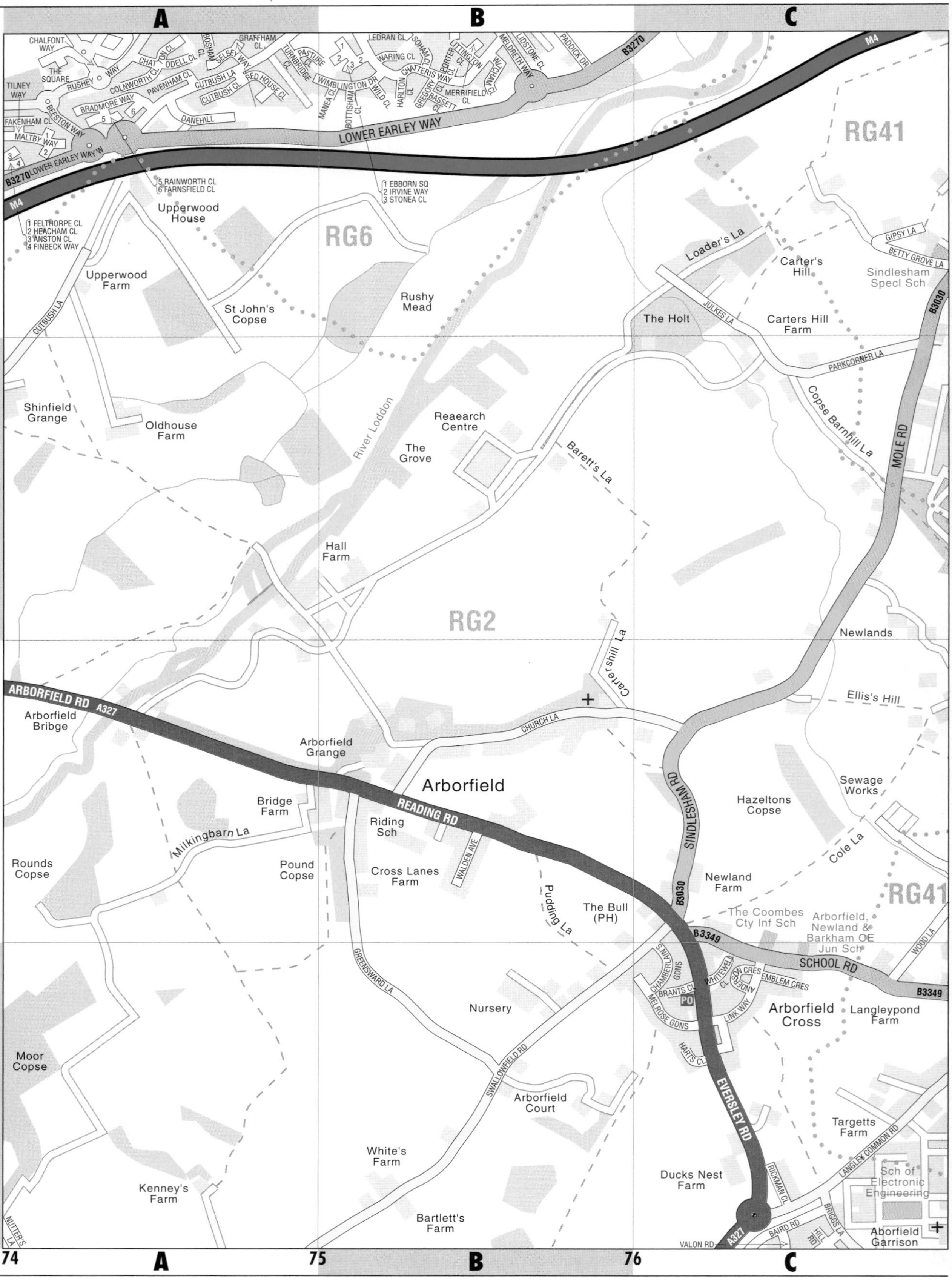


113 140

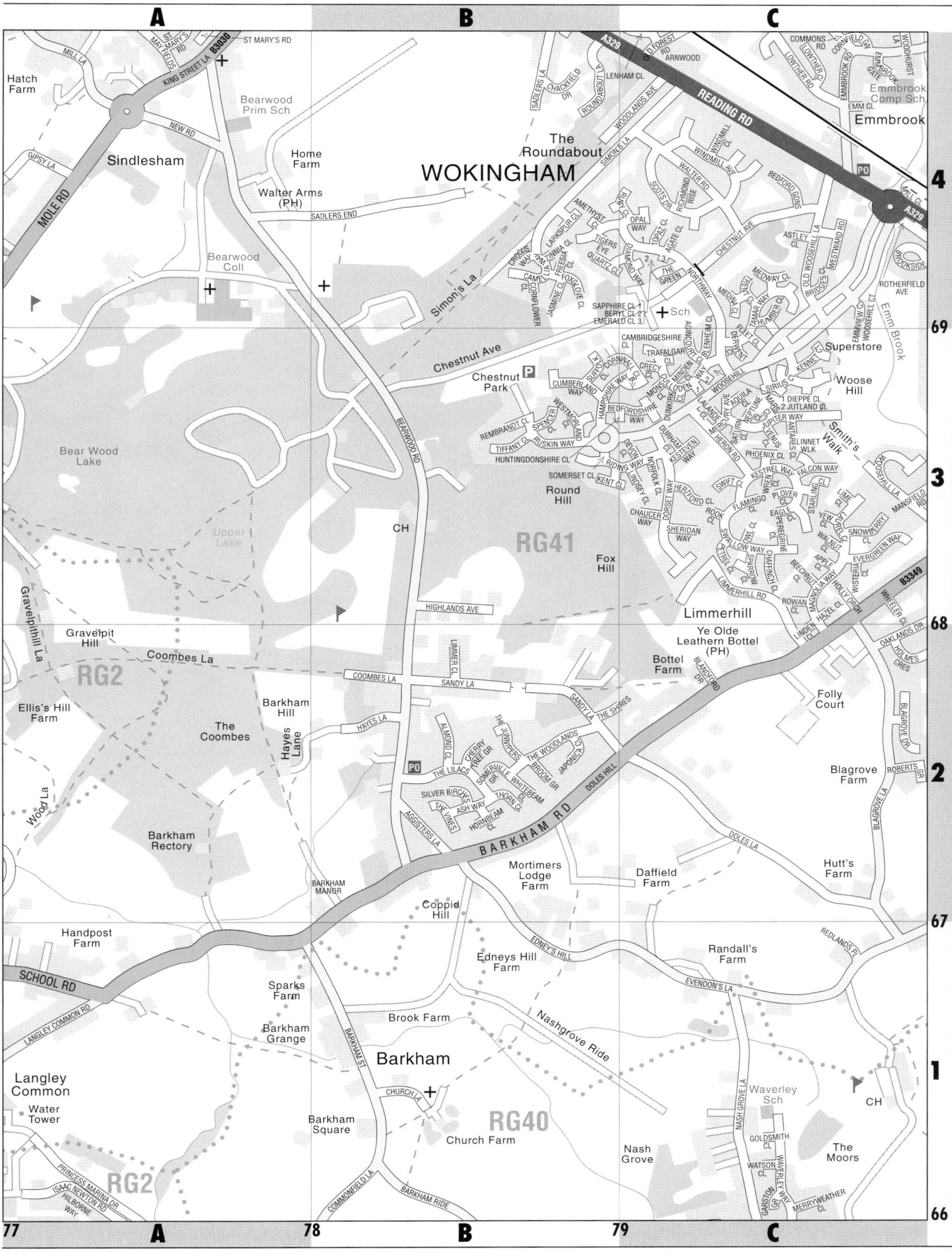
A
B
C
Hatch Farm
Sindlesham
MILL LA
KING STREET LA
B3030
ST MARY'S RD
MAYFIELDS
NEW RD
GIPSY LA
MOLE RD
Bearwood Prim Sch
Home Farm
Walter Arms (PH)
SADLERS END
Bearwood Coll
WOKINGHAM
The Roundabout
SADLERS LA
CHACKFIELD DR
ROUNDABOUT LA
LENHAM CL
A329
OLD FOREST RD
ARNWOOD
READING RD
WOODLANDS AVE
SIMON'S LA
Simon's La
COMMONS RD
LOWTHER RD
CORNFIELD GN
EMMBROOK RD
EMMBROOK GATE
WOODHURST LA
Emmbrook Comp Sch
EMM CL
Emmbrook
PO
WINDMILL CL
WINDMILL AVE
WALTER RD
SCOTS DR
RICHMOND RISE
BEDFORD GDNS
MILL CL
AMETHYST CL
RUBY CL
OPAL WAY
TOPAZ CL
AGATE CL
TIGERS EYE
QUARTZ CL
DIAMOND WAY
THE GREEN
NORTHWAY
CHESTNUT AVE
ASTLEY CL
OLD WOOSEHILL LA
WESTWARD RD
BROOKSIDE
LARKSPUR CL
ZINNIA CL
IVY CL
CROCUS WAY
CAMEL CL
CORNFLOWER
FREESIA CL
JASMINE CL
FOXGLOVE CL
MEDWAY CL
MEDINA CL
TRENT CL
TAMAR WAY
HUMBER CL
BRIDGES CL
ROTHERFIELD AVE
SAPPHIRE CL 1
BERYL CL 2
EMERALD CL 3
Sch
Chestnut Ave
Chestnut Park
P
CAMBRIDGESHIRE CL
TRAFALGAR CL
AGINCOURT CL
BLENHEIM CL
DERWENT CL
FLEET CL
EMMVIEW CL
WOOSEHILL CT
Superstore
Emm Brook
CUMBERLAND WAY
SUFFOLK CL
CORNWALL CL
HAMPSHIRE WAY
CRECY CL
MONS CL
MINDEN CL
LODEN CL
DUNKIRK CL
WOOSEHILL
LALANDE CL
SIRIUS CL
KENNET CL
Woose Hill
1 DIEPPE CL
2 JUTLAND CL
REMBRANDT CL
SPENCER CL
WESTMORLAND CL
BEDFORDSHIRE WAY
MERCURY AVE
AQUILA CL
NEPTUNE CL
MARS CL
JUPITER WAY
ANTARES CL
VENUS CL
SATURN CL
TIFFANY CL
RUSKIN WAY
HUNTINGDONSHIRE CL
DEVON CL
DURHAM CL
KESTEVEN WAY
HERON RD
LINNET WLK
Smith's Walk
PHOENIX CL
FALCON WAY
KESTREL WAY
SOMERSET CL
KENT CL
RIDING WAY
LINDSEY CL
NORFOLK CL
Bear Wood Lake
BEARWOOD RD
Round Hill
CHAUCER WAY
DORSET WAY
HERTFORD CL
SWIFT CL
FLAMINGO CL
WREN CL
PLOVER CL
EAGLE CL
STARLING CL
LIME CL
YEW CL
CYPRESS CL
MANSFIELD RD
WOOSEHILL LA
SNOWBERRY CL
WALNUT CL
Upper Lake
CH
RG41
SHERIDAN WAY
ROOK CL
SWALLOW WAY
OWL CL
PEREGRINE CL
EVERGREEN WAY
Fox Hill
EGRET CL
SPARROW CL
CHAFFINCH CL
BEECHNUT CL
APPLE CL
MAGNOLIA WAY
WISTERIA CL
HOLLY ORCH
LIMMERHILL RD
ROWAN CL
HAZEL CL
WHEELER CL
B3349
LINDEN CL
Limmerhill
HIGHLANDS AVE
Gravelpit Hill
Gravelpithill La
Coombes La
RG2
LIMMER CL
Ye Olde Leathern Bottel (PH)
OAKLANDS DR
HOLMES CRES
COOMBES LA
SANDY LA
Bottel Farm
BLANDFORD DR
Ellis's Hill Farm
Barkham Hill
The Coombes
Hayes Lane
HAYES LA
THE SHIRES
Folly Court
BLAGROVE DR
ALMOND CL
CHERRY TREE GR
THE JUNIPERS
THE WOODLANDS
JAPONICA CL
PO
THE LILACS
SOMERVILLE GR
BROOM GR
WHITEBEAM CL
DOLES HILL
Blagrove Farm
ROBERTS GR
BLAGROVE LA
Wood La
SILVER BIRCHES
THE VINES
ASH WAY
HORNBEAM CL
THORN CL
Barkham Rectory
AGGISTERS LA
BARKHAM RD
DOLES LA
Hutt's Farm
Mortimers Lodge Farm
Daffield Farm
BARKHAM MANOR
Coppid Hill
Handpost Farm
EDNEY'S HILL
Edneys Hill Farm
Randall's Farm
REDLANDS PL
SCHOOL RD
Sparks Farm
EVENDON'S LA
LANGLEY COMMON RD
Brook Farm
Barkham Grange
Nashgrove Ride
BARKHAM ST
Barkham
Langley Common
Water Tower
CHURCH LA
Waverley Sch
CH
Barkham Square
RG40
Church Farm
NASH GROVE LA
GOLDSMITH CL
The Moors
Nash Grove
WATSON CL
WAVERLEY WAY
PRINCESS MARINA DR
ISAAC NEWTON RD
HILBORNE WAY
RG2
COMMONFIELD LA
BARKHAM RIDE
GARSTON GR
MERRYWEATHER CL
4
69
3
68
2
67
1
66
77
78
79

115
89

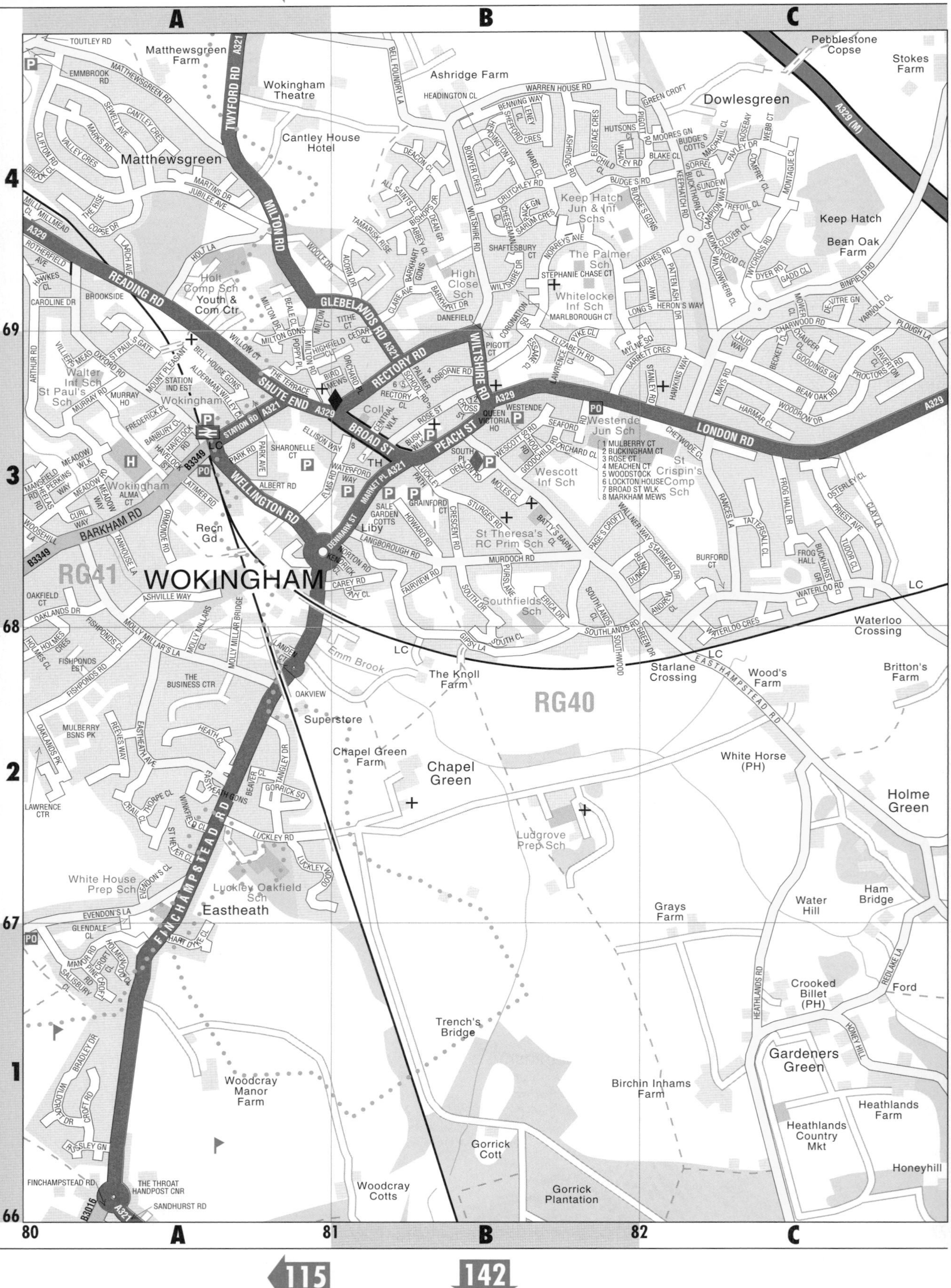


115
142

90
118

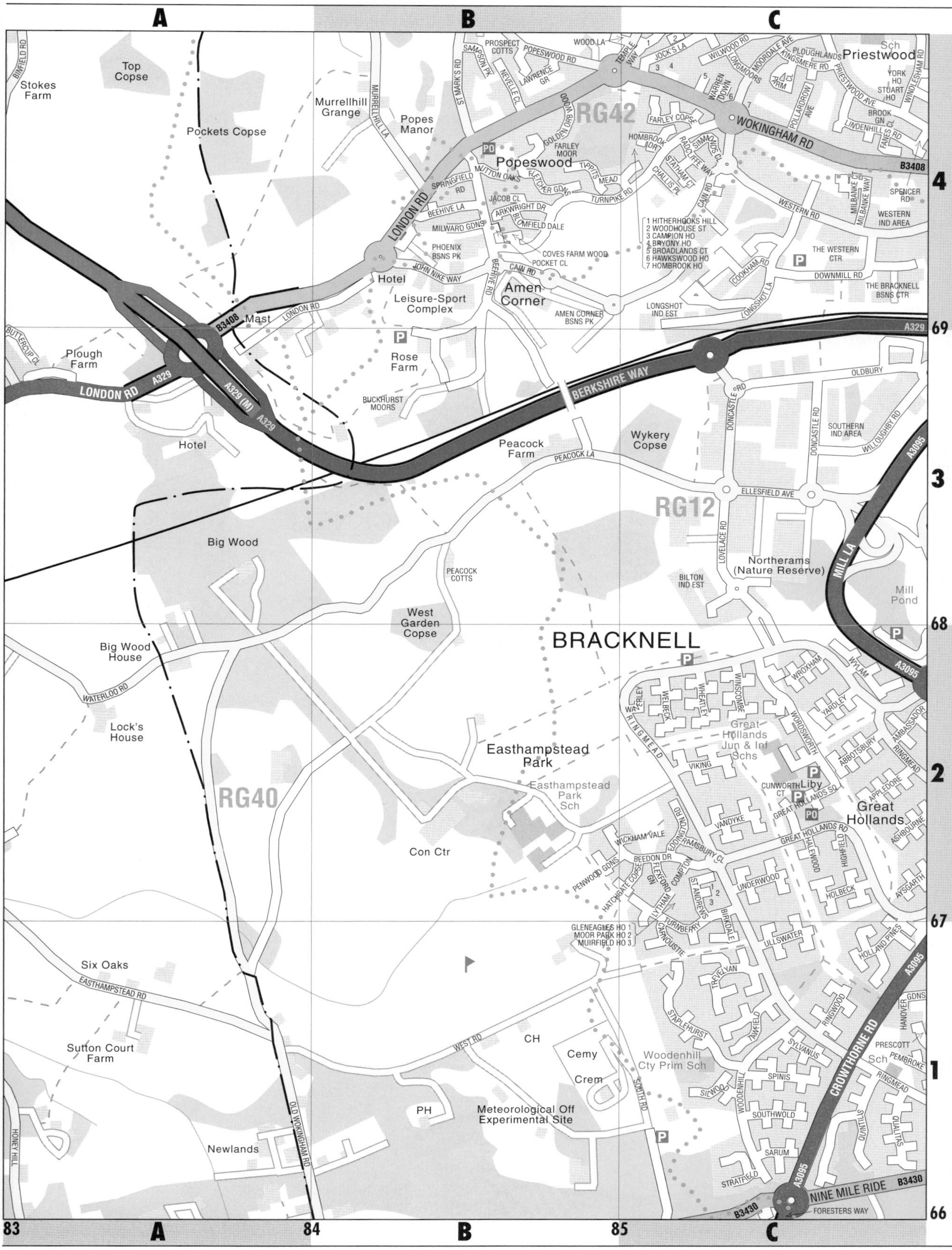


143
118

A4
1 PRIESTWOOD SQ
2 SALTIRE GDNS
3 WINDLEBROOK GN
4 APPLETREE PL
5 PORTMAN CL
6 HART CL
7 BIRCHETTS CL
8 ASHRIDGE GN

117

B4
1 LYNWOOD CHASE
2 DENE CL
3 LAKESIDE
4 EDMONDS CT

91

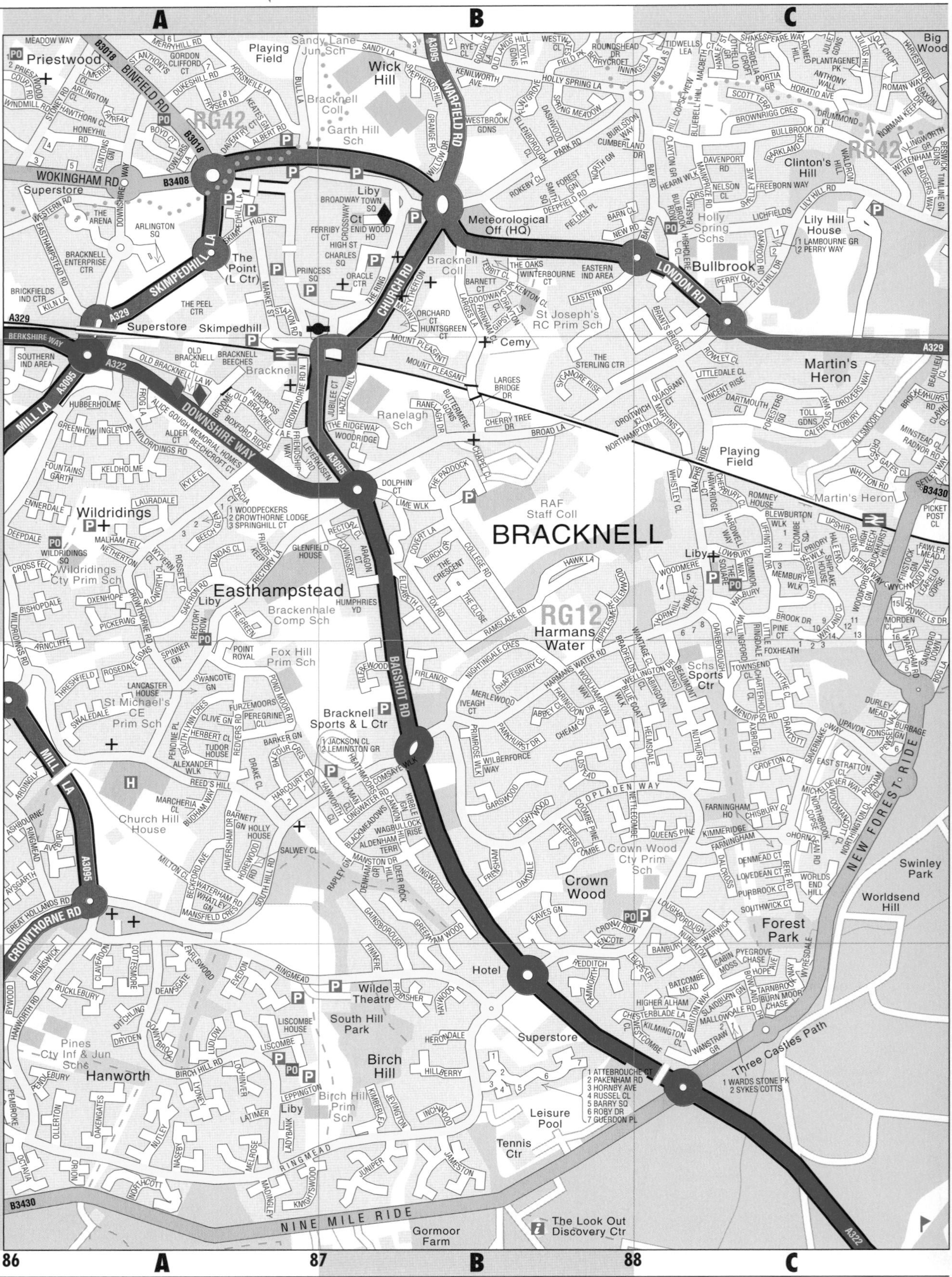


117
144

C2
1 MULBERRY CT
2 ROWAN
3 LINDEN
4 LYTCHET MINSTER CL
5 STOKEFORD CL
6 FROXFIELD DOWN

C3
1 HOWORTH CT
2 BOVENEY HO
3 BOULTERS HO
4 HEATHERMOUNT
5 HAMBLEDEN CT
6 CLEEVE HO
7 RUSHY HO
8 CULHAM HO
9 THE WILLOWS
10 CEDARS
11 MAPEL CT
12 GREENWOOD
13 LARCHWOOD
14 THE FIRS
15 CHARLBURY CL
16 HOLTON HEATH
17 BLOXWORTH CL

92
120

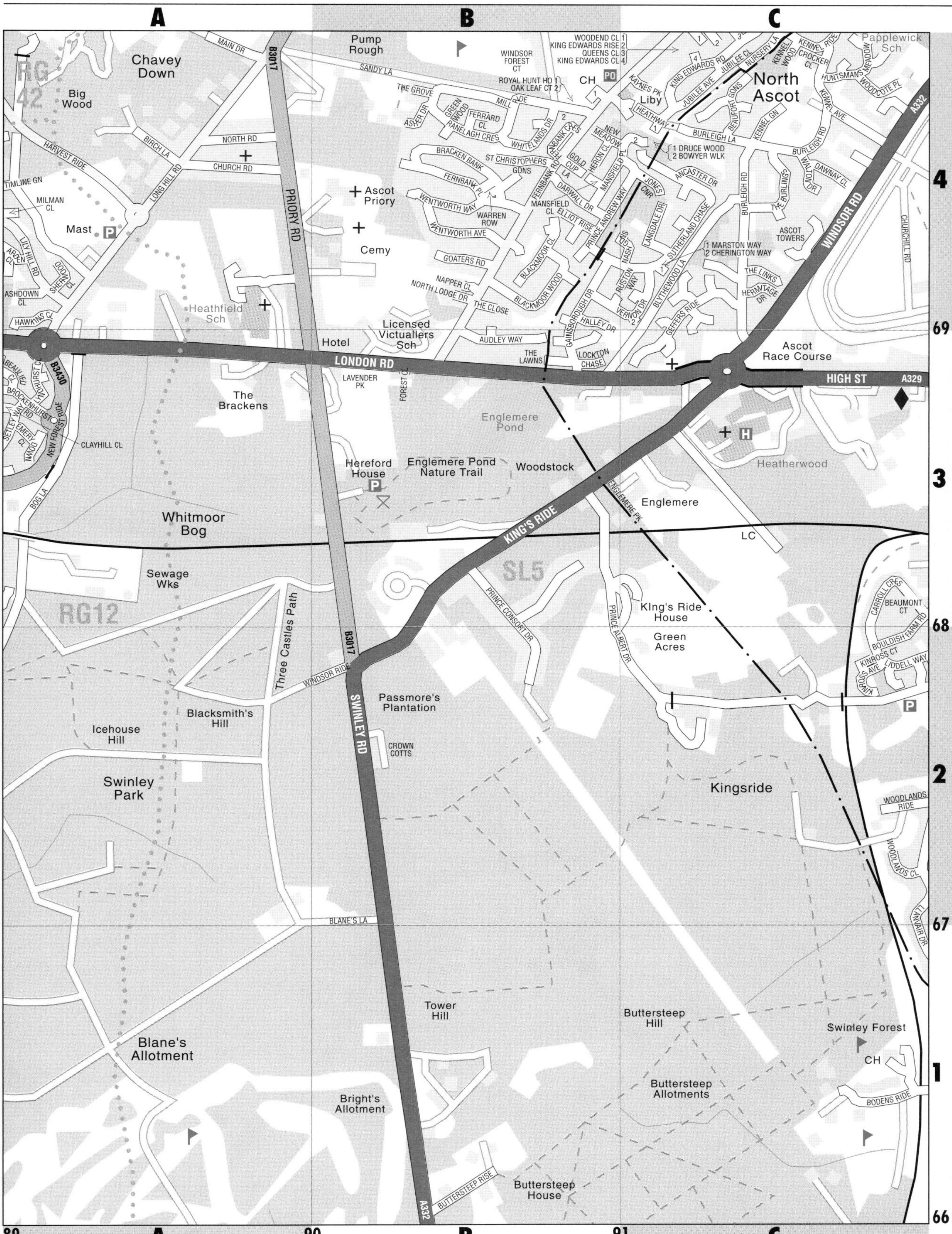


145
120

119
93

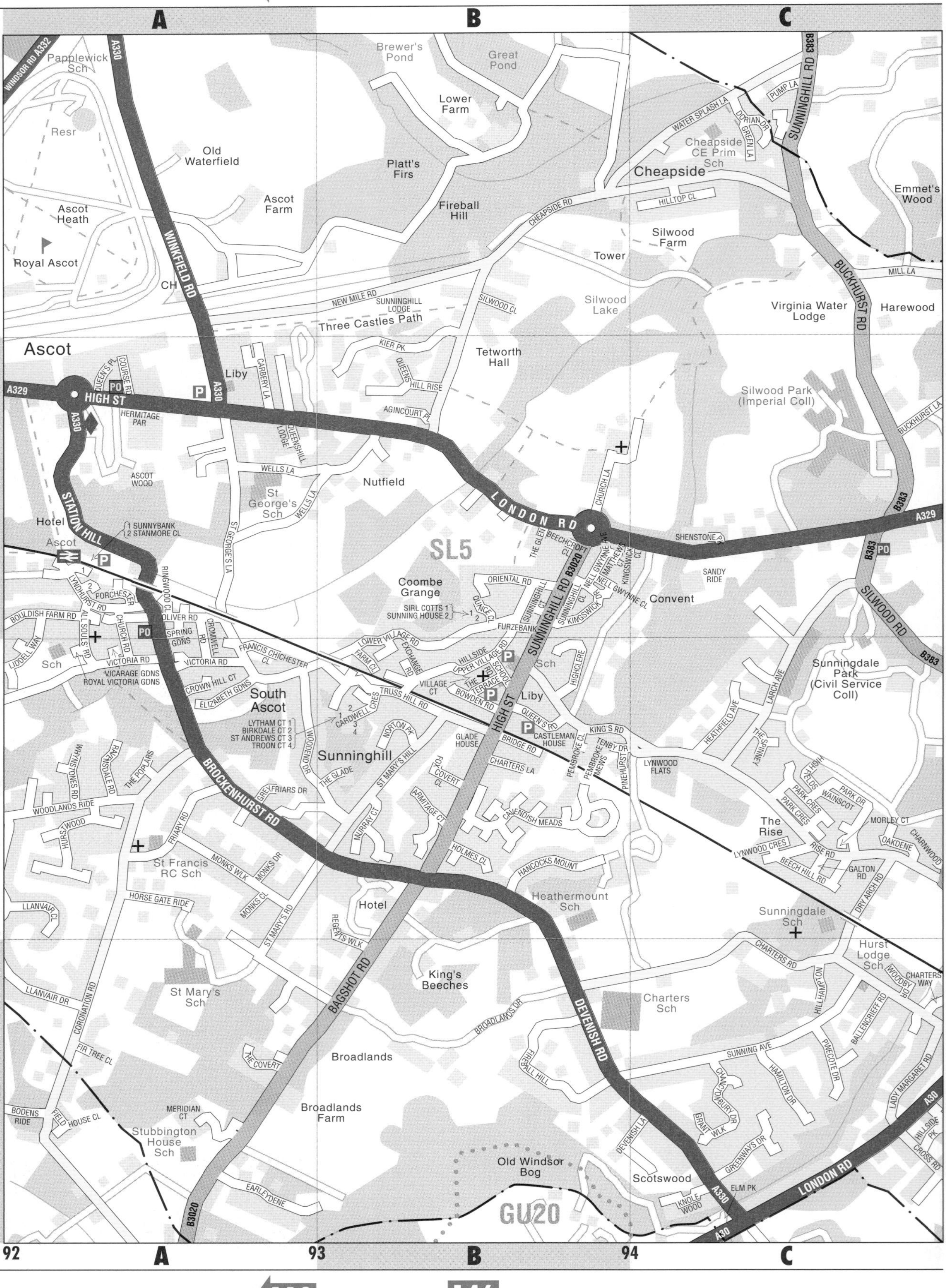


119
146

94
122

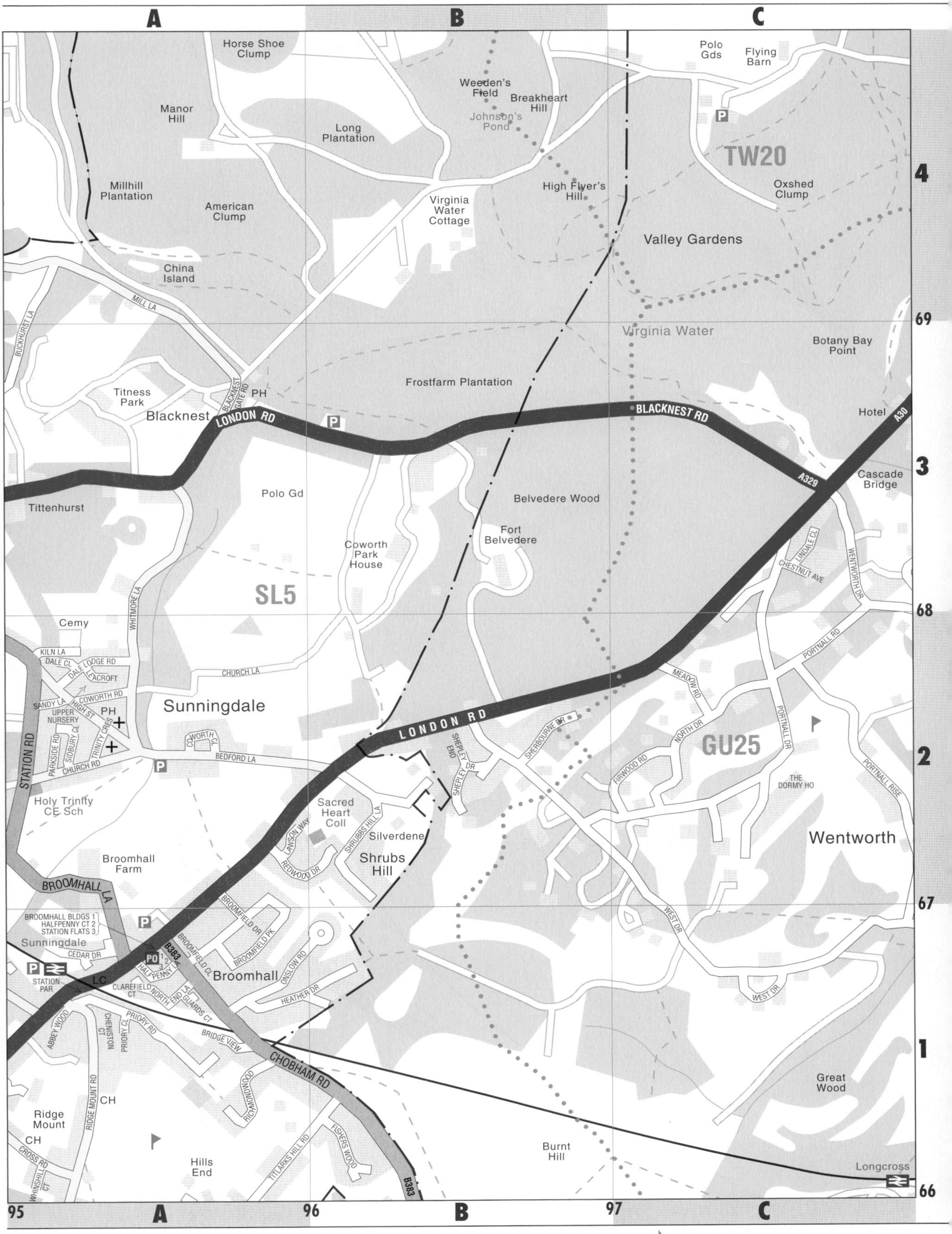
A
B
C
Horse Shoe Clump
Polo Gds
Flying Barn
Weeden's Field
Breakheart Hill
Johnson's Pond
Manor Hill
Long Plantation
TW20
Millhill Plantation
American Clump
Virginia Water Cottage
High Flyer's Hill
Oxshed Clump
Valley Gardens
4
China Island
MILL LA
BUCKHURST LA
69
Virginia Water
Botany Bay Point
Frostfarm Plantation
Titness Park
BLACKNEST GATE RD
PH
Blacknest
LONDON RD
BLACKNEST RD
Hotel
A30
A329
3
Tittenhurst
Polo Gd
Belvedere Wood
Cascade Bridge
Fort Belvedere
Coworth Park House
LINDALE CL
CHESTNUT AVE
WENTWORTH DR
SL5
WHITMORE LA
Cemy
68
KILN LA
DALE CL
DALE LODGE RD
ACROFT
CHURCH LA
MEADOW RD
PORTNALL RD
COWORTH RD
SANDY LA
HIGH ST
UPPER NURSERY
TRINITY CRES
Sunningdale
PH
LONDON RD
SHERBOURNE DR
NORTH DR
PORTNALL DR
GU25
STATION RD
PARKSIDE RD
SIDBURY CL
COWORTH CL
BEDFORD LA
SHEPLEY END
SHEPLEY DR
FIRWOOD RD
PORTNALL RISE
2
CHURCH RD
THE DORMY HO
Holy Trinity CE Sch
Sacred Heart Coll
LAWSON WAY
SHRUBBS HILL LA
Silverdene
Wentworth
Broomhall Farm
Shrubs Hill
REDWOOD DR
BROOMHALL LA
BROOMFIELD DR
67
BROOMHALL BLDGS 1
HALFPENNY CT 2
STATION FLATS 3
BROOMFIELD PK
WEST DR
Sunningdale
B383
BROOMFIELD CL
CEDAR DR
PO
ONSLOW RD
STATION PAR
LC
HALFPENNY
Broomhall
CLAREFIELD CT
NORTH END LA
GUARDS CT
HEATHER DR
WEST DR
ABBEY WOOD
CHENISTON CT
PRIORY CL
PRIORY RD
BRIDGE VIEW
1
CHOBHAM RD
RIDGEMOUNT RD
CH
RICHMONDWOOD
Great Wood
Ridge Mount
CH
Burnt Hill
CROSS RD
TITLARKS HILL RD
FISHERS WOOD
Hills End
WHINSHILL CT
B383
Longcross
66
95
A
96
B
97
C

122

121
95

TW20
Egham Wick Plantations
Wick Pond
Totem Pole
Woodlee
Virginia Water Plantations
LONDON RD
American Comm Sch
GLENWOOD
Callow Hill
Great Wood
Whitehall Farm
Stroude
Highmoor Farm
The Dell
Stroude Farm
The Clockcase
Merlewood
Allot Gdns
Christchurch CE Fst Sch
Virginia Water
The Royal Standard (PH)
CHRISTCHURCH RD
General's Copse
St Ann's Heath
Home Farm
Virginia Water Prep Sch
Broom Hill
Liby
GU25
Wentworth Club
CH
The Bourne
SANDHILLS LA
St Ann's Heath Cty Mid Sch
Waterloo Bridge
Trumps Green Cty Fst Sch
Harpesford
1 FAIRVIEW COTTS
2 THE PARADE
The Stag & Hounds (PH)
Trumps Green
Knowle Hill
Beech Wood
Westwood
Knowle Grove
Trumps Farm
LYNE PLACE MANOR
Longcross Bridge
Hersham Copse
KT16
Works
M3
A30
B389

121

96
124

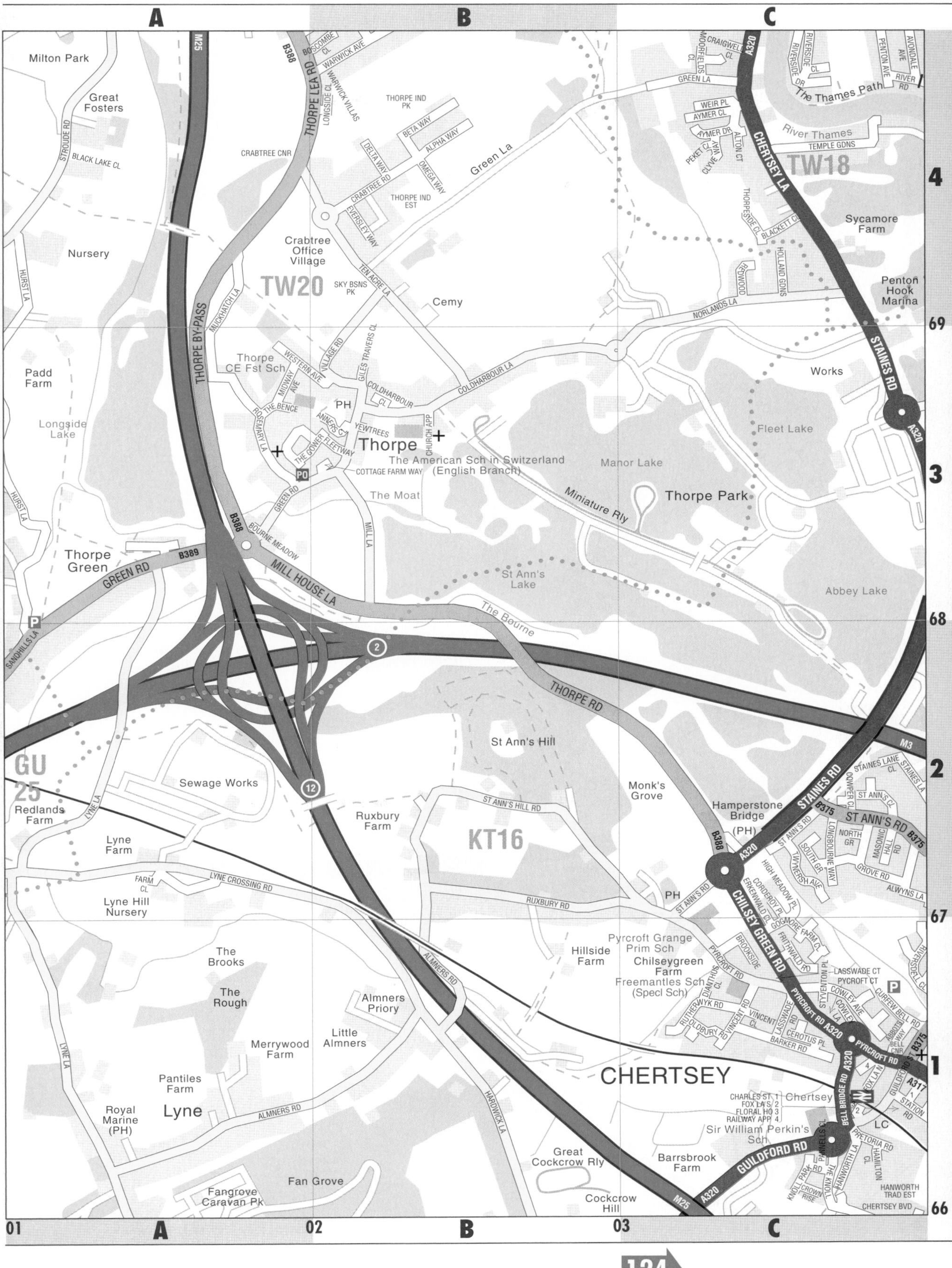
A
B
C
4
69
3
68
2
67
1
66
01
02
03
Milton Park
Great Fosters
STROUDE RD
BLACK LAKE CL
Nursery
HURST LA
Padd Farm
Longside Lake
Thorpe Green
GREEN RD
B389
SANDHILLS LA
GU 25
Redlands Farm
LYNE LA
Lyne Farm
FARM CL
LYNE CROSSING RD
Lyne Hill Nursery
Sewage Works
The Brooks
The Rough
Merrywood Farm
Pantiles Farm
Royal Marine (PH)
Lyne
ALMNERS RD
Fangrove Caravan Pk
Fan Grove
M25
B388
THORPE LEA RD
BOSCOMBE CL
WARWICK AVE
LONGSIDE CL
WARWICK VILLAS
THORPE IND PK
BETA WAY
ALPHA WAY
DELTA WAY
CRABTREE CNR
CRABTREE RD
OMEGA WAY
THORPE IND EST
EVERSLEY WAY
Green La
Crabtree Office Village
TW20
SKY BSNS PK
TEN ACRE LA
Cemy
MUCKHATCH LA
THORPE BY-PASS
Thorpe CE Fst Sch
WESTERN AVE
MIDWAY AVE
VILLAGE RD
GILES TRAVERS CL
COLDHARBOUR CL
COLDHARBOUR LA
PH
THE BENCE
ROSEMARY LA
ANNERS CL
YEWTREES
CHURCH APP
THE GOWER
FLEETWAY
Thorpe
PO
COTTAGE FARM WAY
The American Sch in Switzerland (English Branch)
The Moat
GREEN RD
MILL LA
BOURNE MEADOW
MILL HOUSE LA
The Bourne
St Ann's Lake
Manor Lake
Miniature Rly
Thorpe Park
Fleet Lake
Abbey Lake
THORPE RD
St Ann's Hill
Ruxbury Farm
ST ANN'S HILL RD
KT16
Monk's Grove
RUXBURY RD
Hillside Farm
ALMNERS RD
Almners Priory
Little Almners
HARDWICK LA
Great Cockcrow Rly
Cockcrow Hill
CHERTSEY
Pyrcroft Grange Prim Sch
Chilseygreen Farm
Freemantles Sch (Specl Sch)
Barrsbrook Farm
Sir William Perkin's Sch
CRAIGWELL CL
MOORFIELDS CL
GREEN LA
A320
RIVERSIDE CL
RIVERSIDE DR
PENTON AVE
AVONDALE AVE
RIVER RD
The Thames Path
WEIR PL
AYMER CL
AYMER DR
PEKET CL
CLYVE WAY
ALTON CT
River Thames
TEMPLE GDNS
CHERTSEY LA
TW18
THORPESIDE CL
BLACKETT CL
HOLLAND GDNS
REDWOOD
Sycamore Farm
Penton Hook Marina
NORLANDS LA
Works
STAINES RD
M3
STAINES LANE CL
STAINES LA
COWPER CL
ST ANN'S CL
Hamperstone Bridge (PH)
B375
ST ANN'S RD
NORTH GR
MASONIC HALL RD
SOUTH GR
LONGBOURNE WAY
TWYNERSH AVE
GROVE RD
ALWYNS LA
ST ANN'S RD
HIGH MEADOW PL
CORDEROY PL
ERKENWALD CL
CHILSEY GREEN RD
GOGMORE FARM CL
FRITHWALD RD
BROOKSIDE
PYRCROFT RD
DIANTHUS CL
STYVENTON PL
LASSWADE CT
PYRCROFT CT
COWLEY AVE
COWLEY LA
CURFEW BELL RD
RIVERSDELL CL
RUTHERWYK RD
OLDBURY RD
VINCENT RD
VINCENT CL
LASSWADE RD
CEROTUS PL
BARKER RD
BELL CNR
P
FOX LA N
GUILDFORD ST
A317
STATION RD
CHARLES ST 1
FOX LA S 2
FLORAL HO 3
RAILWAY APP 4
Chertsey
BELL BRIDGE RD
LC
GUILDFORD RD
PANNELLS CL
PRETORIA RD
HAMILTON CL
HANWORTH LA
THE KNOLL
KNOLL PARK RD
CROWN RISE
HANWORTH TRAD EST
CHERTSEY BVD

123
97

A
B
C
4
69
3
68
2
67
1
66
04
05
06
TW15
TW18
TW17
KT16
KT15
KT13
Greenfield Nurseries
Gravel Pit
Queen Mary Resr
Nursery
Penton Hook Island
Penton Hook
Manor Farm
Laleham CE Prim Sch
Penton Hook Marina
Penton Park Est
Recn Gd
Laleham
Shepperton Studios
Laleham Nurseries
Laleham Park
Laleham Burway
Laleham Abbey
Resr
Camping Site
Gravel Pit
Abbey Mead
Abbey Chase
Abbey Chase Farm
CHERTSEY
Chertsey Mus
Abbeyfields
Riverscroft
Camping Site
Stepgates Prim Sch
Dumsey Eyot
Mead Farm
Chertsey Bridge
Picnic Area
St Anne's RC Prim Sch
Marina
Chertsey Meads
Dockett Eddy
Salesian Sch
Liby
STAINES RD
ASHFORD RD
THE BROADWAY
SHEPPERTON RD
LALEHAM RD
LITTLETON LA
CHERTSEY BRIDGE RD
CHERTSEY RD
BRIDGE RD
LONDON ST
WINDSOR ST
EASTWORTH RD
FORDWATER RD
WEIR RD
HERIOT RD
River Thames
The Thames Path
Burway Ditch
Abbey River
River Ash
Sweep's Ditch
The Bourne
M3
B376
B377
B375
B387
A320
A317
1 ONSLOW MEWS
2 WINDSOR PL
3 ALWYNS CL
4 ALWYNS LA
5 WILLATS CL
A1
1 FOUNDRY MEWS
2 BEOMONDS ROW
3 WHITE HART ROW
4 GALSWORTHY RD
5 BEOMONDS
6 CHERTSEY WLK
7 STANWAY COTTS
8 HOLLY CT
9 CAVENDISH CT
10 BLAKES CT
NELSON CT
REED PLACE BSNS PK
LABURNHAM CT
HANWORTH TRAD EST
FORDWATER TRAD EST
DOCKETT MOORINGS

123

98

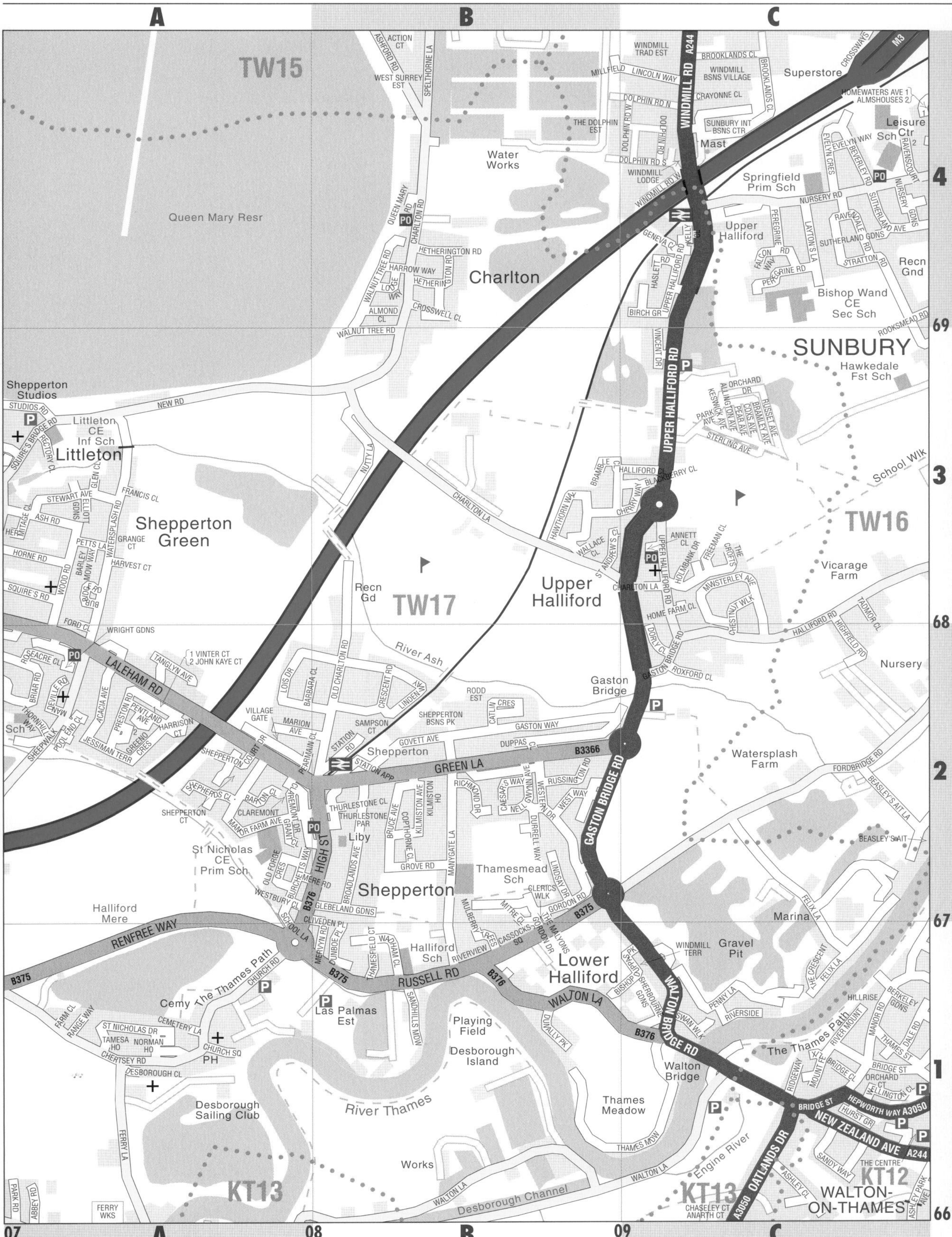
A
B
C
4
69
3
68
2
67
1
66
07
08
09
TW15
TW16
TW17
KT13
KT12
Queen Mary Resr
Water Works
Charlton
SUNBURY
Upper Halliford
Shepperton Green
Littleton
Shepperton
Lower Halliford
WALTON-ON-THAMES
Shepperton Studios
Littleton CE Inf Sch
Springfield Prim Sch
Bishop Wand CE Sec Sch
Hawkedale Fst Sch
Leisure Ctr
Sch
Recn Gnd
Recn Gd
Superstore
Mast
Vicarage Farm
Watersplash Farm
Nursery
Gaston Bridge
Thamesmead Sch
St Nicholas CE Prim Sch
Liby
Halliford Sch
Halliford Mere
Las Palmas Est
Playing Field
Desborough Island
Desborough Sailing Club
Desborough Channel
River Thames
River Ash
Engine River
The Thames Path
Cemy
PH
Works
FERRY WKS
Thames Meadow
Walton Bridge
Marina
Gravel Pit
School Wlk
WINDMILL TRAD EST
WINDMILL BSNS VILLAGE
SUNBURY INT BSNS CTR
THE DOLPHIN EST
SHEPPERTON BSNS PK
RODD EST
VILLAGE GATE
WINDMILL RD
A244
M3
A3050
B3366
B375
B376
UPPER HALLIFORD RD
GASTON BRIDGE RD
WALTON BRIDGE RD
WALTON LA
RUSSELL RD
RENFREE WAY
HIGH ST
GREEN LA
LALEHAM RD
NEW RD
CHARLTON LA
CHARLTON RD
NUTTY LA
SPELTHORNE LA
ASHFORD RD
WEST SURREY EST
ACTION CT
HETHERINGTON RD
WALNUT TREE RD
CROSSWELL CL
ALMOND CL
HARROW WAY
NURSERY RD
SUTHERLAND GDNS
PEREGRINE RD
LAYTON'S LA
STRATTON RD
ROOKSMEAD RD
BROOKLANDS CL
BROOKLANDS RD
LINCOLN WAY
CRAYONNE CL
DOLPHIN RD
CROSSWAYS
HOMEWATERS AVE
ALMSHOUSES
EVELYN WAY
EVELYN CRES
BEVERLEY RD
RAVENSCOURT
NURSERY GDNS
GENEVA CL
BIRCH GR
VINCENT DR
HASLETT RD
ORCHARD DR
RUSSELL AVE
STERLING AVE
HALLIFORD CL
BLACKBERRY CL
HAWTHORN WAY
CHERRY WAY
WALLACE CL
ST ANDREW'S CL
HOLMBANK DR
FREEMAN CL
THE CROFTS
ANNETT CL
HOME FARM CL
DORLY CL
ROXFORD CL
CHESTNUT WLK
MINSTERLEY AVE
HALLIFORD RD
HIGHFIELD RD
TADMOR CL
FORDBRIDGE RD
BEASLEY'S AIT LA
BEASLEY'S AIT
FELIX LA
THE CRESCENT
HILLRISE
BERKELEY GDNS
MANOR RD
THAMES ST
DALE RD
RIVER MOUNT
BRIDGE ST
ORCHARD CT
WELLINGTON CL
HEPWORTH WAY
NEW ZEALAND AVE
HURST GR
SANDY WAY
THE CENTRE
ASHLEY PARK AVE
ASHLEY CL
OATLANDS DR
CHASELEY CT
ANARTH CT
RIDGEWAY
MOUNT PL
PENNY LA
RIVERSIDE
SWAN WLK
WINDMILL TERR
BISHOP DUPPAS PK
SHERBOURNE GDNS
THAMES MDW
WALTON LA
DUNALLY PK
SANDHILLS MDW
STUDIOS RD
SQUIRE'S BRIDGE RD
RECTORY CL
GLEN CL
STEWART AVE
ELLIOTT GDNS
ASH RD
HORNE RD
SQUIRE'S RD
WOOD RD
FRANCIS CL
WATERSPLASH RD
GRANGE CT
HARVEST CT
PETTS LA
BARLEY MOW WAY
FORD CL
WRIGHT GDNS
1 VINTER CT
2 JOHN KAYE CT
TANGLYN AVE
SEACRE CL
BRIAR RD
DEVILLE RD
THORNHILL WAY
SHEEPWALK
POOL END CL
ACACIA AVE
PRESTON RD
PENTLAND AVE
HARRISON CT
JESSIMAN TERR
GREENO CRES
SHEPPERTON COURT DR
SHEPHERDS CL
SHEPPERTON CT
CLAREMONT
MANOR FARM AVE
BARTON CL
OLD FORGE CRES
BURCHETTS WAY
WESTBURY CL
SCHOOL LA
MARION AVE
STATION RD
STATION APP
PEARMAIN CL
LOIS DR
BARBARA CL
OLD CHARLTON RD
CRESCENT RD
LINDEN WAY
SAMPSON CT
GOVETT AVE
CATLIN CRES
GASTON WAY
DUPPAS CL
THURLESTONE CL
THURLESTONE PAR
BRUCE AVE
COPTHORNE CL
KILMISTON AVE
KILMISTON HO
RICHMOND DR
CAESAR'S WAY
NELL GWYNN AVE
WESTERN DR
RUSSINGTON RD
WEST WAY
DURRELL WAY
LINDSAY DR
MANYGATE LA
BROADLANDS AVE
GROVE RD
MERE RD
GLEBELAND GDNS
CLIVEDEN PL
MERVYN RD
DUNBOE PL
THAMESFIELD CT
WADHAM CL
MULBERRY CRES
RIVERVIEW
CASSOCKS SQ
MITRE CL
CLERICS WLK
GORDON RD
GORDON DR
THE MALYONS
CHURCH RD
FARM CL
RANGE WAY
ST NICHOLAS DR
CEMETERY LA
TAMESA HO
NORMAN HO
CHURCH SQ
CHERTSEY RD
DESBOROUGH CL
FERRY LA
PARK RD
ABBEY RD
PO
P

100

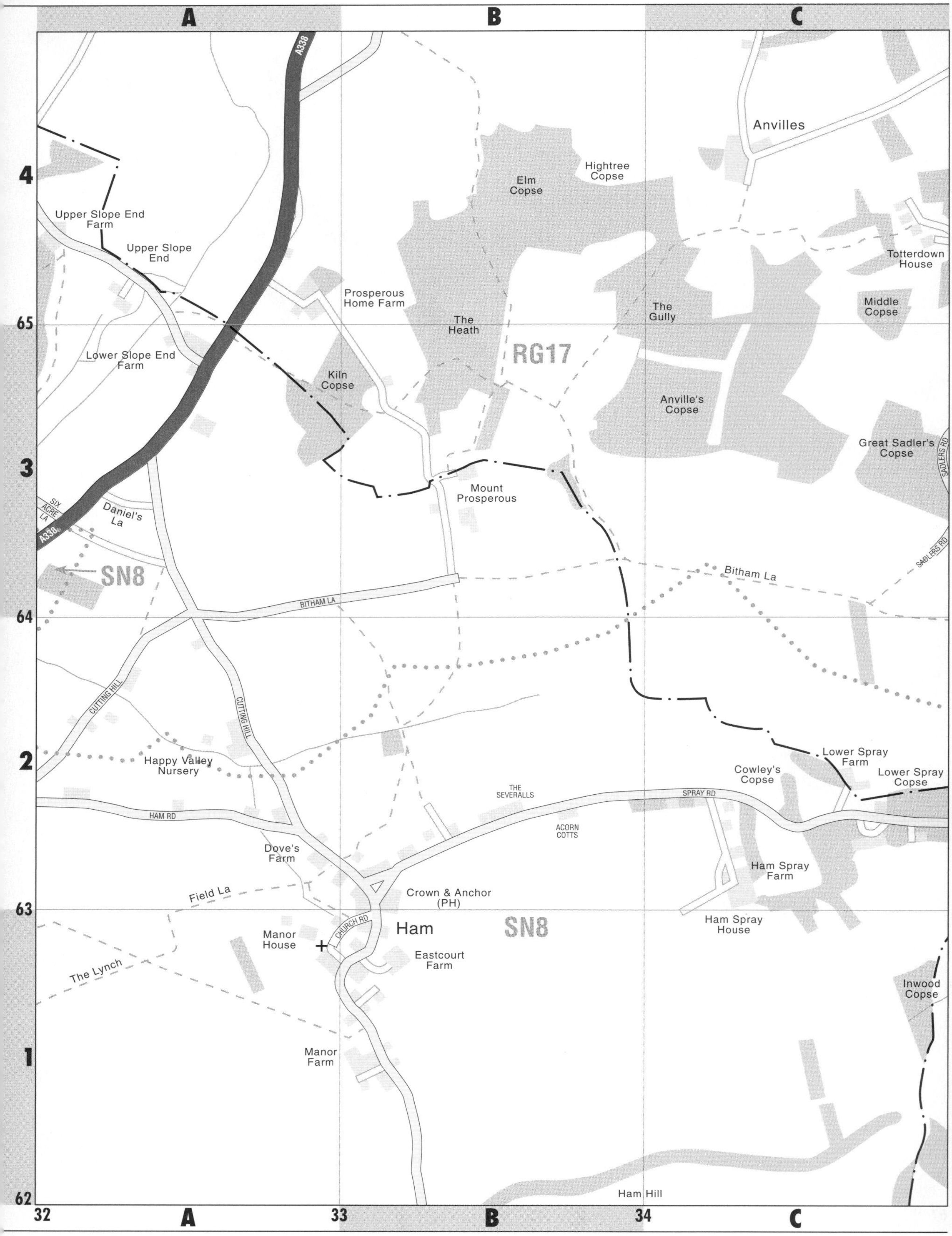
A
B
C
4
65
3
64
2
63
1
62
32
33
34
A338
Anvilles
Hightree
Copse
Elm
Copse
Upper Slope End
Farm
Upper Slope
End
Totterdown
House
Prosperous
Home Farm
The
Gully
Middle
Copse
The
Heath
RG17
Lower Slope End
Farm
Kiln
Copse
Anville's
Copse
Great Sadler's
Copse
SADLERS RD
Mount
Prosperous
SIX
ACRE
LA
Daniel's
La
SN8
Bitham La
BITHAM LA
CUTTING HILL
Happy Valley
Nursery
Lower Spray
Farm
Cowley's
Copse
Lower Spray
Copse
THE
SEVERALLS
SPRAY RD
HAM RD
ACORN
COTTS
Dove's
Farm
Ham Spray
Farm
Field La
Crown & Anchor
(PH)
CHURCH RD
Ham
SN8
Ham Spray
House
Manor
House
Eastcourt
Farm
The Lynch
Inwood
Copse
Manor
Farm
Ham Hill

101
128

147
128

127
102

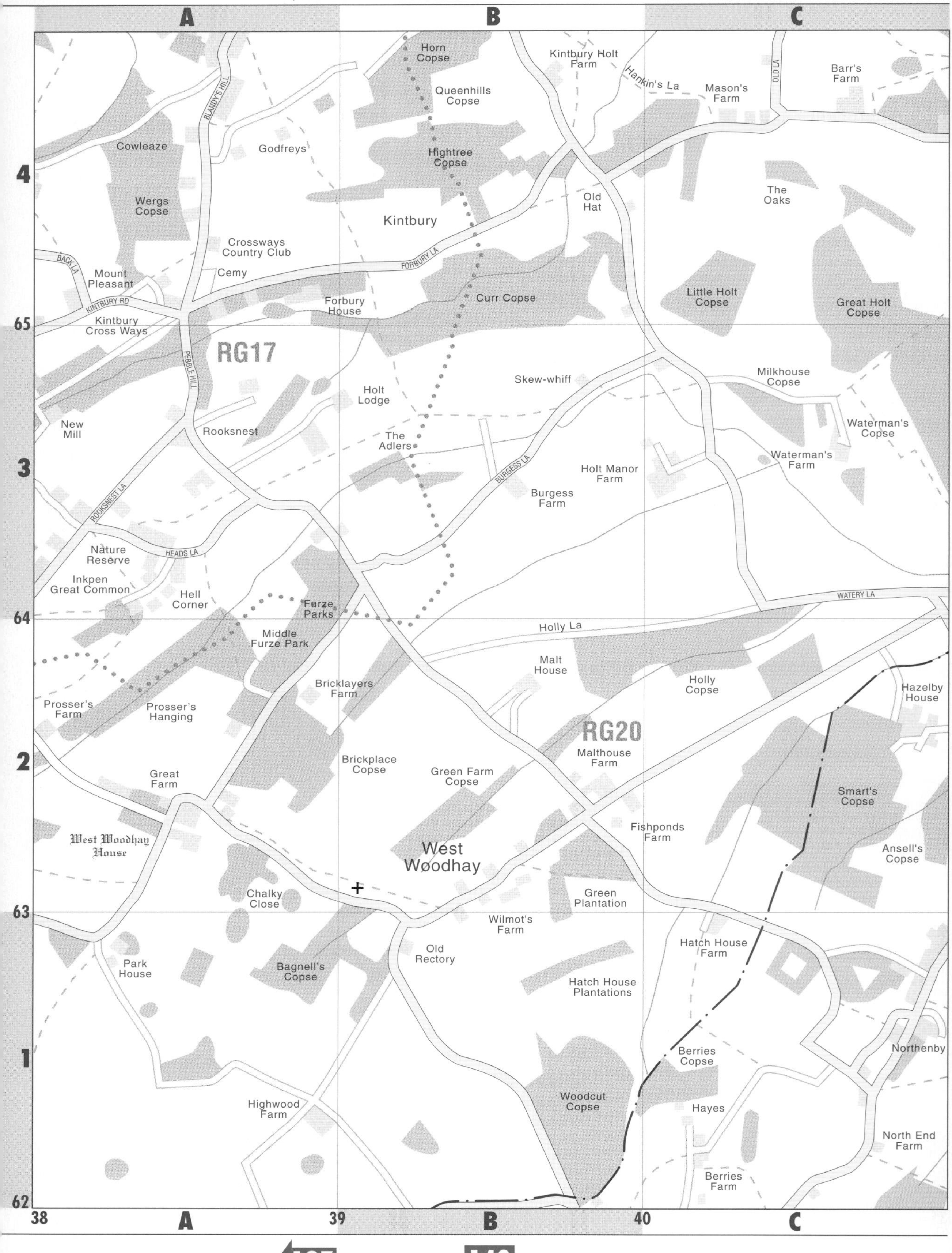


127
148

103
130

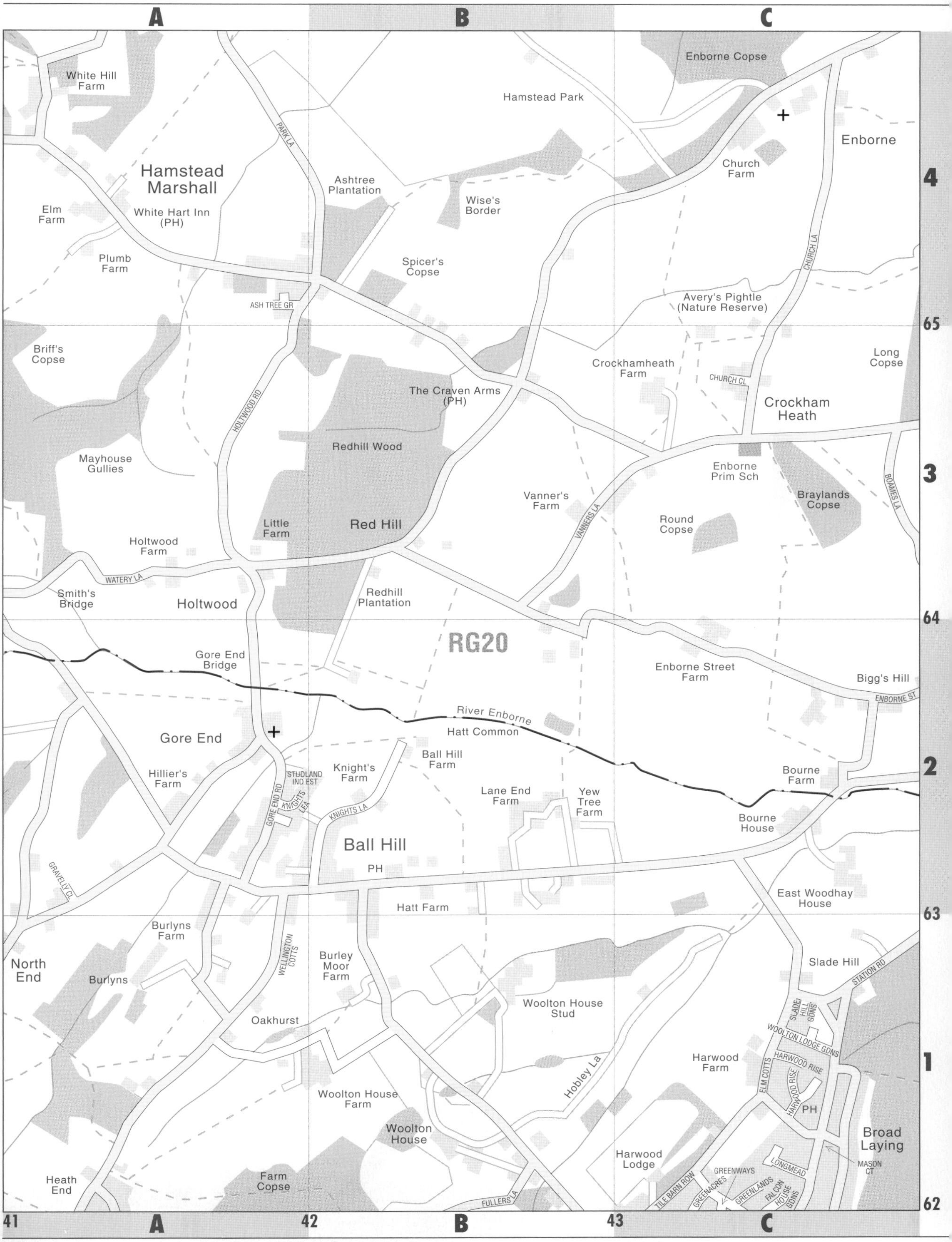
A
B
C
White Hill Farm
Enborne Copse
Hamstead Park
Enborne
Church Farm
Hamstead Marshall
Ashtree Plantation
Elm Farm
White Hart Inn (PH)
Wise's Border
PARK LA
Plumb Farm
Spicer's Copse
CHURCH LA
ASH TREE GR
Avery's Pightle (Nature Reserve)
Briff's Copse
Crockhamheath Farm
Long Copse
CHURCH CL
The Craven Arms (PH)
Crockham Heath
HOLTWOOD RD
Redhill Wood
Mayhouse Gullies
Enborne Prim Sch
Vanner's Farm
Braylands Copse
BOAMES LA
Round Copse
VANNERS LA
Little Farm
Red Hill
Holtwood Farm
WATERY LA
Redhill Plantation
Smith's Bridge
Holtwood
RG20
Gore End Bridge
Enborne Street Farm
Bigg's Hill
ENBORNE ST
River Enborne
Hatt Common
Gore End
Ball Hill Farm
Knight's Farm
Hillier's Farm
STUDLAND IND EST
Bourne Farm
Lane End Farm
Yew Tree Farm
GORE END RD
KNIGHTS LEA
KNIGHTS LA
Bourne House
Ball Hill
PH
GRAVELLY CL
East Woodhay House
Hatt Farm
Burlyns Farm
North End
WELLINGTON COTTS
Burley Moor Farm
Slade Hill
Burlyns
STATION RD
Woolton House Stud
SLADE HILL GDNS
Oakhurst
WOOLTON LODGE GDNS
Harwood Farm
HARWOOD RISE
Hobley La
ELM COTTS
Woolton House Farm
Woolton House
Broad Laying
Harwood Lodge
LONGMEAD
MASON CT
Heath End
Farm Copse
GREENWAYS
TILE BARN ROW
GREENACRES
GREENLANDS
FALCON HOUSE GDNS
FULLERS LA
4
65
3
64
2
63
1
62
41
42
43

130

129
104

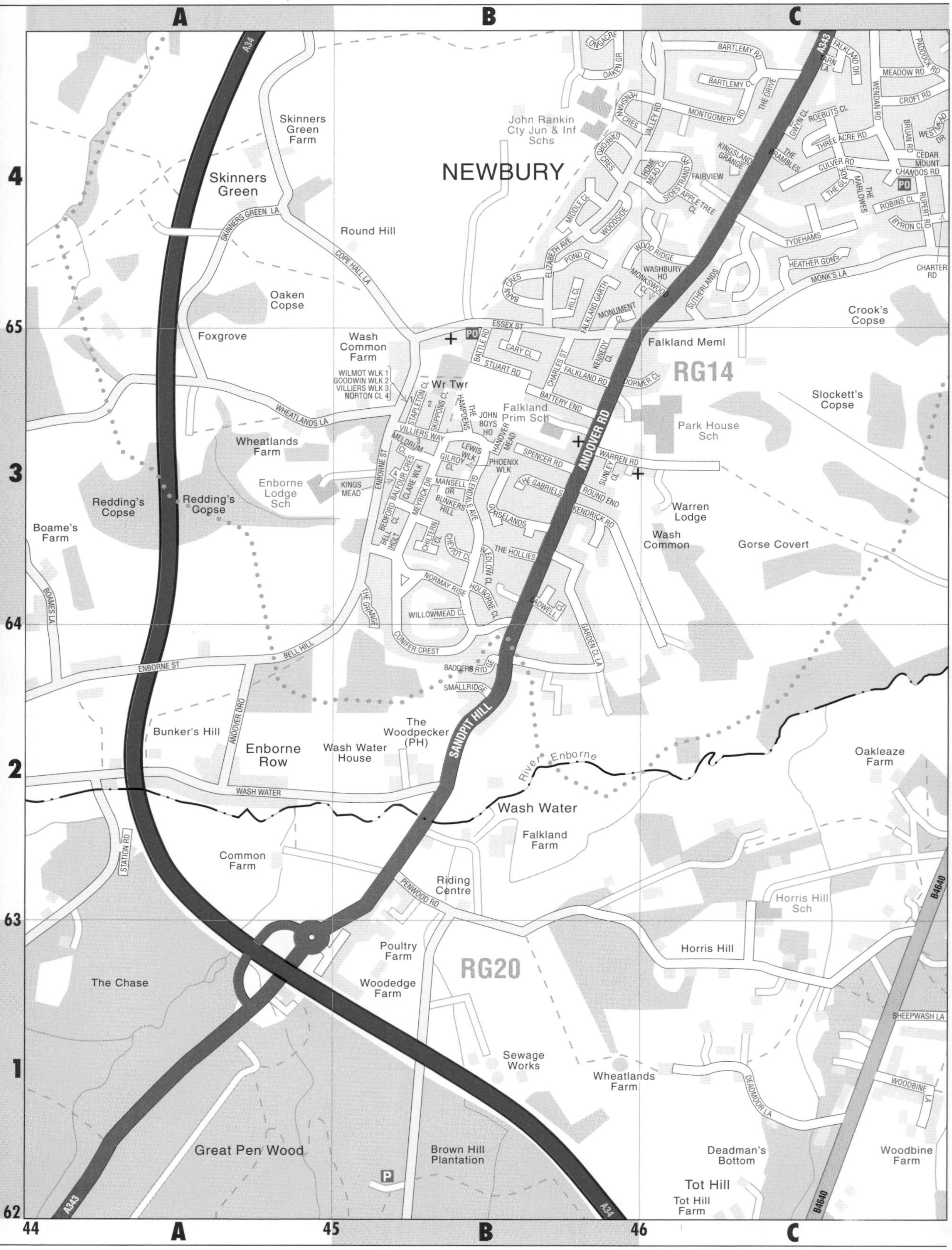
A
B
C
4
3
2
1
65
64
63
62
44
45
46
NEWBURY
RG14
RG20
Skinners Green Farm
Skinners Green
SKINNERS GREEN LA
Round Hill
COPE HALL LA
Oaken Copse
Foxgrove
Wash Common Farm
John Rankin Cty Jun & Inf Schs
WILMOT WLK 1
GOODWIN WLK 2
VILLIERS WLK 3
NORTON CL 4
Wr Twr
WHEATLANDS LA
Wheatlands Farm
Enborne Lodge Sch
Redding's Copse
Boame's Farm
BOAMES LA
ENBORNE ST
BELL HILL
Bunker's Hill
ANDOVER DRO
Enborne Row
Wash Water House
The Woodpecker (PH)
SANDPIT HILL
WASH WATER
River Enborne
Wash Water
Falkland Farm
Common Farm
STATION RD
Riding Centre
PENWOOD RD
Poultry Farm
Woodedge Farm
The Chase
Great Pen Wood
Brown Hill Plantation
Sewage Works
Wheatlands Farm
DEADMOOR LA
Deadman's Bottom
Tot Hill
Tot Hill Farm
Woodbine Farm
WOODBINE LA
SHEEPWASH LA
Horris Hill
Horris Hill Sch
Oakleaze Farm
Gorse Covert
Wash Common
Warren Lodge
Park House Sch
Slockett's Copse
Crook's Copse
Falkland Meml
Falkland Prim Sch
ANDOVER RD
ESSEX ST
CARY CL
STUART RD
BATTLE RD
CHARLES ST
FALKLAND RD
KENNEDY CL
DORMER CL
BATTERY END
SPENCER RD
WARREN RD
SUNLEY CL
ROUND END
THE GABRIELS
KENDRICK RD
GORSELANDS
THE HOLLIES
CADWELL CL
GARDEN CL LA
BADGERS RIDGE
SMALLRIDGE
CONIFER CREST
WILLOWMEAD CL
HOLBORNE CL
BLEDLOW CL
NORMAY RISE
CHEVIOT CL
CHILTERN CL
BELL HOLT
BEDFORD CL
BALFOUR CRES
CLARE WLK
METRICK DR
MANSELL DR
BUNKERS HILL
GLENDALE AVE
GILROY CL
LEWIS WLK
PHOENIX WLK
HANOVER MEAD
JOHN BOYS HO
THE HAMPDENS
SKIPPONS CL
STAPLETON CL
VILLIERS WAY
MELDRUM CL
ENBORNE ST
KINGS MEAD
THE GRANGE
BARN CRES
ELIZABETH AVE
POND CL
HILL CL
FALKLAND GARTH
MONUMENT CL
MIDDLE CL
WOODSIDE
GARFORD CRES
HENSHAW CRES
VALLEY RD
HOME MEAD CL
SIDESTRAND RD
APPLE TREE CL
FAIRVIEW
WOOD RIDGE
WASHBURY HO
MONKSWOOD CL
SUTHERLANDS
LONGACRE
OAKEN GR
BARTLEMY RD
BARTLEMY CL
MONTGOMERY RD
THE DRIVE
KINGSLAND GRANGE
THE BRAMBLES
GWYN CL
ROEBUTS CL
THREE ACRE RD
CULVER RD
THE GLADE
THE MARLOWES
TYDEHAMS
HEATHER GDNS
MONK'S LA
ROBINS CL
BYRON CL
RUPERT RD
CHANDOS RD
CEDAR MOUNT
BRUAN RD
WESTMEAD DR
CROFT RD
MEADOW RD
PADDOCK RD
WENDAN RD
FALKLAND DR
TARN LA
CHARTER RD
A34
A343
B4640
PO
P

105
132

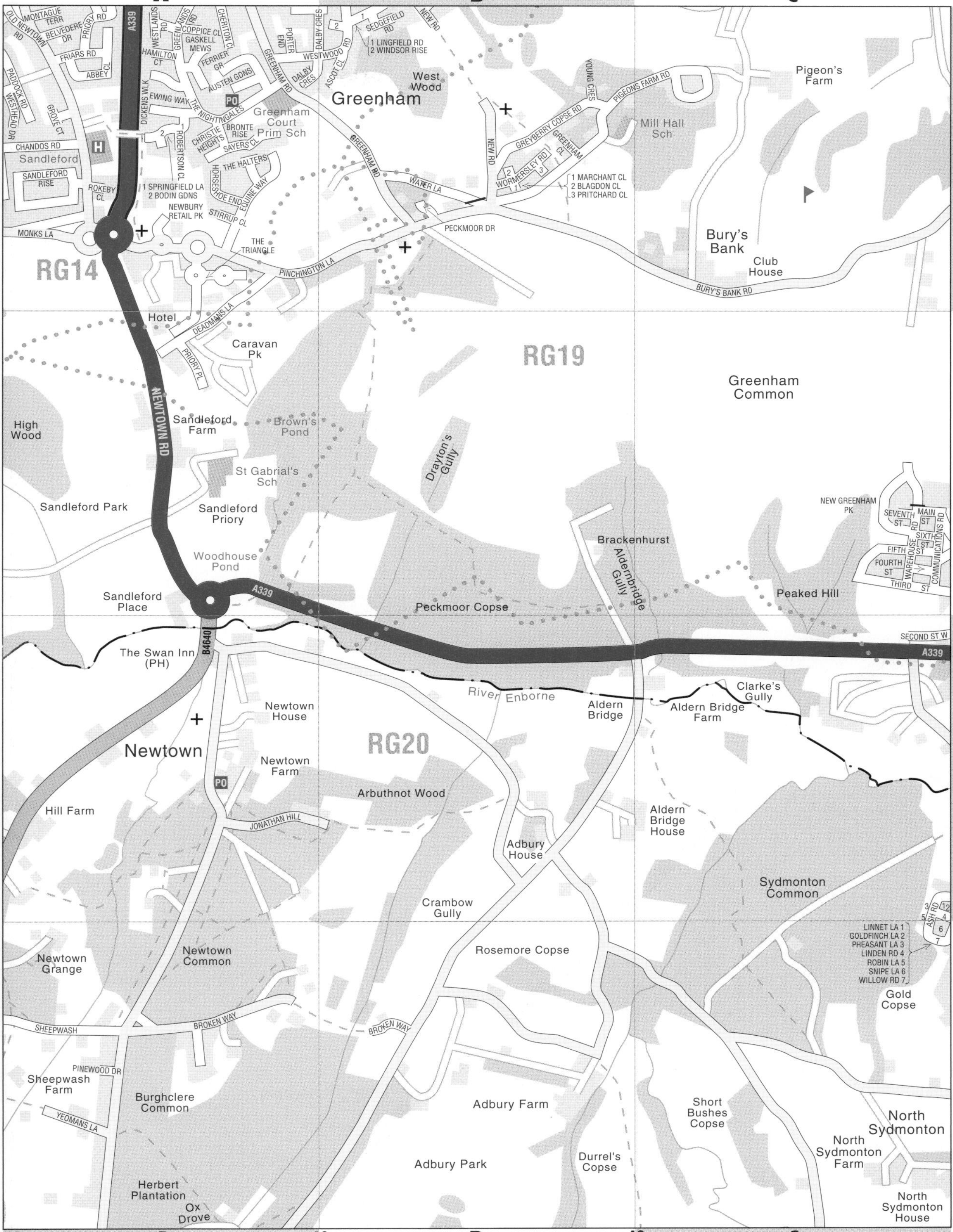
A
B
C
Greenham
West Wood
Greenham Court Prim Sch
Mill Hall Sch
Pigeon's Farm
Sandleford
RG14
RG19
RG20
Bury's Bank
Club House
BURY'S BANK RD
PINCHINGTON LA
PECKMOOR DR
WATER LA
NEWTOWN RD
A339
B4640
Hotel
Caravan Pk
High Wood
Sandleford Farm
Brown's Pond
St Gabrial's Sch
Sandleford Park
Sandleford Priory
Woodhouse Pond
Sandleford Place
Greenham Common
Drayton's Gully
Brackenhurst
Aldermbridge Gully
NEW GREENHAM PK
Peaked Hill
Peckmoor Copse
The Swan Inn (PH)
River Enborne
Aldern Bridge
Aldern Bridge Farm
Clarke's Gully
Newtown House
Newtown
Newtown Farm
Arbuthnot Wood
Hill Farm
JONATHAN HILL
Aldern Bridge House
Adbury House
Sydmonton Common
Crambow Gully
Rosemore Copse
Newtown Grange
Newtown Common
LINNET LA 1
GOLDFINCH LA 2
PHEASANT LA 3
LINDEN RD 4
ROBIN LA 5
SNIPE LA 6
WILLOW RD 7
Gold Copse
SHEEPWASH
BROKEN WAY
PINEWOOD DR
Sheepwash Farm
YEOMANS LA
Burghclere Common
Adbury Farm
Short Bushes Copse
North Sydmonton
North Sydmonton Farm
Adbury Park
Durrel's Copse
Herbert Plantation
Ox Drove
North Sydmonton House
1 SPRINGFIELD LA
2 BODIN GDNS
1 MARCHANT CL
2 BLAGDON CL
3 PRITCHARD CL
1 LINGFIELD RD
2 WINDSOR RISE
4
3
2
1
65
64
63
62
47
48
49

132

131
106

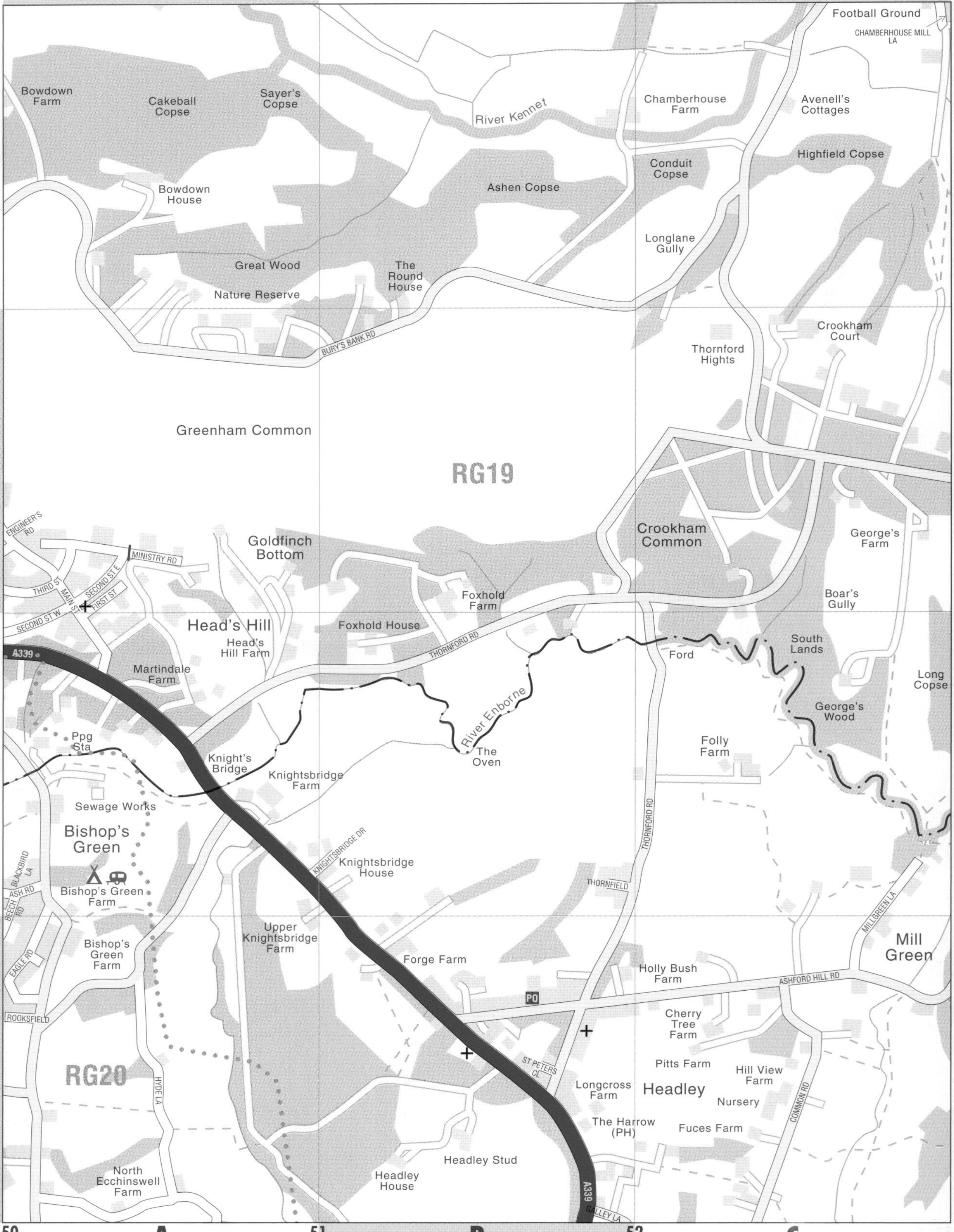
A
B
C
4
65
3
64
2
63
1
62
50
51
52
Football Ground
CHAMBERHOUSE MILL LA
Bowdown Farm
Cakeball Copse
Sayer's Copse
River Kennet
Chamberhouse Farm
Avenell's Cottages
Conduit Copse
Highfield Copse
Bowdown House
Ashen Copse
Longlane Gully
Great Wood
The Round House
Nature Reserve
BURY'S BANK RD
Crookham Court
Thornford Hights
Greenham Common
RG19
Crookham Common
George's Farm
ENGINEER'S RD
MINISTRY RD
Goldfinch Bottom
THIRD ST
SECOND ST E
MAIN ST
FIRST ST
SECOND ST W
Head's Hill
Head's Hill Farm
Foxhold Farm
Foxhold House
THORNFORD RD
Boar's Gully
South Lands
A339
Martindale Farm
Ford
Long Copse
George's Wood
River Enborne
Ppg Sta
Knight's Bridge
The Oven
Folly Farm
Knightsbridge Farm
Sewage Works
Bishop's Green
KNIGHTSBRIDGE DR
Knightsbridge House
THORNFORD RD
BLACKBIRD LA
ASH RD
BEECH RD
Bishop's Green Farm
THORNFIELD
MILLGREEN LA
Upper Knightsbridge Farm
Mill Green
Bishop's Green Farm
EAGLE RD
Forge Farm
Holly Bush Farm
ASHFORD HILL RD
PO
ROOKSFIELD
Cherry Tree Farm
Pitts Farm
ST PETERS CL
RG20
HYDE LA
Hill View Farm
Longcross Farm
Headley
Nursery
COMMON RD
The Harrow (PH)
Fuces Farm
North Ecchinswell Farm
Headley Stud
Headley House
GALLEY LA

131

107
134

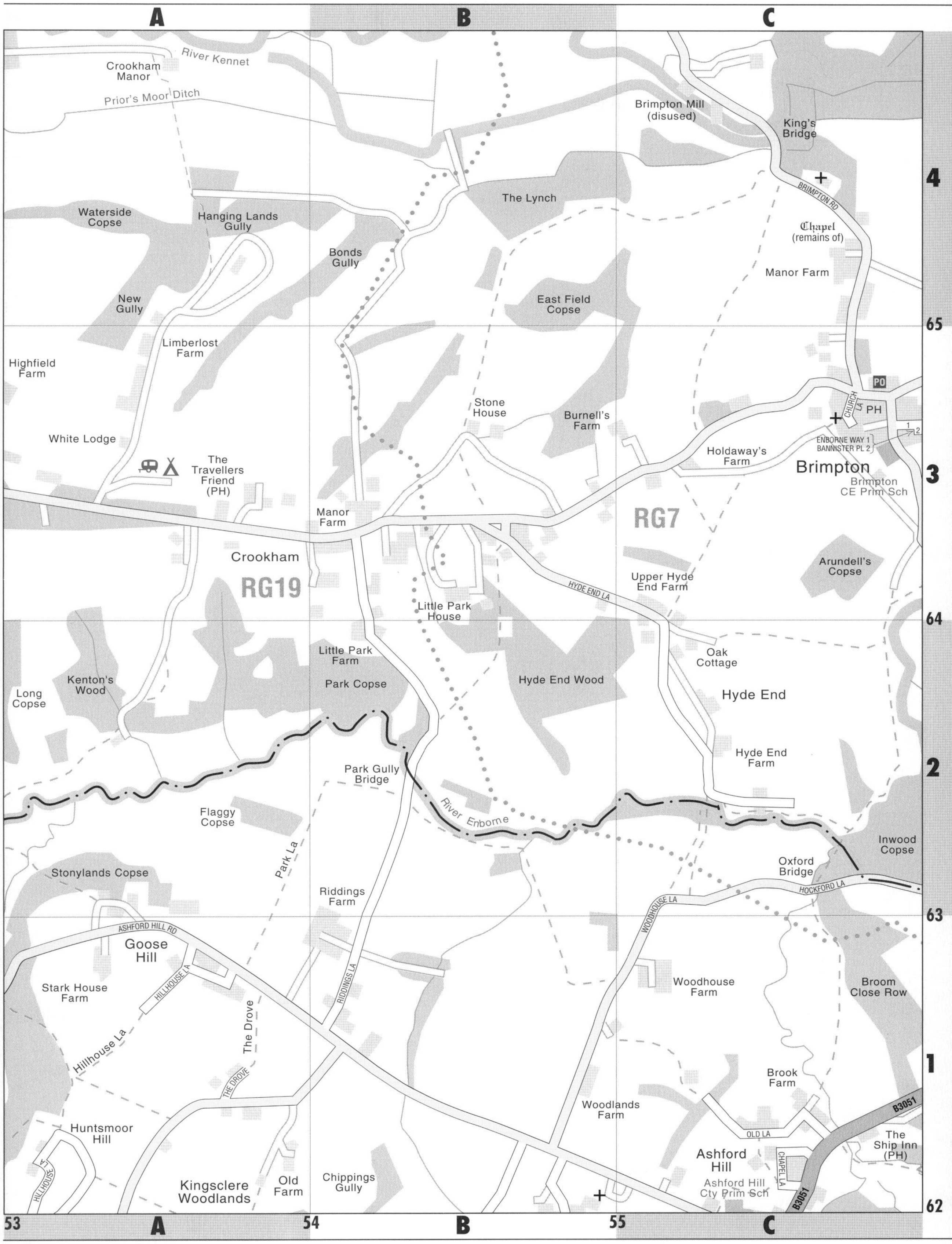
A
B
C
River Kennet
Crookham Manor
Prior's Moor Ditch
Brimpton Mill (disused)
King's Bridge
BRIMPTON RD
Chapel (remains of)
The Lynch
Waterside Copse
Hanging Lands Gully
Bonds Gully
Manor Farm
East Field Copse
New Gully
Limberlost Farm
Highfield Farm
Stone House
Burnell's Farm
PO
CHURCH LA
PH
ENBORNE WAY 1
BANNISTER PL 2
Holdaway's Farm
Brimpton
Brimpton CE Prim Sch
White Lodge
The Travellers Friend (PH)
Manor Farm
RG7
Crookham
RG19
Arundell's Copse
Upper Hyde End Farm
HYDE END LA
Little Park House
Oak Cottage
Little Park Farm
Park Copse
Hyde End Wood
Hyde End
Long Copse
Kenton's Wood
Hyde End Farm
Park Gully Bridge
River Enborne
Flaggy Copse
Inwood Copse
Oxford Bridge
HOCKFORD LA
Park La
Stonylands Copse
Riddings Farm
WOODHOUSE LA
ASHFORD HILL RD
Goose Hill
HILLHOUSE LA
Stark House Farm
RIDDINGS LA
Woodhouse Farm
Broom Close Row
The Drove
Hillhouse La
THE DROVE
Brook Farm
Woodlands Farm
B3051
Huntsmoor Hill
OLD LA
The Ship Inn (PH)
Ashford Hill
CHAPEL LA
HILLHOUSE
Kingsclere Woodlands
Old Farm
Chippings Gully
Ashford Hill Cty Prim Sch
B3051
4
65
3
64
2
63
1
62
53
54
55

134

133
108

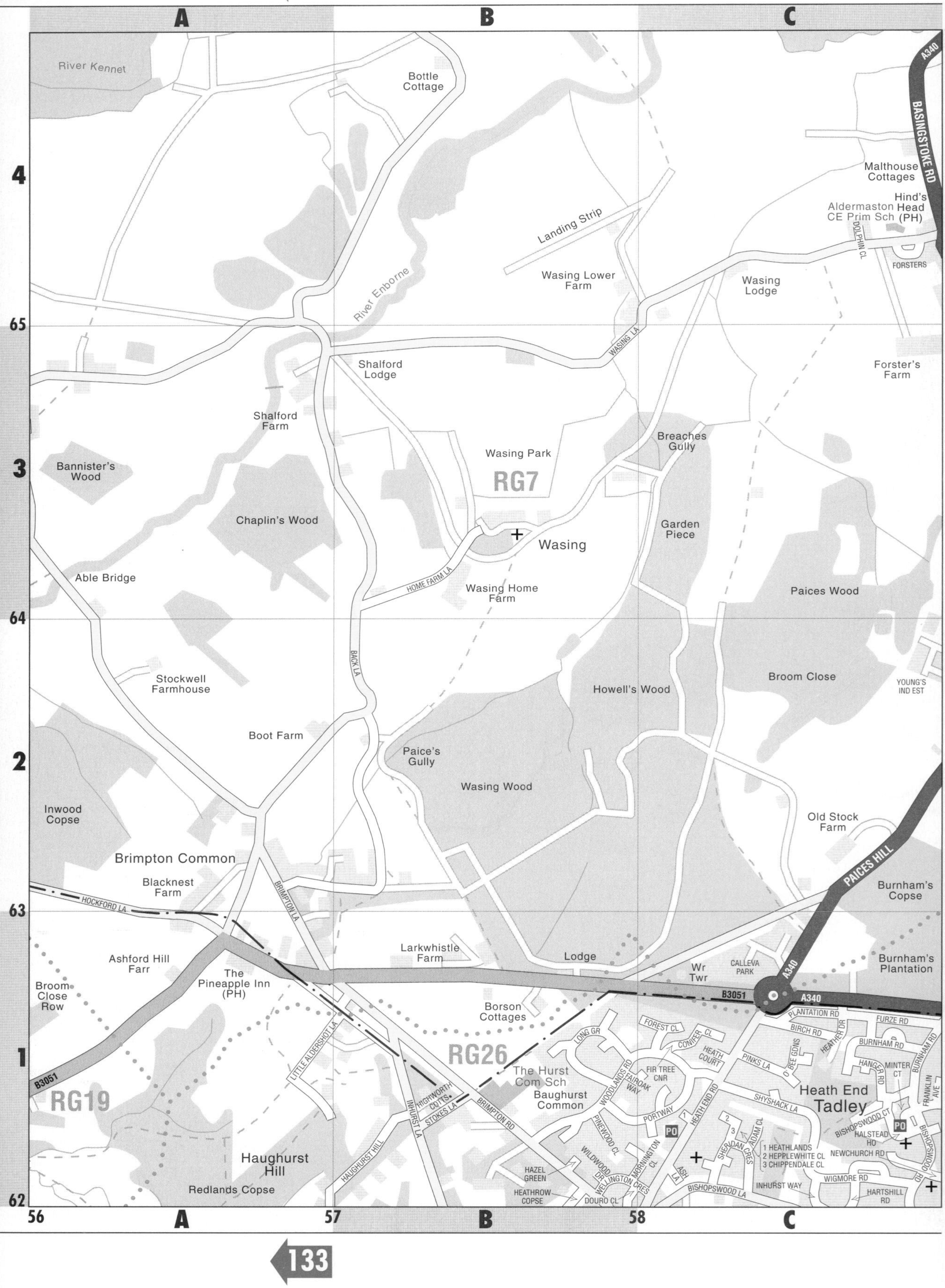
A
B
C
River Kennet
Bottle Cottage
A340
BASINGSTOKE RD
4
Malthouse Cottages
Hind's Head (PH)
Aldermaston CE Prim Sch
DOLPHIN CL
FORSTERS
Landing Strip
Wasing Lower Farm
Wasing Lodge
River Enborne
65
WASING LA
Shalford Lodge
Forster's Farm
Shalford Farm
Breaches Gully
Wasing Park
3
Bannister's Wood
RG7
Chaplin's Wood
Garden Piece
Wasing
Able Bridge
HOME FARM LA
Wasing Home Farm
Paices Wood
64
BACK LA
Stockwell Farmhouse
Howell's Wood
Broom Close
YOUNG'S IND EST
Boot Farm
Paice's Gully
2
Wasing Wood
Inwood Copse
Old Stock Farm
Brimpton Common
PAICES HILL
Blacknest Farm
BRIMPTON LA
Burnham's Copse
HOCKFORD LA
63
Ashford Hill Farr
Larkwhistle Farm
Lodge
Burnham's Plantation
Broom Close Row
The Pineapple Inn (PH)
Wr Twr
CALLEVA PARK
B3051
A340
Borson Cottages
PLANTATION RD
FURZE RD
LITTLE ALDERSHOT LA
RG26
LONG GR
FOREST CL
CONIFER CL
BIRCH RD
HEATHER DR
BURNHAM RD
1
HEATH COURT
BEE GDNS
HANGER RD
MINTER CT
BURNHAM RD
B3051
RG19
The Hurst Com Sch
WOODLANDS RD
FIR TREE CNR
FAIROAK WAY
PINKS LA
Heath End
FRANKLIN AVE
HIGHWORTH COTTS
STOKES LA
BRIMPTON RD
Baughurst Common
HEATH END RD
SHYSHACK LA
Tadley
INHURST LA
PORTWAY
PO
ADAM CL
BISHOPSWOOD CT
HALSTEAD RD
BISHOPSWOOD RD
PO
PINEWOOD CL
SHERIDAN CRES
1 HEATHLANDS
2 HEPPLEWHITE CL
3 CHIPPENDALE CL
NEWCHURCH RD
Haughurst Hill
HAUGHURST HILL
WILDWOOD DR
MORNINGTON CL
HAZEL GREEN
WELLINGTON CRES
ASH LA
INHURST WAY
WIGMORE RD
Redlands Copse
HEATHROW COPSE
DOURO CL
BISHOPSWOOD LA
HARTSHILL RD
62
56
A
57
B
58
C

133

109
136

A
B
C
4
3
2
1
65
64
63
62
59
60
61
A340
Aqua Vitae Copse
Fisherman's Cottage
Sawmill
Upper Lodge Farm
Upper Church Farm
The Old Rectory
FISHERMAN'S LA
Padworth Gully
RECTORY RD
PO
Aldermaston
Church Farm
Springhill Farm
Wrays Farm
Hatch Farm House
THE STREET
CONGREVE CL
CHURCH RD
SPRING LA
Portland House
The Birches
REDLANE HILL
Court Farm
Wr Twr
RAGHILL
Raghill Farm
PAICES HILL
Harbourhill Copse
Black Pightle
Old Warren
RED LA
CHAPEL LA
RG7
WELSHMAN'S RD
Little Heath
VALENTINE WOOD IND EST
Decoy Pond
SOKE RD
Aldermaston Soke
Upper Moor's Gully
THIRD AVE
SECOND AVE
FIRST AVE
RAVENSWING MOBILE HOME PK
Soke Pig Farm
WINKWORTH LA
PH
White House Farm
FALCON FIELDS
ALMSWOOD RD
PELICAN RD
WAKEFORD CT
PRIORS RD
SILCHESTER RD
WAKEFORD CL
KNOLLYS RD
THE BURROWS
SARUM RD
SPENCER CL
CHURCH RD
JUBILEE CL
SPRINGFIELD RD
OAKFIELD RD
CLAPPS GATE RD
ERSKINE CL
Pamber Heath
MEON CL
BRACKENWOOD DR
RG26
Tadley Court
IMPSTONE RD
FRANKLIN AVE
TURBARY GDNS
Liby
ILEX CL
Burnham Copse Jun & Inf Schs
BISHOPS CL
MULFORDS HILL
STACEY'S IND EST
BROADHALF PENNY LA
TADLEY COMMON RD
CHURCH RD
VALLEY WAY
ROMANS GATE
GLENDALE RD
HONEYBOTTOM RD
THE PARADE
Tadley Common
THE GLEN
NEWCHURCH RD
OAK TREE CL
HILLCREST
PAMBER HEATH RD
WESTLYN RD
EASTLYN RD
SEARING WAY
NEWTOWN
SILVERDALE RD
MOUNT PLEASANT
BLAKE'S LA
SYMPSON RD
HEATH RD
BEAVERS CL
HUNTSMOOR RD
SOUTHDOWN RD
STANFIELD
GORSELANDS
ARNEWOOD AVE
BURNEY BIT

136

135
110

A
B
C
4
65
3
64
2
63
1
62
62
63
64
Oval Pond
Ufton Park
Brent's Gully
Cowpond Piece
Four Houses Corner
ISLAND FARM RD
Mast
Wr Twr
Roundoak Piece
CAMP RD
Gibbet Piece
Five Oaken
SILVER LA
LONGMOOR LA
Mowbray's Piece
The Croft
MAY'S LA
PADWORTH RD
Holden's Firs
The Round Oak (PH)
Fifty Acre Piece
COLLEGE PIECE
RECTORY RD
THE CRES
GROVES LEA
BRIARLEA RD
PINE DR
VICTORIA RD
Hundred Acre Piece
Pickling Yard Plantation
STEPHENS FIRS
RAMPTONS LA
Padworth Common
Pond Bay
SWEETZER'S PIECE
LEIGHFIELD
CROFT RD
BIRCHLAND CL
STEPHEN'S CL
STEPHEN'S RD
GLENAPP GRANGE
ST CATHERINE'S HILL
RAVENSWORTH RD
Stockwell's Piece
Chaplin's Copse
BIRCH LA
LANESWOOD
WEST END RD
Burnt Common
Budd's Firs
Turner's Arms (PH)
STANMORE GDNS
LOVES WOOD
DRURY LA
CHAPEL RD
RG7
Summerlug
WELSHMAN'S RD
ROWLAND'S CL
THE BRIDGES
West End Farm
TURK'S LA
Simms's Copse
Fox Hill
Lovegrove's Farm
SIMMS FARM LA
BACK LA
Mortimer West End
Simms Stud Farm
Benyon's Inclosure
West End Brook
Red Lion (PH)
Alders Slade
Nine Acre Copse
Simms's Plantation
Hungry Hill
Pond Farm
Stone Hill
Catthaw Lands Copse
Kiln Yard Copse
WALL LA
SOKE RD
Catthawlands Farm
The Drove
SILCHESTER RD
KINGS RD
Calleva Mus
Silchester CE Prim Sch
SCHOOL LA
CALLEVA ROMAN TOWN (remains of)
Manor Farm
CLAPPERS FARM RD
PAMBER RD
BRAMLEY RD
Silchester Common
Calleva Arms (PH)
Silchester
CHURCH LA
LITTLE LONDON RD
DUKES RIDE
ROMAN FIELD
WHISTLERS LA
Silchester Hall

135

111
138

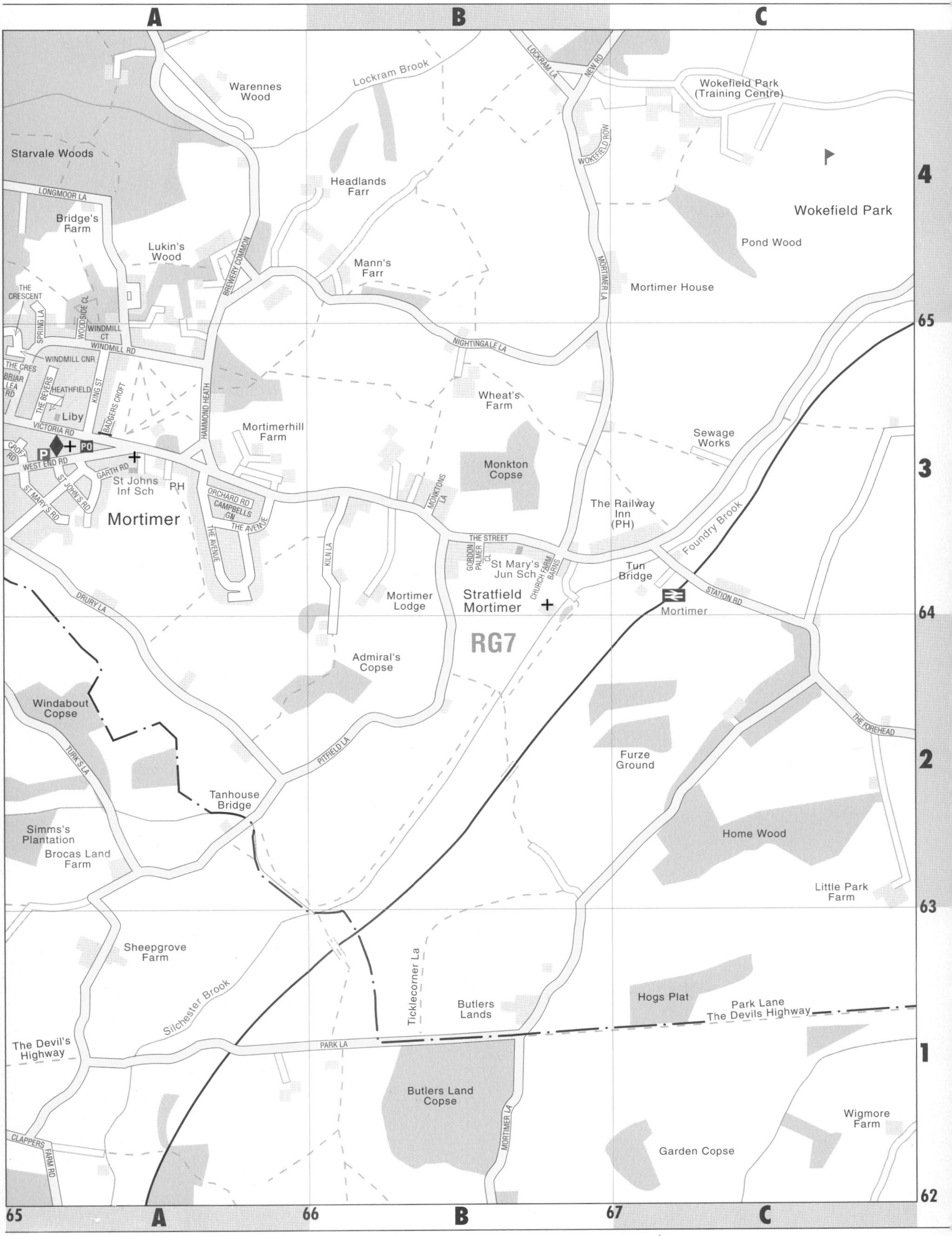
A
B
C
Warennes Wood
Lockram Brook
LOCKRAM LA
NEW RD
Wokefield Park (Training Centre)
Starvale Woods
Headlands Farr
WOKEFIELD ROW
4
LONGMOOR LA
Wokefield Park
Bridge's Farm
Lukin's Wood
BREWERY COMMON
Mann's Farr
Pond Wood
MORTIMER LA
Mortimer House
THE CRESCENT
SPRING LA
WOODSIDE CL
WINDMILL CT
WINDMILL RD
NIGHTINGALE LA
65
WINDMILL CNR
THE CRES
BRIAR LEA RD
THE BEVERS
HEATHFIELD
KING ST
BADGERS CROFT
HAMMOND HEATH
Wheat's Farm
Liby
VICTORIA RD
Mortimerhill Farm
Sewage Works
CROFT RD
PO
WEST END RD
GARTH RD
Monkton Copse
3
St Johns Inf Sch
PH
ST JOHN'S RD
ST MARY'S RD
ORCHARD RD
CAMPBELLS GN
THE AVENUE
MONKTONS LA
The Railway Inn (PH)
Mortimer
Foundry Brook
THE STREET
KILN LA
GORDON PALMER CL
St Mary's Jun Sch
CHURCH FARM BARNS
Tun Bridge
DRURY LA
Mortimer Lodge
Stratfield Mortimer
STATION RD
Mortimer
64
RG7
Admiral's Copse
Windabout Copse
THE FOREHEAD
PITFIELD LA
TURK'S LA
Furze Ground
2
Tanhouse Bridge
Simms's Plantation
Home Wood
Brocas Land Farm
Little Park Farm
63
Sheepgrove Farm
Ticklecorner La
Silchester Brook
Butlers Lands
Hogs Plat
Park Lane
The Devils Highway
The Devil's Highway
PARK LA
1
Butlers Land Copse
Wigmore Farm
CLAPPERS FARM RD
MORTIMER LA
Garden Copse
62
65
66
67

137
112

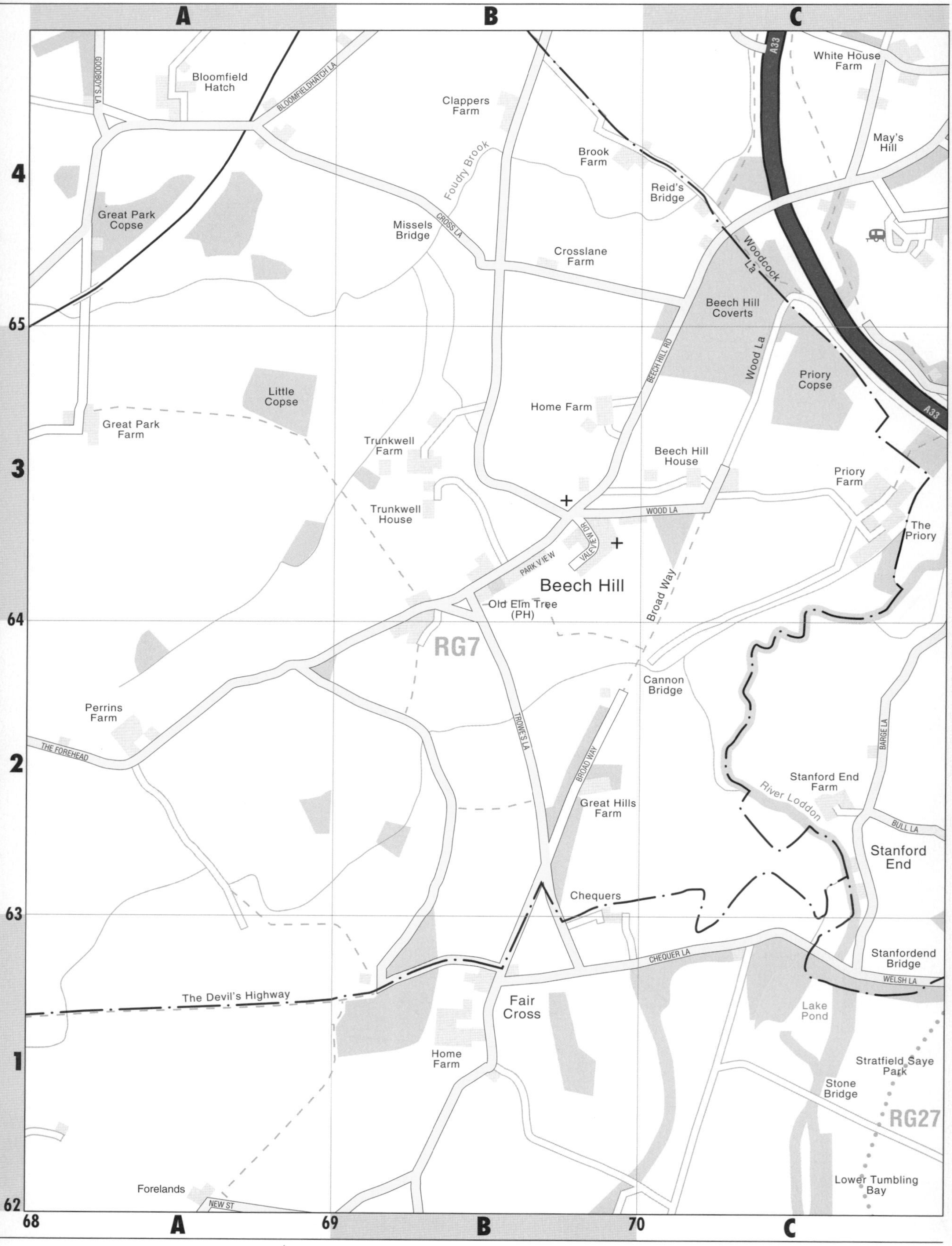
A
B
C
4
65
3
64
2
63
1
62
68
69
70
Goodboy's La
Bloomfield Hatch
Bloomfieldhatch La
Clappers Farm
White House Farm
A33
May's Hill
Brook Farm
Reid's Bridge
Foudry Brook
Great Park Copse
Missels Bridge
Cross La
Crosslane Farm
Woodcock La
Beech Hill Coverts
Wood La
Beech Hill Rd
Little Copse
Priory Copse
Home Farm
Great Park Farm
Trunkwell Farm
Beech Hill House
Priory Farm
Trunkwell House
Wood La
The Priory
Valeview Dr
Park View
Beech Hill
Broad Way
Old Elm Tree (PH)
RG7
Cannon Bridge
Perrins Farm
The Forehead
Trowe's La
Barge La
Broad Way
Stanford End Farm
River Loddon
Great Hills Farm
Bull La
Stanford End
Chequers
Chequer La
Stanfordend Bridge
Welsh La
The Devil's Highway
Fair Cross
Lake Pond
Home Farm
Stratfield Saye Park
Stone Bridge
RG27
Lower Tumbling Bay
Forelands
New St

137

113
140

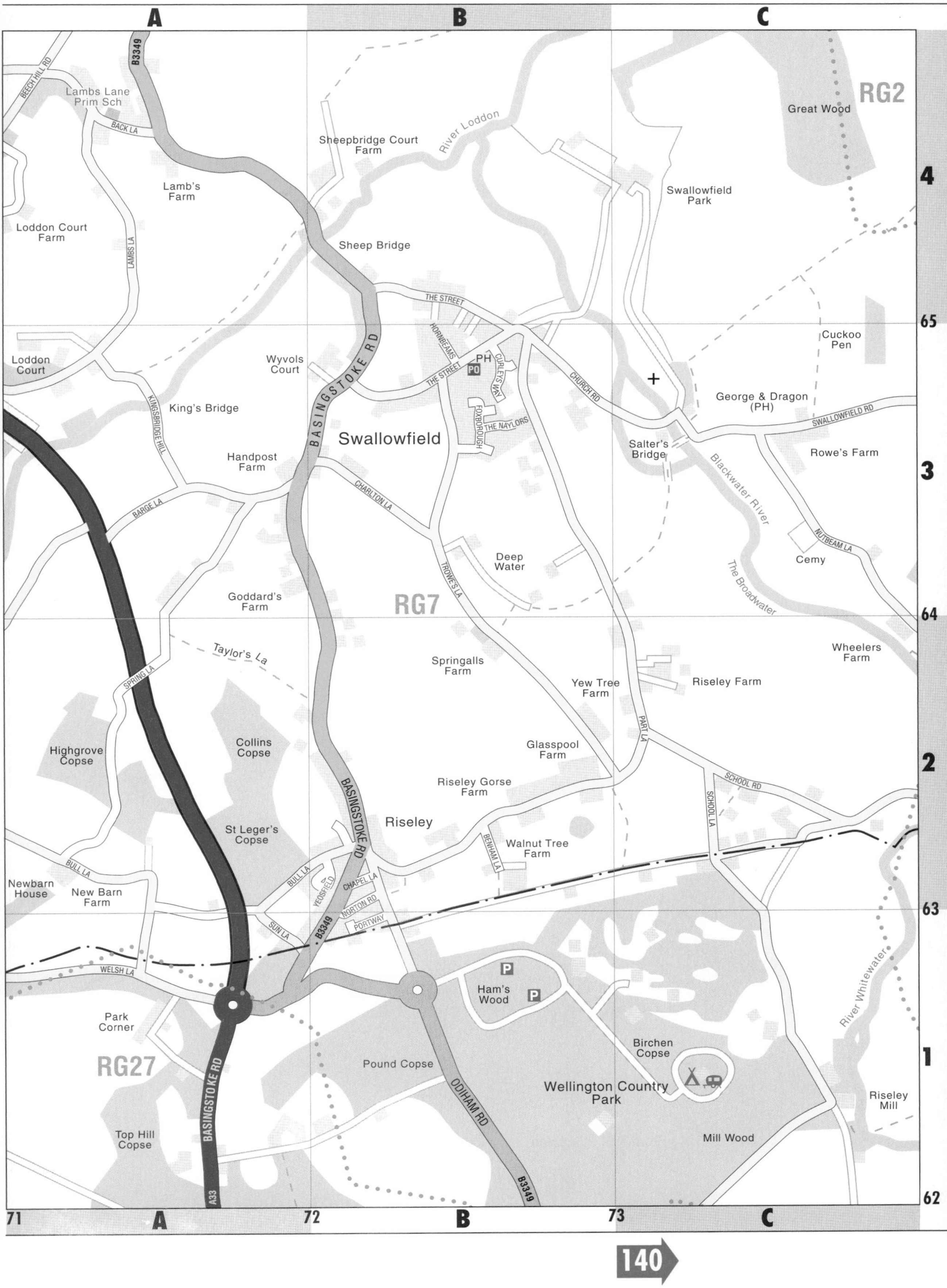
A
B
C
Lambs Lane Prim Sch
BEECH HILL RD
BACK LA
B3349
Lamb's Farm
Loddon Court Farm
LAMBS LA
Sheepbridge Court Farm
River Loddon
Sheep Bridge
Swallowfield Park
Great Wood
RG2
THE STREET
Loddon Court
Wyvols Court
King's Bridge
KINGSBRIDGE HILL
HORNBEAMS
PH
PO
CURLEYS WAY
THE STREET
BASINGSTOKE RD
CHURCH RD
Cuckoo Pen
George & Dragon (PH)
SWALLOWFIELD RD
FOXBOROUGH
THE NAYLORS
Swallowfield
Salter's Bridge
Rowe's Farm
Blackwater River
Handpost Farm
BARGE LA
CHARLTON LA
Deep Water
NUTBEAM LA
Cemy
The Broadwater
Goddard's Farm
TROWE'S LA
RG7
Taylor's La
Springalls Farm
Yew Tree Farm
Riseley Farm
Wheelers Farm
SPRING LA
PART LA
Highgrove Copse
Collins Copse
Glasspool Farm
SCHOOL RD
SCHOOL LA
Riseley Gorse Farm
BASINGSTOKE RD
Riseley
St Leger's Copse
Walnut Tree Farm
BENHAM LA
BULL LA
BULL LA
YEOSFIELD
CHAPEL LA
NORTON RD
PORTWAY
Newbarn House
New Barn Farm
SUN LA
B3349
WELSH LA
P
Ham's Wood
P
Park Corner
River Whitewater
RG27
Birchen Copse
Pound Copse
ODIHAM RD
Wellington Country Park
Riseley Mill
BASINGSTOKE RD
Top Hill Copse
Mill Wood
A33
B3349
4
65
3
64
2
63
1
62
71
72
73
A
B
C

140

139
114

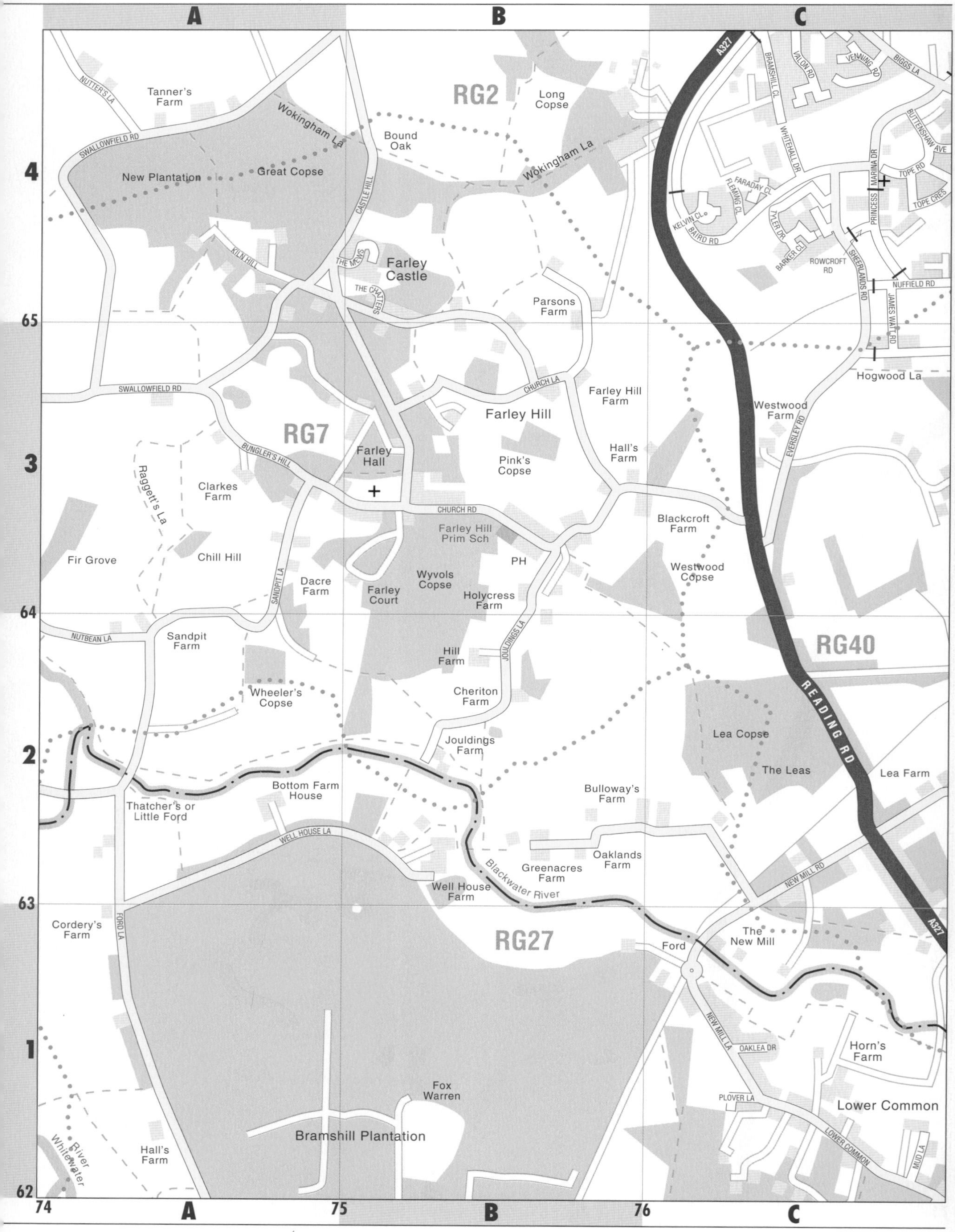
A
B
C
A
B
C
4
65
3
64
2
63
1
62
74
75
76
RG2
RG7
RG40
RG27
Tanner's Farm
NUTTER'S LA
SWALLOWFIELD RD
Wokingham La
New Plantation
Great Copse
Bound Oak
Long Copse
Wokingham La
CASTLE HILL
KILN HILL
THE MEWS
Farley Castle
THE CHATTERS
Parsons Farm
SWALLOWFIELD RD
CHURCH LA
Farley Hill
Farley Hill Farm
BUNGLER'S HILL
Farley Hall
Pink's Copse
Hall's Farm
Raggett's La
Clarkes Farm
CHURCH RD
Farley Hill Prim Sch
Blackcroft Farm
Chill Hill
Fir Grove
PH
Westwood Copse
SANDPIT LA
Dacre Farm
Farley Court
Wyvols Copse
Holycress Farm
JOULDINGS LA
NUTBEAN LA
Sandpit Farm
Hill Farm
Wheeler's Copse
Cheriton Farm
Jouldings Farm
Lea Copse
The Leas
Lea Farm
READING RD
Bottom Farm House
Thatcher's or Little Ford
Bulloway's Farm
WELL HOUSE LA
Greenacres Farm
Oaklands Farm
Blackwater River
Well House Farm
NEW MILL RD
Cordery's Farm
FORD LA
Ford
The New Mill
A327
A327
BRAMSHILL CL
VALON RD
VENNING RD
BIGGS LA
WHITEHALL DR
BUTTENSHAW AVE
TOPE RD
TOPE CRES
MARINA DR
PRINCESS
FARADAY CL
FLEMING CL
KELVIN CL
BAIRD RD
TYLER DR
BARKER CL
ROWCROFT RD
SHEERLANDS RD
NUFFIELD RD
JAMES WATT RD
Hogwood La
Westwood Farm
EVERSLEY RD
NEW MILL LA
OAKLEA DR
Horn's Farm
Fox Warren
PLOVER LA
Lower Common
LOWER COMMON
MUD LA
Bramshill Plantation
River Whitewater
Hall's Farm

139

115
142

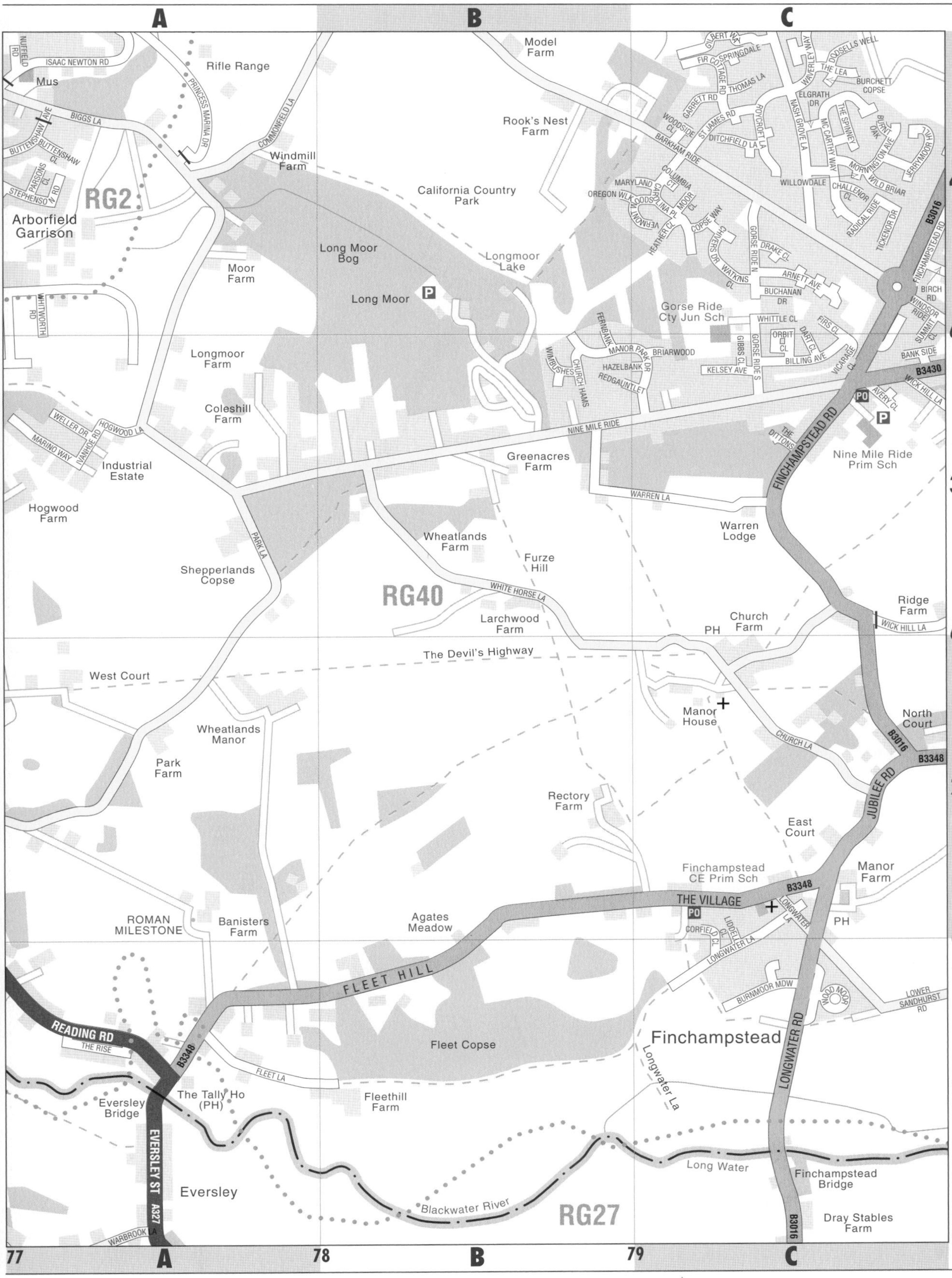
A
B
C
Model Farm
Rifle Range
Mus
ISAAC NEWTON RD
NUFFIELD RD
PRINCESS MARINA DR
COMMONFIELD LA
BIGGS LA
BUTTENSHAW AVE
BUTTENSHAW CL
PARSONS CL
STEPHENSON RD
RG2
Arborfield Garrison
Windmill Farm
Rook's Nest Farm
California Country Park
Long Moor Bog
Longmoor Lake
Moor Farm
Long Moor
P
WHITWORTH RD
GILBERT WAY
FIR COTTAGE RD
SPRINGDALE
THOMAS LA
GARRETT RD
WOODSIDE CL
ST JAMES RD
ROYCROFT LA
DITCHFIELD LA
BARKHAM RIDE
WAVERLEY WAY
DODSELLS WELL
THE LEA
BURCHETT COPSE
ELGRATH DR
NASH GROVE LA
MC CARTHY WAY
THE SPINNEY
BURNT OAK
MORNINGTON AVE
JERRYMOOR HILL
WILLOWDALE
CHALLENOR CL
WILD BRIAR
RADICAL RIDE
TICKENOR DR
MARYLAND
COLUMBIA CT
OREGON WLK
CAROLINA PL
MOOR CL
WOODS
VERMONT
COPSE WAY
HEATHER CL
CHIVERS DR
GORSE RIDE N
DRAKE CL
WATKINS CL
ARNETT AVE
BUCHANAN DR
B3016
FINCHAMPSTEAD RD
BIRCH RD
WINDSOR RIDE
SUMMIT CL
Gorse Ride Cty Jun Sch
WHITTLE CL
ORBIT CL
DART CL
FIRS CL
FERNBANK
MANOR PARK DR
BRIARWOOD
GIBBS CL
GORSE RIDE S
BILLING AVE
VICARAGE CL
BANK SIDE
B3430
WICK HILL LA
WIMBUSHES
CHURCH HAMS
HAZELBANK
REDGAUNTLET
KELSEY AVE
AVERY CL
PO
Longmoor Farm
Coleshill Farm
WELLER DR
HOGWOOD LA
MARINO WAY
IVANHOE RD
Industrial Estate
NINE MILE RIDE
Greenacres Farm
THE DITTONS
Nine Mile Ride Prim Sch
Hogwood Farm
WARREN LA
Warren Lodge
PARK LA
Shepperlands Copse
Wheatlands Farm
Furze Hill
RG40
WHITE HORSE LA
Larchwood Farm
Ridge Farm
Church Farm
PH
The Devil's Highway
West Court
Manor House
North Court
CHURCH LA
Wheatlands Manor
Park Farm
B3348
JUBILEE RD
Rectory Farm
East Court
Manor Farm
Finchampstead CE Prim Sch
THE VILLAGE
ROMAN MILESTONE
Banisters Farm
Agates Meadow
CORFIELD CL
LIDDELL CL
LONGWATER LA
FLEET HILL
BURNMOOR MDW
WOOD MOOR
LOWER SANDHURST RD
READING RD
THE RISE
Fleet Copse
Finchampstead
LONGWATER RD
FLEET LA
The Tally Ho (PH)
Eversley Bridge
Fleethill Farm
Longwater La
EVERSLEY ST
A327
Long Water
Finchampstead Bridge
Eversley
Blackwater River
RG27
Dray Stables Farm
WARBROOK LA
4
65
3
64
2
63
1
62
77
78
79

142

141 116

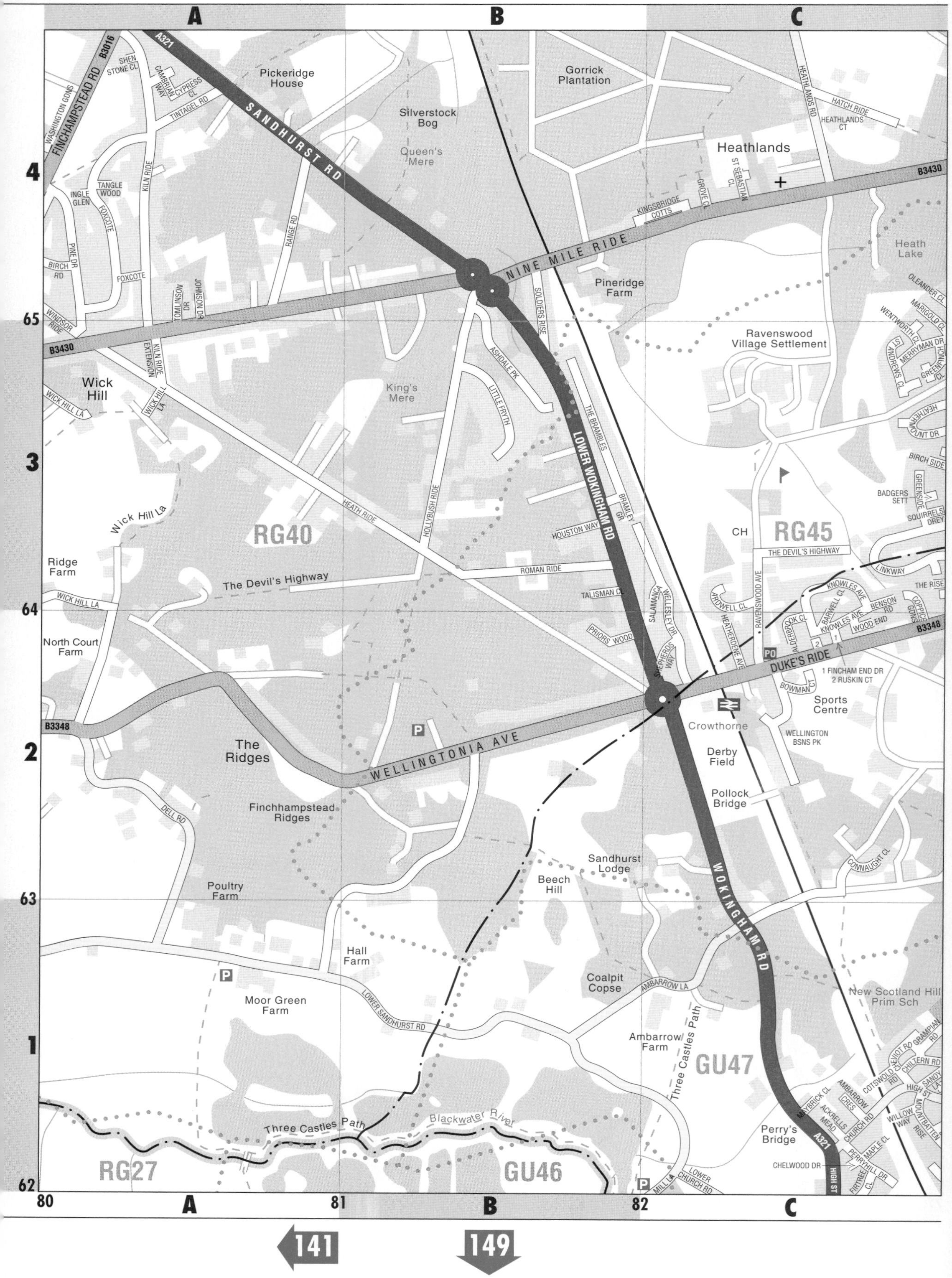


141 149

117
144

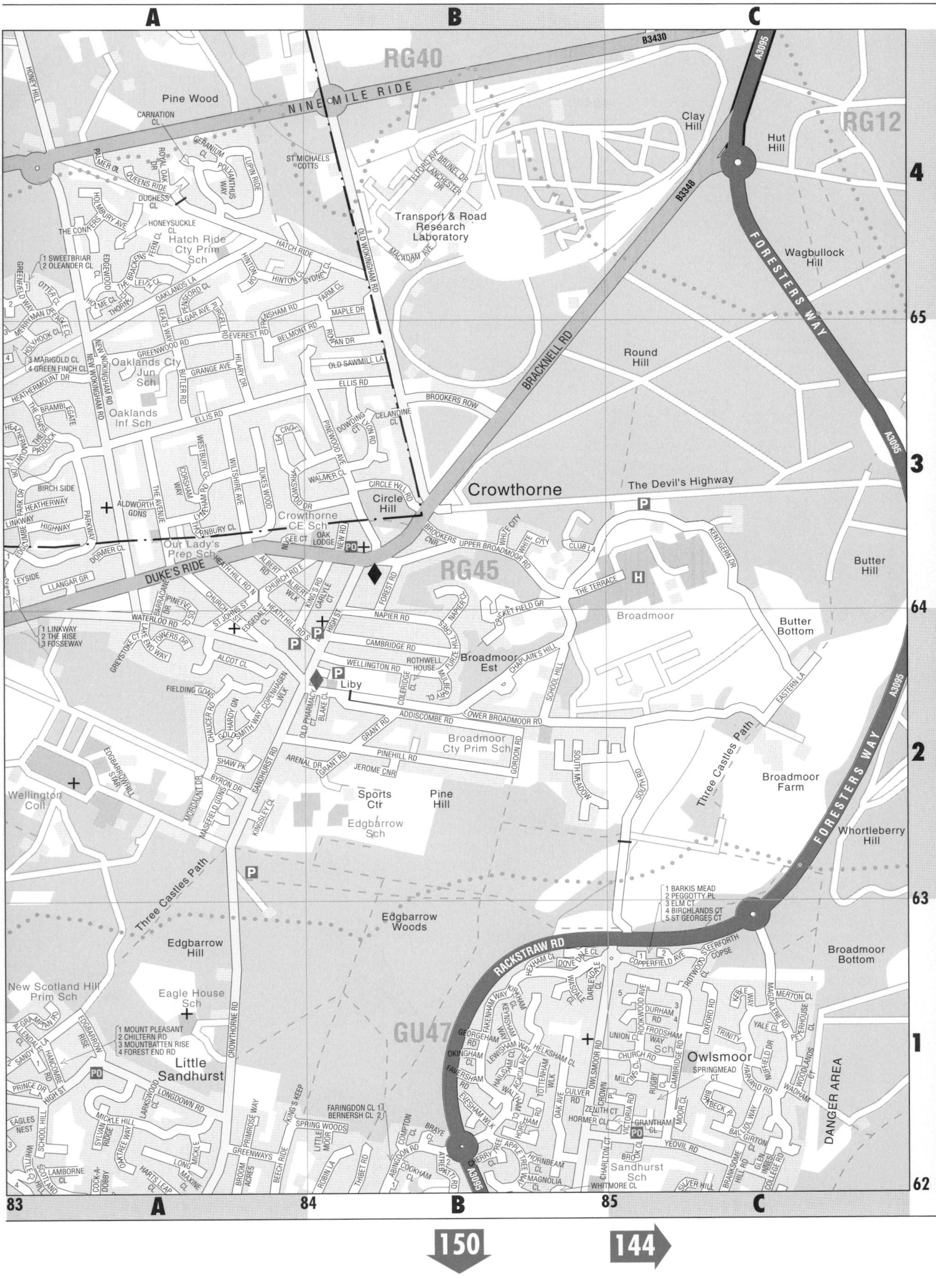


150
144

143
118

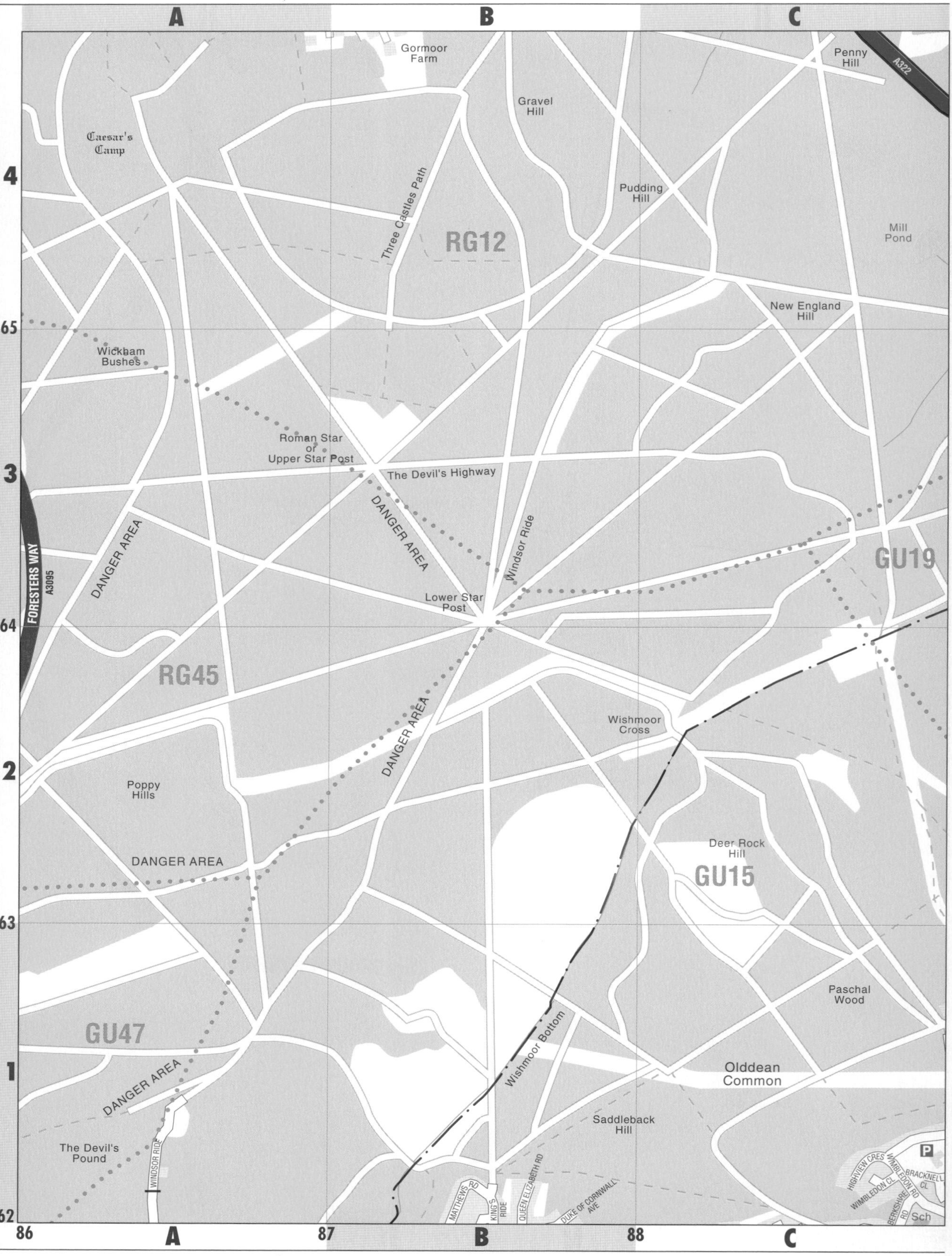


143
151

119
146

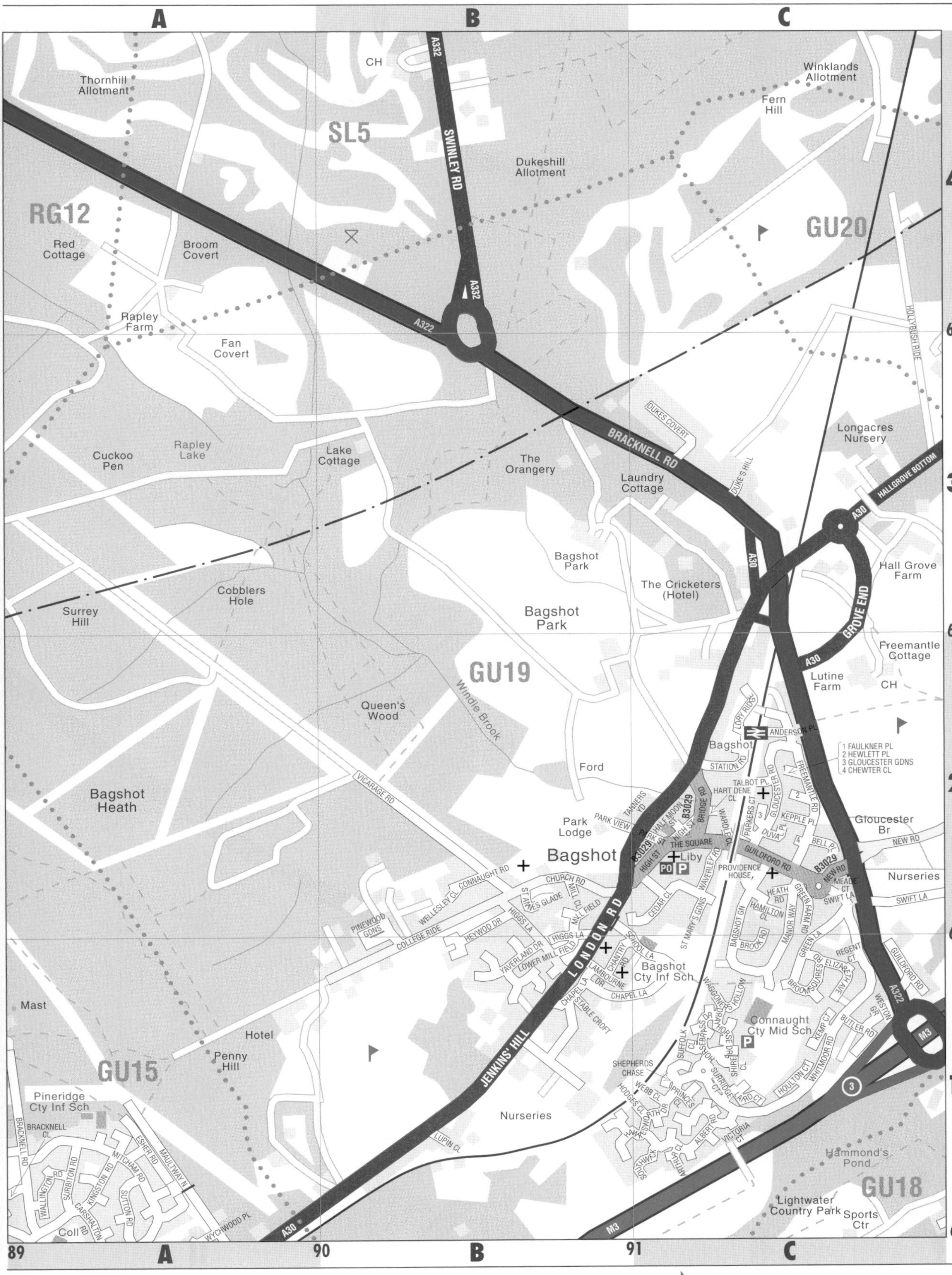


152
146

145
120

145
153

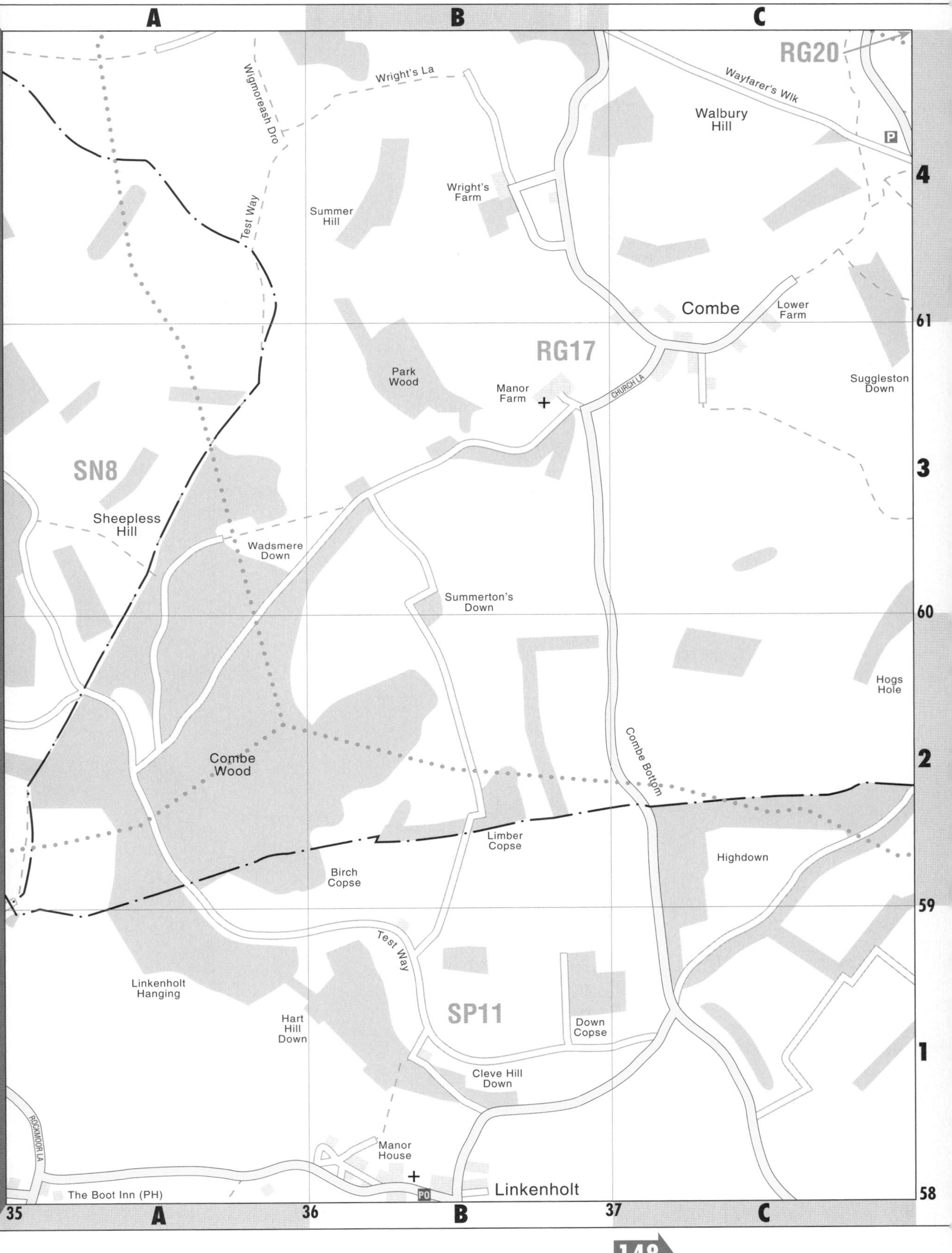
A
B
C
RG20
Wayfarer's Wlk
Walbury Hill
Wright's La
Wigmoreash Dro
Test Way
Summer Hill
Wright's Farm
4
Combe
Lower Farm
61
RG17
Park Wood
Manor Farm
CHURCH LA
Suggleston Down
SN8
3
Sheepless Hill
Wadsmere Down
Summerton's Down
60
Hogs Hole
Combe Bottom
Combe Wood
2
Limber Copse
Highdown
Birch Copse
59
Test Way
Linkenholt Hanging
SP11
Hart Hill Down
Down Copse
1
Cleve Hill Down
ROCKMOOR LA
Manor House
Linkenholt
The Boot Inn (PH)
PO
58
35
36
37
A
B
C

147
128

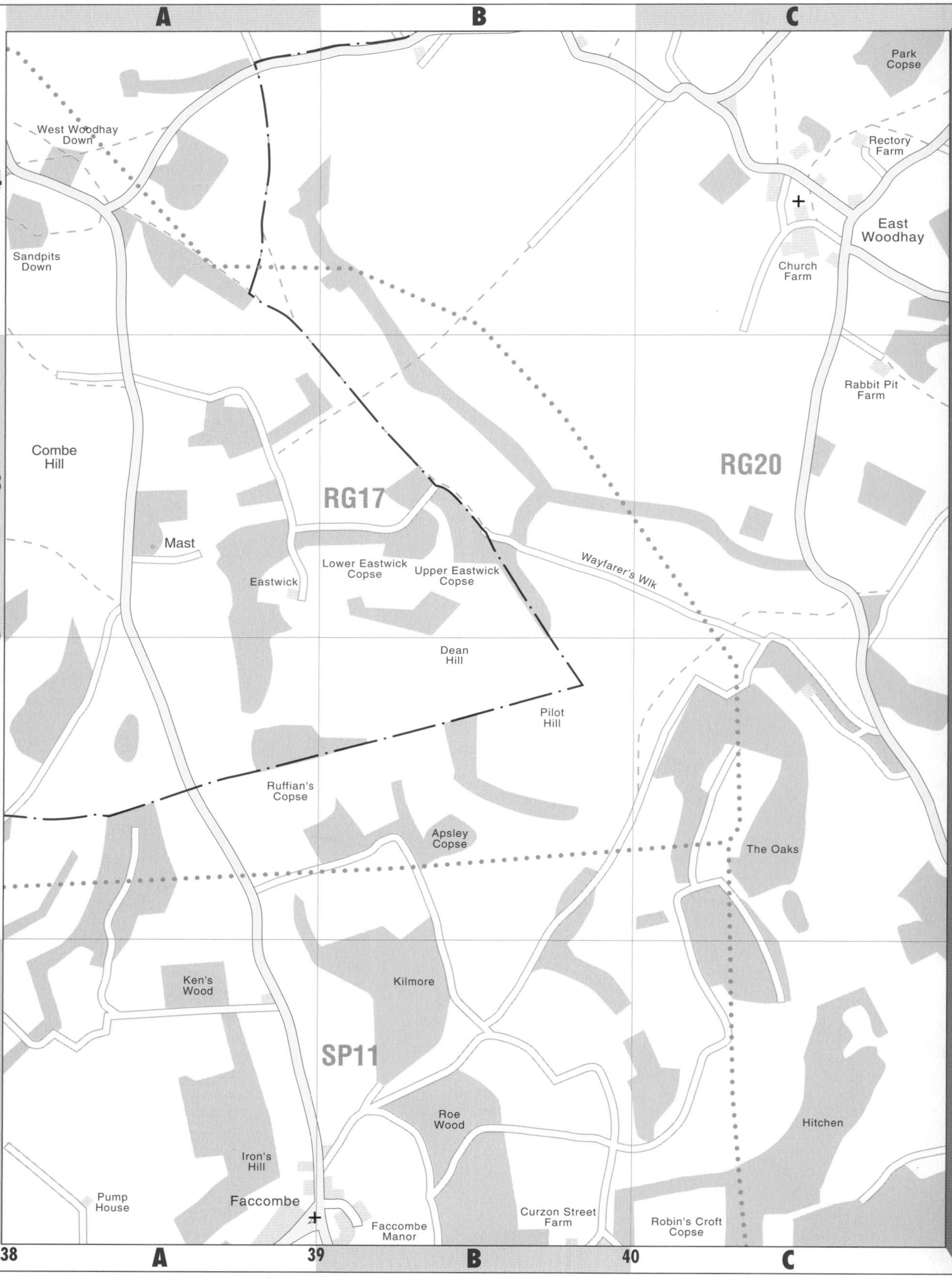
A
B
C
4
61
3
60
2
59
1
58
38
39
40
West Woodhay Down
Sandpits Down
Park Copse
Rectory Farm
East Woodhay
Church Farm
Rabbit Pit Farm
Combe Hill
RG17
RG20
Mast
Eastwick
Lower Eastwick Copse
Upper Eastwick Copse
Wayfarer's Wlk
Dean Hill
Pilot Hill
Ruffian's Copse
Apsley Copse
The Oaks
Ken's Wood
Kilmore
SP11
Roe Wood
Hitchen
Iron's Hill
Pump House
Faccombe
Faccombe Manor
Curzon Street Farm
Robin's Croft Copse

147

142
150


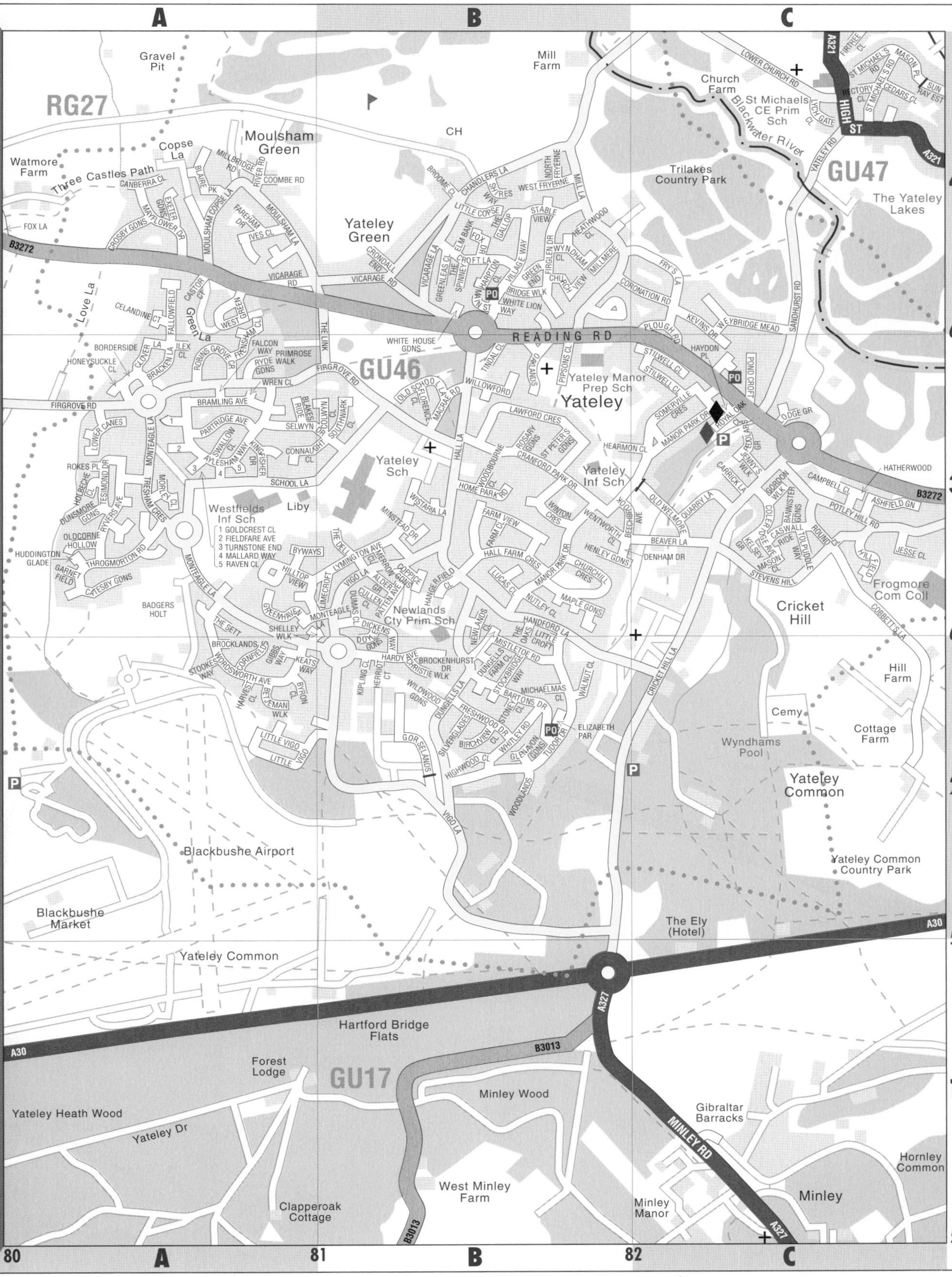
A
B
C
4
3
2
1
61
60
59
58
80
81
82
RG27
GU46
GU47
GU17
Gravel Pit
Mill Farm
Church Farm
St Michaels CE Prim Sch
Blackwater River
Trilakes Country Park
The Yateley Lakes
Moulsham Green
Copse La
Watmore Farm
Three Castles Path
Yateley Green
CH
READING RD
B3272
A321
HIGH ST
Yateley
Yateley Manor Prep Sch
Yateley Inf Sch
Yateley Sch
Westfields Inf Sch
1 GOLDCREST CL
2 FIELDFARE AVE
3 TURNSTONE END
4 MALLARD WAY
5 RAVEN CL
Liby
Newlands Cty Prim Sch
Frogmore Com Coll
Cricket Hill
Hill Farm
Cemy
Cottage Farm
Wyndhams Pool
Yateley Common
Yateley Common Country Park
Blackbushe Airport
Blackbushe Market
The Ely (Hotel)
A30
A327
B3013
Hartford Bridge Flats
Forest Lodge
Minley Wood
Yateley Heath Wood
Yateley Dr
Gibraltar Barracks
MINLEY RD
Hornley Common
Minley
West Minley Farm
Clapperoak Cottage
Minley Manor
Badgers Holt
Love La
Green La
FIRGROVE RD
MONTEAGLE LA
VIGO LA
CRICKET HILL LA
HALL LA
THE LINK
VICARAGE RD
SANDHURST RD
LOWER CHURCH RD
YATELEY RD
CHANDLERS LA
STEVENS HILL
COBBETT'S LA
BEAVER LA
SCHOOL LA
FOX LA

150

149
143

B4
1 MULBERRY CL
2 MAY CL
3 SHRIVENHAM CL
4 CENTURION CL
5 CHAFFINCH CL
6 TARBAT CT
7 ROCKFIELD WAY
8 BALINTORE CT

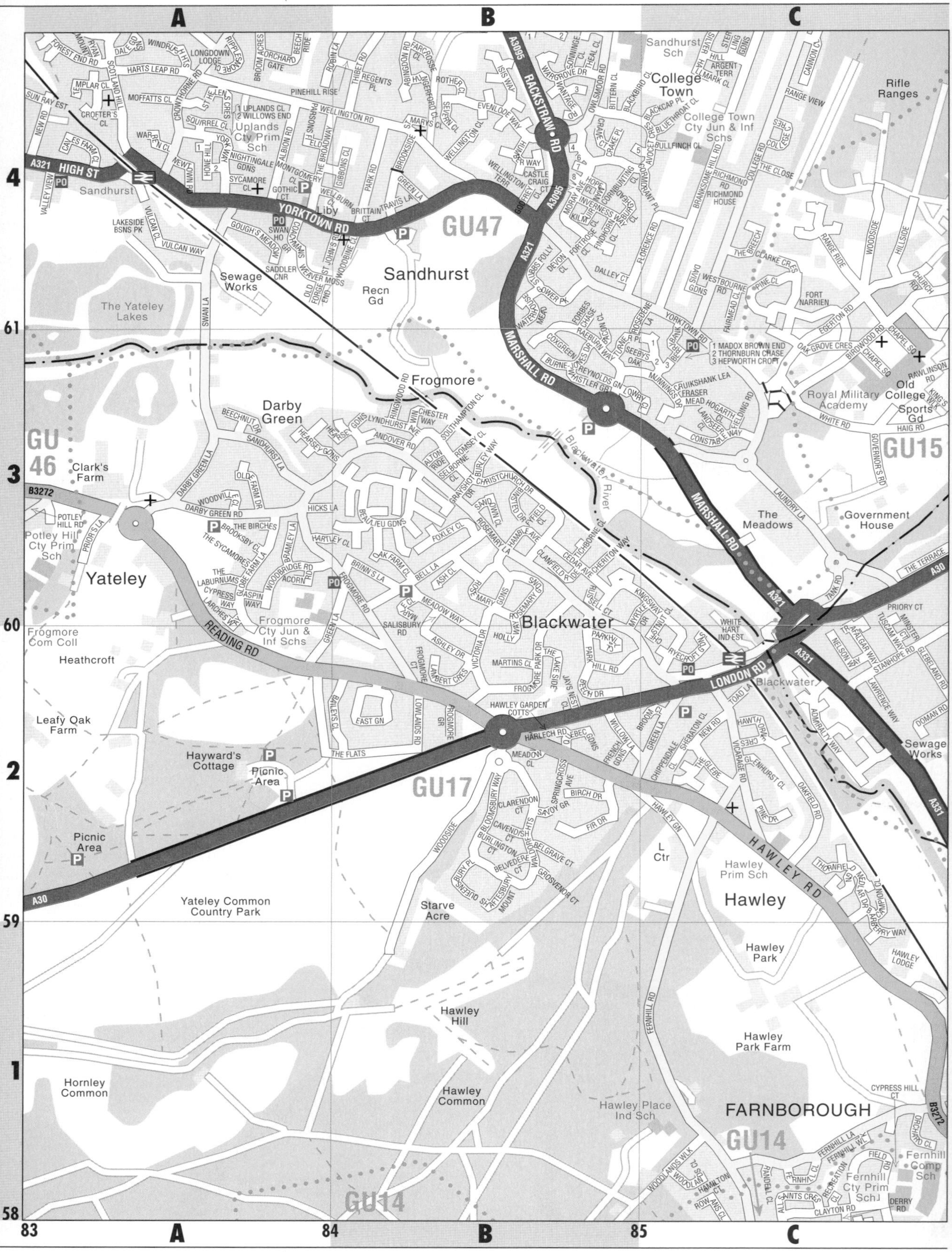


149

144
152

A B C

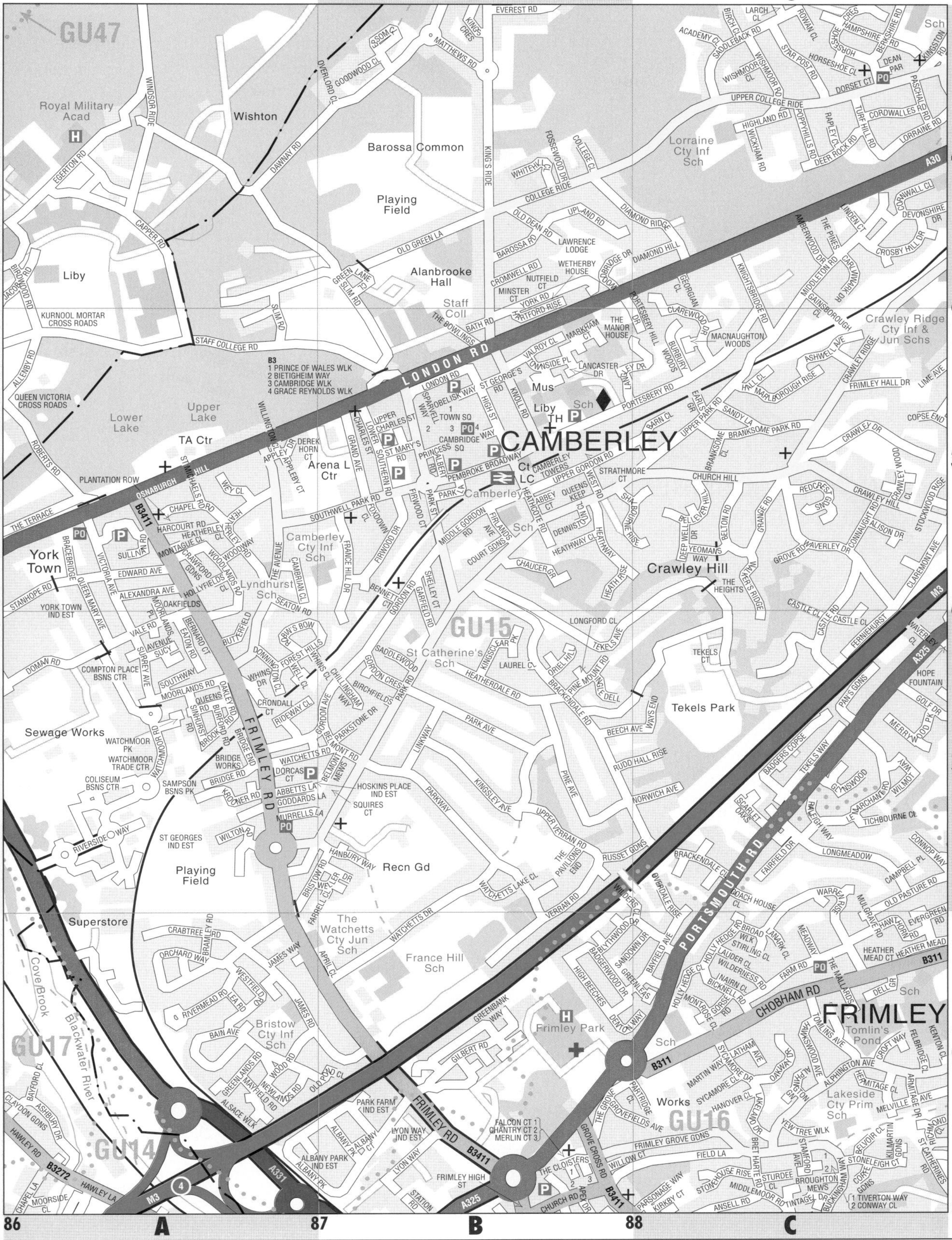


86 A 87 B 88 C

152

151
145

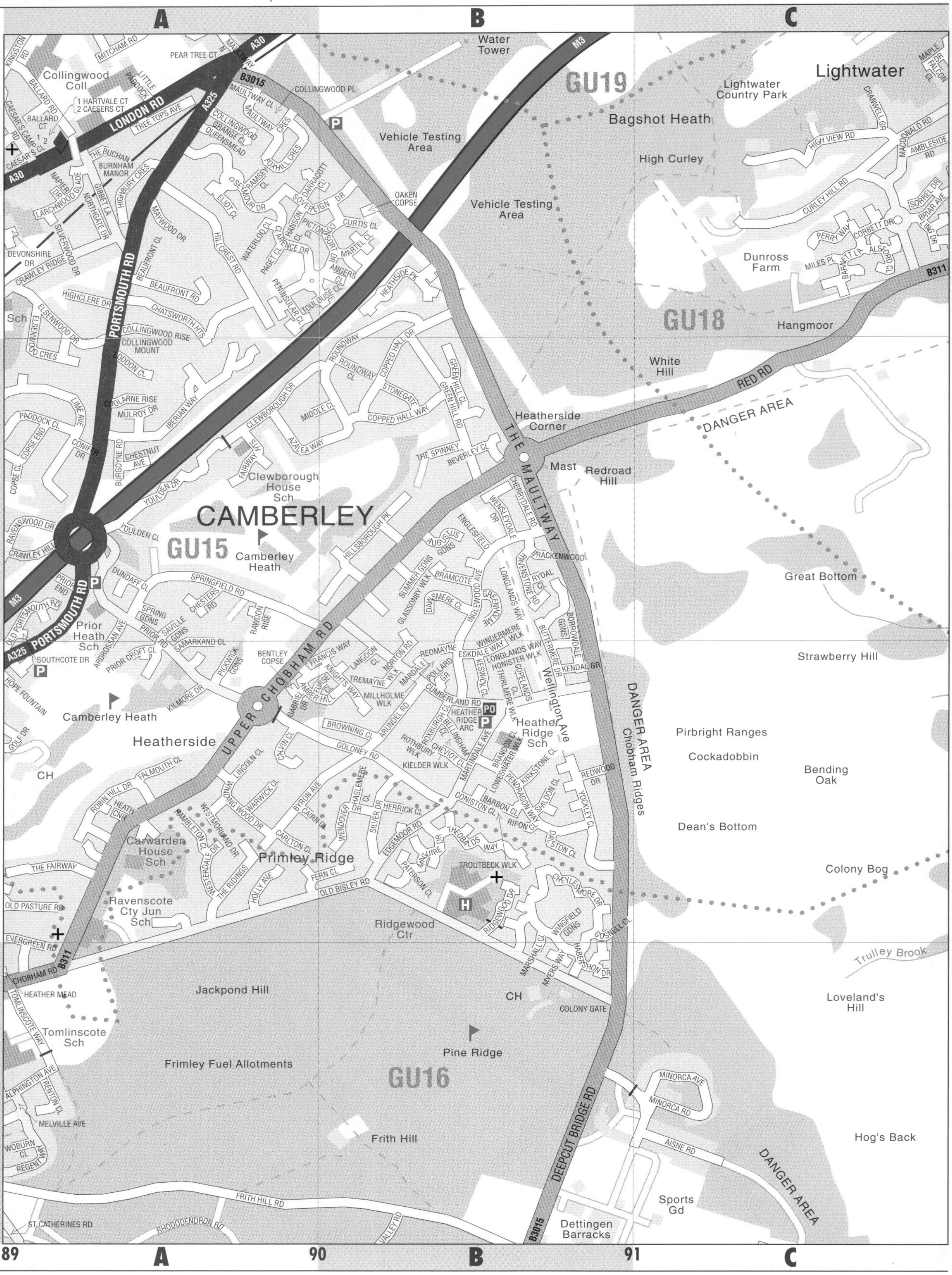
A
B
C
Lightwater
Lightwater Country Park
Bagshot Heath
High Curley
GU19
Water Tower
Vehicle Testing Area
Vehicle Testing Area
Collingwood Coll
Dunross Farm
GU18
Hangmoor
White Hill
RED RD
DANGER AREA
Heatherside Corner
THE MAULTWAY
Mast
Redroad Hill
Clewborough House Sch
CAMBERLEY
GU15
Camberley Heath
Great Bottom
Prior Heath Sch
Strawberry Hill
Camberley Heath
Heatherside
UPPER CHOBHAM RD
Heather Ridge Sch
Wellington Ave
DANGER AREA
Chobham Ridges
Pirbright Ranges
Cockadobbin
Bending Oak
Dean's Bottom
Carwarden House Sch
Frimley Ridge
Colony Bog
Ravenscote Cty Jun Sch
Ridgewood Ctr
Trulley Brook
Jackpond Hill
Loveland's Hill
Tomlinscote Sch
Pine Ridge
Frimley Fuel Allotments
GU16
Frith Hill
DEEPCUT BRIDGE RD
Hog's Back
Sports Gd
Dettingen Barracks
LONDON RD
PORTSMOUTH RD
CHOBHAM RD
OLD BISLEY RD
FRITH HILL RD
MINORCA AVE
MINORCA RD
AISNE RD
COLONY GATE
A30
A325
M3
B3015
B311
4
3
2
1
61
60
59
58
89
90
91

151

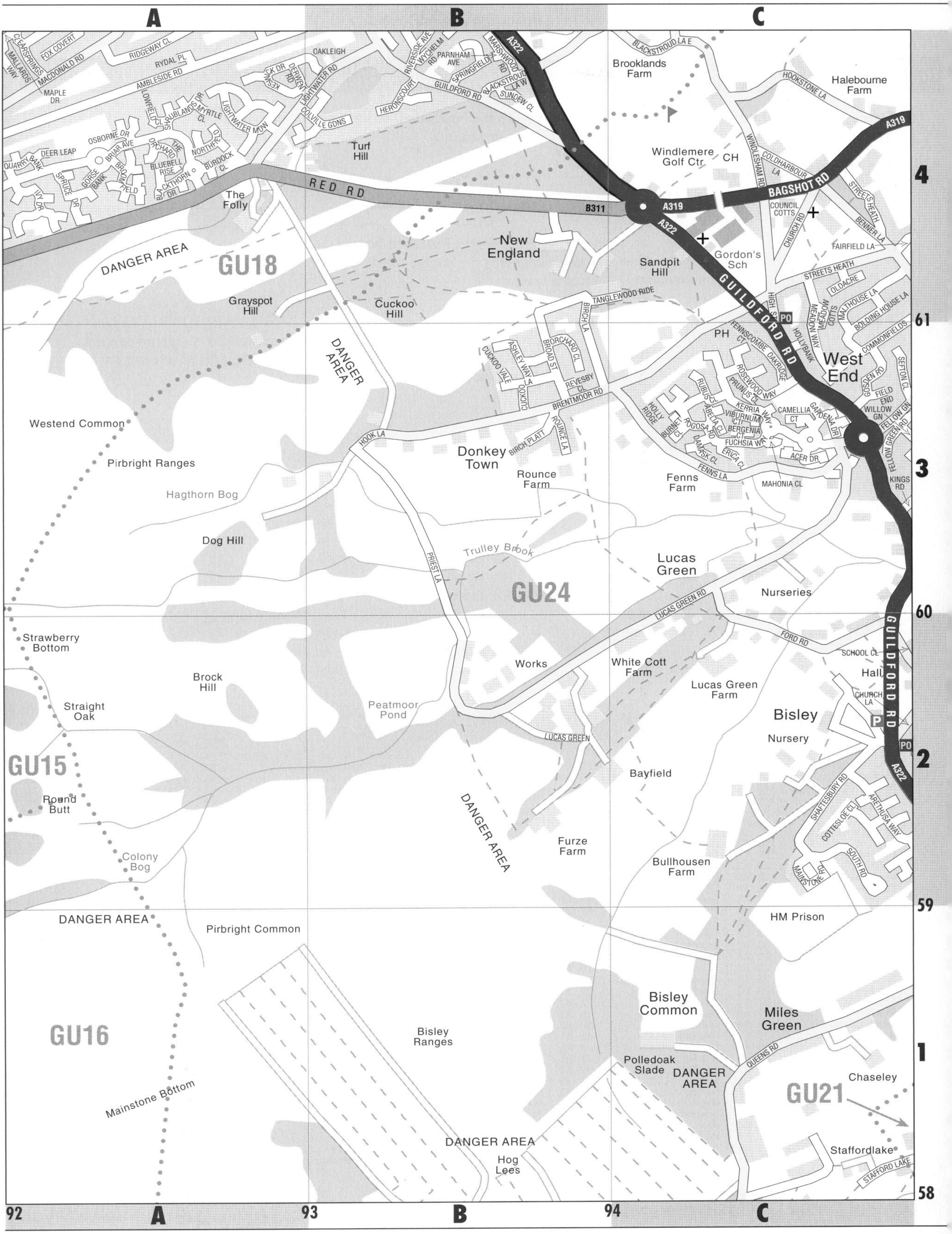
A
B
C
4
3
2
1
61
60
59
58
92
93
94
GU18
GU24
GU15
GU16
GU21
RED RD
GUILDFORD RD
BAGSHOT RD
A322
A319
B311
The Folly
Turf Hill
New England
Brooklands Farm
Halebourne Farm
Windlemere Golf Ctr
CH
Sandpit Hill
Gordon's Sch
Grayspot Hill
Cuckoo Hill
DANGER AREA
West End
PH
PO
Westend Common
Pirbright Ranges
Hagthorn Bog
Donkey Town
Rounce Farm
Fenns Farm
Dog Hill
Trulley Brook
Lucas Green
Nurseries
Strawberry Bottom
Works
White Cott Farm
Lucas Green Farm
Brock Hill
Straight Oak
Peatmoor Pond
Bisley
Hall
Nursery
Round Butt
Bayfield
Colony Bog
Furze Farm
Bullhousen Farm
HM Prison
Pirbright Common
Bisley Common
Miles Green
Bisley Ranges
Polledoak Slade
Chaseley
Mainstone Bottom
Staffordlake
Hog Lees
HOOK LA
PRIEST LA
LUCAS GREEN RD
LUCAS GREEN
FORD RD
SCHOOL CL
CHURCH LA
QUEENS RD
STAFFORD LAKE
BRENTMOOR RD
TANGLEWOOD RIDE
BIRCH LA
FENNS LA
MAHONIA CL
ACER DR
HOOKSTONE LA
COLDHARBOUR LA
WINDLESHAM RD
CHURCH RD
COUNCIL COTTS
STREETS HEATH
FAIRFIELD LA
BENNER LA
HIGH ST
HOLLYBANK
MEADOW WAY
OLDACRE
MALTHOUSE LA
BOLDING HOUSE LA
COMMONFIELDS
SEFTON CL
GOSDEN RD
FIELD END
WILLOW GN
FELLOW GN
KINGS RD
SHAFTESBURY RD
ARETHUSA WAY
COTTESLOE CL
SOUTH RD
MAINSTONE RD
BLACKSTROUD LA E
BLACKSTROUD LA W
SUNDEW CL
GUILDFORD RD
HERONSCOURT
COLVILLE GDNS
LIGHTWATER RD
OAKLEIGH
RIDGEWAY CL
RYDAL PL
AMBLESIDE RD
MACDONALD RD
FOX COVERT
CLEARSPRINGS
MALLARDS WAY
MAPLE DR
DEER LEAP
OSBORNE DR
BRIAR AVE
QUARRY BANK
IVY DR
SPRUCE DR
GORSE BANK
BLUEBELL RISE
HAWTHORN DR
BURDOCK CL
NORTHFIELD
LIGHTWATER MDW
MYRTLE CL
LOWFIELD CL
ORCHARD
CUCKOO VALE
ASHLEY WAY
BROAD ST
ORCHARD CL
REVESBY CL
ROUNCE LA
BIRCH PLATT
CUCKOO LA
HOLLY RIDGE
BURNET CL
RUBUS CL
ROGOSA RD
DAMASK CL
ERICA CL
FUCHSIA WAY
BERGENIA CT
VIBURNUM CT
KERRIA WAY
PRUNUS CL
ROSEWOOD WAY
FENNSCOMBE CT
OAKRIDGE
CAMELLIA CT
GARDENIA DR
MARSHWOOD RD
SPRINGFIELD
PARNHAM AVE
WYCHELM RD
RIVERSIDE AVE
DERWENT RD
KESWICK DR

# Index

**Street names are listed alphabetically and show the locality, the Postcode District, the page number and a reference to the square in which the name falls on the map page**

**Garden Mews** **8** Reading RG30..............**85** B3

**Full street name**
This may have been abbreviated on the map

**Location number**
If present, this indicates the street's position on a congested area of the map instead of the name

**Town, village or locality** in which the street falls.

**Postcode District** for the street name

**Page number** of the map on which the street name appears

**Grid square** in which the centre of the street falls

**Schools, hospitals,sports centres, railway stations, shopping centres, industrial estates, public amenities and otherplaces of interest are also listed. These are highlighted in** magenta

## Abbreviations used in the index

| | |
|---|---|
| App | **Approach** |
| Arc | **Arcade** |
| Ave | **Avenue** |
| Bvd | **Boulevard** |
| Bldgs | **Buildings** |
| Bsns Pk | **Business Park** |
| Bsns Ctr | **Business Centre** |
| Bglws | **Bungalows** |
| Cswy | **Causeway** |
| Ctr | **Centre** |
| Cir | **Circus** |
| Cl | **Close** |
| Comm | **Common** |
| Cnr | **Corner** |
| Cotts | **Cottages** |
| Ct | **Court** |
| Ctyd | **Courtyard** |
| Cres | **Crescent** |
| Dr | **Drive** |
| Dro | **Drove** |
| E | **East** |
| Emb | **Embankment** |
| Espl | **Esplanade** |
| Est | **Estate** |
| Gdns | **Gardens** |
| Gn | **Green** |
| Gr | **Grove** |
| Hts | **Heights** |
| Ind Est | **Industrial Estate** |
| Intc | **Interchange** |
| Junc | **Junction** |
| La | **Lane** |
| N | **North** |
| Orch | **Orchard** |
| Par | **Parade** |
| Pk | **Park** |
| Pas | **Passage** |
| Pl | **Place** |
| Prec | **Precinct** |
| Prom | **Promenade** |
| Ret Pk | **Retail Park** |
| Rd | **Road** |
| Rdbt | **Roundabout** |
| S | **South** |
| Sq | **Square** |
| Strs | **Stairs** |
| Stps | **Steps** |
| St | **Street, Saint** |
| Terr | **Terrace** |
| Trad | **Trading Est** |
| Wlk | **Walk** |
| W | **West** |
| Yd | **Yard** |

## Town and village index

Aldermaston.........135 A3
Aldworth.............32 A2
Arborfield...........114 B1
Ascot ..............120 A1
Ashampstead .........54 A3
Ashford..............97 A3
Aston Tirrold..........12 C4
Bagshot ............145 B1
Ball Hill.............129 C1
Barkham............115 A1
Beech Hill...........138 A1
Beedon...............51 B4
Beenham ...........108 C3
Binfield...............90 A1
Bisham ...............18 A1
Bisley ..............153 C2
Blackwater ..........150 A2
Blewbury .............12 A3
Bourne End.............3 A1
Boxford...............76 A1
Bracknell ...........118 B2
Bradfield..............82 A1
Brands Hill ............69 A4
Brightwalton...........28 B1
Brimpton ...........133 C3
Bucklebury ...........80 A1
Burchett's Green ......38 A3
Burghfield Common ...110 B1
Burnham..............21 A1
Camberley ..........151 A1
Caversham ...........59 A1
Chaddleworth.........49 A2
Charlton ............125 B4
Charvil ..............61 A1
Chertsey............124 A1
Chieveley ............51 A1
Chilton ..............10 B4
Chilton Foliat .........73 A4
Cholsey...............14 A4
Cold Ash............106 A4
Colnbrook............69 A3
Combe .............147 C3
Compton.............31 B2
Cookham ............20 A3
Crowthorne .........143 A4
Datchet...............68 A3
Dorney ..............41 A2
Earley ...............87 A1
East Bedfont..........98 A3
East Garston..........47 A2
East Ilsley ............30 A3
Egham ..............96 A1
Englefield Green.......95 A1
Eton .................67 B4
Farnborough (Berks) ...28 A4
Farnborough (Hants) . .150 C1
Farnham Common .....22 A1
Fawley (Berks)........27 B2
Fawley (Bucks).........15 A3
Feltham .............98 B2
Finchampstead.......141 A1
Flackwell Heath ........3 A3
Frimley .............151 B1
Froxfield.............99 A1
Fulmer ..............23 A3
Goring ..............34 A3
Great Shefford ........48 A1
Greenham...........131 B4
Ham ...............126 A2
Hambleden...........16 A4
Hampstead Norreys ....52 C3
Hamstead Marshall....129 A4
Harlington ...........71 A1
Harmondsworth .......70 A2
Hatton ..............71 B1
Headley ............132 C1
Henley-on-T..........15 A2
Hermitage ...........79 A1
Holyport ............65 A4
Horton ..............69 A1
Hungerford..........100 A2
Hungerford Newtown...74 A2
Hurley...............17 A1
Hurst ...............88 B2
Inkpen .............127 B2
Iver.................44 A3
Iver Heath............23 B1
Kintbury ............102 A1
Knowl Hill............37 A3
Laleham ............124 A4
Lambourn............25 A1
Leckhampstead .......49 C3
Letcombe Bassett.......6 B4
Lightwater ..........152 C4
Linkenholt ..........147 A1
Little Marlow ..........2 A2
Littleton ............125 A2
Littlewick Green.......38 A2
Lower Basildon........34 A1
Lower Halliford.......125 A1
Lyne ...............123 A1
Maidenhead ..........39 A1
Mapledurham .........57 C3
Marlow ................1 A1
Marlow Bottom..........1 A3
Medmenham .........17 A2
Mortimer ...........137 A3
Moulsford............13 B2
Newbury............104 B1
Newell Green .........92 A3
Newtown ...........131 C1
North Ascot .........119 C4
Oakley Green .........66 A1
Old Windsor ..........95 A3
Padworth ...........109 B2
Pangbourne ..........56 A1
Peasemore...........50 A4
Poyle ...............69 B3
Purley on T...........57 A1
Reading .............86 A2
Remenham Hill........16 A1
Sandhurst...........150 A4
Shefford Woodlands....74 B4
Shepperton..........125 A1
Shinfield............113 A1
Shiplake .............35 A1
Silchester...........136 A1
Slough ..............42 A3
Sonning .............60 C1
South Stoke ..........14 A2
Staines ..............96 B3
Stanford Dingley.......81 B2
Stanwell .............97 A3
Stockcross ..........104 A4
Stoke Poges ..........22 C1
Streatley.............34 A3
Sulham...............56 C3
Sulhamstead.........110 B1
Sunbury ............125 C3
Sunningdale .........121 A1
Swallowfield.........139 A1
Tadley..............134 A1
Taplow ..............20 C1
Thatcham ...........106 A1
Theale ..............83 A1
Thorpe .............123 A3
Thorpe Lea............96 A1
Tidmarsh ............56 A1
Twyford..............61 A3
Upper Basildon........55 A3
Upper Halliford.......125 B3
Virginia Water .......122 A2
Waltham St Lawrence...62 A4
Walton-on-T ........125 C1
Wargrave ............36 B1
Wentworth ..........121 A1
West End ...........153 C3
West Ilsley ...........10 A1
West Woodhay .......128 A3
Whitchurch-on-T.......56 B4
White Waltham........63 A3
Wickham ............75 B2
Windlesham .........146 A2
Windsor .............67 A2
Winkfield ............92 A1
Winnersh ............88 A1
Winterbourne.........77 B3
Wokingham .........116 A1
Wooburn Green ........3 B2
Wooburn Moor.........3 C4
Woodley .............88 A3
Woolhampton........108 B1
Wraysbury ...........68 B1
Yateley .............149 A2
Yattendon............53 A1

## 3


3 Acre Mobile Home Pk SL0 44 A4


## A


Abattoirs Rd RG1 86 A4
Abberbury Cl RG14 104 C3
Abbetts La GU15 151 A2
Abbey Cl Bracknell RG12 118 B2
Newbury RG14 131 A4
Slough SL1 41 C3
Wokingham RG40 116 B4
Abbey Cotts SL7 17 A2
Abbey Ct Camberley GU15 151 B3
Chertsey KT16 124 A1
Abbey Dr TW18 124 B3
Abbey Gdns KT16 124 A2
Abbey Gn KT16 124 A2
Abbey Jun Sch RG1 86 B3
Abbey Lodge TW18 96 C2
Abbey Pk RG7 110 C2
Abbey Rd Bourne End SL8 2 C3
Chertsey KT16 124 A1
Lower Halliford TW17 125 A1
Virginia Water GU25 122 B3
Abbey River Cotts KT16 124 B2
Abbey Sq RG1 86 A4
Abbey St RG1 86 A4
Abbey Way SL7 18 B3
Abbey Wood SL5 121 A1
Abbot Cl TW18 97 B1
Abbot's Wlk SL4 66 C3
Abbots Dr GU25 122 B3
Abbots Rd
Burghfield Common RG7 110 C1
Newbury RG14 105 A1
Abbots Way KT16 123 C1
Abbots Wlk RG1 86 A4
Abbotsbury RG12 117 C2
Abbotsbury Ct 3 RG30 85 A4
Abbotsmead Pl RG4 59 A1
Abbotts Way SL1 41 B3
Abelia Cl GU24 153 C3
Abell Gdns SL6 19 A1
Aberaman RG4 58 C3
Aberdeen Ave SL1 42 A3
Aberford Cl RG30 85 B4
Abex Rd RG14 105 B2
Abingdon Cl RG12 118 C2
Abingdon Dr RG4 59 B3
Abingdon Rd
East Isley RG20 30 C4
Sandhurst GU47 143 B1
Abingdon Wlk SL6 19 C2
Abington SL3 69 B4
Abney Court Dr SL8 3 A1
Abotts Mead OX10 14 A4
Abrahams Rd RG9 15 B2
Acacia RG9 15 B1
Acacia Ave Littleton TW17 125 A2
Sandhurst GU47 143 B1
Wraysbury TW19 68 C2
Acacia Ct RG12 118 A3
Acacia Mews UB7 70 B4
Acacia Rd Reading RG1 86 B3
Staines TW18 97 A2
Academy Cl GU15 151 C4
Accommodation La UB7 70 B4
Acer Dr GU24 153 C3
Ackrells Mead GU47 142 C1
Acorn Cotts SN8 126 B2
Acorn Dr Thatcham RG18 106 B3
Wokingham RG40 116 B4
Acorn Gr UB3 71 C4
Acorn Rd GU17 150 A3
Acorn Wlk RG31 84 B3
Acre Bsns Pk RG2 113 A4
Acre Pas SL4 67 B3
Acre Rd RG2 113 A4
Acre The SL7 1 C1
Action Ct TW15 125 B4
Adam Cl Slough SL1 42 A3
Tadley RG26 134 C1
Adam Ct RG9 15 C1
Adams Way RG6 86 C1
Addington Cl SL4 67 A2
Addington Rd RG1 86 B3
Addington Specl Sch RG5 87 C3
Addiscombe Chase RG31 57 A2
Addiscombe Rd RG45 143 B2
Addison Cl SL0 44 C3
Addison Ct SL6 20 A1
Addison Rd RG1 59 A1
Adelaide Cl SL1 42 A2
Adelaide Rd Ashford TW15 97 B2
Reading RG6 87 A3
Adelaide Sq SL4 67 B3
Adelphi Gdns SL1 42 C2
Adey's Cl RG14 105 A1
Adkins Rd RG10 62 C4
Admirals Ct RG2 86 A3
Admiralty Way GU15 150 C2
Admoor La RG7 82 B1
Adwell Dr RG6 87 B1
Adwell Sq RG9 15 B1
Adwood Ct RG19 106 C2
Aeriel Bsns Pk RG17 45 C2
Agar Cres RG42 91 A1
Agars Pl SL3 68 A4
Agate Cl RG41 115 C4
Aggisters La RG41 115 B2
Agincourt Cl RG41 115 C3
Agincourt Pl SL5 120 B3
Agricola Way RG19 106 C1
Ainsdale Cres RG30 85 A2
Aintree RG17 25 A1
Aintree Cl Newbury RG14 105 B1
Poyle SL3 69 C3
Air Forces Meml TW20 95 B2
Airport Way TW19 70 A2
Aisne Rd GU16 152 C1
Ajax Ave SL1 42 A3
Alan Pl RG30 85 A3
Alan Way SL3 43 C4
Alandale Cl RG2 113 B4
Albain Cres TW15 97 C3
Albany Ct GU16 151 B1
Albany Park Dr RG41 88 A2
Albany Park Ind Est
GU15 151 B1
Albany Pk Frimley GU15 151 B1
Poyle SL3 69 B4
Albany Pl TW20 96 A2
Albany Rd Old Windsor SL4 68 A1
Reading RG30 85 B4
Windsor SL4 67 B3
Alben Rd RG42 90 B2
Albert Ave KT16 124 A3
Albert Cl 28 SL1 42 C2
Albert Illsley Cl RG31 84 B4
Albert Pl SL4 42 A1
Albert Rd Ashford TW15 97 C2
Bagshot GU19 145 C1
Bracknell RG42 118 A4
Camberley GU15 151 B3
Caversham RG4 58 C2
Crowthorne RG45 143 A3
Englefield Green TW20 95 B1
Henley-on-T RG9 15 C1
19 Newbury RG14 105 A2
Windsor SL4 67 C2
Wokingham RG40 116 A3
Albert St Maidenhead SL6 39 C4
Slough SL1 42 C2
Windsor SL4 67 A3
Albert Wlk RG45 143 A3
Albion SL3 44 A1
Albion Cl SL2 43 A3
Albion Cotts SL6 19 B4
Albion Pl 2 SL4 67 A3
Albion Rd GU47 150 A4
Albion Terr RG1 86 B4
Albury Cl RG30 58 B1
Albury Gdns RG31 84 C2
Alcot Cl RG45 143 A2
Aldborough Spur SL1 42 C4
Aldbourne Ave RG6 87 A2
Aldbourne Cl RG17 100 B3
Aldbourne Rd SL1 41 A4
Aldeburgh Cl RG4 59 B4
Aldebury Rd SL6 19 C1
Alden View SL4 66 B3
Aldenham Cl RG4 59 B3
Aldenham Terr RG12 118 B2
Alder Bridge Steiner Sch
RG7 109 B2
Alder Cl
Englefield Green TW20 95 C2
Newbury RG14 105 B2
Slough SL1 41 C3
Alder Ct RG12 118 A3
Alder Dr Earley RG6 87 B1
Reading RG31 84 B3
Alder Glade RG7 110 C2
Alder Gr GU46 149 B3
Alderbourne La SL3 23 C4
Alderbrook Cl RG45 142 C2
Alderbury Rd SL3 43 C2
Alderbury Rd W SL3 43 C2
Alderfield Cl RG7 83 C2
Alderley Cl RG5 60 C1
Alderman Willey Cl
RG41 116 A3
Aldermaston
CE Prim Sch RG7 134 C4
Aldermaston Sta RG7 109 B2
Alderney Ct 27 RG1 86 B4
Alderney Gdns RG41 88 B1
Alders The RG18 106 B2
Alderside Wlk TW20 95 C2
Aldin Ave N SL1 43 A2
Aldin Ave S SL1 43 A2
Aldous Ho TW18 96 C2
Aldridge Rd SL2 22 A1
Aldryington Prim Sch
RG6 87 A2
Aldwick Dr SL6 39 B3
Aldworth Cl
Bracknell RG12 118 A3
Reading RG30 85 B3
Aldworth Gdns RG45 143 A3
Aldworth Rd
Compton RG20 31 C2
Upper Basildon RG8 55 A3
Aldwyn Ct TW20 95 A1
Alexander Ct 24 RG1 85 C4
Alexander Fst Sch SL4 66 B2
Alexander Rd Egham TW20 96 B2
Thatcham RG19 106 C1
Alexander Wlk RG12 118 A2
Alexandra Ave GU15 151 A3
Alexandra Cl Ashford TW15 98 B1
Staines TW18 97 B1
Alexandra Ct TW15 98 B1
Alexandra Rd
Ashford TW15 98 C1
Englefield Green TW20 95 B1
Maidenhead SL6 39 B4
Reading RG1 86 B3
Slough SL1 42 B2
Windsor SL4 67 B3
Alford Cl RG30 84 B4
Alfred Davis Ct SL7 1 B2
Alfred St RG1 85 C4
Alfred Sutton Prim Sch
RG1 86 C3
Alice Gough Memorial
Homes RG12 118 A3
Alice La SL1 21 A1
Alison Cl RG7 110 C1
Alison Dr GU15 151 C3
All Hallows Rd RG4 59 B2
All Saints' Ave SL6 39 B4
All Saints CE Inf Sch RG1 85 C4
All Saints CE Jun Sch SL6 39 B3
All Saints Cl RG40 116 B4
All Saints Cres GU14 150 C1
All Saints Ct RG30 85 C3
All Saints Rd GU18 146 B1
All Saints Rise RG42 91 C1
All Souls Cotts SL3 43 C4
All Souls' Rd SL5 120 A3
Allanson Rd SL7 1 C2
Allcot Cl TW14 98 C4
Allcroft Rd RG1 86 B3
Allenby Rd Maidenhead SL6 39 A4
Sandhurst GU15 151 A3
Allendale Cl GU47 143 A1
Allendale Rd RG6 87 A2
Allerds Rd SL2 22 A2
Alleyns La SL6 19 B4
Allhusen Gdns SL3 23 C4
Alliance Ct TW15 98 B2
Allington Ave TW17 125 C3
Allington Ct SL2 42 C3
Allison Ct 17 RG1 85 C4
Allison Gdns RG8 57 B3
Allkins Ct SL4 67 B3
Allnatt Ave RG41 88 B1
Allonby Cl RG6 87 B1
Allsmoor La RG12 118 C3
Allyn Cl TW18 96 C1
Alma Ct Burnham SL1 21 B1
Eton SL4 41 C1
Wokingham RG41 116 A3
Alma Rd Eton SL4 41 C1
Windsor SL4 67 B3
Alma St RG30 85 B4
Almners Rd KT16 123 A1
Almond Ave RG14 105 A3
Almond Cl Charlton TW17 125 B4
Englefield Green TW20 95 A1
Windsor SL4 67 A3
Wokingham RG41 115 B2
Almond Dr Caversham RG4 59 C2
Thatcham RG18 106 B2
Almond Rd SL1 21 B1
Almons Way SL2 43 A4
Almshouses Eton SL4 67 B4
Reading RG1 86 A4
Sunbury TW16 125 C4
Almswood Rd RG26 135 A1
Alpha Ho 4 RG1 86 B3
Alpha St N SL1 43 A2
Alpha St S SL1 42 C2
Alpha Way TW20 123 B4
Alphington Ave GU16 151 C1
Alphington Gn GU16 151 C1
Alphington Rd RG2 113 A4
Alpine St RG1 86 A3
Alsace Wlk GU15 151 A1
Alsford Cl GU18 152 C4
Alston Gdns SL6 39 C4
Alston Mews RG19 106 B1
Alston Wlk RG4 59 B1
Altmore SL6 38 C2
Alton Ct TW18 123 C4
Alton Ride GU17 150 B3
Altona Way SL1 42 A4
Altwood Bailey SL6 39 A3
Altwood CE Comp Sch
SL6 39 A3
Altwood Cl
Maidenhead SL6 39 A3
Slough SL1 41 C4
Altwood Dr SL6 39 A3
Altwood Rd SL6 39 A3
Alvista Ave SL6 41 A4
Alwyn Inf Sch SL6 39 A4
Alwyn Rd SL6 39 A4
Alwyns Cl KT16 124 A2
Alwyns La KT16 124 A2
Alyson Ct 2 SL6 19 C1
Amanda Ct Ashford TW15 97 C3
Slough SL3 43 B2
Ambarrow Cres GU47 142 C1
Ambarrow La GU47 142 C1
Ambassador RG12 117 C2
Amber Cl RG6 87 B2
Amber Ct TW18 96 C2
Amber Hill GU15 152 A2
Amberley Cl RG14 104 C2
Amberley Ct SL6 20 B2
Amberley Dr RG10 61 B3
Amberley Pl 20 SL4 67 B3
Amberley Rd SL2 41 C4
Amberwood Dr GU15 151 C4
Amblecote Rd RG30 85 A4
Ambleside Cl RG5 87 C4
Ambleside Dr TW14 98 C4
Ambleside Rd GU18 153 A4
Ambleside Way TW20 96 A1
Ambrook Rd RG2 113 A4
Ambrose Pl RG1 85 C4
Ambury Rd RG8 32 C2
Amen Corner Bsns Pk
RG12 117 B4
Amerden Cl SL6 40 B4
Amerden La SL6 40 B4
Amerden Way SL1 42 A2
American Comm Sch
GU25 122 B4
American Magna Carta
Meml TW20 95 B3
American Sch in
Switzerland (English
Branch) The TW20 123 B3
Amersham Rd RG4 59 B1
Amethyst Cl RG41 115 B4
Amethyst La RG30 85 B3
Amherst Rd RG6 87 A3
Amity Rd RG1 86 C4
Amity St RG1 86 C4
Ammanford RG4 58 C3
Amners Farm Rd RG30 112 A4
Ampere Rd RG14 105 A2
Anarth Ct KT13 125 C1
Ancaster Dr SL5 119 C4
Ancastle Gr RG9 15 B1
Andermans SL4 66 B3
Anderson Ave RG6 87 A3
Anderson Cres RG2 114 C1
Anderson Dr TW15 98 B2
Anderson Pl GU19 145 C2
Andover Cl
East Bedfont TW14 98 C4
Reading RG31 57 B1
Andover Ct TW19 97 B4
Andover Dro RG20 130 A2
Andover Rd
Blackwater GU17 150 B3
Newbury RG14 130 B3
Andrew Cl RG40 116 C3
Andrews Cl RG7 83 C2
Andrews Rd RG6 87 A2
Andrews Reach SL8 3 A1
Andrews Way SL7 1 B4
Angel Ct 2 RG14 105 A2
Angel Mead RG7 108 B1
Angel Pl RG42 90 B1
Angers Cl GU15 152 B4
Angle Field Rd RG4 59 B2
Anglers Way RG1 86 B4
Anglesey Cl TW15 98 A3
Angus Cl RG31 84 C2
Annadale RG18 79 B1
Anne Cl SL6 19 C1
Anneforde Pl RG42 91 A1
Anners Cl TW20 123 B3
Annesley Gdns RG41 88 B2
Annett Cl TW17 125 C3
Annie Brookes Cl TW18 96 B3
Ansculf Rd SL2 22 A1
Ansell Rd GU16 151 C1
Anslow Pl SL1 41 B4
Anson Cres RG2 113 B4
Anson Ct TW15 97 C4
Anson Wlk RG2 113 B4
Anstey Pl RG7 111 A2
Anstey Rd 6 RG1 86 A4
Anston Cl RG6 114 A4
Antares Cl RG41 115 C3
Anthian Cl RG5 88 A4
Anthony Wall RG42 118 C4
Anthony Way SL1 41 B3
Antrim Rd RG5 87 B3
Anvil Ct Slough SL3 44 A1
Thatcham RG18 106 B2
Apex Dr GU16 151 B1
Aplin Way GU18 146 A1
Apple Cl Purley on T RG31 57 A2
Wokingham RG41 115 C3
Apple Tree Cl RG14 130 C4
Apple Tree Way GU47 143 B1
Appleby Ct GU15 151 A3
Appleby End RG30 85 A4
Appleby Gdns TW14 98 C4
Applecroft SL6 39 B2
Appledore RG12 117 C2
Appleford Cl RG19 106 B1
Appleford Rd RG30 85 A3
Appleton Ho 34 RG1 86 B4
Appletree La
Shinfield RG7 113 A1
Slough SL3 43 B2
Appletree Pl 4 RG42 118 A4
Appley Dr GU15 151 A3
Approach Rd
Ashford TW15 98 B1
Taplow SL6 40 C4
April Cl GU15 151 B1
Apsey Ct RG42 90 C1
Apsley Cotts SL6 19 C4
Apsley Ho SL1 43 A2
Aquila Cl RG41 115 C3
Aragon Cl TW16 98 C1
Aragon Ct RG12 118 B3
Arbor La RG41 88 A2
Arbor Mdws RG41 88 A2
Arborfield Cl SL1 42 C2
Arborfield, Newland &
Barkham CE Jun Sch
RG2 114 C1
Arborfield Rd RG2 113 C2
Arbour Cl RG1 85 C3
Arbour Vale Sch SL2 42 C4
Arc The RG1 86 A4
Arcade The Goring RG8 34 B3
Newbury RG14 105 A2
Archangel Way RG18 106 C2
Archer Cl SL6 39 B4
Archway Rd RG4 59 A1
Arden Cl RG12 119 A4
Ardingly RG12 118 A2
Ardler Rd RG4 59 B1
Ardrossan Ave GU15 152 A3
Ardrossan Cl SL2 22 B1
Ardwell Cl RG45 142 C3
Arena L Ctr GU15 151 B3
Arena The RG12 118 A4
Arenal Dr RG45 143 B2
Arethusa Way GU24 153 C2
Argent Cl TW20 96 B1
Argent Terr GU47 150 C4
Argosy Gdns TW18 96 C1
Argosy La TW19 97 B4
Argyle Rd Newbury RG14 104 C1
Reading RG1 85 C4
Argyle St RG1 85 C4
Argyll Ave SL1 42 A3
Aries Ho HP10 3 A4
Arkle Ave RG19 105 C2
Arkley Ct SL6 40 B1
Arkwright Dr RG42 117 B4
Arkwright Rd Poyle SL3 69 C3
Reading RG2 86 A2
Arlington Bsns Pk RG7 84 A2
Arlington Cl
Bracknell RG42 118 A4
Maidenhead SL6 39 A4
Arlington Rd TW15 97 C2
Arlington Sq RG12 118 A4
Armadale Ct RG30 85 B3
Armitage Ct SL5 120 B2
Armitage Dr GU16 151 C1
Armour Hill RG31 57 B1
Armour Rd RG31 57 B1
Armour Wlk RG31 57 B1
Armstrong Rd TW20 95 B1
Armstrong Way RG5 88 A4
Arncliffe RG12 118 A2
Arndale Way TW20 96 A2
Arnett Ave RG40 141 C4
Arnewood Ave RG26 135 B1
Arnhem Rd RG14 105 A2
Arnold Rd TW18 97 B1
Arnside Cl RG10 61 B4
Arnwood RG41 115 C4
Arrowhead Rd RG7 83 C1
Arrowsmith Way RG19 106 C1
Artemis Ho RG14 105 A2
Arthur Cl GU19 145 C1
Arthur Pl RG1 86 B4
Arthur Rd Newbury RG14 104 C1
Slough SL1 42 B2
Windsor SL4 67 B3
Wokingham RG41 116 A3
Arthurstone Birches RG42 90 B2
Artillery Mews RG30 85 B3
Arun Cl RG41 88 A1
Arun Ct RG30 85 B3
Arundel Cl SL6 39 A4
Arundel Ct SL3 43 B1
Arundel Rd Frimley GU15 152 B2
Woodley RG5 87 C4
Ascot Heath Inf Sch SL5 92 C1
Ascot Heath Jun Sch SL5 92 C1
Ascot Race Course SL5 119 C3
Ascot Rd
East Bedfont TW14 98 A3
Holyport SL6 65 A4
Newell Green RG42 91 C4
Ascot Sta SL5 120 A3
Ascot Twrs SL5 119 C4
Ascot Wood SL5 120 A3
Ash Cl Blackwater GU17 150 B3
Brightwalton RG20 28 B2
Slough SL3 44 A2
Ash Copse RG4 59 C4
Ash Ct Ashford TW15 98 B2
Caversham RG4 59 A2
16 Newbury RG14 105 A2
Ash Gate RG18 106 C2
Ash Gn RG2 113 B4
Ash Gr Bradfield RG7 82 A1
East Bedfont TW14 98 C4
Staines TW18 97 B1
Stoke Poges SL2 22 C3
Ash La
Burghfield Common RG7 111 A2
Tadley RG26 134 C1
Windsor SL4 66 B3
Ash Lodge 6 TW16 98 C1
Ash Rd Littleton TW17 125 A3
Newtown RG20 131 C1
Reading RG30 84 C4
Ash Terr RG18 106 A4
Ash Tree Gr RG20 129 A4
Ash Way RG41 115 B2
Ashampstead Rd
Bradfield RG7 82 A4
Reading RG30 85 A2
Upper Basildon RG8 55 A3
Ashbourne RG12 117 C2
Ashbourne Gr SL6 39 B2
Ashbourne Ho 5 SL1 42 C2
Ashbourne Way RG19 106 A2
Ashbrook Rd SL4 95 A4
Ashburton Rd RG2 86 B1
Ashbury Dr
Farnborough (Hants) GU17 151 A1
Reading RG31 84 B4
Ashby Ct RG2 113 A4
Ashby Way UB7 71 A4
Ashcroft Cl RG4 58 C3
Ashcroft Ct SL1 21 A2
Ashcroft Rd SL6 39 B4
Ashdale Cl TW19 97 C3
Ashdale Pk RG40 142 B3
Ashdene Cl TW15 98 B1
Ashdene Ho TW20 95 B1
Ashdown SL6 20 A2
Ashdown Cl RG12 119 A4

Ashdown Ho [13] RG30 85 C3
Ashen Cross SL3 44 A4
Ashenden Wlk SL2 22 B4
Asher Dr SL5 119 B4
Ashes The RG7 113 A1
Ashfield Gn GU46 149 C3
Ashford Ave TW15 98 A1
Ashford CE Prim Sch TW15 98 A1
Ashford Cl TW15 97 C2
Ashford Cres TW15 97 C3
Ashford High Sch The TW15 97 C3
Ashford Hill Cty Prim Sch RG19 133 C1
Ashford Hill Rd RG19 132 C1
Ashford Hospl TW15 97 C3
Ashford Ind Est TW15 98 B2
Ashford La SL4 41 A2
Ashford Manor Golf Club TW15 97 C1
Ashford Park Cty Prim Sch TW15 97 B2
Ashford Rd
Feltham TW13, TW15 98 C3
Littleton TW15 98 B1
Staines TW18 124 B4
Ashford Sta TW15 97 C3
Ashgrove Rd TW15 98 B2
Ashlea Ho TW15 97 C2
Ashleigh Ave TW20 96 B1
Ashley HP10 3 C4
Ashley Cl Earley RG6 87 A1
Walton-on-T KT12, KT13 125 C1
Ashley Ct SL6 40 A4
Ashley Dr GU17 150 B2
Ashley Hill Pl RG10 36 C4
Ashley Park Ave KT12 125 C1
Ashley Pk SL6 20 A1
Ashley Rd RG1 85 C3
Ashley Way GU24 153 B3
Ashman Rd RG19 107 A2
Ashmead Sch RG2 86 B1
Ashmere Cl RG31 84 B2
Ashmere Terr RG30 85 C4
Ashmore Green Rd RG18 106 A4
Ashmore Rd RG2 86 B1
Ashridge Ct [7] RG14 105 A1
Ashridge Gn [3] RG42 118 A4
Ashridge Rd RG40 116 B4
Ashton Cl RG31 84 B4
Ashton Pl Kintbury RG17 102 A1
Maidenhead SL6 39 A3
Ashton Rd Newbury RG14 105 A1
Wokingham RG41 88 C1
Ashtree Ct TW15 98 A2
Ashtrees Rd RG5 87 C4
Ashurst Dr TW17 124 C3
Ashview Cl TW15 97 C2
Ashview Gdns TW15 97 C2
Ashville Way RG41 116 A3
Ashwell Ave GU15 151 C3
Ashwell Ct TW15 97 C3
Ashwood RG5 87 B2
Ashwood Cl RG31 84 A3
Ashwood Dr RG14 105 B2
Ashwood Rd TW20 95 A1
Ashworth Dr RG19 106 B1
Askew Dr RG7 113 A2
Aspect Park Golf Ctr RG9 16 B1
Aspen Cl Slough SL2 42 A4
Staines TW18 96 C3
Aspen Gdns TW15 98 B2
Aspin Way GU17 150 A3
Astleham Rd TW17 124 C3
Astley Cl RG41 115 C4
Aston Ave RG31 84 A4
Aston Cl RG8 56 B3
Aston Ct RG30 85 A3
Aston Ferry La RG9 16 B3
Aston La RG9 16 B2
Aston Mead SL4 66 C3
Aston St OX11 12 C4
Aston Villas SL2 22 B4
Astor Cl Maidenhead SL6 40 A3
Winnersh RG41 88 B2
Astra Mead RG42 92 A1
Atfield Gr GU20 146 B2
Atherton Cl Reading RG30 84 C4
Stanwell TW19 70 B1
Atherton Cres RG17 100 B3
Atherton Ct SL4 67 B4
Atherton Pl RG17 25 A2
Atherton Rd RG17 100 B3
Athlone Cl SL6 19 C1
Atrebatti Rd GU47 143 B1
Atte La RG42 91 B1
Attebrouche Ct RG12 118 B1
Auburn Ct RG4 59 A1
Auckland Cl SL6 40 A4
Auckland Rd RG6 87 A3
Auclum Cl RG7 111 A1
Auclum La RG7 111 A1
Audley Cl RG14 105 B3
Audley Dr SL6 39 A3
Audley St RG30 85 C4
Audley Way SL5 119 B3
Augur Cl TW18 96 C2
August End Reading RG30 85 B4
Slough SL3 43 C4
Augustine Cl SL3 69 C2
Augustine Wlk RG42 91 C1
Augustus Gdns GU15 152 B3
Austen Gdns RG14 131 A4
Austin Rd RG5 87 C3
Austins Gate SL6 38 C4
Australia Ave SL6 39 C4
Australia Rd SL1 43 A2
Auton Pl RG9 35 B4
Autumn Cl Caversham RG4 59 B4
Slough SL1 41 C3
Autumn Wlk
Maidenhead SL6 39 A3
Wargrave RG10 36 B1
Avalon Rd Bourne End SL8 3 A3
Earley RG6 87 B2
Avebury Bracknell RG12 118 A2
Slough SL1 42 A3
Avebury Sq RG1 86 B3
Aveley Wlk [26] RG1 86 A3
Avenue Rd Egham TW18 96 B2
Feltham TW13 98 C3
Maidenhead SL6 40 A3
Avenue Sch The RG2 86 B2
Avenue Sucy GU15 151 A2
Avenue The Bourne End SL8 3 A2
Camberley GU15 151 A3
Crowthorne RG45 143 A3
Datchet SL3 68 A3
Egham TW20 96 A2
Farnham Common SL2 22 A4
Lightwater GU18 146 A1
Maidenhead SL6 20 B2
Mortimer RG7 137 A3
North Ascot SL5 92 C1
Old Windsor SL4 68 A1
Staines TW18 124 A4
Wraysbury TW19 68 B2
Averil Ct SL6 41 B4
Avery Cl RG40 141 C3
Avington Cl RG31 84 A4
Avocet Cres GU47 150 C4
Avocet Ct [4] RG1 86 A3
Avon Cl Reading RG31 84 C3
Slough SL1 41 C3
Avon Gr RG12 91 B1
Avon Pl RG1 86 B4
Avon Rd TW16 98 C1
Avon Way RG7 109 C3
Avondale SL6 19 B1
Avondale Ave TW18 96 C1
Avondale Rd TW15, TW19 97 B3
Avonway RG14 105 B2
Axbridge RG12 118 C2
Axbridge Rd RG2 86 B1
Ayebridges Ave TW20 96 B1
Aylesbury Cres SL1 42 B4
Aylesford Way RG19 107 A1
Aylesham Way GU46 149 A3
Aylesworth Ave SL2 22 A1
Aylesworth Spur SL4 95 A4
Aylsham Cl RG30 84 C4
Aymer Cl TW18 123 C4
Aymer Dr TW18 123 C4
Ayrton Senna Rd RG31 84 B4
Aysgarth RG12 118 A2
Aysgarth Pk SL6 40 A1
Azalea Cl RG41 88 A1
Azalea Way Frimley GU15 152 A3
Slough SL3 43 C4

## B

Babbington Rd RG2 113 B3
Bachelors Acre SL4 67 B3
Back La Beenham RG7 109 A4
Brimpton RG7 134 B2
Kintbury RG17 127 C4
Shinfield RG7 139 A4
Silchester RG7 136 B2
Stanford Dingley RG7 81 C2
Back St RG17 47 B3
Backsideans RG10 36 B1
Bacon Cl GU47 150 B3
Bad Godesberg Way SL6 39 C4
Baden Cl TW18 97 A1
Bader Gdns SL1 42 A2
Bader Way The RG5 88 A3
Badgebury Rise SL7 1 B4
Badgemoor La RG9 15 B2
Badgemore Cty Prim Sch RG9 15 B1
Badger Cl SL6 39 B2
Badger Dr
Lightwater GU18 146 A1
Twyford RG10 61 B4
Badgers Cl TW15 97 C2
Badgers Copse GU15 151 C2
Badgers Croft RG7 137 A3
Badgers Glade RG7 111 A1
Badgers Hill GU25 122 B2
Badgers Holt GU46 149 A3
Badgers Ridge RG20 130 B2
Badgers Rise RG4 59 A3
Badgers Sett RG45 142 C3
Badgers Way
Bracknell RG12 118 C4
Marlow Bottom SL7 1 B4
Badgers Wlk RG9 36 A2
Badgers Wood SL2 22 B4
Badgerwood Dr GU16 151 B1
Badminton Rd SL6 39 A3
Bagnols Way RG14 104 C1
Bagshot Cty Inf Sch GU19 145 C1
Bagshot Gn GU19 145 C2
Bagshot Rd Ascot SL5 120 B1
Bracknell RG12 118 B2
Englefield Green TW20 95 B1
West End GU24 153 C4
Bagshot Sta GU19 145 C2
Baigents La GU20 146 B2
Bailey Cl Maidenhead SL6 39 C4
Windsor SL4 67 A3
Bailey Ho [7] SL8 3 A2
Bailey's La RG10 62 C2
Baileys Cl GU17 150 B2
Baily Ave RG18 106 A2
Bain Ave GU15 151 A1
Bainbridge Rd RG31 84 A2
Bainhurst Cotts SL6 38 A3
Baird Cl SL1 42 A2
Baird Rd RG2 140 C4
Bakeham La TW20 95 B1
Baker St Aston Tirrold OX11 12 C4
Reading RG1 85 C4
Baker's Orch HP10 3 C3
Bakers Ct TW19 70 B1
Bakers La SL6 38 C4
Baldwin Rd SL1 21 B1
Baldwin's Shore SL4 67 B4
Balfour Cres
Bracknell RG12 118 A2
Newbury RG14 130 B3
Balfour Dr RG31 84 A2
Balfour Pl SL7 1 B2
Balintore Ct [8] GU47 150 B4
Ball Pit Rd RG20 30 A3
Ballamoor Cl RG31 84 A2
Ballard Ct GU15 152 A4
Ballard Gn SL4 66 C4
Ballard Rd GU15 152 A4
Ballencrieff Rd SL5 120 C1
Balliol Rd RG4 58 B2
Balliol Way GU47 143 C1
Balme Cl RG10 61 A2
Balmoral SL6 19 A1
Balmoral Cl SL1 41 C4
Balmoral Gdns SL4 67 B2
Balmoral Grange TW18 124 A4
Balmore Dr RG4 59 A2
Balmore Ho RG4 59 A2
Balmore Pk RG4 59 A2
Bamburgh Cl RG2 86 B2
Bamford Pl RG31 84 A2
Banbury RG12 118 C1
Banbury Ave SL1 41 C4
Banbury Cl RG41 116 A3
Banbury Gdns RG4 59 B2
Bancroft Cl TW15 98 A2
Bancroft Pl RG31 84 A2
Band La [1] TW20 96 A2
Bangors Cl SL0 44 C4
Bangors Rd S SL0 44 C4
Bank Side RG40 141 C3
Banks Spur SL1 42 A2
Bankside Cl RG2 86 B1
Bannard Rd SL6 39 A3
Bannister Cl SL3 43 C2
Bannister Gdns GU46 149 C3
Bannister Pl RG7 133 C3
Bannister Rd RG7 110 C1
Barbara Cl TW17 125 A2
Barbaras Mdw RG31 57 A1
Barbel Cl RG6 87 A4
Barber Cl RG10 88 C4
Barberry Way GU17 150 C1
Barbon Cl GU15 152 B2
Barbrook Cl RG31 57 B2
Barchester Rd SL3 43 C2
Barclay Rd RG31 84 B2
Barclose Ave RG4 59 B2
Bardney Cl SL6 39 B2
Bardolphs Cl RG4 58 B4
Bardown RG20 51 A1
Barefoot Cl RG31 57 A1
Barfield Rd RG18 106 A2
Barge La RG7 139 A3
Bargeman Rd SL6 39 C3
Barholm Cl RG6 87 C1
Barkby RG6 87 B1
Barker Cl RG2 140 C4
Barker Ct RG10 88 C4
Barker Gn RG12 118 A2
Barker Rd KT16 123 C1
Barkham Manor RG41 115 B2
Barkham Rd
Barkham RG41 115 B2
Wokingham RG41 116 A3
Barkham Ride
Barkham RG40 115 B1
Wokingham RG40 141 C4
Barkham St RG40 115 B1
Barkhart Dr RG40 116 B4
Barkhart Gdns RG40 116 B4
Barkis Mead GU47 143 C1
Barkwith Cl RG6 87 C1
Barley Cl RG19 106 C1
Barley Fields HP10 3 C4
Barley Mead RG42 91 C1
Barley Mow Rd TW20 95 B2
Barley Mow Way TW17 125 A3
Barley Way [6] SL7 1 B1
Barley Wlk RG31 84 A3
Barn Cl Ashford TW15 98 A2
Bracknell RG12 118 B4
Camberley GU15 151 C3
Farnham Common SL2 22 A4
Kintbury RG17 102 A1
Maidenhead SL6 19 C1
Reading RG30 85 B2
Barn Cotts RG17 74 B4
Barn Cres RG14 130 B4
Barn Dr SL6 39 A2
Barn La RG9 15 B2
Barn Owl Way RG7 111 A2
Barnard Cl RG4 59 B3
Barnards Hill SL7 1 B1
Barnes Way SL0 44 C3
Barnett Ct RG12 118 B4
Barnett Gn RG12 118 A2
Barnett La GU18 152 C4
Barnfield Iver SL0 44 C4
Slough SL1 41 B3
Barnfield Cl SL6 19 C3
Barnhill Cl SL7 1 B2
Barnhill Gdns SL7 1 B2
Barnhill Rd SL7 1 B2
Barnsdale Rd RG2 86 B2
Barnway TW20 95 B2
Barnwood Cl RG30 85 C4
Baroma Way RG9 15 C1
Baron Ct RG30 85 C4
Barons Mead RG9 15 B1
Barons Way TW20 96 B1
Barossa Rd GU15 151 B4
Barr's Rd SL6 41 A4
Barracane Dr RG45 143 A3
Barrack La SL4 67 B3
Barracks La RG7 113 A1
Barrett Cres RG40 116 C3
Barrington Cl RG6 87 A3
Barrington Ct TW18 96 C1
Barrington Ho RG2 113 A4
Barrington Way RG30 85 C3
Barry Ave SL4 67 B4
Barry Pl RG1 86 A4
Barry Sq RG12 118 B1
Barry Terr TW15 97 C3
Barry View SL4 66 B3
Bartelotts Rd SL2 21 C1
Bartholemew Pl RG42 91 C1
Bartholomew Ct RG14 104 C1
Bartholomew St RG14 104 C1
Bartlemy Cl RG14 130 C4
Bartlemy Rd RG14 130 C4
Bartletts La SL6 65 A4
Barton Cl TW17 125 A2
Barton Rd Reading RG31 84 A4
Slough SL3 43 C2
Bartons Dr GU46 149 B2
Barwell Cl RG45 142 C2
Basemoors RG12 118 C4
Basford Way SL4 66 B2
Basil Cl RG6 86 C1
Basildon CE Prim Sch RG8 55 A3
Basingstoke Rd
Aldermaston RG7 109 A1
Reading RG2 86 A2
Swallowfield RG7 139 B3
Baskerville La RG9 36 A2
Baslow Rd RG41 88 A1
Basmore La RG9 36 A2
Bass Mead SL6 19 C3
Bassett Cl RG6 114 B4
Bassett Rd OX12 6 C4
Bassett Way SL2 21 C1
Batcombe Mead RG12 118 C1
Bates Cl SL3 43 C4
Bath Ct SL6 39 B3
Bath Rd Camberley GU15 151 B3
Froxfield SN8,RG17 99 B2
Harlington TW6, UB3 71 C4
Harmondsworth TW6, UB7 70 C3
Hungerford RG17 100 C4
Knowl Hill RG10 37 B2
Littlewick Green SL6 38 B3
Maidenhead SL6 39 B3
Newbury RG14 104 B2
Poyle SL3, UB7 69 C3
Reading RG30, RG31 85 B3
Slough SL1,SL6 41 B3
Sonning RG4 60 C1
Thatcham RG7,RG19 107 B1
Woolhampton RG7 108 B1
Bathurst Cl SL0 44 C2
Bathurst Rd RG41 88 A1
Bathurst Wlk SL0 44 C2
Battery End RG14 130 B3
Battle Cl RG14 104 B2
Battle Hospl RG30 85 B4
Battle Prim Sch RG30 85 B4
Battle Rd Goring RG8 34 C4
Newbury RG14 130 B3
Battle St RG1 85 C4
Battlemead Cl SL6 20 B2
Batty's Barn Cl RG40 116 B3
Baxendales The RG14 105 B1
Baxter Cl SL1 42 C2
Bay Cl RG6 86 C1
Bay Dr RG12 118 C4
Bay Rd RG12 118 C4
Bay Tree Ct SL1 21 B1
Bay Tree Rise RG31 84 B3
Baydon Dr RG1 85 C3
Baydon Rd RG17 24 C1
Bayfield Ave GU16 151 C1
Bayford Cl GU17 151 A1
Bayford Dr RG31 84 C2
Bayley Cres SL1 41 A4
Bayley Ct RG41 88 A1
Baylis Court Sch SL1,SL2 42 B4
Baylis Par SL1 42 C4
Baylis Rd SL1 42 C3
Bayliss Rd RG10 36 B1
Baysfarm Ct TW6, UB7 70 B3
Beach's Ho TW18 97 A2
Beacon Ct Colnbrook SW3 69 B4
[3] Reading RG30 85 B3
Beacon Rd TW19, TW6 71 A1
Beacon Rdbt TW6 71 A1
Beaconsfield Cotts SL8 3 A1
Beaconsfield Rd SL2 22 B3
Beaconsfield Way RG6 87 A1
Beacontree Plaza RG2 86 A1
Beal's La RG31 84 A4
Beale Cl RG40 116 A4
Beale Park Wildlife Pk RG8 55 C4
Beales Farm Rd RG17 25 A1
Bean Oak Rd RG40 116 C3
Beancroft Rd RG19 106 B1
Bear La Newbury RG14 105 A2
Wargrave RG10 37 A2
Beard's Rd TW15 98 C1
Bearfield La RG17 73 A4
Bears Rails Pk SL4 94 C4
Bearwater RG17 100 B3
Bearwood Coll RG41 115 A4
Bearwood Path RG41 88 A1
Bearwood Prim Sch RG41 115 A4
Bearwood Rd RG41 115 B3
Beasley's Ait TW16,TW17 125 C2
Beasley's Ait La TW16, TW17 125 C2
Beattie Cl TW14 98 C4
Beatty Dr RG30 84 C4
Beauchief Cl RG6 113 C4
Beaufield Cl RG5 87 B4
Beaufort Cl SL7 1 C1
Beaufort Gdns Marlow SL7 1 C1
North Ascot SL5 119 C4
Beaufort Pl SL6 40 B2
Beauforts TW20 95 B2
Beaufront Cl GU15 152 A4
Beaufront Rd GU15 152 A4
Beaulieu Cl
Bracknell RG12 119 A3
Datchet SL3 68 A3
Beaulieu Gdns GU17 150 B3
Beaumaris Ct SL1 42 B4
Beaumont Cl SL6 39 A2
Beaumont Cotts [1] SL4 67 B3
Beaumont Ct Ascot SL5 119 C3
Slough SL3 43 B4
Beaumont Dr TW15 98 B2
Beaumont Gdns RG12 118 C2
Beaumont Rd Slough SL2 42 B4
Windsor SL4 67 B3
Beaumont Rise SL7 1 C1
Beaver Cl RG41 116 A2
Beaver La GU46 149 C3
Beaver Way RG5 88 A4
Beavers Cl RG26 135 A1
Beck Ct RG1 86 B3
Beckett Cl RG40 116 C3
Beckford Ave RG12 118 A2
Beckford Cl RG41 88 C1
Beckford Ct RG19 106 B2
Beckfords RG8 55 A3
Beckins Way HP10 3 B4
Bede Wlk RG2 86 B2
Bedfont Cl TW14 71 B1
Bedfont Court Est TW19 70 A2
Bedfont Ct TW19 70 A2
Bedfont Green Cl TW14 98 B4
Bedfont Ho TW14 98 C4
Bedfont Ind Pk N TW15 98 B3
Bedfont Inf Sch TW14 71 C1
Bedfont Jun Sch TW14 71 C1
Bedfont La TW14, TW13 98 C4
Bedfont Lakes Ctry Pk TW14 98 B3
Bedfont Rd
Feltham TW13, TW14 98 B3
Stanwell TW19 70 C1
Bedford Ave SL1 42 A4
Bedford Cl Maidenhead SL6 39 A2
Newbury RG14 130 B3
Bedford Dr SL2 22 A3
Bedford Gdns RG41 115 C4
Bedford La SL5 121 A2
Bedford Rd RG1 85 C4
Bedfordshire Down RG42 91 C1
Bedfordshire Way RG41 115 C3
Bedwins La SL6 19 A3
Beech RG9 15 B1
Beech Ave GU15 151 B2
Beech Cl Ashford TW15 98 B2
Burghfield Common RG30 111 A2
Hampstead Norreys RG18 53 A3
Maidenhead SL6 39 A4
Stanwell TW19 97 B4
Beech Ct Caversham RG4 59 A2
[1] Marlow SL7 1 C1
[15] Newbury RG14 105 A2
Beech Dr GU17 150 B2
Beech Glen RG12 118 A3
Beech Hill Rd
Beech Hill RG7 138 C3
Sunningdale SL5 120 C2
Beech La RG6 87 A1
Beech Lodge TW18 96 C2
Beech Rd
East Bedfont TW14 98 C4
Mapledurham RG4 58 B4
Newtown RG20 132 A2
Purley on T RG8 57 A3
Reading RG2 86 C1
Slough SL3 43 C2
Beech Ride GU47 143 A1
Beech Tree La TW18 124 A4
Beech Wlk RG19 106 C1
Beecham Rd RG30 85 B4
Beechbrook Ave GU46 149 B3
Beechcroft RG18 53 A3
Beechcroft Cl SL5 120 B3
Beechcroft Ct RG12 118 A3
Beeches Dr SL2 22 A4
Beeches Rd SL2 22 A4
Beeches The Goring RG8 34 A3
Reading RG31 57 B2
Staines TW18 97 A2

Beechfield RG18 80 B4
Beechingstoke 4 SL7 1 C2
Beechmont Ave GU25 122 B2
Beechnut Cl RG41 115 C3
Beechnut Dr GU17 150 A3
Beechtree Ave
Englefield Green TW20 95 A1
Marlow Bottom SL7 1 B3
Beechwood Ave
Reading RG31 84 B4
Staines TW18 97 A1
Woodley RG5 87 B4
Beechwood Cl SL5 92 C1
Beechwood Dr
Maidenhead SL6 39 A3
Marlow SL7 18 A4
Beechwood Gdns SL1 42 C2
Beechwood Prim Schs
RG5 87 C4
Beechwood Rd Slough SL2 42 B4
Wentworth GU25 122 A1
Beechwood Sec Sch SL2 22 A1
Beedon CE Prim Sch
RG20 51 B4
Beedon Dr RG12 117 C2
Beehive La RG12 117 B4
Beehive Rd
Bracknell RG12, RG42 117 B4
Staines TW18 96 C2
Beenham Cty Prim Sch
RG7 108 C3
Beeston Way RG6 114 A4
Beggars Hill Rd RG10 61 A1
Beighton Cl RG6 113 C4
Belfast Ave SL1 42 B4
Belford Ct 13 RG1 86 A3
Belgrave Ct GU17 150 B2
Belgrave Par SL1 42 C3
Belgrave Rd SL1 42 C3
Belgravia Ct 22 RG30 85 B3
Bell Bridge Rd KT16 123 C1
Bell Bsns Ctr SL6 39 C3
Bell Cl SL2 43 A4
Bell Cnr KT16 123 C1
Bell Ct SL6 17 C2
Bell Foundry La RG40 116 B4
Bell Hill RG14 130 A2
Bell Holt RG14 130 B3
Bell House Gdns RG41 116 A3
Bell La Aldworth RG8 32 C2
Blackwater GU17 150 B3
Eton SL4 41 C1
Henley-on-T RG9 15 C2
Inkpen RG17 127 B2
Bell Pl GU19 145 C2
Bell St Henley-on-T RG9 15 C1
Maidenhead SL6 39 C3
Bell View SL4 66 C3
Bell View Cl SL4 66 C3
Bell Weir Cl TW19 96 A3
Belle Ave RG6 87 A3
Belle Vue Cl TW18 124 A4
Belle Vue Rd
Henley-on-T RG9 35 B4
Reading RG1 85 C4
Belleisle RG8 57 A3
Bellever Hill GU15 151 C3
Bellevue Terr 15 RG1 85 C4
Bellingham Cl GU15 152 B2
Bellingham Wlk RG4 59 A3
Bellman Ct 1 RG1 86 A4
Bells Hill SL2 23 A2
Bells Hill Gn SL2 23 A3
Bells La SL3 69 A2
Bellsfield Ct SL4 41 C1
Bellswood La SL0 44 A4
Belmont SL2 42 A4
Belmont Cotts SL3 69 B4
Belmont Cres SL6 39 B4
Belmont Dr SL6 39 B4
Belmont Mews GU15 151 B2
Belmont Park Ave SL6 39 B4
Belmont Park Rd SL6 39 B4
Belmont Rd
Camberley GU15 151 B2
Crowthorne RG45 143 A3
Maidenhead SL6 39 B4
Reading RG30 85 B4
Belmont Vale SL6 39 B4
Belton Rd GU15 151 C3
Belvedere Ct GU17 150 B2
Belvedere Dr RG14 131 A4
Belvedere Mans SL1 42 B2
Belvedere Wlk RG41 88 A2
Belvoir Cl GU16 151 C1
Bembridge Ct 20 SL1 42 C2
Bembridge Pl RG1 86 B4
Benbricke Gn RG42 91 A1
Bence The TW20 123 A3
Bencombe Rd SL7 1 C3
Benedict Dr TW14 98 B4
Benedict Gn RG42 91 C1
Benen-Stock Rd TW19 70 A1
Benetfeld Rd RG42 90 A1
Benett Cl RG14 104 C3
Benett Gdns RG14 104 C3
Benham Chase RG20 103 C3
Benham Hill
Newbury RG18 105 C2
Thatcham RG18 106 A2
Benham La RG7 139 B2
Benhams La RG9 15 C4
Benjamin Ct TW15 98 B1
Benner La GU24 153 C4
Bennet Ct RG2 86 A1
Bennet Rd RG2 86 A1
Bennett Ct GU15 151 B3
Bennetts Cl SL1 42 A3
Bennetts Hill RG7,RG30 111 B4
Benning Cl SL4 66 B2
Bennings Cl RG42 91 A1
Bensington Ct TW14 71 B1
Benson Cl Reading RG2 86 B2
Slough SL2 43 A3
Benson Rd RG45 142 C3
Bentley Copse GU15 152 A2
Bentley Pk SL2 21 B2
Bentley Rd SL1 42 A3
Benyon Ct RG1 85 C3
Benyon Mews RG1 85 C3
Beomonds 5 KT16 124 A1
Beomonds Row 2 KT16 124 A1
Bere Court Rd RG8 56 A2
Bere Rd RG12 118 C2
Beresford Ave SL2 43 B3
Beresford Rd RG30 85 C4
Bergenia Ct GU24 153 C3
Berkeley Ave RG1 85 C3
Berkeley Cl TW19 96 B3
Berkeley Ct 1 RG1 85 C3
Berkeley Dr SL4 93 A4
Berkeley Gdns KT12 125 C1
Berkeley Mews SL7 1 C1
Berkeley Rd RG14 104 C1
Berkley Cl SL6 39 A4
Berkshire Ave SL1 42 A4
Berkshire Bsns Ctr RG19 107 A1
Berkshire Coll
of Agriculture SL6 18 A1
Berkshire Coll
of Agriculture
(Hall Place) SL6 38 A4
Berkshire Dr Reading RG31 84 B4
Thatcham RG19 107 A1
Berkshire Ind Hospl RG1 85 C3
Berkshire Lodge 1 SL6 39 C3
Berkshire Rd
Camberley GU15 151 C4
Henley-on-T RG9 35 B4
Berkshire Way RG12 117 B3
Bernadine Cl RG42 91 C1
Bernard Ct GU15 151 A2
Berners Cl SL1 41 C3
Bernersh Cl GU47 143 B1
Berries Rd SL6 20 A4
Berry Field SL2 43 B4
Berry Hill SL6 40 B4
Berry Hill Ct SL6 40 B4
Berrybank GU47 150 C3
Berrycroft RG12 118 B4
Berrylands Rd RG4 59 A2
Berrys La RG30 85 A1
Berrys Rd RG7 107 B3
Berryscroft Ct TW18 97 B1
Berryscroft Rd TW18 97 B1
Berstead Cl 3 RG6 87 A1
Berwick Ave SL1 42 A3
Berwick Cl SL7 1 B2
Berwick La SL7 1 B2
Berwick Rd SL7 1 B2
Berwyn Ho RG2 113 B4
Beryl Cl RG41 115 C4
Bessels Way OX11 12 A4
Bestobell Rd SL1 42 B4
Beswick Gdns RG12 118 C4
Beta Ho 6 RG30 85 B3
Beta Way TW20 123 B4
Betam Rd RG1 86 B4
Betchworth Ave RG6 87 A2
Bethany Waye TW14 98 C4
Bethesda Cl RG8 55 A3
Bethesda St RG8 55 A4
Betjeman Wlk GU46 149 A2
Betteridge Rd RG19 106 C1
Betty Grove La RG41 114 C4
Beverley Cl Frimley GU15 152 B3
Marlow SL7 1 A1
Thatcham RG18 106 B2
Beverley Ct SL1 43 A2
Beverley Gdns
Maidenhead SL6 19 A1
Wargrave RG10 36 C1
Beverley Rd Reading RG31 57 B1
Sunbury TW16 125 C4
Bevers The RG7 137 A3
Bexley Ct RG30 85 B3
Bexley St SL4 67 B3
Bibury Cl RG5 87 B2
Bicknell Rd GU16 151 C1
Biddles Cl 6 SL1 41 C3
Bideford Cl RG5 87 B3
Bideford Spur SL2 22 A1
Bier Path The RG8 14 A2
Bietigheim Way 2 GU15 151 B3
Big Barn Gr RG42 91 B1
Big La RG17 25 A2
Bigbury Gdns RG2 86 B2
Bigfrith La SL6 19 A3
Biggs La RG2,RG40 141 A4
Bill Hill Pk RG41 89 A2
Billet La SL0, SL3 44 A4
Billet Rd TW18, TW19 97 A3
Billing Ave RG40 141 C3
Billingbear La RG42 90 A3
Billington Way RG18 106 B3
Bilton Ind Est RG12 117 C3
Binbrook Cl RG6 87 B1
Binbury Row TW18 96 C2
Binfield CE Prim Sch
RG42 90 B1
Binfield Park Hospl RG42 90 B2
Binfield Rd
Bracknell, Priestwood RG42 91 A1
Wokingham RG40 116 C4
Bingham Dr TW18 97 B1
Bingham Rd SL1 41 A4
Binghams The SL6 40 A2
Bingley Gr RG5 60 C1
Binsted Dr GU17 150 B3
Birch Ave RG30 85 A4
Birch Cl GU15 151 C4
Birch Copse Prim Sch
RG31 84 B4
Birch Dr GU17 150 B2
Birch Gn Reading RG2 113 B4
Staines TW18 97 A2
Birch Gr Bracknell RG12 118 B3
Slough SL2 42 A4
Upper Halliford TW17 125 C4
Windsor SL4 66 B3
Birch Hill Prim Sch
RG12 118 A1
Birch Hill Rd RG12 118 A1
Birch La Mortimer RG7 136 C3
West End GU24 153 B4
Winkfield RG12, SL5 119 A4
Birch Platt GU24 153 B3
Birch Rd
Burghfield Common RG7 111 A2
Tadley RG26 134 C1
Windlesham GU20 146 C2
Wokingham RG40 142 A4
Birch Side RG45 143 A3
Birch Tree View GU18 146 A1
Birch View RG2 86 C1
Birches The
Blackwater GU17 150 A3
Goring RG8 34 A3
Birchetts Cl 2 RG42 118 A4
Birchfields GU15 151 B2
Birchington Rd SL4 67 A3
Birchland Cl RG7 136 C3
Birchlands Ct GU47 143 C1
Birchmead RG41 88 B1
Birchview Cl GU46 149 B2
Birchwood Cl RG4 59 B3
Birchwood Dr GU18 146 B1
Birchwood Rd RG14 105 B2
Birchwoods The RG31 84 A4
Bird Mews RG40 116 A3
Bird Mount Cotts SL4 67 B4
Birdhill Ave RG2 86 B1
Birds La RG7 107 C2
Birdwood Rd
Maidenhead SL6 39 A4
Sandhurst GU15 150 C3
Birkbeck Pl GU47 143 C1
Birkdale RG12 117 C1
Birkdale Ct SL5 120 B2
Birkhall Cl RG31 84 B3
Birley Rd SL1 42 B4
Biscuit Way RG2 112 C4
Bisham Abbey National
Sports Ctr SL7 18 B4
Bisham CE Prim Sch SL7 18 B4
Bisham Ct Bisham SL7 18 C3
19 Slough SL1 42 C2
Bisham Gn SL7 18 C3
Bishop Ct SL6 39 B3
Bishop Ctr The SL6 40 C4
Bishop Duppas Pk TW17 125 C1
Bishop Wand CE Sec Sch
TW16 125 C4
Bishop's La SL4 92 A4
Bishopdale RG12 118 A3
Bishops Cl RG26 135 A1
Bishops Ct TW16 98 C1
Bishops Dr
East Bedfont TW14 71 B1
Wokingham RG40 116 B4
Bishops Farm Cl SL4 66 A3
Bishops Gr GU20 146 B2
Bishops Orch SL2 22 A1
Bishops Rd Bradfield RG7 81 C2
Reading RG6 87 A3
Bishops Way TW20 96 B1
Bishops Wlk HP10 3 C4
Bishopseate Sch TW20 95 A3
Bishopsgate Rd TW20 95 A3
Bishopswood Ct RG26 134 C1
Bishopswood La RG26 134 C1
Bishopswood Rd RG26 134 C1
Bispham Ct 2 RG1 86 B3
Bissley Dr SL6 39 A2
Bitham La Ham RG17 126 A3
Inkpen RG17 127 A2
Bitham Rd OX12 8 B4
Bittern Cl GU47 150 B4
Bitterne Ave RG31 84 A3
Bix Hill RG9 15 A3
Bix La SL6 38 C4
Black Boy La SL6 17 B2
Black Butts Cotts SL6 20 A4
Black Horse Cl SL4 66 B3
Black Lake Cl TW20 123 A4
Black Park Ctry Pk SL3 23 C2
Black Park Rd SL3 23 C2
Blackberry Cl TW17 125 C3
Blackbird Cl
Burghfield Common RG7 111 A2
Sandhurst GU47 150 B4
Blackbird La RG20 132 A2
Blackburn Trad Est TW19 70 C1
Blackcap Pl GU47 150 C4
Blackdown Way RG19 106 B1
Blackett Cl TW18 123 C4
Blacklands Rd RG7 107 B3
Blackley Cl RG6 87 C2
Blackmeadows RG12 118 B2
Blackmoor Cl SL5 119 B4
Blackmoor Wood SL5 119 B4
Blacknest Gate Rd SL5 121 A3
Blacknest Rd GU25, SL5 121 C3
Blackpond La SL2 22 A2
Blacksmith Row SL3 44 A1
Blacksmith's La TW18 124 B3
Blacksmiths La KT16 124 A1
Blackstroud La E
GU18, GU24 153 C4
Blackstroud La W GU18 153 B4
Blackthorn Cl Earley RG6 87 A4
Purley on T RG31 57 A1
Blackthorn Dell SL3 43 B2
Blackthorn Dr
Lightwater GU18 153 A4
Thatcham RG18 106 B3
Blackthorne Cres SL3 69 C3
Blackthorne Rd SL3 69 C2
Blackwater Cl
Caversham RG4 59 C2
Shinfield RG7 113 A1
Blackwater Rise RG31 84 A2
Blackwater Sta GU17 150 C2
Blaenant RG4 58 C3
Blaenavon RG4 58 C3
Blagdon Cl RG19 131 B4
Blagdon Rd RG2 86 B1
Blagrave La RG4 58 B2
Blagrave Rise RG31 84 B3
Blagrave St RG1 86 A4
Blagrove Dr RG41 115 C2
Blagrove La RG41 115 C2
Blair Rd SL1 42 C3
Blaire Pk GU46 149 A4
Blake Cl Crowthorne RG45 143 B2
Wokingham RG40 116 C4
Blakeney Ct SL6 19 C1
Blakeney Fields RG17 48 A2
Blakes Cotts Reading RG1 86 B4
Wargrave RG10 37 A1
Blakes Ct 10 KT16 124 A1
Blakes La Tadley RG26 135 B1
Wargrave RG10 37 A1
Blakes Lock Mus RG1 86 B4
Blakes Rd RG10 36 C2
Blakes Ride GU46 149 A3
Blamire Dr RG42 90 C1
Blanchard Cl RG5 88 A4
Blandford Cl SL3 43 B2
Blandford Dr RG41 115 C2
Blandford Rd RG2 113 B4
Blandford Rd N SL3 43 B2
Blandford Rd S SL3 43 B2
Blands Cl RG7 110 C1
Blandy Rd RG9 35 B4
Blandys Hill RG17 128 A4
Blandys La RG8 55 A3
Blane's La SL5 119 B2
Blatchs Cl RG7 83 B2
Blay's La TW20 95 A1
Blays Cl TW20 95 B1
Bledlow Cl RG14 130 B3
Blenheim Cl Slough SL3 43 C3
Wokingham RG41 115 C3
Blenheim Cotts RG18 106 A4
Blenheim Ct Egham TW18 96 B2
19 Reading RG1 86 A3
Blenheim Gdns RG1 86 C3
Blenheim Rd
Caversham RG4 59 A2
Maidenhead SL6 39 A4
Newbury RG14 104 C1
Reading RG1 86 C3
Slough SL3 43 B1
Blenheim Terr 1 RG1 86 A3
Bletchmore Cl UB3 71 B4
Blewburton Wlk RG12 118 C3
Blewbury Dr RG31 84 A4
Blewbury Hill OX11 12 A4
Blinco La SL3 43 C4
Blind La
Bourne End HP10, SL8 3 A3
Lambourn RG17 25 A1
Blomfield Dale RG42 117 B4
Blondell Cl UB7 70 B4
Bloomfield Dr RG12 91 B1
Bloomfield Rd SL6 39 A3
Bloomfieldhatch La
Beech Hill RG7 138 A4
Shinfield RG7 112 C1
Bloomsbury Way GU17 150 B2
Blossom Ave RG7 83 C2
Blossom La RG7 83 C2
Blount Cres RG42 90 C1
Bloxworth Cl 17 RG12 118 C3
Blue Ball La TW20 95 C2
Blue Coat Wlk RG12 118 B2
Bluebell Dr RG7 110 C2
Bluebell Hill RG12 118 C4
Bluebell Mdw RG41 88 B2
Bluebell Rise GU18 153 A4
Bluebell Way RG18 106 B3
Bluecoats RG18 106 B2
Bluethroat Cl GU47 150 C4
Blumfield Cres SL1 41 C4
Blumfield Ct SL1 21 B1
Blundell's Rd RG30 84 C4
Blunden Dr SL3 44 B1
Blunts Ave UB7 71 A4
Blyth Ave RG19 106 C1
Blyth Wlk 31 RG1 86 A3
Blythe Cl SL0 44 C4
Blythewood La SL5 119 C4
Blythwood Dr GU16 151 B1
Boames La RG20 129 C3
Boarlands Cl SL1 41 C3
Boathouse Reach RG9 15 C1
Bobgreen Ct RG2 113 B3
Bobmore La SL7 1 C2
Bockhampton Rd RG17 25 B1
Bockmer La SL7 17 A4
Bodens Ride SL5 119 C1
Bodin Gdns RG14 131 A4
Bodmin Ave SL2 42 A4
Bodmin Cl RG19 106 B1
Bodmin Rd RG5 87 B3
Body Rd RG1 85 C4
Bog La RG12 119 A3
Bohams Rd OX11 11 B3
Bold's Ct SL2 23 A3
Bolding House La GU24 153 C4
Boldrewood RG7 110 C1
Boleyn Cl TW18 96 C2
Bolingbroke Way RG19 106 C2
Bolney Rd RG9 36 A3
Bolney Trevor Dr RG9 36 A2
Bolton Ave SL4 67 B2
Bolton Cres SL4 67 B2
Bolton Rd SL4 67 B2
Bolton Row RG20 50 B4
Bolton's La UB3 71 B4
Boltons La RG42 90 C1
Bolwell Cl RG10 61 C2
Bomer Cl UB7 71 A4
Bomford Cl RG18 78 C3
Bond St TW20 95 B2
Bone La RG14 105 B2
Bonemill La RG20 104 B1
Bones La RG9 35 A2
Boot End RG2 112 C4
Booth Dr TW18 97 B1
Borderside Slough SL2 43 A4
Yateley GU46 149 A3
Borrowdale Cl TW20 96 A1
Borrowdale Gdns GU15 152 B2
Borrowdale Rd RG41 88 A2
Boscombe Cl TW20 123 B4
Boscowen Way RG19 107 A1
Bosham Cl RG6 114 A4
Boshers Gdns TW20 95 C1
Bosman Dr GU20 146 A3
Bossington Ct TW18 96 C2
Bostock La RG7 83 A1
Boston Ave RG1 85 C3
Boston Dr SL8 3 A2
Boston Gr SL1 42 B4
Boston Rd RG9 35 C4
Bosworth Gdns RG5 87 C2
Botany Cl RG19 106 C2
Botham Dr SL1 42 C2
Bothy The RG10 36 B1
Botmoor Way RG20 48 C4
Bottisham Cl RG6 114 B4
Bottle La Knowl Hill SL6 38 A1
Newell Green RG42 91 A3
Bottom La RG7 110 B4
Bottom Waltons
Caravan Site SL2 21 C2
Bouldish Farm Rd SL5 120 A3
Boult St RG1 86 B4
Boulters Cl
Maidenhead SL6 20 B1
Slough SL1 42 A2
Woodley RG5 87 C4
Boulters Ct SL6 20 B1
Boulters Gdns SL6 20 B1
Boulters Ho 3 RG12 118 C3
Boulters La SL6 20 B1
Boulton Rd RG2 86 A2
Boults Wlk RG2 86 A3
Boundary Cl RG31 84 B3
Boundary La RG4 58 C2
Boundary Pl HP10 3 B4
Boundary Rd
Newbury RG14 105 A1
Staines TW15 97 B2
Taplow SL6 40 C4
Wooburn Green HP10 3 B4
Bourn Cl RG6 87 B1
Bourne Arch RG18 106 A2
Bourne Ave
Chertsey KT16 124 A3
Reading RG2 86 A2
Windsor SL4 67 B2
Bourne Cl Bourne End SL8 3 A3
Reading RG31 84 A2
Bourne End Bsns Ctr 8
SL8 3 A2
Bourne End Rd SL6,SL8 20 C4
Bourne End Sta SL8 3 A2
Bourne Ho TW15 98 A2
Bourne Mdw TW20 123 A3
Bourne Rd Pangbourne RG8 56 C3
Slough SL1 42 B2
Thatcham RG19 106 A2
Wentworth GU25 122 B2
Bourne- Stevens Cl RG1 86 A4
Bourne Vale RG17 100 B3
Bourneside GU25 122 A1
Bourton Cl RG30 84 C4
Bouverie Way SL3 43 C1
Boveney Cl SL1 42 A2
Boveney Ho 2 RG12 118 C3
Boveney New Rd SL4 41 C1
Boveney Rd SL4 41 B1
Bovingdon Hts SL7 1 A1
Bowden Cl TW14 98 C4
Bowden Rd SL5 120 B2
Bowdown Ct RG14 104 C1
Bower Ct 3 SL1 41 C3
Bower Way SL1 41 C3
Bowes Rd Egham TW18 96 C1
Thatcham RG19 106 B1
Bowes-Lyon Cl 7 SL4 67 B3
Bowfell Cl RG31 57 B1
Bowland Dr RG12 118 C1
Bowling Ct RG9 15 B2

Bowling Green La RG8 57 A3
Bowling Green Rd RG18 106 A3
Bowlings The GU15 151 B3
Bowman Ct RG45 142 C2
Bowmans Cl SL1 21 A2
Bowry Dr TW19 68 C1
Bowyer Cres RG40 116 B4
Bowyer Dr SL1 41 C3
Bowyer Wlk SL5 119 C4
Bowyers La RG42 91 B3
Boxford Ridge RG12 118 A3
Boxshall Ct RG14 104 C1
Boyd Ct RG42 118 A4
Boyn Hill Ave SL6 39 B3
Boyn Hill Cl SL6 39 B3
Boyn Hill Rd SL6 39 B3
Boyn Valley Rd SL6 39 B3
Boyndon Rd SL6 39 B4
Boyne Hill CE Inf Sch SL6 39 B3
Bracebridge GU15 151 A3
Bracken Bank SL5 119 B4
Bracken Cl Ashford TW16 98 C1
Farnham Common SL2 22 B4
Purley on T RG31 57 B1
Bracken Copse RG17 127 C3
Bracken La GU46 149 A3
Bracken Rd SL6 39 B2
Bracken Way
Burghfield Common RG7 111 A1
Flackwell Heath HP10 3 A4
Brackendale Cl GU15 151 C2
Brackendale Rd GU15 151 B2
Brackenforde SL3 43 B2
Brackenhale Comp Sch RG12 118 A3
Brackens The RG45 143 A4
Brackenwood
Burghfield Common RG7 110 C1
Frimley GU15 152 B3
Brackenwood Dr RG26 135 A1
Brackley Ho TW18 96 C2
Bracknell Beeches RG12 118 A3
Bracknell Bsns Ctr The RG12 117 C4
Bracknell Cl GU15 144 C1
Bracknell Coll
Bracknell RG12 118 B4
Bracknell, Wick Hill RG12 118 B4
Bracknell Enterprise Ctr RG12 118 A4
Bracknell Rd
Bagshot GU19 145 C3
Camberley GU15 145 A1
Crowthorne RG45 143 B3
Winkfield RG42 92 A3
Bracknell Sports & L Ctr RG12 118 B2
Bracknell Sta RG12 118 A3
Brackstone Cl RG4 59 B1
Bradbury Gdns SL3 23 B4
Bradcutts La SL6 19 C4
Bradenham La SL7 18 B3
Bradfield CE Prim Sch RG7 82 A1
Bradfield Coll RG7 82 B3
Bradfields RG12 118 B2
Bradford Rd SL1 42 A4
Brading Way RG8 57 B3
Bradley Cl RG17 102 A1
Bradley Dr RG40 116 A1
Bradley Rd SL1 42 C3
Bradley-Moore Sq RG18 106 C3
Bradmore Way RG6 114 A4
Bradshaw Cl SL4 66 C3
Bradwell Rd RG31 57 B2
Braemar SL6 63 B4
Braemar Ct 1 SL7 1 B1
Braemar Gdns SL1 42 A2
Braemore Cl RG19 106 B1
Brakendale Way RG6 87 A3
Bramber Ct SL1 42 A3
Bramber Mews RG4 59 C2
Bramble Cl TW17 125 B3
Bramble Cres RG30 84 C4
Bramble Dr SL6 39 A2
Brambledown TW18 124 A4
Bramblegate RG45 143 A3
Brambles The
Crowthorne RG45 142 B3
Newbury RG14 130 C4
Bramblings RG4 58 C3
Bramcote GU15 152 B3
Bramley Ave TW17 125 C3
Bramley Chase SL6 39 B2
Bramley Cl Chertsey KT16 124 A1
Earley RG6 87 A2
Maidenhead SL6 39 B2
Staines TW18 97 B1
Bramley Gr RG45 142 B3
Bramley La GU17 150 A3
Bramley Rd
Camberley GU15 151 A1
Silchester RG7 136 A1
Bramling Ave GU46 149 A3
Brammas Cl SL1 42 B2
Brampton Chase RG9 36 A2
Brampton Ct SL6 40 A4
Bramshaw Rd RG30 58 A1
Bramshill Cl RG2 140 C4
Bramwell Cl RG19 106 C1
Bran Cl RG30 84 C4
Brandon Ave RG5 88 A4
Brandon Cl GU15 152 B2
Brands Rd SL3 69 A4
Branksome Cl GU15 151 C3
Branksome Ct 19 RG1 85 C4
Branksome Hill Rd GU47 150 C4
Branksome Park Rd GU15 151 C3
Brants Bridge RG12 118 C4
Brants Cl RG2 114 C1
Braunfels Wlk RG14 104 C1
Bravington Cl TW17 124 C2
Bray Cl SL6 40 B2
Bray Ct SL6 40 B1
Bray Rd Maidenhead SL6 40 A3
Reading RG30 85 A2
Braybank SL6 40 B2
Braybrooke Dr RG10 88 C4
Braybrooke Gdns RG10 36 B1
Braybrooke Rd
Bracknell RG42 91 A1
Wargrave RG10 36 B1
Braye Cl GU47 143 B1
Brayfield Rd SL6 40 B2
Brayford Rd RG2 113 B4
Braywick Park & Nature Ctr SL6 40 A2
Braywick Rd SL6 40 A2
Braywood Ave TW20 96 A1
Braywood CE Fst Sch SL4 65 C3
Braywood Cotts SL4 66 A3
Braziers La SL4, SL5 92 B2
Breach Sq RG17 100 B2
Breadcroft La SL6 38 C2
Breadcroft Rd SL6 38 C2
Bream Cl SL7 18 B4
Brean Wlk RG6 87 A1
Brechin Ct 3 RG1 86 B3
Brecon Ct SL1 42 B2
Brecon Rd RG5 87 C4
Bredon Rd RG41 88 C1
Bredward Cl SL1 21 A1
Breech The GU47 150 C4
Breedons Hill RG8 56 B3
Bremer Rd TW18, TW19 97 A3
Brendon Cl Harlington UB3 71 B4
Reading RG30 57 C1
Brent Cl RG19 106 B1
Brent Gdns RG2 86 A2
Brent Rd SL8 3 A2
Brentmoor Rd GU24 153 B3
Brerewood RG6 86 C1
Bret Harte Rd GU16 151 C1
Brew Tower SL7 1 B1
Brewery Comm RG7 137 A4
Brewhouse Hill SN8 99 A2
Briants Ave RG4 59 B1
Briants Piece RG18 79 A3
Briar Ave GU18 153 A4
Briar Cl Burnham SL6 41 A4
Caversham RG4 59 A3
Briar Dene SL6 19 B1
Briar Glen SL6 19 C3
Briar Rd TW17 125 A2
Briar Way SL2 42 A4
Briarlea Rd RG7 136 C3
Briars Cl RG8 56 C3
Briars The Slough SL3 43 C1
Stanwell TW19 70 A1
Briarwood RG40 141 C3
Briarwood Cl TW13 98 C3
Brickfield La Burnham SL1 21 A2
Harlington UB3 71 B4
Brickfields Ind Ctr RG12 118 A4
Bridge Ave Cookham SL6 19 C3
Maidenhead SL6 40 A4
Bridge Cl Slough SL1 41 C3
Staines TW18 96 C2
Walton-on-T KT12 125 C1
Bridge Ct SL6 40 B4
Bridge End GU15 151 A2
Bridge Gdns TW15 98 B1
Bridge La GU25, KT16 122 C2
Bridge Rd Ascot SL5 120 B2
Bagshot GU19 145 C2
Camberley GU15 151 A2
Chertsey KT16 124 A1
Maidenhead SL6 40 A4
Bridge St Caversham RG4 59 A1
Colnbrook SL3 69 B4
Hungerford RG17 100 B3
Maidenhead SL6 40 A4
Newbury RG14 105 A2
Reading RG1 86 A4
Staines TW18 96 C2
Walton-on-T KT12 125 C1
Bridge View SL5 121 A1
Bridge Walk GU46 149 B4
Bridge Works GU15 151 A2
Bridgeman Ct 5 SL4 67 A3
Bridgeman Dr SL4 67 A3
Bridges Cl RG41 115 C4
Bridges The RG7 136 B3
Bridgestone Dr SL8 3 B2
Bridgewater Cl RG30 58 B1
Bridgewater Ct SL3 44 A1
Bridgewater Terr SL4 67 B3
Bridgewater Way SL4 67 B3
Bridle Cl SL6 19 C1
Bridle Rd SL6 19 C1
Bridlepath Way TW14 98 C4
Bridlington Spur SL1 42 A2
Bridport Cl RG6 87 B1
Bridport Way SL2 22 A1
Brierley Pl RG31 57 B2
Briff La RG7 107 B4
Brigham Rd RG1 59 A1
Brighton Rd RG6 87 A3
Brighton Spur SL2 22 A1
Brightside Ave TW18 97 B1
Brightwalton CE Prim Sch RG20 28 B2
Brigidine Sch The SL4 67 B2
Brill Cl Caversham RG4 59 A2
Maidenhead SL6 39 B2
Marlow SL7 1 B1
Brimblecombe Cl RG41 89 A1
Brimpton CE Prim Sch RG7 133 C3
Brimpton La RG7 134 A2
Brimpton Rd
Brimpton RG7 133 C4
Reading RG30 85 A2
Tadley RG26 134 B1
Brinkworth Pl SL4 95 A4
Brinn's La GU17 150 B3
Briony Ho RG2 113 A4
Brisbane Rd RG30 85 A4
Bristol Cl TW19 70 C1
Bristol Ct 10 TW19 70 C1
Bristol Way SL1 42 C3
Bristow Ct Caversham RG4 59 A1
Marlow SL7 2 A2
Bristow Cty Inf Sch GU15 151 A1
Bristow Rd GU15 151 A2
Britannia Ind Est SL3 69 C3
Britannia Way TW19 97 B4
Brittain Ct GU47 150 B4
Britten Rd RG2 86 A3
Britwell Rd SL1 21 B1
Brixham Rd RG2 86 A1
Broad Hinton RG10 61 C2
Broad La Bracknell RG12 118 B3
Bucklebury RG7 107 B3
Wooburn Green HP10 3 C3
Broad Ley's SL4 66 C4
Broad Oak Ashford TW16 98 C1
Slough SL2 22 B1
Broad Oak Ct SL2 22 B1
Broad Platts SL3 43 B2
Broad St East Isley RG20 30 C4
Reading RG1 86 A4
West End GU24 153 B3
Wokingham RG40 116 B3
Broad St Wlk RG40 116 B3
Broad Street Mall The RG1 86 A4
Broad Way RG7 138 B2
Broad Wlk GU16 151 C1
Broadacre TW18 97 A2
Broadcommon Rd RG10 89 A4
Broadhalfpenny La RG26 135 B1
Broadlands Ave TW17 125 B2
Broadlands Cl RG31 84 B3
Broadlands Ct RG42 117 C4
Broadlands Dr SL5 120 B1
Broadley Gn GU20 146 B2
Broadmark Rd SL2 43 A3
Broadmeadow End RG18 106 C2
Broadmoor Cty Prim Sch RG45 143 B2
Broadmoor Hospl RG45 143 C3
Broadmoor La RG10, SL6 63 A3
Broadrick Heath RG42 91 C1
Broadview Est TW19 98 A4
Broadwater Cl TW19 95 C4
Broadwater La RG10 61 C1
Broadwater Pk SL6 40 C1
Broadwater Rd RG10 61 C2
Broadway Bracknell RG12 118 B4
Maidenhead SL6 39 C4
Staines TW18 97 A1
Thatcham RG19 106 B2
Winkfield SL4 93 A4
Broadway Ctyd RG19 106 B2
Broadway Mall 6 SL6 39 C4
Broadway Rd GU18,GU20 146 B1
Broadway The
Laleham TW18 124 B4
Lambourn RG17 25 A2
12 Newbury RG14 105 A2
Sandhurst GU47 150 A4
Brocas Rd RG7 110 C1
Brocas St SL4 67 B4
Brocas Terr SL4 67 B4
Brock Gdns RG30 85 B4
Brock La SL6 39 C4
Brock La Mall 7 SL6 39 C4
Brock Way GU25 122 B3
Brockenhurst Dr GU46 149 B3
Brockenhurst Rd
Ascot SL5 120 A2
Bracknell RG12 119 A3
Brockhurst & Marlston House Prep Schs RG18 79 C2
Brocklands GU46 149 A2
Brockley Cl RG30 85 A4
Brocks La RG7 & RG18 80 A2
Brocks Way RG9 36 A2
Brockway SL3 44 A1
Broken Furlong SL4 42 A1
Broken Way RG20 131 A1
Bromley Wlk RG30 84 C4
Brompton Cl 9 RG6 87 B1
Brompton Dr SL6 19 B1
Bromycroft Rd SL2 22 A1
Bronte Rise RG14 131 A4
Brook Cl Sandhurst GU47 143 C1
Stanwell TW19 97 C4
Wokingham RG41 116 A4
Brook Cres SL1 41 C4
Brook Dr Ashford TW16 98 C1
Bracknell RG12 118 C3
Reading RG30 112 C4
Brook Gn RG42 117 C4
Brook Ho SL1 42 B2
Brook La RG10 62 C2
Brook Path SL1 41 C3
Brook Rd Bagshot GU19 145 C1
Camberley GU15 151 A2
Brook St Twyford RG10 61 B2
Windsor SL4 67 B3
Brook St W RG1 86 A3
Brookbank HP10 3 B2
Brookdene Cl SL6 19 C1
Brooke Furmston Pl SL7 1 C2
Brooke Pl RG42 90 B2
Brookers Cnr RG45 143 B3
Brookers Hill RG2 113 B3
Brookers Row RG45 143 B3
Brookfield Ho SL3 68 B3
Brookfield Rd HP10 3 B2
Brookfields Specl Sch RG31 57 B2
Brookhouse Dr HP10 3 B2
Brooklands Cl TW16 125 C4
Brooklyn Dr RG4 59 A3
Brookmill The RG1 85 C3
Brooks Rd RG18 106 C2
Brooksby Cl GU17 150 A3
Brooksby Rd RG31 57 B1
Brookside Chertsey KT16 123 C1
Colnbrook SL3 69 B4
Reading RG31 84 C2
Sandhurst GU47 150 B4
Slough SL3 43 C4
Wokingham RG41 115 C4
Brookside Ave
Staines TW15 97 B2
Wraysbury TW19 68 C2
Brookside Cl RG6 87 B1
Brookway RG14 105 C1
Broom Acres GU47 143 A1
Broom Cl
Blackwater GU17 150 C2
Reading RG31 84 B3
Broom Field GU18 153 A4
Broom Gr RG41 115 B2
Broom Hill Cookham SL6 19 C3
Stoke Poges SL2 23 A3
Broom Ho SL3 43 C1
Broome Cl GU46 149 B4
Broome Ct RG12 118 A3
Broome Lodge TW18 97 A2
Broomfield TW18 97 A1
Broomfield Cl SL5 121 A1
Broomfield Dr SL5 121 A2
Broomfield Pk SL5 121 A1
Broomfield Rd RG30 84 C4
Broomhall Bldgs SL5 121 A1
Broomhall La SL5 121 A2
Broomsquires Rd GU19 145 C1
Broughton Cl RG30 58 B1
Broughton Mews GU16 151 C1
Brownfield Gdns SL6 39 C3
Browngraves Rd UB3 71 B4
Browning Cl
Frimley GU15 152 B2
Thatcham RG18 106 B2
Brownlow Dr RG42 91 B1
Brownlow Rd RG1 85 C4
Brownrigg Cres RG12 118 C4
Brownrigg Rd TW15 98 A2
Browns Ct SL1 41 C3
Brownsfield Rd RG18 106 B2
Bruan Rd RG14 130 C4
Bruce Ave TW17 125 B2
Bruce Cl SL1 42 A3
Bruce Rd RG5 87 B4
Bruce Wlk SL4 66 B3
Brucewood Par SL7 1 C3
Brudenell SL4 66 C2
Brummell Rd RG14 104 C3
Brunel Cl SL6 39 C3
Brunel Ctr SL6 39 B3
Brunel Dr
Crowthorne RG45 143 B4
Woodley RG5 60 C1
Brunel Rd Maidenhead SL6 39 B3
Reading RG30 85 A2
Theale RG7 83 C1
Brunel Ret Pk RG2 86 A2
Brunel Univ (Runnymede Campus) TW20 95 B3
Brunel Way SL1 42 C3
Brunswick RG12 118 A1
Brunswick Hill RG1 85 C4
Brunswick Lodge 12 RG1 85 C4
Brunswick St RG1 85 C3
Bruton Way RG12 118 C1
Bryant Ave SL2 42 C4
Bryants La RG18 53 C1
Bryants Pl RG8 57 A3
Brybur Cl RG2 113 B4
Bryer Pl SL4 66 B2
Bryony Ho RG42 117 C4
Bryony Way TW16 98 C1
Bsns Village The SL2 43 A3
Buccaneer Cl RG5 88 A4
Buccleuch Rd SL3 68 A4
Buchan The GU15 152 A4
Buchanan Dr RG40 141 C4
Buchanan Sq RG19 106 C1
Buck Side RG4 59 A1
Buckden Cl RG5 88 A3
Buckfield Ct SL0 44 C2
Buckham Hill RG17 & RG20 48 B3
Buckhurst Gr RG40 116 C3
Buckhurst Hill RG12 118 C3
Buckhurst La SL5 121 A3
Buckhurst Moors RG12 117 B3
Buckhurst Rd SL5 120 C4
Buckhurst Way RG6 87 A2
Buckingham Ave SL1 42 A4
Buckingham Ave E SL1 42 B4
Buckingham Ct
Staines TW18 97 A2
Wokingham RG40 116 B3
Buckingham Dr RG4 59 A3
Buckingham Gate SL7 17 B4
Buckingham Gdns 12 SL1 42 C2
Buckingham Ho 4 SL6 39 C3
Buckingham Rd RG14 104 C1
Buckingham Way GU16 151 C1
Buckland Ave SL2 43 A2
Buckland Cres SL4 66 C3
Buckland Cty Jun & Inf Sch TW18 97 B1
Buckland Gate SL3 23 A1
Buckland Rd RG2 86 A2
Buckle La RG42 91 A3
Bucklebury RG12 118 A1
Bucklebury CE Prim Sch RG7 107 B3
Bucklebury Cl SL6 40 B1
Bucklebury Farm Pk RG7 80 B1
Bucknell Ave RG8 56 C3
Bucknell Cl RG31 84 C2
Buckthorn Cl RG40 116 C4
Budebury Rd TW18 97 A2
Budge's Cotts RG40 116 C4
Budge's Gdns RG40 116 C4
Budge's Rd RG40 116 B4
Budham Way RG12 118 A2
Buffins SL6 20 C1
Bulbrook Row RG12 118 C4
Bulkeley Ave SL4 67 A2
Bulkeley Cl TW20 95 B2
Bull La Bracknell RG42 118 A4
Swallowfield RG7 139 A2
Bull Meadow The RG8 33 C3
Bullbrook Dr RG12 118 C4
Bullfinch Cl GU47 150 C4
Bulmershe Rd RG1 86 C3
Bulpit La RG17 100 B2
Bulstrode Pl SL1 42 C2
Bunby Rd SL2 22 C3
Bunces Cl SL4 42 A1
Bunces La RG7 111 A1
Bundy's Way TW18 96 C1
Bungalow Dr RG31 84 B4
Bunglers Hill RG7 140 A3
Bunkers Hill RG14 130 B3
Bunten Meade SL1 42 A3
Bunyan Ct 12 RG1 86 A3
Burbage Gn RG12 118 C2
Burbidge Cl RG31 84 C2
Burbidge Rd TW17 125 A3
Burbury Woods GU15 151 C3
Burchell Rd RG14 104 C3
Burchett Copse RG40 141 C4
Burchett's Green CE Inf Sch SL6 38 A4
Burchett's Green Rd SL6 18 B1
Burchetts Green La SL6 38 B3
Burchetts Green Rd SL6 38 A4
Burchetts Way TW17 125 A2
Burcombe Way RG4 59 A2
Burcot Gdns SL6 19 C2
Burdens Heath RG7 107 A3
Burdett Ct RG2 86 B2
Burdock Cl
Burghfield Common RG7 111 A1
Lightwater GU18 153 A4
Burfield Rd SL4, TW19 95 A4
Burford Cl SL7 1 B3
Burford Ct 11 Reading RG1 85 C4
Wokingham RG40 116 C3
Burford Cty Comb Sch SL7 1 B3
Burford Gdns SL1 41 B4
Burford Rd GU15 151 A2
Burfords RG17 47 B3
Burges Way TW18 97 A2
Burgess Cl RG5 87 B2
Burgess La RG17,RG20 128 B3
Burgett Rd SL1 42 A2
Burghead Cl GU47 150 B4
Burghfield Rd RG30 85 A2
Burghfield St Mary's CE Prim Sch RG30 111 B3
Burgoyne Rd
Ashford TW16 98 C1
Camberley GU15 152 A3
Burleigh Gdns TW15 98 B2
Burleigh La SL5 119 C4
Burleigh Mews RG4 59 B3
Burleigh Rd SL5 119 C4
Burley Orch KT16 124 A2
Burley Way GU17 150 B3
Burlingham Cl RG2 113 B3
Burlings The SL5 119 C4
Burlington Ave SL1 42 C2
Burlington Cl TW14 98 B4
Burlington Ct
Blackwater GU17 150 B2
1 Slough SL1 42 C2
Burlington Rd
Burnham SL1 21 A1
Reading RG30 84 B4
2 Slough SL1 42 C2
Burlsdon Way RG12 118 C4
Burn Moor Chase RG12 118 C1
Burn Wlk SL1 21 A1
Burne-Jones Dr GU47 150 B3
Burnet Cl GU24 153 C3
Burnetts Rd SL4 66 C3
Burney Bit RG26 135 C1
Burnham Beeches (Nature Reserve) SL2 22 A4
Burnham Cl Bourne End SL8 3 A2
Windsor SL4 66 B3
Burnham Copse Jun & Inf Schs RG26 135 A1

Burnham Gr RG42 91 B1
Burnham Gram Sch SL1 21 B1
Burnham La SL1 41 C4
Burnham Manor GU15 152 A4
Burnham Rd RG26 134 C1
Burnham Rise RG4 59 B4
Burnham Sta SL1 41 B4
Burnham Upper Sch SL1 41 A4
Burniston Cl RG6 87 C1
Burnmoor Mdw RG27 141 C1
Burns Cl RG5 87 C2
Burns Wlk RG18 106 B2
Burnt Oak Cookham SL6 19 C4
Wokingham RG40 141 C4
Burnt Pollard La GU18 146 C1
Burnthouse Gdns RG42 91 C1
Burnthouse La RG7,RG30 112 A3
Burrcroft Rd RG30 85 A3
Burrell Rd RG20 31 C2
Burroughs Cres SL8 3 A2
Burroway Rd SL3 44 A2
Burrows Hill Cl
TW19, TW6 70 B2
Burrows The RG26 135 A1
Burton Cl Twyford RG10 61 C1
Windlesham GU20 146 B2
Burton Way SL4 66 C2
Burtons Hill RG17 102 A1
Burway Cres KT16 124 A3
Burwell Cl RG6 87 B1
Burys Bank Rd RG19 132 B3
Bush Rd TW17 124 C2
Bush Wlk RG40 116 B3
Business Ctr The RG41 116 A2
Butchers La SL6 63 B4
Bute St RG30 85 A3
Butler Ct 5 SL7 1 C2
Butler Rd Bagshot GU19 145 C1
Crowthorne RG45 143 A3
Butlers Cl SL4 66 B3
Butson Cl RG14 104 C2
Buttenshaw Ave RG2 141 A4
Buttenshaw Cl RG2 141 A4
Butter Market RG1 86 A4
Buttercup Cl RG40 117 A3
Buttercup Pl RG18 106 B2
Buttercup Sq TW19 97 B4
Butterfield
Camberley GU15 151 A2
Wooburn Green HP10 3 B2
Buttermere Ave SL1 41 B4
Buttermere Cl TW14 98 C4
Buttermere Dr GU15 152 B2
Buttermere Gdns RG12 118 B3
Buttermere Way TW20 96 A1
Buttersteep Rise
GU20, SL5 119 B1
Butts Furlong RG20 28 B2
Butts Hill Rd RG5 87 C4
Buxton Ave RG4 58 C2
Buxton Rd TW15 97 B2
Bybend Cl SL2 22 A2
Byefield Rd RG30 85 A2
Byeways Cl RG10 37 C2
Byland Dr SL6 40 A1
Byreton Cl RG6 87 A1
Byron SL3 44 A1
Byron Ave GU15 152 A2
Byron Cl 6 Marlow SL7 1 C2
Newbury RG14 130 C4
Twyford RG10 61 C2
Yateley GU46 149 A2
Byron Dr RG45 143 A2
Byron Rd Earley RG6 87 A4
Twyford RG10 61 C2
Bythorn Cl RG6 87 C1
Byways Burnham SL1 41 A4
Yateley GU46 149 A3
Bywood RG12 118 A1
Byworth Cl RG2 113 A4

## C

Cabin Moss RG12 118 C1
Cabrera Ave GU25 122 B2
Cabrera Cl GU25 122 B2
Cadbury Cl TW16 98 C1
Cadbury Rd TW16 98 C1
Caddy Cl 4 TW20 96 A2
Cadogan Cl Holyport SL6 65 A4
Reading RG30 84 C4
Cadwell Dr SL6 39 B2
Caesar's Camp Rd GU15 152 A4
Caesar's Cl GU15 152 A4
Caesar's Way TW17 125 B2
Caesars Gate RG42 91 C1
Caesers Ct GU15 152 A4
Cages Wood Dr SL2 22 A4
Cain Rd RG12, RG42 117 C4
Cain's La TW14 71 C1
Cairn Cl GU15 152 A2
Cairngorm Pl SL2 22 B1
Cairngorm Rd RG19 106 B1
Caistor Cl RG31 84 A2
Calard Dr RG18 106 A3
Calbourne Dr RG31 84 B2
Calbroke Rd SL2 21 C1
Calcot Ct RG31 84 C3
Calcot Place Dr RG31 84 C2
Caldbeck Dr RG5 87 C4
Calder Cl Maidenhead SL6 19 C1
Reading RG30 84 C4
Calder Ct Maidenhead SL6 19 B1
Slough SL3 43 C1
Calder Way SL3 69 C2
Caldicott Prep Sch SL2 22 A3
Caldwell Rd GU20 146 B3
Caledonia Rd TW19 97 C4
Caleta Cl RG4 59 B1
Calfridus Way RG12 118 C3
California Ctry Pk RG2 141 B4
Calleva Mus RG7 136 A1
Calleva Pk RG7 134 C1
Calleva Roman Town
RG7 136 B1
Callington Rd RG2 86 B1
Callins La RG10 63 A2
Callis Farm Cl TW19 70 C1
Callow Hill GU25, TW20 122 B4
Calshot Pl RG31 84 B2
Calshot Rd TW6 71 A3
Calshot Way TW6 71 A3
Calvin Cl GU15 152 A2
Camberley Cty Inf Sch
GU15 151 B3
Camberley Heath
Golf Course GU15 152 A3
Camberley Rd TW6 71 A2
Camberley Sta GU15 151 B3
Camberley Towers GU15 151 B3
Camborne Cl Earley RG6 87 A1
Harmondsworth TW6 71 A2
Camborne Cres TW6 71 A2
Camborne Rd TW6 71 A2
Camborne Way TW6 71 A2
Cambria Ct Slough SL3 43 A2
Staines TW18 96 C2
Cambria Gdns TW19 97 C4
Cambrian Cl GU15 151 A3
Cambrian Way
Reading RG31 84 B2
Wokingham RG40 142 A4
Cambridge Ave
Burnham SL1 21 A2
Slough SL1 42 A4
Cambridge Cl UB7 70 B4
Cambridge Ho 2 SL4 67 B3
Cambridge Rd
Crowthorne RG45 143 B2
Littleton TW15 98 B1
Marlow SL7 1 B1
Sandhurst GU47 143 C1
Cambridge Sq GU15 151 B3
Cambridge St 1 RG1 85 C4
Cambridge Wlk 3 GU15 151 B3
Cambridgeshire Cl
Bracknell RG42 91 C1
Wokingham RG41 115 C3
Camden Pl Bourne End SL8 3 A2
Reading RG31 84 A2
Camden Rd SL6 19 B1
Camelford Cl RG2 86 A1
Camellia Ct GU24 153 C3
Camellia Way RG41 115 B4
Camgate Est TW19 97 C4
Camilla Cl TW16 98 C1
Camley Gdns SL6 39 A4
Camley Park Dr SL6 38 C4
Camm Ave SL4 66 C2
Camp Rd RG7 110 B1
Campbell Cl GU46 149 C3
Campbell Pl GU16 151 C2
Campbell Rd RG5 87 B3
Campbells Gn RG7 137 A3
Camperdown SL6 20 A1
Camperdown Ho 38 SL4 67 B3
Campion Cl GU17 150 C2
Campion Ho RG42 117 C4
Campion Way RG40 116 C4
Canada Rd SL1 43 A2
Canal View Rd RG14 105 B2
Canal Walk RG17 100 B3
Canal Way RG1 86 B4
Canal Wharf SL3 44 A2
Canberra Cl GU46 149 A4
Canberra Rd TW6 71 A2
Candleford Cl RG12 91 B1
Candover Cl UB7 70 B4
Canford Ct RG30 85 B4
Cannock Cl SL6 40 A3
Cannock Way RG6 87 B1
Cannon Cl GU47 150 C4
Cannon Court Rd SL6 19 B2
Cannon Hill RG12 118 B2
Cannon Hill Cl SL6 40 B1
Cannon La SL6 38 C2
Cannon St 3 RG1 85 C4
Cannondown Rd SL6 19 C3
Canon Hill Dr SL6 40 A2
Canon Hill Way SL6 40 A1
Canon's Cloisters SL4 67 B4
Canopus Way TW19 97 C4
Cansfield End RG14 104 C2
Canterbury Ave SL2 22 B1
Canterbury Ct TW15 97 C2
Canterbury Rd RG2 86 B2
Cantley Cres RG41 116 A4
Cantley House Hotel
RG40 116 A4
Cape Villas SL0 44 C4
Capper Rd GU15 151 A4
Capricorn Ho HP10 3 A4
Captains Gorse RG8 54 C3
Caraway Rd RG6 87 A1
Carbery La SL5 120 A3
Carbinswood La RG7 108 A3
Cardiff Rd RG1 58 C1
Cardigan Cl SL1 41 C3
Cardigan Gdns RG1 86 C3
Cardigan Rd RG1 86 C3
Cardinal Cl RG4 59 A1
Cardinal's Wlk TW16 98 C1
Cardinals Wlk SL6 41 B4
Cardwell Cres SL5 120 B2
Carew Rd TW15 98 B1
Carey Cl SL4 67 A2
Carey Rd RG40 116 B3
Carey St RG1 85 C4
Cariad Ct RG8 34 A4
Carisbrooke Cl
Caversham RG4 59 B3
Maidenhead SL6 39 B3
Carisbrooke Ct SL1 42 C3
Carland Cl RG6 87 A1
Carlesgill Pl RG9 35 C4
Carlile Gdns RG10 61 B3
Carlinwark Dr GU15 151 C4
Carlisle Rd Reading RG31 57 C2
Slough SL1 42 B3
Carlton Cl Frimley GU15 152 A2
Woodley RG5 87 C3
Carlton Ct TW18 97 A2
Carlton Ho TW19 70 B1
Carlton Rd Ashford TW16 98 C1
Caversham RG4 58 C3
Slough SL2 43 A3
Carlyle Ct RG45 143 B3
Carlyle Rd TW18 97 A1
Carmarthen Rd SL1 42 C3
Carmela Ct TW15 98 B1
Carnarvon Rd RG1 86 C3
Carnation Cl RG45 143 A4
Carnation Dr RG42 92 A1
Carnegie Rd RG14 105 A1
Carnoustie RG12 117 C1
Carnoustie Ct 23 RG1 86 B4
Carolina Pl RG40 141 C4
Caroline Ct Ashford TW15 98 A1
Marlow SL7 1 C2
Caroline Dr RG41 116 A4
Caroline Pl UB3 71 C4
Caroline St 7 RG1 85 C4
Carrick Gdns RG5 87 B4
Carrick La GU46 149 C3
Carrington Ave HP10 3 A4
Carrington Cty Mid Sch The
HP10 3 A4
Carrington Rd SL1 42 C3
Carroll Cres SL5 119 C3
Carron Cl RG30 85 A4
Carsdale Cl RG1 85 C3
Carshalton Rd GU15 145 A1
Carshalton Way RG6 87 B1
Carston Gr RG31 84 C2
Carter Cl SL4 67 A3
Carters Hill RG40 & RG42 90 A2
Carters Rise RG31 84 C2
Cartmel Dr RG5 87 B3
Carwarden House Sch
GU15 152 A2
Cary Cl RG14 130 B3
Casey Ct RG7 81 B2
Cassia Dr RG6 86 C1
Cassiobury Ave TW14 98 C4
Cassocks Sq TW17 125 B1
Castle Ave SL3 68 A4
Castle Cl 3 Charlton TW16 98 C1
Frimley GU15 151 C2
Castle Cres RG1 85 C3
Castle Ct SL6 39 B4
Castle Dr SL6 39 B4
Castle End Rd RG10 62 A4
Castle Farm Caravan Site
SL4 66 B3
Castle Gr RG14 104 C3
Castle Hill Maidenhead SL6 39 C4
Reading RG1 85 C3
Swallowfield RG7 140 B4
Windsor SL4 67 C3
Castle Hill Rd TW20 95 B3
Castle Hill Terr SL6 39 C4
Castle Ind Pk RG14 105 B3
Castle La RG14 104 C3
Castle Lodge SL6 39 C4
Castle Mews SL6 39 C4
Castle Rd GU15 151 C2
Castle St Reading RG1 86 A4
Slough SL1 42 C2
Castlecraig Ct GU47 150 B4
Castleman Ho SL5 120 B2
Castleton Ct SL7 1 C1
Castleview Comb Sch
SL3 43 B1
Castleview Ho 11 SL4 67 B3
Castleview Rd SL3 43 B1
Castor Ct GU46 149 A4
Caswall Cl RG42 90 B1
Caswall Ride GU46 149 C3
Catalina Cl RG5 88 A4
Catalina Rd TW6 71 A2
Catcliffe Way RG6 113 C4
Catena Rise GU18 146 A1
Catesby Gdns GU46 149 A3
Catherine Dr TW16 98 C1
Catherine Rd RG14 105 A1
Catherine St RG30 85 C4
Catlin Cres TW17 125 B2
Catmore Rd RG20 29 B4
Causeway Est TW20 96 B2
Causeway The
Caversham RG4 59 B1
Egham TW18, TW20 96 B2
Maidenhead SL6 40 B2
Marlow SL7 1 C1
Causmans Way RG31 57 B1
Cavalier Cl Newbury RG14 105 B3
Theale RG7 83 B1
Cavalier Ct TW15 98 B1
Cavalry Cres SL4 67 B2
Cavendish Cl
Ashford TW16 98 C1
Burnham SL6 41 A4
Cavendish Ct
Ashford TW16 98 C1
Blackwater GU17 150 B2
9 Chertsey KT16 124 A1
Newbury RG14 105 C3
Poyle SL3 69 C3
Cavendish Gdns RG41 88 A2
Cavendish Meads SL5 120 B2
Cavendish Rd
Ashford TW16 98 C1
Caversham RG4 59 B3
Caversham Hill RG4 59 A2
Caversham Park Dr RG4 59 B3
Caversham Park Prim Sch
RG4 59 B3
Caversham Park Rd RG4 59 C3
Caversham Prim Sch
RG4 59 A2
Caversham Rd RG1 59 A1
Caversham Wharf RG1 59 A1
Caves Farm Cl GU47 150 A4
Cawcott Dr SL4 66 C3
Cawsam Gdns RG4 59 B2
Caxton Cl RG30 58 B1
Caxton Ct RG9 15 C1
Cecil Aldin Dr RG31 57 B2
Cecil Cl TW15 98 B1
Cecil Rd Ashford TW15 98 B1
Iver SL0 44 C4
Cecil Way SL2 21 C1
Cedar RG9 15 B1
Cedar Ave GU17 150 B3
Cedar Chase SL6 20 B1
Cedar Cl Bagshot GU19 145 C2
Laleham TW18 124 B3
Wokingham RG40 116 B3
Cedar Ct Egham TW20 96 A2
Maidenhead SL6 39 B4
Marlow SL7 1 C1
6 Windsor SL4 67 A3
Cedar Dr Bracknell RG42 91 B1
Cookham SL6 19 C4
Marlow Bottom SL7 1 B4
Pangbourne RG8 56 B2
Sunningdale SL5 121 A1
Cedar Gr RG19 106 B2
Cedar Ho TW16 98 C1
Cedar Mount RG14 130 C4
Cedar Pl RG5 87 C3
Cedar Rd
East Bedfont TW14 98 B4
Reading RG2 86 C1
Cedar Way Charlton TW16 98 C1
Slough SL3 43 C1
Cedar Wood Cres RG4 59 A2
Cedars 10 RG12 118 C3
Cedars Cl GU47 149 C4
Cedars Rd SL6 40 A4
Cedars The RG31 57 B1
Celandine Cl RG45 143 B3
Celandine Ct GU46 149 A4
Celandine Gr RG18 106 C2
Celia Cres TW15 97 B1
Cell Farm SL4 68 A1
Cell Farm Ave SL4 68 A1
Celsea Pl OX10 14 A4
Cemetery La TW17 125 A1
Centenary Bsns Pk RG9 15 C1
Central Dr SL1 41 C3
Central Est SL6 39 C4
Central La SL4 93 A4
Central Way SL4 93 A4
Central Wlk RG40 116 B3
Centre The
Farnham Common SL2 22 B3
Walton-on-T KT12 125 C1
Centurion Cl Reading RG1 86 A3
4 Sandhurst GU47 150 B4
Century Dr RG7 113 B1
Century Rd TW20 96 B2
Cerotus Pl KT16 123 C1
Chackfield Dr RG41 115 B4
Chaddleworth St Andrews
CE Prim Sch
RG20 49 A4
Chaffinch Cl Reading RG31 84 A4
5 Sandhurst GU47 150 B4
Wokingham RG41 115 C3
Chagford Rd RG2 86 A1
Chain St RG1 86 A4
Chainhill Rd Ox12 8 A4
Chalcott SL1 42 C2
Chalcraft Cl RG9 35 B4
Chalfont Cl RG6 87 A1
Chalfont Ct RG6 87 A1
Chalfont Way RG6 87 A1
Chalford HP10 3 C3
Chalford Rd RG14 104 C1
Chalgrove Cl SL6 40 A3
Chalgrove Way RG4 59 A3
Chalk Hill
Aston Tirrold OX11 12 C4
Shiplake RG9 35 B3
Chalk Pit La SL1 21 A2
Chalklands SL8 3 A2
Chalkpit La SL7 1 A2
Challenge Rd TW15 98 B3
Challenor Cl RG40 141 C4
Challis Pl RG42 117 C4
Challow Ct SL6 19 B1
Chalmers Rd TW15 98 A2
Chalmers Rd E TW15 98 B2
Chalvey Cty Fst Sch SL1 42 B2
Chalvey Gdns SL1 42 C2
Chalvey Gr SL1 42 A2
Chalvey Pk SL1 42 C2
Chalvey Rd E SL1 42 C2
Chalvey Rd W SL1 42 B2
Chamberhouse Mill Rd
RG19 106 C1
Chamberlains Gdns RG2 114 C1
Chambers The 20 RG1 86 A4
Champion Rd RG4 59 B1
Chancel Mans RG42 91 B1
Chancellors Way The
RG6 86 C2
Chancery Mews 25 RG1 85 C4
Chancery Pl SL4 67 B4
Chanctonbury Dr SL5 120 C1
Chandlers Cl TW14 98 C4
Chandlers La GU46 149 B4
Chandos Mall 16 SL1 42 C2
Chandos Rd Egham TW18 96 B2
Newbury RG14 131 A4
Chantry Cl SL4 67 A3
Chantry Ct GU16 151 B1
Chantry Mead RG17 100 B3
Chantry Rd Bagshot GU19 145 B1
Chertsey KT16 124 B1
Chapel Arches SL6 40 A4
Chapel Cl Bracknell RG12 118 B3
South Stoke RG8 14 B2
Chapel Ct
Hungerford RG17 100 B3
Maidenhead SL6 39 B2
18 Reading RG1 86 A4
Thatcham RG18 106 C2
Chapel Hill Reading RG31 84 B4
Windsor SL4 67 B3
Chapel La
Ashampstead RG8 54 A4
Bagshot GU19 145 B1
Binfield RG42 90 B1
Blewbury OX11 12 A4
Farnborough (Hants) GU14 151 A1
Headley RG19 133 C1
Hermitage RG18 79 B4
Hermitage, Curridge RG18 78 C2
Lambourn RG17 25 A2
Shinfield RG7 113 A1
Silchester RG7 135 C3
Stoke Poges SL2 23 A3
Swallowfield RG7 139 B2
Yattendon RG18 53 C1
Chapel Rd
Camberley GU15 151 A3
Flackwell Heath HP10 3 A4
Silchester RG7 136 B3
Stockcross RG20 103 C3
Chapel Row RG10 61 B2
Chapel Sq
Sandhurst GU15 150 C3
Virginia Water GU25 122 C3
Chapel St Marlow SL7 1 C1
Slough SL1 42 C2
Thatcham RG18 106 B2
Chapels Cl SL1 41 C3
Chaplain's Hill RG45 143 B2
Chaplin Cres TW16 98 C1
Chapman La HP10, SL8 3 A3
Chapman Wlk RG18 106 A2
Chapter Mews SL4 67 B4
Charadon Cl RG2 86 A3
Chard Cl RG5 87 C3
Charfield Ct RG1 86 C4
Charlbury Cl 15 RG12 118 C3
Charlecombe Ct TW18 97 A2
Charles Ct TW15 98 B2
Charles Evans Way RG4 59 B1
Charles Gdns SL2 43 A4
Charles Ho 9 SL4 67 B3
Charles Pl 26 RG1 86 B4
Charles Rd Cholsey OX10 14 A4
Staines TW18 97 B1
Charles Sq RG12 118 B4
Charles St Chertsey KT16 123 C1
Newbury RG14 130 B3
Reading RG1 85 C4
Windsor SL4 67 B3
Charlock Cl RG18 106 C3
Charlotte Cl RG18 79 A3
Charlton SL4 66 B3
Charlton Cl SL1 42 A2
Charlton Ct GU47 143 B1
Charlton La
Swallowfield RG7 139 B3
Upper Halliford TW17 125 B3
Charlton Pl
Newbury RG14 105 A2
2 Windsor SL4 66 B3
Charlton Rd TW17 125 B4
Charlton Row 5 SL4 66 B3
Charlton Sq 4 SL4 66 B3
Charlton Way SL4 66 B3
Charlton Wlk 3 SL4 66 B3
Charlville Dr RG31 84 A2
Charmwood Cl RG14 104 C3
Charnham Ct RG17 100 C3
Charnham La RG17 100 B3
Charnham Pk RG17 100 B4
Charnham St RG17 100 B3
Charnwood SL5 120 C2
Charrington Rd RG31 84 B2
Charta Rd TW20 96 B2
Charter Cl SL1 42 C2
Charter Rd Newbury RG14 130 C4
Slough SL1 41 C3
Charterhouse Cl RG12 118 C2
Charters La SL5 120 B2
Charters Rd SL5 120 C1
Charters Sch SL5 120 B1
Charters Way SL5 120 C1
Charvil House Rd RG10 61 A3

Charvil La RG4 .60 C2
Charvil Meadow Rd RG10 .61 A3
Charwood Rd RG40 .116 C4
Chase Gdns RG42 .90 B2
Chase The
Crowthorne RG45 .143 A3
Maidenhead SL6 .19 B2
Marlow SL7 .2 A2
Newbury RG14 .104 C4
Reading RG31 .84 B2
Chaseley Ct KT13 .125 C1
Chaseside Ave RG10 .61 B4
Chaseside Gdns KT16 .124 A1
Chatfield SL2 .42 A4
Chatham Ct 3 SL1 .43 A2
Chatham St RG1 .85 C4
Chatsworth Ave RG41 .88 A1
Chatsworth Cl
Caversham RG4 .59 B3
Maidenhead SL6 .39 B3
Chatsworth Hts GU15 .152 A4
Chatteris Way RG6 .114 B4
Chattern Ct TW15 .98 A2
Chattern Hill TW15 .98 A2
Chattern Rd TW15 .98 B2
Chatters The RG7 .140 B4
Chatton Cl RG6 .114 A4
Chaucer Cl Caversham RG4 .59 A3
Windsor SL4 .67 B2
Wokingham RG40 .116 C3
Chaucer Cres RG14 .104 C3
Chaucer Ct TW18 .96 B2
Chaucer Gr GU15 .151 B3
Chaucer Rd Ashford TW15 .97 C2
Crowthorne RG45 .143 A2
Chaucer Way RG41 .115 C3
Chauntry Cl SL6 .40 B3
Chauntry Rd SL6 .40 A3
Chavey Down Rd RG42 .92 A1
Chawridge La SL4 .92 B4
Chazey Cl RG4 .58 B4
Chazey Rd RG4 .58 B2
Cheam Cl RG12 .118 B2
Cheap St Compton RG20 .31 C3
Newbury RG14 .105 A1
Cheapside RG1 .86 A4
Cheapside CE Prim Sch
SL5 .120 C4
Cheapside Rd SL5 .120 B4
Cheddar Rd TW6 .71 A3
Cheddington Cl RG30 .84 C3
Cheeseman Cl RG40 .116 B4
Chelford Way RG4 .58 C2
Chelmsford Ct 35 SL4 .67 B3
Chelsea Cl RG30 .84 C4
Chelwood Dr GU47 .142 C1
Chelwood Rd RG6 .87 A1
Cheney Cl RG42 .90 B1
Cheniston Ct SL5 .121 A1
Cheniston Gr SL6 .38 C4
Chepstow Rd RG31 .57 B1
Chequer La RG7 .138 C1
Chequers Orch SL0 .44 C4
Chequers Way RG5 .87 B4
Cherbury Cl RG12 .118 C3
Cherington Gate SL6 .19 A1
Cherington Way SL5 .119 C4
Cheriton Ave RG10 .61 B3
Cheriton Cl RG14 .131 A4
Cheriton Ct 2 RG1 .86 A3
Cheriton Way GU17 .150 B3
Cherries The SL2 .43 A4
Cherry Ave SL3 .43 B2
Cherry Cl Caversham RG4 .59 B4
Flackwell Heath HP10 .3 A4
Newbury RG14 .104 C2
Cherry Cnr HP10 .3 A4
Cherry Garden La SL6 .38 C2
Cherry Gr RG17 .100 B3
Cherry Orch
Great Shefford RG17 .48 A2
Staines TW18 .97 A2
Stoke Poges SL2 .23 A3
Cherry Rise HP10 .3 A4
Cherry Tree Ave TW18 .97 A1
Cherry Tree Cl GU47 .143 B1
Cherry Tree Dr RG12 .118 B3
Cherry Tree Gr RG41 .115 B2
Cherry Tree La SL3 .23 C3
Cherry Tree Rd SL2 .22 B3
Cherry Way Horton SL3 .69 B2
Upper Halliford TW17 .125 C3
Cherrydale Rd GU15 .152 B3
Cherrygarden La SL6 .63 C4
Cherrywood Ave TW20 .95 A1
Cherrywood Gdns HP10 .3 A4
Chertsey Bridge Rd
KT16, TW18 .124 B1
Chertsey Bvd KT16 .123 C1
Chertsey La TW18 .96 C1
Chertsey Mus KT16 .124 A1
Chertsey Rd
Ashford TW15 &TW16 .98 B1
Feltham TW13 &TW16 .98 C2
Lower Halliford TW17 .125 A1
Shepperton TW17 .124 C1
Windlesham GU20 .146 C3
Chertsey Sta KT16 .123 C1
Chertsey Wlk 6 KT16 .124 A1
Chervil Way RG7 .111 A1
Cherwell Cl Brands Hill SL3 .69 A4
Maidenhead SL6 .40 A4
Cherwell Cres 18 RG1 .85 C4
Cherwell Rd Bourne End SL8 .3 A2
Caversham RG4 .59 A3
Cheseridge Rd RG20 .31 B2
Cheshire Ct SL1 .43 A2
Cheshire Pk RG42 .91 C1
Chessholme Ct TW16 .98 C1
Chessholme Rd TW15 .98 B1
Chester Cl Ashford TW15 .98 B2
Newbury RG14 .105 B1
Chester Rd Harlington TW6 .71 A2
Slough SL1 .42 B4
Chester St Caversham RG4 .59 A1
Reading RG30 .85 B4
Chesterblade La RG12 .118 C1
Chesterfield Mews TW15 .97 C2
Chesterfield Rd
Ashford TW15 .97 C2
Newbury RG14 .105 A1
Chesterman St RG1 .86 A3
Chesterment Way RG6 .87 B1
Chesters Rd GU15 .152 A3
Chesterton Dr TW19 .97 C4
Chesterton Rd RG18 .106 B3
Chestnut Ave
Camberley GU15 .152 A3
Caversham RG4 .59 C2
Slough SL3 .43 C2
Wentworth GU25 .121 C3
Wokingham RG41 .115 C4
Chestnut Cl
Ashford, Chattern Hill TW15 .98 A2
Ashford, Felthamhill TW16 .98 C1
Blackwater GU17 .150 C2
Englefield Green TW20 .95 B1
Harlington UB7 .71 A4
Maidenhead SL6 .20 A1
Medmenham SL7 .17 B4
Theale RG7 .83 C2
Chestnut Cres
Newbury RG14 .105 A2
Shinfield RG2 .113 C2
Chestnut Ct 17 RG14 .105 A2
Chestnut Dr
Burghfield Common RG30 .111 A2
Englefield Green TW20 .95 B1
Windsor SL4 .66 C2
Chestnut Gr
Purley on T RG8 .57 B3
Staines TW18 .97 B1
Chestnut La RG17 .25 C2
Chestnut Manor Cl TW18 .97 A2
Chestnut Pk SL4 .40 C2
Chestnut Rd TW15 .98 A2
Chestnut Wlk
Hungerford RG17 .100 B2
Upper Halliford TW17 .125 C3
Chestnuts The RG9 .36 A2
Chetwode Cl RG40 .116 C3
Cheveley Gdns SL1 .21 B2
Cheviot Cl Frimley GU15 .152 B2
Harlington UB3 .71 B4
Maidenhead SL6 .40 A3
Newbury RG14 .130 B3
Cheviot Dr RG10 .61 A2
Cheviot Rd
Sandhurst GU47 .142 C1
Slough SL3 .44 A1
Chewter Cl GU19 .145 C2
Chewter La GU20 .146 A3
Cheylesmore Dr GU16 .152 B2
Cheyne Rd TW15 .98 B1
Chichester Ct Slough SL1 .43 A2
Stanwell TW19 .97 C4
Chichester Rd RG30 .84 C4
Chicory Cl RG6 .86 C1
Chieveley Cl RG31 .84 B4
Chieveley Prim Sch RG20 .78 A4
Chilbolton TW20 .95 C2
Chilcombe Way RG6 .87 B1
Child Cl RG40 .116 B4
Child St RG17 .25 A2
Childrey Way RG31 .84 A4
Chillingham Way GU15 .151 B2
Chilsey Green Rd KT16 .123 C1
Chiltern Cl
Henley-on-T RG9 .35 A4
Newbury RG14 .130 B3
Staines TW18 .97 A2
Chiltern Coll The RG4 .59 A2
Chiltern Cres RG6 .87 A4
Chiltern Ct Caversham RG4 .59 A3
Windsor SL4 .67 A3
Chiltern Ct Mews SL4 .67 A3
Chiltern Dr RG10 .61 A2
Chiltern End Cl RG9 .35 B4
Chiltern Gn HP10 .3 A4
Chiltern Rd Burnham SL1 .41 A4
Caversham RG4 .59 B2
Maidenhead SL6 .40 A3
Marlow SL7 .1 B1
Sandhurst GU47 .142 C1
Chiltern View RG8 .57 B3
Chiltern Wlk RG8 .56 C3
Chilterns Cl HP10 .3 A4
Chilterns Pk SL8 .3 A3
Chilton Ct SL6 .41 B4
Chilton Cty Prim Sch
OX11 .10 B4
Chilton Foliat CE Prim Sch
RG17 .73 A1
Chilton Way RG17 .100 B3
Chilwick Rd SL2 .21 C1
Chippendale Cl
Blackwater GU17 .150 C2
Tadley RG26 .134 C1
Chippenham Cl RG6 .113 C4
Chisbury Cl RG12 .118 C2
Chiswick Lodge 2 SL7 .1 B1
Chitterfield Gate UB7 .71 A4
Chittering Cl RG6 .87 B1
Chive Rd RG6 .87 A1
Chivers Dr RG40 .141 C4
Chives Pl RG42 .91 B1
Chobham La GU25 .122 A1
Chobham Rd
Frimley GU16 .151 C1
Sunningdale SL5 .121 A1
Choke La SL6 .19 A2
Cholmeley Pl RG1 .86 C4
Cholmeley Rd RG1 .86 C4
Cholmeley Terr RG1 .86 C4
Cholsey Rd RG19 .106 C2
Choseley Cl RG10 .37 C2
Choseley Rd RG10 .37 C2
Chrislaine Cl TW19 .70 B1
Christ the King
RC Prim Sch RG2 .113 B4
Christ the King RC Sch
TW19 .70 C1
Christchurch CE Fst Sch
GU25 .122 A3
Christchurch Cotts
GU25 .122 A3
Christchurch Ct 10 RG1 .86 B3
Christchurch Dr GU17 .150 B3
Christchurch Gdns RG2 .86 B3
Christchurch Rd
Harlington TW6 .71 A2
Reading RG2 .86 B3
Virginia Water GU25 .122 B3
Christian Sq SL4 .67 B3
Christie Cl GU18 .146 B1
Christie Hts RG14 .131 A4
Christie Wlk GU46 .149 B2
Christmas La 2 SL2 .22 B4
Christopher Ct
Ashford TW15 .97 C2
Newbury RG14 .105 A1
Christopher Ho 6 SL2 .22 B4
Chudleigh Gdns RG2 .86 B1
Church App TW20 .123 B3
Church Ave RG9 .15 C1
Church Cl Eton SL4 .67 B4
Hamstead Marshall RG20 .129 C3
Laleham TW18 .124 B3
Lambourn RG17 .25 A1
Maidenhead SL6 .39 B3
Winnersh RG41 .88 B1
Church Cotts SL6 .20 C1
Church Croft RG17 .100 B3
Church Dr SL6 .40 B2
Church End La RG30 .84 C4
Church Farm Barns RG7 .137 B3
Church Gate RG19 .106 B2
Church Gr SL3 .43 B4
Church Hams RG40 .141 B3
Church Hill Binfield RG42 .90 B3
Camberley GU15 .151 C3
Chilton OX11 .10 B4
Hurst RG10 .88 C3
Woolhampton RG7 .107 C2
Church Hill House Hospl
RG12 .118 A2
Church La Arborfield RG2 .114 B2
Ascot SL5 .120 B3
Ashampstead RG8 .54 A3
Barkham RG40 .115 B1
Binfield RG42 .90 B2
Bisley GU24 .153 C2
Brimpton RG7 .133 C3
Burghfield Common RG30 .111 C3
Caversham RG4 .59 C4
Chieveley RG20 .51 A1
Combe RG17 .147 C3
Finchampstead RG40 .141 C2
Hamstead Marshall RG20 .129 C4
Hungerford RG17 .100 B3
Maidenhead SL6 .40 B2
Newbury RG14 .104 B2
Newell Green RG42 .91 B3
Padworth RG7 .110 B2
Reading RG2 .113 B3
Shiplake RG9 .35 C1
Silchester RG7 .136 C1
Slough SL2, SL3 .43 B4
Stoke Poges SL2 .22 C1
Sunningdale SL5 .121 A2
Swallowfield RG7 .140 B3
Thatcham RG19 .106 B2
Twyford RG10 .61 C3
17 Windsor SL4 .67 B3
Yattendon RG18 .53 C1
Church Mews
Purley on T RG8 .57 B3
Woodley RG5 .87 C4
Church Par TW15 .97 C2
Church Path SL6 .40 B2
Church Rd
Aldermaston RG7 .135 A4
Arborfield RG7 .140 B3
Ascot SL5 .120 A3
Ashford TW15 .97 C2
Bagshot GU19 .145 B2
Blewbury OX11 .12 A4
Bracknell RG12 .118 B4
Caversham RG4 .59 A1
Cookham SL6 .19 A3
Earley RG6 .87 A3
Egham TW20 .96 A2
Farnham Common SL2 .22 B1
Frimley GU16 .151 B1
Froxfield SN8 .99 A3
Ham SN8 .126 B1
Little Marlow SL7 .2 B3
Lower Halliford TW17 .125 A1
Maidenhead SL6 .40 A3
Newbury RG14 .105 A3
Old Windsor SL4 .68 A1
Church Rd *continued*
Pangbourne RG8 .56 B3
Sandhurst GU15 .150 C4
Sandhurst,
Owlsmoor GU47 .143 C1
Silchester RG26 .135 C1
Stockcross RG20 .103 C3
Sunningdale SL5 .121 A2
Swallowfield RG7 .139 B3
West End GU24 .153 C4
Windlesham GU20 .146 B2
Winkfield SL4 .92 B3
Winkfield, Chavey Down SL5 119 A4
Woodley RG5 .87 C4
Church Rd E RG45 .143 A3
Church Row SL3 .23 B4
Church Side RG20 .30 C3
Church Sq TW17 .125 A1
Church St
Burnham SL1 .21 B1
Caversham RG4 .59 A1
Crowthorne RG45 .143 A2
Froxfield SN8 .99 A1
Great Shefford RG17 .48 A2
Hampstead Norreys RG18 .52 C3
Henley-on-T RG9 .15 B1
Hungerford RG17 .100 B3
Kintbury RG17 .102 A1
Reading RG1 .86 A3
Slough SL1 .42 B2
Slough, Upton Park SL1 .42 C2
Staines TW18 .96 C2
Theale RG7 .83 B2
Twyford RG10 .61 B2
Wargrave RG10 .36 B1
15 Windsor SL4 .67 B3
Church Street Mews RG7 .83 B2
Church Terr
8 Reading RG1 .86 A3
Windsor SL4 .66 C3
Church View
Beenham RG7 .109 A3
8 Slough SL1 .43 A2
White Waltham SL6 .63 C4
Yateley GU46 .149 B4
Church Views SL6 .39 C4
Church Way RG17 .100 B3
Church Wlk KT16 .124 A2
Churchend Prim Sch
RG30 .84 C3
Churchfield Mews SL2 .43 A4
Churchill Cl
East Bedfont TW14 .98 C4
Flackwell Heath HP10 .3 A4
Reading RG2 .86 A1
Churchill Cres GU46 .149 B3
Churchill Ct TW18 .97 B1
Churchill Dr Marlow SL7 .1 C2
Winnersh RG41 .88 A1
Churchill Rd
North Ascot SL5 .119 C4
Slough SL3 .43 C1
Churchmead Sch SL3 .68 A4
Churchward Wlk RG31 .84 C2
Churchway RG20 .10 A1
Churn Rd RG20 .31 B3
Cinnamon Cl RG6 .86 C1
Cintra Ave RG2 .86 B3
Cintra Cl RG1 .86 B3
Cippenham Inf Sch SL1 .41 B3
Cippenham La SL1 .42 A3
Cippenham Mid Sch SL1 .41 C3
Circle Hill Rd RG45 .143 B3
Circuit La RG30 .85 B3
City Rd RG31 .84 A4
Clacy Gn RG42 .91 A1
Claires Court Sch SL6 .20 A1
Clandon Ave TW20 .96 B1
Clanfield Cres RG31 .57 B1
Clanfield Ride GU17 .150 B3
Clappers Farm Rd RG7 .136 C1
Clappers Mdw SL6 .20 B1
Clapps Gate Rd RG26 .135 C1
Clapton App HP10 .3 B4
Clare Ave RG40 .116 B4
Clare Dr SL2 .22 A4
Clare Gdns TW20 .96 A2
Clare Rd Maidenhead SL6 .39 B3
Slough SL6 .41 B4
Stanwell TW19 .97 C4
Clare Wlk RG14 .130 B3
Claredon Cl RG41 .88 B1
Clarefield Cl SL6 .19 A1
Clarefield Ct SL5 .121 A1
Clarefield Dr SL6 .19 A1
Claremont Poyle SL3 .69 B3
Shepperton TW17 .125 A2
Claremont Ave GU15 .151 C3
Claremont Dr TW17 .125 A2
Claremont Gdns SL7 .1 C1
Claremont Rd
Egham TW18 .96 B2
Marlow SL7 .1 C1
Windsor SL4 .67 B3
Clarence Cres SL4 .67 B3
Clarence Ct Egham TW20 .95 C1
Maidenhead SL6 .39 C4
Windsor SL4 .67 A3
Clarence Dr
Camberley GU15 .152 A4
Englefield Green TW20 .95 B2
Clarence Lodge TW20 .95 B2
Clarence Rd
Henley-on-T RG9 .15 B1
Windsor SL4 .67 A3
Clarence St Egham TW20 .95 C1
Staines TW18 .96 C2
Clarence Way RG31 .84 A2
Clarendon Ct
Blackwater GU17 .150 B2
Slough SL2 .43 A3
Clarendon Cty Prim Sch
TW15 .97 C2
Clarendon Gdns RG14 .105 A2
Clarendon Rd
Ashford TW15 .97 C2
Reading RG6 .87 A3
Clares Green Rd RG7 .113 A2
Clarewood Dr GU15 .151 C3
Clarke Cres GU15 .150 C4
Clarks Gdns RG17 .100 B3
Classics The RG17 .25 A1
Claverdon RG12 .118 A1
Clay Cl Flackwell Heath HP10 .3 A4
Purley on T RG31 .57 A1
Clay Cnr KT16 .124 A1
Clay Hill Cres RG14 .105 B3
Clay La Beenham RG7 .108 C3
Wokingham RG40 .116 C3
Claycots Inf Sch SL2 .22 A1
Claycots Jun Sch SL2 .22 A1
Claydon Ct
2 Caversham RG4 .59 A1
Staines TW18 .97 A2
Claydon Gdns GU17 .151 A1
Clayhall La SL4 .67 C1
Clayhill Cl RG12 .119 A3
Clayhill Rd RG7,RG30 .111 A2
Clayton Ct SL3 .44 A2
Clayton Gr RG12 .118 C4
Clayton Rd GU14 .150 C1
Clayton Wlk RG2 .86 B2
Claytons Cty Comb Sch
SL8 .3 A3
Claytons Mdw SL8 .3 A2
Cleares Pasture SL1 .21 A1
Clearsprings GU18 .153 A4
Cleeve Ct TW14 .98 C4
Cleeve Down RG8 .34 B4
Cleeve Ho 6 RG12 .118 C3
Cleeve Rd RG8 .34 A4
Clements Cl Shinfield RG7 .113 A1
Slough SL1 .43 A2
Clements Mead RG31 .57 A1
Clements Rd RG9 .15 B2
Clent Rd RG2 .86 A2
Cleopatra Pl RG42 .91 C1
Clerewater Pl RG19 .105 C2
Clerics Wlk TW17 .125 B2
Cleve Ct RG8 .34 A4
Clevedon Dr RG6 .87 A1
Clevedon Rd RG31 .57 C2
Clevehurst Cl SL2 .23 A3
Cleveland RG10 .61 A2
Cleveland Cl
Maidenhead SL6 .40 A3
Wooburn Green HP10 .3 C4
Cleveland Dr TW18 .124 A4
Cleveland Gr RG14 .104 C2
Cleveland Pk TW19 .70 C1
Clevemede RG8 .34 B4
Cleves Ct SL4 .66 C2
Cleves Way TW16 .98 C1
Clewborough Dr GU15 .152 A3
Clewborough House Sch
GU15 .152 A3
Clewer Ave SL4 .67 A3
Clewer Ct Rd SL4 .67 A4
Clewer Fields SL4 .67 B3
Clewer Green CE Fst Sch
SL4 .67 A2
Clewer Hill Rd SL4 .66 C2
Clewer New Town SL4 .67 A3
Clewer Pk SL4 .67 A4
Clifford Gr TW15 .98 A2
Clifford Way SL8 .3 A3
Clifton Cl SL6 .40 A2
Clifton Ct 8 TW19 .70 C1
Clifton Lodge Eton SL4 .42 A1
10 Slough SL1 .43 A2
Clifton Park Rd RG4 .59 A1
Clifton Rd Harlington TW6 .71 A2
Newbury RG14 .104 C1
Slough SL1 .43 A2
Wokingham RG41 .116 A4
Clifton Rise
Wargrave RG10 .36 C1
Windsor SL4 .66 B3
Clifton St RG1 .85 C4
Clintons Gn RG42 .118 A4
Clive Ct SL1 .42 B2
Clive Gn RG12 .118 A2
Clivedale Rd RG5 .87 C2
Cliveden SL6 .20 C4
Cliveden Mead SL6 .20 B1
Cliveden Pl TW17 .125 B2
Cliveden Rd SL6 .20 C2
Clivemont Rd SL6 .39 C4
Clockhouse La
TW14, TW15 .98 A3
Clockhouse La E TW20 .96 A1
Clockhouse La W TW20 .96 A1
Cloister Mews RG7 .83 C2
Cloisters The
Caversham RG4 .59 A2
Frimley GU16 .151 B1
Clonmel Cl RG4 .59 B1
Clonmel Way SL1 .21 A1
Close End RG17 .25 A1
Close The
Aston Tirrold OX11 .12 C4
Bourne End SL8 .3 A3
Bracknell RG12 .118 B3
Burghfield Common RG7 .111 A2
Burnham SL1 .41 B3
Great Shefford RG17 .48 A2

Close The *continued*
Hampstead Norreys RG18 52 C3
Henley-on-T RG9 35 B4
Lightwater GU18 146 A1
North Ascot SL5 119 B4
Sandhurst GU47 150 C4
Thatcham RG18 106 A2
Virginia Water GU25 122 B2
Woodley RG5 87 C3
Clough Dr RG18 78 C3
Clove Cl RG6 86 C1
Clover Cl RG40 116 C4
Clover La GU46 149 A3
Club La RG45 143 B3
Clumps The TW13,TW15 98 B2
Clyde Rd TW19 97 C4
Clyve Way TW18 123 C4
Coach Ho The HP10 3 C3
Coach House Cl GU16 151 C2
Coach Rd SL5 92 C1
Coach Ride SL7 1 B2
Coachman's Lodge 28 SL4 67 B3
Coachmans Ct RG14 105 A2
Coachmans Gr GU47 150 A4
Coalmans Way SL1,SL6 41 A4
Coalport Way RG30 57 C1
Cobb Cl SL3 68 B3
Cobbetts La GU46,GU17 149 C3
Cobblers Cl SL2 22 A2
Cobham Cl SL1 41 C3
Cobham Rd RG5 87 C4
Cochrane Cl RG19 106 C2
Cochrane Pl GU20 146 B3
Cock La RG7 82 A1
Cock's La RG42, SL4 92 A3
Cock-A-Dobby GU47 143 A1
Cockett Rd SL3 43 C2
Cockney Hill RG30 84 C3
Cody Cl RG5 88 A4
Coe Spur SL1 42 A2
Coftards SL2 43 B4
Cokers Ct 2 SL8 3 A2
Cold Ash Hill RG18 106 B4
Cold Ash St Mark's CE Prim Sch RG18 79 B1
Cold Grove Cotts SL6 20 C1
Coldharbour Cl
Henley-on-T RG9 35 B4
Thorpe TW20 123 B3
Coldharbour La
Thorpe TW20 123 B3
West End GU24 153 C4
Coldharbour Rd RG17 100 B2
Coldicutt St RG4 59 B1
Coldmoorholme La SL8 2 C2
Colemans Moor La RG5 87 C3
Colemans Moor Rd RG5 88 A3
Colenorton Cres SL4 41 C1
Coleridge Ave GU46 149 C3
Coleridge Cl
Crowthorne RG45 143 B2
Twyford RG10 61 C2
Coleridge Cres SL3 69 C3
Coleridge Rd TW15 97 C2
Coley Ave RG1 85 C3
Coley Hill RG1 85 C3
Coley Park Prim Sch RG1 85 C3
Coley Park Rd RG1 85 C3
Coley Pl RG1 86 A3
Coley Prim Sch RG1 86 A3
Colin Way SL1 42 A2
Coliseum Bsns Ctr GU15 151 A2
Collaroy Glen RG18 106 B4
Collaroy Rd RG18 106 B4
College Ave Egham TW20 96 A1
Maidenhead SL6 39 C4
Slough SL1 42 C2
College Cl GU15 151 B4
College Cres
Sandhurst GU47 150 C4
Windsor SL4 67 B3
College Glen SL6 39 B4
College Piece RG7 136 C3
College Rd
Bracknell RG12 118 B3
Maidenhead SL6 39 C4
Reading RG6 86 C3
Sandhurst GU47 150 C4
Slough SL1 41 C3
College Ride
Bagshot GU19 145 B1
Camberley GU15 151 B4
College Rise SL6 39 B4
College Town Cty Inf Sch GU47 150 C4
College Town Cty Jun Sch GU47 150 C4
College Way Ashford TW15 97 C2
East Garston RG17 47 B3
Colleton Cty Prim Sch The RG10 61 C2
Colleton Dr RG10 61 C2
Collier Cl SL6 19 C1
Colliers Way RG30 85 A4
Collingwood Coll GU15 152 A4
Collingwood Grange Cl GU15 152 A4
Collingwood Mount GU15 152 A3
Collingwood Pl GU15 152 A4
Collingwood Rise GU15 152 A4
Collingwood Wlk RG31 84 A4
Collins Cl RG14 105 B2
Collins Dr RG18 78 C3
Collinswood Rd 1 SL2 22 B4
Collis St RG2 86 A3
Colliston Wlk RG31 84 C2
Collum Green Rd SL2 23 A4
Coln Cl SL6 39 C4
Coln Trad Est SL3 69 C3
Colnbrook By-Pass
Colnbrook SL3, UB7 69 B4
Harmondsworth UB7 70 B4
Colnbrook CE Prim Sch SL3 69 B4
Colnbrook Ct SL3 69 C3
Colndale Rd SL3 69 C3
Colne Bank SL3, TW19 69 B2
Colne Orch SL0 44 C3
Colne Reach TW19 69 C1
Colne Way TW19 96 A3
Colnebridge Cl TW18 96 C2
Colnworth Cl RG6 114 A4
Colonel's La KT16 124 A2
Colonial Rd
East Bedfont TW14 98 C4
Slough SL1 43 A2
Colonnade SL6 40 A4
Colony Gate GU16 152 B1
Colston Cl RG31 84 B2
Colthrop La RG19 107 A1
Colthrop Way RG19 107 A1
Coltsfoot Cl RG7 111 A2
Columbia Ct RG40 141 C4
Colville Gdns GU18 153 B4
Colwyn Cl GU46 149 B3
Colyer Cl RG18 79 B4
Colyton Way RG8 57 B3
Combe Rd RG30 84 C4
Combe View RG17 100 B2
Combermere Cl SL4 67 A3
Comet Rd TW19 97 B4
Comet Way RG5 88 A4
Comfrey Cl RG40 116 C4
Commercial Rd
Reading RG2 86 A1
Staines TW18 97 A1
Common Hill RG7 82 C2
Common La
Brightwalton RG20 28 B3
Eton SL4 42 B1
Common Rd Dorney SL4 41 B1
Eton SL4 42 A1
Flackwell Heath HP10 3 A4
Headley RG19 132 C1
Slough SL3 44 A1
Common The HP10 3 A4
Common Wood SL2 22 B4
Commonfield La RG40 141 A4
Commonfields GU24 153 C3
Commons Rd RG41 88 C1
Communications Rd RG19 131 C3
Compton Ave RG31 84 A4
Compton CE Prim Sch RG20 31 C2
Compton Cl
Bracknell RG12 117 C2
Earley RG6 87 B2
Sandhurst GU47 143 B1
Compton Ct SL1 41 C4
Compton Dr SL6 39 A4
Compton Manor RG20 31 B2
Compton Place Bsns Ctr GU15 151 A2
Comsaye Wlk RG12 118 B2
Concorde Rd SL6 39 B2
Concorde Way Slough SL1 42 B2
Woodley RG5 88 A4
Condor Cl RG31 57 B2
Condor Rd TW18 124 B3
Conegar Ct SL1 42 C3
Coney Grange RG42 91 A1
Coneygree Cl RG6 87 A1
Congreve Cl RG7 135 A4
Conifer Cl RG26 134 C1
Conifer Crest RG14 130 B2
Conifer Dr
Camberley GU15 152 A3
Purley on T RG31 57 A1
Conifer La TW20 96 B2
Conifers The
Crowthorne RG45 143 A4
Maidenhead SL6 39 A4
Coningham Rd RG2 113 B3
Coningsby RG12 118 B3
Coningsby Cl SL6 39 B2
Coningsby La SL6 65 B3
Conisboro Ave RG4 58 C3
Conisboro Way RG4 58 C3
Coniston Cl Frimley GU15 152 B2
Thatcham RG19 106 A2
Woodley RG5 87 C3
Coniston Cres SL1 41 B4
Coniston Ct
Lightwater GU18 146 A1
18 Newbury RG14 105 A2
Coniston Dr RG30 57 C1
Coniston Way TW20 96 A1
Conkers SL6 40 A4
Connaught Ave TW15 97 C2
Connaught Cl
Crowthorne RG45 142 C2
Maidenhead SL6 19 C1
Reading RG30 85 B4
Yateley GU46 149 A3
Connaught Cty Mid Sch GU19 145 C1
Connaught Rd
Bagshot GU19 145 B2
Camberley GU15 151 C3
Newbury RG14 105 A2
Reading RG30 85 B4
Slough SL1 43 A2
Conniston Cl SL7 1 A1
Connop Way GU16 151 C2
Consort Dr GU15 152 B4
Constable Cl RG5 88 A4
Constable Way GU47 150 C3
Constitution Rd RG30 85 A4
Consul Cl RG5 88 A3
Control Tower Rd TW6 71 A2
Convent Lodge TW15 98 A2
Convent Rd Ashford TW15 98 A2
Windsor SL4 67 A3
Conway Cl GU16 151 C1
Conway Dr Ashford TW15 98 B1
Thatcham RG18 106 A3
Conway Rd Burnham SL6 41 A4
Harlington TW6 71 A2
Reading RG31 84 B3
Cooke Rise RG42 91 A1
Cookham Cl GU47 143 B1
Cookham Dean Bottom La SL6 19 B4
Cookham Dean CE Prim Sch SL6 19 A4
Cookham Lodge 15 SL6 39 C3
Cookham Rd
Bracknell RG12 117 C4
Maidenhead SL6 19 C2
Cookham Rise Cty Prim Sch SL6 19 C3
Cookham Sta SL6 19 C4
Coolarne Rise GU15 152 A3
Coolgardie Rd TW15 98 B2
Coombe Ct RG19 106 C2
Coombe Hill OX12 28 A4
Coombe Pine RG12 118 B2
Coombe Rd Compton RG20 31 C1
Yateley GU46 149 A4
Coombe Sq RG19 106 C2
Coombe The RG8 33 C3
Coombes Cty Inf Sch The RG2 114 C2
Coombes La RG41 115 B2
Coombesbury La RG20 76 B1
Cooper Cl RG2 113 B4
Cooper Rd Henley-on-T RG9 15 B2
Windlesham GU20 146 B2
Cooper Way SL1 42 A2
Cooper's Hill La TW20 95 B2
Coopers Cl TW18 96 C2
Coopers Cres RG18 106 B2
Cope Ct SL6 39 B4
Cope Hall La RG14 130 B4
Copelands Cl GU15 152 B2
Copenhagen Cl RG2 113 B4
Copenhagen Wlk RG45 143 A2
Copped Hall Dr GU15 152 B3
Copped Hall Way GU15 152 B3
Copper Beech Cl SL4 66 B3
Copperage Rd OX12 9 A1
Copperdale Cl RG6 86 C2
Copperfield Ave GU47 143 C1
Copperfields
Ashford TW16 98 C1
Reading RG4 58 C2
Coppermill Rd TW19 69 A1
Coppice Cl RG14 131 A4
Coppice Dr TW19 95 B4
Coppice Gdns
Crowthorne RG45 142 C3
Yateley GU46 149 B3
Coppice Gn RG42 90 C1
Coppice Rd RG5 87 C2
Coppice The TW15 98 A1
Coppins La SL0 44 C4
Copse Ave RG4 59 C2
Copse Cl Camberley GU15 152 A3
Marlow SL7 1 B1
Purley on T RG31 57 B2
Slough SL1 41 C3
Copse Dr RG41 116 A4
Copse End GU15 152 A3
Copse Mead RG5 60 C1
Copse The RG10 36 C2
Copse Way RG40 141 C4
Copthall Ho SL6 40 A4
Copthorn Cl SL6 39 A2
Copthorne Chase TW15 97 C2
Copthorne Cl TW17 125 B2
Copthorne Dr GU18 146 A1
Corbett Dr GU18 152 C4
Corbett Gdns RG5 87 C4
Corbridge Rd RG2 86 B2
Corby Cl RG5 61 A1
Corby Dr TW20 95 B1
Cordelia Croft RG42 118 C4
Cordelia Gdns TW19 97 C4
Cordelia Rd TW19 97 C4
Corderoy Cl RG19 106 C1
Corderoy Pl KT16 123 C2
Cordwalles Cty Jun Sch GU15 151 C4
Cordwalles Rd GU15 151 C4
Cordwallis Est SL6 39 C4
Cordwallis Pk SL6 39 C4
Cordwallis Rd SL6 39 C4
Cordwallis St SL6 39 C4
Cores End Rd SL8 3 A2
Corfe Gdns Frimley GU16 151 C1
Slough SL1 42 A3
Corfe Mews RG4 59 C2
Corfe Pl SL6 39 B4
Corfield Cl RG40 141 C2
Coriander Way RG6 86 C1
Corinne Cl RG2 86 A1
Cormorant Pl GU47 150 C4
Corn Croft RG42 91 C1
Cornbunting Cl GU47 150 B4
Cornel Ho 1 SL4 67 B2
Cornerside TW15 98 B1
Cornfield Gn RG41 115 C4
Cornfield Rd RG5 88 A4
Cornfields GU46 149 A2
Cornflower Cl RG41 115 B4
Cornwall Ave SL2 22 B1
Cornwall Cl Bracknell RG42 91 C1
Camberley GU15 151 C4
Eton SL4 41 C1
Maidenhead SL6 19 C1
Purley on T RG31 57 A2
Wokingham RG41 115 B3
Cornwall Lodge 11 SL6 39 C3
Cornwall Way TW18 96 C1
Cornwell Rd SL4 68 A1
Cornwood Gdns RG2 86 B2
Coronation Ave SL3 43 C4
Coronation Rd Ascot SL5 120 A1
Littlewick Green SL6 38 A3
Yateley GU46 149 C4
Coronation Sq
Reading RG30 85 A2
Wokingham RG40 116 B4
Corporation Cotts 1 RG14 105 A2
Corrie Gdns GU25 122 B1
Corsair Cl TW19 97 C4
Corsair Rd TW19 97 C4
Corsham Rd RG31 84 C2
Corsham Way RG45 143 A3
Corwen Rd RG30 84 C4
Coster Cl RG14 104 B3
Costers Cotts SL8 3 A1
Cotswold Cl
Maidenhead SL6 40 A3
Slough SL1 42 A2
Staines TW18 97 A2
Cotswold Rd GU47 142 C1
Cotswold Way RG31 57 B1
Cottage Farm Way TW20 123 B3
Cottage La RG30 85 B1
Cotterell Cl RG42 91 A1
Cotterell Gdns RG10 61 C2
Cottesbrooke Cl SL3 69 B3
Cottesloe Cl GU24 153 C2
Cottesmore RG12 118 A1
Cottesmore Rd RG5 87 B3
Coulson Way SL1 41 A4
Council Cotts GU24 153 C4
Council Hos RG18 77 B3
Country Life Ho SL3 68 A4
County La RG42 91 C1
Courage Ct RG30 85 A3
Courage Shire Horse Ctr SL6 38 B3
Course Rd SL5 120 A3
Court Cl SL6 40 B1
Court Cres SL1 42 B4
Court Dr SL6 20 B2
Court Farm Ho SL1 42 A3
Court Farm Ind Est TW19 70 C1
Court Garden L Complex SL7 1 B1
Court Gdns GU15 151 B3
Court Hill Rd OX12 7 B4
Court La Burnham SL1 21 B1
Dorney SL4 41 A2
Iver SL0 44 C3
Court Rd SL6 20 B2
Court The RG18 106 B2
Courtenay Dr RG4 59 A4
Courtfield Dr SL6 39 B3
Courtfield Rd TW15 98 A1
Courthouse Cty Jun Sch SL6 39 A4
Courthouse Rd SL6 39 B4
Courtlands 14 SL6 39 C3
Courtlands Ave SL3 43 B1
Courtlands Hill RG8 56 B2
Courtlands Rd RG14 105 A1
Courtney Rd TW6 71 A2
Courts Rd RG6 87 A2
Courtyard The
17 Bourne End SL8 3 A2
Theale RG7 83 C2
Coventry Rd RG1 86 C4
Coverdale Way SL2 21 C1
Covert La RG12 118 B3
Covert The SL5 120 A1
Coves Farm Wood RG42 117 B4
Cow La East Isley RG20 30 C4
Moulsford OX10 13 C2
Reading RG1 58 C1
Cowley Ave KT16 123 C1
Cowley La KT16 123 C1
Coworth Cl SL5 121 A2
Coworth Rd SL5 121 A2
Cowper Cl KT16 123 C2
Cowper Rd SL2 22 A1
Cowper Way RG30 85 B2
Cowslade RG14 104 B3
Cowslip Cl RG31 84 A3
Cowslip Cres RG18 106 C3
Cox Green Comp Sch SL6 39 A2
Cox Green La SL6 39 B2
Cox Green Rd SL6 39 B2
Coxborrow Cl SL6 19 C4
Coxeter Rd RG14 104 C2
Coxgreen GU47 150 B3
Coxs Ave TW17 125 C3
Coxs La RG7 107 B2
Crabtree Cl RG18 78 C3
Crabtree Cnr TW20 123 A4
Crabtree La RG18 78 C3
Crabtree Office Village TW20 123 B4
Crabtree Rd
Camberley GU15 151 A1
Thorpe TW20 123 B4
Craddock Rd RG2 86 A2
Crafnant Ct TW15 97 C2
Crafts End OX11 10 C4
Craig Ave RG30 85 A4
Craigwell Cl TW18 123 C4
Crail Cl RG41 116 A2
Crake Pl GU47 150 B4
Cramond Ct TW14 98 C4
Cranbourne Ave
Reading RG31 84 B2
Windsor SL4 66 C3
Cranbourne Cl SL1 42 B3
Cranbourne Cotts SL4 93 A3
Cranbourne Gdns RG30 58 A1
Cranbourne Prim Sch SL5 93 A2
Cranbourne Rd SL1 42 B3
Cranbrook Dr SL6 19 B1
Cranbury Rd RG30 85 B4
Crane Ct GU47 150 B4
Crane Rd TW19 71 A1
Crane Wharf 14 RG1 86 A4
Craneswater UB3 71 C4
Cranford Ave TW19 97 C4
Cranford Cl Hurst RG10 88 C4
Stanwell TW19 97 C4
Cranford House Sch OX10 13 C3
Cranford La
Harlington TW6 71 C3
Harlington UB3 71 C4
Hatton TW6 71 C2
Cranford Mews 10 RG1 86 A3
Cranford Park Dr GU46 149 B3
Cranleigh Rd TW13 98 C2
Cranmer Cl RG31 57 A2
Cranwell Gr
Lightwater GU18 152 C4
Littleton TW17 124 C3
Cranwell Rd TW6 71 A3
Craufurd Ct SL6 39 C4
Craufurd Rise SL6 39 C4
Craven Cl RG17 102 A1
Craven Dene RG14 105 A2
Craven Rd Inkpen RG17 127 A3
Newbury RG14 104 C1
Reading RG1 86 B3
Craven Way RG17 102 A1
Crawford Cl RG6 87 A2
Crawford Gdns GU15 151 A3
Crawford Pl RG14 104 C2
Crawley Chase RG42 92 A1
Crawley Dr GU15 151 C3
Crawley Hill GU15 151 C3
Crawley Ridge GU15 151 C3
Crawley Ridge Cty Inf Sch GU15 151 C3
Crawley Ridge Cty Jun Sch GU15 151 C4
Crawley Wood Cl GU15 151 C3
Crawshay Dr RG4 59 A4
Crayle St SL2 22 A1
Crayonne Cl TW16 125 C4
Crazies Hill CE Prim Sch RG10 36 C3
Crecy Cl RG41 115 C3
Crediton Cl RG5 88 A3
Cree's Mdw GU20 146 B2
Creighton Ct RG2 86 B2
Cremyll Rd RG1 58 C1
Crendon Ct RG4 59 A1
Crescent Ct TW18 96 C2
Crescent Dale SL6 39 C3
Crescent Dr SL6 39 C4
Crescent Rd
Reading, Tilehurst RG31 57 B1
Reading, Whiteknights RG1 86 C3
Shepperton TW17 125 B2
Wokingham RG40 116 B3
Crescent The
Ashford TW15 97 C2
Bracknell RG12 118 B3
Chertsey KT16 124 A3
Earley RG6 87 B2
Egham TW20 95 C1
Harlington UB3 71 B4
Kintbury RG17 102 A1
Lower Halliford TW17 125 C1
Maidenhead SL6 39 C4
Mortimer RG7 137 A3
Padworth RG7 109 B2
Shiplake RG9 36 A2
Slough SL1 42 C2
Theale RG7 83 C2
Crescent Villas 5 SL4 67 B3
Cress Rd SL1 42 A2
Cressex Cl RG42 90 B1
Cressida Chase RG42 91 C1
Cressingham Rd RG2 86 B1
Cressington Pl SL8 3 A2
Cresswell Rd RG14 105 B2
Cresswell Row SL7 1 B1
Cresswells Mead SL6 40 B1
Crest Cl RG10 61 C3
Crest Ho TW15 98 A2
Crest The RG4 59 B3
Creswell Cl RG2 113 B3
Cricket Field Gr RG45 143 B2
Cricket Hill La GU17,GU46 149 C2
Cricketers RG20 103 C3
Cricketers La
Windlesham GU20 146 B2
Winkfield RG42 92 A2
Crimp Hill SL4, TW20 95 A3
Crisp Gdns RG42 90 C1

Crisp Rd RG9 15 B2
Crispin Cl RG4 58 B3
Crispin Way SL2 22 B4
Crocker Cl SL5 119 C4
Crockford Pl RG42 90 C1
Crockhamwell Rd RG5 87 C3
Crocus Mead RG18 106 C2
Crocus Way RG41 115 B4
Croft Cl Harlington UB3 71 B4
Wokingham RG41 116 A1
Croft Cnr SL4 68 A1
Croft La Newbury RG14 104 C2
Yateley GU46 149 B4
Croft Rd Goring RG8 34 B3
Hungerford RG17 100 B3
Mortimer RG7 136 C3
Newbury RG14 130 C4
Shinfield RG7 113 B1
Wokingham RG40 116 A1
Croft The Bracknell RG42 91 A1
Kintbury RG17 102 A1
Maidenhead SL6 39 B3
Marlow SL7 2 A2
Croft Way GU16 151 C1
Crofter's Cl GU47 150 A4
Crofters SL4 68 A1
Crofthill Rd SL2 22 A1
Crofton Cl RG12 118 C2
Crofts The TW17 125 C3
Cromer Cl RG31 57 B1
Cromer Ct SL1 42 C4
Cromer Rd TW6 71 A3
Cromwell Cl RG9 35 C4
Cromwell Dr SL1 42 C4
Cromwell Gdns SL7 1 C1
Cromwell Pl 21 RG14 105 A2
Cromwell Rd Ascot SL5 120 A2
Camberley GU15 151 B4
Caversham RG4 59 A1
Henley-on-T RG9 35 C4
Maidenhead SL6 39 B4
Marlow SL7 1 C1
Newbury RG14 105 B3
Crondall Ct GU15 151 A2
Crondall End GU46 149 B4
Cropper Cl RG19 107 A2
Crosby Gdns GU46 149 A4
Crosby Hill Dr GU15 151 C4
Crosfields Sch RG2 113 C4
Cross Fell RG12 118 A3
Cross Gates Cl RG12 118 C3
Cross Keys Rd RG8 14 B2
Cross La RG7 138 B4
Cross Oak SL4 67 A3
Cross Rd SL5 121 A1
Cross St Reading RG1 86 A4
Wokingham RG40 116 B3
Crossfields Cl RG2 113 C4
Crossland Rd RG1 86 A4
Crossway RG12 118 B4
Crossways Charlton TW16 98 C1
Egham TW20 96 B1
Woodley RG5 87 C3
Crossways Ct 31 SL4 67 B3
Crosswell Cl TW17 125 B4
Crosthwaite Way SL1 41 B4
Crouch La SL4 92 C4
Crow Piece La SL2 21 C2
Crowfield Dr RG19 106 A2
Crowle Rd RG17 25 A1
Crown Acre Cl RG19 106 B2
Crown Cl SW3 69 B4
Crown Colonnade RG1 86 C4
Crown Cotts
Bracknell SL5 119 B2
Englefield Green TW20 95 A1
Windsor SL4 67 B2
Crown Ct RG19 106 B2
Crown Hill Ct SL5 120 A2
Crown La Burnham SL2 22 A2
Maidenhead SL6 40 A4
Marlow SL7 1 B1
Theale RG7 83 C2
Wentworth GU25 122 B2
Crown Mdw SL3 69 A4
Crown Mead RG19 106 B2
Crown Pl Reading RG1 86 B3
Sandhurst GU47 143 C1
Crown Rd Marlow SL7 1 B1
Wentworth GU25 122 B2
Crown Rise KT16 123 C1
Crown Row RG12 118 B2
Crown St Egham TW20 96 A2
Reading RG1 86 A3
Crown Wood
Cty Prim Sch RG12 118 C2
Crowsley Rd RG9 36 A2
Crowthorne CE Sch
RG45 143 B3
Crowthorne Lodge RG12 118 A3
Crowthorne Rd
Bracknell RG40, RG12 117 C1
Bracknell,
Easthampstead RG12 118 A3
Sandhurst GU47 143 A1
Crowthorne Rd N RG12 118 A3
Crowthorne Sta RG45 142 C2
Croxley Rise SL6 39 B3
Croydon Rd TW6 71 A2
Cruikshank Lea GU47 150 C3
Crummock Cl SL1 41 B4
Crutchley Rd RG40 116 B4
Cuba Cotts SL6 20 A2
Cuckoo La GU24 153 B3
Cuckoo Vale GU24 153 B3
Culford Cl RG6 87 B1
Culham Ct RG30 85 A2
Culham Dr SL6 19 C1
Culham Ho 8 RG12 118 C3
Cullen Cl GU46 149 B3
Cullern's Pass SL6 39 C3
Culley Way SL6 39 A2
Culloden Way RG41 115 C3
Culver Croft RG42 90 C1
Culver La RG6 87 A4
Culver Rd Newbury RG14 130 C4
Reading RG6 86 C3
Sandhurst GU47 143 B1
Cumberland Ave SL2 22 B1
Cumberland Dr RG12 118 C4
Cumberland Lodge SL4 94 B2
Cumberland Rd
Ashford TW15 97 B3
Frimley GU15 152 B2
Reading RG1 86 C4
Cumberland St TW18 96 B2
Cumberland Way RG41 115 B3
Cumbernauld Gdns TW16 98 C2
Cumbrae Cl SL2 43 A3
Cumbria Cl SL6 39 B2
Cumnor Way RG12 118 C3
Cunworth Ct RG12 117 C2
Curfew Bell Rd KT16 123 C1
Curl Way RG41 116 A3
Curlew Cl RG19 106 B2
Curlew Dr RG31 84 B3
Curley Hill Rd GU18 152 C4
Curleys Way RG7 139 B3
Curling Way RG14 105 B2
Curls La SL6 39 C2
Curls Rd SL6 39 B2
Curnock Ct RG14 104 C1
Curridge Gn RG18 78 C3
Curridge Piece RG18 78 C3
Curridge Prim Sch RG18 78 B2
Curridge Rd RG18 78 B2
Curriers La SL1 21 B4
Curtis Cl GU15 152 B4
Curtis Rd RG31 84 B2
Curzon Mall 15 SL1 42 C2
Curzon St RG30 85 C4
Cutbush Cl RG6 114 A4
Cutbush La RG2 & RG6 114 A4
Cutting Hill SN8,RG17 126 A2
Cuttings The RG18 52 C3
Cwmcarn RG4 58 C3
Cygnet Cl RG19 106 A2
Cygnets The TW18 96 C2
Cypress Cl RG40 142 A4
Cypress Hill Ct GU14 150 C1
Cypress Ho SL3 44 A1
Cypress Rd RG5 88 A3
Cypress Way GU17 150 A3
Cypress Wlk TW20 95 A1

D

Dacre Ave RG4 59 C2
Dagmar Rd SL4 67 B3
Dair House Sch SL2 22 B2
Dairy Ct SL6 65 A4
Dairy La RG9 16 A4
Dalby Cres RG14 131 A4
Dalcross RG12 118 C2
Dale Cl SL5 121 A2
Dale Ct SL1 42 B2
Dale Gdns GU47 150 A4
Dale Lodge Rd SL5 121 A2
Dale Rd Ashford TW16 98 C1
Reading RG2 86 A3
Walton-on-T KT12 125 C1
Daleham Ave TW20 96 A1
Dalley Ct GU47 150 B4
Dalston Cl GU15 152 B2
Dalton Cl RG30 84 C4
Damask Cl GU24 153 C3
Damer Gdns RG9 35 C4
Damson Gr SL1 42 B2
Dandridge Cl SL3 43 B1
Dandridge Dr SL8 3 B2
Dane Rd TW15 98 B1
Danefield RG40 116 B3
Danehill RG6 114 A4
Danehurst Cl TW20 95 C1
Danes Ct SL6 39 B4
Danes Gdns SL6 19 C3
Danesfield Sch SL7 17 C4
Danvers Cl RG19 106 B1
Danywern Dr RG41 88 B1
Darby Green La GU17 150 A3
Darby Green Rd GU17 150 A3
Darby La RG8 55 A3
Darby Vale RG42 91 A1
Darell Rd RG4 58 C2
Dark La Bradfield RG7 82 B4
Purley on T RG31 57 A1
Wargrave RG10 36 B1
Wickham RG17 101 A4
Darleydale Cl GU47 143 B1
Darling's La SL6 18 C1
Darracott Cl GU15 152 A4
Darrell Cl SL3 43 C1
Dart Cl Brands Hill SL3 69 A4
Thatcham RG18 106 A3
Wokingham RG40 141 C3
Dartington Ave RG5 87 B2
Dartington Cl RG30 84 C4
Dartmouth Cl RG12 118 C3
Dartmouth Ct 27 SL1 42 C2
Dartmouth Terr 1 RG1 86 B3
Darvill's La SL1 42 B2
Darvills La RG10 62 C1
Darwall Dr SL5 119 B4
Darwin Cl RG2 86 A1
Darwin Rd SL3 43 C2
Dashwood Cl
Bracknell RG12 118 B4
Slough SL3 43 B1
Datchet Pl SL3 68 A3
Datchet Rd Horton SL3 68 C2
Old Windsor SL4 68 A2
Slough SL3 42 C1
Windsor SL4 67 B4
Datchet Sta SL3 68 A3
Dauntless Rd RG7 111 A2
Davenport Rd RG12 118 C4
Daventry Cl SL3 69 C3
Daventry Ct RG42 118 A4
David Cl UB3 71 C4
David Ct TW18 97 A2
David Rd SL3 69 C3
David Smith Ct RG31 84 C3
Davis Cl SL7 1 C1
Davis Gdns GU47 150 C4
Davis St RG10 88 B3
Davis Way RG10 88 B2
Davy Cl RG40 116 B3
Dawes East Rd SL1 21 B1
Dawes Moor Cl SL2 43 B4
Dawley Ride SL3 69 C3
Dawlish Rd RG2 86 B1
Dawn Redwood Cl SL3 69 A2
Dawnay Cl SL5 119 C4
Dawnay Rd GU15 151 A4
Daws Ct SL0 44 C4
Dawsmere Cl GU15 152 B3
Dawson Cl SL4 67 A3
Daytona Dr RG19 107 A1
Dayworth Mews RG30 85 B4
De Beauvoir Rd RG1 86 C3
De Bohun Rd RG1 86 A4
De Havilland Way TW19 70 C1
De Montfort Gr RG17 100 B2
De Montfort Rd
Newbury RG14 104 C3
Reading RG1 59 A1
De Ros Pl TW20 96 A1
De-Vitre Gn RG40 116 C4
Deacon Cl RG40 116 B4
Deacon Ct SL4 66 B3
Deacon Way RG30 58 A1
Deaconfield RG8 14 B2
Deacons La RG18 79 B4
Deadman's La RG7 83 B2
Deadmans La RG14, RG19 131 A3
Deadmoor La RG20 130 C1
Deal Ave SL1 41 C4
Dean Cl SL4 66 B2
Dean Gr RG40 116 B4
Dean La SL6 19 B4
Dean Par GU15 151 C4
Dean St SL7 1 B1
Dean's Cloisters SL4 67 B4
Deanfield Ave RG9 15 B1
Deanfield Cl SL7 1 B2
Deanfield Rd RG9 15 B1
Deans Cl SL2 23 A2
Deans Ct GU20 146 B2
Deans Farm RG4 59 B1
Deansfield Cl SL6 19 B1
Deansgate RG12 118 A1
Deansgate Rd RG1 86 A3
Decies Way SL2 23 A2
Dedmere Ct SL7 1 C1
Dedmere Rd SL7 1 C1
Dedmere Rise SL7 1 C1
Dedworth Dr SL4 66 C3
Dedworth Green Fst Sch
SL4 66 C3
Dedworth Manor SL4 66 C3
Dedworth Mid Sch SL4 66 C3
Dedworth Rd SL4 66 B3
Dee Rd RG30 85 A4
Deena Cl SL1 41 C3
Deep Field SL3 68 A4
Deep Well Dr GU15 151 C3
Deepcut Bridge Rd
GU16 152 B1
Deepdale RG12 118 A3
Deepdene Cl RG1 85 C4
Deepfield Rd RG12 118 B4
Deer Leap GU18 153 A4
Deer Rock Hill RG12 118 B2
Deer Rock Rd GU15 151 C4
Deerhurst Ave RG41 88 B1
Deerhurst Cl RG31 84 C2
Deerswood SL6 20 A1
Defford Cl RG41 88 C1
Delafield Dr RG31 84 B2
Delaford Cl SL0 44 C4
Delamere Ho 8 RG1 85 C3
Delamere Rd RG6 87 A4
Delane Dr RG41 88 A1
Delaney Cl RG30 84 C4
Delft Cl RG30 84 C4
Dell Cl SL2 22 B4
Dell Gr GU16 151 C1
Dell Rd
Finchampstead RG40 142 A2
Purley on T RG31 57 B1
Dell The
Englefield Green TW20 95 A3
Maidenhead SL6 38 C1
9 Reading RG1 86 B4
Yateley GU46 149 B3
Deller St RG42 90 C1
Dellwood Com Hospl
RG30 85 B3
Delph The RG6 87 B1
Delta Way TW20 123 B4
Delwood Pk RG4 58 C2
Denbeigh Pl RG1 58 C1
Denborough Cres SL6 39 B3
Denbury Gdns RG2 113 B4
Denby Way RG30 57 C1
Dencliffe TW15 98 A2
Dene Cl 2 Bracknell RG12 118 B4
Earley RG6 87 A2
Dene Hollow OX11 10 C4
Dene Way RG14 105 A3
Denefield Sch RG31 57 A2
Denford La RG17 101 B4
Denham Cl SL6 39 B3
Denham Dr GU46 149 B3
Denham Gr RG12 118 B2
Denham Rd TW20 96 A2
Denison Rd TW13 98 C2
Denly Way GU18 146 B1
Denman Dr TW15 98 A1
Denmark Ave RG5 61 A1
Denmark Rd
Newbury RG14 105 A2
Reading RG1 86 B3
Denmark St
Maidenhead SL6 39 C4
Wokingham RG40 116 B3
Denmead Ct RG12 118 C2
Dennis Cl TW15 98 B1
Dennis Way SL1 41 B3
Dennistoun Cl GU15 151 B3
Dennose Cl RG6 87 A1
Denny Rd SL3 43 C1
Denton Cl RG19 106 B1
Denton Ct SL7 1 C2
Denton Rd RG40 116 B3
Denton Way GU16 151 B1
Depot Rd SL6 40 A3
Derby Cl RG17 25 A1
Derby Rd Caversham RG4 59 A2
Newbury RG14 104 C1
Derby St RG1 85 C4
Derbyshire Gn RG42 91 C1
Derek Horn Ct GU15 151 A3
Derek Rd SL6 40 B4
Deri Dene Cl 2 TW19 70 C1
Derrick Cl RG31 84 B2
Derry Rd GU14 150 C1
Derwent Ave RG30 57 C1
Derwent Cl
East Bedfont TW14 98 C4
Wokingham RG41 115 C3
Derwent Dr Burnham SL1 41 B4
Maidenhead SL6 39 B4
Derwent Rd
Lightwater GU18 153 A4
Thatcham RG19 106 A2
Thorpe Lea TW20 96 A1
Desborough Cl TW17 125 A1
Desborough Sch SL6 39 C3
Deseronto Wharf Ind Est
SL3 43 C2
Desford Way TW15 97 C3
Devenish La SL5 120 B1
Devenish Rd SL5 120 B1
Devereux Rd SL4 67 B3
Deverills Way SL3 44 B1
Deveron Dr RG30 85 A4
Devil's La TW20 96 B1
Devils Highway The
RG45 142 C3
Devitt Cl RG2 86 C1
Devon Ave SL1 42 B4
Devon Chase RG42 91 C1
Devon Cl Sandhurst GU47 150 B4
Wokingham RG41 115 C3
Devon Dr RG4 59 C2
Devonshire Cl SL2 22 A2
Devonshire Dr GU15 151 C4
Devonshire Gdns RG31 57 A2
Devonshire Gn SL2 22 A2
Devonshire Lodge 10 SL6 39 C3
Devonshire Pk RG2 86 C1
Dewberry Down RG18 106 C2
Dewe La RG30 84 C1
Dhoon Rise SL6 39 C3
Diamedes Ave TW19 97 B4
Diamond Cotts RG10 37 B3
Diamond Hill GU15 151 C4
Diamond Rd SL1 43 A2
Diamond Ridge GU15 151 C4
Diamond Way RG41 115 C4
Diana Cl SL3 43 C4
Dianthus Ct KT16 123 C1
Dianthus Pl RG42 92 A1
Dick Turpin Way TW14 71 C2
Dickens Cl RG4 59 B1
Dickens Way GU46 149 B3
Dickens Wlk RG14 131 A4
Dido Rd OX11 9 C4
Dieppe Cl RG41 115 C3
Digby Rd RG14 104 C2
Dines Way RG18 79 B4
Dingle Rd TW15 98 A2
Dinton Pastures Ctry Pk
RG10 88 B3
Disraeli Ct SL3 69 A4
Ditchfield La RG40 141 C4
Ditchling RG12 118 A1
Ditton Park Rd SL3 68 C4
Ditton Rd Datchet SL3 68 B4
Slough SL3 68 C4
Dittons The RG40 141 C3
Divine Mercy Coll RG9 15 C3
Dobson's La RG9 15 B4
Dockett Eddy La TW17 124 C1
Dockett Moorings KT16 124 C1
Doctors La RG18 79 A3
Doddington Cl RG6 87 B1
Dodsells Well RG40 141 C4
Dodsfield Rd SL2 22 A1
Dog La RG8 54 A3
Doghurst Ave UB3 71 A4
Doghurst Dr UB7 71 A4
Dogkennel La OX12 27 B2
Doles Hill RG41 115 B2
Doles La RG41 115 C2
Dolman Rd RG14 105 A2
Dolphin Cl Brimpton RG7 134 C4
Winnersh RG41 88 B1
Dolphin Ct Bracknell RG12 118 B3
Slough SL1 43 A2
Stanwell TW19 97 A3
Dolphin Ct N TW19 97 A3
Dolphin Est The TW16 125 B4
Dolphin Rd
Charlton TW16 125 C4
Slough SL1 43 A2
Dolphin Rd N TW16 125 C4
Dolphin Rd S TW16 125 C4
Dolphin Rd W TW16 125 C4
Doman Rd GU15 151 A2
Domoney Cl RG19 106 C2
Don Cl RG30 85 A4
Donaldson Way RG5 88 A4
Doncastle Rd RG12 117 C3
Donegal Cl RG4 59 B2
Donkey Dr SL8 3 A2
Donkey La SL8 3 A2
Donkin Hill RG4 59 B2
Donnington Castle RG14 104 C4
Donnington Cl
Bucklebury RG7 108 B4
Camberley GU15 151 A2
Donnington Gdns
Maidenhead SL6 19 C1
Reading RG1 86 C3
Donnington Lodge RG14 104 C4
Donnington Pl RG41 88 B1
Donnington Rd RG1 86 B3
Donnington Sq RG14 104 C3
Donnybrook RG12 118 A1
Dorcas Ct GU15 151 A2
Dorchester Cl SL6 19 A1
Dorchester Ct
Reading RG30 85 B3
Staines TW18 97 A2
Dorchester Dr TW14 71 C1
Dorian Dr SL5 120 C4
Doris Rd TW15 98 B1
Dorking Way RG31 84 A2
Dorly Cl TW17 125 C2
Dormer Cl
Crowthorne RG45 143 A3
Newbury RG14 130 C3
Dormy Ho The GU25 121 C2
Dornels SL2 43 B4
Dorney Ct SL4 41 A2
Dorney Cty Comb Sch
SL4 40 C2
Dorney Lake Rowing Ctr
SL4 66 A4
Dorney Reach Rd SL4 40 C2
Dorney Wood Rd SL1 21 B3
Dorothy Ct RG14 105 B2
Dorothy St 20 RG1 86 A3
Dorset Ct GU15 151 C4
Dorset Lodge 9 SL6 39 C3
Dorset Rd Ashford TW15 97 B3
Windsor SL4 67 B3
Dorset St RG30 85 B4
Dorset Vale RG42 91 C1
Dorset Way RG41 115 C3
Douai Sch RG7 108 C3
Doublet Cl RG19 106 A2
Douglas Ct Earley RG6 87 A2
Marlow SL7 2 A2
Douglas Grange RG10 88 B2
Douglas La TW19 68 C1
Douglas Rd
Caversham RG4 59 B1
Slough SL2 42 B4
Stanwell TW19 70 B1
Doultons The TW18 97 A1
Douro Cl RG26 134 B1
Dove Cl RG6 113 C4
Dove Ct TW19 97 C4
Dove House Cres SL2 21 C1
Dovecote Rd RG2 113 A4
Dovedale Cl
Caversham RG4 58 C2
Sandhurst GU47 143 B1
Dover Rd SL1 41 C4
Dover St RG1 86 A3
Doveton Way RG14 105 A2
Dowding Cl RG5 88 A4
Dowding Ct RG45 143 B3
Dower Pk SL4 66 C2
Down Pl SL4 66 A4
Downe House Sch RG18 79 A2
Downend La RG20 51 A1
Downfield La SL6 63 B3
Downfield Rd RG10 63 A2
Downham Ct RG2 86 C1
Downing Path SL2 21 C1
Downing Rd RG31 84 B4
Downlands RG17 47 B3
Downmill Rd RG12 117 C4
Downs Cl RG17 46 C4
Downs Rd Aldworth RG20 32 A2
Slough SL3 43 B2
Downs Sch The RG20 31 B2
Downs View OX11 12 C4
Downs Way Chilton OX11 9 C4
Purley on T RG31 57 B1
Downshire Cl RG17 48 A2
Downshire Sq RG1 85 C3

**Downshire Way**
Bracknell, Priestwood RG12 118 A3
Bracknell, Skimpedhill RG12, RG42 118 A4
**Downside** OX11 10 B4
**Downsway Sch** RG31 57 B2
**Doyle Gdns** GU46 149 B2
**Drain Hill** RG17 25 A2
**Drake Ave** Slough SL3 43 B1
Staines TW18 96 C2
**Drake Cl** Bracknell RG12 118 A2
Wokingham RG40 141 C4
**Draper Cl** RG19 106 B1
**Draycott** RG12 118 C2
**Drayhorse Dr** GU19 145 C1
**Drayton Cl** RG12 118 B4
**Drayton Rd** RG30 85 A4
**Dresden Way** RG30 57 C1
**Drew Mdw** SL2 22 B4
**Drewett Cl** RG2 113 B3
**Drift Rd** Holyport SL4,SL6 65 B2
Oakley Green SL4 66 A1
**Drift Way** SL3 69 B4
**Driftway Cl** 4 RG6 87 B1
**Drill Hall Rd** KT16 124 A1
**Drive The** Ashford TW15 98 B1
Bourne End SL8 2 C2
Datchet SL3 68 A3
Earley RG6 87 A4
Newbury RG14 130 C4
Slough SL3 43 C2
Virginia Water GU25 122 C2
Wraysbury TW19 68 B1
**Droitwich Cl** RG12 118 C3
**Dromepath** RG41 88 A2
**Dropmore Rd** SL1 21 B3
**Drove La** RG18 79 B1
**Drove The** RG19 133 A1
**Drovers Way**
Bracknell RG12 118 C3
Woodley RG5 87 C3
**Druce Way** RG19 106 B2
**Druce Wood** SL5 119 C4
**Drummond Cl** RG12 118 C4
**Drummond Ho** 4 SL4 67 B2
**Drury La** RG7 137 A3
**Dry Arch Rd** SL5 120 C2
**Dryden** RG12 118 A1
**Dryden Cl** RG18 106 B3
**Du Pre Wlk** HP10 3 B2
**Duchess Cl** RG45 143 A4
**Duchess St** SL1 41 C3
**Dudley Cl** RG31 57 C1
**Dudley Ct** SL1 43 A2
**Dudley Mews** RG31 57 C1
**Dudley Rd** Ashford TW15 97 C2
East Bedfont TW14 98 B4
**Duffield La** SL2 22 C3
**Duffield Pk** SL2 23 A1
**Duffield Rd** RG5 60 C1
**Dugdale Ho** TW20 96 B2
**Duke Of Cornwall Ave** GU15 144 B1
**Duke St** Eton SL4 67 B4
Henley-on-T RG9 15 C1
Reading RG1 86 A4
**Duke's Hill** GU19 145 C3
**Duke's La**
Old Windsor SL4, SL5 94 A2
Winkfield SL5 93 C1
**Duke's Ride** RG45 143 A3
**Dukes Cl** TW15 98 B2
**Dukes Covert** GU19 145 C3
**Dukes Pl** SL7 1 B1
**Dukes Ride** RG7 136 A1
**Dukes Wood** RG45 143 A3
**Dukeshill Rd** RG42 118 A4
**Dulnan Cl** RG30 85 A4
**Dulverton Gdns** RG2 86 B1
**Dumas Cl** GU46 149 B3
**Dumbarton Way** RG4 59 C3
**Dunally Pk** TW17 125 B1
**Dunaways Cl** RG6 87 B2
**Dunbar Cl** SL2 43 A3
**Dunbar Dr** RG5 88 A3
**Dunboe Pl** TW17 125 B1
**Duncan Dr** RG40 116 C3
**Duncan Gdns**
Purley on T RG8 57 B2
Staines TW18 97 A1
**Duncan Rd** RG5 87 C3
**Duncannon Cres** SL4 66 B2
**Duncombe Ct** TW18 96 C1
**Duncroft** SL4 66 C2
**Duncroft Manor** TW18 96 C3
**Dundaff Cl** GU15 152 A3
**Dundas Cl** RG12 118 A3
**Dundee Rd** SL1 42 A4
**Dundela Cl** RG5 87 C3
**Dunford Pl** RG42 90 C1
**Dungells Farm Cl** GU46 149 B2
**Dungells La** GU46 149 B2
**Dungrovehill La** SL6 18 B2
**Dunholme Cl** RG6 87 C1
**Dunholme End** SL6 39 B2
**Dunkirk Cl** RG41 115 C3
**Dunleary Ct** 13 RG30 85 B3
**Dunluce Gdns** RG8 56 C3
**Dunn Cres** RG17 102 A1
**Dunnock Way** RG10 36 C2
**Dunoon Cl** RG31 84 C2
**Dunsfold Rd** RG30 84 C4
**Dunsmore Gdns** GU46 149 A3
**Dunstable Ho** 11 SL7 1 C1
**Dunstall Cl** RG31 84 B4
**Dunstan Ct** TW18 97 A2
**Dunstan Park Inf Sch** RG18 106 B2
**Dunstan Rd** RG18 106 C2
**Dunstans Dr** RG41 88 A1
**Dunster Cl** RG4 59 B3
**Dunster Gdns** SL1 42 A3
**Dunt Ave** RG10 88 C2
**Dunt La** RG10 88 C2
**Dunwood Ct** SL6 39 B3
**Duppas Cl** TW17 125 B2
**Dupre Cl** SL1 41 C2
**Durand Rd** RG6 87 A1
**Durant Way** RG31 57 B2
**Durham Ave** SL1 42 A4
**Durham Cl** Reading RG2 113 B4
Wokingham RG41 115 C3
**Durham Rd** GU47 143 C1
**Durley Mead** RG12 118 C2
**Durrell Way** TW17 125 B2
**Dutch Barn Cl** TW19 70 B1
**Dutton Way** SL0 44 C4
**Duval Pl** GU19 145 C2
**Dwyer Rd** RG30 85 A2
**Dyer Straits** OX12 9 C4
**Dyers Ct** RG5 87 B4
**Dyson Cl** SL4 67 A2
**Dysons Cl** RG14 104 C2
**Dysonswood La** RG4 58 C4


## E


**Eagle Cl** Crowthorne RG45 143 A4
Wokingham RG41 115 C3
**Eagle House Sch** GU47 143 A1
**Eagle Rd** RG20 132 A1
**Eagles Nest** GU47 143 A1
**Earle Croft** RG42 91 B1
**Earley Hill Rd** RG6 87 A3
**Earley Pl** RG1 86 A4
**Earley Sta** RG6 87 B2
**Earleydene** SL5 120 A1
**Earls Gr** GU15 151 C3
**Earls La** SL1 41 C3
**Earlsfield** SL6 40 B1
**Earlsfield Cl** RG4 59 C2
**Earlswood** RG12 118 A1
**Easby La** RG6 87 B1
**Easington Dr** RG6 87 C1
**East Berkshire Coll**
Maidenhead SL6 39 B3
Slough SL3 44 A2
Windsor SL4 67 B3
**East Burnham Cotts** SL2 22 A2
**East Burnham La** SL2 22 A2
**East Cres** SL4 66 C3
**East Dr** Reading RG31 84 C3
Stoke Poges SL2 22 C1
Wentworth GU25 122 A2
**East Gn** GU17 150 B2
**East La** RG20 51 A1
**East Paddock** SL6 18 C3
**East Park Farm Dr** RG10 61 A2
**East Ramp** TW6 71 A3
**East Rd** East Bedfont TW14 98 B4
Maidenhead SL6 39 C4
**East Ridge** SL8 3 A2
**East St** RG1 86 A4
**East Stratton Cl** RG12 118 C2
**East View Cl** RG10 36 C1
**East View Rd** RG10 36 C1
**Eastbourne Rd** SL1 42 A4
**Eastbridge** SL2 43 A3
**Eastbury Ave** RG31 84 A4
**Eastbury Ct** RG42 90 C1
**Eastbury Pk** RG41 88 B1
**Eastbury Shute** RG17 46 C1
**Eastchurch Rd** TW6 71 C2
**Eastchurch Road Rdbt** TW6 71 C3
**Eastcourt Ave** RG6 87 A3
**Eastcroft** SL2 22 A1
**Eastern Ave**
Chertsey KT16 124 A3
Reading RG1 86 C3
**Eastern Dr** SL8 3 B2
**Eastern Ind Area** RG12 118 B4
**Eastern La** RG45 143 C2
**Eastern Perimeter Rd**
Hatton TW14 71 C2
Hatton TW6 71 C3
**Eastern Rd** RG12 118 B4
**Eastfield** OX11 12 A4
**Eastfield Cl** 4 SL1 43 A2
**Eastfield La** RG8 56 B4
**Eastfield Rd** SL1 41 A4
**Easthampstead Park Sch** RG12 117 B2
**Easthampstead Rd**
Bracknell RG12 118 A4
Wokingham RG40 116 C2
**Eastheath Ave** RG41 116 A2
**Eastheath Gdns** RG41 116 A2
**Eastleigh Rd** TW6 71 C2
**Eastlyn Rd** RG26 135 C1
**Easton Hill** RG20 76 A2
**Eastwood Ct** 1 SL7 1 C2
**Eastwood Rd** RG5 87 C2
**Eastworth Rd** KT15, KT16 124 A1
**Eaton Pl** RG1 85 C4
**Eaton Rd** GU15 151 A2
**Ebborn Sq** RG6 114 B4
**Ebsworth Cl** SL6 20 B2
**Eccles Cl** RG4 59 B1
**Echelford Cty Mid Sch** TW15 98 A2
**Echelforde Dr** TW15 98 A2
**Eddington Hill** RG17 100 C4
**Eddington Rd** RG12 117 C2
**Eddystone Wlk** TW19 97 C4
**Eden Cl** SL3 44 A1
**Eden Way** RG41 88 A1
**Edenhall Cl** RG31 57 B2
**Edenham Cl** RG6 87 C1
**Edenham Cres** RG1 85 C3
**Edgar Milward Cl** RG30 58 A1
**Edgar Wallace Pl** SL8 3 A3
**Edgbarrow Rise** GU47 143 A1
**Edgbarrow Sch** RG45 143 B2
**Edgbarrowhill Star** RG45 143 A2
**Edgcumbe Park Dr** RG45 143 A3
**Edgecombe La** RG14 105 B3
**Edgedale Cl** RG45 143 A3
**Edgehill St** RG1 86 A3
**Edgell Cl** GU25 122 C3
**Edgell Rd** TW18 96 C2
**Edgemoor Rd** GU16 152 B2
**Edgewood Cl** RG45 143 A4
**Edinburgh Ave** SL1 42 A4
**Edinburgh Dr** TW18 97 B1
**Edinburgh Rd**
Maidenhead SL6 19 C1
Marlow SL7 1 C2
Reading RG30 85 C4
**Edith Rd** SL6 39 A4
**Edmonds Ct** 4 RG12 118 B4
**Edmunds Way** SL2 43 A4
**Edneys Hill** RG41 115 B1
**Edward Ave** GU15 151 A3
**Edward Ct** TW18 97 B1
**Edward Pauling Ho** TW14 98 C4
**Edward Pauling Prim Sch** TW13 98 C3
**Edward Pl** 25 RG1 86 B4
**Edward Rd** Hatton TW14 71 C1
Twyford RG10 61 A3
Windlesham GU20 146 B2
**Edward Way** TW15 97 C3
**Edwards Ct** SL1 42 C2
**Edwards Hill** RG17 25 A1
**Edwin Cl** RG19 106 C2
**Eeklo Pl** RG14 105 A1
**Egerton Rd** Reading RG2 86 C1
Sandhurst GU15 150 C4
Slough SL2 21 C1
**Egham By-Pass** TW20 96 A2
**Egham Hill** TW20 95 B1
**Egham Hill Rdbt** TW20 95 C2
**Egham Mus** TW20 96 A2
**Egham Sta** TW20 96 A2
**Eghams Ct** 9 SL8 3 A2
**Egremont Dr** RG6 87 B2
**Egremont Gdns** SL1 42 A3
**Egypt La** SL2 22 A4
**Eight Acres** SL1 41 A1
**Eight Bells** RG14 104 C1
**Eisenhower Ave** RG20 49 A2
**Elan Cl** RG30 84 C4
**Elbow Mdw** SL3 69 C3
**Eldart Cl** RG30 85 A4
**Elder Cl** RG31 57 B1
**Elderberry Way** RG6 87 B1
**Elderfield Cres** OX11 10 B4
**Elderfield Rd** SL2 22 C3
**Eldon Pl** RG1 86 B4
**Eldon Rd** RG1 86 A4
**Eldon Sq** RG1 86 B4
**Eldon St** RG1 86 B4
**Eldon Terr** RG1 86 B4
**Eldrick Ct** TW14 98 B4
**Elford Cl** RG6 87 B1
**Elgar Ave** RG45 143 A4
**Elgar Rd** RG2 86 A3
**Elgar Rd S** RG2 86 A2
**Elgarth Dr** RG40 141 C4
**Elgin Ave** TW15 98 B1
**Elgin Cres** TW6 71 C3
**Elgin Ho** SL3 69 C3
**Eliot Cl** Camberley GU15 152 A4
Caversham RG4 59 A2
Thatcham RG18 106 B3
**Elizabeth Ave**
Bagshot GU19 145 C1
Newbury RG14 130 B4
Staines TW18 97 B1
**Elizabeth Cl**
Bracknell RG12 118 B3
Cookham SL6 19 C4
Henley-on-T RG9 35 A4
**Elizabeth Ct** 9 Slough SL1 43 A2
Wargrave RG10 36 B2
**Elizabeth Gdns** Ascot SL5 120 A2
Kintbury RG17 102 A1
**Elizabeth Ho** TW15 97 C2
**Elizabeth Mews** 18 RG1 86 A3
**Elizabeth Par** GU46 149 B2
**Elizabeth Rd**
Henley-on-T RG9 35 A4
Marlow SL7 1 C2
Wokingham RG40 116 B3
**Elizabeth Rout Cl** RG7 113 B1
**Elizabeth Way** SL2 22 C2
**Elizabeth Wlk** 28 RG1 86 A3
**Elizabethan Cl** TW19 97 B4
**Elizabethan Way** TW19 97 B4
**Ellenborough Cl** RG12 118 B4
**Ellerton Cl** RG7 83 C2
**Ellesfield Ave** RG12 117 C3
**Ellesmere Cl** RG4 59 A2
**Ellies Mews** TW15 97 C3
**Elliman Ave** SL2 42 C3
**Ellington Ct** SL6 40 B4
**Ellington Gdns** SL6 40 B4
**Ellington Pk** SL6 19 C1
**Ellington Prim Sch** SL6 19 C1
**Ellington Rd** Feltham TW13 98 C2
**Ellington Rd** *continued*
Taplow SL6 40 B4
**Elliot Dr** SL7 1 C2
**Elliot Rise** SL5 119 B4
**Elliots Way** RG4 59 A1
**Elliott Gdns** TW17 125 A3
**Ellis Ave** SL1 42 C2
**Ellis Rd** RG45 143 A3
**Ellison Cl** SL4 66 C2
**Ellison Ho** 23 SL4 67 B3
**Ellison Way** RG40 116 A3
**Elm Bank** GU46 149 B4
**Elm Cl**
Farnham Common SL2 22 B3
Stanwell TW19 97 B4
**Elm Cotts** RG20 129 C1
**Elm Croft** SL3 68 B3
**Elm Ct** 9 Charlton TW16 98 C1
Sandhurst GU47 143 C1
**Elm Dr**
Burghfield Common RG30 111 A3
Winkfield SL4 93 A4
**Elm Gr** Maidenhead SL6 39 C4
Thatcham RG18 106 A3
**Elm La** Bourne End SL8 2 C3
Earley RG6 86 C1
**Elm Lodge Ave** RG30 85 B4
**Elm Park Rd** RG30 85 B4
**Elm Pk** Reading RG30 85 B4
Sunningdale SL5 120 C1
**Elm Rd** Earley RG2 & RG6 86 C1
East Bedfont TW14 98 B4
Mapledurham RG4 58 B4
Windsor SL4 67 A2
**Elm Tree Cl** TW15 98 A2
**Elmar Gn** SL2 22 A1
**Elmbank Ave** TW20 95 A1
**Elmcroft** RG8 34 B3
**Elmcroft Cl** TW14 71 C1
**Elmcroft Dr** TW15 98 A2
**Elmdon Rd** TW6 71 C2
**Elmhurst Ballet Sch** GU15 151 B3
**Elmhurst Ct** SL3 44 A2
**Elmhurst Rd** Goring RG8 34 B4
Reading RG1 86 B3
Slough SL3 44 A2
Thatcham RG18 106 A3
**Elmleigh Ct** RG4 59 B2
**Elmley Cl** RG41 88 C1
**Elms Ave** RG19 106 C2
**Elms Dr** SL8 3 B2
**Elms Rd** RG40 116 A3
**Elms The** TW15 98 A2
**Elmshott La** SL1 41 C3
**Elmsleigh Ctr The** TW18 96 C2
**Elmsleigh Rd** TW18 96 C2
**Elmslie Ct** SL6 39 C4
**Elmstone Dr** RG31 57 B1
**Elmsway** TW15 98 A2
**Elmwood** SL6 20 A2
**Elmwood Rd** SL2 43 A3
**Elsenwood Cres** GU15 152 A3
**Elsenwood Dr** GU15 152 A4
**Elsinore Ave** TW19 97 C4
**Elsley Rd** RG31 57 C2
**Elstow Ave** RG4 59 B3
**Elstree Cl** RG31 57 B1
**Elstree Sch** RG7 108 B2
**Elsworth Cl** TW14 98 C4
**Eltham Ave** Caversham RG4 59 C3
Slough SL1 41 C2
**Elton Dr** SL6 39 B4
**Elvaston Way** RG30 85 A4
**Elveden Cl** RG6 87 C1
**Elvendon Rd** RG8 34 B4
**Elwell Cl** TW20 96 A1
**Ely Ave** SL1 42 B4
**Ely Rd** Hatton TW6 71 C3
Theale RG7 83 C2
**Embankment The** TW19 95 B4
**Ember Rd** SL3 44 A2
**Emblem Cres** RG2 114 C1
**Embrook Way** RG31 84 A2
**Emerald Cl** RG41 115 C4
**Emerald Ct** SL1 42 C2
**Emerson Ct** HP10 3 C3
**Emery Acres** RG8 55 A3
**Emery Down Cl** RG12 119 A3
**Emlyns Bldgs** SL4 67 B4
**Emm Cl** RG41 115 C4
**Emma La** RG10 36 C1
**Emmbrook Comp Sch** RG41 115 C4
**Emmbrook Ct** RG2 86 C1
**Emmbrook Gate** RG41 115 C4
**Emmbrook Inf Sch** RG41 88 C1
**Emmbrook Jun Sch** RG41 88 C1
**Emmbrook Rd** RG41 115 C4
**Emmbrook Vale** RG41 89 A1
**Emmer Green Ct** RG4 59 B3
**Emmer Green Prim Sch** RG4 59 A3
**Emmets Nest** RG42 90 B1
**Emmets Pk** RG42 90 B1
**Emmview Cl** RG41 115 C4
**Empress Rd** RG31 84 B3
**Enborne Cl** RG31 84 B4
**Enborne Gate** RG14 104 B1
**Enborne Gdns** RG12 91 B1
**Enborne Gr** RG14 104 C1
**Enborne Lodge Sch** RG14 130 A3
**Enborne Pl** RG14 104 C1
**Enborne Prim Sch** RG20 129 C3
**Enborne Rd** RG14 104 B1
**Enborne St**
Hamstead Marshall RG20 130 A2
**Enborne St** *continued*
Newbury RG14 130 B3
**Enborne Way** RG7 133 C3
**Enfield Rd** TW6 71 C3
**Enfield Road Rdbt** TW6 71 C3
**Engineers Rd** RG19 132 A3
**Englefield CE Prim Sch** RG7 83 A2
**Englefield Cl** TW20 95 B1
**Englefield Green Sch** TW20 95 B2
**Englefield Rd** RG7 83 B2
**Engleheart Dr** TW14 71 C1
**Englehurst** TW20 95 B1
**Englemere Pk** SL5 119 B3
**Englemere Pond Nature Trail** SL5 119 B3
**Englemere Rd** RG42 90 C1
**Englesfield** GU15 152 B3
**English Gdns** TW19 68 B1
**English Martyrs RC Prim Sch** RG30 85 A4
**Enid Wood Ho** RG12 118 B4
**Ennerdale** RG12 118 A3
**Ennerdale Cl** TW14 98 C4
**Ennerdale Cres** SL1 41 B4
**Ennerdale Rd** RG2 86 B2
**Ennerdale Way** RG19 106 A2
**Ensign Cl** TW19 97 B4
**Ensign Way** TW19 97 B4
**Enstone Rd** RG5 88 A4
**Enterprise Way** RG19 107 A1
**EP Collier Prim Sch** RG1 59 A1
**Epping Cl** RG1 85 C4
**Epping Ho** 6 RG1 85 C3
**Epping Way** RG12 118 C3
**Epsom Cl** GU15 151 B4
**Epsom Cres** RG14 105 A1
**Epsom Ct** RG1 85 C3
**Epsom Sq** TW6 71 C3
**Equine Way** RG14 131 A4
**Eric Ave** RG4 59 A3
**Erica Cl** Slough SL1 41 C3
West End GU24 153 C3
**Erica Dr** RG40 116 B3
**Eriswell Cl** RG6 87 C1
**Erkenwald Cl** KT16 123 C2
**Erleigh Court Dr** RG6 87 A4
**Erleigh Court Gdns** RG6 87 A4
**Erleigh Dene** RG14 104 C1
**Erleigh Rd** RG1 86 B3
**Ermin St** Lambourn RG17 46 B1
Stockcross RG20 103 B4
Wickham RG20 75 B2
**Ermin Wlk** RG19 106 A2
**Errington Dr** SL4 67 A3
**Erskine Cl** RG26 135 C1
**Escot Rd** TW16 98 C1
**Esher Cres** TW6 71 C3
**Esher Rd** GU15 145 A1
**Eskdale Gdns** SL6 40 A1
**Eskdale Rd** RG41 88 A2
**Eskdale Way** GU15 152 B2
**Eskin Cl** RG30 85 A4
**Essame Cl** RG40 116 B3
**Essex Ave** SL2 42 B4
**Essex Pl** RG17 25 A2
**Essex Rise** RG42 91 C1
**Essex St** Newbury RG14 130 B4
Reading RG2 86 A3
**Ethel Rd** TW15 97 C2
**Eton Cl** SL3 68 A4
**Eton Coll** SL4 67 B4
**Eton Ct** Eton SL4 67 B4
Staines TW18 96 C2
**Eton End PNEU Sch** SL3 68 A4
**Eton Pl** SL7 1 B1
**Eton Porny CE Comb Sch** SL4 67 B4
**Eton Rd** Datchet SL3 68 A4
Harlington UB3 71 C4
**Eton Sq** SL4 67 B4
**Eton Wick CE Fst Sch** SL4 42 A1
**Eton Wick Rd** SL4 42 A1
**Eton Wlk** 22 SL1 42 C2
**European Weather Ctr** RG2 113 B4
**Eustace Cres** RG40 116 B4
**Evedon** RG12 118 A1
**Evelyn Cres** TW16 125 C4
**Evelyn Ct** RG5 87 C3
**Evelyn Way** TW16 125 C4
**Evendon's Cl** RG41 116 A2
**Evendon's La**
Barkham RG41 115 C1
Wokingham RG41 116 A2
**Evenlode** SL6 39 C4
**Evenlode Rd** SL8 3 A2
**Evenlode Way** GU47 150 B4
**Everard Ave** SL1 42 C2
**Everest Rd**
Camberley GU15 151 B4
Crowthorne RG45 143 A3
Stanwell TW19 97 C4
**Evergreen Ct** TW19 97 B4
**Evergreen Dr** RG31 84 C2
**Evergreen Rd** GU16 152 A2
**Evergreen Way**
Stanwell TW19 97 B4
Wokingham RG41 115 C3
**Everington La** RG18 53 A1
**Everland Rd** RG17 100 B3
**Eversley Rd**
Arborfield RG2 114 C1
Barkham RG40 140 C3

Eversley St RG27 141 A1
Eversley Way TW20 123 B4
Evesham Rd RG4 59 A3
Evesham Wlk GU47 143 B1
Evreham Rd SL0 44 C4
Evreux Cl RG19 106 C1
Ewing Way RG14 131 A4
Exbourne Rd RG2 113 B4
Exchange Rd SL5 120 B2
Exeforde Ave TW15 98 A2
Exeter Ct RG2 113 A4
Exeter Gdns GU46 149 A4
Exeter Rd TW6 71 C2
Exeter Way Hatton TW6 71 C3
Theale RG7 83 C2
Exmoor Rd RG19 106 B2
Explorer Ave TW19 97 C4
Expressway RG14 105 C1
Exwick Sq RG2 113 B4
Eylham RG8 57 A3
Eynsford Cl RG4 59 C3
Eynsham Rd RG5 87 C4
Eyre Gn SL2 22 A1

## F

Fagg's Rd TW14 71 C2
Fair Close Ho 1 RG14 105 A1
Fair Lawn Gn RG2 86 C1
Fair Mile RG9 15 B2
Fair Mile Hospl OX10 14 A4
Fair View Cotts SL6 19 C4
Fairacre SL6 39 B3
Fairacres Ind Est SL4 66 B3
Faircroft SL2 22 A1
Faircross RG12 118 A3
Faircross Quarters RG18 78 C3
Faircross Rd RG30 85 B3
Fairfax RG42 118 A4
Fairfax Cl RG4 59 A2
Fairfax Pl RG14 105 C3
Fairfield RG20 31 B2
Fairfield App TW19 68 B1
Fairfield Ave Datchet SL3 68 B4
Farnham Common SL2 22 A2
Staines TW18 96 C2
Fairfield Cl SL3 68 B4
Fairfield Dr GU16 151 C2
Fairfield La GU24 153 C4
Fairfield Rd Burnham SL1 21 B1
Goring RG8 34 B4
Wraysbury TW19 68 B1
Fairfields RG17 100 B3
Fairford Rd
Maidenhead SL6 39 C4
Purley on T RG31 57 B1
Fairhaven TW20 95 C2
Fairhaven Ct 1 TW20 95 C2
Fairholme TW14 98 C4
Fairholme Jun & Inf Schs
TW14 98 B4
Fairholme Rd TW15 97 C2
Fairlawn Pk SL4 66 C2
Fairlawns Cl TW18 97 A1
Fairlea SL6 39 A2
Fairlie Rd SL1 42 A4
Fairlight Ave SL4 67 B3
Fairlop Cl RG31 84 B2
Fairmead Cl GU47 150 C4
Fairmead Rd RG2 113 C3
Fairmile Ct RG9 15 B2
Fairoak Way RG26 134 B1
Fairsted Cl RG30 85 A4
Fairview RG14 130 C4
Fairview Ave RG6 87 A3
Fairview Cotts GU25 122 B2
Fairview Ct TW15 98 A2
Fairview Dr TW17 124 C2
Fairview Est RG9 35 C4
Fairview Rd Burnham SL6 41 A4
Hungerford RG17 100 B3
Slough SL2 21 C1
Wokingham RG40 116 B3
Fairwater Dr RG5 87 B3
Fairway KT16 124 A1
Fairway Ave RG30 84 B3
Fairway Dr RG10 61 A3
Fairway Hts GU15 152 A3
Fairway The Burnham SL1 21 B2
Flackwell Heath HP10 3 B4
Frimley GU15 152 A2
Maidenhead SL6 39 A2
Fairways TW15 98 A1
Faithfull Cl RG42 91 A1
Fakenham Cl RG6 114 A4
Fakenham Way GU47 143 B1
Falaise TW20 95 C2
Falcon Ave RG2 86 C1
Falcon Cl GU18 152 C4
Falcon Ct GU16 151 B1
Falcon Dr TW19 70 C1
Falcon Fields RG26 135 A1
Falcon House Gdns
RG20 129 C1
Falcon Way
Sunbury TW16 125 C4
Wokingham RG41 115 C3
Yateley GU46 149 A3
Falcons Croft HP10 3 C4
Falconwood TW20 95 C2
Falkland Dr RG14 130 C4
Falkland Garth RG14 130 B4
Falkland Ho SL6 39 C4
Falkland Prim Sch RG14 130 B3
Falkland Rd
Caversham RG4 59 A1
Newbury RG14 130 B3
Fallowfield GU46 149 A4
Fallowfield Cl RG4 59 A2
Falmouth Cl GU15 152 A2
Falmouth Rd
Reading RG2 113 B4
Slough SL1 42 A4
Falmouth Way RG19 106 C2
Falstaff Ave RG6 86 C1
Fane Way SL6 39 B3
Fanes Cl RG42 117 C4
Fannys La RG7 80 B1
Faraday Cl Arborfield RG2 140 C4
Slough SL2 42 A4
Faraday Rd
Newbury RG14 105 A2
Slough SL2 42 A4
Farcrosse Cl GU47 150 B4
Fareham Dr GU46 149 A4
Faringdon Cl GU47 143 B1
Faringdon Dr RG12 118 B2
Faringdon Wlk RG30 85 A2
Farleigh Mews RG4 59 C3
Farley Copse RG42 117 C4
Farley Hill Prim Sch
RG7 140 B3
Farley Moor RG42 117 B4
Farley Villas KT16 124 A1
Farm Cl Ascot SL5 120 B2
Bracknell RG42 117 C4
Crowthorne RG45 143 B4
Egham TW18 96 C2
Lower Halliford TW17 125 A1
Lyne KT16 123 A2
Maidenhead SL6 40 B1
Maidenhead, Highway SL6 39 A4
Purley on T RG8 57 B3
Yateley GU46 149 B3
Farm Cres SL2 43 B4
Farm Dr Old Windsor SL4 68 A1
Reading RG31 84 A3
Farm Lea HP10 3 C4
Farm Rd Bourne End SL8 2 C2
Burnham SL6 41 A3
Frimley GU16 151 C1
Goring RG8 34 B3
Henley-on-T RG9 35 C4
Maidenhead SL6 39 A4
Staines TW18 97 A1
Farm View GU46 149 B3
Farm Way TW19 69 C1
Farm Yd SL4 67 B4
Farman Cl RG5 88 A4
Farmer's Rd TW18 96 C2
Farmers Cl Maidenhead SL6 39 A2
Reading RG2 113 B3
Farmers End RG10 61 A2
Farmers Gate RG18 106 B3
Farmers Way SL6 39 A2
Farmiloe Cl RG8 57 B2
Farnburn Ave SL1 42 A4
Farnell Rd TW18 97 A3
Farnham Cl RG12 118 B4
Farnham Common
Cty Inf Sch SL2 22 A4
Farnham Common
Cty Jun Sch SL2 22 B4
Farnham Common Ho 3
SL2 22 B4
Farnham Dr RG4 59 C2
Farnham La SL2 22 A2
Farnham Park La SL2 22 B2
Farnham Rd SL1, SL2 42 B4
Farningham RG12 118 C2
Farningham Ho RG12 118 C2
Farnsfield Cl RG6 114 A4
Farrell Cl GU15 151 B2
Farrer Theatre SL4 42 B1
Farrier Ct 11 SL8 3 A2
Farriers Cl RG5 87 C4
Farriers La RG20 30 C4
Farrowdene Rd RG2 113 B4
Farthing Green La SL2 23 A2
Farthingales The SL6 40 A4
Fatherson Rd RG1 86 B4
Faulkner Pl GU19 145 C2
Faversham Rd GU47 143 B1
Fawcett Cres RG5 87 B3
Fawcett Rd SL4 67 A3
Fawler Mead RG12 118 C3
Fawley Bottom Rd RG9 15 A4
Fawley Cl SL6 19 B1
Fawley Ct RG9 15 C3
Fawley Mews 2 RG1 85 C3
Fawley Rd RG30 85 B3
Fawns Manor Cl TW14 98 B4
Fawns Manor Rd TW14 98 B4
Fawsley Cl SL3 69 C4
Faygate Way RG6 87 A1
Feathers La TW19 96 A3
Felbridge Cl GU16 151 C1
Felbridge Ct UB3 71 B4
Felix La TW17 125 C2
Felixstowe Cl RG6 87 B1
Fellow Gn GU24 153 C3
Fellow Green Rd GU24 153 C3
Fellowes Ct UB3 71 B4
Fells The RG31 84 A3
Felstead Cl RG6 86 C2
Feltham Hill
Jun & Inf Schs TW13 98 C3
Feltham Hill Rd TW15 98 B1
Feltham Rd TW15 98 B2
Felthorpe Cl RG6 114 A4
Felton Way RG31 84 B4
Fencote RG12 118 B2
Fennel Cl Earley RG6 86 C1
Newbury RG14 105 B3
Fenns La GU24 153 C3
Fennscombe Ct GU24 153 C3
Fenton Ave TW18 97 B2
Fern Cl Crowthorne RG45 143 A4
Frimley GU16 152 B2
Reading RG31 84 B3
Fern Dr SL6 41 A4
Fern Glen RG31 57 B1
Fern Wlk Ashford TW15 97 B2
Reading RG31 84 B3
Fernbank RG40 141 B4
Fernbank Cres SL5 119 B4
Fernbank Pl SL5 119 B4
Fernbank Rd SL5 119 B4
Fernbrook Rd RG4 58 C3
Ferndale Ave RG30 85 A2
Ferndale Cl RG31 57 C2
Ferndale Ct RG19 106 B2
Ferndale Pk SL6 65 C4
Ferndale Rd TW15 97 C2
Ferne Cl RG8 34 B4
Fernery The TW18 96 C2
Fernhill Cl Bracknell RG42 90 C1
Farnborough (Hants) GU17 150 C1
Fernhill Comp Sch
GU14 150 C1
Fernhill Cty Prim Sch
GU14 150 C1
Fernhill La GU17 150 C1
Fernhill Rd GU14,GU17 150 C1
Fernhill Wlk GU17 150 C1
Fernhurst Rd
Ashford TW15 98 B2
Reading RG31 84 B2
Ferniehurst GU15 151 C2
Fernley Ct SL6 19 B1
Ferrard Cl SL5 119 B4
Ferrers Cl SL1 41 C3
Ferriby Ct RG12 118 B4
Ferrier Gr RG14 131 A4
Ferry Ave TW18 96 C1
Ferry End SL6 40 B2
Ferry La Bourne End SL8 3 A1
Chertsey KT16 124 A2
Cookham SL6 20 A4
Goring RG8 34 A3
Hambleden RG9 16 B3
Laleham TW18 124 B3
Lower Halliford TW16,TW17 125 A1
Medmenham SL7 17 A3
South Stoke RG8 14 A2
Wargrave RG10 36 B1
Wraysbury TW19 96 A3
Ferry Rd Maidenhead SL6 40 B2
South Stoke RG8 14 B2
Ferry Wks TW17 125 A1
Festival Cotts SL3 69 B4
Fettiplace RG17 48 A2
Fidlers La RG20 30 C4
Fidlers Wlk RG10 36 C1
Field Cl
Burghfield Common RG7 111 A1
Harlington UB3 71 B4
Field End GU24 153 C3
Field House Cl SL5 120 A1
Field Hurst SL3 43 C1
Field La GU16 151 C1
Field Pk RG12 118 B4
Field Rd
Farnborough (Hants) GU14 150 C1
Peasemore RG20 29 B1
Reading RG1 86 A3
Field View Caversham RG4 59 A2
Egham TW20 96 B2
Feltham TW13 98 B3
Fielden Pl RG12 118 B4
Fieldfare Ave GU46 149 A3
Fieldhead Gdns SL8 3 A2
Fieldhouse Ind Est SL7 1 C1
Fieldhouse La SL7 1 C1
Fieldhouse Way SL7 1 C1
Fielding Gdns
Crowthorne RG45 143 A2
Slough SL3 43 B2
Fielding Rd
Maidenhead SL6 39 A4
Sandhurst GU47 150 C3
Fieldings The SL6 65 A4
Fieldridge RG14 105 B3
Fields The SL1 42 B2
Fieldview Ct TW18 97 A1
Fieldway RG41 88 B1
Fifehead Cl TW15 97 C1
Fifield Cotts SL6 65 B3
Fifield La SL4,SL6 65 B2
Fifield Rd SL6 65 B4
Fifth Rd RG14 104 C1
Fifth St RG19 131 C3
Filbert Dr RG31 84 B4
Filey Rd RG1 86 C4
Filey Spur SL1 42 A2
Filmer Rd SL4 66 B3
Finbeck Way RG6 113 C4
Finch Ct SL6 39 B3
Finch Rd RG6 87 B2
Finch Way RG7 111 A2
Fincham End Dr RG45 142 C2
Finchampstead
CE Prim Sch RG40 141 C2
Finchampstead Rd
Finchampstead RG40 141 C3
Finchampstead RG40 142 A4
Wokingham RG41, RG40 116 A2
Findhorn Cl GU47 150 B4
Fineleigh Ct SL1 42 C3
Finmere RG12 118 B1
Finney Dr GU20 146 B2
Finstock Cl RG6 87 B1
Finstock Gn RG12 118 C3
Fir Cottage Rd RG40 141 C4
Fir Dr GU17 150 B2
Fir Tree Ave SL2 22 C1
Fir Tree Cl SL5 120 A1
Fir Tree Cnr RG26 134 C1
Fir Tree Cotts RG20 10 A1
Fir Tree La RG14 105 C2
Fir Tree Paddock RG20 10 A1
Fir Tree Pl TW15 98 A2
Fir Tree Prim Sch RG14 105 C2
Firbank Pl TW20 95 A1
Fircroft Cl Reading RG31 57 B1
Stoke Poges SL2 23 A3
Fireball Hill SL5 120 B1
Firglen Dr GU46 149 B4
Firgrove Rd RG27,GU46 149 B3
Firlands RG12 118 B2
Firlands Ave GU15 151 B3
Firmstone Cl RG6 87 B1
Firs Ave SL4 66 C2
Firs Cl RG40 141 C4
Firs Dr SL3 43 C3
Firs End RG7 111 A1
Firs La Maidenhead SL6 38 C2
Reading RG30 85 B3
Firs Rd RG31 84 B3
Firs The 14 Bracknell RG12 118 C3
Inkpen RG17 127 C3
Maidenhead SL6 39 C4
Reading RG30 85 C3
Thatcham RG18 106 A2
First Ave Marlow SL7 2 A1
Tadley RG7 135 B1
First Cres SL1 42 B4
First St RG19 132 A3
Firtree Cl GU47 142 C1
Firview Cl SL7 1 C1
Firwood Ct GU15 151 B3
Firwood Dr GU15 151 B3
Firwood Rd GU25 121 C2
Fisher Gn RG42 90 A1
Fisherman's Way SL8 3 A2
Fishermans La RG7 135 A4
Fishermans Retreat SL7 1 C1
Fishers Cotts RG4 59 B3
Fishers Ct RG4 59 B3
Fishers La RG18 79 A1
Fishers Wood SL5 121 B1
Fishery Rd SL6 40 B3
Fishguard Spur SL1 43 A2
Fishponds Cl RG41 116 A2
Fishponds Est RG41 116 A2
Fishponds Rd RG41 116 A2
Fitzrobert Pl TW20 96 A1
Fitzroy Cres RG5 88 A3
Five Acre RG31 57 A1
Five Acres HP10 3 C4
Flag Staff Sq RG19 106 C1
Flambards RG4 59 B1
Flamborough Cl RG6 87 C1
Flamborough Spur SL1 42 A2
Flamingo Cl RG41 115 C3
Flanders Ct TW20 96 B2
Flats The GU17 150 B2
Flaxman Cl RG6 86 C1
Flecker Cl RG18 106 B3
Fleet Cl RG41 115 C3
Fleet Hill RG40 141 B1
Fleet La RG40 141 A1
Fleetbrook Ho SL3 68 B3
Fleetham Gdns RG6 87 B1
Fleetway TW20 123 B3
Fleetwood Cl RG14 105 B3
Fleetwood Ct 7 TW19 70 C1
Fleetwood Rd SL2 42 C3
Fleming Cl RG2 140 C4
Fleming Rd RG14 105 A2
Flemish Fields KT16 124 A1
Fletcher Gdns RG42 117 B4
Flexford Gn RG12 117 C2
Flintgrove RG12 118 B4
Flintjack Pl RG17 25 A1
Flintlock Cl TW19 70 A2
Flodden Dr RG31 84 B2
Floral Ho KT16 123 C1
Floral Way RG18 106 C3
Floreat Gdns RG14 104 C1
Florence Ave SL6 40 A4
Florence Cl GU46 149 B3
Florence Cotts SL4 92 B4
Florence Ct 19 RG30 85 B3
Florence Gdns TW18 97 A1
Florence Rd GU47 150 C4
Florence Wlk RG1 86 B4
Florian Gdns RG30 85 A3
Florida Ct Reading RG30 85 C3
Staines TW18 97 A2
Flowers Hill RG8 56 B2
Flowers Piece RG8 54 A3
Fobney St RG1 86 A4
Fokerham Rd RG19 106 C1
Folder's La RG42 91 B1
Foliejohn Way SL6 38 C1
Folkestone Ct SL3 44 A1
Follet Cl SL4 68 A1
Folly La RG7,RG30 110 C3
Folly Rd Inkpen RG17 127 C3
Lambourn RG17 25 A2
Folly The RG14 105 A1
Fontmell Cl TW15 98 A2
Fontmell Pk TW15 98 A2
Fontwell Cl SL6 39 A4
Fontwell Dr RG30 84 C3
Fontwell Rd RG14 105 A1
Forbes Chase GU47 150 B4
Forbury Ho 6 RG30 85 A4
Forbury La RG17,RG20 128 B4
Forbury Rd RG1 86 B4
Forbury Ret Pk RG1 86 B4
Forbury The RG1 86 A4
Ford Cl Ashford TW15 97 C1
Littleton TW17 125 A2
Ford La RG7 140 A1
Ford Rd Ashford TW15 97 C2
Bisley GU24 153 C2
Chertsey KT16 124 A1
Fordbridge Ct TW15 97 C1
Fordbridge Rd
Ashford TW15 97 C2
Upper Halliford
TW16, TW17 125 C2
Fordham Way RG6 87 B1
Fordingbridge Cl KT16 124 A1
Fordwater Rd KT15, KT16 124 A1
Fordwater Trad Est
KT16 124 B1
Fordwells Dr RG12 118 C3
Forehead The RG7 137 C2
Forest Cl Bracknell SL5 119 B3
Tadley RG26 134 C1
Forest Comp Sch The
RG41 88 B1
Forest Dean RG2 113 B4
Forest Dr TW16 98 C1
Forest End Rd GU47 150 A4
Forest Gn RG12 118 A4
Forest Green Rd SL6 65 B3
Forest Hill RG30 57 C1
Forest Hills GU15 151 A2
Forest Rd Binfield RG42 90 B2
Crowthorne RG45 143 B3
Windsor SL4 93 C4
Windsor, Dedworth SL4 66 C3
Winkfield RG42, SL5 92 B1
Forest View Cotts SL6 65 B3
Foresters Sq RG12 118 C3
Foresters Way RG45 143 C4
Forge Cl Caversham RG4 59 B1
Kintbury RG17 102 A1
Forge Cotts SN8 99 A3
Forge Dr SL2 22 B3
Forge Hill RG18 53 B3
Forge The Harlington UB3 71 B4
Hungerford RG17 100 B3
Forlease Cl SL6 40 A3
Forlease Dr SL6 40 A3
Forlease Rd SL6 40 A3
Formby Cl Earley RG6 87 C2
Slough SL3 44 B1
Forndon Cl RG6 87 C1
Forsters RG7 134 C4
Fort Narrien GU15 150 C4
Fortrose Cl GU47 150 B4
Fortrose Wlk RG31 84 C2
Forty Green Dr SL7 1 A1
Fosseway RG45 143 A3
Fossewood Dr GU15 151 B4
Foster Ave SL4 66 C2
Fosters Gr GU20 146 A3
Fosters La RG5 87 C3
Fosters Path SL2 21 C1
Fotherby Ct SL6 40 A3
Fotheringay Gdns SL1 42 A3
Foundation Pk SL6 38 C2
Foundry Ct KT16 124 A1
Foundry Ho RG17 100 C4
Foundry La SL3 69 A2
Foundry Mews 1 KT16 124 A1
Foundry Pl 6 RG1 86 A3
Fountain Gdns SL4 67 B2
Fountains Garth RG12 118 A3
Fourth Ave SL7 2 A1
Fourth St RG19 131 C3
Fowler Cl RG6 87 A2
Fowlers La RG42 118 A4
Fox Cl RG7 111 A2
Fox Covert GU18 153 A4
Fox Covert Cl SL5 120 B2
Fox Dr GU46 149 B4
Fox Hill Prim Sch RG12 118 A2
Fox La RG27 149 A4
Fox La N KT16 123 C1
Fox La S KT16 123 C1
Fox Rd Bracknell RG12 118 B3
Slough SL3 43 B1
Foxborough RG7 139 B3
Foxborough Cl SL3 44 A1
Foxborough Ct SL6 39 C2
Foxborough Prim Sch
SL3 44 A1
Foxbury RG17 25 A1
Foxcombe Dr RG31 84 B4
Foxcote RG40 142 A4
Foxdown Cl GU15 151 B3
Foxes Piece SL7 1 C2
Foxes Piece Comb Sch SL7 1 C2
Foxes Wlk RG10 61 A2
Foxglove Cl Stanwell TW19 97 B4
Winkfield RG42 92 A1
Wokingham RG41 115 B4
Foxglove Gdns 4 RG1 85 C4
Foxglove Way
Thatcham RG18 106 B3
Thatcham RG18 106 C3
Foxhays Rd RG2 113 B4
Foxheath RG12 118 C2
Foxherne SL3 43 B2
Foxhill Cl RG4 60 A3
Foxhill Cres GU15 152 A4
Foxhill La RG4 59 C3
Foxhill Rd RG1 86 C3
Foxhollow Dr SL2 22 B4
Foxhunt Gr RG31 84 C2

**Foxhunter Way** RG19 105 C2
**Foxleigh Ct** TW18 96 B2
**Foxley Cl** GU17 150 B3
**Foxley La** RG42 90 B1
Foxley PNEU Sch RG10 63 A1
**Framewood Manor** SL2 23 B3
**Framewood Rd** SL2, SL3 23 B3
**Framlingham Dr** RG4 59 C3
**Frampton Cl** RG5 60 C1
**France Hill Dr** GU15 151 B3
France Hill Sch GU15 151 B1
**Frances Ave** SL6 20 B1
**Frances Rd** SL4 67 B3
**Frances The** RG18 106 B2
Francis Baily Prim Sch
RG19 106 C2
**Francis Chichester Cl**
SL5 120 A2
**Francis Cl** TW17 125 A3
**Francis Gdns** RG42 91 B1
**Francis St** RG1 86 A3
**Francis Way** Burnham SL1 41 B3
Frimley GU15 152 B2
**Francomes Field** RG17 25 B1
**Frank Lunnon Cl** SL8 3 B2
**Frank Sutton Way** SL1 42 B3
**Franklin Ave** Slough SL2 42 A4
Tadley RG26 135 A1
**Franklin Ct** 21 RG1 85 C4
**Franklin St** RG1 85 C4
**Franklyn Cres** SL4 66 B2
**Frascati Way** SL6 39 C4
**Fraser Ave** RG4 59 B3
**Fraser Mead** GU47 150 C3
**Fraser Rd** RG42 118 A4
**Frederick Ho** TW15 97 C2
**Frederick Pl** RG41 116 A3
**Free Prae Rd** KT16 124 A1
**Freeborn Way** RG12 118 C4
**Freeman Cl** TW17 125 C3
**Freemans Cl**
Hungerford RG17 100 B3
Stoke Poges SL2 23 A3
**Freemantle Rd** GU19 145 C2
Freemantles Sch
(Specl Sch) KT16 123 C1
**Freesia Cl** RG41 115 B4
**French Gdns** GU17 150 B2
**Frenchum Gdns** SL1 41 C3
**Frensham** RG12 118 B2
**Frensham Cl** GU46 149 A3
**Frensham Gn** RG2 86 C1
**Frensham Rd** RG45 143 A4
**Frensham Wlk** SL2 22 B3
**Freshfield Cl** RG6 87 C2
**Freshfields La** RG20 51 A1
**Freshwater Rd** RG1 86 C4
**Freshwood Dr** GU46 149 B2
**Friar St** RG1 86 A4
**Friars Keep** RG12 118 A3
**Friars Rd** Newbury RG14 131 A4
Virginia Water GU25 122 B3
**Friars Way** KT16 124 A2
**Friars Wlk** 3 RG1 86 A4
**Friary Dr** TW19 68 B1
**Friary Rd** Ascot SL5 120 A2
Wraysbury TW19 95 B4
**Friary The** SL4 68 B1
**Friday St** RG9 15 C1
**Friendship Way** RG12 118 A3
**Frieth Cl** RG6 87 A1
**Frilsham Rd** RG30 85 A2
**Frimley Cl** RG5 87 B4
**Frimley Grove Gdns**
GU16 151 C1
**Frimley Hall Dr** GU15 151 C3
**Frimley High St** GU16 151 B1
Frimley Park Hospl
GU16 151 B1
**Frimley Rd**
Camberley GU15 151 A2
Frimley GU15, GU16 151 B1
**Fringford Cl** RG6 87 B1
**Frith Hill Rd** GU16 152 A1
**Frithe The** SL2 43 A4
**Frithwald Rd** KT16 123 C1
**Frobisher** RG12 118 B1
**Frobisher Cres** TW19 97 C4
**Frobisher Gdns** TW19 97 C4
**Frodsham Way** GU47 143 C1
**Frog Hall** RG40 116 C3
**Frog Hall Dr** RG40 116 C3
**Frog La** RG12 118 A3
**Frogmill** SL6 17 B2
**Frogmill Ct** SL6 17 B2
**Frogmore Cl** SL1 42 A2
Frogmore Com Coll
GU46 149 C3
**Frogmore Ct** GU17 150 B2
Frogmore Cty Inf Sch
GU17 150 A3
Frogmore Cty Jun Sch
GU17 150 A3
**Frogmore Gr** GU17 150 B2
**Frogmore Park Dr** GU17 150 B2
**Frogmore Rd** GU17 150 B3
**Frogmore Way** RG30 85 A3
**Fromer Rd** HP10 3 B2
**Fromont Dr** RG19 106 B2
**Fromow Gdns** GU20 146 B2
**Front St** RG17 47 B3
Frouds Bridge Marina
RG7 108 C1
**Frouds La** RG7 109 A1
**Froxfield Ave** RG1 85 C3
**Froxfield Down** 6 RG12 118 C2
**Fruen Rd** TW14 98 C4
**Fry Ct** RG4 59 A2
**Frymley Hill** SL4 66 B3
**Frys La** GU46 149 C4
**Fuchsia Cl** RG31 84 B3
**Fuchsia Way** GU24 153 C3
**Fullbrook Cl**
Maidenhead SL6 40 A4
Wokingham RG41 89 A1
**Fullbrook Cres** RG31 57 B2
**Fuller Cl** RG19 106 C1
**Fullers La** Ball Hill RG20 129 B1
Burghfield Common RG7 112 A2
**Fullers Yd** SL6 20 A1
**Fulmead Rd** RG30 85 B4
**Fulmer Chase** SL3 23 B4
**Fulmer Cl** RG6 87 A1
**Fulmer Common Rd** SL3 23 C3
Fulmer Cty Fst Sch SL3 23 C4
**Fulmer Rd** SL3 23 C4
**Furlong Cl** SL8 3 A2
**Furlong Rd** SL8 3 A2
**Furness** SL4 66 B3
**Furness Pl** 8 SL4 66 B3
**Furness Row** 9 SL4 66 B3
**Furness Sq** 6 SL4 66 B3
**Furness Way** SL4 66 B3
**Furness Wlk** 7 SL4 66 B3
**Furnival Ave** SL2 42 A4
**Furnival Cl** GU25 122 B2
**Furrow Way** SL6 39 A2
**Furse Cl** GU15 152 B2
**Furze Hill Cres** RG45 143 B2
Furze Platt Cty Inf Sch
SL6 19 B1
Furze Platt Cty Jun Sch
SL6 19 B1
Furze Platt Halt SL6 19 C1
**Furze Platt Rd** SL6 19 A1
Furze Platt Sch SL6 19 B1
**Furze Rd** Maidenhead SL6 19 B1
Tadley RG26 134 C1
**Furzebank** SL5 120 B3
**Furzedown Cl** TW20 95 C1
**Furzemoors** RG12 118 A2
**Furzen Cl** SL2 22 A1
**Fuzzens Wlk** SL4 66 C3
**Fydlers Cl** SL5 93 A1
**Fyfield Cl** GU17 150 B3
**Fyfield Rd** RG19 106 B1
**Fylingdales** RG19 106 B1

## G

**Gables Ave** TW15 97 C2
**Gables Cl** Datchet SL3 68 A4
Maidenhead SL6 40 A4
**Gables Way** RG19 107 B1
**Gabriel Dr** GU15 152 A2
**Gabriels The** RG14 130 B3
**Gage Cl** SL6 39 C2
**Gainsborough**
Bracknell RG12 118 B2
Cookham SL6 19 C3
**Gainsborough Ave** RG17 102 A1
**Gainsborough Cl**
Camberley GU15 151 C4
Woodley RG5 88 A3
**Gainsborough Cres** RG9 35 B4
**Gainsborough Dr**
Maidenhead SL6 39 B2
North Ascot SL5 119 B4
**Gainsborough Hill** RG9 35 B4
**Gainsborough Rd**
Henley-on-T RG9 35 B4
Reading RG30 85 A3
**Gairn Cl** RG30 85 A4
**Galahad Cl** SL1 42 A2
**Gale Dr** GU18 146 A1
**Galley La** RG19 132 B1
**Galleymead Rd** SL3 69 C3
**Gallop The** GU46 149 B4
**Gallops The** RG20 30 C3
**Galloway Chase** SL2 43 A3
Galloway Ctr The RG14 105 C1
**Galloway Ho** 7 RG1 85 C3
**Gallys Rd** SL4 66 B3
**Galsworthy Dr** RG4 59 C3
**Galsworthy Rd** 4 KT16 124 A1
**Galton Rd** SL5 120 C2
**Galvin Rd** SL1 42 B3
**Garde Rd** RG4 60 C2
**Garden Cl** Ashford TW15 98 B1
Maidenhead SL6 39 A3
**Garden Close La** RG14 130 B2
**Garden Cotts** SL3 69 B4
**Garden Mews**
8 Reading RG30 85 B3
Slough SL1 42 C3
**Gardeners La** RG8 55 B2
**Gardenia Dr** GU24 153 C3
**Gardens The** Hatton TW14 71 B1
South Stoke RG8 14 B2
**Gardner Ho** SL6 19 C1
**Gardner Rd** SL6 19 C1
**Gardners Rd** RG42 92 A1
**Garfield Pl** 26 SL4 67 B3
**Garfield Rd** GU15 151 B3
**Garford Cres** RG14 130 B4
Garland Jnr Sch RG7 111 A2
**Garlands Cl** RG7 111 A1
**Garnet Cl** SL1 42 A2
**Garnet Ct** SL7 1 B1
**Garnet Field** GU46 149 A3
**Garnet Hill** 7 RG1 86 A3
**Garnet St** RG1 86 A3
**Garrard Rd** SL2 21 C1
**Garrard St** RG1 86 A4
**Garrett Rd** RG40 141 C4
**Garrick Cl** TW18 97 A1
**Garson La** TW19 95 B4
**Garson's La** SL4 92 A4
**Garston Cl** RG30 85 A2
**Garston Cres** RG31 84 A3
**Garston Gr** RG40 115 C1
**Garswood** RG12 118 B2
**Garth Cl** RG41 88 B1
Garth Hill Sch RG12 118 B4
**Garth Rd** RG7 137 A3
**Garth Sq** RG42 91 A1
**Gas La** SL6 40 A2
**Gas Works Rd** RG1 86 B4
**Gascon's Gr** SL2 22 A1
**Gaskell Mews** RG14 131 A4
**Gaskells End** RG4 58 B4
**Gaston Bridge Rd**
Shepperton TW17 125 B2
Upper Halliford TW17 125 C2
**Gaston Way** TW17 125 B2
**Gatcombe Cl** RG31 84 B2
**Gatehampton Rd** RG8 34 B3
**Gatewick Cl** SL1 42 C3
**Gatward Ave** SL6 39 A2
**Gaveston Rd** SL2 21 C1
**Gayhurst Cl** RG4 59 B3
**Gays La** SL6 65 A4
**Gaywood Dr** RG14 105 B2
**Gazelle Cl** RG41 88 A2
**Geffers Ride** SL5 119 C4
**Gelder Dr** RG6 87 B1
**Genesis Cl** TW19 97 C4
**Geneva Cl** TW17 125 C4
Geoffrey Field
Jun & Inf Schs RG2 113 B4
**Geoffreyson Rd** RG4 58 C3
**George Cl** SL7 1 C2
**George Green Rd** SL3 43 C4
George Palmer Inf Sch
RG2 86 B2
George Palmer Jun Sch
RG2 86 B2
**George St** Caversham RG4 59 A1
Reading RG1 85 C4
Staines TW18 96 C2
**George V Pl** SL4 67 B4
**Georgeham Rd** GU47 143 B1
**Georges Dr** HP10 3 B4
**Georgian Cl**
Camberley GU15 151 C4
Staines TW18 97 A2
**Geranium Cl** RG45 143 A4
**Gerrards Cross Rd** SL2 23 A4
**Gervaise Cl** SL1 41 C3
**Gibbet La** GU15 152 A4
**Gibbins La** RG42 91 B2
**Gibbons Cl** GU47 150 B4
**Gibbs Cl** RG40 141 C3
**Gibbs Way** GU46 149 A2
**Gibraltar La** SL6 2 B1
**Gibson Ct** SL3 43 C1
**Gibson Pl** TW19 70 B1
**Gifford Cl** RG4 59 C3
**Gifford Ho** 2 RG4 59 B1
**Gilbert Ct** RG18 106 B2
**Gilbert Rd** GU15 151 B1
**Gilbert Way** RG40 141 C4
**Gilbey Wlk** HP10 3 B2
**Gilchrist Way** SL6 38 A3
**Giles Travers Cl** TW20 123 B3
**Gill Rise** RG42 91 B1
**Gillette Way** RG2 86 A1
**Gilliat Rd** SL1 42 C3
**Gilliatt Cl** SL0 44 C4
**Gillotts Cl** RG9 35 A4
**Gillotts La** RG9 35 A4
Gillotts Sch RG9 35 A4
**Gilman Cres** SL4 66 B2
**Gilmore Cl** SL3 43 B2
**Gilmore Cres** TW15 98 A1
**Gilpin Way** UB3 71 B4
**Gilroy Cl** RG14 130 B3
**Gilson Ct** SL4 95 B4
**Gingells Farm Rd** RG10 61 A3
**Gipsy La** Arborfield RG41 114 C4
Bracknell RG12 118 B4
Earley RG6 87 B2
Hungerford RG17 100 C4
Reading RG30 57 C1
Wokingham RG40 116 B2
Wokingham,
Sindlesham RG41 115 A4
**Girton Cl** GU47 143 C1
**Glade Ho** Ascot SL5 120 B2
3 Marlow SL7 1 C1
**Glade Rd** SL7 1 C1
**Glade The** Ascot SL5 120 B2
Newbury RG14 130 C4
Purley on T RG8 57 B2
Staines TW18 97 A1
**Gladridge Cl** RG6 87 B2
**Gladstone Cl** RG17 102 A1
Gladstone Ind Est SL6 39 C4
**Gladstone La** RG18 106 B4
**Gladstone Way** SL1 42 A3
**Glaisdale** RG19 106 B1
**Glamis Way** RG31 84 A2
**Glanmor Rd** SL2 43 A3
**Glanty The** TW20 96 A2
**Glasgow Rd** SL1 42 A4
**Glassonby Wlk** GU15 152 B3
**Glebe Cl** Dorney SL6 40 C2
Lightwater GU18 146 B1
Moulsford OX10 13 C3
**Glebe Cotts** RG8 14 B2
**Glebe Field** RG20 49 A4
**Glebe Gdns** RG4 60 C2
**Glebe La** Sonning RG4 60 C2
**Glebe La** *continued*
Stockcross RG20 103 C3
**Glebe Pl** RG17 73 A1
**Glebe Rd** Egham TW20 96 B1
Maidenhead SL6 40 A3
Old Windsor SL4 68 A1
Purley on T RG8 57 A3
Reading RG2 86 B3
Staines TW18 97 A2
**Glebe Ride** RG8 34 A3
**Glebe The** Aldworth RG8 32 C2
Blackwater GU17 150 C2
**Glebefields** RG14 105 A3
**Glebeland Gdns** TW17 125 B2
**Glebeland Rd** GU15 150 C2
**Glebelands** RG19 106 B2
**Glebelands Rd** RG40 116 B4
**Glebewood** RG12 118 B2
**Glen Ave** TW15 98 A2
**Glen Cl** TW17 125 A3
**Glen Ct** TW18 96 C1
**Glen Innes** GU47 143 C1
**Glen The** Ascot SL5 120 B3
Silchester RG26 135 C1
Slough SL3 43 B1
**Glenalmond Ho** TW15 97 C3
**Glenapp Grange** RG7 136 C3
**Glenavon Gdns** Slough SL3 43 B2
Yateley GU46 149 B2
**Glenbeigh Terr** RG1 85 C3
**Glendale Ave** RG14 130 B3
**Glendale Cl** RG41 116 A2
**Glendale Rd** RG26 135 A1
**Glendevon Rd** RG5 87 C4
**Gleneagles Cl** TW19 70 B1
**Gleneagles Ct** 32 RG1 86 B4
**Gleneagles Ho** RG12 117 C2
**Glenfield Ho** RG12 118 B3
**Glenfield Rd** TW15 98 B1
**Glenhaven Dr** TW19 70 A1
**Glenhurst Cl** GU17 150 C2
**Glenmore Cl** RG19 106 B1
**Glenn Miller Cl** RG20 49 A3
**Glennon Cl** RG30 85 B2
**Glenrhondda** RG4 58 C3
**Glenrosa Rd** RG30 85 A4
**Glentworth Pl** SL1 42 B3
**Glenwood** Bracknell RG12 118 B3
Virginia Water GU25 122 B4
**Glenwood Dr** RG31 84 B4
**Globe Farm La** GU17 150 A3
**Glory Cl** HP10 3 C4
**Glory Hill La** HP9 3 C4
**Glory Mill La** HP10 3 C4
**Gloucester Ave** SL1 42 B4
**Gloucester Cres** TW18 97 B1
**Gloucester Ct** RG30 85 B4
**Gloucester Dr** TW18, TW19 96 B3
**Gloucester Gdns** GU19 145 C2
**Gloucester Pl**
Bracknell RG42 91 C1
Windsor SL4 67 B3
**Gloucester Rd**
Bagshot GU19 145 C2
Maidenhead SL6 19 C1
Newbury RG14 104 C1
Reading RG30 85 B4
**Gloucestershire Lea** RG42 91 C1
**Glyme Wlk** RG31 84 C2
**Glyncastle** RG4 58 C3
**Glynswood** GU15 151 C2
**Glynwood Ho** SL6 40 A4
**Goaters Rd** SL5 119 B4
**Goddard Cl**
Littleton TW17 124 C3
Shinfield RG2 113 C3
**Goddard Ct** RG41 88 A1
**Goddard Dr** RG7 107 C2
**Goddards La** GU15 151 A2
**Goddington Rd** SL8 3 A3
**Godfrey Cl** GU47 150 B4
Godolphin Inf Sch SL1 42 B4
Godolphin Jun Sch SL1 42 B4
**Godolphin Rd** SL1 42 B3
**Godstow Cl** RG5 87 C4
**Goffs Rd** TW15 98 B1
**Gogmore Farm Cl** KT16 123 C1
**Gogmore La** KT16 124 A1
**Gold Cup La** SL5 119 B4
**Goldcrest Cl** GU46 149 A3
**Goldcrest Way** RG31 84 A3
**Golden Ball La** SL6 19 A2
**Golden Oak** SL2 22 B3
**Golden Orb Wood** RG42 117 B4
**Goldfinch La** RG20 131 C2
**Golding Cl** RG19 106 C2
**Goldney Rd** GU15 152 B2
**Goldsmid Rd** RG1 85 C4
**Goldsmith Cl**
Thatcham RG18 106 B3
Wokingham RG40 115 C1
**Goldsmith Way** RG45 143 A2
**Goldsworthy Way** SL1 41 B4
**Goldthorpe Gdns** RG6 113 C4
**Goldwell Dr** RG14 104 C2
**Golf Dr** GU15 151 C2
**Gooch Cl** RG10 61 C2
**Goodboys La** RG7 112 A1
**Goodchild Rd** RG40 116 B3
**Goodings Gn** RG40 116 C3
**Goodings La** RG17 47 A2
**Goodliffe Gdns** RG31 57 B2
**Goodman Pk** SL2 43 B3
**Goodman Pl** TW18 96 C2
**Goodrich Cl** RG4 59 C3
**Goodways Dr** RG12 118 B4
**Goodwin Cl** RG31 84 C2
**Goodwin Mdws** HP10 3 C3
**Goodwin Rd** SL2 21 C1
**Goodwin Wlk** RG14 130 B3
**Goodwood Cl**
Burghfield Common RG7 111 A1
Camberley GU15 151 B4
**Goodwood Rise** SL7 1 B4
**Goodwood Way** RG14 105 B1
**Goose Cnr** RG42 91 C2
**Goose Gn**
Farnham Common SL2 22 A2
Lambourn RG17 25 A2
**Goose Green Way** RG19 106 B2
**Goose La** RG20 49 C3
**Gordon Ave** GU15 151 B2
**Gordon Cl** TW18 97 A1
**Gordon Clifford Ct** RG42 118 A4
**Gordon Cres**
Camberley GU15 151 B2
Compton RG20 31 B2
**Gordon Ct** 8 RG14 105 A1
**Gordon Dr** TW17 125 B1
**Gordon Palmer Cl** RG7 137 B3
**Gordon Palmer Ct** RG30 85 B4
**Gordon Pl** RG30 85 B4
**Gordon Rd** Ashford TW15 97 C3
Camberley GU15 151 B3
Crowthorne RG45 143 B2
Maidenhead SL6 39 B4
Newbury RG14 105 A1
Shepperton TW17 125 B2
Thatcham RG18 106 A3
Windsor SL4 66 C3
**Gordon Wlk** GU46 149 C3
Gordon's Sch GU24 153 C4
**Gore End Rd** RG20 129 A2
**Gore Rd** SL1 21 A1
**Gore The** SL1 21 A1
Goring CE Prim Sch RG8 34 B4
**Goring La** RG7 111 A1
**Goring Rd** TW18 96 C2
Goring & Streatley Sta
RG8 34 B3
**Gorrick Sq** RG41 116 A2
**Gorse Bank** GU18 153 A4
**Gorse Cottage Dr** RG18 79 B1
**Gorse Dr** RG5 88 A4
**Gorse Hill La** GU25 122 B3
**Gorse Hill Rd** GU25 122 B3
**Gorse Meade** SL1 42 A3
**Gorse Pl** RG42 92 A1
**Gorse Rd** Cookham SL6 19 C3
Frimley GU16 151 C1
Gorse Ride Cty Jun Sch
RG40 141 C4
**Gorse Ride N** RG40 141 C4
**Gorse Ride S** RG40 141 C3
**Gorselands**
Caversham RG4 59 A3
Newbury RG14 130 B3
Tadley RG26 135 B1
Yateley GU46 149 B2
**Gosbrook Ho** 1 RG4 59 B1
**Gosbrook Rd** RG4 59 A1
**Gosden Rd** GU24 153 C3
**Gosforth Cl** RG6 87 B1
**Goslar Way** SL4 67 A3
**Gosling Gn** SL3 43 C2
**Gosling Rd** SL3 43 C2
**Gosnell Cl** GU16 152 B2
**Gossmore Cl** SL7 1 C1
**Gossmore La** SL7 1 C1
**Gossmore Wlk** SL7 1 C1
**Goswell Hill** SL4 67 B3
**Goswell Rd** SL4 67 B3
**Gothic Ct** Harlington UB3 71 B4
Sandhurst GU47 150 A4
**Gough's La**
Bracknell RG12 118 B4
Newell Green RG12 91 B1
**Gough's Mdw** GU47 150 A4
**Goughs Barn La** RG42 91 A4
**Gould Cl** RG14 105 A2
**Gould Rd** TW14 98 C4
**Goulders Cotts** RG10 36 C4
**Governor's Rd** GU15 150 C3
**Govett Ave** TW17 125 B2
**Govett Gr** GU20 146 B3
**Gower Pk** GU47 150 B4
**Gower St** RG1 85 C4
**Gower The** TW20 123 B3
**Gowings Gn** SL1 41 C2
**Grace Ct** SL1 42 B3
**Grace Reynolds Wlk** 4
GU15 151 B3
**Graces La** RG20 78 A4
**Graffham Cl** RG6 114 A4
**Grafton Cl** Maidenhead SL6 19 C1
Slough SL3 43 C4
**Grafton Ct** TW14 98 B4
**Grafton Rd** RG30 84 B4
**Graham Cl** Blewbury OX11 12 A4
Maidenhead SL6 39 B3
Reading RG31 84 C2
**Graham Rd** Cookham SL6 19 C3
Windlesham GU20 146 B2
**Grahame Ave** RG8 56 B3
**Grainford Ct** RG40 116 B3
**Grampian Cl** UB3 71 B4
**Grampian Rd** GU47 143 A1
**Grampian Way** SL3 44 A1
**Gramps Hill** OX12 6 C3
**Granby Ct** RG1 86 C4
**Granby End** RG7 111 A2
**Granby Gdns** RG1 86 C4
**Grand Ave** GU15 151 B3

**Grange Ave**
Crowthorne RG45 . . . . . . . .143 A3
Reading RG6 . . . . . . . . . . . .87 A3
**Grange Cl** Goring RG8 . . . . .34 A3
Wraysbury TW19 . . . . . . . . .68 C1
**Grange Ct** Earley RG6 . . . . . .87 A4
Egham TW20 . . . . . . . . . . . .95 C2
Littleton TW17 . . . . . . . . . .125 A3
Newbury RG14 . . . . . . . . . .105 A1
Staines TW18 . . . . . . . . . . . .97 A2
**Grange Dr** HP10 . . . . . . . . . . .3 B2
**Grange Gdns** SL2 . . . . . . . . .22 B4
**Grange La** SL6 . . . . . . . . . . .19 C4
**Grange Pl** TW18 . . . . . . . . .124 B4
**Grange Rd** Bracknell RG12 .118 B4
Camberley GU15 . . . . . . . . .151 C3
Cookham SL6 . . . . . . . . . . . .19 C4
Egham TW20 . . . . . . . . . . . .95 C2
Henley-on-T RG9 . . . . . . . . . .15 C1
**Grange The** Burnham SL1 . . .21 B1
Caversham RG4 . . . . . . . . . . .58 B3
Newbury RG14 . . . . . . . . . .130 B3
Old Windsor SL4 . . . . . . . . . .68 A1
**Grange Way** SL0 . . . . . . . . . .44 C4
**Grangely Cl** RG31 . . . . . . . . .84 B2
**Grangewood** SL3 . . . . . . . . .43 B4
**Grant Ave** SL1 . . . . . . . . . . .42 C4
**Grant Cl** TW17 . . . . . . . . . .125 A2
**Grant Ho** 5 SL8 . . . . . . . . . . .3 A2
**Grant Rd** RG45 . . . . . . . . . .143 B2
**Grant Wlk** SL5 . . . . . . . . . .120 C1
**Grantham Cl** GU47 . . . . . . .143 C1
**Grantham Ho** 5 TW16 . . . . .98 C1
**Grantham Rd** RG30 . . . . . . .84 C2
**Granthams The** RG17 . . . . .25 A2
**Grantley Hts** 3 RG1 . . . . . . .86 B4
**Granville Ave** SL2 . . . . . . . . .42 B4
**Granville Rd** RG30 . . . . . . . .85 A3
**Grasholm Way** SL3 . . . . . . .44 B1
**Grasmere** SL4 . . . . . . . . . . . .66 C4
**Grasmere Ave**
Reading RG30 . . . . . . . . . . . .57 C1
Slough SL2 . . . . . . . . . . . . . .43 A3
**Grasmere Cl**
East Bedfont TW14 . . . . . . . .98 C4
Thorpe Lea TW20 . . . . . . . . .96 A1
**Grasmere Par** SL2 . . . . . . . .43 A3
**Grasmere Rd** GU18 . . . . . .146 A1
**Grass Hill** RG4 . . . . . . . . . . .58 C2
**Grassington Pl** RG19 . . . . .106 B2
**Grassmead** RG19 . . . . . . . .106 C1
**Grassmere Cl** RG41 . . . . . . .88 A1
**Grassy La** SL6 . . . . . . . . . . .39 C4
**Grattan Ct** SL7 . . . . . . . . . . . .2 A2
**Gratton Dr** SL4 . . . . . . . . . . .66 C2
**Gratton Rd** RG2 . . . . . . . . .113 B4
**Gratwicke Rd** RG30 . . . . . . .84 C4
**Gravel Hill** Caversham RG4 .59 A3
Henley-on-T RG9 . . . . . . . . . .15 B1
Stockcross RG20 . . . . . . . .103 C3
**Gravel Rd** RG9 . . . . . . . . . . .35 A1
**Gravelly Cl** RG20 . . . . . . . .129 A2
**Graveney Dr** RG4 . . . . . . . . .58 C2
**Gravett Cl** RG9 . . . . . . . . . . .35 B4
**Gray Ct** SL4 . . . . . . . . . . . . .66 B3
**Gray's Mon** SL2 . . . . . . . . . .22 C1
**Gray's Pl** SL2 . . . . . . . . . . . .42 C3
**Gray's Rd** SL1 . . . . . . . . . . .42 C3
**Grayling Cl** SL7 . . . . . . . . . . .18 B4
**Grayling Ct** 4 RG1 . . . . . . . .59 A1
**Grays Cres** RG5 . . . . . . . . . .87 B4
**Grays La** TW15 . . . . . . . . . . .98 A2
**Grays Park Rd** SL2 . . . . . . .23 A1
**Grayshot Dr** GU17 . . . . . . .150 B3
Grazeley Parochial
Prim Sch RG7 . . . . . . . . . .112 C1
**Grazeley Rd** RG7 . . . . . . . .113 A2
**Great Auclum Pl** RG7 . . . .111 A1
**Great Barn Ct** RG19 . . . . . .106 B2
**Great Hill Cres** SL6 . . . . . . .39 B3
Great Hollands
Jun & Inf Sch RG12 . . . .117 C2
**Great Hollands Rd** RG12 .117 C2
**Great Hollands Sq** RG12 .117 C2
**Great Knollys St** RG1 . . . . .85 C4
**Great Lea** RG7 . . . . . . . . . .113 A3
Great Marlow Sch SL7 . . . . .1 C2
**Great Severals** RG17 . . . . .102 A1
**Great South-West Rd**
East Bedfont TW14 . . . . . . . .98 B4
Hatton TW6, TW14 . . . . . . . .71 B1
**Grebe Ct** TW18 . . . . . . . . . .97 A2
**Green Acre Mount** RG30 . .84 B4
Green Bsns Ctr The TW20 .96 B2
**Green Cl** Burnham SL6 . . . . .41 A4
Maidenhead SL6 . . . . . . . . . .19 C1
**Green Cres** HP10 . . . . . . . . . .3 B4
**Green Croft** RG40 . . . . . . .116 C4
**Green Ct** TW16 . . . . . . . . . . .98 C1
**Green Dr** RG40 . . . . . . . . . .116 C2
**Green Dragon La** HP10 . . . . .3 A4
**Green End** GU46 . . . . . . . . .149 B4
**Green End Cl** RG7 . . . . . . .113 A1
**Green Farm Rd** GU19 . . . .145 C2
**Green Farm Rise** SN8 . . . . . .99 A3
**Green Finch Cl** RG45 . . . .142 C3
**Green Hill Cl** GU15 . . . . . .152 B3
**Green Hill Rd** GU15 . . . . . .152 B3
**Green La** Ascot SL5 . . . . . .120 C4
Ashford TW16 . . . . . . . . . . . .98 C1
Bagshot GU19 . . . . . . . . . .145 C1
Blackwater GU17 . . . . . . . . .150 A2
Blackwater, Hawley GU17 . .150 C2
Bradfield RG7 . . . . . . . . . . . .81 C2
Burghfield Common RG30 . . .85 A1
**Green La** *continued*
Burnham SL1 . . . . . . . . . . . .21 B2
Caversham RG9 . . . . . . . . . .35 A1
Chieveley RG20 . . . . . . . . . .78 A4
Datchet SL3 . . . . . . . . . . . . .68 A3
Egham TW20 . . . . . . . . . . . .96 A2
Farnham Common SL2 . . . . .22 A3
Henley-on-T RG9 . . . . . . . . . .35 B4
Holyport SL6 . . . . . . . . . . . .64 A3
Hurst RG10 . . . . . . . . . . . . .88 C2
Littlewick Green SL6 . . . . . .38 A3
Maidenhead SL6 . . . . . . . . . .40 A3
Newbury RG14 . . . . . . . . . .104 C1
Padworth RG7 . . . . . . . . . .110 B1
Pangbourne RG8 . . . . . . . . . .56 B3
Sandhurst GU47 . . . . . . . . .150 B4
Shepperton TW17 . . . . . . . .125 B2
Thatcham RG19 . . . . . . . . . .106 B2
Thorpe TW18 . . . . . . . . . . .123 C4
Windsor SL4 . . . . . . . . . . . .67 A3
Wokingham RG41 . . . . . . . . .88 B1
**Green Lane Cl** GU15 . . . . .151 B4
**Green Lane Ct** SL1 . . . . . . . .21 B1
**Green Leas** TW16 . . . . . . . . .98 C1
**Green Leas Cl** TW16 . . . . . .98 C1
**Green Leys** SL6 . . . . . . . . . .19 C1
**Green Pk** TW18 . . . . . . . . . .96 C3
**Green Rd** Reading RG6 . . . . .87 A3
Thorpe TW20 . . . . . . . . . . .123 A3
**Green The**
Bracknell RG12 . . . . . . . . . .118 A3
Burnham SL1 . . . . . . . . . . . . .21 A1
Chilton OX11 . . . . . . . . . . . .10 C4
Datchet SL3 . . . . . . . . . . . . .68 A4
Kintbury RG17 . . . . . . . . . .102 A1
Slough SL1 . . . . . . . . . . . . . .42 B2
Staines TW18 . . . . . . . . . . . .97 B2
Theale RG7 . . . . . . . . . . . . .83 B1
Wokingham RG41 . . . . . . . .115 C4
Wooburn Green HP10 . . . . . . .3 C3
Wraysbury TW19 . . . . . . . . . .68 C1
**Green Verges** SL7 . . . . . . . . .1 C2
**Green Wood** SL5 . . . . . . . .119 B4
**Greenacre** SL4 . . . . . . . . . . .66 C3
**Greenacre Ct** TW20 . . . . . . .95 B1
**Greenacres** RG20 . . . . . . . .129 C1
**Greenacres Ave** RG41 . . . . .88 A2
**Greenacres La** RG41 . . . . . .88 A2
**Greenaway Terr** TW19 . . . . .97 C4
**Greenbank Way** GU15 . . . .151 B1
**Greencroft Gdns** RG30 . . . .84 C2
**Greendale Mews** SL2 . . . . .43 A3
**Greene Fielde End** TW18 . .97 B1
**Greenfern Ave** SL1 . . . . . . .41 B4
**Greenfield Way** RG45 . . . .143 A4
**Greenfields** SL6 . . . . . . . . . .40 A3
**Greenfields Rd** RG2 . . . . .113 A4
**Greenfinch Cl** RG31 . . . . . . .84 A3
**Greenham Cl**
Greenham RG19 . . . . . . . . .131 B4
Woodley RG5 . . . . . . . . . . . .88 A3
Greenham Court
Prim Sch RG14 . . . . . . . . .131 A4
**Greenham Mill** RG14 . . . . .105 A2
**Greenham Rd** RG14 . . . . . .105 A1
**Greenham Wood** RG12 . . .118 B2
**Greenhaven** GU46 . . . . . . .149 A3
**Greenholme** GU15 . . . . . . .152 B3
**Greenhow** RG12 . . . . . . . .118 A3
**Greenidge Cl** 5 RG1 . . . . . .85 C3
**Greenlake Terr** TW18 . . . . .97 A1
**Greenlands** Ball Hill RG20 .129 C1
Flackwell Heath HP10 . . . . . . .3 A4
**Greenlands Ct**
Maidenhead SL6 . . . . . . . . . .39 A4
Staines TW18 . . . . . . . . . . . .97 A2
**Greenlands Rd**
Camberley GU15 . . . . . . . . .151 A1
Newbury RG14 . . . . . . . . . .105 A1
Staines TW18 . . . . . . . . . . . .97 A2
**Greenleaf Ct** SL3 . . . . . . . . .68 A4
**Greenleas** GU16 . . . . . . . . .151 C1
**Greenleas Ave** RG4 . . . . . . .59 A4
**Greenleas Cl** GU46 . . . . . .149 B4
**Greenleaves Ct** TW15 . . . . .98 A1
**Greeno Cres** TW17 . . . . . .125 A2
**Greenock Rd** SL1 . . . . . . . . .42 A4
**Greenside** Bourne End SL8 . . .3 A3
Crowthorne RG45 . . . . . . . .142 C3
Slough SL2 . . . . . . . . . . . . . .42 A4
**Greensward La** RG2 . . . . .114 B1
**Greenview Ct** TW15 . . . . . . .97 C2
**Greenway Dr** TW18 . . . . . .124 B4
**Greenway The**
Fawley OX12 . . . . . . . . . . . .27 B4
Slough SL1 . . . . . . . . . . . . . .41 B3
**Greenways** Ball Hill RG20 . .129 C1
Egham TW20 . . . . . . . . . . . .95 C2
Lambourn RG17 . . . . . . . . . .25 A1
Sandhurst GU47 . . . . . . . . .143 A1
**Greenways Dr**
Maidenhead SL6 . . . . . . . . . .39 A4
Sunningdale SL5 . . . . . . . . .120 C1
**Greenwood** 12 RG12 . . . . . .118 C3
**Greenwood Gr** RG41 . . . . . .88 B2
**Greenwood Rd**
Crowthorne RG45 . . . . . . . .143 A3
Reading RG30 . . . . . . . . . . . .84 C3
**Gregory Cl** RG6 . . . . . . . . .114 B4
**Gregory Dr** SL4 . . . . . . . . . .68 A1
**Grenfell Ave** SL6 . . . . . . . . .39 C3
**Grenfell Pl** SL6 . . . . . . . . . .39 C3
**Grenfell Rd** SL6 . . . . . . . . . .39 C3
**Grenville Cl** SL1 . . . . . . . . . .21 A2
**Gresham Ct** TW18 . . . . . . . .97 A2
**Gresham Rd** Slough SL1 . . .42 A4
Staines TW18 . . . . . . . . . . . .97 A2
**Gresham Way** RG30 . . . . . . .58 A1
**Greyberry Copse Rd**
RG19 . . . . . . . . . . . . . . . . .131 B4
**Greyfriars Dr** SL5 . . . . . . .120 A2
**Greyfriars Rd** RG1 . . . . . . . .86 A4
**Greys Ct** 6 RG1 . . . . . . . . . .86 B4
**Greys Hill** RG9 . . . . . . . . . . .15 B1
**Greys Rd** RG9 . . . . . . . . . . .15 B1
**Greystoke Ct** RG45 . . . . . .143 A2
**Greystoke Ho** 9 RG1 . . . . .85 C3
**Greystoke Rd**
Caversham RG4 . . . . . . . . . .59 B2
Slough SL2 . . . . . . . . . . . . . .41 C4
**Griffin Cl** Maidenhead SL6 . .39 C3
Slough SL1 . . . . . . . . . . . . . .42 B2
**Griffiths Cl** RG19 . . . . . . . .106 C1
**Grindle Cl** RG18 . . . . . . . .106 B3
**Gringer Hill** SL6 . . . . . . . . . .39 C4
**Groombridge Pl** RG14 . . .104 C3
**Grosvenor Ct**
Blackwater GU17 . . . . . . . .150 B2
Slough SL1 . . . . . . . . . . . . . .42 C4
**Grosvenor Dr** SL6 . . . . . . . .40 B4
**Grosvenor Lawn** RG14 . . .104 C1
**Grosvenor Rd**
Caversham RG4 . . . . . . . . . .59 B2
Staines TW18 . . . . . . . . . . . .97 A1
**Grove Cl** Old Windsor SL4 . . .95 A4
2 Slough SL1 . . . . . . . . . . . .43 A2
Wokingham RG40 . . . . . . . .142 C4
**Grove Cotts** RG4 . . . . . . . . .59 A3
**Grove Cross Rd** GU16 . . . .151 B1
**Grove Ct** Egham TW20 . . . . .96 A2
Maidenhead SL6 . . . . . . . . . .39 B4
Newbury RG14 . . . . . . . . . .131 A4
Grove Cty Prim Sch The
GU16 . . . . . . . . . . . . . . . . .151 C1
**Grove End** GU19 . . . . . . . .145 C3
**Grove Hill** RG4 . . . . . . . . . . .59 A2
**Grove Ho** Ashford TW15 . . . .97 C2
Old Windsor SL4 . . . . . . . . . .95 B4
**Grove La** RG42 . . . . . . . . . . .92 A2
**Grove Pk** SL6 . . . . . . . . . . . .63 C4
**Grove Rd** Burnham SL1 . . . .21 C2
Camberley GU15 . . . . . . . . .151 C3
Caversham RG4 . . . . . . . . . .59 A3
Chertsey KT16 . . . . . . . . . .123 C2
Henley-on-T RG9 . . . . . . . . . .15 C1
Maidenhead SL6 . . . . . . . . . .39 C4
Newbury RG14 . . . . . . . . . .104 C3
Shepperton TW17 . . . . . . . .125 B2
Windsor SL4 . . . . . . . . . . . .67 B3
**Grove The** Egham TW20 . . . .96 A2
Frimley GU16 . . . . . . . . . . .151 B1
Medmenham SL7 . . . . . . . . .17 C3
North Ascot SL5 . . . . . . . . .119 B4
Reading RG1 . . . . . . . . . . . . .86 B4
Slough SL1 . . . . . . . . . . . . . .43 A2
Thatcham RG18 . . . . . . . . .106 B2
Twyford RG10 . . . . . . . . . . . .61 B3
**Grovebarns** TW18 . . . . . . . .97 A1
**Grovefields Ave** GU16 . . . .151 B1
**Groveland Pl** RG30 . . . . . . .85 A4
**Groveland Rd** RG14 . . . . . .104 C3
**Grovelands Ave** RG41 . . . . .88 B1
**Grovelands Cl** RG41 . . . . . . .88 B2
**Grovelands Rd**
Reading RG30 . . . . . . . . . . . .85 A4
Shinfield RG7 . . . . . . . . . . .113 B1
**Groveley Rd** TW13, TW16 . . .98 C2
**Groves Cl** SL8 . . . . . . . . . . . .3 B2
**Groves Lea** RG7 . . . . . . . .136 C3
**Groves The** RG17 . . . . . . . . .73 A1
**Groves Way** SL6 . . . . . . . . .19 C3
**Grovestile Waye** TW14 . . . .98 B4
**Grubwood La** SL6 . . . . . . . .19 A4
**Guards Club Rd** SL6 . . . . . .40 B4
**Guards Ct** SL5 . . . . . . . . . .121 A1
**Guards Rd** SL4 . . . . . . . . . . .66 B3
**Guards Wlk** 1 SL4 . . . . . . . .66 B3
**Guerdon Pl** RG12 . . . . . . . .118 B1
**Guildford Ave** TW13 . . . . . .98 C3
**Guildford Rd**
Bagshot GU19 . . . . . . . . . .145 C1
Bagshot GU19 . . . . . . . . . .145 C2
Bisley GU24 . . . . . . . . . . . .153 C2
Chertsey KT16 . . . . . . . . . .123 C1
Lightwater GU18 . . . . . . . . .146 A1
West End GU24 . . . . . . . . .153 C4
**Guildford St**
Chertsey KT16 . . . . . . . . . .124 A1
Staines TW18 . . . . . . . . . . . .97 A1
**Gullane Ct** 31 RG1 . . . . . . . .86 B4
**Gun St** RG1 . . . . . . . . . . . . .86 A4
**Gunthorpe Rd** SL7 . . . . . . . .2 A2
**Gurney Cl** RG4 . . . . . . . . . . .58 B3
**Gurney Dr** RG4 . . . . . . . . . . .58 B3
**Gwendale** SL6 . . . . . . . . . . .19 B1
**Gwendoline Ct** TW15 . . . . . .97 C2
**Gweneth Ct** SL7 . . . . . . . . . . .1 B2
**Gwent Cl** SL6 . . . . . . . . . . . .39 A2
**Gwyn Cl** RG14 . . . . . . . . . .130 C4
**Gwynne Cl**
Purley on T RG31 . . . . . . . . .57 B2
Windsor SL4 . . . . . . . . . . . .66 C3
**Gwyns Piece** RG17 . . . . . . . .25 A2
**Gypsy La** Marlow SL7 . . . . . . .1 C2
Stoke Poges SL2 . . . . . . . . .22 C4


## H


**Habershon Dr** GU16 . . . . .152 B1
**Haddenhurst Ct** RG42 . . . . .90 B1
**Haddon Dr** RG5 . . . . . . . . . .87 C4
**Haddon Rd** SL6 . . . . . . . . . .39 B3
**Hadfield Rd** TW19 . . . . . . . .70 B1
**Hadleigh Rise** RG4 . . . . . . .59 C3
**Hadley Ct** SL3 . . . . . . . . . . .69 C3
**Hadlow Ct** SL1 . . . . . . . . . .42 B3
**Hadrian Cl** TW19 . . . . . . . . .97 C4
**Hadrian Way** TW19 . . . . . . .97 B4
**Hadrian Wlk E** RG2 . . . . . . .86 B2
**Hadrian Wlk W** RG2 . . . . . .86 B2
**Hafod** RG4 . . . . . . . . . . . . .58 C3
**Hag Hill La** SL6 . . . . . . . . . .41 A4
**Hag Hill Rise** SL6 . . . . . . . .41 A4
**Hagley Rd** RG2 . . . . . . . . . .86 A2
**Haig Dr** SL1 . . . . . . . . . . . . .42 A2
**Haig Rd** GU15 . . . . . . . . . .150 C3
**Hailey La** RG20 . . . . . . . . . .29 C1
**Haileybury Ct** SL4 . . . . . . . .67 A2
**Hailsham Cl** GU47 . . . . . . .143 B1
**Halcyon Ct** TW18 . . . . . . . .124 A4
**Halcyon Terr** RG30 . . . . . . .84 C4
**Haldane Rd** RG4 . . . . . . . . .58 C3
**Hale** SL4 . . . . . . . . . . . . . . . .66 C3
**Hale End** RG12 . . . . . . . . . .118 C3
**Hale St** TW18 . . . . . . . . . . . .96 C2
**Halewood** RG12 . . . . . . . . .117 C2
**Half Mile Rd** RG17 . . . . . . . .46 A1
**Half Moon St** GU19 . . . . . .145 C2
**Halfacre Cl** RG7 . . . . . . . . .113 A2
**Halfpenny Ct** SL5 . . . . . . . .121 A1
**Halfpenny La** Cholsey OX10 .13 B3
Sunningdale SL5 . . . . . . . . .121 A1
**Halfway Hos** SL6 . . . . . . . . .19 C2
**Halifax Cl** SL6 . . . . . . . . . . .39 A4
**Halifax Pl** RG18 . . . . . . . . .106 B2
**Halifax Rd** SL6 . . . . . . . . . . .39 A4
**Halifax Way** SL6 . . . . . . . . .39 A4
**Halkingcroft** SL3 . . . . . . . . .43 B2
**Hall Cl** GU15 . . . . . . . . . . .151 C3
**Hall Ct** SL3 . . . . . . . . . . . . . .68 A4
**Hall Farm Cres** GU46 . . . . .149 B3
Hall Grove (Sch) GU19 . . .146 A3
**Hall La** Harlington UB3 . . . . .71 B4
Yateley GU46 . . . . . . . . . . .149 B3
**Hall Mdw** SL1 . . . . . . . . . . . .21 A2
**Hall Place La** SL6 . . . . . . . . .38 A4
**Hallbrook Gdns** RG42 . . . . .90 C1
**Halldore Hill** SL6 . . . . . . . . .19 C4
**Halley Dr** SL5 . . . . . . . . . . .119 B4
**Hallgrove Bottom** GU19 . .145 C3
**Halliford Cl** TW17 . . . . . . .125 C3
**Halliford Rd** TW16, TW17 .125 C3
Halliford Sch TW17 . . . . . .125 B1
**Hallmark Cl** GU47 . . . . . . .150 C4
**Halls La** Earley RG2 . . . . . . .86 C1
Waltham St Lawrence RG10 .63 A4
**Halls Rd** RG30 . . . . . . . . . . .84 B3
**Hallsmead Ct** 3 RG1 . . . . . .59 A1
**Halpin Cl** RG31 . . . . . . . . . .84 B2
**Halstead Cl** RG5 . . . . . . . . .87 C4
**Halstead Ho** RG26 . . . . . . .134 C1
**Halters The** RG14 . . . . . . .131 A4
**Ham Island** SL4 . . . . . . . . . .68 B2
**Ham La**
Englefield Green TW20 . . . . .95 A2
Old Windsor SL4 . . . . . . . . . .68 B2
**Ham Rd** SN8 . . . . . . . . . . . .126 A2
**Hamble Ave** GU17 . . . . . . .150 B3
**Hamble Ct** 16 RG1 . . . . . . . .86 A3
**Hambleden Ct** RG12 . . . . .118 C3
**Hambleden Mill** RG9 . . . . . .16 B4
**Hambleden Pl** RG9 . . . . . . .16 B3
**Hambleden Rise** RG9 . . . . .16 B4
**Hambleden Wlk** SL6 . . . . . .19 C1
**Hambledon Cl** RG6 . . . . . . .87 C1
**Hambleton** TW19 . . . . . . . . .95 B4
**Hambleton Cl** GU16 . . . . . .152 A2
**Hamblin Mdw** RG17 . . . . . .100 C4
**Hambridge Rd** RG14 . . . . .105 B1
**Hamfield Cotts** SL6 . . . . . .19 C4
**Hamilton Ave** RG9 . . . . . . . .15 C1
**Hamilton Cl** TW13 . . . . . . . .98 C2
**Hamilton Cl** GU19 . . . . . . .145 C2
**Hamilton Cl** KT16 . . . . . . . .123 C1
**Hamilton Ct**
Farnborough (Hants) GU17 .150 C1
Newbury RG14 . . . . . . . . . .131 A4
**Hamilton Dr** SL5 . . . . . . . .120 C1
**Hamilton Gdns** SL1 . . . . . . .21 A1
**Hamilton Pk** SL6 . . . . . . . . .39 A3
**Hamilton Rd** Feltham TW13 .98 C2
Reading RG1 . . . . . . . . . . . . .86 C3
Slough SL1 . . . . . . . . . . . . . .42 A4
Wargrave RG10 . . . . . . . . . .36 C1
**Hamlet St** RG42 . . . . . . . . .118 C4
**Hammond Cl** RG19 . . . . . .106 C1
**Hammond Ct** RG42 . . . . . . .91 A1
**Hammond End** SL2 . . . . . . .22 A4
Hammond Jun Sch
GU18 . . . . . . . . . . . . . . . . .146 A1
**Hammond Way** GU18 . . . .146 A1
**Hammonds Heath** RG7 . . .137 A3
**Hampden Cl** SL2 . . . . . . . . .23 A1
**Hampden Rd**
Caversham RG4 . . . . . . . . . .59 A1
Maidenhead SL6 . . . . . . . . . .39 A4
Slough SL3 . . . . . . . . . . . . . .43 C2
**Hampdens The** RG14 . . . . .130 B3
**Hampshire Ave** SL1 . . . . . . .42 B4
**Hampshire Lodge** 8 SL6 . .39 C3
**Hampshire Rd** GU15 . . . . .151 C4
**Hampshire Rise** RG42 . . . . .91 C1
**Hampshire Way** RG41 . . . .115 B3
**Hampshire Wlk** RG31 . . . . .84 A4
**Hampstead Ct** RG30 . . . . . .85 A4
**Hampstead Hill** RG9 . . . . . .60 B4
Hampstead Norreys
CE Prim Sch RG18 . . . . . . .52 C3
**Hampstead Norreys Rd**
RG18 . . . . . . . . . . . . . . . . . .79 A4
**Hampton Ho** SL3 . . . . . . . . .69 B4
**Hampton Rd** RG14 . . . . . .104 C1
**Hampton Twrs** 4 RG30 . . . .85 B3
**Hanbury Cl** SL1 . . . . . . . . . .41 A4
**Hanbury Dr** RG31 . . . . . . . .84 B2
**Hanbury Way** GU15 . . . . . .151 B2
**Hanbury Wlk** RG19 . . . . . .106 B1
**Hancocks Mount** SL5 . . . .120 B2
**Hancombe Rd** GU47 . . . . .143 A1
**Handford La** GU46 . . . . . .149 B3
**Hanger Rd** RG26 . . . . . . . .134 C1
**Hangerfield Cl** GU46 . . . . .149 B3
**Hangmans Stone La** RG20 .49 A3
**Hanley Cl** SL4 . . . . . . . . . . .66 B3
**Hannibal Rd** TW19 . . . . . . . .97 C4
**Hanningtons Way** RG7 . . .111 B2
**Hanover Cl**
Englefield Green TW20 . . . . .95 B1
Frimley GU16 . . . . . . . . . . .151 C1
Slough SL1 . . . . . . . . . . . . . .43 A2
Windsor SL4 . . . . . . . . . . . .66 C3
**Hanover Ct** Caversham RG4 .59 B3
Reading RG30 . . . . . . . . . . . .84 C3
**Hanover Gdns** RG12 . . . . .117 C1
**Hanover Mead**
Maidenhead SL6 . . . . . . . . . .40 B2
Newbury RG14 . . . . . . . . . .130 B3
**Hanover Way** SL4 . . . . . . . .66 C3
**Hanson Cl** GU15 . . . . . . . .152 A4
**Hanwood Cl** RG5 . . . . . . . . .87 B4
**Hanworth Cl** RG12 . . . . . . .118 B2
**Hanworth La** KT16 . . . . . . .123 C1
**Hanworth Rd** RG12 . . . . . .118 A1
Hanworth Trad Est KT16 .123 C1
**Harborough Cl** SL1 . . . . . . .41 B3
**Harbury Ct** RG14 . . . . . . . .105 A1
**Harcourt** TW19 . . . . . . . . . .68 C1
**Harcourt Cl** Dorney SL4 . . . .40 C2
Egham TW20 . . . . . . . . . . . .96 B1
Henley-on-T RG9 . . . . . . . . . .15 B1
**Harcourt Dr** RG6 . . . . . . . . .86 C2
**Harcourt Rd**
Bracknell RG12 . . . . . . . . . .118 A2
Camberley GU15 . . . . . . . . .151 A3
Dorney SL4 . . . . . . . . . . . . .40 C2
Windsor SL4 . . . . . . . . . . . .66 C3
**Hardell Cl** TW20 . . . . . . . . .96 A2
**Harding Rd** RG5 . . . . . . . . .87 B4
**Hardwell Way** RG12 . . . . . .118 C3
**Hardwick Cl** SL6 . . . . . . . . .39 A4
**Hardwick La** KT16 . . . . . . .123 B1
**Hardwick Rd** Reading RG30 .84 C4
Whitchurch-on-T RG8 . . . . . .56 B4
**Hardy Ave** GU46 . . . . . . . . .149 B2
**Hardy Cl** Caversham RG4 . . .59 B1
Slough SL1 . . . . . . . . . . . . . .42 A3
Thatcham RG18 . . . . . . . . .106 B3
**Hardy Gn** RG45 . . . . . . . . .143 A2
**Hare Shoots** SL6 . . . . . . . . .39 C3
**Harebell Dr** RG18 . . . . . . .106 C3
**Harefield Cl** RG41 . . . . . . . .88 B1
**Harefield Rd** SL6 . . . . . . . . .39 A4
**Harewood Dr** RG18 . . . . . .106 B4
**Harewood Pl** SL1 . . . . . . . . .43 A2
**Hargrave Rd** SL6 . . . . . . . . .39 B4
**Hargreaves Way** RG31 . . . .84 C2
**Harkness Rd** SL1 . . . . . . . . .41 A4
**Harlech Ave** RG4 . . . . . . . . .59 B3
**Harlech Rd** GU17 . . . . . . .150 B2
**Harley Rd** RG4 . . . . . . . . . . .59 A1
**Harlington Cl** UB3 . . . . . . .71 B4
**Harlington Cnr** UB3 . . . . . .71 B3
**Harlton Cl** RG6 . . . . . . . . .114 B4
Harmans Water
Cty Inf Sch RG12 . . . . . . .118 C2
Harmans Water
Cty Jun Sch RG12 . . . . . .118 C2
**Harmans Water Rd** RG12 .118 B2
**Harmar Cl** RG40 . . . . . . . .116 C3
**Harmondsworth La** UB7 . . .70 C4
Harmondsworth Prim Sch
UB7 . . . . . . . . . . . . . . . . . . .70 B4
**Harness Cl** RG2 . . . . . . . . .113 A3
**Harold Rd** RG17 . . . . . . . . .102 A1
**Harpesford Ave** GU25 . . . .122 B2
**Harpsden Rd** RG9 . . . . . . . .35 C4
**Harpsden Way** RG9 . . . . . . .35 C4
**Harpton Cl** GU46 . . . . . . . .149 B4
**Harrier Cl** RG5 . . . . . . . . . .88 A3
**Harrington Cl** Earley RG6 . .87 B1
Newbury RG14 . . . . . . . . . .105 C3
Windsor SL4 . . . . . . . . . . . .66 C2
**Harris Arc** 5 RG1 . . . . . . . .86 A4
**Harris Cl** Lambourn RG17 . . .25 A2
Woodley RG5 . . . . . . . . . . . .88 A4
**Harrison Cl** RG10 . . . . . . . .61 C2
**Harrison Ct** TW17 . . . . . . .125 A2
**Harrison Way** SL1 . . . . . . . .41 B3
**Harrogate Ct** SL3 . . . . . . . .44 A1
**Harrogate Rd** RG4 . . . . . . . .58 C2
**Harrow Bottom Rd** GU25 .122 C2
**Harrow Cl** SL6 . . . . . . . . . . .19 C1
**Harrow Ct** RG1 . . . . . . . . . .85 C3
**Harrow La** SL6 . . . . . . . . . . .19 C1
Harrow Mkt The SL3 . . . . . .44 A2
**Harrow Rd**
Ashford TW14,TW15 . . . . . .98 A3
Slough SL3 . . . . . . . . . . . . . .43 C2
**Harrow Way** TW17 . . . . . . .125 B4
**Harry Tee Ct** 11 RG1 . . . . . .86 B4
**Hart Cl** 6 RG42 . . . . . . . . .118 A4
**Hart Dene Cl** GU19 . . . . . .145 C2
**Hart Dyke Cl** RG41 . . . . . .116 A1
**Hart St** Henley-on-T RG9 . . . .15 C1
Reading RG1 . . . . . . . . . . . . .85 C4
**Hartford Rise** GU15 . . . . . .151 B3
**Hartigan Pl** RG5 . . . . . . . . .88 A4
**Hartland Cl** SL1 . . . . . . . . . .42 B3
**Hartland Rd** RG2 . . . . . . . . .86 B1
**Hartley Cl**
Blackwater GU17 . . . . . . . .150 A3

Hartley Cl *continued*
Stoke Poges SL3 23 B2
Hartley Copse SL4 68 A1
Hartley Court Rd RG7 112 C3
Hartley Way RG18 106 C2
Hartmead Rd RG19 106 C2
Harts Cl RG2 114 C1
Harts Hill Rd RG18 106 C2
Harts La RG7 110 B3
Harts Leap Cl GU47 143 A1
Harts Leap Rd GU47 150 A4
Hartsbourne Rd RG6 87 A2
Hartshill Rd RG26 134 C1
Hartslock Ct RG8 56 A3
Hartslock View RG8 34 C1
Hartslock Way RG31 57 B1
Hartvale Ct GU15 152 A4
Harvard Cl RG5 88 A4
Harvard Rd GU47 143 C1
Harvest Cl Reading RG31 84 A3
Yateley GU46 149 A2
Harvest Ct TW17 125 A3
Harvest Gn RG14 104 C1
Harvest Hill SL8 3 B1
Harvest Hill Rd SL6 39 C2
Harvest Rd TW20 95 B1
Harvest Ride
Bracknell RG42 91 B1
Winkfield RG12, RG42, SL5 119 A4
Harvey Ho 11 RG30 85 B3
Harvey Rd SL3 44 A2
Harwell Int Bsns Ctr OX11 9 C4
Harwich Cl 8 RG6 87 B1
Harwich Rd SL1 42 A4
Harwood Gdns SL4 95 A4
Harwood Rd SL7 1 B1
Harwood Rise RG20 129 C1
Haslemere Cl GU16 152 B2
Haslemere Rd SL4 67 A3
Haslett Rd TW17 125 C4
Hasting Cl SL6 40 B1
Hastings Mdw SL2 23 A2
Hatch Cl RG7 108 B4
Hatch End GU20 146 B2
Hatch Gate La RG10 37 A3
Hatch La Bucklebury RG7 108 B4
Burghfield Common RG30 111 B3
Harmondsworth TW6, UB7 70 B4
Windsor SL4 67 A3
Hatch Ride
Crowthorne RG45 143 A4
Wokingham RG40 142 C4
Hatch Ride Cty Prim Sch
RG45 143 A4
Hatch The SL4 66 B4
Hatchet La SL4, SL5 93 A3
Hatchets La RG18 80 B4
Hatchett Rd TW14 98 B4
Hatchgate Cl RG18 106 B4
Hatchgate Copse RG12 117 C2
Hatchgate Gdns SL1 21 B1
Hatchley RG2 113 B4
Hatfield Cl SL6 39 B3
Hatfield Ct RG31 84 A2
Hatfield Rd SL1 43 A2
Hatford Rd RG30 85 A2
Hatherley Rd RG1 86 C3
Hatherwood GU46 149 C3
Hatt Cl RG20 50 B4
Hatton Ave SL2 22 B1
Hatton Cross Rdbt TW6 71 C2
Hatton Cross Sta TW6 71 C2
Hatton Ct SL4 67 B3
Hatton Hill
Ashampstead RG8 54 A4
Windlesham GU20 146 B3
Hatton Rd
East Bedfont TW14 98 B4
Hatton TW14, TW6 71 C1
Haughurst Hill RG26 134 B1
Havelock Cres SL6 39 A4
Havelock Rd
Maidenhead SL6 39 A4
Wokingham RG41 116 A3
Havelock St RG41 116 A3
Haven Ct 21 RG1 86 B4
Haven Of Rest SL6 40 A4
Haven Rd TW15 98 A3
Haven The RG17 102 A1
Haversham Dr RG12 118 A2
Haw La Aldworth RG8 32 C1
Ashampstead RG8,RG18 53 C4
Hawk La RG12 118 B3
Hawkchurch Rd RG2 113 B4
Hawkedale Fst Sch
TW16 125 C3
Hawkedon Prim Sch RG6 87 C1
Hawkedon Way RG6 87 C1
Hawker Ct SL3 44 A2
Hawker Way RG5 88 A4
Hawkes Cl RG41 116 A4
Hawkes Leap GU20 146 A3
Hawkesbury Dr RG31 84 C2
Hawkesworth Dr GU19 145 C1
Hawkins Cl RG12 119 A4
Hawkins Way RG40 116 C3
Hawkridge Ct RG12 118 C3
Hawks Hill SL8 3 B1
Hawkshill Rd SL2 22 A1
Hawksway TW18 96 C3
Hawkswood Ave GU16 151 C1
Hawkswood Ho RG42 117 C4
Hawkswood La SL9 23 C4
Hawksworth Rd RG7 111 A2
Hawley Cl RG31 84 B2
Hawley Garden Cotts
GU17 150 B2
Hawley Gn GU17 150 C2
Hawley La GU14,GU17 151 A1
Hawley Lodge GU17 150 C1
Hawley Place Ind Sch
GU17 150 C1
Hawley Prim Sch GU17 150 C2
Hawley Rd GU17 150 C2
Hawley Way TW15 98 A2
Hawthorn Cl
Bracknell RG42 118 A4
Marlow SL7 1 C2
Hawthorn Gdns RG2 86 C1
Hawthorn La Burnham SL2 22 A3
Newell Green, Hawthorn Hill
RG42 91 C4
Newell Green,
Nuptown RG42 92 A4
Hawthorn Rd
Frimley GU16 151 C1
Newbury RG14 105 A2
Hawthorn Way
Sonning RG4 60 C2
Upper Halliford TW17 125 B3
Hawthorne Ave SL4 93 A3
Hawthorne Cres
Blackwater GU17 150 C2
Slough SL1 42 C4
Hawthorne Ct TW19 97 B4
Hawthorne Dr SL4 93 A4
Hawthorne Rd
Caversham RG4 59 C2
Egham TW20 96 B2
Hawthorne Way
Great Shefford RG17 48 A2
Stanwell TW19 97 B4
Winkfield SL4 93 A4
Hawthornes RG31 57 A2
Hawthorns Prim Sch The
RG41 115 C4
Hawthorns The
Charvil RG10 61 A2
Flackwell Heath HP10 3 A4
Poyle SL3 69 C3
Wooburn Green HP10 3 C3
Hawtrey Cl SL1 43 A2
Hawtrey Rd SL4 67 B3
Hay La SL3 23 B4
Hay Rd RG1 85 C3
Haydon Ct SL6 39 C3
Haydon Pl GU46 149 C3
Hayes La RG41 115 B2
Hayes Pl SL7 1 B1
Hayfield Cl RG31 84 B4
Hayfield Ct RG17 46 C3
Hayley Gn RG42 91 C2
Haymill Rd SL1,SL2 21 B1
Haynes Cl SL3 43 C1
Hayse Hill SL4 66 B3
Hayward Pl SL8 3 B1
Haywards Cl RG9 15 B1
Haywards Mead SL4 41 C1
Haywards The RG18 106 B2
Haywood RG12 118 B1
Haywood Ct RG1 86 C4
Haywood Way RG30 84 C3
Hazel Cl
Burghfield Common RG30 111 A3
Englefield Green TW20 95 A1
Marlow Bottom SL7 1 B3
Wokingham RG41 115 C3
Hazel Cres RG2 86 C1
Hazel Dr RG5 87 B3
Hazel Gn RG26 134 B1
Hazel Gr Staines TW18 97 B1
Thatcham RG18 106 B3
Hazel Rd RG8 57 B2
Hazelbank RG40 141 C3
Hazelbank Ct KT16 124 B1
Hazelbank Rd KT16 124 B1
Hazeldene RG20 51 A1
Hazelhurst Rd SL1 21 B2
Hazell Cl SL6 39 C4
Hazell Hill RG12 118 B3
Hazell Way SL2 22 C3
Hazelmere Cl TW14 71 C1
Hazelmere Rd SL2 43 A3
Hazels Paddock RG18 106 B4
Hazelwood Cl RG31 57 B1
Hazelwood La RG42 90 C2
Heacham Cl RG6 114 A4
Headington Cl
Maidenhead SL6 39 A4
Wokingham RG40 116 B4
Headington Dr RG40 116 B4
Headington Rd SL6 39 A4
Headley Cl RG5 88 A4
Headley Park Ind Est RG5 87 C4
Headley Rd RG5 87 C4
Headley Rd E RG5 88 A4
Heads La RG17 128 A3
Heardman Cl RG19 106 C1
Hearmon Cl GU46 149 C3
Hearn Rd RG5 87 C3
Hearn Wlk RG12 118 C4
Hearne Dr SL6 40 A1
Hearsey Gdns GU17 150 B3
Heath Cl Harlington UB3 71 B4
Stanwell TW19 70 B1
Virginia Water GU25 122 B3
Wokingham RG41 116 A2
Heath Cnr GU15 152 A2
Heath Ct RG26 134 C1
Heath Dr RG9 35 A1
Heath End Rd RG26 134 C1
Heath Gr TW16 98 C1
Heath Hill Rd N RG45 143 A3
Heath Hill Rd S RG45 143 A2
Heath La RG18 106 B3
Heath Rd Bagshot GU19 145 C2
Heath Rd *continued*
Bradfield RG7 82 A1
Reading RG6 87 A3
Silchester RG26 135 C1
Wooburn Moor HP9 3 C4
Heath Ride RG40,RG45 142 B3
Heath Rise
Camberley GU15 151 B3
Virginia Water GU25 122 B3
Heathacre SL3 69 C3
Heathcote SL6 40 A1
Heathcote Ct 2 SL4 67 B2
Heathcote Rd GU15 151 B3
Heathcroft Ave TW16 98 C1
Heather Cl RG40 141 C4
Heather Dr
Sunningdale SL5 121 A1
Tadley RG26 134 C1
Thatcham RG18 106 B3
Heather Gdns RG14 130 C4
Heather Mead GU16 151 C1
Heather Mead Ct GU16 151 C1
Heather Ridge Arc GU15 152 B2
Heather Ridge
Cty Inf Sch GU15 152 B2
Heatherdale Rd GU15 151 B2
Heatherden Cl RG2 113 B4
Heatherdene Ave RG45 142 C2
Heatherley Cl GU15 151 A3
Heatherley Rd GU15 151 A3
Heathermount 4 RG12 118 C3
Heathermount Dr RG45 143 A3
Heathermount Sch SL5 120 B2
Heathers The TW19 97 C4
Heatherside Dr GU25 122 A2
Heatherway RG45 143 A3
Heatherwood Hospl SL5 119 C3
Heathfield RG7 137 A3
Heathfield Ave Ascot SL5 120 C2
Reading RG30 84 B3
Shiplake RG9 35 A1
Heathfield Cl RG9 35 A1
Heathfield Ct TW15 97 C3
Heathfield Rd SL1 3 C1
Heathfield Sch SL5 119 A4
Heathfields RG20 78 A4
Heathlands RG26 134 C1
Heathlands Country Mkt
RG40 116 C1
Heathlands Ct RG40 142 C4
Heathlands Dr SL6 39 A3
Heathlands Rd RG40 116 C1
Heathmoors RG12 118 B2
Heathpark Dr GU20 146 C2
Heathrow Airport London
TW6 71 A3
Heathrow Airport Visitor Ctr
TW6 71 B3
Heathrow Bvd UB7 70 C4
Heathrow Central Sta
TW6 71 A2
Heathrow Cl TW6 70 A3
Heathrow Copse RG26 134 B1
Heathrow Sch UB7 70 C4
Heathrow Terminal 4 Sta
TW6 71 B1
Heathside Pk GU15 152 B4
Heathway
Camberley GU15 151 B3
North Ascot SL5 119 C4
Reading RG31 84 B4
Heathway Cl GU15 151 B3
Heathwood Cl GU46 149 B4
Heavens Lea SL8 3 B1
Hebbecastle Down RG42 91 B1
Hebden Cl RG19 106 B1
Hedge Lea HP10 3 B4
Hedgeway RG14 105 B2
Hedingham Mews SL6 39 B4
Hedley Rd HP10 3 A4
Hedsor Hill SL8 3 B1
Hedsor La HP10,SL1 3 C1
Hedsor Rd SL8 3 A1
Hedsor View Cotts SL6 19 C4
Heelas Rd RG41 116 A3
Heights The
Camberley GU15 151 C3
Marlow SL7 18 A4
Helen Cotts SL4 66 B3
Helena Rd SL4 67 B3
Helgiford Gdns TW16 98 C1
Helksham Cl GU47 143 B1
Hellyer Way SL8 3 B2
Helmsdale RG12 118 C2
Helmsdale Cl RG30 85 A4
Helston Gdns RG2 86 A1
Helston La SL4 67 A3
Helvellyn Cl TW20 96 A1
Hemdean Hill RG4 59 A2
Hemdean House Sch RG4 59 A2
Hemdean Rd RG4 59 A2
Hemdean Rise RG4 59 A2
Hemming Way SL2 22 A1
Hemmyng Cnr RG42 91 B1
Hempson Ave SL3 43 B2
Hemsdale SL6 19 A1
Hemwood Rd SL4 66 B2
Hencroft St N SL1 42 C2
Hencroft St S SL1 42 C2
Hendon Terr TW15 98 B1
Hendon Way TW19 70 B1
Hendons Way SL6 40 A1
Hengrave Cl RG6 87 C1
Henley Cres TW15 97 B3
Henley Coll The
(Deanfield Bldgs) RG9 15 B1
Henley Coll The
(Rotherfield Bldgs) RG9 15 B1
Henley Coll The
(Southfield Bldgs) RG9 15 B1
Henley Gdns GU46 149 B3
Henley Lodge 12 SL6 39 C3
Henley Rd Bisham SL6 18 A1
Caversham RG9 59 B2
Hurley SL6 17 B2
Marlow SL7 18 A4
Shiplake RG9 60 B4
Slough SL1 41 C4
Henley Trinity Prim Sch
RG9 15 B1
Henley Wood Rd RG6 87 B2
Henley-on-Thames Sta
RG9 15 C1
Henry Ct 24 RG1 86 B4
Henry Rd SL1 42 B2
Henry St RG1 86 A3
Henrys The RG18 106 B2
Henshaw Cres RG14 130 B4
Hensworth Rd TW15 97 B2
Henwick Cl RG18 106 A3
Henwick La RG18 106 A2
Henwood Copse RG8 55 A3
Hepplewhite Cl RG26 134 C1
Hepworth Croft GU47 150 C3
Hepworth Way KT12 125 C1
Herald Way RG5 88 A3
Herbert Cl RG12 118 A2
Hereford Cl TW18 124 A4
Herewood Cl RG14 104 C2
Heriot Rd KT16 124 A1
Heritage Ct 2
Egham TW20 96 A2
27 Reading RG1 85 C4
Hermitage Cl
Frimley GU16 151 C1
Littleton TW17 125 A3
Slough SL3 43 B2
Hermitage Ct TW18 96 C2
Hermitage Cty Prim Sch
RG18 79 A4
Hermitage Dr
North Ascot SL5 119 C4
Twyford RG10 61 B3
Hermitage La SL4 67 A2
Hermitage Par SL5 120 A3
Hermitage Rd RG18 79 A1
Hermitage The
Feltham TW13 98 C3
Lambourn RG17 46 C4
Hermits Cl RG7 111 A2
Hermits Hill RG7,RG30 111 B2
Herndon Cl TW20 96 A2
Heroes Wlk RG2 113 A4
Heron Cl SL5 119 B4
Heron Ct Staines TW18 97 A2
Stanwell TW19 97 C4
Heron Dr Slough SL3 44 A1
Twyford RG10 61 C3
Heron Ho RG14 105 B2
Heron Island RG4 59 B1
Heron Rd RG41 115 C3
Heron Shaw RG8 34 B4
Heron Way
Burghfield Common RG1 85 C2
Padworth RG7 109 A2
Thatcham RG19 106 A2
Heron's Way RG40 116 C4
Herondale RG12 118 B1
Heronfield TW20 95 B1
Herongate RG17 100 B4
Herons Pl SL7 1 C2
Heronscourt GU18 153 B4
Herrick Cl GU16 152 B2
Herrings La GU20 146 B2
Herriot Ct GU46 149 B4
Herschel Gram Sch SL1 42 B4
Herschel Grange RG42 91 B2
Herschel Park Dr SL1 42 C2
Herschel St SL1 42 C2
Hertford Cl Caversham RG4 59 B3
Wokingham RG41 115 C3
Hetherington Cl SL2 21 C1
Hetherington Rd TW17 125 B4
Hever Cl SL6 39 B3
Hewett Ave RG4 58 B2
Hewett Cl RG4 58 B2
Hewgate Ct RG9 15 C1
Hewlett Pl GU19 145 C2
Hexham Cl GU47 143 B1
Hexham Rd RG2 86 B2
Heynes Gn SL6 39 A2
Heywod Dr GU19 145 B2
Heywood Ave SL6 39 A1
Heywood Court Cl SL6 39 A1
Heywood Gdns SL6 39 A1
Hibbert Rd SL6 40 A2
Hibbert's Alley 25 SL4 67 B3
Hickox Ct HP10 3 C4
Hicks La GU17 150 A3
Higgs La GU19 145 B2
High Beech RG12 118 C3
High Beeches GU16 151 B1
High Close Sch RG40 116 B4
High Fields SL5 120 C2
High Heavens Wood SL7 1 B4
High Mdw RG4 58 B2
High Meadow Pl KT16 123 C2
High Rd SL6 19 C3
High St Ascot SL5 120 A3
Ascot, Sunninghill SL5 120 B2
Bagshot GU19 145 C2
Boxford RG20 76 A1
Bracknell RG12 118 A4
Burnham SL1 21 B1
Camberley GU15 151 B3
Chieveley RG20 51 A1
High St *continued*
Colnbrook SL3 69 B4
Compton RG20 31 B2
Cookham SL6 20 A4
Crowthorne RG45 143 B2
Datchet SL3 68 A3
East Isley RG20 30 C4
4 Egham TW20 95 C2
Eton SL4 67 B4
Feltham TW13 98 C3
Goring RG8 34 B3
Harlington UB3 71 B4
Harmondsworth UB7 70 B4
Hungerford RG17 100 B3
Iver SL0 44 C4
Kintbury RG17 102 A1
Lambourn RG17 25 A1
Lambourn, Upper
Lambourn RG17 24 C3
Maidenhead SL6 40 B2
Marlow SL7 1 C1
Pangbourne RG8 56 B3
Reading RG1 86 A4
Sandhurst GU47 149 C4
Sandhurst,
Little Sandhurst GU47 143 A1
Shepperton TW17 125 B2
Slough, Langley SL3 44 A1
Slough, Upton SL1 42 C2
Sonning RG4 60 B2
Staines TW18 96 C2
Stanwell TW19 70 B1
Streatley RG8 34 A3
Sunningdale SL5 121 A2
Taplow SL6 20 C1
Thatcham RG19 106 B2
Theale RG7 83 C2
Twyford RG10 61 B2
Wargrave RG10 36 B1
West End GU24 153 C4
Whitchurch-on-T RG8 56 B4
Windsor SL4 67 B3
Wraysbury TW19 68 C1
High St Mall 1 SL6 39 C4
High Street Harlington
UB3 71 B4
High Town Rd SL6 39 C4
High Tree Dr RG6 87 A3
High View Cl SL7 1 B4
High View Rd GU18 152 C4
Highbeeches Cl SL7 1 B4
Highbridge Cl RG4 59 C3
Highbridge Wharf 13 RG1 86 A4
Highbury Cres GU15 152 A4
Highbury Rd RG31 84 A4
Highclere SL5 120 B2
Highclere Cl RG12 118 C4
Highclere Dr GU15 152 A4
Highcliffe Cl RG5 60 C1
Highdown Ave RG4 59 A3
Highdown Hill Rd RG4 59 A3
Highdown Sixth Form
Comp Sch RG4 59 A3
Higher Alham RG12 118 C1
Highfield Bracknell RG12 117 C2
Earley RG6 87 A1
Highfield Ave RG14 105 A1
Highfield Cl
Englefield Green TW20 95 B1
Wokingham RG40 116 A3
Highfield Ct
Burghfield Common RG7 111 A2
Burnham SL2 22 A2
Englefield Green TW20 95 B1
Highfield La SL6 39 A2
Highfield Pk Marlow SL7 1 A1
Wargrave RG10 36 C2
Highfield Rd Bourne End SL8 3 A2
Chertsey KT16 124 A1
Englefield Green TW20 95 B1
Flackwell Heath HP10 3 A4
Maidenhead SL6 39 A4
Newbury RG14 104 C1
Purley on T RG31 57 B2
Upper Halliford TW16 125 C2
Windsor SL4 66 C2
Highgate Rd RG5 87 B3
Highgrove Pk SL6 39 C4
Highgrove Pl RG10 61 C3
Highgrove St RG1 86 B3
Highgrove Terr RG1 86 A3
Highland Pk TW13 98 C2
Highland Rd GU15 151 C4
Highlands HP10 3 A4
Highlands Ave RG41 115 B3
Highlands La RG9 35 A4
Highlands Sch The RG31 57 B1
Highlands The SL2 22 B4
Highlea Ave HP10 3 A4
Highmead Cl RG2 86 C1
Highmoor Rd RG4 58 C2
Highview GU21 84 A3
Highview Cres GU15 144 C1
Highway RG45 143 A3
Highway Ave SL6 39 A3
Highway Rd SL6 39 A3
Highwayman's Ridge
GU20 146 A3
Highwood Cl
Newbury RG14 105 A3
Yateley GU46 149 B2
Highwoods Cl SL7 1 B4
Highwoods Dr SL7 1 B4
Highworth Cotts RG26 134 B1
Highworth Way RG31 57 A1

Hilary Cl RG2 113 B4
Hilary Dr RG45 143 A3
Hilary Ho 10 RG14 105 A1
Hilborne Way RG2 115 A1
Hilbury Rd RG6 87 A2
Hilcot Rd RG30 85 B4
Hildens Dr RG31 84 B4
Hill Cl Newbury RG14 130 B4
Wooburn Green HP10 3 C4
Hill Copse View RG12 118 C4
Hill Cres RG7 108 B2
Hill Farm App HP10 3 C4
Hill Farm Rd
Marlow Bottom SL7 1 C3
Taplow SL6 20 C1
Hill Gdns RG8 34 A3
Hill Lands RG10 36 B1
Hill Piece OX11 10 C4
Hill Pl SL2 22 A3
Hill Prim Sch The RG4 59 B3
Hill Rd Arborfield RG2 114 C1
Newbury RG14 104 C2
Hill Side RG1 86 B3
Hill St RG1 86 A3
Hill Top Dr SL7 1 A1
Hill View Rd TW19 68 B1
Hillary Ct TW19 97 C4
Hillary Rd SL3 43 C2
Hillberry RG12 118 B1
Hillbrow RG2 86 C1
Hillcrest
Hampstead Norreys RG18 52 C3
Tadley RG26 135 A1
Hillcrest Ave SL6 19 C3
Hillcrest Rd GU15 152 A4
Hilldrop La RG17 46 A2
Hillersdon SL2 43 A4
Hillfield GU46 149 C3
Hillgreen La RG20 50 B4
Hillhampton SL5 120 C1
Hillhouse La RG19 133 A1
Hillingdon Ave TW19 97 C4
Hillmead Ct SL6 40 C4
Hillrise Brands Hill SL3 69 A4
Walton-on-T KT12 125 C1
Hills La SL6 19 B4
Hillsborough Pk GU15 152 B3
Hillside Ascot SL5 120 B2
Burghfield Common RG7 111 B2
East Garston RG17 47 B3
Maidenhead SL6 39 B3
Sandhurst GU15 150 C4
Slough SL1 42 C2
Wentworth GU25 122 B2
Whitchurch-on-T RG8 56 B4
Hillside Dr RG42 90 B1
Hillside Pk Earley RG2 86 C1
Sunningdale SL5 120 C1
Hillside Rd Earley RG6 87 B2
Hungerford RG17 100 B2
Marlow SL7 1 C2
Hilltop Cl SL5 120 C4
Hilltop Fst Sch SL4 66 C2
Hilltop Rd Caversham RG4 58 B3
Earley RG6 87 A4
Twyford RG10 61 C4
Hilltop View GU46 149 A3
Hillview Cl RG31 57 A1
Hilmanton RG6 113 C4
Hilperton Rd 3 SL1 42 C2
Hindhead Rd RG6 87 A2
Hinksey Cl SL3 44 A2
Hinton Cl RG45 143 A4
Hinton Dr RG45 143 A4
Hinton Pk RG10 61 C1
Hinton Rd Hurst RG10 62 A1
Slough SL1 41 C3
Hintonhatch Cnr RG10 62 A1
Hirstwood RG30 57 C1
Hirtes Ave RG2 113 C3
Hitcham Ho SL1 21 A1
Hitcham La Burnham SL1 21 A1
Taplow SL1,SL6 20 C1
Hitcham Rd SL1,SL6 41 A4
Hitchcock Cl TW17 124 C3
Hitherhooks Hill RG42 90 C1
Hithermoor Rd TW19 70 A1
Hobart Ct SL7 2 A2
Hobbis Dr SL6 39 A3
Hockett La SL6 19 A3
Hockford La RG7 134 A2
Hockham Rd RG20 31 C3
Hockley La SL2 23 A3
Hodge La SL5 93 A2
Hodgedale La RG10 37 B3
Hodges Cl GU19 145 C1
Hodsoll Rd RG1 85 C4
Hoe Benham La RG20 102 C4
Hogarth Ave Ashford TW15 98 B1
Reading RG30 84 C3
Hogarth Cl
Sandhurst GU47 150 C3
Slough SL1 41 C3
Hogfair La SL1 21 B1
Hogmoor La RG10 61 C1
Hogoak La SL4 92 A4
Hogwood La RG40 141 A3
Holbeche Cl GU46 149 A3
Holbeck RG12 117 C2
Holberton Rd RG2 113 B4
Holborn Hill OX12 6 B4
Holborne Cl RG14 130 B3
Holbrook Ct TW20 96 B2
Holbrook Mdw TW20 96 B1
Holford Cl RG31 84 B4
Holkam Cl RG30 84 C4
Holkham Cl RG30 57 C1
Holland Ct TW15 97 C1
Holland Gdns TW20 123 C4
Holland Pines RG12 117 C1
Holland Rd Marlow SL7 1 C2
Reading RG30 84 B4
Hollands The RG19 106 C2
Hollicombe Cl RG30 84 C4
Hollies The RG14 130 B3
Hollington Pl RG19 106 B2
Hollins Wlk RG30 85 B3
Hollow Hill La SL0 44 B3
Hollow La Shinfield RG2 113 C3
Virginia Water GU25 122 B3
Holloway Dr GU25 122 C3
Holloway La UB7 70 C4
Holly Ave GU16 152 A2
Holly Cl
Englefield Green TW20 95 A1
Farnham Common SL2 22 B4
Holly Cres SL4 66 B3
Holly Ct 8 KT16 124 A1
Holly Dr Maidenhead SL6 39 C4
Windsor SL4 67 C1
Holly Hedge Cl GU16 151 C1
Holly Hedge Rd GU16 151 C1
Holly Ho RG12 118 A2
Holly La RG8 54 A3
Holly Orch RG41 115 C3
Holly Rd RG5 88 A3
Holly Ridge GU24 153 C3
Holly Spring Cty Inf Sch
RG12 118 C4
Holly Spring Cty Jun Sch
RG12 118 C4
Holly Spring La RG12 118 B4
Holly Way GU17 150 B2
Holly Wlk SL4 93 C2
Hollybank GU24 153 C3
Hollybush Hill SL2 23 A3
Hollybush La Cookham SL6 19 A3
Iver SL0 44 A4
Sulhamstead RG7 110 C2
Hollybush Ride
Windlesham GU19,GU20 145 C3
Wokingham RG40,RG45 142 B3
Hollycombe TW20 95 B2
Hollycroft Cl UB7 71 A4
Hollycroft Gdns UB7 71 A4
Hollydale Cl RG2 86 C1
Hollyfields Cl GU15 151 A3
Hollym Cl RG6 87 C1
Holmanleaze SL6 40 A4
Holmbank Dr TW17 125 C3
Holmbury Ave RG45 143 A4
Holmdale SL2 43 B3
Holmdene RG7 111 A2
Holme Cl RG45 143 A4
Holme Park Farm La RG4 60 B1
Holmemoor Dr RG4 60 C1
Holmes Cl Ascot SL5 120 B2
Wokingham RG41 116 A2
Holmes Cres RG41 116 A2
Holmes Rd RG6 87 A3
Holmewood Cl RG41 116 A1
Holmlea Rd Datchet SL3 68 B3
Goring RG8 34 B3
Holmlea Wlk SL3 68 B3
Holmsdale Cl SL0 44 C4
Holmwood Ave RG30 84 C2
Holmwood Cl SL6 39 A3
Holsworthy Cl RG6 87 C2
Holt Comp Sch RG41 116 A4
Holt La Brightwalton RG20 49 C4
Wokingham RG41 116 A4
Holt Rd RG17 102 A1
Holt The RG8 57 B2
Holton Heath 16 RG12 118 C3
Holtspur Ave HP10 3 C4
Holtspur La HP10 3 C3
Holtwood Rd RG20 129 A3
Holy Family RC Sch SL3 43 C1
Holy Trinity CE Mid Sch
SL7 1 B2
Holy Trinity CE Sch SL5 121 A2
Holy Trinity Prim Sch
SL6 20 A4
Holybrook Cres RG30 85 A2
Holybrook Rd RG1 85 C3
Holyhook Cl RG45 143 A3
Holyport CE Prim Sch
SL6 65 A4
Holyport Manor Sch SL6 64 C3
Holyport Rd SL6 40 A1
Holyport St SL6 65 A4
Holyrood Cl RG4 59 B3
Holywell Cl TW19 97 C4
Holywell Ct RG19 106 B2
Holywell Way TW19 97 C4
Hombrook Dr RG42 117 C4
Hombrook Ho RG42 117 C4
Home Croft RG31 57 A1
Home Farm Cl
Reading RG2 86 B2
Upper Halliford TW17 125 C3
Home Farm La RG7 134 B3
Home Farm Way SL3 23 B2
Home Mdw SL2 22 B2
Home Mead Cl RG14 130 C4
Home Meadow Dr HP10 3 A4
Home Park Rd GU46 149 B3
Home Wood SL7 17 C3
Homefield Way RG17 100 B3
Homelands Way RG9 15 B1
Homer Fst Sch SL4 66 B3
Homers Rd SL4 66 B3
Homeside Cl SL6 19 C1
Homestead Rd
Maidenhead SL6 39 B2
Staines TW15 97 A1
Homewaters Ave TW16 125 C4
Homewood SL3 43 B4
Hone Hill GU47 150 A4
Honesty Bottom RG20 28 B1
Honey End La RG30 85 A3
Honey Hill
Lambourn RG17 25 A2
Wokingham RG40 117 A1
Honey La SL6 17 C1
Honey Meadow Cl RG4 59 C1
Honeybottom Rd RG26 135 A1
Honeyfields RG17 100 B3
Honeyhill Rd RG42 118 A4
Honeysuckle Cl
Crowthorne RG45 143 A4
Iver SL0 44 B4
Yateley GU46 149 A3
Honister Wlk GU15 152 B2
Honiton Rd RG2 86 B1
Honnor Rd TW18 97 B1
Hook End La RG8 34 A1
Hook La GU24 153 B3
Hook Mill La GU18 146 B1
Hookstone La GU24 153 C4
Hoops Way RG2 112 C4
Hop Gdns RG9 15 B1
Hope Ave RG12 118 C1
Hope Fountain GU15 152 A2
Hopeman Cl GU47 150 B4
Hopwood Cl RG14 105 B2
Horatio Ave RG42 118 C4
Horewood Rd RG12 118 A2
Horizon West Ind Est
RG14 105 B2
Hormer Cl GU47 143 B1
Horn St RG20 31 C3
Hornbeam Cl
Purley on T RG8 57 B3
Sandhurst GU47 143 B1
Wokingham RG41 115 B2
Hornbeam Dr RG6 87 B1
Hornbeam Gdns 7 SL1 43 A2
Hornbeam Pightle RG7 111 A2
Hornbeams RG7 139 B3
Hornby Ave RG12 118 B1
Horncastle Dr RG30 84 C3
Horndean Rd RG12 118 C2
Horne Rd Littleton TW17 125 A3
Thatcham RG19 106 C1
Hornsea Cl RG30 57 C1
Horris Hill Sch RG20 130 C2
Horse Cl The RG4 59 B2
Horse Gate Ride SL5 120 A2
Horsebrass Dr GU19 145 C1
Horseguards Dr SL6 40 A4
Horsell Ct KT16 124 A1
Horsemoor Cl SL3 44 A1
Horseshoe Cl GU15 151 C4
Horseshoe Cloisters 12
SL4 67 B3
Horseshoe Cres
Burghfield Common RG7 111 A2
Camberley GU15 151 C4
Horseshoe End RG14 131 A4
Horseshoe Hill SL1 21 B4
Horseshoe Pk RG8 56 B3
Horseshoe Rd RG8 56 B3
Horsham Rd
East Bedfont TW14 71 B1
Sandhurst GU47 143 B1
Horsnape Gdns RG42 90 A1
Horsneile La RG42 118 A4
Horton Cl SL6 20 B1
Horton Gdns SL3 68 C2
Horton Grange SL6 20 B1
Horton Rd Datchet SL3 68 B3
Horton SL3 69 A3
Poyle SL3, TW19 69 C2
Stanwell TW19 70 A1
Horton Trad Est SL3 69 A2
Hose Hill RG7,RG30 111 A4
Hosier St RG1 86 A4
Hoskins Place Ind Est
GU15 151 A2
Houlton Ct GU19 145 C1
Houston Ct 33 SL4 67 B3
Houston Way RG45 142 B3
Howard Ave SL2 42 C4
Howard Cl TW16 98 C1
Howard Ct SL8 3 A2
Howard Rd
Newbury RG14 105 A1
Wokingham RG40 116 B3
Howard St RG1 85 C4
Howarth Rd SL6 40 A3
Howe La RG42 63 C1
Howell Cl RG42 91 B1
Howgate Dr RG8 34 B4
Howorth Ct 1 RG12 118 C3
Howth Dr RG5 87 B4
Hoylake Cl SL1 41 C2
Hrmondsworth Moor
Ctry Pk UB7 70 A4
Hubbard Cl RG10 61 C1
Hubberholme RG12 118 A3
Hubert Rd SL3 43 B2
Huckleberry Cl RG8 57 B2
Huddington Glade GU46 149 A3
Hudson Rd Harlington UB3 71 B4
Woodley RG5 87 C3
Hugh Faringdon RC Sch
(Specl Resource Aspergers
Syndrome) RG30 85 B3
Hugh Fraser Dr RG31 84 B3
Hughenden Rd SL1 42 B4
Hughendon Cl SL6 39 B3
Hughes Rd Ashford TW15 98 B1
Wokingham RG40 116 C4
Hull Cl SL1 42 B2
Humber Cl
Thatcham RG18 106 A3
Wokingham RG41 115 C4
Humber Way
Sandhurst GU47 150 B4
Slough SL3 44 A1
Hummer Rd TW20 96 A2
Humphreys La RG17 47 B3
Humphries Yd RG12 118 B3
Hungerford Ave SL2 42 C4
Hungerford Cl GU47 150 B4
Hungerford Dr
Maidenhead SL6 19 C2
Reading RG1 85 C3
Hungerford Hill
East Garston RG17 47 C1
Lambourn RG17 25 A1
Hungerford La
Bradfield RG7 81 C1
Waltham St Lawrence RG10 62 C1
Hungerford Newtown
RG17 74 A2
Hungerford Prim Sch
RG17 100 B3
Hungerford Rd RG17 101 C2
Hungerford Sta RG17 100 C3
Hunstanton Cl SW3 69 B4
Hunt's La SL6 20 C2
Hunter Ct SL1 41 B4
Hunter's Ct RG5 87 C3
Huntercombe Cl SL6 41 B4
Huntercombe La N SL6 41 B4
Huntercombe La S SL6 41 B3
Hunters Chase RG4 58 C3
Hunters Hill RG7 110 C2
Hunters Mdw RG17 48 A2
Hunters Mews SL4 67 B3
Hunters Way
Shinfield RG7 113 A1
Slough SL1 41 C2
Huntingdonshire Cl
RG41 115 B3
Huntingfield Way TW20 96 B1
Huntington Cl RG6 87 C1
Huntley Ct RG1 86 C3
Huntsgreen Ct RG12 118 B4
Huntsmans Mdw SL5 119 C4
Huntsmoor Rd RG26 135 A1
Huntswood La SL1,SL6 20 C2
Hurford Dr RG19 106 C2
Hurley Ct RG12 118 C3
Hurley High St SL6 17 C2
Hurley La SL6 18 A2
Hurricane Way Slough SL3 44 B1
Woodley RG5 88 A4
Hursley Cl RG30 84 C4
Hurst Com Sch The
RG26 134 B1
Hurst Gr KT12 125 C1
Hurst La TW20 123 A3
Hurst Lodge Sch SL5 120 C1
Hurst Park Rd RG10 61 C1
Hurst Rd Slough SL1 41 B4
Twyford RG10 61 C2
Hurst Way RG2 112 C4
Hurstdene Ave TW18 97 A1
Hurstfield Dr SL6 41 A4
Hurstwood SL5 120 A2
Huscarle Way RG31 57 B2
Huson Rd RG42 91 B2
Hutsons Cl RG40 116 B4
Hutton Cl Earley RG6 87 A1
Newbury RG14 105 A2
Windlesham GU20 146 B2
Hyde Cl TW15 98 C1
Hyde End La
Brimpton RG7 133 B3
Shinfield RG7 113 B2
Hyde End Rd RG7 113 B1
Hyde Gn SL7 1 C1
Hyde La RG20 132 A1
Hyde Terr TW15 98 C1
Hydes The RG31 57 B2
Hyland Ho 10 SL8 3 A2
Hylle Cl SL4 66 C3
Hyperion Way RG2 86 A2
Hythe Cl RG12 118 C2
Hythe Cty Prim Sch TW18 96 B2
Hythe End Rd TW19 96 A3
Hythe Field Ave TW20 96 B1
Hythe Park Rd TW20 96 B1
Hythe Rd TW18 96 B2
Hythe The TW18 96 C2

I

Ian Mikardo Way RG4 59 B1
Iberian Way GU15 152 A3
Ibotson Ct SL3 69 C3
Ibstock Cl RG30 85 A4
Ibstone Ave RG4 59 C3
Icarus Ct 18 RG1 86 B4
Icknield Pl RG8 34 B4
Icknield Rd RG8 34 B4
Iden Ct RG14 105 A2
Iffley Ct TW18 96 C2
Ilbury Cl RG2 113 C3
Ilchester Cl SL6 39 B3
Ilchester Ct 6 RG14 105 A1
Ilchester Mews RG4 59 C3
Ilex Cl
Englefield Green TW20 95 A1
Silchester RG26 135 C1
Ilex Cl *continued*
Yateley GU46 149 A3
Ilfracombe Way RG6 87 C2
Ilkley Rd RG4 58 C2
Ilkley Way RG19 106 B1
Illingworth SL4 66 C2
Illingworth Ave RG4 59 C3
Illingworth Gr RG12 118 C4
Ilsley Prim Sch The RG20 30 C3
Ilsley Rd RG20 31 B2
Imperial Ct
Henley-on-T RG9 15 C1
Windsor SL4 67 A2
Imperial Ho GU25 122 C2
Imperial Rd
East Bedfont TW14 98 C4
Windsor SL4 67 A3
Imperial Way RG2 113 A4
Impstone Rd RG26 135 C1
In The Ray SL6 40 A4
Inchwood RG12 118 B1
India Rd SL1 43 A2
Ingle Dell GU15 151 B2
Ingle Glen RG40 142 A4
Ingleglen SL2 22 A4
Ingleside SL3 69 C3
Ingleton RG12 118 A3
Inglewood Ave GU15 152 B3
Inglewood Ct RG30 85 B3
Inglewood Rd RG17 101 C1
Inhurst La RG26 134 B1
Inhurst Way RG26 134 C1
Inkerman Rd SL4 41 C1
Inkpen Cl RG30 85 A2
Inkpen Prim Sch RG17 127 B3
Inkpen Rd
Hungerford RG17 100 C2
Inkpen RG17 127 A4
Kintbury RG17 102 A1
Inner Ring E TW6 71 A2
Inner Ring W TW6 71 A2
Innings La
White Waltham SL6 63 B4
Winkfield RG12 118 C4
Inniscrown Ho SL3 68 A4
Institute Rd Marlow SL7 1 C1
Taplow SL6 40 C4
Instow Rd RG6 87 A1
Invergordon Cl RG31 84 C2
Inverness Way GU47 150 B4
Invicta Cl TW14 98 C4
Inwood Cl SL6 19 A3
Iona Cres SL1 41 C4
Ipswich Rd SL1 42 A4
Irish Hill Rd RG17 102 A1
Irvine Ho SL4 66 C3
Irvine Pl GU25 122 C2
Irvine Way RG6 114 B4
Isaac Newton Rd RG2 115 A1
Isis Cl RG41 88 A1
Isis Ct RG1 59 A1
Isis Way Bourne End SL8 3 A2
Sandhurst GU47 150 B4
Island Cl TW18 96 C2
Island Farm Rd RG7 110 B1
Island Rd RG2 85 C1
Islandstone La RG10 89 A3
Islet Park Dr SL6 20 B2
Islet Park Ho SL6 20 B2
Islet Pk SL6 20 B2
Islet Rd SL6 20 B2
Isobel Ho 12 TW16 98 C1
Ivanhoe Rd RG40 141 A3
Iveagh Ct RG12 118 B2
Iver Cty Fst Sch SL0 44 C4
Iver Cty Mid Sch SL0 44 C4
Iver Lodge SL0 44 C4
Iver Sta SL0 44 C2
Iverdale Cl SL0 44 B3
Iverna Gdns TW14 71 B1
Ives Cl GU46 149 A4
Ives Rd SL3 44 A2
Ivy Cl SL6 65 A4
Ivy Cres SL1 41 C3
Ivy Dr GU18 153 A4
Ivybank RG31 57 B1
Ivydene Rd RG30 58 B1

J

Jack Price Ct 25 RG1 86 A3
Jack St RG14 105 A2
Jackson Cl RG12 118 A2
Jackson Ind Est SL8 3 A1
Jacob Cl Bracknell RG42 117 B4
Windsor SL4 66 C3
Jacob Rd GU15 151 A4
Jakes Ho SL6 40 A4
James Butcher Dr RG7 83 C2
James Cl SL7 1 C2
James Ct 21 RG30 85 B3
James Elliman Cty Inf Sch
SL2 42 C4
James Elliman Cty Mid Sch
SL2 42 C4
James Rd GU15 151 A1
James St Reading RG1 85 C4
Windsor SL4 67 B3
James Watt Rd RG2 140 C4
James Way GU15 151 A1
James's La RG7,RG30 111 C2
Jameston RG12 118 B1
Jamnagar Cl TW18 96 C1
Janson Ct RG1 85 C3
Japonica Cl RG41 115 B2
Jaques's La RG7 110 C3
Jardine Cotts SL2 23 A4

Jarratt Ho SL4 67 A2
Jarry Ct SL7 1 C2
Jarvis Dr RG10 61 B3
Jasmine Cl RG41 115 B4
Jay Cl RG6 87 A1
Jays Nest Cl GU17 150 B2
Jayworth Ho RG1 86 C4
Jedburgh Cl RG19 106 C2
Jefferson Cl
Caversham RG4 59 B4
Slough SL3 44 A1
Jeffries Ct SL8 3 A1
Jellicoe Cl SL1 42 A2
Jenkins Cl RG30 85 B3
Jenkins' Hill London Rd
GU19 145 B1
Jenner Wlk RG31 84 A4
Jennery La SL1 21 B1
Jennetts Cl RG7 81 C2
Jennings Field HP10 3 B4
Jennings Wharf SL4 67 B4
Jennys Wlk GU46 149 C3
Jerome Cl SL7 1 C2
Jerome Cnr GU47 143 B2
Jerome Rd RG5 87 C3
Jerrymoor Hill RG40 141 C4
Jesmond Dene RG14 104 C2
Jesse Cl GU46 149 C3
Jesse Terr RG1 85 C4
Jessiman Terr TW17 125 A2
Jevington RG12 118 B1
Jig's La N RG42 91 C1
Jig's La S Bracknell RG42 91 C1
Winkfield RG42 118 C4
Job's La SL6 19 A4
Jock's La Binfield RG42 90 C1
Bracknell RG42 117 C4
Joel Cl RG6 87 A2
Johannes Ct 5 RG30 85 B3
John Balliol Ct 29 RG1 86 B4
John Boys Ho RG14 130 B3
John Childs Cl RG14 105 A1
John Hunt Cl RG19 106 C1
John Kaye Ct TW17 125 A2
John Kimber's
Almshouses RG14 104 C2
John Nike Way RG12 117 B4
John Norgate Ho RG18 105 C2
John O'Gaunt Sch RG17 100 B2
John Rankin Cty Inf Sch
RG14 130 B4
John Rankin Cty Jun Sch
RG14 130 B4
John Taylor Ct SL1 42 B3
Johnson Dr RG40 142 A4
Johnsons La RG18 106 B4
Jonathan Ct SL6 39 C4
Jonathan Hill RG20 131 A2
Jonathan Miller Sch The
SL1 41 C4
Jones Cnr SL5 119 C4
Jordan Cl Caversham RG4 59 C3
Shinfield RG7 113 B1
Jordans Cl TW19 97 B4
Jordans La RG7 110 C1
Joseph Ct RG42 91 C1
Josephine Ct RG1 85 C3
Jouldings La RG7 140 B2
Jourdelay's Pas SL4 67 B4
Journeys End SL2 42 C4
Jubilee Ave
North Ascot SL5 119 C4
Wokingham RG41 116 A4
Jubilee Cl
North Ascot SL5 119 C4
Silchester RG26 135 C1
Stanwell TW19 97 B4
Jubilee Ct Bracknell RG12 118 B3
Staines TW18 97 A2
Thatcham RG19 106 A2
Jubilee Rd
Finchampstead RG40 141 C2
Littlewick Green SL6 38 A3
Newbury RG14 105 A1
Reading RG6 87 A3
Jubilee Sq RG1 86 A3
Jubilee Way TW14 98 C4
Judy's Pas SL4 42 B1
Juliet Gdns RG42 118 C4
Julius Hill RG42 118 C4
Julkes La RG2 114 C4
Junction Rd Ashford TW15 98 B2
Lightwater GU18 146 A1
Reading RG1 86 C3
Junction Terr RG14 105 B1
Juniper RG12 118 B1
Juniper Ct SL1 43 A2
Juniper Dr SL6 40 A4
Juniper Gdns TW16 98 C1
Juniper Hill Cty Comb Sch
HP10 3 A4
Juniper La HP10 3 B4
Juniper Rd SL7 1 B3
Juniper Way RG31 57 B1
Junnipers The RG41 115 B2
Jupiter Way RG41 115 C3
Justice Cl RG19 106 C1
Jutland Cl RG41 115 C3
Jutland Ho SL4 66 C3
Jutland Pl TW20 96 B2

## K

Katesgrove La RG1 86 A3
Katesgrove Prim Sch RG1 86 A3
Kathleen Saunders Ct
RG7 83 C2
Kaynes Pk SL5 119 C4
Kaywood Cl SL3 43 B2
Keane Cl RG5 87 C4
Kearsley Rd RG30 85 B3
Keates Gn RG42 118 A4
Keats Cl RG5 87 C2
Keats La SL4 67 B4
Keats Rd RG5 87 C2
Keats Way
Crowthorne RG45 143 A3
Yateley GU46 149 A2
Keble Rd SL6 39 C4
Keble Way GU47 143 C1
Keel Dr SL1 42 B2
Keeler Cl SL4 66 C2
Keep Hatch Inf Sch
RG40 116 B4
Keep Hatch Jun Sch
RG40 116 B4
Keepers Combe RG12 118 B2
Keepers Farm Cl SL4 66 C3
Keepers Terr GU25 122 A2
Keepers Wlk GU25 122 B2
Keephatch Rd RG40 116 C4
Keighley Cl RG19 106 B1
Kelburne Cl RG41 88 B2
Keldholme RG12 118 A3
Kelly Cl TW17 125 C4
Kelmscott Cl RG4 58 C2
Kelpatrick Rd SL1 41 B4
Kelsey Ave RG40 141 C3
Kelsey Cl SL6 39 B2
Kelsey Gr GU46 149 C3
Kelso Mews RG4 59 C3
Kelton Cl RG6 87 C1
Kelvedon Way RG4 58 C3
Kelvin Cl RG2 140 C4
Kelvin Rd RG14 105 A2
Kemble Ct RG31 84 B2
Kemerton Cl RG31 84 B2
Kemp Ct GU19 145 C1
Kempe Cl SL3 44 B1
Kempton Cl RG14 105 B1
Kemsley Chase SL2 22 B2
Kenavon Dr RG1 86 B4
Kendal Ave Caversham RG4 59 C3
Shinfield RG2 113 C3
Kendal Cl
East Bedfont TW14 98 C4
Slough SL2 43 A3
Thatcham RG18 106 B2
Kendal Dr SL2 43 A3
Kendal Gr GU15 152 B2
Kendrick Cl RG40 116 B3
Kendrick Ct 5 RG1 86 B3
Kendrick Girls' Gram Sch
RG1 86 B4
Kendrick Rd
Newbury RG14 130 B3
Reading RG1 86 B3
Slough SL3 43 A2
Kenilworth Ave
Bracknell RG12 118 B4
Reading RG30 85 B3
Kenilworth Ct SL1 42 C2
Kenilworth Gdns TW18 97 B2
Kenilworth Rd
TW15, TW19 97 B3
Kenneally SL4 66 B3
Kenneally Cl 11 SL4 66 B3
Kenneally Pl 12 SL4 66 B3
Kenneally Row 13 SL4 66 B3
Kenneally Wlk 10 SL4 66 B3
Kennedy Cl
Farnham Common SL2 22 B3
Maidenhead SL6 39 B3
Marlow SL7 1 C2
Newbury RG14 130 B3
Kennedy Ct TW15 98 B2
Kennedy Dr RG8 56 C3
Kennedy Gdns RG6 87 A2
Kennedy Ho SL1 41 B3
Kennel Ave SL5 119 C4
Kennel Cl SL5 92 C1
Kennel Gn SL5 119 C4
Kennel La Bracknell RG42 91 A1
Cookham SL6 19 B4
Windlesham GU20 146 B3
Kennel Lane Sch RG42 91 A1
Kennel Ride SL5 92 C1
Kennel Wood SL5 119 C4
Kennet & Avon Canal
Visitor Ctr RG7 109 B2
Kennet Cl RG19 106 C2
Kennet Ct
Hungerford RG17 100 C4
4 Newbury RG14 105 A1
Wokingham RG41 115 C3
Kennet Ctr The RG14 105 A1
Kennet Pl
Burghfield Common RG7 111 A2
Chilton Foliat RG17 73 A1
10 Newbury RG14 105 A2
Kennet Rd Kintbury RG17 102 A1
Maidenhead SL6 39 C4
Newbury RG14 104 C1
Kennet Sch RG19 106 C2
Kennet Side
Newbury RG14 105 B2
12 Reading RG1 86 B4
Kennet St RG1 86 B4
Kennet Valley Prim Sch
RG31 84 C2
Kennet Way RG17 100 C4
Kennett Rd Bourne End SL8 3 A2
Slough SL3 44 A2
Kensington Cl RG6 87 A1
Kensington Rd RG30 85 B4
Kent Ave SL1 42 B4
Kent Cl Staines TW18 97 B1
Wokingham RG41 115 B3
Kent Folly RG42 91 C1
Kent Lodge 6 SL6 39 C3
Kent Rd Reading RG30 85 B4
Windlesham GU20 146 B3
Kent Way SL6 19 C1
Kentigern Dr RG45 143 C3
Kenton Cl Bracknell RG12 118 B4
Frimley GU16 151 C1
Marlow SL7 1 C1
Kenton Rd RG6 87 B2
Kenton's La SL4 66 C3
Kentons La RG10 36 B4
Kentwood Cl RG30 57 C1
Kentwood Hill RG31 57 C1
Kenwood Cl
Harmondsworth UB7 71 A4
Maidenhead SL6 39 A4
Kenworth Gr GU18 146 A1
Keppel Spur SL4 95 A4
Keppel St SL4 67 B3
Kepple Pl GU19 145 C2
Kernham Dr RG31 57 B2
Kerria Way GU24 153 C3
Kerris Way RG6 87 A1
Kersey Cres RG14 104 C3
Kesteven Way RG41 115 C3
Keston Cl RG4 59 B1
Kestrel Ave TW18 96 C3
Kestrel Cl RG19 106 A2
Kestrel Path SL2 21 C1
Kestrel Way
Burghfield Common RG7 111 A2
Reading RG30 85 A2
Wokingham RG41 115 C3
Keswick Ave TW17 125 C3
Keswick Cl Frimley GU15 152 B2
Reading RG30 84 B4
Keswick Ct SL2 42 C3
Keswick Dr GU18 153 A4
Keswick Gdns RG5 87 C3
Keswick Rd TW20 96 A1
Ketcher Gn RG42 90 B2
Kettering Cl RG31 84 C2
Kevins Dr GU46 149 C4
Keynsham Way GU47 143 B1
Keys La SL6 39 C3
Kibble Gn RG12 118 B2
Kibblewhite Cres RG10 61 B3
Kidderminster Rd SL2 22 A1
Kidmore End Rd RG4 59 A4
Kidmore Rd RG4 58 C3
Kidwells Cl SL6 39 C4
Kidwells Park Dr SL6 39 C4
Kielder Wlk GU15 152 B2
Kier Pk SL5 120 B3
Kilburn Cl RG31 84 B2
Kildare Gdns RG4 59 B2
Killarney Dr SL6 39 C4
Killigrew Ho 4 TW16 98 C1
Killross Rd TW14 98 B4
Kilmartin Gdns GU16 151 C1
Kilmington Cl RG12 118 C1
Kilmiston Ave TW17 125 B2
Kilmiston Ho TW17 125 B2
Kilmore Dr GU15 152 A2
Kilmuir Cl GU47 150 B4
Kiln Cl Harlington UB3 71 B4
Hermitage RG18 79 B4
Kiln Croft Cl SL7 2 A2
Kiln Dr RG18 78 C3
Kiln Hill RG7 140 A4
Kiln La Bourne End SL8,HP10 3 B2
Bracknell RG12 118 A4
Mortimer RG7 137 B3
Reading RG31 84 A4
Shiplake RG9 35 B1
Sunningdale SL5 121 A2
Winkfield SL5 93 A1
Kiln Pl SL6 19 A2
Kiln Rd Caversham RG4 59 B4
Newbury RG14 105 B3
Kiln Ride
Upper Basildon RG8 54 C3
Wokingham RG40 142 A4
Kiln Ride Extension
RG40 142 A3
Kiln Terr RG18 78 C3
Kiln View Rd RG2 86 B1
Kilnsea Dr RG6 87 B1
Kilowna Cl RG10 61 A2
Kilross Rd TW14 98 C4
Kimber Cl SL4 67 A2
Kimber's Cl RG14 104 C2
Kimber's La SL6 39 C2
Kimberley RG12 118 B1
Kimberley Cl
4 Reading RG1 85 C3
Slough SL3 43 C1
Kimbers Dr Burnham SL1 21 B1
Newbury RG14 104 B3
Kimmeridge RG12 118 C2
Kimpton Cl RG6 113 C4
Kinburn Dr TW20 95 C2
King Acre Ct TW18 96 C3
King Edward Ct 14 SL4 67 B3
King Edward St SL1 42 B2
King Edward VII Ave
SL4, SL3 67 C4
King Edward VII Hospl
SL4 67 B2
King Edwards Cl SL5 119 C4
King Edwards Rd SL5 119 C4
King Edwards Rise SL5 119 C4
King George Cl TW16 98 C2
King James Way RG9 35 B4
King John's Cl TW19 68 B1
King John's Palace SL3 69 B3
King St Chertsey KT16 124 A1
Maidenhead SL6 39 C3
Mortimer RG7 137 A3
Reading RG1 86 A4
King Stable St SL4 67 B4
King Street La RG41 88 B1
King's Ave TW16 98 C1
King's Cl TW18 97 B1
King's Court Cty Fst Sch
SL4 95 A4
King's Gr SL6 39 C3
King's Keep GU47 143 A1
King's Rd Ascot SL5 120 B2
Crowthorne RG45 143 B3
Egham TW20 96 A2
Henley-on-T RG9 15 B1
Slough SL1 42 C2
Windsor SL4 67 B2
Windsor SL4 67 B3
King's Ride Bracknell SL5 119 B3
Camberley GU15 151 B4
King's Road Ho 27 SL4 67 B3
King's Wlk GU15 150 C3
Kingfisher Cl RG7 109 A2
Kingfisher Court Ind Est
RG14 105 B2
Kingfisher Ct Slough SL2 22 A1
Twyford RG10 61 C2
Kingfisher Dr
Staines TW18 96 C2
Woodley RG5 87 B3
Yateley GU46 149 A3
Kingfisher Pl RG1 86 A4
Kinghorn La SL6 19 B2
Kinghorn Pk SL6 19 B2
Kings Cl RG9 15 B1
Kings Cres GU15 151 B4
Kings La Cookham SL6 19 A4
Englefield Green TW20 95 A1
Windlesham GU20 146 C3
Kings Mead RG14 130 B3
Kings Meadow Rd RG1 86 A4
Kings Rd Caversham RG4 59 B1
Newbury RG14 105 A1
Reading RG1 86 B4
Silchester RG7 136 A1
West End GU24 153 C3
Kings Rd W RG14 105 A1
Kings Reach Ct 17 RG1 86 A4
Kings Terr SL3 69 A4
Kings Wlk 4
Maidenhead SL6 39 C4
Reading RG1 86 A4
Kings Wood SL7 17 B4
Kingsbridge Cotts RG40 142 C4
Kingsbridge Hill RG7 139 A3
Kingsbridge Rd
Newbury RG14 104 C1
Reading RG2 86 B1
Kingsbury Cres TW18 96 B2
Kingsbury Dr SL4 95 A4
Kingsclear Pk GU15 151 B2
Kingscroft Cty Inf Sch
TW18 97 A2
Kingscroft Cty Jun Sch
TW18 97 A1
Kingscroft La RG42 92 A3
Kingsdown Cl RG6 87 A1
Kingsfield SL4 66 B3
Kingsford Cl RG5 88 A3
Kingsgate Pl 20 RG1 86 B4
Kingsgate St RG1 86 B4
Kingsland Grange RG14 130 C4
Kingsley Ave
Camberley GU15 151 B2
Englefield Green TW20 95 A1
Kingsley Cl Charvil RG10 61 A3
Crowthorne RG45 143 A2
Newbury RG14 105 A3
Reading RG2 113 A4
Kingsley Dr SL7 1 B3
Kingsley Path SL2 21 B1
Kingsmere Rd RG42 117 C4
Kingston Ave TW14 71 C1
Kingston Cres TW15 97 B1
Kingston Gdns RG2 86 B1
Kingston La RG7 110 B3
Kingston Rd
Ashford TW15, TW17 97 C1
Camberley GU15 145 A1
Staines TW15, TW18 97 A1
Kingsway
Blackwater GU17 150 C3
Caversham RG4 59 C3
Farnham Common SL2 22 B3
Iver SL0 44 C4
Stanwell TW19 97 C4
Thatcham RG19 106 C1
Kingswick Cl SL5 120 B3
Kingswick Dr SL5 120 B3
Kingswood Cl TW20 95 B2
Kingswood Creek TW19 68 B1
Kingswood Ct
Maidenhead SL6 39 C3
17 Reading RG30 85 B3
Kingswood Hall of
Residence TW20 95 B2
Kingswood Ho SL1 42 B4
Kingswood Par SL7 1 B3
Kingswood Rise TW20 95 B2
Kinnaird Cl SL1 41 B4
Kinross Ave SL5 119 C2
Kinross Cl TW16 98 C2
Kinross Ct SL5 119 C2
Kinross Dr TW16 98 C2
Kinson Rd RG30 58 A1
Kintbury Rd RG17 127 C3
Kintbury Sq RG17 102 A1
Kintbury Sta RG17 102 A2
Kinver Wlk 30 RG1 86 A3
Kipling Cl Thatcham RG18 106 B3
Woodley RG5 87 C2
Yateley GU46 149 B2
Kipling Ct SL4 67 A3
Kirkby Ct GU16 151 C1
Kirkfell Cl RG31 57 B1
Kirkham Cl Caversham RG4 59 C3
Sandhurst GU47 143 B1
Kirkstall Ct RG31 84 B2
Kirkstone Cl GU15 152 B2
Kirkwall Spur SL1 42 C4
Kirkwood Cres RG7 110 C2
Kirton Cl RG30 85 A4
Kirtons Farm Rd
RG2 & RG30 85 B1
Kitsmead La GU25 122 B1
Kittiwake Cl RG5 88 A4
Kitwood Dr RG6 87 C1
Klondyke SL7 1 B1
Knapp Rd TW15 97 C2
Knapp The RG6 87 A2
Knappe Cl RG9 35 B4
Knighton Cl RG4 59 A2
Knights Cl Egham TW20 96 B1
Windsor SL4 66 B3
Knights La RG20 129 B2
Knights Lea RG20 129 A2
Knights Pl 32 SL4 67 B3
Knights Way
Caversham RG4 59 A3
Frimley GU15 152 B2
Knightsbridge Cres TW18 97 A1
Knightsbridge Dr RG19 132 A2
Knightsbridge Rd GU15 151 C4
Knightswood RG12 118 A1
Knole Wood SL5 120 C1
Knoll Cl OX12 6 C4
Knoll Park Rd KT16 123 C1
Knoll Rd GU15 151 B3
Knoll The Chertsey KT16 123 C1
Purley on T RG31 57 A1
Knollmead RG31 84 B2
Knollys Rd RG26 135 C1
Knolton Way SL2 43 B4
Knossington Cl RG6 87 B1
Knott La RG7 109 A2
Knowl Hill CE Prim Sch
RG10 37 C2
Knowl Hill Terr RG10 37 C2
Knowle Cl RG4 58 B2
Knowle Gn TW18 97 A2
Knowle Gr GU25 122 B1
Knowle Grove Cl GU25 122 B1
Knowle Hill GU25 122 B1
Knowle Park Ave TW18 97 A2
Knowle Rd RG5 87 C2
Knowles Ave RG45 142 C3
Knowsley Cl SL6 19 A1
Knowsley Rd RG31 57 B2
Knox Gn RG42 90 B2
Kola Ho SL2 43 A3
Korda Cl TW17 124 C3
Krooner Rd GU15 151 A2
Kurnool Mortar
Cross Roads GU15 151 A3
Kybes La RG7,RG30 112 B3
Kyftle Court Flat RG14 104 C1
Kyle Cl RG12 118 A3

## L

La Roche Cl SL3 43 B2
Laburnham Ct KT16 124 A1
Laburnham Rd
Maidenhead SL6 39 C3
Winnersh RG41 88 B1
Laburnum Cl SL7 1 C2
Laburnum Gdns RG2 86 C1
Laburnum Gr
Brands Hill SL3 69 A4
Newbury RG14 105 A2
Laburnum Pl TW20 95 A1
Laburnum Rd KT16 124 A1
Laburnum Way TW19 97 C4
Laburnums The GU17 150 A3
Lacewood Gdns RG2 86 C1
Lacey Cl TW20 96 B1
Ladbroke Cl RG5 87 C3
Ladbrooke Rd SL1 42 B2
Ladwell Cl RG14 130 B3
Lady Jane Ct RG4 59 B2
Lady Margaret Rd SL5 120 C1
Ladybank RG12 118 A1
Ladyday Pl SL1 42 B3
Ladymask Cl RG31 84 C2
Laffords The RG7 82 A1
Laggan Rd SL6 19 C1
Laggan Sq SL6 19 C1
Laird Ct GU19 145 C1
Lake Ave SL1 42 B3
Lake End Ct SL6 41 A4
Lake End Rd SL4,SL6 41 A3
Lake End Way RG45 143 A2
Lake Rd GU25 122 A3
Lake Side The GU17 150 B2
Lake View SL6 20 A1
Lakeland Dr GU16 151 C1
Lakes The SL7 18 A3
Lakeside
3 Bracknell RG42 118 B4

**Lakeside** *continued*
Earley RG6 .87 A2
Maidenhead SL6 .20 A1
Lakeside Bsns Pk GU47 .150 A4
Lakeside Cty Prim Sch GU16 .151 C1
**Lakeside Dr** SL2 .22 C2
Lakeside Est SL3 .70 A4
**Lakeside Rd** SL3 .69 C4
**Lalande Cl** RG41 .115 C3
Laleham CE Prim Sch TW18 .124 B4
**Laleham Rd**
Shepperton TW17 .125 A2
Staines TW18 .96 C1
**Laleham Reach** KT16 .124 A3
**Laleys Gn** RG18 .78 C2
**Lamb Cl** RG18 .106 B3
**Lambdens Hill** RG7 .109 B4
**Lambert Ave** SL3 .43 C2
**Lambert Cres** GU17 .150 B2
**Lambeth Ct** RG30 .84 C4
**Lambfields** RG7 .83 B2
**Lambly Hill** GU25 .122 C3
**Lamborne Cl** GU47 .143 A1
**Lambourn Ct** RG14 .105 A2
**Lambourn Pl** RG17 .25 A2
**Lambourn Rd** RG20 .104 B3
**Lambourne Cl** RG31 .84 B4
**Lambourne Dr**
Bagshot GU19 .145 B1
Maidenhead SL6 .39 B2
**Lambourne Gdns** RG6 .87 B2
**Lambourne Gr** RG12 .118 C4
**Lambridge La** RG9 .15 B2
**Lambridge Wood Rd** RG9 .15 A2
**Lambs La** RG7 .139 A4
Lambs Lane Prim Sch RG7 .139 A4
**Lambwood Hill** RG7 .112 B1
**Lamerton Rd** RG2 .86 B4
**Lamesley Ho** SL6 .39 C3
**Lammas Ave** 30 SL4 .67 B3
**Lammas Ct** Stanwell TW19 .96 B3
Windsor SL4 .67 B3
**Lammas Dr** TW18 .96 B2
**Lammas Mead** RG42 .90 C1
**Lammas Rd** SL1 .41 B4
**Lamorna Cres** RG31 .57 B1
**Lamp Acres** RG14 .105 A3
**Lamplighters Wlk** RG31 .84 C2
**Lamsden Way** RG7 .111 A2
**Lanark Cl** Frimley GU16 .151 C1
Woodley RG5 .88 A3
**Lancashire Hill** RG42 .91 C1
**Lancaster Ave** SL2 .22 B1
**Lancaster Cl**
Englefield Green TW20 .95 B2
8 Reading RG1 .86 B3
Stanwell TW19 .70 C1
Thatcham RG18 .106 B2
**Lancaster Ct** Reading RG2 .86 C1
Stanwell TW19 .97 C4
**Lancaster Dr** GU15 .151 B3
**Lancaster Gdns** RG6 .87 A2
**Lancaster Ho** RG12 .118 A2
**Lancaster Rd** SL6 .39 A4
**Lancaster Sq** RG17 .100 B2
**Lancastria Mews** SL6 .39 B4
**Lancelot Cl** SL1 .42 A2
**Lanchester Dr** RG45 .143 B4
**Lancing Cl** RG30 .85 B4
**Lancing Rd** TW13 .98 C3
**Landen Ct** RG40 .116 A2
**Landon Way** TW15 .98 A1
**Landrake Cres** RG2 .86 B1
**Landseer Cl** GU47 .150 C3
**Landsend La** RG10 .61 A1
**Lane End Cl** RG2 .113 C3
**Lane The** Chertsey KT16 .124 A3
Chilton OX11 .10 C4
Virginia Water GU25 .122 C3
**Laneswood** RG7 .136 C3
**Langborough Rd** RG40 .116 B3
**Langdale Cl** SL6 .40 A3
**Langdale Dr** SL5 .119 C4
**Langdale Gdns** RG6 .86 C1
**Langdon Cl** GU15 .152 B2
**Langford Cl** RG4 .59 B3
**Langham Pl** TW20 .95 C2
**Langhams Way** RG10 .36 C1
**Langley Broom** SL3 .43 C1
Langley Bsns Ctr SL3 .44 A2
Langley Bsns Pk SL3 .44 A2
**Langley Cnr** SL3 .23 C3
**Langley Common Rd**
RG2, RG40 .114 C1
**Langley Cres** UB3 .71 C4
**Langley Dr** GU15 .151 B3
Langley Gram Sch SL3 .43 C1
**Langley Hill** RG31 .84 B3
**Langley Hill Cl** RG31 .84 B3
Langley Manor Sch SL3 .43 C3
**Langley Park Rd** SL0 .44 B3
**Langley Rd** Slough SL3 .43 B2
Staines TW18 .96 C1
Langley Sta SL3 .44 A2
**Langley Way** SL7 .1 B1
Langley Wood Sec Sch SL3 .43 C2
**Langton Cl** Maidenhead SL6 .39 B4
Slough SL1 .41 B3
**Langton Way** TW20 .96 B1
**Langton's Mdw** SL2 .22 B3
**Langworthy End** SL6 .65 A4
**Langworthy La** SL6 .65 A4
**Laniver Cl** RG6 .87 A1
**Lansdowne Ave** SL1 .42 C3
**Lansdowne Ct** SL1 .42 C3
**Lansdowne Gdns** RG7 .113 B1
**Lansdowne Rd**
Reading RG30 .84 B4
Staines TW18 .97 A1
**Lanterns Wlk** SL6 .40 A4
**Lapwing Cl** RG31 .84 B3
**Larbert Cotts** SL6 .38 A3
**Larch Ave** Ascot SL5 .120 C2
Wokingham RG41 .116 A4
**Larch Cl**
Burghfield Common RG30 .111 A2
Camberley GU15 .151 C4
Newbury RG14 .104 B3
Slough SL2 .42 A4
**Larch Ct** RG4 .59 A2
**Larch Dr** RG5 .87 C3
**Larches Way** GU17 .150 A3
Larchfield Prim Sch SL6 .39 C2
**Larchfield Rd** SL6 .39 C3
**Larchmoor Pk** SL2 .23 A4
**Larchside Cl** RG7 .113 A1
**Larchwood** 13 RG12 .118 C3
**Larchwood Dr** TW20 .95 A1
**Larchwood Glade** GU15 .152 A4
**Larges Bridge Dr** RG12 .118 B3
**Larges La** RG12 .118 B4
**Larissa Cl** RG31 .57 C1
**Lark Ave** TW18 .96 C3
**Larkham Cl** TW13 .98 C3
**Larkings La** SL2 .23 A2
**Larks-Meade** RG6 .87 A1
**Larksfield** TW20 .95 B1
**Larkspur Cl** RG41 .115 B4
**Larkspur Gdns** RG18 .106 C2
**Larkswood Cl**
Reading RG31 .57 B2
Sandhurst GU47 .143 A1
**Larkswood Dr** RG45 .143 A3
**Lascelles Ho** 11 SL1 .43 A2
**Lascelles Rd** SL3 .43 A2
**Lashbrook Mead** RG9 .36 A2
**Lashbrook Rd** RG9 .36 A2
**Lassell Gdns** SL6 .40 A4
**Lasswade Ct** KT16 .123 C1
**Lasswade Rd** KT16 .123 C1
**Lastingham Ct** TW18 .97 A1
**Latham Ave** GU16 .151 C1
**Latimer** RG12 .118 A1
**Latimer Dr** RG31 .84 B2
**Latimer Rd** RG41 .116 A3
**Latton Cl** OX11 .10 C4
**Laud Cl** Newbury RG14 .105 B3
Reading RG2 .86 A3
**Laud Way** RG40 .116 C3
**Laud's Cl** RG9 .15 B1
**Lauder Cl** GU16 .151 C1
**Lauderdale Ho** TW18 .96 C2
**Launceston Ave** RG4 .59 C3
**Launcestone Cl** RG6 .87 A1
**Laundry La** GU47 .150 C3
**Lauradale** RG12 .118 A3
**Laurel Ave**
Englefield Green TW20 .95 A2
Slough SL3 .43 C2
**Laurel Cl** Camberley GU15 .151 B2
Poyle SL3 .69 C4
Wokingham RG41 .115 C3
**Laurel Dr** RG31 .84 A4
**Laurels The** RG8 .56 B3
**Laurence Ct** SL7 .1 B1
**Lauser Rd** TW19 .97 B4
**Lavender Pk** SL5 .119 B3
**Lavenham Dr** RG5 .87 C4
**Lawford Cres** GU46 .149 B3
**Lawkland** SL2 .22 B1
**Lawn Cl** SL3 .68 B4
**Lawn The** SL3 .68 B3
**Lawns The**
North Ascot SL5 .119 B3
Reading RG2 .86 B2
**Lawrence Cl** RG40 .116 B3
**Lawrence Cres** GU20 .146 B2
**Lawrence Ct** SL4 .67 B3
Lawrence Ctr RG41 .116 A2
**Lawrence Gr** RG42 .117 B4
**Lawrence Lodge** GU15 .151 B4
**Lawrence Mead** RG17 .102 A1
**Lawrence Rd** RG30 .85 A4
**Lawrence Way**
Camberley GU15 .150 C2
Slough SL1 .41 B4
**Lawrences La** RG18 .106 B3
**Lawrences Way** RG18 .106 B3
**Lawson Dr** RG4 .58 C3
**Lawson La** OX11 .10 C4
**Lawson Rd** RG9 .35 C4
**Lawson Way** SL5 .121 A2
**Laxton Gn** SL6 .39 B2
**Layburn Cres** SL3 .69 A4
**Laylands Gn** RG17 .102 A1
**Layton Rise** RG31 .57 B2
**Layton's La** TW16 .125 C4
**Lazare Ct** TW18 .96 C2
**Le Marchant Rd**
GU15, GU16 .151 C2
**Lea Cl** Marlow Bottom SL7 .1 B3
Reading RG30 .85 A2
**Lea Croft** RG45 .143 A3
Lea Fst Sch SL2 .43 A3
Lea Mid Sch SL2 .43 A3
**Lea Rd** GU15 .151 A1
**Lea The** Thorpe Lea TW20 .96 B1
Wokingham RG40 .141 C4
**Lea View** RG18 .79 B4
**Leacroft** Staines TW18 .97 A2
Sunningdale SL5 .121 A2
**Leacroft Cl** TW18 .97 A2
**Leacroft Rd** SL0 .44 C4
**Leafield Copse** RG12 .118 C3
**Leaholme Gdns** SL1 .41 B4
**Leander Pl** RG31 .84 B2
**Leas Dr** SL0 .44 C4
**Leaver Rd** RG9 .15 B1
**Leaves Gn** RG12 .118 B2
**Ledbury Cl** RG30 .58 A1
**Ledbury Dr** RG31 .84 B2
**Ledger La** SL6 .65 B3
**Ledger's Rd** SL1 .42 B2
**Ledran Cl** RG6 .87 B1
**Lee Ct** RG5 .87 C4
**Lee La** SL6 .18 C1
**Leeds Rd** SL1 .42 C3
**Lees Cl** SL6 .39 A3
**Lees Gdns** SL6 .39 A3
**Lees Wlk** SL7 .1 B1
**Leeson Gdns** SL4 .41 C1
Legoland Windsor SL4 .66 B1
**Leicester** RG12 .118 C1
**Leicester Cl** RG9 .15 B2
**Leigh Field** RG7 .136 C3
**Leigh Pk** SL3 .68 A4
**Leigh Rd** SL1 .42 A3
**Leigh Sq** SL4 .66 B3
**Leighton Ct** RG2 .86 C2
**Leighton Gdns** SL6 .20 A1
**Leighton Ho** 5 SL7 .1 C1
Leighton Park Sch RG2 .86 C2
**Leiston Cl** 7 RG6 .87 B1
**Leiston Spur** SL1 .42 C4
**Leith Cl** Crowthorne RG45 .143 A4
Slough SL1 .43 A3
**Lemart Cl** RG30 .84 C4
**Lemington Gr** RG12 .118 A2
**Leney Cl** RG40 .116 B4
**Lenham Cl** RG41 .88 C1
**Lennox Cl** RG31 .84 A2
**Lennox Rd** RG6 .87 A3
**Lent Gn** SL1 .21 A1
**Lent Green La** SL1 .21 A1
Lent Rise Cty Comb Sch SL1 .41 A4
**Lent Rise Rd** SL1 .21 A1
**Leopold Mall** 14 SL1 .42 C2
**Leopold Wlk** RG1 .86 B4
**Leppington** RG12 .118 A1
**Lerwick Dr** SL1 .42 C4
**Lesford Rd** RG1 .85 C3
**Lesley Ct** 16 RG30 .85 B3
**Leslie Southern Ct** RG14 .105 A2
**Lesters Rd** SL6 .19 B3
**Letchworth Ave** TW14 .98 C4
**Letcombe Ct** 17 RG1 .86 A3
**Letcombe Sq** RG12 .118 C3
**Letcombe St** RG1 .86 A4
**Leverkusen Rd** RG12 .118 A3
**Leverton La** RG17 .73 A1
**Lewendon Rd** RG14 .104 C3
**Lewington Mews** RG17 .100 B2
**Lewins Farm Ct** 4 SL1 .41 C3
**Lewins Way** SL1 .41 C3
**Lewis Wlk** RG14 .130 B3
**Lewisham Way** GU47 .143 B1
**Lexington Ave** SL6 .39 B3
**Lexington Gr** RG2 .113 B3
**Leyburn Cl** RG5 .88 A4
**Leycester Cl** GU20 .146 A3
**Leyland Gdns** RG2 .113 C3
**Leylands La** TW19 .70 A1
**Leys Gdns** RG14 .104 C2
**Leyside** RG45 .143 A3
**Libra Ho** HP10 .3 A4
**Library Par** RG5 .87 C4
Licensed Victuallers Sch SL5 .119 B3
**Lichfield Cl** 1 RG6 .87 B1
**Lichfield Rd** SL3 .68 B3
**Lichfields** RG12 .118 C4
**Liddell** SL4 .66 B2
**Liddell Cl** RG40 .141 C2
**Liddell Pl** SL4 .66 B2
**Liddell Sq** 14 SL4 .66 B3
**Liddell Way** Ascot SL5 .119 C2
Windsor SL4 .66 B2
**Lido Rd** OX11 .9 C4
**Lidstone Cl** RG6 .114 B4
**Liebenrood Rd** RG30 .85 B3
**Lightlands La** SL6 .19 C3
Lightwater Ctry Pk GU18 .145 C1
**Lightwater Mdw** GU18 .153 A4
**Lightwater Rd** GU18 .153 B4
Lightwater Village Sch GU18 .146 A1
**Lightwood** RG12 .118 B2
**Lilac Cl** RG8 .57 B3
**Lilac Ct** SL2 .21 C1
**Lilac Wlk** RG31 .84 B3
**Lilacs The** RG41 .115 B2
**Lilley Way** SL1 .41 C3
**Lillibrooke Cres** SL6 .39 A2
**Lily Hill Dr** RG12 .118 C4
**Lily Hill Rd** RG12 .118 C4
**Lima Ct** RG1 .85 C3
**Lime Ave** Camberley GU15 .152 A3
Winkfield SL4 .93 C3
**Lime Barn** 4 SL7 .1 B1
**Lime Cl** Newbury RG14 .105 B2
Wokingham RG41 .115 C3
**Lime Lo** 7 TW16 .98 C1
**Lime Tree Rd** RG8 .34 A3
**Lime Tree Wlk** GU25 .122 C3
**Lime Wlk** Bracknell RG12 .118 B3
Maidenhead SL6 .39 A4
**Limecroft** GU46 .149 B3
**Limefield Cl** RG6 .87 C2
**Limerick Cl** RG42 .118 A4
**Limes Cl** TW15 .98 A2
**Limes Rd** TW20 .95 C2
**Limes The** SL4 .66 B3
**Limmer Cl** RG41 .115 B2
**Limmerhill Rd** RG41 .115 C3
**Lincoln Cl** Frimley GU15 .152 A2
Winnersh RG41 .88 A2
**Lincoln Ct** Newbury RG14 .104 C1
24 Slough SL1 .42 C2
**Lincoln Gdns** RG10 .61 B3
**Lincoln Hatch La** SL1 .21 B1
**Lincoln Rd**
Maidenhead SL6 .39 A4
Reading RG2 .86 B2
**Lincoln Way**
Charlton TW16 .125 C4
Slough SL1 .41 B3
**Lincolnshire Gdns** RG42 .91 C1
**Lind Cl** RG6 .87 A1
**Lindale Cl** GU25 .121 C3
**Lindberg Way** RG5 .61 A1
**Linden** 3 Bracknell RG12 .118 C2
Slough SL3 .44 A1
**Linden Ave** SL6 .19 B1
**Linden Cl** Holyport SL6 .65 A4
Newbury RG14 .104 C2
Wokingham RG41 .115 C2
**Linden Ct**
Camberley GU15 .151 C4
Englefield Green TW20 .95 A1
**Linden Dr** SL2 .22 B2
**Linden Pl** TW18 .96 C2
**Linden Rd** Newtown RG20 .131 C2
Reading RG2 .86 C1
Woodley RG5 .87 B2
**Linden Way** TW17 .125 B2
**Lindenhill Rd** RG42 .117 C4
**Lindores Rd** SL6 .65 A4
**Lindsay Cl** TW19 .70 B1
**Lindsay Dr** TW17 .125 B2
**Lindsey Cl** RG41 .115 C3
**Lindsey Gdns** TW14 .98 B4
**Lines Rd** RG10 .88 C3
**Ling Dr** GU18 .152 C4
**Lingfield Rd** RG14 .131 B4
**Lingholm Cl**
Maidenhead SL6 .39 B3
Reading RG30 .84 C3
**Lingwood** RG12 .118 B2
**Link Ho** 2 RG14 .105 A1
**Link Rd** Datchet SL3 .68 B3
East Bedfont TW14 .98 C4
Newbury RG14 .105 A1
**Link The** Slough SL2 .43 A4
Yateley GU46 .149 B4
**Link Way** Arborfield RG2 .114 C1
Staines TW18 .97 A1
Thatcham RG18 .106 A2
**Links Dr** RG30 .85 A4
**Links Rd** Ashford TW15 .97 C2
Flackwell Heath HP10 .3 B4
**Links The** SL5 .119 C4
**Links Way** HP10 .3 A4
**Linkscroft Ave** TW15 .98 A1
**Linkswood Rd** SL1 .21 B2
**Linkway** Camberley GU15 .151 B2
Crowthorne RG45 .142 C3
**Linnet Cl** RG31 .84 A3
**Linnet La** RG20 .131 C2
**Linnet Wlk** RG41 .115 C3
**Lintott Ct** TW19 .70 B1
**Lion Cl** TW17 .124 C3
**Lipscomb Cl** RG18 .79 A3
**Lipscombe Cl** RG14 .104 C2
**Liquel Cl** RG17 .100 B2
**Liscombe** RG12 .118 A1
**Liscombe Ho** RG12 .118 A1
**Lisle Cl** RG14 .104 C3
**Lismore Cl** RG5 .87 C2
**Lismore Ct** TW18 .97 A2
**Lismore Pk** SL2 .42 C4
**Lisset Rd** SL6 .40 A3
**Lister Cl** RG8 .57 B3
**Liston Ct** 3 SL7 .1 B1
**Liston Rd** SL7 .1 B1
**Litcham Spur** SL1 .42 B4
**Lithgow's Rd** TW14, TW6 .71 C2
**Littington Cl** RG6 .114 B4
**Little Aldershot La** RG26 .134 A1
**Little Boltons** 7 SL7 .1 C1
**Little Bowden La** RG8 .55 C2
**Little Buntings** SL4 .66 C2
**Little Chapels Way** SL1 .42 A2
**Little Cl** HP10 .3 A3
**Little Copse** GU46 .149 B4
**Little Croft** GU46 .149 B2
**Little Croft Rd** RG8 .34 B3
**Little Elms** UB3 .71 B4
**Little Fryth** RG40 .142 B3
**Little Glebe** RG4 .60 C2
**Little Heath Rd** RG31 .84 A4
Little Heath Sch RG31 .84 A4
**Little Hill Rd** RG10 .88 B2
**Little Johns La** RG30 .85 B4
**Little La** RG7 .107 B3
**Little London Rd** RG7 .136 A1
Little Marlow CE Fst Sch SL7 .2 B3
**Little Marlow Rd** SL7 .1 C2
**Little Moor** GU47 .143 B1
**Little Oak Dr** RG31 .84 B4
**Little Paddock** GU15 .152 A4
**Little Ringdale** RG12 .118 C3
**Little Saffron** RG18 .79 A3
**Little St** 2 RG1 .85 C4
**Little Sutton La**
Brands Hill SL3 .69 A4
Slough, Sutton SL3 .44 B1
**Little Vigo** GU46 .149 A2
**Little Woodlands** SL4 .66 C2
**Littlebrook Ave** SL2 .41 C4
**Littlecote Dr** RG1 .85 C3
**Littlecote Rd** SN8 .99 A3
**Littlecroft Rd** 2 TW20 .95 C2
**Littledale Cl** RG12 .118 C3
**Littledown Cotts** SL1 .42 C3
**Littledown Rd** SL1 .42 C3
Littledown Sch SL1 .42 C3
**Littlefield Ct** UB7 .70 B4
**Littlefield Gn** SL6 .63 C3
**Littlejohns La** RG30 .58 B1
**Littleport Spur** SL1 .42 C4
**Littlestead Cl** RG4 .59 C3
Littleton CE Inf Sch TW17 .125 A3
**Littleton La** TW17, TW18 .124 C2
**Littleton Rd** TW15 .98 B1
Littlewick Green Montessori Sch SL6 .38 B2
**Litton Rd** RG2 .86 B1
**Liverpool Rd** Reading RG1 .86 C4
Slough SL1 .42 A4
**Livery Cl** RG1 .86 A4
**Livingstone Ct** TW19 .97 C4
**Livingstone Gdns** RG5 .87 C3
**Livingstone Rd** RG14 .105 A1
**Llangar Gr** RG45 .143 A3
**Llanvair Cl** SL5 .120 A2
**Llanvair Dr** SL5 .119 C2
**Llewellyn Pk** RG10 .61 B3
**Lochinvar Cl** SL1 .42 A2
**Lochinver** RG12 .118 A1
**Lock Ave** SL6 .20 B1
**Lock Bridge Rd** SL8 .3 A2
**Lock La** SL6 .39 B2
**Lock Mead** SL6 .20 B1
**Lock Path** SL4 .66 B4
**Lock Pl** RG1 .86 B4
**Lock Rd** SL7 .1 C1
**Lockbridge Ct** SL6 .40 B4
**Locke Gdns** SL3 .43 B2
**Lockets Cl** SL4 .66 B3
**Lockram La** RG7 .111 B1
**Locks Ride** SL5 .92 B1
**Lockside Ct** RG7 .109 B2
**Locksley Ct** 25 SL1 .42 C2
**Lockstile Mead** RG8 .34 B3
**Lockstile Way** RG8 .34 B3
**Lockton Chase** SL5 .119 B3
**Lockton Ho** RG40 .116 B3
**Loddon Bridge Rd** RG5 .87 C3
**Loddon Cl** GU15 .152 A3
**Loddon Dr** Charvil RG10 .61 A4
Maidenhead SL6 .39 B4
**Loddon Hall Rd** RG10 .61 C3
Loddon Inf Sch The RG6 .87 B2
Loddon Jun Sch RG6 .87 B2
**Loddon Rd** SL8 .3 A2
**Loddon Spur** SL1 .42 C4
**Loddon Vale Ctr** RG5 .88 A4
**Lodge Cl**
Englefield Green TW20 .95 B2
Marlow SL7 .1 C1
Slough SL1 .42 B2
**Lodge Gr** GU46 .149 C3
**Lodge Rd** RG10 .88 C4
**Lodge The** RG14 .105 A2
**Lodge Way** Ashford TW15 .97 C3
Charlton TW17 .125 B4
Windsor SL4 .66 C2
**Lodgings of the Military Knights** 18 SL4 .67 B3
**Logan Cl** RG30 .84 C4
**Lois Dr** TW17 .125 A2
**Lomond Ave** RG4 .59 C3
**London Rd** Ascot SL5 .120 B3
Ashford TW15, TW18, TW19, TW14 .97 B3
Bagshot GU15,GU19 .145 B1
Blackwater GU15,GU17 .150 C2
Blewbury OX11 .11 C4
Bracknell RG12, SL5 .119 B3
Bracknell, Binfield RG12, RG42 .117 B4
Brands Hill SL3 .69 A4
Camberley GU15 .151 B3
Datchet SL3 .68 B4
Earley RG6 .87 A4
Englefield Green TW20 .95 B1
Newbury RG14 .105 B2
Reading RG1 .86 B4
Slough SL3 .43 C1
Sunningdale, Blacknest SL5 .121 A3
Sunningdale, Shrubs Hill SL5, GU25 .121 B2
Thatcham RG18 .106 C2
Twyford RG10 .61 C3
Virginia Water GU25, TW20 .122 A4
Windlesham GU19,GU20,SL5 GU19,GU20,SL5 .146 B4
Woodley RG4,RG5 .60 B1
**London St** Chertsey KT16 .124 A1
Reading RG1 .86 A4
**Loneacre** GU20 .146 C2
**Long Barn La** RG2 .86 B2
**Long Cl**
Farnham Common SL2 .22 A3
Kintbury RG17 .102 A1
Long Close Sch SL3 .43 A2
**Long Dr** SL1 .21 B1
**Long Furlong Dr** SL2 .21 C1
**Long Gr** RG26 .134 B1

**Long Grove** RG7 107 B3
**Long Half Acre** SL6 38 A2
**Long Hedge** RG17 25 B1
**Long Hill Rd** RG12, SL5 119 A4
**Long La** Brightwalton RG20 28 C2
Cookham SL6 19 B3
Hermitage RG14, RG18 78 C1
Holyport, Braywoodside SL6 64 B2
Holyport, Touchen-end SL6 64 C3
Newbury RG18 105 B4
Purley on T RG31 57 A2
Stanwell TW15, TW19 97 C4
Long Lane Prim Sch
RG31 57 A2
**Long Mickle** GU47 143 A1
**Long Readings La** SL2 22 A1
**Long Water Dr** RG30 112 B4
**Long Wlk The** SL4 94 B4
**Long's Way** RG40 116 C4
**Longacre** RG14 130 B4
**Longbourne Way** KT16 123 C2
**Longbridge Rd** RG19 106 C1
**Longcroft Rd** RG19 106 C1
Longcross Sta GU25 121 C1
**Longdon Rd** RG41 88 B1
**Longdown Lodge** GU47 150 A4
**Longdown Rd** GU47 143 A1
**Longfield Rd** RG10 61 B3
**Longford Ave**
Feltham TW14 71 C1
Stanwell TW19 97 C4
**Longford Cl** GU15 151 B2
**Longford Rdbt** TW6, UB7 70 A3
Longford Sch TW14 98 C4
**Longford Way** TW19 97 C4
**Longhurst Cl** RG4 59 B2
**Longlands Way** GU15 152 B3
**Longleat Dr** RG31 57 A2
**Longleat Gdns** SL6 39 B3
**Longleat Way** TW14 98 B4
**Longmead** Ball Hill RG20 129 C1
Windsor SL4 66 C3
**Longmead La** SL1 21 B3
**Longmeadow** GU15, GU16 151 C2
**Longmoor La** RG7 137 A4
**Longmoors** RG42 117 C4
**Longmore Rd** RG2 113 B3
**Longridge Cl** RG30 85 A4
Longridge Scout Boating
Activity Ctr SL7 18 C4
Longshot Ind Est RG12 117 C4
**Longshot La** RG12 117 C4
**Longside Cl** TW20 123 B4
**Longview** HP9 3 C4
**Longwater Dr** RG30 85 C1
**Longwater La** RG27,RG40 141 C2
**Longwater Rd**
Bracknell RG12 118 B2
Finchampstead RG40 141 C1
**Longworth Ave** RG31 84 A4
**Longworth Dr** SL6 20 B1
**Lonsdale Cl** SL6 20 A1
**Lonsdale Way** SL6 40 B1
Look Out Discovery Ctr
The RG12 118 B1
**Loosen Dr** SL6 39 A2
**Lord Knyvett Cl** TW19 70 B1
**Loring Rd** SL4 66 C3
**Lorne Cl** SL1 42 A2
**Lorne Pl** RG1 85 C4
**Lorne St** RG1 85 C4
Lorraine Cty Inf Sch
GU15 151 C4
**Lorraine Rd** GU15 151 C4
**Lory Ridge** GU19 145 C2
**Losfield Rd** SL4 66 C3
**Loughborough** RG12 118 C2
**Loundyes Cl** RG18 106 A2
**Lovatt Cl** RG31 84 A4
**Love Green La** SL0 44 C4
**Love Hill La** SL3 44 A3
**Love La** Iver SL0 44 B4
Newbury RG14 105 A3
**Lovedean Ct** RG12 118 C2
**Lovegrove Dr** SL2 21 C1
**Lovejoy La** SL4 66 B3
**Lovel La** SL5 93 A2
**Lovel Rd** SL5 93 A2
**Lovelace Cl** SL6 17 C2
**Lovelace Rd** RG12 117 C3
**Lovell Cl** RG9 35 B4
**Lovells Cl** GU18 146 A1
**Loverock Rd** RG30 58 B1
**Loves Cl** RG7 111 A2
**Loves Wood** RG7 136 C3
**Lovett Gdns** SL6 20 B2
**Lovett Rd** TW20 96 B2
**Lowbrook Dr** SL6 39 A2
Lowbrook Prim Sch SL6 39 A2
**Lowbury** RG12 118 C3
**Lower Armour Rd** RG31 57 B1
**Lower Bglws** RG8 34 B4
**Lower Boyndon Rd** SL6 39 C3
**Lower Britwell Rd** SL2 21 B1
**Lower Broadmoor Rd**
RG45 143 B2
**Lower Brook St** RG1 86 A3
**Lower Canes** GU46 149 A3
**Lower Charles St** GU15 151 B3
**Lower Church Rd** GU47 149 C4
**Lower Cippenham La** SL1 41 C3
**Lower Common** RG27 140 C1
**Lower Cookham Rd** SL6 20 B1
**Lower Earley Way** RG6 114 B4
**Lower Earley Way (N)**
RG6 87 C1
**Lower Earley Way (W)**
RG6 113 C4
**Lower Elmstone Dr** RG31 57 B1
**Lower Farm Ct** RG19 105 C1
**Lower Field Rd** RG1 86 A3
**Lower Henley Rd** RG4 59 B2
**Lower Lees Rd** SL2 22 A1
**Lower Meadow Rd** RG2 86 B1
**Lower Mill Field** GU19 145 B1
**Lower Mount** RG1 86 B3
**Lower Pound La** SL7 1 B1
**Lower Rd** Chilton OX11 10 B4
Cookham SL6 19 C4
**Lower Ridge** SL8 3 A2
**Lower Sandhurst Rd**
RG40,GU47 142 B1
**Lower Ventnor Cotts** SL6 19 B4
**Lower Village Rd** SL5 120 B2
**Lower Way** RG19 106 A2
**Lower Wokingham Rd**
RG40, RG45 142 B3
**Lowes Cl** RG9 36 A2
**Lowestoft Cl** RG6 87 B1
**Lowestoft Dr** SL1 41 B4
**Loweswater Wlk** GU15 152 B2
**Lowfield Cl** GU18 153 A4
**Lowfield Ct** RG4 59 B3
**Lowfield Gn** RG4 59 C2
**Lowfield Rd** RG4 59 B3
**Lowlands Rd**
Blackwater GU17 150 B2
Stanwell TW19 70 B1
**Lowry Cl** GU47 150 B3
**Lowther Cl** RG41 115 C4
**Lowther Rd** RG41 115 C4
**Loxwood** RG6 87 B1
**Loxwood Cl** TW14 98 C4
**Lucan Dr** TW18 97 B1
**Lucas Cl** GU46 149 B3
**Lucas Gn** GU24 153 B2
**Lucas Green Rd** GU24 153 C3
**Lucey Cl** RG31 57 A2
**Lucie Ave** TW15 98 A1
Luckley Oakfield Sch
RG40 116 A2
**Luckley Path** RG40 116 B3
**Luckley Rd** RG41 116 A2
**Luckley Wood** RG41 116 A2
**Luckmore Dr** RG6 87 A2
**Lud Lodge** TW15 97 C3
**Luddington Ave**
GU25, TW20 122 C4
Ludgrove Prep Sch
RG40 116 B2
**Ludlow** RG12 118 A1
**Ludlow Cl** RG14 105 C3
**Ludlow Ho** SL6 39 C3
**Ludlow Rd** SL6 39 C3
**Luff Cl** SL4 66 C2
**Luker Ave** RG9 15 B2
**Lulworth Rd** RG2 113 B4
**Lunds Farm Rd** RG5 88 A4
**Lundy Ct** SL1 41 C3
**Lundy La** RG30 85 B4
**Lupin Cl** GU19 145 B1
**Lupin Ride** RG45 143 A4
**Luscombe Cl** RG4 59 B2
**Lutman La** SL6 19 C1
**Lutmans Haven** RG10 37 C3
**Lutterworth Cl** RG42 91 B1
**Lutton Cl** RG6 113 C4
**Lych Gate Cl** GU47 149 C4
**Lycroft Cl** RG8 34 B4
**Lydbury** RG12 118 C3
**Lydford Ave** SL2 42 B4
**Lydford Rd** RG1 86 C3
**Lydney** RG12 118 A1
**Lydsey Cl** SL2 22 A1
**Lyefield Ct** RG4 59 A3
**Lyell Place E** SL4 66 B2
**Lyell Place W** SL4 66 B2
**Lyell Rd** SL4 66 B2
**Lyell Walk E** SL4 66 B2
**Lyell Walk W** SL4 66 B2
**Lyme Gr** RG31 57 B1
**Lymington Ave** GU46 149 B3
**Lymington Gate** RG4 58 C3
**Lynch Hill La** SL2 21 C1
Lynch Hill Sch SL2 21 C1
**Lynch La** RG17 25 A2
**Lynchets View** RG17 24 C3
**Lynden Mews** RG2 86 A3
**Lyndhurst Ave**
Blackwater GU17 150 B3
Cookham SL6 19 C3
**Lyndhurst Cl** RG12 119 A3
**Lyndhurst Rd** Ascot SL5 120 A3
Goring RG8 34 B3
Reading RG30 58 A1
Lyndhurst Sch GU15 151 A3
**Lyndwood Dr** SL4 68 A1
**Lyndwood Par** SL4 68 A1
**Lyne Cl** GU25 122 C2
**Lyne Crossing Rd**
KT16, GU25 123 A2
**Lyne Ct** GU25 122 C1
**Lyne La** KT16,TW20,GU25 123 A2
**Lyne Place Manor** GU25 122 C1
**Lyne Rd** GU25 122 C2
**Lynegrove Ave** TW15 98 B2
**Lyneham Gdns** SL6 19 A1
**Lyneham Rd** RG45 143 A3
**Lynmouth Ct** RG1 59 A1
**Lynmouth Rd** RG1 59 A1
**Lynn Cl** TW15 98 B2
**Lynton Cl** RG5 87 B3
**Lynton Ct** 4 RG14 105 A2
**Lynton Gn** SL6 39 C4
**Lynwood Ave** Egham TW20 95 C1
Slough SL3 43 B2
**Lynwood Chase** 1 RG12 118 B4
**Lynwood Cres** SL5 120 C2
**Lynwood Ct** TW15 97 C2
**Lynwood Flats** SL5 120 C2
**Lyon Cl** RG19 106 C1
**Lyon Oaks** RG42 91 A1
**Lyon Rd** RG45 143 B3
**Lyon Sq** RG30 85 A4
**Lyon Way** GU16 151 B1
Lyon Way Ind Est GU16 151 B1
**Lysander Cl** RG5 88 A4
**Lysander Mead** SL6 40 B4
**Lytchet Minster Cl** 4
RG12 118 C2
**Lytham** RG12 117 C2
**Lytham Cl** RG30 85 B2
**Lytham Ct** SL5 120 B2
**Lytham End** RG31 57 A2
**Lytham Rd** RG5 87 C4

## M

**Macadam Ave** RG45 143 B4
**Macbeth Ct** RG42 118 C4
**Macdonald Rd** GU18 153 A4
**Mace Cl** RG6 87 A1
**Mackay Cl** RG31 84 C2
Mackenzie Mall 10 SL1 42 C2
**Mackenzie St** 9 SL1 42 C2
**Macklin Cl** RG17 100 B3
**Macnaughton Woods**
GU15 151 C3
**Macphail Cl** RG40 116 C4
**Macrae Rd** GU46 149 B3
**Maddle Rd** RG17 24 B4
**Madeira Pl** 3 RG14 105 A1
Madejski Stad RG2 112 C4
**Madingley** RG12 118 A1
**Madox Brown End** GU47 150 C3
**Mafeking Rd** TW19 96 A3
**Magdalene Rd**
Littleton TW17 124 C3
Sandhurst GU47 143 C1
**Magill Ct** RG7 113 A1
**Magna Carta La** TW19 95 C4
Magna Carta Sch TW18 96 B1
**Magna Rd** TW20 95 A1
**Magnolia Cl** GU47 143 B1
**Magnolia Ct** RG5 88 A4
**Magnolia Gdns** SL3 43 B2
**Magnolia Way** RG41 115 C3
**Magpie Cl** RG19 106 A2
**Magpie Way** Reading RG31 84 A3
Slough SL2 21 C1
**Maguire Dr** GU16 152 B2
**Mahonia Cl** GU24 153 C3
Maiden Erlegh Comp Sch
RG6 87 A2
**Maiden Erlegh Dr** RG6 87 A2
**Maiden Lane Ctr** 5 RG6 87 B1
**Maiden Pl** RG6 87 B1
**Maiden's Gn** SL4 92 A3
Maidenhead Coll Claires
Court Girls SL6 39 C4
**Maidenhead Court Pk**
SL6 20 A2
Maidenhead Office Pk
SL6 38 C1
**Maidenhead Rd**
Binfield RG40 89 B2
Cookham SL6 19 C3
Newell Green RG42 91 A3
Windsor SL4 66 C4
Maidenhead Sta SL6 39 C3
**Maidensfield** RG41 88 B1
**Main Dr** Bracknell RG42 91 C1
Iver SL0 44 C2
Winkfield RG12, SL5 119 A4
**Main St** Chilton OX11 10 B4
Greenham RG19 131 C3
Newtown RG19 132 A3
Yateley GU46 149 B4
**Mainprize Rd** RG12 118 C4
**Mainstone Rd** GU24 153 C2
**Maise Webster Cl** TW19 97 B4
**Maitland Rd** RG1 85 C4
**Maiwand Gdns** RG31 84 B4
**Maize La** RG42 91 C1
**Majendie Cl** RG14 104 B3
**Major's Farm Rd**
Brands Hill SL3 69 A4
Datchet SL3 68 B4
**Makepiece Rd** RG42 91 A1
**Maker Cl** RG30 85 A2
**Makins Rd** RG9 35 A4
**Malders La** SL6 19 B2
**Maldon Cl** RG30 85 B3
**Malet Cl** TW20 96 B1
**Malham Fell** RG12 118 A3
**Malham Rd** RG19 106 B2
**Mallard Cl** Earley RG6 87 A2
Twyford RG10 61 C2
**Mallard Ct** RG14 104 C2
**Mallard Dr** SL1 41 C3
**Mallard Row** RG1 86 A4
**Mallard Way**
Padworth RG7 109 A2
Yateley GU46 149 A3
**Mallards The**
Frimley GU16 151 C1
Great Shefford RG17 48 A2
Laleham TW18 124 A4
**Mallards Way** GU18 153 A4
**Mallory Ave** RG4 59 B3
**Mallow Pk** SL6 19 B1
**Mallowdale Rd** RG12 118 C1
**Malone Rd** RG5 87 B3
**Malpas Rd** SL2 43 A3
**Malt Hill** Egham TW20 95 C2
Newell Green RG42 91 C3
**Malt Ho** SL4 95 A4
**Malt House Cl** SL4 95 A4
**Malt Shovel La** RG17 24 C2
**Maltby Way** RG6 114 A4
**Malthouse Cl** RG19 106 C1
**Malthouse La** 8
Reading RG1 85 C4
West End GU24 153 C4
**Malthouse Way** 7 SL7 1 B1
**Maltings Pl** 8 RG1 86 A4
**Maltings The** Staines TW18 96 C2
Thatcham RG19 106 C1
West Ilsley RG20 10 A1
**Malton Ave** SL1 42 A3
**Malvern Cl** RG5 87 C3
**Malvern Ct** Brands Hill SL3 69 A4
Newbury RG14 104 C1
Reading RG1 86 B3
**Malvern Rd** Harlington UB3 71 C4
Maidenhead SL6 19 B1
**Malvern Way** RG10 61 B4
**Malyons The** TW17 125 B2
**Man's Hill** RG7 111 B1
**Managua Cl** RG4 59 C1
**Manchester Rd** RG1 86 C4
**Mandarin Ct** RG14 105 B1
**Mandela Ct** 15 RG1 86 B4
**Mandeville Cl** RG30 84 C3
**Mandeville Ct** TW20 96 A2
**Mandeville Rd** TW17 125 A2
**Manea Cl** RG6 114 B4
**Manfield Cl** SL2 22 A1
**Manners Rd** RG5 87 B4
**Mannock Way** RG5 88 A4
**Manor Bglws** RG20 31 B2
**Manor Cl** RG42 91 A1
**Manor Cres** RG20 31 B2
**Manor Ct** Marlow SL7 1 B2
Slough, Cippenham SL1 41 C3
29 Slough, Upton Park SL1 42 C2
**Manor Farm Ave** TW17 125 A2
**Manor Farm Cl** SL4 66 C2
**Manor Farm Cotts** SL4 68 A1
**Manor Farm Ct** TW20 96 A2
**Manor Farm Ho** SL4 66 C2
**Manor Farm La**
Egham TW20 96 A2
Tidmarsh RG8 56 B1
**Manor Farm Rd** RG2 86 A1
**Manor Gdns** HP10 3 C3
**Manor Gr** SL6 65 B3
**Manor House Dr** SL5 93 A1
**Manor House La** SL3 68 A3
**Manor House The** GU15 151 B3
**Manor La** Chieveley RG20 51 A1
Harlington UB3 71 B4
Hermitage RG18 79 A4
Leckhampstead RG20 49 C2
Maidenhead SL6 39 C2
Newbury RG14 105 C3
**Manor Leaze** TW20 96 A2
**Manor Park Cl** RG30 84 B3
**Manor Park Dr**
Wokingham RG40 141 C3
Yateley GU46 149 B3
**Manor Pk** Froxfield SN8 99 A2
Staines TW18 96 B3
**Manor Pl** Newbury RG14 104 B3
Staines TW18 97 A2
Manor Prim Sch RG30 85 A2
**Manor Rd** Ashford TW15 98 A2
Goring RG8 34 A3
Henley-on-T RG9 35 B3
Letcombe Bassett OX12 7 B3
Maidenhead SL6 39 C2
Walton-on-T KT12 125 C1
Whitchurch-on-T RG8 56 B4
Windsor SL4 66 C3
Wokingham RG41 116 A1
**Manor Way** Bagshot GU19 145 C2
Egham TW20 95 C1
Holyport SL6 65 A4
**Manor Wood Gate** RG9 36 A2
Manorcroft Sch TW20 96 A1
**Manorcrofts Rd** TW20 96 A1
**Manse Cl** UB3 71 B4
**Mansel Cl** SL2 43 A4
**Mansell Cl** SL4 66 C3
**Mansell Ct** RG2 86 C1
**Mansell Dr** RG14 130 B3
**Mansfield Cl** SL5 119 B4
**Mansfield Cres** RG12 118 A2
**Mansfield Pl** SL5 119 B4
**Mansfield Rd**
Reading RG1 85 C3
Wokingham RG41 116 A3
**Mansion House St** 24
RG14 105 A2
**Mansion La** SL0 44 B3
**Manston Dr** RG12 118 B2
**Mant Cl** RG20 75 B3
**Manygate La** TW17 125 B2
**Mapel Ct** 11 RG12 118 C3
**Maple Cl** Blackwater GU17 150 B3
Maidenhead SL6 39 B3
Sandhurst GU47 142 C1
Winnersh RG41 88 B2
**Maple Cres**
Newbury RG14 105 A2
Slough SL2 43 A3
**Maple Ct**
Englefield Green TW20 95 A1
Goring RG8 34 A3
Marlow SL7 1 C2
Windsor SL4 67 B2
**Maple Dr**
Crowthorne RG45 143 B4
Lightwater GU18 152 C4
**Maple Gdns** Reading RG2 86 C1
Stanwell TW19 97 C3
Yateley GU46 149 B3
**Maple La** RG8 55 A3
**Maple Rise** SL7 1 C2
**Mapledene** RG4 58 C2
**Mapledurham Dr** RG8 57 B3
Mapledurham Ho RG31 57 C3
**Mapledurham View** RG31 57 B1
Mapledurham Watermill
RG31 57 C3
**Mapledurham Wlk** SL6 19 C2
**Maples The** 15 SL8 3 A2
**Maplin Pk** SL3 44 A2
**Marathon Cl** RG5 88 A4
**Marbeck Cl** SL4 66 B3
**Marbull Way** RG42 91 A1
**Marchant Cl** RG19 131 B4
**Marchant Ct** SL7 2 A2
**Marcheria Cl** RG12 118 A2
**Marchwood Ave** RG4 59 B4
**Marcia Ct** SL1 41 C3
**Marconi Rd** RG14 105 A2
**Marcus Cl** RG30 85 A4
**Mardale** GU15 152 B2
**Mardy** RG4 58 C3
**Mare La** RG10 63 C2
**Marefield** RG6 87 B1
**Marefield Rd** SL7 1 B1
**Marescroft Rd** SL2 21 C1
**Mareshall Ave** RG42 91 A1
**Marfleet Cl** RG6 87 C1
**Margaret Cl** Reading RG2 113 B4
Staines TW18 97 B1
**Maria Ct** 15 RG30 85 B3
**Marie Davis Ct** 21 RG1 86 A4
**Marigold Cl** RG45 142 C3
**Marina Cl** KT16 124 B1
**Marina Way** SL1 41 B3
**Mariners La** RG7 82 A2
**Marino Way** RG40 141 A3
**Marion Ave** TW17 125 A2
**Marish Ct** SL3 44 A2
Marish Cty Fst Sch SL3 44 A2
Marish Jun Sch SL3 44 A2
Marish Wharf Ind Est SL3 43 C2
Marjory Kinnon Sch
TW14 71 C1
**Markby Way** RG6 87 C1
**Market La** SL3 44 B2
**Market Pl** Colnbrook SL3 69 B4
Henley-on-T RG9 15 B1
25 Newbury RG14 105 A2
Reading RG1 86 A4
Wokingham RG40 116 B3
**Market Sq** Marlow SL7 1 B1
Staines TW18 96 C2
**Market St** Bracknell RG12 118 A4
Maidenhead SL6 39 C4
Newbury RG14 105 A1
18 Windsor SL4 67 B3
**Market Way** 15 RG1 86 A4
Markham Centre
Trad Est The RG7 83 C1
**Markham Ct** GU15 151 B3
**Markham Mews** RG40 116 B3
**Marks Rd** RG41 116 A4
**Marlborough Ave** RG1 86 B3
**Marlborough Cl** SL6 39 A3
**Marlborough Ct**
Reading RG1 85 C3
Slough SL1 41 C4
Wokingham RG40 116 B4
**Marlborough Ho**
5 Maidenhead SL6 39 C3
Reading RG1 86 B3
**Marlborough Rd**
Ashford TW15 97 C2
Maidenhead SL6 39 A3
Slough SL3 43 C1
**Marlborough Rise** GU15 151 C3
**Marlborough Way** RG31 84 A2
**Marley Croft** TW18 96 C3
**Marlin Cl** TW16 98 C1
**Marlin Ct** SL7 1 B1
**Marling Cl** RG31 57 B1
**Marlow Bottom** SL7 1 B3
**Marlow Bridge La** SL7 18 C4
Marlow CE Inf Sch SL7 1 B2
Marlow Com Hospl SL7 1 C1
**Marlow Lodge** 13 SL6 39 C3
**Marlow Mill** SL7 1 C1
**Marlow Rd** Bisham SL7 18 B4
Bisham SL6 18 C2
Henley-on-T RG9 15 C2
Little Marlow SL7,SL8 2 B3
Maidenhead SL6 39 C4
Marlow Bottom SL7 1 A4
Marlow Sta SL7 1 C1
**Marlowes The** RG14 130 C4
**Marlston Rd** RG18 79 B3
**Marmion Rd** RG9 35 C4
**Marquis Pl** RG1 86 C4
**Marriott Cl** TW14 71 B1
**Mars Cl** RG41 115 C3
**Marsack St** RG4 59 B1
**Marsh Ct** RG30 85 B4
**Marsh La**
Hungerford RG17 100 A3
Newbury RG14 105 A2
Taplow SL6 40 C3
**Marsh Rd** RG18 106 C2

Marshall Cl Frimley GU16 .152 B1
Purley on T RG8 .57 B2
Marshall Ho 4 RG30 .85 A4
Marshall Rd GU47 .150 B3
Marshalls Ct RG14 .104 B3
Marsham Ho RG42 .91 A1
Marshaw Ct RG2 .86 B2
Marshfield SL3 .68 B3
Marshgate Trad Est SL6 .41 A4
Marshland Sq RG4 .59 A3
Marshwood Rd GU18 .153 B4
Marston Dr RG14 .105 B3
Marston Way SL5 .119 C4
Martel Cl GU15 .152 B4
Marten Pl RG31 .57 A2
Martin Cl Windsor SL4 .66 B3
Woodley RG5 .87 C3
Martin Rd Maidenhead SL6 .39 C4
Slough SL1 .42 C2
Martin Way GU16 .151 C1
Martin's Heron Sta RG12 .118 C3
Martin's Plain SL2 .22 C2
Martindale Ave GU15 .152 B2
Martineau La RG10 .88 C4
Martins Cl GU17 .150 B2
Martins Dr RG41 .116 A4
Martins La RG12 .118 C3
Martins The RG19 .106 C1
Marunden Gn SL2 .21 C1
Mary Drew Almshouse The TW20 .95 B1
Mary Hare Gram Sch for the Deaf The RG18 .77 C2
Mary Mead RG42 .91 B1
Mary Morgan Ct SL2 .42 B4
Maryland RG40 .141 C4
Maryside SL3 .43 C2
Mascoll Path SL2 .21 C1
Masefield Gdns RG45 .143 A2
Masefield Rd RG18 .106 B2
Masefield Way TW19 .97 C4
Mason Cl GU46 .149 C3
Mason Ct Ball Hill RG20 .129 C1
6 Reading RG1 .85 C4
Mason Pl GU47 .149 C4
Mason St RG1 .85 C4
Mason's Ct SL1 .41 C3
Masonic Hall Rd KT16 .123 C2
Masons Rd SL1 .41 C3
Master Cl RG5 .88 A4
Mathisen Way SL3 .69 C3
Matlock Rd RG4 .58 C2
Matson Dr RG9 .15 C1
Matthew Arnold Cl TW18 .97 B1
Matthew Arnold Sch The TW18 .97 B1
Matthews Chase RG42 .90 C1
Matthews Cl RG19 .106 A2
Matthews Ct SL5 .120 B3
Matthews La TW18 .96 C2
Matthews Rd GU15 .151 B4
Matthewsgreen Rd RG41 .116 A4
Maudsley Ho SL6 .40 A4
Maultway Cl GU15 .152 A4
Maultway Cres GU15 .152 A4
Maultway N GU15 .145 A1
Maultway The GU15, GU16 .152 B3
Mawbray Cl RG6 .87 B1
Maxine Cl GU47 .143 A1
Maxwell Cl RG5 .87 C4
Maxwell Rd TW15 .98 B1
May Cl 2 GU47 .150 B4
May Fields RG41 .115 A4
May Pk RG31 .84 C2
May Tree Cl SL7 .1 B3
May's La RG7 .136 A4
Maybrick Cl GU47 .142 C1
Maybury Cl SL1 .41 B4
Mayfair RG30 .84 B4
Mayfair Dr RG14 .104 C1
Mayfield Ave RG31 .84 A2
Mayfield Cl TW15 .98 A1
Mayfield Cotts RG20 .31 B2
Mayfield Dr RG4 .59 B2
Mayfield Gdns TW18 .96 C1
Mayfield Rd
Camberley GU15 .151 A1
Wooburn Green HP10 .3 C3
Mayflower Ct 16 RG1 .86 A4
Mayflower Dr GU46 .149 A4
Mayflower Way SL2 .22 B4
Maynard Cl RG18 .106 B3
Maynard Ct Staines TW18 .97 A2
Windsor SL4 .67 A3
Mayors La RG14 .105 A1
Mayow Cl RG19 .106 C1
Maypole Rd SL6 .41 A4
Mays Cl RG6 .87 A3
Mays La RG6 .87 A3
Mays Rd RG40 .116 C3
Maywood Dr GU15 .152 A4
McCarthy Way RG40 .141 C4
McCraes Wlk RG10 .36 B1
Mckay Trad Est SL3 .69 C3
McNair Cl RG6 .87 A1
Meachen Ct RG40 .116 B3
Mead Ave SL3 .44 A2
Mead Cl Egham TW20 .96 A1
7 Marlow SL7 .1 C2
Peasemore RG20 .50 B4
Reading RG31 .84 A3
Slough SL3 .44 A2
Mead Ct TW20 .96 B1
Mead Haze SL6 .20 B1
Mead La Chertsey KT16 .124 B1
Lower Basildon RG8 .34 C1
Upper Basildon RG8 .55 B3
Mead The RG17 .48 A2
Mead Way SL1 .41 B4
Mead Wlk SL3 .44 A2
Meade Ct GU19 .145 C2
Meadfield Ave SL3 .44 A2
Meadfield Rd SL3 .44 A2
Meadhurst Pk TW16 .98 C1
Meadhurst Rd KT16 .124 A1
Meadhurst Sports Club TW16 .98 C2
Meadow Bank 16 SL8 .3 A2
Meadow Cl
Blackwater GU17 .150 B2
Compton RG20 .31 C3
Goring RG8 .34 B3
Marlow SL7 .1 C1
Moulsford OX10 .13 C2
Old Windsor SL4 .68 A1
Thatcham RG19 .106 B2
Meadow Cotts GU24 .153 C4
Meadow Ct TW18 .96 C3
Meadow Gdns TW18 .96 B2
Meadow La SL4 .67 B4
Meadow Rd Ashford TW15 .98 B2
Earley RG6 .87 B2
Henley-on-T RG9 .15 C1
Newbury RG14 .130 C4
Reading RG1 .58 C1
Slough SL3 .43 C2
Wentworth GU25 .121 C2
Wokingham RG41 .116 A3
Meadow Vale Prim Sch
Binfield RG42 .90 C1
Bracknell RG42 .117 C4
Meadow View
Marlow Bottom SL7 .1 C3
Winnersh RG41 .88 B2
Meadow View La SL6 .64 C4
Meadow Way
Blackwater GU17 .150 B3
Bracknell RG42 .91 A1
Dorney SL4 .40 C2
Holyport SL6 .65 B3
Old Windsor SL4 .68 A1
Theale RG7 .83 B2
West End GU24 .153 C3
Wokingham RG41 .116 A3
Meadow Wlk RG41 .116 A3
Meadowbank Rd GU18 .146 B1
Meadowbrook Cl SL3 .69 C3
Meadowbrook Montessori Sch RG42 .91 C2
Meadowcroft Rd RG2 .113 B4
Meadowlea Cl UB7 .70 B4
Meadows Cty Comb Sch The HP10 .3 C4
Meadows The
Flackwell Heath HP10 .3 A4
Sandhurst GU47 .150 C3
Meadowside RG31 .57 A1
Meadowside Rd RG8 .56 B3
Meadowsweet Cl RG18 .106 C2
Meadowview TW19 .69 C1
Meads The 4 SL4 .67 A3
Meadway Ashford TW15 .98 A2
Frimley GU16 .151 C1
Staines TW18 .97 A1
Meadway Cl TW18 .97 A1
Meadway Comp Sch RG30 .84 C4
Meadway Prec RG30 .85 A3
Meadway The RG30 .84 C4
Meare Est HP10 .3 C4
Mearings The RG30 .111 C3
Measham Way RG6 .87 B1
Meashill Way OX11 .9 C4
Meavy Gdns RG2 .86 A1
Medallion Pl SL6 .40 A4
Mede Cl TW19 .95 B4
Mede Ct TW18 .96 C3
Medina Cl RG41 .115 C4
Medlake Rd TW20 .96 B1
Medlar Dr GU17 .150 C2
Medway Cl
Thatcham RG18 .106 A3
Wokingham RG41 .115 C4
Medway Ct RG30 .85 B3
Melbourne Ave Slough SL1 .42 B4
Winnersh RG41 .88 B1
Melbury Cl KT16 .124 A1
Meldreth Way RG6 .87 B1
Meldrum Cl RG14 .130 B3
Melford Gn RG4 .59 C3
Melksham Cl RG6 .113 C4
Melling Cl RG6 .87 C2
Mellor Wlk 27 RG1 .86 A3
Melody Cl RG41 .88 B2
Melrose RG12 .118 A1
Melrose Ave RG6 .87 A3
Melrose Gdns RG2 .114 C1
Melton Ct SL6 .39 C3
Melville Ave GU16 .151 C1
Membury Wlk RG12 .118 C3
Memorial Ave RG9 .35 C1
Mendip Cl Charvil RG10 .61 A2
Harlington UB3 .71 B4
Slough SL3 .44 A1
Mendip Dr RG31 .84 A3
Mendip Rd RG12 .118 C2
Menpes Rd RG31 .57 B2
Meon Cl RG26 .135 A1
Merchants Pl RG1 .86 A4
Mercia Rd SL6 .39 B2
Mercian Way SL1 .41 B3
Mercury Ave RG41 .115 C3
Mere Cl SL7 .1 C1
Mere Rd
Shepperton TW17 .125 A2
Slough SL1 .42 C2
Mereoak La RG7 .112 C2
Meridian Ct SL5 .120 A1
Merlewood RG12 .118 B2
Merlin Cl SL3 .69 A4
Merlin Clove RG42 .92 A1
Merlin Ct Frimley GU16 .151 B1
Maidenhead SL6 .39 A4
Mermaid Cl RG41 .88 A1
Merrifield Cl RG6 .114 B4
Merrivale Gdns RG2 .86 A1
Merron Cl GU46 .149 B3
Merryhill Green Hill RG41 .88 B2
Merryhill Rd RG42 .118 A4
Merryman Dr RG45 .143 A4
Merryweather Cl RG40 .115 C1
Merrywood Pk GU15 .151 C2
Mersey Way RG18 .106 A3
Merthyr Vale RG4 .59 A3
Merton Cl Maidenhead SL6 .39 B2
Sandhurst GU47 .143 C1
Merton Rd SL1 .43 A2
Merton Rd N RG2 .86 A1
Merton Rd S RG2 .86 A1
Mervyn Rd TW17 .125 B1
Merwin Way SL4 .66 B2
Metcalf Rd TW15 .98 A2
Meteor Cl RG5 .88 A4
Meteorological Off (HQ) RG12 .118 B4
Meteorological Office Coll RG2 .113 B4
Metro Ctr The RG41 .89 A1
Mews The Newbury RG14 .104 C1
Reading RG1 .86 C3
Swallowfield RG7 .140 B4
Mey Cl RG31 .84 B3
Meyrick Dr RG14 .130 B3
Mezel Hill Cotts SL4 .94 B2
Michael Rd SL6 .39 B3
Michaelmas Cl GU46 .149 B2
Micheldever Way RG12 .118 C2
Michelet Cl GU18 .146 A1
Micklands Prim Sch RG4 .59 B2
Micklands Rd RG4 .59 C2
Mickle Hill GU47 .143 A1
Micro Ctr The RG2 .86 A1
Midcroft SL2 .22 A1
Middle Cl Frimley GU15 .152 B3
Newbury RG14 .130 B4
Middle Gn Slough SL3 .43 C3
Staines TW18 .97 B1
Middle Gordon Rd GU15 .151 B3
Middle Hill TW20 .95 B2
Middle Walk SL1 .21 B1
Middlefields RG10 .61 C3
Middlegreen Rd SL3 .43 B3
Middlegreen Trad Est SL3 .43 B2
Middlemoor Rd GU16 .151 C1
Middleton Ct RG14 .105 C3
Middleton Rd GU15 .151 C4
Middletons Cl RG17 .100 C4
Midsummer Mdw RG4 .58 C3
Midway Ave
Chertsey KT16 .124 A3
Thorpe TW20 .123 A3
Midway Cl TW18 .97 A3
Midwinter Cl RG30 .84 C4
Milbanke Ct RG12 .117 C4
Milbanke Way RG12 .117 C4
Mildenhall Cl RG6 .87 B1
Mildenhall Rd SL1 .42 C4
Mile Elm SL7 .2 A2
Miles Pl GU18 .152 C4
Miles Way RG5 .88 A4
Milestone Ave
Charvil RG10 .61 A3
Sonning RG4 .60 C2
Milestone Cres RG10 .61 A2
Milestone View Ct RG4 .59 C2
Milestone Way RG4 .59 B3
Milford Ct SL1 .43 A2
Milford Rd RG1 .58 C1
Milkhouse Rd RG20 .103 B2
Mill Bank RG17 .102 A2
Mill Cl Bagshot GU19 .145 B2
Wokingham RG41 .116 A4
Mill Ct SL3 .69 B2
Mill End RG9 .16 B4
Mill Farm Ave TW16 .98 C1
Mill Field GU19 .145 B2
Mill Gn Binfield RG42 .90 C1
Caversham RG4 .59 B1
Mill Hall Sch RG20 .131 B4
Mill House La KT16 .123 A3
Mill La Ascot SL5 .121 A4
Bracknell RG12 .117 C3
Cookham SL6 .20 B4
Earley RG6 .87 C2
Earley, Sindlesham RG6 .87 C1
Henley-on-T RG9 .35 C4
Horton SL3 .69 B2
Hurley SL6 .17 C2
Lambourn RG17 .25 B1
Newbury RG14 .105 A2
Padworth RG7 .109 B1
Reading RG1 .86 A4
Reading, Horncastle RG31 .84 C2
Shiplake RG9 .36 A1
Taplow SL6 .40 B4
Thorpe TW20 .123 B3
Windsor SL4 .67 A4
Mill La *continued*
Winnersh RG41 .87 C1
Yateley GU46 .149 B4
Mill Mead TW18 .96 C2
Mill Pl SL3 .68 B3
Mill Pond Rd GU20 .146 A3
Mill Rd
Burghfield Common RG30 .84 C1
Caversham RG4 .59 B1
Goring RG8 .34 B4
Marlow SL7 .1 C1
Shiplake RG9 .36 A2
Mill Reef Cl RG19 .105 C2
Mill Ride SL5 .119 B4
Mill St Colnbrook SL3 .69 B4
Slough SL2 .42 C3
Millbank SL7 .1 C1
Millbank Cres RG5 .87 C3
Millboard Rd SL8 .3 A2
Millbridge Rd GU46 .149 A4
Millbrook Way SL3 .69 C3
Milldown Ave RG8 .34 B4
Milldown Rd RG8 .34 B4
Miller's Ct TW20 .96 B1
Miller's La SL4 .68 A1
Millers Cl Goring RG8 .34 A4
Staines TW18 .97 A2
Millers Ct RG4 .59 B1
Millers Field RG17 .48 A2
Millers Gr RG31 .84 C2
Milley La RG10 .62 A4
Milley Rd RG10 .62 C3
Millfield Charlton TW16 .125 B4
Lambourn RG17 .25 A1
Millgreen La RG19 .132 C1
Millholme Wlk GU15 .152 B2
Millins Cl GU47 .143 C1
Millmead RG41 .116 A4
Millmere GU46 .149 B4
Mills Spur SL4 .95 A4
Millside SL8 .3 B2
Millstream Ho RG14 .105 B2
Millstream La SL1 .41 C3
Millstream Way HP10 .3 C4
Millworth La RG2 .113 C2
Milman Cl RG12 .119 A4
Milman Rd RG2 .86 A3
Milner Rd SL1 .41 A4
Milsom Cl RG2 .113 C3
Milton Cl Bracknell RG12 .118 A2
Henley-on-T RG9 .15 B1
Horton SL3 .69 A2
Milton Ct RG40 .116 A4
Milton Dr Littleton TW17 .124 C3
Wokingham RG40 .116 A4
Milton Gdns
Stanwell TW19 .97 C4
Wokingham RG40 .116 A3
Milton Rd Earley RG6 .87 A4
Egham TW20 .95 C2
Slough SL2 .22 B1
Wokingham RG40, RG41 .116 A3
Milton Way RG10 .61 C3
Milverton Cl SL6 .39 A2
Milward Gdns RG12 .117 B4
Mina Ave SL3 .43 B2
Minchin Gn RG42 .90 B2
Minden Cl RG41 .115 C3
Minerva Cl TW19 .70 A1
Ministry Rd RG19 .132 A3
Minley Rd GU17 .149 C1
Minniecroft Rd SL1 .21 A1
Minorca Ave GU16 .152 C1
Minorca Rd GU16 .152 C1
Minstead Cl RG12 .118 C3
Minstead Dr GU46 .149 B3
Minster Ct
Camberley GU15 .151 B4
Camberley, York Town GU15 .150 C2
Minster St RG1 .86 A4
Minster Way SL3 .43 C2
Minsterley Ave TW16, TW17 .125 C3
Mint Cl RG6 .86 C1
Minter Ct RG26 .134 C1
Minton Cl RG30 .84 C4
Minton Rise SL6 .41 A4
Mirador Cres SL2 .43 B3
Mire La RG10 .62 B2
Misbourne Ct SL3 .44 A1
Missenden Cl TW14 .98 C4
Missenden Gdns SL1 .41 A4
Mistletoe Rd GU46 .149 B2
Mitcham Cl RG2 .86 A3
Mitcham Rd GU15 .145 A1
Mitchell Cl SL1 .42 A2
Mitchell Way RG5 .88 A4
Mitford Cl RG2 .113 B4
Mitre Cl TW17 .125 B2
Mitre Pl RG42 .91 A1
Mixnams La KT16 .124 A3
Moat Dr SL2 .43 B4
Modbury Gdns RG2 .86 B1
Moffatts Cl GU47 .150 A4
Moffy Hill SL6 .19 C1
Mohawk Way RG5 .88 A4
Mole Rd RG41 .114 C3
Moles Cl RG40 .116 B3
Mollison Cl RG5 .88 A4
Molly Millar Bridge RG41 .116 A2
Molly Millar's La RG41 .116 A2
Molly Millars Cl RG40 .116 A2
Molyneux Rd GU20 .146 B2
Molyns Mews 7 SL1 .41 C3
Monarch Cl TW14 .98 C4
Monck Ct 7 RG30 .85 B3
Mondial Way UB3 .71 B4
Moneyrow Gn SL6 .65 A4
Monkey Island La
Holyport SL6 .65 C4
Maidenhead SL6 .40 C1
Monkley Ct 5 RG4 .59 B1
Monks Cl SL5 .120 A2
Monks Dr SL5 .120 A2
Monks Hollow SL7 .1 C3
Monks La RG14 .130 C4
Monks Rd
Virginia Water GU25 .122 B3
Windsor SL4 .66 B3
Monks Way
Harmondsworth UB7 .70 C4
Reading RG30 .85 B3
Staines TW18 .97 B1
Monks Wlk SL5 .120 A2
Monksbarn RG2 .86 B1
Monksfield Way SL2 .22 A1
Monkshood Cl RG40 .116 C4
Monkswood Cl RG14 .130 C4
Monkswood Ct 6 SL7 .1 C1
Monktons La RG7 .137 B3
Monmouth Ct 5 RG1 .59 A1
Mons Cl RG41 .115 C3
Mons Wlk TW20 .96 B2
Monsell Gdns TW18 .96 C2
Montacute Dr RG19 .106 C1
Montagu Rd SL3 .68 A3
Montague Cl
Camberley GU15 .151 A3
Lightwater GU18 .146 A1
Wokingham RG40 .116 C4
Montague Ho (Coll) RG40 .116 B3
Montague Rd SL1 .42 C3
Montague St
Caversham RG4 .59 B1
Reading RG1 .86 B4
Montague Terr RG14 .131 A4
Monteagle La
Yateley GU46 .149 A3
Yateley GU46 .149 B3
Montem Inf Sch The SL1 .42 A2
Montem La SL1 .42 B2
Montgomery Cl GU47 .150 A4
Montgomery Dr RG7 .113 A1
Montgomery Pl SL2 .43 B4
Montgomery Rd RG14 .130 C4
Montpelier Ct SL4 .67 B3
Montpelier Dr RG4 .59 B3
Montrose Ave Datchet SL3 .68 B4
Slough SL1 .42 A4
Montrose Cl Ashford TW15 .98 B2
Frimley GU16 .151 C1
Montrose Dr SL6 .39 A3
Montrose Ho 2 RG1 .86 A4
Montrose Rd TW14 .71 B1
Montrose Way SL3 .68 B4
Montrose Wlk RG31 .84 C2
Monument Cl RG14 .130 B4
Monycrower Dr SL6 .39 C4
Moor Cl Sandhurst GU47 .143 C1
Wokingham RG40 .141 C4
Moor Copse Cl RG6 .87 A2
Moor End SL6 .40 B1
Moor Furlong SL1 .41 C3
Moor La
Harmondsworth UB7 .70 B4
Maidenhead SL6 .19 C1
Newbury RG14 .104 C2
Staines TW18, TW19 .96 B3
Moor Park Ho RG12 .117 C2
Moor Pl GU20 .146 A3
Moorbridge Rd SL6 .40 A4
Moordale Ave RG42 .90 C1
Moore Cl SL1 .42 A2
Moore Grove Cres TW20 .95 C1
Moores Gn RG40 .116 C4
Moores La SL4 .41 C1
Moores Pl RG17 .100 B3
Moorfield Terr SL6 .40 A4
Moorfields Cl TW18 .123 C4
Moorhayes Dr TW18 .124 B3
Moorhen Dr RG6 .87 A1
Moorings The SL4 .95 B4
Moorland Rd UB7 .70 B4
Moorlands Dr SL6 .38 C4
Moorlands Pl GU15 .151 A3
Moorlands Prim Sch RG30 .84 C4
Moorlands Rd GU15 .151 A2
Moormede Cres TW18 .96 C2
Moors The Pangbourne RG8 .56 B3
Thatcham RG19 .106 B1
Moorside HP10 .3 C4
Moorside Cl
Farnborough (Hants) GU14 .151 A1
Maidenhead SL6 .19 C1
Moorstown Ct 7 SL1 .42 C2
Moray Ave GU47 .150 B4
Moray Dr SL2 .43 A4
Mordaunt Dr RG45 .143 A2
Morden Cl RG12 .118 C3
Moreau Wlk SL3 .43 C4
Morecambe Ave RG4 .58 C3
Moreland Ave SL3 .69 B4
Moreland Cl SL3 .69 B4
Moreleigh Cl RG2 .113 A4
Morella Cl GU25 .122 B3
Morello Dr SL3 .43 C3
Moreton Ct RG1 .86 B3
Moreton Way SL1 .41 B3
Morgan Ct TW15 .98 A2
Morgan Rd RG1 .86 B3
Moriston Cl RG30 .85 A4
Morlais RG4 .59 A3

Morlands Ave RG30 85 A3
Morley Cl Slough SL3 43 C2
Yateley GU46 149 A3
Morley Ct SL5 120 C2
Morley Pl RG17 100 B3
Mornington Ave RG40 141 C4
Mornington Cl RG26 134 C1
Mornington Rd TW15 98 B2
Morpeth Cl RG2 86 B2
Morrell Ct TW18 97 A2
Morrice Cl SL3 44 A1
Morris Ct SL4 66 C3
Morris Pl 5 SL7 1 B1
Morriss Ct 14 RG1 86 B4
Mortaine Rd TW15 97 B3
Mortimer Cl RG2 113 B4
Mortimer La RG7 137 B4
Mortimer Rd SL3 43 B2
Mortimer Sta RG7 137 C3
Morton Pl RG7 83 C2
Moss Cl RG4 59 B2
Mossy Vale SL6 19 B1
Mostyn Ho RG42 91 A1
Moulsford Prep Sch OX10 14 A3
Moulsham Copse La GU46 149 A4
Moulsham La GU46 149 A4
Moundsfield Way SL1 41 C2
Mount Cl
Farnham Common SL2 22 B4
Newbury RG14 105 A1
Mount Cl The GU25 122 B2
Mount Felix KT12 125 C1
Mount La Bracknell RG12 118 B4
Chaddleworth RG20 49 A4
Mount Lee TW20 95 C2
Mount Pleasant
Bracknell RG12 118 B3
Reading RG1 86 A3
Sandhurst GU47 143 A1
Tadley RG26 135 A1
Wokingham RG41 116 A3
Mount Pleasant Cl GU18 146 A1
Mount Pleasant Cotts
12 Bourne End SL8 3 A2
Englefield Green TW20 95 B1
Mount Pleasant Gr RG1 86 A3
Mount Rd RG18 106 C2
Mount St RG2 86 A3
Mount The Caversham RG4 58 C2
Reading RG1 86 B3
Wentworth GU25 122 B2
Mount View RG9 15 B1
Mount View Ct RG9 15 B1
Mountain Ash SL7 1 B3
Mountbatten Cl
Newbury RG14 105 B3
6 Slough SL1 43 A2
Mountbatten Rise GU47 142 C1
Mountbatten Sq 8 SL4 67 B3
Mountfield RG8 34 B4
Mounts Hill SL4, SL5 93 B2
Mountsfield Cl TW19 70 A1
Mowbray Cres TW20 96 A2
Mowbray Dr RG30 85 A4
Mower Cl RG40 116 C4
Moyleen Rise SL7 1 B1
Muckhatch La TW20 123 A4
Mud La
Finchampstead RG27 140 C1
Peasemore RG20 50 B3
Muirfield Cl RG1 86 B4
Muirfield Ho RG12 117 C2
Mulberry Ave TW19 97 C4
Mulberry Bsns Pk RG41 116 A2
Mulberry Cl
Crowthorne RG45 143 B2
1 Sandhurst GU47 150 B4
Woodley RG5 87 C3
Mulberry Ct
1 Bracknell RG12 118 C2
Newbury RG14 104 C2
Wokingham RG40 116 B3
Mulberry Dr SL3 43 C1
Mulberry Ho RG42 91 A1
Mulberry Trees TW17 125 B1
Mulberry Way RG7 83 C2
Mulberry Wlk SL6 39 B4
Mulfords Hill RG26 135 A1
Mulgrave Rd GU16 151 C1
Mullens Rd TW20 96 B2
Mullion Ct 22 RG1 85 C4
Mulroy Dr GU15 152 A3
Mumbery Hill RG10 36 C1
Muncaster Cl TW15 98 A2
Muncaster Rd TW15 98 A2
Munces Rd SL7 1 B3
Munday Ct RG42 90 C1
Mundaydean La SL7 1 A2
Mundesley Spur SL1 42 C4
Mundesley St RG1 86 A3
Munkle Marsh RG19 107 A2
Munnings Dr GU47 150 C3
Munro Ave RG5 87 C2
Murdoch Cl TW18 97 A2
Murdoch Rd RG40 116 B3
Murray Ct SL5 120 B2
Murray Ho RG41 116 A3
Murray Rd RG41 116 A3
Murrellhill La RG42 117 B4
Murrells La GU15 151 A2
Murrin Rd SL6 39 B4
Mus of Berkshire Aviation The RG5 88 A3
Mus of English Rural Life RG2 86 C2
Mus of Reading RG1 86 A4
Mushroom Castle La RG42 92 A1
Mustard La RG4 60 C1
Mustard Mill Rd TW18 96 C2
Muswell Cl RG7 83 C2
Mutton Oaks RG12 117 B4
Myers Way GU16 152 B1
Mylne Sq RG40 116 B3
Mylum Cl RG2 113 B3
Myrke The SL3 42 C1
Myrtle Ave TW14 71 C1
Myrtle Cl
Burghfield Common RG7 111 A2
Lightwater GU18 153 A4
Poyle SL3 69 C3
Purley on T RG31 57 B2
Myrtle Cres SL2 42 C3
Myrtle Dr GU17 150 B3
Myton Wlk RG7 83 C2

## N

Nabbs Hill Cl RG31 84 B3
Nairn Cl GU16 151 C1
Nalderhill Rd RG20 103 A3
Napier Cl RG45 143 B3
Napier Dr GU15 152 A4
Napier Lodge TW15 98 B1
Napier Rd Ashford TW15 98 B1
Crowthorne RG45 143 B2
Harmondsworth TW6 70 B3
Maidenhead SL6 39 A3
Reading RG1 86 B4
Napier Wlk TW15 98 B1
Napper Cl SL5 119 B4
Narromine Dr RG31 84 C2
Naseby RG12 118 A1
Naseby Rise RG14 105 B3
Nash Cl RG6 87 A2
Nash Gdns SL5 119 C4
Nash Grove La RG40 115 C1
Nash Pk RG42 90 A1
Nash Rd SL3 44 A1
Nashdom La SL1 21 A3
Natalie Cl TW14 98 B4
Nathan Ct 20 RG1 85 C4
Naylors The RG7 139 B3
Neath Gdns RG30 84 C4
Needham Cl SL4 66 C3
Neil Cl TW15 98 B2
Nell Gwynn Ave TW17 125 B2
Nell Gwynne Ave SL5 120 B3
Nell Gwynne Cl SL5 120 B3
Nelson Cl Bracknell RG12 118 C4
East Bedfont TW14 98 C4
Slough SL3 43 B1
Nelson Ct KT16 124 A1
Nelson Rd Ashford TW15 97 C2
Caversham RG4 59 B1
Harmondsworth TW6 70 C3
Windsor SL4 66 C2
Nelson Terr 22 RG1 86 A3
Nelson Way GU15 150 C2
Nelson's La RG10 89 A3
Nene Rd TW6, UB7 71 A3
Neptune Cl RG41 115 C3
Neptune Rd TW6 71 B3
Neptune Way SL1 41 C2
Netherton RG12 118 A3
Netley Cl RG4 59 C3
Nettlecombe RG12 118 B2
Nettleton Rd TW6 71 A3
Neve Ho SL6 39 C4
Nevelle Cl RG42 117 B4
Neville Cl Stoke Poges SL2 22 C3
Waltham St Lawrence RG10 62 C3
Neville Ct SL1 21 B1
Neville Dr RG19 106 C2
Nevis Rd RG31 57 B2
New Bath Rd RG10 61 B3
New Bldgs RG7 81 B2
New Bright St 5 RG1 86 A3
New Christ Church CE Prim Sch RG1 86 A3
New Cl RG9 16 A4
New Ct SL7 1 B1
New Forest Ride RG12 118 C2
New Greenham Pk RG19 131 C3
New Hill RG8 57 B3
New Lane Hill RG30 84 C3
New Mdw SL5 119 B4
New Mile Rd SL5 120 B4
New Mill La RG27 140 C1
New Mill Rd RG27 140 C2
New Par TW15 97 C2
New Park Rd TW15 98 B2
New Rd Bagshot GU19 145 C2
Blackwater GU17 150 C2
Bourne End SL8 3 A2
Bracknell RG12 118 B4
Burghfield Common RG7 111 C1
Cookham SL6 19 C4
Crowthorne RG45 143 B3
Datchet SL3 68 B3
East Bedfont TW14 71 B1
Egham TW18 96 B2
Harlington UB3 71 B4
Holyport SL6 65 A4
Hurley SL6 17 C2
Littleton TW17 125 A3
Marlow Bottom SL7 1 B3
Newbury RG14 105 B1
North Ascot SL5 92 C1
Reading RG1 86 B3
Sandhurst GU47 150 A4
Shiplake RG9 36 A2
Slough SL3 44 A2
New Rd *continued*
Twyford RG10 61 B4
Twyford, Ruscombe RG10 61 C3
Windlesham GU19,GU20 146 A2
Wokingham RG41 115 A4
New Road Hill RG7 108 A2
New Scotland Hill Prim Sch GU47 143 A1
New Sq East Bedfont TW14 98 B4
Slough SL1 42 C2
New St Beech Hill RG7 138 A1
Henley-on-T RG9 15 C1
Staines TW18 97 A2
New Town Prim Sch RG1 86 B4
New Way RG7 82 A1
New Wickham La TW20 96 A1
New Wokingham Rd RG45 143 A3
New Zealand Ave KT12 125 C1
Newall Rd TW6 71 B3
Newalls Rise RG10 36 C1
Newark Rd GU20 146 A3
Newark St RG1 86 A3
Newberry Cres SL4 66 B3
Newbery Cl RG31 57 B1
Newbery Way SL1 42 B2
Newbold Coll RG42 90 B1
Newbold Rd RG14 104 B3
Newbold Sch RG42 90 B1
Newbolt Cl RG18 106 B3
Newbury Cl RG10 61 A2
Newbury Coll RG14 104 C2
Newbury District Hospl RG14 104 C1
Newbury District Mus RG14 105 A2
Newbury Dr SL6 40 A3
Newbury Hill RG18 52 C3
Newbury La RG20 31 B2
Newbury Rd
Great Shefford RG17 48 A1
Harmondsworth TW6 70 C3
Hermitage RG18 79 A3
Lambourn RG17 25 B1
Newbury Ret Pk RG14 131 A4
Newbury St
Kintbury RG17 102 A1
Lambourn RG17 25 A1
Newbury Sta RG14 105 A1
Newcastle Rd RG2 86 B2
Newchurch Rd Slough SL2 41 C4
Tadley RG26 135 A1
Newell Gn RG42 91 B2
Newfield Gdns SL7 1 C2
Newfield Rd SL7 1 C2
Newfield Way SL7 1 C1
Newhaven Cres TW15 98 B2
Newhaven Spur SL2 22 A1
Newhurst Gdns RG42 91 B2
Newlands Ave RG4 59 A2
Newlands Cl GU46 149 B3
Newlands Cty Prim Sch GU46 149 B3
Newlands Dr
Maidenhead SL6 39 A4
Poyle SL3 69 C2
Newlands Rd GU15 151 A1
Newlands Sch SL6 39 A4
Newlyn Gdns RG2 86 A1
Newmarket Cl 10 RG6 87 B1
Newport Cl 11 RG14 105 A2
Newport Dr RG42 91 A1
Newport Rd
Harmondsworth TW6 71 A3
Newbury RG14 105 A2
Reading RG1 59 A1
Slough SL2 21 C1
Newquay Dr RG6 87 A1
Newstead Rise RG2 86 C1
Newton Ave RG4 59 B3
Newton Cl SL3 43 C2
Newton Ct SL4 68 A1
Newton La SL4 68 A1
Newton Side Orch SL4 68 A1
Newtonside SL4 68 A1
Newtown RG26 135 A1
Newtown Gdns RG9 35 C4
Newtown Rd
Henley-on-T RG9 35 C4
Marlow SL7 1 C2
Newbury RG14 & RG20 131 A3
Sandhurst GU47 150 A4
Niagara Rd RG9 35 C4
Nicholas Ct 23 RG1 85 C4
Nicholas Gdns SL1 41 C3
Nicholas Rd RG9 35 A4
Nicholls SL4 66 B2
Nicholls Wlk SL4 66 B2
Nicholson Wlk 3 TW20 96 A2
Nicholsons Ctr 5 SL6 39 C4
Nicholsons La SL6 39 C4
Nideggen Cl RG19 106 B2
Nightingale Cres RG12 118 B2
Nightingale Gdns GU47 150 A4
Nightingale Ho 3 RG1 85 C3
Nightingale La
Maidenhead SL6 19 B2
Mortimer RG7 137 B3
Nightingale Pk SL2 21 C3
Nightingale Pl SL6 19 C4
Nightingale Rd RG5 87 B2
Nightingale Wlk SL4 67 B2
Nightingales The
Newbury RG14 131 A4
Stanwell TW19 97 C4
Nimrod Cl RG5 88 A4
Nimrod Way RG2 86 A3
Nine Acres SL1 41 C3
Nine Elms Cl TW14 98 C4
Nine Mile Ride
Bracknell RG12, RG40 117 C1
Crowthorne RG40 142 B4
Nine Mile Ride Prim Sch RG40 141 C3
Nire Rd RG4 59 C1
Nixey Cl SL1 43 A2
No 4 RG30 85 B3
Noakes Hill RG8 54 A4
Nobel Dr UB3 71 C4
Noble Rd RG9 35 C4
Nobles Way TW20 95 C1
Nodmore RG20 49 A4
Norcot Rd RG30 84 C4
Norden Cl SL6 39 B2
Norden Mdws SL6 39 B3
Norden Rd SL6 39 B3
Nores Rd RG2 113 B4
Norfolk Ave SL1 42 B4
Norfolk Chase RG42 91 C1
Norfolk Cl RG41 115 C3
Norfolk Park Cotts SL6 39 C4
Norfolk Rd Maidenhead SL6 39 C4
Reading RG30 85 B4
Norland Dr HP10 3 B4
Norland Nursery Training Coll RG17 101 B4
Norlands RG18 106 B3
Norlands La TW18, TW20 123 C4
Norman Ave RG9 15 C1
Norman Ct TW18 97 A2
Norman Ho TW17 125 A1
Norman Keep RG42 118 C4
Norman Pl RG1 59 A1
Norman Rd Ashford TW15 98 B1
Caversham RG4 59 B2
Normandy Wlk TW20 96 B2
Normanhurst TW15 98 A2
Normans The SL2 43 A4
Normanstead Rd RG31 84 B4
Normay Rise RG14 130 B3
Normoor Rd RG7 110 C1
Norreys Ave RG40 116 B4
Norreys Dr SL6 39 B2
Norris Field RG20 49 A4
Norris Ho SL6 39 C4
Norris La RG20 49 A4
Norris Rd Reading RG6 87 A3
Staines TW18 96 C2
North Burnham Cl SL1 21 A2
North Cl East Bedfont TW14 71 B1
Medmenham SL7 17 B4
Windsor SL4 66 C3
North Cotts SL2 22 B1
North Croft HP10 3 C3
North Dr Sulhamstead RG7 110 B4
Wentworth GU25 121 C2
North End La SL5 121 A1
North Farm Cl RG17 25 B2
North Fryerne GU46 149 B4
North Gn Bracknell RG12 118 B4
3 Maidenhead SL6 19 C1
Slough SL1 42 C3
North Gr KT16 123 C2
North Hatton Rd TW6 71 B3
North Links Rd HP10 3 A4
North Lodge Dr SL5 119 B4
North Lodge Mews RG30 85 B2
North Pk SL0 44 B2
North Rd
East Bedfont TW14 71 B1
Maidenhead SL6 39 C4
Moulsford OX10 13 C2
Winkfield SL5 119 A4
North Row SL3 23 C4
North St Caversham RG4 59 A1
Egham TW20 95 C1
Reading RG1 85 C4
Winkfield SL4 93 A3
North Standen Rd RG17 100 A2
North Star La SL6 39 B3
North Town Cl 1 SL6 19 C1
North Town Mead 4 SL6 19 C1
North Town Moor SL6 19 C1
North Town Rd SL6 19 C1
North View Gdns 8 RG14 105 A2
North Wlk RG7 83 C2
Northam Cl RG6 87 C2
Northampton Ave SL1 42 B4
Northampton Cl RG12 118 C3
Northborough Rd SL2 22 A1
Northbourne Cl RG6 87 A1
Northbrook Copse RG12 118 C2
Northbrook Pl RG14 105 A2
Northbrook Rd RG4 59 B3
Northbrook St RG14 105 A2
Northbury Ave RG10 61 C3
Northbury La RG10 61 C3
Northcott RG12 118 A1
Northcourt Ave RG2 86 B2
Northcroft SL2 22 A1
Northcroft Cl TW20 95 A2
Northcroft Gdns TW20 95 A2
Northcroft La RG14 104 C2
Northcroft Rd TW20 95 A2
Northcroft Terr RG14 104 C2
Northcroft Villas TW20 95 A2
Northdean 5 SL6 19 C1
Northend Cl HP10 3 B4
Northern Ave RG14 105 A3
Northern Hts SL8 3 A3
Northern Perimeter Rd TW6 71 B3
Northern Perimeter Road (W) TW6 70 B3
Northern Rd SL2 22 B1
Northern Way RG2 85 C1
Northern Woods HP10 3 B4
Northfield GU18 153 A4
Northfield Ave RG9 36 A2
Northfield Ct
Henley-on-T RG9 15 B2
Staines TW18 124 A4
Northfield End RG9 15 B2
Northfield Rd Eton SL4 41 C1
Maidenhead SL6 19 C1
Reading RG1 59 A1
Shiplake RG9 36 A2
Staines TW18 124 A4
Thatcham RG18 106 A2
Northfields Chieveley RG20 51 A2
Lambourn RG17 25 A2
Northfields Terr RG17 25 B2
Northgate Dr GU15 152 A4
Northington Cl RG12 118 C2
Northlands Dr SL1 21 B2
Northmead Rd SL2 41 C4
Northolt Rd TW6 70 C3
Northrop Rd TW6 71 C3
Northumberland Ave RG2 86 B2
Northumberland Cl
Bracknell RG42 91 C1
Stanwell TW19 70 C1
Northumberland Cres TW14 71 C1
Northumbria Rd SL6 39 A2
Northview RG17 100 B3
Northview Hts RG17 100 B3
Northway Newbury RG14 105 A1
Thatcham RG18 106 B3
Wokingham RG41 115 C4
Northwood Dr RG14 105 B2
Northwood Rd TW6 70 B3
Norton Cl RG14 130 B3
Norton Pk SL5 120 B2
Norton Rd Frimley GU15 152 B2
Reading RG1 86 C4
Swallowfield RG7 139 B2
Wokingham RG40 116 B3
Woodley RG5 87 C3
Norway Dr SL2 43 A4
Norwich Ave GU15 151 C2
Norwich Dr RG5 87 B4
Norwich Ho SL6 39 C4
Norwood Cres TW6 71 B3
Norwood Rd RG1 86 C4
Notley End TW20 95 B1
Notton Way RG6 113 C4
Nuffield Dr GU47 143 C1
Nuffield Rd Barkham, Arborfield Garrison RG2 140 C4
Barkham, Langley Common RG2 141 A4
Nugee Ct RG45 143 A3
Nugent Cl SL7 1 C2
Nuneaton RG12 118 C2
Nunhide La RG8,RG31 83 C3
Nuns Acre RG8 34 A4
Nuns Wlk GU25 122 B2
Nuptown La RG42 91 C4
Nursery Cl Hurst RG10 88 C4
Shiplake RG9 36 A2
Nursery Gdns
Purley on T RG8 57 A3
Staines TW18 97 A1
Sunbury TW16 125 C4
Nursery La
North Ascot SL5 119 C4
Slough SL3 43 B3
Nursery Rd Burnham SL6 41 A4
Sunbury TW16 125 C4
Nursery Way TW19 68 B1
Nursery Wlk SL7 1 A1
Nut La RG10 62 C3
Nutbean La RG7 139 C3
Nutbourne Ct TW18 96 C1
Nutfield Ct GU15 151 B4
Nuthatch Dr RG6 87 A2
Nuthurst RG12 118 C2
Nutley RG12 118 A1
Nutley Cl GU46 149 B3
Nutmeg Cl RG6 86 C1
Nutter's La RG2 140 A4
Nuttingtons RG20 49 C3
Nutty La TW17 125 B3

## O

O' Bee Gdns RG26 134 C1
Oak Ave Egham TW20 96 B1
Sandhurst GU47 143 B1
Oak Dr
Burghfield Common RG7 110 C1
Newbury RG14 104 C1
Woodley RG5 88 A3
Oak End Way RG7 109 B2
Oak Farm Cl GU17 150 B3
Oak Gn RG2 113 B4
Oak Grove Cres GU15 150 C3
Oak Hill SN8 99 B2
Oak La
Englefield Green TW20 95 B3
Windsor SL4 67 A3
Oak Leaf Ct SL5 119 B4
Oak Lo 8 TW16 98 C1
Oak Lodge RG45 143 B3
Oak Stubbs La SL4 40 C2
Oak Tree Ave SL7 1 B2
Oak Tree Cl Marlow SL7 1 B2
Tadley RG26 135 A1

**Oak Tree Cl** *continued*
Wentworth GU25 122 B2
**Oak Tree Copse** RG31 57 C2
**Oak Tree Dr** TW20 95 B2
**Oak Tree Rd** Marlow SL7 1 B2
Reading RG31 57 C1
Thatcham RG19 106 C1
**Oak Tree Wlk** RG8 57 B3
**Oak View** RG31 84 B4
**Oak Way**
East Bedfont TW14 98 C4
Woodley RG5 87 B2
**Oakdale** RG12 118 B2
**Oakdale Cl** RG31 84 B4
**Oakdale Wlk** RG5 88 A4
**Oakdene**
Burghfield Common RG7 111 A1
Sunningdale SL5 120 C2
**Oaken Copse** GU15 152 B4
**Oaken Gr** Maidenhead SL6 19 B1
Newbury RG14 130 B4
**Oakengates** RG12 118 A1
**Oakes Ct** RG17 100 B3
**Oakfield** RG1 86 B3
**Oakfield Ave** SL1 42 A3
**Oakfield Ct** RG41 116 A3
Oakfield Cty Fst Sch SL4 67 A3
**Oakfield Rd** Ashford TW15 98 A2
Blackwater GU17 150 C2
Bourne End SL8 3 A2
Silchester RG26 135 C1
**Oakfields** GU15 151 A3
**Oakhall Ct** TW16 98 C2
**Oakhall Dr** TW16 98 C2
**Oakham Cl** RG31 57 B1
**Oakhurst** SL6 20 A2
**Oaklands** Reading RG1 86 B3
Yateley GU46 149 B3
**Oaklands Cl** SL5 92 C1
Oaklands Cty Jun Sch RG45 143 A3
**Oaklands Dr**
North Ascot SL5 92 C1
Wokingham RG41 116 A3
Wokingham RG41 116 A3
Oaklands Inf Sch RG45 143 A3
**Oaklands La** RG45 143 A4
**Oaklands Pk** RG41 116 A2
**Oaklea Dr** RG27 140 C1
**Oakleigh** GU18 153 B4
**Oakley** HP10 3 C4
**Oakley Cres** SL1 42 C3
**Oakley Green Rd** SL4 66 A3
**Oakley Rd**
Camberley GU15 151 A2
Caversham RG4 58 C2
Newbury RG14 105 B2
**Oakmede Pl** RG42 90 B1
**Oakridge** GU24 153 C3
**Oaks Rd** Shiplake RG9 36 A2
Stanwell TW19 70 B1
**Oaks The** Bracknell RG12 118 B4
Staines TW18 96 C2
Yateley GU46 149 B3
**Oakside Way** RG2 113 C4
**Oaktree Way** GU47 143 A1
**Oakview** RG40 116 A2
**Oakway Dr** GU16 151 C1
**Oakwood Rd**
Bracknell RG12 118 C4
Virginia Water GU25 122 B2
Windlesham GU20 146 C2
**Oareborough** RG12 118 C2
**Oast Ct** TW18 96 C2
**Oast House Cl** TW19 95 C4
**Oatlands Dr** Slough SL1 42 B4
Walton-on-T KT13 125 C1
**Oatlands Rd** RG2 113 C3
**Oban Ct** SL1 42 B2
**Oban Gdns** RG5 87 C2
**Obelisk Way** GU15 151 B3
**Oberon Way** TW17 124 C3
**Ockwells Rd** SL6 39 B1
**Octavia** RG12 118 A1
**Octavia Way** TW18 97 A1
**Oddfellows Rd** RG14 104 C1
**Odell Cl** RG6 114 A4
**Odencroft Rd** SL2 22 A1
**Odiham Ave** RG4 59 C3
**Odiham Rd** RG7 139 B1
**Odney La** SL6 20 A4
**Ogmore Cl** RG30 84 C4
**Okingham Cl** GU47 143 B1
**Old Acre La** RG10 61 A3
**Old Barn Cl** RG4 59 A3
**Old Bath Rd** Charvil RG10 61 A3
Newbury RG14 104 C2
Sonning RG4 60 B1
**Old Bisley Rd** GU16 152 B2
**Old Bothampstead Rd** RG20 51 B3
**Old Bracknell Cl** RG12 118 A3
**Old Bracknell La E** RG12 118 A3
**Old Bracknell La W** RG12 118 A3
**Old Charlton Rd** TW17 125 B2
**Old Court Cl** SL6 39 A2
**Old Crown** 11 SL1 42 C2
**Old Dean Rd** GU15 151 B4
**Old Elm Dr** RG30 84 B4
**Old Farm Cres** RG31 57 B1
**Old Farm Dr** RG12 91 B1
**Old Ferry Dr** TW19 68 B1
**Old Fives Ct** SL1 21 A1
**Old Forest Rd** RG41 88 C1
**Old Forge Cl** SL6 40 A2
**Old Forge Cres** TW17 125 A2
**Old Forge End** GU47 150 A4
**Old Green La** GU15 151 B4
**Old Hayward La** RG17 73 B1
**Old House Ct** SL3 43 B4
**Old Kennels Ct** RG30 85 A3
**Old Kiln Rd** HP10 3 A4
**Old La**
Hamstead Marshall RG20 102 C1
Headley RG19 133 C1
**Old La The** RG1 85 C3
**Old Lands Hill** RG12 118 B4
**Old Marsh La** SL6 40 C2
**Old Mill Ct** RG10 61 B3
**Old Mill La** SL6 40 B2
**Old Moor La** HP10 3 C4
**Old Newtown Rd** RG14 104 C1
**Old Nursery Pl** TW15 98 A2
**Old Orchard The** RG31 84 C2
**Old Palace Ct** SL3 69 B3
**Old Pasture Rd** GU16, GU15 151 C2
**Old Pharmacy Ct** RG45 143 B2
**Old Pond Cl** GU15 151 B1
**Old Portsmouth Rd** GU15 152 A3
**Old Post Office La** 10 SL6 39 C4
**Old Priory La** RG42 91 B1
**Old Sawmill La** RG45 143 B3
**Old Sawmills The** RG17 127 C3
**Old School Ct** TW19 95 C4
**Old School La** GU46 149 B3
**Old School The**
Hampstead Norreys RG18 52 C3
Wooburn Green HP10 3 B2
**Old School Yd The** RG17 25 A1
**Old Slade La** SL0 44 C1
**Old St** Chieveley RG18 51 C1
Chieveley, Beedon Common RG20 51 B3
Hermitage RG18 78 C4
Old Station Bsns Pk RG20 31 C2
**Old Station Way** HP10 3 C3
**Old Station Yd The** RG17 25 A1
**Old Vicarage Way** HP10 3 B2
**Old Watery La** HP10 3 C4
**Old Well Ct** RG4 60 B2
**Old Welmore** GU46 149 C3
**Old Whitley Wood La** RG2 113 B3
**Old Wokingham Rd** RG40,RG45 143 B4
**Old Woosehill La** RG41 115 C4
**Oldacre** GU24 153 C4
**Oldacres** SL6 40 A4
**Oldbury** RG12 117 C3
**Oldbury Rd** KT16 123 C1
**Oldcorne Hollow** GU46 149 A3
**Olde Farm Dr** GU17 150 A3
**Oldean Cl** RG31 57 B1
**Oldershaw Mews** SL6 39 A4
**Oldfield Cl** RG6 87 A4
Oldfield Prim Sch SL6 40 A3
**Oldfield Rd** SL6 40 A3
Oldfield Rd Ind Est SL6 40 A4
**Oldhouse La** GU18 146 B1
**Oldstead** RG12 118 B2
**Oldway La** SL1 41 B3
**Oleander Cl** RG45 143 A4
**Oliver Dr** RG31 84 B3
**Oliver Rd** SL5 120 A3
**Oliver's Paddock** SL7 1 B3
**Ollerton** RG12 118 A1
**Omega Way** TW20 123 B4
**Omer's Rise** RG7 110 C2
**One Pin La** SL2 22 B4
**Onslow Dr** SL5 93 A1
**Onslow Gdns** RG4 59 B2
**Onslow Lodge** TW18 96 C1
**Onslow Mews** KT16 124 A2
**Onslow Rd** SL5 121 A1
**Opal Ct** SL3 23 B1
**Opal Way** RG41 115 C4
**Opendale Rd** SL1 41 A4
**Opladen Way** RG12 118 C2
Oracle Ctr RG1 118 B4
Oracle Ctr The RG1 86 A4
**Oracle Parkway**
Reading RG6 86 C4
Sonning RG6 60 A1
**Orbit Cl** RG40 141 C3
**Orchard Ave** Ashford TW15 98 B1
Hatton TW14 71 B1
Slough SL1 41 B4
Windsor SL4 67 A3
**Orchard Chase** RG10 88 C4
**Orchard Cl** Ashford TW15 98 B1
Farnborough (Hants) GU17 150 C1
Henley-on-T RG9 15 C1
Hermitage RG18 79 B4
Maidenhead SL6 40 A2
Newbury RG14 105 B3
Purley on T RG31 57 B2
Shinfield RG7 113 A1
Shiplake RG9 35 C1
West End GU24 153 B3
Wokingham RG40 116 B3
Woolhampton RG7 108 B1
**Orchard Ct**
Bracknell RG12 118 B4
Harmondsworth UB7 70 B4
Reading RG2 113 B4
Thatcham RG19 106 C2
Walton-on-T KT12 125 C1
**Orchard Dr** Sunbury TW17 125 C3
Wooburn Green HP10 3 B2
**Orchard Est** RG10 61 C3
**Orchard Gate**
Farnham Common SL2 22 B4
Sandhurst GU47 150 A4
**Orchard Gr** Caversham RG4 59 C2
Flackwell Heath HP10 3 A4
Maidenhead SL6 39 B4
**Orchard Hill** Bourne End SL8 3 A1
Windlesham GU20 146 B2
**Orchard Ho** 6 SL8 3 A2
**Orchard Park Cl** RG17 100 B2
**Orchard Pl** RG40 116 B3
**Orchard Rd** Hurst RG10 88 C4
Mortimer RG7 137 A3
Old Windsor SL4 68 A1
**Orchard St** RG1 86 A3
**Orchard The**
Flackwell Heath HP10 3 A4
Lightwater GU18 153 A4
Marlow SL7 1 C2
Theale RG7 83 C2
Virginia Water GU25 122 C2
**Orchard Way**
Ashford TW15 97 C3
Camberley GU15 151 A1
Slough SL3 43 C3
**Orchardene** RG14 105 A2
**Orchards The** TW15 98 B2
**Orchardville** SL1 21 A1
**Orchids The** OX11 10 B4
**Oregon Ave** RG31 57 B2
**Oregon Wlk** RG40 141 C4
**Oriel Hill** GU15 151 B2
**Oriental Rd** SL5 120 B3
**Orion** RG12 118 A1
**Orkney Cl** RG31 84 C2
**Orkney Ct** SL6 20 C3
**Ormathwaites Cnr** RG42 91 C1
**Ormonde Rd** RG41 116 A3
**Ormsby St** RG1 85 C4
**Orrin Cl** RG30 85 A4
**Orts Rd** Newbury RG14 105 A1
Reading RG1 86 B4
**Orville Cl** RG5 88 A4
**Orwell Cl** Caversham RG4 58 C2
Windsor SL4 67 B2
**Osborne Ave** TW19 97 C4
**Osborne Dr** GU18 153 A4
**Osborne La** RG42 91 B2
**Osborne Mews** SL4 67 B3
**Osborne Rd** Egham TW20 95 C1
Reading RG30 85 A4
Windsor SL4 67 B2
Wokingham RG40 116 B3
**Osborne St** SL1 42 C2
**Osbourne Ct** SL4 67 B3
**Osier Pl** TW20 96 B1
**Osman's Cl** RG42 92 A1
**Osnaburgh Hill** GU15 151 A3
**Osney Rd** SL6 19 C1
**Osprey Ct** 4 RG1 86 B4
**Osterley Cl** RG40 116 C3
**Osterley Dr** RG4 59 C3
**Ostler Gate** SL6 19 B1
**Oswald Cl** RG42 91 B1
**Othello Gr** RG42 118 C4
**Otter Cl** RG45 143 A4
Our Lady of Peace RC Inf Sch SL1 41 B4
Our Lady of Peace RC Mid Sch SL1 41 B4
Our Lady of the Rosary RC Sch TW18 97 A1
Our Lady's Prep Sch RG45 143 A3
**Ouseley Lodge** TW19 95 B4
**Ouseley Rd** TW19 95 B4
**Overbridge Sq** RG14 105 C2
**Overbury Ave** RG41 88 C1
**Overdale Rise** GU16 151 C2
**Overdown Rd** RG31 57 B2
**Overlanders End** RG31 57 C2
**Overlord Cl** GU15 151 B4
**Owen Rd** Newbury RG14 105 A3
Windlesham GU20 146 B3
**Owl Cl** RG41 115 C3
Owlsmoor Cty Prim Sch GU47 143 C1
**Owlsmoor Rd** GU47 143 B1
**Owston** RG6 87 B1
**Oxenhope** RG12 118 A3
**Oxford Ave** Burnham SL1 21 A2
Harlington UB3 71 C4
Slough SL1 41 C4
**Oxford Cl** TW15 98 B1
**Oxford Rd** Marlow SL7 1 B1
Newbury RG14 104 C3
Reading RG30 58 A1
Sandhurst GU47 143 C1
Windsor SL4 67 B3
Wokingham RG41 116 A3
**Oxford Rd E** SL4 67 B3
Oxford Road Prim Sch RG1 85 C4
**Oxford St** Caversham RG4 59 A1
Hungerford RG17 100 C4
Lambourn RG17 25 A2
Newbury RG14 104 C2

## P

**Pacific Cl** TW14 98 C4
**Pack & Prime La** RG9 15 B1
**Packman Dr** RG10 61 B3
**Padbury Cl** TW14 98 B4
**Padbury Oaks** UB7 70 A3
**Paddick Cl** RG4 60 C2
**Paddick Dr** RG6 87 B1
**Paddock Cl**
Camberley GU15 152 A3
Maidenhead SL6 39 A1
**Paddock Cotts** SL6 39 A1
**Paddock Hts** RG10 61 C2
**Paddock Rd**
Caversham RG4 59 B1
Newbury RG14 130 C4
**Paddock The**
Bracknell RG12 118 B3
Crowthorne RG45 143 A3
Datchet SL3 68 A3
Maidenhead SL6 19 B1
Newbury RG14 105 B1
**Paddocks The** HP10 3 A4
**Paddocks Way** KT16 124 A1
**Padley Ct** 7 RG1 86 B4
**Padstow Cl** SL3 43 C2
**Padstow Gdns** RG2 86 A1
**Padstow Wlk** TW14 98 C4
**Padworth La** RG7 109 C2
Padworth Prep Sch RG7 109 C1
**Padworth Rd** RG7 136 B4
**Page Rd** TW14 71 B1
**Page's Croft** RG40 116 B3
**Paget Cl** Camberley GU15 152 A4
Marlow SL7 1 C2
**Paget Dr** SL6 39 A2
**Paget Rd** SL3 43 C1
**Pagoda The** SL6 20 A1
**Paice Gn** RG40 116 B4
**Paices Hill** RG7 135 A3
**Pakenham Rd** RG12 118 B1
**Palace Cl** SL1 41 C3
**Paley St** SL6 64 A3
Palmer CE Jun Sch The RG40 116 B4
**Palmer Cl**
Crowthorne RG40 143 A4
Peasemore RG20 50 B4
**Palmer Park Ave** RG6 87 A3
**Palmer School Rd** RG40 116 B3
**Palmera Ave** RG31 84 B2
**Palmers Cl** SL6 39 A2
**Palmers Hill** RG8 54 B3
**Palmers La**
Burghfield Common RG7 111 A1
Burghfield Common, Poundgreen RG7 112 A2
**Palmerston Ave** SL3 43 A2
**Palmerstone Rd** RG6 87 A3
**Pamber Heath Rd** RG26 135 C1
**Pamber Rd** RG7 136 A1
**Pamela Row** SL6 65 A4
**Pan's Gdns** GU15 151 C2
**Panbourne Hill** RG8 56 B3
Pangbourne Coll RG8 56 A2
Pangbourne Prim Sch RG8 56 C3
**Pangbourne Rd** RG8 55 B2
**Pangbourne St** 2 RG30 85 A4
Pangbourne Sta RG8 56 B3
**Pankhurst Dr** RG12 118 B2
**Pannells Cl** KT16 123 C1
**Pantile Row** SL3 44 A1
**Papist Way** OX10 13 C4
Papplewick Sch SL5 120 A1
**Paprika Cl** RG6 86 C1
**Par The** SL2 22 B3
**Parade The** Ashford TW16 98 C1
Bourne End SL8 3 A2
Earley RG6 87 A2
Egham TW18 96 B2
Reading RG30 85 B3
Tadley RG26 135 A1
Wentworth GU25 122 B2
Windsor SL4 66 B3
Woodley RG5 87 C4
**Paradise Mews** RG9 15 B1
**Paradise Rd** RG9 15 B1
**Paradise Way** RG7 108 B4
**Park Ave** Camberley GU15 151 B2
Egham TW20 96 B1
Staines TW18 97 A1
Thatcham RG18 106 B2
Upper Halliford TW17 125 C3
Wokingham RG40 116 A3
Wraysbury TW19 68 B2
**Park Cl** SL4 67 B3
**Park Close Cotts** TW20 94 C2
**Park Cnr** SL4 66 C2
**Park Cres** Reading RG30 85 A3
Sunningdale SL5 120 C2
**Park Dr** SL5 120 C2
**Park End** RG14 105 A2
Park Farm Ind Est GU15 151 B1
**Park Gr** RG30 85 A3
**Park Ho** SL6 39 C3
Park House Sch RG14 130 C3
**Park La** Barkham RG40 141 A3
Beech Hill RG7 137 B1
Binfield RG42 90 C1
Burnham SL1 21 C4
Camberley GU15 151 B3
Charvil RG10 61 A2
Horton SL3 69 A2
Newbury RG14 105 A2
Reading RG31 84 B4
Slough SL3 43 A2
Stockcross RG20 103 A1
Thatcham RG18 106 B2
Winkfield SL4 93 A4
Park Lane Prim Sch RG31 84 B4
Park Lane Prim Sch Annexe RG31 84 B4
**Park Lawn** SL2 22 B1
**Park Mews** TW19 97 C4
**Park Rd** Ashford TW15 98 A2
**Park Rd** *continued*
Bracknell RG12 118 B4
Camberley GU15 151 B2
Egham TW20 96 A2
Henley-on-T RG9 15 C1
Lower Halliford TW17 125 A1
Sandhurst GU47 150 B4
Stanwell TW19 70 B1
Stoke Poges SL2 22 C2
Wokingham RG40 116 A3
**Park St** Bagshot GU19 145 C2
Camberley GU15 151 B3
Hungerford RG17 100 B3
Maidenhead SL6 39 C4
Newbury RG14 105 A2
Poyle SL3 69 B3
Slough SL1 42 C2
Windsor SL4 67 B3
**Park Terr** RG14 105 A2
**Park The** RG17 25 A2
**Park View** Bagshot GU19 145 B2
Beech Hill RG7 138 B3
**Park View Dr N** RG10 61 A3
**Park View Dr S** RG10 61 A2
**Park Wall La** RG8 34 B1
**Park Way**
Hungerford RG17 100 C2
Newbury RG14 105 A2
**Park Wlk** RG8 57 B3
**Parkcorner La** RG41 114 C3
**Parker's La** RG42 92 A3
**Parkers Ct** GU19 145 C2
**Parkgate** SL1 21 B1
**Parkhill Cl** GU17 150 B2
**Parkhill Dr** RG31 57 B1
**Parkhill Rd** GU17 150 B2
**Parkhouse La** RG30 85 B3
**Parkhouse Mews** 9 RG30 85 B3
**Parkhurst** 20 RG30 85 B3
**Parkland Ave** SL3 43 B1
**Parkland Dr** RG12 118 C4
**Parkland Gr** TW15 98 A2
**Parkland Rd** TW15 98 A2
**Parkside** Henley-on-T RG9 15 B1
Maidenhead SL6 19 B1
**Parkside Rd** Reading RG30 85 B3
Sunningdale SL5 121 A2
Thatcham RG18 106 B3
**Parkside Wlk** SL1 43 A2
**Parkstone Dr** GU15 151 B2
**Parkview**
Flackwell Heath HP10 3 A4
Maidenhead SL6 39 C4
**Parkview Chase** SL1 41 C4
**Parkway** Camberley GU15 151 B2
Crowthorne RG45 143 A3
Marlow SL7 2 A2
**Parkway Dr** RG4 60 C2
Parlaunt Park Comb Sch SL3 44 A2
**Parlaunt Rd** SL3 44 A1
**Parliament La** SL6 20 C3
**Parnham Ave** GU18 153 B4
**Parry Gn N** SL3 43 C1
**Parry Gn S** SL3 44 A1
**Parsley Cl** RG6 86 C1
**Parson's Wood La** SL2 22 B3
**Parsonage Gdns** SL7 1 C1
**Parsonage La**
Farnham Common SL2 22 B2
Hungerford RG17 100 B3
Lambourn RG17 25 A2
Windsor SL4 67 A3
**Parsonage Pl** RG17 25 A2
**Parsonage Rd** TW20 95 B2
**Parsonage Way** GU16 151 C1
**Parsons Cl** Barkham RG2 141 A4
Newbury RG14 104 C1
Parsons Down Jun & Inf Schs RG19 106 A2
**Parsons Field** GU47 150 A4
**Part La** RG7 139 C2
**Parthia Cl** RG1 86 A3
**Partridge Ave** GU46 149 A3
**Partridge Cl** GU16 151 C1
**Partridge Dr** RG31 84 B3
**Partridge Mead** SL6 19 C1
**Paschal Rd** GU15 151 C4
**Pasture Cl** RG6 114 A4
**Patches Field** SL7 1 C3
**Paterson Cl** GU16 152 B2
**Pates Manor Dr** TW14 98 B4
**Patricia Cl** SL1 41 C3
**Patrick Gdns** RG42 91 C1
**Patrick Rd** RG4 59 A1
**Patriot Pl** RG1 86 B4
**Patten Ash Dr** RG40 116 C4
**Patten Ave** GU46 149 B3
**Pavenham Cl** RG6 114 A4
**Pavilion Gdns** TW18 97 A1
**Pavilions End The** GU15 151 B2
**Pavy Cl** RG19 106 C1
**Paxton Ave** SL1 42 B2
**Payley Dr** RG40 116 C4
**Paynesdown Rd** RG19 106 A2
**Peace La** SL6 19 C3
**Peach St** RG40 116 B3
**Peachy Dr** RG19 106 C1
**Peacock Ave** TW14 98 B4
**Peacock Cotts** RG12 117 B3
**Peacock La** RG12 117 B3
**Peacock Rd** SL7 2 A2
**Pear Ave** TW17 125 C3
**Pear Tree Ct** GU15 152 A4
**Pear Tree La** RG14 105 B3
**Pear Tree Rd** TW15 98 B2
**Pearce Cl** SL6 19 C1
**Pearce Dr** SL6 19 C4

Pearce Rd SL6 19 C1
Pearces Orch RG9 15 B2
Pearl Gdns SL1 42 A3
Pearmain Cl TW17 125 A2
Pearmans Glade RG2 113 C4
Pearson Rd RG4 60 B2
Pearson Way RG5 87 C3
Peartree Cl SL1 41 C3
Peascod Pl 21 SL4 67 B3
Peascod St SL4 67 B3
Pease Hill RG7 107 C4
Peasemore Hill RG20 50 A4
Pebble Hill RG17 128 A3
Peckmoor Dr RG19 131 B4
Peddlars Gr GU46 149 C3
Peel Cl Caversham RG4 59 B1
Windsor SL4 67 A2
Woodley RG5 88 A4
Peel Ct SL1 42 A4
Peel Ctr The RG12 118 A4
Peel Ho TW20 95 C1
Pegasus Cl RG19 106 A2
Pegasus Ct RG31 84 B4
Peggotty Pl GU47 143 C1
Pegs Green Cl RG30 85 A3
Peket Cl TW18 123 C4
Pelham Ct Maidenhead SL6 39 C4
12 Reading RG30 85 B3
Staines TW18 97 A2
Pelican La RG14 105 A2
Pelican Rd RG26 135 C1
Pell St RG1 86 A3
Pelling Hill SL4 95 A4
Pemberton Gdns RG31 84 B2
Pemberton Rd SL2 21 C1
Pembroke RG12 118 A1
Pembroke Broadway GU15 151 B3
Pembroke Cl Ascot SL5 120 B2
Burghfield Common RG7 111 B2
Pembroke Ho 3 RG4 59 B1
Pembroke Mews SL5 120 B2
Pembroke Pl RG4 59 B2
Pembroke Rd 22 RG14 105 A2
Pembury Ct UB3 71 B4
Pendals Cl RG18 52 C3
Pendeen Ct SL1 42 A3
Pendell Ave UB3 71 C4
Pendennis Ave RG4 59 C3
Pendine Pl RG12 118 A2
Pendlebury RG12 118 A1
Pendragon Ct RG30 85 B3
Pendragon Way GU15 152 B2
Pendred Rd RG2 113 B3
Peninsular Cl GU15 152 A4
Peninsular Cl TW14 71 C1
Penling Cl SL6 19 C3
Penn Cl RG4 59 A3
Penn Ct 8 SL7 1 C1
Penn Mdw SL2 22 C2
Penn Rd Newbury RG14 104 B3
Slough SL2 22 B1
Pennfields RG10 61 C3
Pennine Cl RG31 84 A3
Pennine Rd SL2 42 A4
Pennine Way Charvil RG10 61 A2
Harlington UB3 71 B4
Penny La TW17 125 C1
Pennylets Gn SL2 23 A3
Pennypiece RG8 34 B4
Pennyroyal Ct RG1 86 A3
Penroath Ave RG30 85 B3
Penrose Ave RG5 87 C3
Penrose Cl RG14 104 C3
Penrose Ct TW20 95 B1
Pensford Cl RG45 143 A4
Penshurst Rd SL6 39 B3
Pentangle The 13 RG14 105 A2
Pentland Ave TW17 125 A2
Pentland Cl RG30 84 C3
Pentland Pl RG19 106 B1
Pentland Rd SL2 42 A4
Pentlands The RG17 102 B1
Penton Ave TW18 123 C4
Penton Ct TW18 96 C1
Penton Hall TW18 124 A4
Penton Hall Dr TW18 124 A4
Penton Hook Marina
Chertsey KT16 124 A3
Egham TW18 123 C4
Penton Hook Rd TW18 124 A4
Penton Rd TW18 96 C1
Penwood Ct SL6 39 A4
Penwood Gdns RG12 117 B2
Penwood La SL7 1 B1
Penwood Rd RG20 130 B2
Penyston Rd SL6 39 B4
Penzance Spur SL2 22 A1
Peppard La RG9 35 C4
Peppard Rd RG4 59 B4
Pepper La RG2 86 C2
Pepys Cl SL3 69 A4
Perch Cl SL7 18 B4
Percival Rd TW13 98 C3
Percy Ave TW15 98 A2
Percy Bryant Rd TW16 98 C1
Percy Pl SL3 68 A3
Peregrine Cl
Bracknell RG12 118 A2
Wokingham RG41 115 C3
Peregrine Rd TW16 125 C4
Periam Cl RG9 35 B4
Perkins Ct TW15 97 C2
Perkins Way RG41 116 A3
Perrin Cl TW15 97 C2
Perry Ho SL1 21 A1
Perry Oaks RG12 118 C4
Perry Oaks Dr TW6, UB7 70 B3
Perry Way Bracknell RG12 118 C4
Lightwater GU18 152 C4
Perrycroft SL4 66 C2
Perryfields Way SL1 21 A1
Perryhill Dr GU47 142 C1
Perryman Way SL2 21 C1
Perseverance Hill RG9 35 A3
Perth Ave SL1 42 A4
Perth Cl RG5 61 A1
Perth Trad Est SL1 42 A4
Peterhead Mews SL3 44 A1
Peterhouse Cl GU47 143 C1
Petersfield Ave Slough SL2 43 A3
Staines TW18 97 B1
Petersfield Rd TW18 97 B2
Petrel Cl RG41 115 C3
Petts La TW17 125 A3
Petty Pl SL6 39 B2
Petworth Ave RG30 84 C2
Petworth Ct Reading RG1 85 C3
Windsor SL4 67 A3
Pevensey Ave RG4 59 C3
Pevensey Ct RG2 86 C1
Pevensey Rd SL2 42 A4
Pewsey Vale RG12 118 C2
Pheasant Cl RG41 88 B1
Pheasant La RG20 131 C2
Pheasants Croft SL6 39 A2
Pheasants Ridge SL7 1 B4
Philbye Mews SL1 41 C2
Philip Dr HP10 3 B4
Philip Rd TW18 97 B1
Phillimore Rd RG4 59 B4
Phillips Cl RG5 61 A1
Phipps Cl SL6 39 A1
Phipps Rd SL1 41 C4
Phoebe Ct RG1 86 A3
Phoenix Bsns Pk RG12 117 B4
Phoenix Cl RG41 115 C3
Phoenix Ct SL6 39 B2
Phoenix Pl TW18 97 A2
Phoenix Wlk RG14 130 B3
Phyllis Court Dr RG9 15 C2
Pickering RG12 118 A3
Picket Post Cl RG12 118 C3
Picketts La RG8 55 C2
Pickford Dr SL3 43 C3
Pickins Piece SL3 69 A3
Pickwell Cl RG6 87 B1
Pickwick Gdns GU15 152 A2
Picton Cl GU15 152 A4
Picton Way RG4 59 A2
Piercefield RG31 84 B2
Pierces Hill RG31 57 B1
Pierson Rd SL4 66 B3
Pigeonhouse La SL4, SL5 92 C2
Pigeons Farm Rd RG19 131 B4
Piggott Sch The RG10 61 B4
Piggotts Rd 4 RG4 59 B1
Pightle The RG7 111 C2
Pigott Ct RG40 116 B3
Pigott Rd RG40 116 C4
Pike Cl SL7 18 B4
Pike St RG14 105 A2
Pikeshaw Way RG31 57 B1
Pimento Dr RG6 86 C1
Pimpernel Pl RG18 106 C2
Pincents Kiln Ind Est RG31 84 A2
Pincents La RG31 84 A3
Pinchcut RG7 111 A2
Pinchington La RG14 & RG19 131 A4
Pindar Pl RG14 105 C3
Pine Ave GU15 151 B2
Pine Cl Maidenhead SL6 39 A4
Sandhurst GU15 150 C4
Pine Croft Rd RG41 116 A1
Pine Ct RG12 118 C3
Pine Dr Blackwater GU17 150 C2
Mortimer RG7 136 C3
Wokingham RG40 142 A4
Pine Gr Twyford RG10 61 B3
Windlesham GU20 146 B2
Pine Mount Rd GU15 151 B2
Pine Ridge RG14 105 B3
Pine Ridge Golf Ctr GU16 152 B1
Pine Ridge Rd RG7 111 A2
Pine Trees Bsns Pk TW18 96 C2
Pine Way TW20 95 A1
Pinecote Dr SL5 120 C1
Pinecroft SL7 1 B2
Pinefields Cl RG45 143 A2
Pinehill Rd RG45 143 B2
Pinehill Rise GU47 150 B4
Pinehurst SL5 120 B2
Pinel Cl GU25 122 C3
Piner Cotts SL4 66 C2
Pineridge Cty Inf Sch GU15 145 A1
Pineridge Gdns 10 RG30 85 B3
Pines Cty Inf Sch RG12 118 A1
Pines Cty Jun Sch RG12 118 A1
Pines The
Camberley GU15 151 C4
Twyford RG10 61 C4
Pinetree Ct RG4 59 A3
Pinewood Ave RG45 143 B3
Pinewood Cl RG26 134 B1
Pinewood Dr
Caversham RG4 58 C3
Newtown RG20 131 A1
Staines TW18 97 A2
Pinewood Gdns GU19 145 B2
Pinewood Mews TW19 70 B1
Pinewood Rd GU25 122 A3
Pingewood Cl RG30 85 A1
Pingewood Rd RG30 85 A1
Pingewood Rd S RG7,RG30 112 B4
Pinglestone Cl TW6, UB7 70 C4
Pink La SL1 21 A2
Pinkneys Dr SL6 38 C4
Pinkneys Rd SL6 39 A4
Pinks La RG26 134 C1
Piper's End GU25 122 B3
Pipers Cl SL1 21 B1
Pipers Ct Burnham SL1 21 B1
Thatcham RG19 107 A1
Pipers Way RG19 107 A1
Pipit Cl RG19 106 A2
Pippins Ct TW15 98 A1
Pippins The SL3 43 C3
Pipsons Cl GU46 149 B3
Pitch Pl RG42 90 B2
Pitcroft Ave RG6 87 A3
Pitfield La RG7 137 B2
Pitford Rd RG5 88 A4
Pitts Cl RG42 90 B1
Pitts La RG6 87 A4
Pitts Rd SL1 42 B3
Plackett Way SL1 41 B3
Plaines Cl SL1 41 C3
Plaitinson Rd RG2 113 B3
Planes The KT16 124 B1
Plantagenet Pk RG42 118 C4
Plantation Cl RG18 78 C3
Plantation Rd Chilton OX12 9 C4
Tadley RG26 134 C1
Plantation Row GU15 151 A3
Platt Ct RG17 100 C2
Platt La RG17 45 B3
Play Platt RG7 83 B2
Players Gn RG5 87 C3
Playhatch Rd RG4 60 A3
Plough La Shiplake RG9 35 C1
Stoke Poges SL2 23 A2
Wokingham RG40 116 C3
Plough Rd GU46 149 C4
Ploughlands RG42 117 C4
Ploughlees La SL1 42 C3
Plover Cl Staines TW18 96 C3
Wokingham RG41 115 C3
Plover La RG27 140 C1
Plowden Way RG9 35 C1
Plummery The 1 RG1 86 B4
Plumpton Rd RG14 105 B1
Plumtrees RG6 87 A1
Pluto Cl SL1 41 C2
Pluto Rd OX11 9 C4
Plymouth Ave RG5 87 B3
Plymouth Rd SL1 41 C4
Plympton Cl RG6 87 C2
Pocket Cl RG12 117 B4
Pococks La SL4 42 C1
Poffley Pl RG19 107 A2
Point (L Ctr) The RG12 118 A4
Point Royal RG12 118 A2
Pointers Cl RG20 51 A1
Points The SL6 39 A2
Polehampton CE Inf Sch RG10 61 B3
Polehampton Cl RG10 61 B2
Polehampton Jun Sch RG10 61 C3
Pollard Cl SL4 68 A1
Pollard Gr GU15 152 B2
Pollardrow Ave RG42 117 C4
Pollards Way RG31 84 B2
Polsted Rd RG31 57 B1
Polyanthus Way RG45 143 A4
Polygon Bsns Ctr SL3 69 C3
Pond Cl RG14 130 B4
Pond Croft GU46 149 C3
Pond Head La RG6 87 B2
Pond La Hermitage RG18 79 B4
Mapledurham RG4 58 A3
Pond Moor Rd RG12 118 A2
Pond Rd TW20 96 B1
Pondside Cl UB3 71 B4
Pool End Cl TW17 125 A2
Pool La Slough SL1 42 C3
Waltham St Lawrence RG10 63 A3
Poole Cl RG30 85 A4
Pooley Ave TW20 96 A2
Pooley Green Cl TW20 96 B2
Pooley Green Rd TW20 96 B2
Poolmans Rd SL4 66 B2
Pope Cl TW14 98 C4
Popes Cl SL3 69 B4
Popes La SL6 19 B4
Popeswood Rd RG42 117 B4
Popham Cl RG12 118 C2
Poplar Ave Reading RG30 84 C3
Windlesham GU20 146 A3
Poplar Cl SL3 69 C3
Poplar Gdns RG2 86 C1
Poplar Ho SL3 43 C1
Poplar La Hurst RG10 62 A1
Winnersh RG41 88 B2
Poplar Pl RG14 105 A3
Poplar Rd TW15 98 B2
Poplars Gr SL6 20 A1
Poplars The SL5 120 A2
Poppy Dr RG18 106 C2
Poppy Pl RG40 116 A3
Poppy Way RG31 84 B3
Poppyhills Rd GU15 151 C4
Porchester SL5 120 A3
Porchester Rd RG14 105 A1
Porchfield Cl RG6 87 A1
Porlock Cl RG19 106 B1
Porlock Pl RG31 84 B2
Port Down RG17 100 C3
Porter Cl RG6 114 B4
Porter End RG14 131 A4
Portesbery Hill Dr GU15 151 C3
Portesbery Rd GU15 151 C3
Portesbery Sch GU15 151 B3
Portia Gr RG42 118 C4
Portland Bsns Ctr SL3 68 A3
Portland Cl SL2 21 B1
Portland Cres TW13 98 B2
Portland Gdns RG30 84 B4
Portland Rd TW15 97 C3
Portlands SL7 1 B1
Portlands Mews 8 SL7 1 B1
Portlock Rd SL6 39 B4
Portman Cl 5 RG42 118 A4
Portman Rd RG30 58 B1
Portmeirion Gdns RG30 57 C1
Portnall Dr GU25 121 C2
Portnall Rd GU25 121 C2
Portnall Rise GU25 121 C2
Portrush Rd RG5 87 B3
Portsmouth Ct SL1 42 C3
Portsmouth Rd GU15 152 A4
Portway Swallowfield RG7 139 B1
Tadley RG26 134 C1
Portway Cl RG1 85 C3
Post Horn Pl RG31 84 C2
Post Office Cotts SL2 23 A3
Post Office La
Burghfield Common RG30 111 B3
Slough SL3 43 B4
Post Office Rd RG17 127 C3
Posting House Mews RG14 104 C2
Potley Hill Cty Prim Sch GU46 150 A3
Potley Hill Rd GU46 149 C3
Pottery La RG17 127 C3
Pottery Rd RG30 57 C1
Poulcott TW19 68 C1
Pound Cres SL7 1 B1
Pound La Hurst RG10 89 A3
Little Marlow SL7 2 B2
Marlow SL7 1 B1
Newbury RG20 104 B2
Sonning RG4 60 C1
Thatcham RG19 106 A2
Windlesham GU20 146 B2
Pound Piece RG17 100 B3
Pound Rd KT16 124 A1
Pound St RG14 104 C1
Pound The Cookham SL6 19 C4
Slough SL1 21 B1
Poundfield La SL6 19 C4
Poundfield Way RG10 61 C2
Powis Cl SL6 39 A2
Powney Rd SL6 39 B4
Poyle 14 Trad Est SL3 69 C2
Poyle Cty Fst Sch SL3 69 C3
Poyle Gdns RG12 118 B4
Poyle La SL1 21 A2
Poyle New Cotts SL3 69 C3
Poyle Rd SL3 69 C3
Poyle Tech Ctr The SL3 69 C3
Poynings SL0 44 C1
Prancing Horse Cl RG19 106 C2
Precinct The TW20 96 A2
Precincts The SL1 21 B1
Prescott RG12 117 C1
Prescott Rd SL3 69 C3
Presentation Coll RG30 85 B3
Preston Pl RG14 105 B3
Preston Rd Littleton TW17 125 A2
Reading RG2 86 A3
Slough SL2 43 B3
Prestwick Ct 36 RG1 86 B4
Prestwood SL2 43 A4
Pretoria Rd KT16 123 C1
Price Gdns RG42 91 A1
Prides Crossing SL5 93 A1
Priest Ave RG40 116 C3
Priest Hill Caversham RG4 59 A2
Englefield Green TW19, SL4 95 B3
Priest La GU24 153 B3
Priestwood Ave RG42 117 C4
Priestwood Court Rd RG42 118 A4
Priestwood Sq 1 RG42 118 A4
Primrose Cl RG8 57 B3
Primrose La RG41 88 B2
Primrose Walk GU46 149 A3
Primrose Way GU47 143 A1
Primrose Wlk RG12 118 B2
Prince Albert Dr SL5 119 B2
Prince Andrew Cl SL6 20 A1
Prince Andrew Rd SL6 20 A1
Prince Andrew Way SL5 119 B4
Prince Consort Cotts SL4 67 B3
Prince Consort Dr SL5 119 B3
Prince Consort's Dr
Old Windsor SL4 94 A3
Winkfield SL4 93 C2
Prince Dr GU47 143 A1
Prince Hold Rd RG19 106 A2
Prince of Wales Ave RG30 85 B4
Prince of Wales Wlk 1 GU15 151 B3
Prince William Ct TW15 97 C2
Prince William Dr RG31 57 B1
Princes Cl Bagshot GU19 145 C1
Eton SL4 41 C1
Princes Ct SL8 3 B2
Princes La RG20 50 B3
Princes Rd Ashford TW15 97 C2
Bourne End SL8 3 B2
Egham TW20 95 C1
Feltham TW13 98 C3
Princes St Reading RG1 86 B4
Slough SL1 43 A2
Princess Ave SL4 67 A2
Princess Christians Hospl SL4 67 B3
Princess Margaret Hospl The SL4 67 B3
Princess Margaret Royal Free Sch The SL4 67 B2
Princess Marina Dr
Barkham, Arborfield Garrison RG2 140 C4
Barkham, Langley Common RG2 115 A1
Princess Sq RG12 118 A4
Princess St SL6 39 C3
Princess Way GU15 151 B3
Prior Croft Cl GU15 152 A2
Prior End GU15 152 A3
Prior Heath Cty Inf Sch GU15 152 A3
Prior Rd GU15 152 A3
Prior's La GU17 150 A3
Priors Cl Maidenhead SL6 40 A1
5 Slough SL1 43 A2
Priors Court Rd RG18 78 C4
Priors Court Specl Sch RG18 78 B4
Priors Ct 21 RG1 86 A3
Priors Rd Tadley RG26 135 A1
Windsor SL4 66 B2
Priors Way SL6 40 A1
Priors Way Ind Est SL6 40 A1
Priors Wood RG45 142 B2
Priory Ave Caversham RG4 59 A1
Hungerford RG17 100 B2
Priory Cl Hungerford RG17 100 B2
Sunningdale SL5 121 A1
Priory Ct Camberley GU15 150 C3
Caversham RG4 59 A1
Egham TW20 96 B1
Winnersh RG41 88 B2
Priory Cty Jun & Inf Sch SL1 41 B4
Priory Gn TW18 97 A2
Priory La RG42 91 B1
Priory Mews TW18 97 A2
Priory Pl Greenham RG19 131 A3
Hungerford RG17 100 B2
Priory Rd Burnham SL1 41 B4
Hungerford RG17 100 B2
Newbury RG14 105 A1
Sunningdale SL5 121 A1
Winkfield SL5 119 A4
Priory The RG41 88 B2
Priory Way Datchet SL3 68 A4
Harmondsworth UB7 70 C4
Priory Wlk RG12 118 C3
Priscilla Ho 18 TW16 98 C1
Pritchard Cl RG19 131 B4
Privet Cl RG6 87 A1
Proctors Rd RG40 116 C3
Progress Bsns Ctr SL1 41 B4
Promenade SL4 67 B4
Promenade Rd RG4 59 A1
Prospect Cotts RG42 117 B4
Prospect Ct RG30 85 A3
Prospect La TW20 95 A2
Prospect Pl Hurley SL6 17 C2
Newbury RG14 105 A1
Staines TW18 96 C2
3 Windsor SL4 67 B2
Prospect Rd
Hungerford RG17 100 B3
Marlow SL7 1 B1
Prospect Sch RG30 85 A3
Prospect St
Caversham RG4 59 A1
Reading RG1 85 C4
Providence Ho GU19 145 C2
Providence La UB3 71 B4
Providence Pl SL6 39 C4
Prudential Bldgs 8 SL1 42 C2
Prune Hill TW20 95 C1
Prunus Cl GU24 153 C3
Pudding Hill RG10 37 B3
Pudding La RG20 28 C1
Puffers Way RG14 104 C1
Pullmans Pl TW18 97 A2
Pump La Ascot SL5 120 C4
Shinfield RG7 112 B1
Pump La N SL7 1 C3
Pump La S SL7 2 A2
Pumpkin Hill SL1 21 C3
Pundles La SL6 63 B3
Purbrook Ct RG12 118 C2
Purcell Rd RG45 143 A4
Purfield Dr RG10 36 C1
Purley CE Inf Sch RG8 57 B3
Purley La RG8 57 B3
Purley Rise RG8 56 C3
Purley Village RG8 56 B3
Purley Way RG8 56 C3
Pursers Farm RG7 113 A2
Purslane RG40 116 B3
Purssell Cl SL6 39 A2
Purton Ct SL2 22 B3
Purton La SL2 22 B3
Putman Pl RG9 15 C1
Pycroft Ct KT16 123 C1
Pyegrove Chase RG12 118 C1
Pyke Cl RG40 116 B3
Pykes Hill RG8 54 B2
Pyle Hill RG14 105 A1
Pyrcroft Grange Prim Sch KT16 123 C2
Pyrcroft Rd KT16 123 C1

## Q

Quadrant Ct RG12 .......118 C3
Quadrant The SL6 ........40 A3
Qualitas RG12 ..........117 C1
Quantock Ave RG4 ........59 B3
Quantock Cl Charvil RG10 ..61 A2
Harlington UB3 ...........71 B4
Slough SL3 ..............44 A1
Quantocks The RG19 .....106 B1
Quarrington Cl RG19 .....106 C1
Quarry Bank GU18 .......153 A4
Quarry La Shiplake RG9 ....36 A2
Yateley GU46 ...........149 C3
Quarry Wood Rd SL6,SL7 ..19 A4
Quarrydale Dr SL7 .........1 C1
Quartz Cl RG41 ..........115 B4
Quaves Rd SL3 ...........43 B2
Quebec Gdns GU17 ......150 B2
Quebec Rd RG9 ...........35 C4
Queen Anne Fst Sch The
SL4 .....................67 B2
Queen Anne's Cl SL4 .....94 A3
Queen Anne's Ct 10 SL4 ...67 B3
Queen Anne's Rd SL4 ......67 B2
Queen Anne's Sch RG4 .....59 A2
Queen Annes Gate RG4 ...59 B2
Queen Charlotte St 19 SL4 67 B3
Queen Cl RG9 .............15 C1
Queen Elizabeth Rd
GU15 ...................144 B1
Queen Mary Ave GU15 ...151 A3
Queen Mary Rd TW17 ....125 B4
Queen St Caversham RG4 ...59 A2
Chertsey KT16 ...........124 A1
Henley-on-T RG9 ..........15 C1
Maidenhead SL6 ...........39 C4
Queen Victoria
Cross Roads GU15 ......151 A3
Queen Victoria Ho RG40 .116 B3
Queen Victoria St RG1 ....86 A4
Queen's Acre SL4 ........67 B2
Queen's Cl
North Ascot SL5 .........119 C4
Old Windsor SL4 ..........68 A1
Queen's Ct Slough SL1 .....42 C3
Staines TW18 .............97 B1
Queen's Gate SL4 .........67 B2
Queen's La 8 SL6 .........39 C4
Queen's Pl SL5 ..........120 A3
Queen's Rd Ascot SL5 ....120 B2
Datchet SL3 ..............68 A4
Egham TW20 .............95 C1
Marlow SL7 ................1 B1
Newbury RG14 ...........105 A1
Slough SL1 ...............42 C3
Windsor SL4 ..............67 B3
Queen's Terr 5 SL4 .......67 B2
Queens Acre Ho 6 SL4 ...67 B2
Queens Cotts RG1 .........86 A4
Queens Ct 11 RG14 ......105 A1
Queens Dr The RG2 & RG6 .86 C2
Queens Hill Rise SL5 ....120 B3
Queens Keep GU15 ......151 B3
Queens Lawns RG1 .......86 B3
Queens Park Gdns TW13 ..98 C3
Queens Pine RG12 .......118 C2
Queens Rd Bisley GU24 ...153 C1
Camberley GU15 .........151 A2
Caversham RG4 ...........59 B1
Eton SL4 .................41 C1
Reading RG1 .............86 B4
Queens Ride RG45 .......143 A4
Queens Way RG17 .......102 B1
Queens Wlk TW15 .........97 B2
Queens Wlk Mall 3 SL6 ..39 C4
Queensborough Dr RG4 ...58 C3
Queensbury Pl GU17 .....150 B2
Queenshill Lodge SL5 ...120 A3
Queensmead
Ashford TW15 .............97 C2
Camberley GU15 .........152 A4
Datchet SL3 ..............68 A3
Queensmere Rd SL1 ......43 A2
Queensway Caversham RG4 .59 B3
Maidenhead SL6 ..........19 C1
Quentin Rd RG5 ..........87 B3
Quentin Way GU25 ......122 A3
Quinbrookes SL2 .........43 B4
Quince Cl SL5 ...........120 B3
Quincy Rd TW20 ..........96 A2
Quinn Ct RG30 ............85 B4
Quintilis RG12 ..........117 C1
Quoiting Sq SL7 ............1 B1
Quoitings Dr SL7 ...........1 B1

## R

R.E.M.E Mus RG2 .......141 A4
Race Course Rd RG14 ...105 A1
Race Course Sta RG14 ..105 B1
Raceview Bsns Ctr RG14 .105 A1
Rachaels Lake View RG42 .91 C1
Rackstraw Rd GU47 .....143 B1
Radbourne Rd RG31 ......84 B2
Radcliffe Way RG42 .....117 C4
Radcot Ave SL3 ..........44 A2
Radcot Cl Maidenhead SL6 ..19 C2
Woodley RG5 .............60 C1
Radical Ride RG40 ......141 C4
Radius Pk TW6 ...........71 C2
Radley Bottom
Hungerford RG17 ........101 B4
Radley Bottom *continued*
Hungerford Newtown RG17 ..74 A2
Radley Cl TW14 ..........98 C4
Radnor Cl RG9 ............15 C1
Radnor Ho 12 RG1 ........85 C3
Radnor Rd Bracknell RG12 .118 C3
Earley RG6 ...............87 B2
Radnor Way SL3 ..........43 C1
Radstock La RG6 .........87 A1
Radstock Prim Sch RG6 ...87 A1
Radstock Rd RG1 .........86 C4
Raeburn Way GU47 ......150 B3
RAF Staff Coll RG12 .....118 B3
Ragdale RG7 ............111 A2
Raggleswood Cl RG6 ......87 B2
Raghill RG7 .............135 B3
Raglan Ct RG2 ...........86 B1
Raglan Gdns RG4 .........59 B2
Ragley Mews RG4 .........59 B3
Ragmans Cl SL7 ............1 B4
Ragstone Rd SL1 .........42 C2
Railside RG7 ............108 C1
Railton Cl RG2 ..........113 B4
Railway App KT16 .......123 C1
Railway Rd RG14 ........105 A1
Railway Terr Egham TW18 ..96 B2
Slough SL2 ...............42 C3
Railways Cotts RG8 .......34 B3
Rainbow Pk RG41 .........88 A1
Rainsborough Chase SL6 .39 A2
Rainworth Cl RG6 .......114 A4
Raleigh Cl Slough SL1 .....42 A3
Woodley RG5 .............87 C3
Raleigh Ct TW18 .........97 A2
Raleigh Rd TW13, TW14 ....98 C3
Raleigh Way GU16 ......151 C2
Ralphs Ride RG12 .......118 C3
Rambler Cl SL6 ...........41 A4
Rambler La SL3 ...........43 B2
Ramptons La RG7 .......136 A3
Ramsay Rd GU20 ........146 C3
Ramsbury Cl RG12 ......117 C2
Ramsbury Dr Earley RG6 ...87 A2
Hungerford RG17 ........100 C3
Ramsey Cl
Camberley GU15 .........152 A4
Earley RG6 ...............87 C1
Ramsey Ct SL2 ...........21 B1
Ramslade Rd RG12 ......118 B3
Rances La RG40 .........116 C3
Randall Cl SL3 ...........43 C1
Randall Ct SL4 ...........68 A1
Randall Mead RG42 .......90 A1
Randell Cl GU17 ........150 C1
Randolph Rd Reading RG1 ..59 A1
Slough SL3 ...............43 C2
Ranelagh Cres SL5 ......119 B4
Ranelagh Dr RG12 ......118 B3
Ranelagh Sch RG12 .....118 B3
Range Rd RG40 .........142 A4
Range Ride GU15 .......150 C4
Range View GU47 .......150 C4
Range Villas TW17 ......124 C1
Range Way TW17 ........125 A1
Rangewood Ave RG30 ....84 C2
Ranikhet Prim Sch RG30 ..85 A4
Rapley Cl GU15 .........151 C4
Rapley Gn RG12 ........118 B2
Ratby Cl RG6 .............87 B1
Raven Cl GU46 ..........149 A3
Ravendale Rd TW16 .....125 C4
Ravenglass Cl RG6 .......87 B2
Ravens Field SL3 .........43 B2
Ravensbourne Ave TW19 ..97 C4
Ravensbourne Dr RG5 .....87 C4
Ravenscote Cty Jun Sch
GU16 ...................152 A2
Ravenscourt Marlow SL7 ....2 A2
Sunbury TW16 ..........125 C4
Ravenscroft Rd RG9 ......15 B1
Ravensdale Mews TW18 ..97 A1
Ravensdale Rd SL5 ......120 A2
Ravensfield TW20 .........95 B1
Ravenshoe Cl SL8 ..........3 A2
Ravenstone Rd GU15 ....152 B3
Ravenswing Mobile
Home Pk RG7 ...........135 B1
Ravenswood Ave RG45 ..142 C3
Ravenswood Dr GU15 ....152 A3
Ravenswood Village
Settlement RG45 .......142 C3
Ravensworth Rd
Mortimer RG7 ...........136 C3
Slough SL2 ...............22 A1
Rawcliffe Ho SL6 .........40 A3
Rawdon Rise GU15 ......152 A3
Rawlinson Rd GU15 ......150 C3
Ray Dr SL6 ...............40 A4
Ray Ho 4 SL8 ..............3 A2
Ray Lea Cl SL6 ...........40 A4
Ray Lea Rd SL6 ...........40 A4
Ray Lodge SL6 ...........40 A4
Ray Lodge Mews SL6 .....40 A4
Ray Mdw SL6 .............20 A1
Ray Mead Ct SL6 .........20 B1
Ray Mead Rd SL6 .........40 B4
Ray Mill Rd E SL6 ........20 A1
Ray Mill Rd W SL6 ........40 A4
Ray Park Ave SL6 .........40 A4
Ray Park La SL6 ..........40 A4
Ray Park Rd SL6 ..........40 A4
Ray St SL6 ...............40 A4
Rayfield SL6 .............40 A4
Raymond Cl SL3 ..........69 C3
Raymond Rd
Maidenhead SL6 ..........39 B4
Slough SL3 ...............44 A2
Rayners Cl SL3 ...........69 B4
Rays Ave SL4 .............66 C4
Raywood Cl UB3 ..........71 B4
Reade Ct SL2 .............22 B3
Reading Alternative Sch
RG1 .....................86 B3
Reading Blue Coat Sch
RG4 .....................60 B2
Reading Bridge RG1 ......86 A4
Reading Coll
of Arts & Tech RG1 ......86 C3
Reading Coll of Tech RG1 .86 B4
Reading Gate Ret Pk RG2 .85 C1
Reading Girls Sch RG2 ....86 B2
Reading Gram Sch RG1 ...86 B3
Reading Link Ret Pk RG2 .86 A3
Reading Rd Aldworth RG8 ..33 A1
Arborfield RG2 ..........114 B2
Blackwater GU17 ........150 A2
Burghfield Common RG7 ..111 A1
Finchampstead RG27 .....140 C2
Goring RG8 ...............34 C3
Henley-on-T RG9 ..........15 C1
Moulsford OX10 ...........14 A4
Pangbourne RG8 ..........56 B3
Streatley RG8 .............34 A3
Wokingham RG41 ........115 C4
Woodley RG5 .............87 B4
Yateley GU46 ............149 B3
Reading St Michael
Cty Prim Sch RG30 ......85 A4
Reading Sta RG1 .........86 A4
Reading West Sta RG30 ...85 C4
Recreation Cl GU14 .....150 C1
Recreation La RG7 ......113 A1
Recreation Rd
Bourne End SL8 ............3 A2
Burghfield Common RG7 ..111 A1
Reading RG30 .............84 C4
Wargrave RG10 ...........36 C1
Rectory Cl Bracknell RG12 .118 B3
Farnham Common SL2 ......22 B1
Littleton TW17 ..........125 A3
Newbury RG14 ..........104 C1
Sandhurst GU47 .........149 C4
Windsor SL4 ..............67 A3
Wokingham RG40 ........116 B3
Rectory La
Aston Tirrold OX11 ........12 C4
Bracknell RG12 ..........118 A3
Letcombe Bassett OX12 .....6 C4
Windlesham GU20 .......146 B2
Rectory Rd Caversham RG4 .59 A1
Padworth RG7 ...........135 C4
Streatley RG8 .............33 B4
Taplow SL6 ...............20 C1
Wokingham RG40 ........116 B3
Rectory Row RG12 ......118 A3
Rectory Terr SL2 ..........22 B2
Red Cottage Dr RG31 .....84 B2
Red Cottage Mews SL3 ...43 B2
Red Cross Rd RG8 ........34 B3
Red Ct SL1 ...............42 C3
Red Hill RG9 .............35 A3
Red House Cl RG6 ......114 A4
Red La RG7 .............135 B3
Red Leaf Cl SL3 ..........43 C3
Red Lion Cotts SL2 .......23 A1
Red Lion Way HP10 ........3 C3
Red Rd GU18, GU24, GU15 .153 B4
Red Rose RG42 ...........90 B2
Red Shute Hill RG18 ......79 A2
Red Shute Ind Est RG18 ...79 A2
Redberry Cl RG4 ..........59 B3
Redcrest Gdns GU15 .....151 C3
Reddington Dr SL3 .......43 C1
Redditch RG12 ..........118 B1
Redfield Ct RG14 ........105 B2
Redford Cl TW13 .........98 C3
Redford Rd SL4 ..........66 B3
Redgauntlet RG40 .......141 B3
Redgrave Pl SL7 ............1 C2
Redhatch Dr RG6 .........87 A1
Redlake La RG40 ........116 C1
Redlands Pl RG40 .......115 C1
Redlands Prim Sch RG1 ...86 C3
Redlands Rd RG1 .........86 B3
Redlane Ct RG1 ...........86 B3
Redlane Hill RG7 ........135 B3
Redleaves Ave TW15 ......98 A1
Redmayne GU15 .........152 B2
Redriff Cl SL6 ............39 B3
Redruth Gdns RG2 ........86 A1
Redshots Cl SL7 ............1 C2
Redvers Rd RG12 .......118 A2
Redwood Burnham SL1 .....21 A2
Egham TW20 ............123 C4
Redwood Ave RG5 ........88 A3
Redwood Dr
Frimley GU15 ...........152 B2
Sunningdale SL5 ........121 A2
Redwood Gdns SL1 .......42 B3
Redwood Mews TW15 .....98 B1
Redwood Way RG31 ......57 B2
Redwoods The SL4 .......67 B2
Reed Cl SL0 ..............44 C4
Reed Place Bsns Pk
TW17 ...................124 C1
Reed Wlk RG14 ..........105 B2
Reed's Hill RG12 ........118 A2
Reeds Ave RG6 ...........86 C2
Reedsfield Cl TW15 .......98 A3
Reedsfield Rd TW15 .......98 A2
Reeve Rd SL6 .............65 A4
Reeves Way RG41 .......116 A2
Reform Rd SL6 ...........40 A4
Regal Ct SL6 .............40 A1
Regatta Ho TW18 .........96 C2
Regency Hts RG4 .........58 C2
Regent Cl Earley RG6 ......87 B1
Hungerford RG17 ........100 B3
Regent Ct Bagshot GU19 ..145 C1
9 Maidenhead SL6 ........39 C4
Reading RG1 .............86 A4
Slough SL1 ...............42 C4
Windsor SL4 ..............67 B3
Regent St RG1 ...........86 C4
Regent Way GU16 .......152 A1
Regents Ct RG14 ........104 C2
Regents Pl GU47 ........150 B4
Regents Wlk SL5 ........120 B1
Regis Cl RG2 ...........113 B4
Regis Ct TW14 ............71 B1
Regnum Dr RG14 ........105 A3
Reid Ave SL6 .............39 C3
Rembrandt Cl RG41 .....115 B3
Rembrandt Way RG1 ......85 C3
Remembrance Rd RG14 ..104 C1
Remenham Church La
RG9 .....................16 A2
Remenham La RG9 ........15 C2
Remenham Terr RG9 ......16 B1
Renault Rd RG5 ..........88 A3
Renfree Way TW17 ......125 A1
Rennie Cl TW15 ..........97 B3
Repton Cl SL6 ............39 B2
Repton Rd RG6 ...........87 B2
Restwold Cl RG30 .........85 B2
Retford Cl RG5 ...........60 C1
Retreat The
Englefield Green TW20 .....95 C2
Holyport SL6 .............65 B4
Revel Rd HP10 .............3 B4
Revesby Cl Maidenhead SL6 .39 B2
West End GU24 ..........153 B3
Rex Ave TW15 ............98 A2
Reynards Cl RG41 ........88 B1
Reynolds Ct RG18 .......106 B2
Reynolds Gn GU47 .......150 B3
Rhigos RG4 ..............58 C3
Rhine Cl RG4 .............59 B1
Rhodes Cl Earley RG6 ......87 C2
Egham TW20 .............96 A2
Rhodes Ct TW20 ..........96 B2
Rhododendron Cl SL5 ....92 C1
Rhododendron Rd GU16 .152 A1
Rhododendron Ride
SL4, TW20 ...............94 C2
Rhododendron Wlk SL5 ...92 C1
Ribbleton Cl RG6 .........87 C2
Ribstone Rd SL6 ..........39 A2
Ricardo Rd SL4 ...........68 A1
Richard Ct TW15 .........97 C2
Richard Nevill Ct 6 RG4 ..59 B1
Richards Cl UB3 ..........71 B4
Richards Way SL1 ........42 A3
Richardson's Lawn Cotts
SL4 .....................94 A3
Richborough Cl RG6 ......87 A1
Richfield Ave RG1 ........58 C1
Richings Way SL0 ........44 C2
Richmond Ave
Feltham TW14 ............71 C1
Thatcham RG19 .........106 A2
Richmond Cl GU16 ......151 C1
Richmond Cres Slough SL1 .43 A3
Staines TW18 .............96 C2
Richmond Dr TW17 ......125 B2
Richmond Ho GU47 .....150 C4
Richmond Rd
Caversham RG4 ...........58 C2
Reading RG30 .............85 B4
Sandhurst GU47 .........150 C4
Staines TW18 .............96 C2
Richmond Rise RG41 ....115 C4
Richmondwood SL5 .....121 A1
Rickman Cl
Arborfield RG2 ..........114 C1
Bracknell RG12 ..........118 B2
Woodley RG5 .............87 B3
Rickman's La SL2 .........22 C3
Riddings La RG19 .......133 B1
Riders La RG7 ..........112 A2
Rideway Cl GU15 .......151 A2
Ridge Hall Cl RG4 ........58 C2
Ridge Mount Rd SL5 .....121 A1
Ridge The Cold Ash RG18 ..106 B4
Lower Basildon RG8 .......34 C1
Upper Basildon RG8 .......55 C4
Ridge Way Iver SL0 .......44 C3
Virginia Water GU25 .....122 C2
Ridgebank SL1 ...........41 C3
Ridgemead Rd TW20 ......95 A3
Ridgemount Cl RG31 .....57 A1
Ridgeway
Walton-on-T KT12 ........125 C1
Wargrave RG10 ...........36 C1
Ridgeway Cl
Hermitage RG18 ..........79 A4
Lightwater GU18 .........153 A4
Marlow SL7 ................1 C2
Ridgeway Prim Sch RG2 ..86 B1
Ridgeway Sch SL6 ........38 C3
Ridgeway The
Bracknell RG12 ..........118 B3
Caversham RG4 ...........59 A2
Letcombe Bassett OX12 .....7 B3
Lightwater GU18 .........146 A1
Marlow SL7 ................1 C2
Woodley RG5 .............87 C3
Ridgeway Trad Est The
SL0 .....................44 C3
Ridgewood Ctr (Hospl)
GU16 ...................152 B2
Ridgewood Dr GU16 .....152 B2
Riding Court Rd SL3 ......68 B4
Riding Ct SL3 ............68 B4
Riding Way RG41 ........115 C3
Ridings The
Caversham RG4 ...........59 B4
Frimley GU16 ...........152 A2
Iver SL0 ..................44 C1
Maidenhead SL6 ..........39 A4
Ridleigh Ct TW15 .........98 A2
Ridlington Cl RG6 ........87 C1
Rigby Lodge SL1 .........42 C4
Righton Cl RG10 ..........61 A2
Riley Rd Marlow SL7 ........1 B1
Reading RG30 .............84 C4
Ring The RG12 ..........118 B4
Ringmead Bracknell,
Great Hollands RG12 .....117 C2
Bracknell, Hanworth RG12 .118 A1
Ringwood RG12 .........117 C1
Ringwood Cl SL5 ........120 A3
Ringwood Rd
Blackwater GU17 ........150 B3
Reading RG30 .............58 A1
Ripley Ave TW20 .........95 C1
Ripley Cl SL3 .............43 C1
Ripley Rd RG30 ...........58 A1
Ripon Cl GU15 ..........152 B2
Ripplesmere RG12 .......118 B3
Ripplesmore Cl GU47 ....150 A4
Ripston Rd TW15 .........98 B2
Risborough Rd SL6 .......39 C4
Rise Rd SL5 .............120 C2
Rise The Caversham RG4 ...59 A2
Cold Ash RG18 ..........106 B4
Crowthorne RG45 .......142 C3
Finchampstead RG40 .....141 A1
Wokingham RG41 ........116 A4
Riseley Rd SL6 ...........39 B4
Rissington Cl RG31 .......57 C2
River Ct SL6 .............40 B4
River Gdns Maidenhead SL6 .40 B2
Purley on T RG8 ..........57 B3
River Mount KT12 .......125 C1
River Park Ave TW18 .....96 B2
River Pk RG14 ..........105 B2
River Rd Caversham RG4 ...58 B2
Reading RG1 .............86 A3
Staines TW18 ...........123 C4
Taplow SL6 ...............40 B3
Yateley GU46 ............149 A4
River & Rowing Mus RG9 .15 C1
River Side Cotts HP10 ......3 C4
River St SL4 .............67 B4
River View HP10 ...........3 A4
River Wlk RG14 .........105 B2
Riverbank TW18 ..........96 C1
Riverdene Dr RG41 .......88 A2
Riverfield Rd TW18 .......96 C1
Rivermead Ct SL7 .........18 B4
Rivermead Ind Est RG19 .106 C1
Rivermead Prim Sch RG5 .87 C3
Rivermead Rd
Camberley GU15 .........151 A1
Woodley RG5 .............87 C3
Riverpark Dr SL7 ...........1 C1
Riversdale SL8 .............3 A1
Riversdale Ct RG1 ........86 C4
Riversdell Cl KT16 ......123 C1
Riverside Bradfield RG7 ...82 B3
Egham TW20 .............96 A3
Lower Halliford TW17 .....125 C1
Wraysbury TW19 ..........95 B4
Riverside Ave GU18 .....153 B4
Riverside Cl TW18 .......123 C4
Riverside Ct 1 RG4 .......59 A1
Riverside Dr Egham TW18 ..96 C2
Staines TW18 ...........123 C4
Riverside Pl TW19 ........70 B1
Riverside Rd Staines TW18 .96 C1
Stanwell TW19 ............70 C1
Riverside Way GU15 .....151 A2
Riverside Wlk SL4 ........67 B4
Riverview TW17 .........125 B1
Riverview Rd RG8 ........56 B3
Riverway
Great Shefford RG17 ......48 A2
Staines TW18 ...........124 A4
Riverwood Ct SL7 .........18 C4
Riverwoods Ave SL7 .......2 A1
Riverwoods Dr SL7 ........2 A1
Rixman Cl SL6 ...........39 B3
Rixon Cl SL3 .............43 C4
Robert Piggott CE Inf Sch
RG10 ....................36 C1
Robert Piggott CE Jun Sch
RG10 ....................36 B1
Robert Sandilands
Prim Sch RG14 .........104 C2
Roberts Cl TW19 ..........70 B1
Roberts Gr RG41 ........115 C2
Roberts Rd GU15 ........151 A3
Roberts Way TW20 ........95 B1
Robertsfield RG19 .......105 C2
Robertson Cl RG14 ......131 A4
Robin Cl RG7 ...........111 A2
Robin Hill Dr GU15 ......152 A2
Robin Hood Cl SL1 .......41 C3
Robin Hood Way RG41 ....88 B2
Robin La Newtown RG20 ..131 C2
Sandhurst GU47 .........143 B1
Robin Par 5 SL2 ..........22 B4
Robin Way Reading RG31 ...84 A3
Staines TW18 .............96 C3
Robin Willis Way SL4 .....68 A1
Robin's Bow GU15 .......151 A2
Robindale Ave RG6 .......87 B2
Robinhood La RG41 ......88 B2
Robins Cl RG14 .........130 C4
Robins Grove Cres GU46 .149 A3
Robins Hill RG17 .......127 C3

Robinson Cl OX11 . . . . . . . .12 A4
Robinson Ct RG6 . . . . . . . . .87 A1
Roby Dr RG12 . . . . . . . . . .118 B1
Rochester Ave
Feltham TW13 . . . . . . . . . . . .98 C3
Woodley RG5 . . . . . . . . . . . .60 C1
Rochester Rd TW20 . . . . . . .96 B1
Rochford Way SL6 . . . . . . . .41 A4
Rochfords Gdns SL2 . . . . . .43 B3
Rockall Ct SL3 . . . . . . . . . .44 A2
Rockbourne Gdns RG30 . . . .58 A1
Rockfel Rd RG17 . . . . . . . . .25 A1
Rockfield Way 7 GU47 . . .150 B4
Rockingham Rd RG14 . . .104 C1
Rockmoor La SP11 . . . . . .147 A1
Rodd Est TW17 . . . . . . . . . .125 B2
Rodney Ct 11 RG1 . . . . . . .86 A3
Rodney Way SL3 . . . . . . . . .69 C3
Rodway Rd RG30 . . . . . . . . .57 C1
Roebuck Est RG42 . . . . . . . .90 B1
Roebuck Gn SL1 . . . . . . . . .41 C3
Roebuck Rise RG31 . . . . . . .57 B2
Roebuts Cl RG14 . . . . . . . .130 C4
Rogers La SL2 . . . . . . . . . . .22 C2
Rogers's La RG17 . . . . . . . . .47 B3
Rogosa Rd GU24 . . . . . . . .153 C3
Rokeby Cl Bracknell RG12 .118 B4
Newbury RG14 . . . . . . . . . .131 A4
Rokeby Dr RG4 . . . . . . . . . .58 B4
Rokes Pl GU46 . . . . . . . . . .149 A3
Rokesby Rd SL2 . . . . . . . . . .21 C1
Rolls La SL6 . . . . . . . . . . . .64 C4
Roman Field RG7 . . . . . . .136 A1
Roman Lea SL6 . . . . . . . . . .19 C4
Roman Ride RG45 . . . . . . .142 B3
Roman Way Bourne End SL8 .3 A2
Earley RG6 . . . . . . . . . . . . . .87 B2
Thatcham RG18 . . . . . . . . .106 A2
Winkfield RG42 . . . . . . . . .118 C4
Romana Ct TW18 . . . . . . . .97 A2
Romano Ct 9 RG14 . . . . .105 A1
Romans Gate RG26 . . . . . .135 C1
Romany Cl RG30 . . . . . . . . .58 A1
Romany La RG30 . . . . . . . . .58 A1
Romeo Hill RG42 . . . . . . . .118 C4
Romney Cl TW15 . . . . . . . . .98 B2
Romney Ct 11 SL7 . . . . . . . . .1 C2
Romney Ho RG12 . . . . . . . .118 C3
Romney Lock Rd SL4 . . . . .67 B4
Romsey Cl
Blackwater GU17 . . . . . . . .150 B3
Slough SL3 . . . . . . . . . . . . .43 C2
Romsey Rd RG30 . . . . . . . . .58 A1
Rona Ct RG30 . . . . . . . . . . .85 A4
Ronaldsay Spur SL1 . . . . . .42 C4
Ronita Ct RG1 . . . . . . . . . . .86 C3
Rood Hill RG20 . . . . . . . . . .76 B2
Rook Cl RG41 . . . . . . . . . . .115 C3
Rook Rd HP10 . . . . . . . . . . . .3 B2
Rookery Ct SL7 . . . . . . . . . . .1 B1
Rookery Rd TW18 . . . . . . . .97 A2
Rookery The RG20 . . . . . . . .50 B4
Rooksfield RG20 . . . . . . . .132 A1
Rooksmead Rd TW16 . . . .125 C4
Rooksnest La RG17 . . . . . .128 A3
Rookswood Bracknell RG42 .91 A1
Stockcross RG20 . . . . . . . .103 C3
Rookwood Ave GU47 . . . .143 C1
Rope Wlk RG19 . . . . . . . . .106 B2
Rosa Ave TW15 . . . . . . . . . .98 A2
Rosary Gdns Ashford TW15 .98 A2
Yateley GU46 . . . . . . . . . . .149 B3
Rose Cl RG5 . . . . . . . . . . . . .88 A4
Rose Cotts SL6 . . . . . . . . . . .39 B2
Rose Ct RG40 . . . . . . . . . . .116 B3
Rose Gdns TW19 . . . . . . . . .97 B4
Rose Hill Binfield RG42 . . . . .90 B2
Burnham SL1 . . . . . . . . . . . .21 A3
Rose Ind Est
Bourne End SL8 . . . . . . . . . . .3 A2
Marlow Bottom SL7 . . . . . . . .1 B3
Rose Kiln La RG1 & RG2 . . .86 A2
Rose La Hurley RG9 . . . . . . .17 A1
Knowl Hill RG10 . . . . . . . . . .37 A4
Rose St RG40 . . . . . . . . . . .116 B3
Rose Wlk Reading RG1 . . . . .86 A4
Slough SL2 . . . . . . . . . . . . . .42 A4
Roseacre Cl TW17 . . . . . . .125 A2
Rosebank Cl SL6 . . . . . . . . .19 C4
Rosebay RG40 . . . . . . . . . .116 C4
Rosebery Rd RG4 . . . . . . . . .58 B4
Rosecroft Way RG2 . . . . . .113 C3
Rosedale RG42 . . . . . . . . . . .90 B2
Rosedale Cres RG6 . . . . . . .87 A4
Rosedale Gdns
Bracknell RG12 . . . . . . . . .118 A2
Thatcham RG19 . . . . . . . . .106 B1
Rosedene La GU47 . . . . . .150 B4
Rosefield Rd TW18 . . . . . . .97 A2
Rosehill Ct SL1 . . . . . . . . . .43 A2
Rosehill Ho RG4 . . . . . . . . . .59 B4
Rosehill Pk RG4 . . . . . . . . . .59 B4
Roseleigh Cl SL6 . . . . . . . . .39 A4
Rosemary Ave RG6 . . . . . . . .86 C1
Rosemary Gdns GU17 . . . .150 B3
Rosemary La
Blackwater GU17 . . . . . . . .150 B3
Thorpe TW20 . . . . . . . . . . .123 A3
Rosemary Terr RG14 . . . . .104 C1
Rosemead KT16 . . . . . . . . .124 A1
Rosemead Ave
Feltham TW13 . . . . . . . . . . .98 C3
Purley on T RG31 . . . . . . . .57 A2
Rosen Ct RG19 . . . . . . . . .106 C2
Rosery The SL8 . . . . . . . . . . .3 A2
Roses La SL4 . . . . . . . . . . . .66 B3
Rosewood RG5 . . . . . . . . . .87 B2
Rosewood Dr TW17 . . . . .124 C2
Rosewood Way
Farnham Common SL2 . . . . . .22 B4
West End GU24 . . . . . . . . .153 C3
Rosier Cl RG19 . . . . . . . . .106 C1
Rosken Gr SL2 . . . . . . . . . . .22 A2
Roslyn Rd RG5 . . . . . . . . . .87 B3
Ross Ho 2 RG30 . . . . . . . . .85 B3
Ross Rd Maidenhead SL6 . . .39 C2
Reading RG1 . . . . . . . . . . . .59 A1
Rossendale Rd RG4 . . . . . . .59 B2
Rossett Cl RG12 . . . . . . . .118 A3
Rossey Pl SL4 . . . . . . . . . . .42 B1
Rossington Pl RG2 . . . . . .113 B4
Rossiter Cl SL3 . . . . . . . . . .43 C1
Rosslea GU20 . . . . . . . . . .146 A3
Rosslyn Cl TW16 . . . . . . . . .98 C1
Rothbury Wlk GU15 . . . . .152 B2
Rother Cl GU47 . . . . . . . . .150 B4
Rotherfield Ave RG41 . . . .116 A4
Rotherfield Cl RG7 . . . . . . .83 C2
Rotherfield Rd RG9 . . . . . . .35 C4
Rotherfield Way RG4 . . . . .59 A2
Rothwell Gdns RG5 . . . . . . .61 A1
Rothwell Ho RG45 . . . . . . .143 B2
Rothwell Wlk RG4 . . . . . . . .59 B1
Rotten Row Hill RG7 . . . . . .81 C2
Roughgrove Copse RG42 . .90 A1
Rounce La GU24 . . . . . . . .153 B3
Round Cl GU46 . . . . . . . . .149 C3
Round End RG14 . . . . . . . .130 B3
Roundabout La RG41 . . . .115 B4
Roundfield RG7 . . . . . . . . .107 A3
Roundhead Rd RG7 . . . . . . .83 B2
Roundshead Dr RG12 . . . .118 B4
Roundway Egham TW20 . . . .96 B2
Frimley GU15 . . . . . . . . . . .152 B3
Roundway Cl GU15 . . . . . .152 B3
Routh Ct TW14 . . . . . . . . . . .98 B4
Routh La RG30 . . . . . . . . . . .84 C3
Row La RG4 . . . . . . . . . . . . .59 C4
Rowallan Cl RG4 . . . . . . . . .59 B3
Rowan 2 RG12 . . . . . . . . .118 C2
Rowan Ave TW20 . . . . . . . . .96 B2
Rowan Cl Camberley GU15 .151 C4
Wokingham RG41 . . . . . . . .115 C3
Rowan Ct RG6 . . . . . . . . . . .87 A1
Rowan Dr
Crowthorne RG45 . . . . . . . .143 B3
Newbury RG14 . . . . . . . . . .105 A3
Woodley RG5 . . . . . . . . . . . .87 C4
Rowan Ho 1 SL8 . . . . . . . . . .3 A2
Rowan Way
Burghfield Common RG30 . .111 A3
Slough SL2 . . . . . . . . . . . . . .42 A4
Rowanhurst Dr SL2 . . . . . . .22 B4
Rowans Cl GU14 . . . . . . . .150 C1
Rowans The TW16 . . . . . . . .98 C2
Rowcroft Rd RG2 . . . . . . . .140 C4
Rowdell Dr RG2 . . . . . . . . . .86 B1
Rowdown RG17 . . . . . . . . . .24 C3
Rowe Ct RG30 . . . . . . . . . . .85 A4
Rowland Cl SL4 . . . . . . . . . .66 B2
Rowland Hill
Almshouses TW15 . . . . . . .98 A2
Rowland Way Earley RG6 . .86 C1
Littleton TW15 . . . . . . . . . . .98 B1
Rowland's Cl RG7 . . . . . . .136 B3
Rowles Paddock RG20 . . . .10 A1
Rowley Cl RG12 . . . . . . . . .118 C3
Rowley La SL3 . . . . . . . . . . .23 B2
Rowley Rd RG2 . . . . . . . . . . .86 A2
Roxborough Way SL6 . . . . .38 C2
Roxburgh Cl GU15 . . . . . . .152 B2
Roxeth Ct TW15 . . . . . . . . . .98 A2
Roxford Cl TW17 . . . . . . . .125 C2
Roxwell Cl SL1 . . . . . . . . . . .41 C3
Roy Cl RG18 . . . . . . . . . . . . .78 C3
Royal Ascot Golf Club
SL5 . . . . . . . . . . . . . . . . . .120 A4
Royal Ave RG31 . . . . . . . . . .84 B3
Royal Berkshire Hospl The
RG1 . . . . . . . . . . . . . . . . . . .86 B3
Royal Cotts SL6 . . . . . . . . . .19 B4
Royal Ct 10 RG1 . . . . . . . . .86 B4
Royal Free Ct 22 SL4 . . . . .67 B3
Royal Holloway Univ
of London TW20 . . . . . . . . .95 B1
Royal Hunt Ho SL5 . . . . . .119 B4
Royal Mans RG9 . . . . . . . . . .15 C1
Royal Military Acad
GU15 . . . . . . . . . . . . . . . . .150 C3
Royal Military Acad
Hospl GU15 . . . . . . . . . . .151 A4
Royal Oak Cl GU46 . . . . . .149 C3
Royal Oak Dr RG45 . . . . . .143 A4
Royal Prim Sch The SL4 . . .94 B2
Royal Victoria Gdns SL5 .120 A2
Royal Way RG2 . . . . . . . . .112 C4
Royal Windsor Race Course
SL4 . . . . . . . . . . . . . . . . . . .66 C4
Roycroft La RG40 . . . . . . .141 C4
Royston Cl RG30 . . . . . . . . .84 C4
Royston Way SL1 . . . . . . . . .41 B4
Rubus Cl GU24 . . . . . . . . . .153 C3
Ruby Cl Slough SL1 . . . . . . .42 A2
Wokingham RG41 . . . . . . . .115 C4
Rudd Hall Rise GU15 . . . .151 C2
Ruddlesway SL4 . . . . . . . . .66 B3
Rudland Cl RG19 . . . . . . . .106 B1
Rudsworth Cl SL3 . . . . . . . .69 B4
Rufus Isaacs Rd RG4 . . . . .59 A1
Rugby Cl GU47 . . . . . . . . . .143 C1
Ruggles-Brise Rd TW15 . . .97 B2
Rumseys La OX11 . . . . . . . .12 A4
Runnemede Rd TW20 . . . . .96 A2
Runnymede Cotts TW19 . . .96 B4
Runnymede Ct TW20 . . . . . .96 A2
Runnymede Rdbt TW20 . . .96 A2
Rupert Cl RG9 . . . . . . . . . . . .15 C2
Rupert House Sch RG9 . . .15 C1
Rupert Rd RG14 . . . . . . . .130 C4
Rupert Sq 19 RG1 . . . . . . . .86 B4
Rupert St RG1 . . . . . . . . . . .86 B4
Rupert Wlk 17 RG1 . . . . . . .86 B4
Rupert's La RG9 . . . . . . . . . .15 C2
Ruscombe Gdns SL3 . . . . . .68 A4
Ruscombe La RG10 . . . . . . .61 C3
Ruscombe Pk RG10 . . . . . . .61 C3
Ruscombe Rd RG10 . . . . . . .61 C3
Ruscombe Way TW14 . . . . .98 C4
Rushall Cl RG6 . . . . . . . . .113 C4
Rusham Park Ave TW20 . . .96 A1
Rusham Rd TW20 . . . . . . . . .95 C1
Rushbrook Rd RG5 . . . . . . .87 B4
Rushburn HP10 . . . . . . . . . . .3 C3
Rushden Dr RG2 . . . . . . . . .86 C1
Rushes The
Maidenhead SL6 . . . . . . . . .40 B3
Marlow SL7 . . . . . . . . . . . . . .18 B4
Rushey Way RG6 . . . . . . . . .87 B1
Rushington Ave SL6 . . . . . .39 C3
Rushmere Pl TW20 . . . . . . .95 C2
Rushmoor Gdns RG31 . . . .84 A2
Rushy Ho 7 RG12 . . . . . . .118 C3
Ruskin Ave TW14 . . . . . . . . .71 C1
Ruskin Ct RG45 . . . . . . . . .142 C2
Ruskin Rd TW18 . . . . . . . . . .96 C1
Ruskin Way RG41 . . . . . . .115 B3
Russel Cl RG12 . . . . . . . . .118 B1
Russell Ct
Blackwater GU17 . . . . . . . .150 B3
Maidenhead SL6 . . . . . . . . . .39 C4
Russell Dr TW19 . . . . . . . . . .70 B1
Russell Ho 3 SL8 . . . . . . . . . .3 A2
Russell Rd
Lower Halliford TW17 . . . . .125 B1
Mapledurham RG4 . . . . . . . .58 B4
Newbury RG14 . . . . . . . . . .104 C1
Russell St Reading RG1 . . . .85 C4
Windsor SL4 . . . . . . . . . . . . .67 B3
Russell Way RG41 . . . . . . . .88 A1
Russet Ave TW16, TW17 . .125 C3
Russet Cl TW19 . . . . . . . . . .69 C1
Russet Gdns GU15 . . . . . . .151 B2
Russet Glade
Burghfield Common RG7 . . .111 A1
Caversham RG4 . . . . . . . . . .59 B4
Russet Rd SL6 . . . . . . . . . . .39 B2
Russington Rd TW17 . . . .125 B2
Russley Gn RG40 . . . . . . . .116 A1
Rustington Cl 5 RG6 . . . . .87 A1
Ruston Way SL5 . . . . . . . . .119 C4
Rutherford Cl SL4 . . . . . . . .66 C3
Rutherford Wlk RG31 . . . . .84 A4
Rutherwyk Rd KT16 . . . . .123 C1
Rutland Ave SL1 . . . . . . . . . .42 B4
Rutland Gate SL6 . . . . . . . . .39 B3
Rutland Pl SL6 . . . . . . . . . . .39 B3
Rutland Rd Maidenhead SL6 .39 B3
Reading RG30 . . . . . . . . . . . .85 B4
Ruxbury Ct TW15 . . . . . . . .97 C3
Ruxbury Rd KT16 . . . . . . .123 B2
Ryan Mount GU47 . . . . . . .150 A4
Ryans Mount SL7 . . . . . . . . . .1 B1
Rycroft SL4 . . . . . . . . . . . . . .66 C2
Rydal Ave RG30 . . . . . . . . . .57 C1
Rydal Cl GU15 . . . . . . . . . .152 B3
Rydal Dr RG19 . . . . . . . . . .106 A2
Rydal Pl GU18 . . . . . . . . . .153 A4
Rydal Way TW20 . . . . . . . . .96 A1
Ryde Gdns GU46 . . . . . . . .149 A3
Ryde The TW18 . . . . . . . . .124 A4
Rydings SL4 . . . . . . . . . . . . .66 C2
Rye Cl Maidenhead SL6 . . . .39 A2
Newell Green RG12 . . . . . . . .91 B1
Winkfield RG12 . . . . . . . . . .118 B4
Rye Ct 1 SL1 . . . . . . . . . . . .43 A2
Rye Gr GU18,GU20 . . . . . . .146 C1
Ryecroft Cl Wargrave RG10 .36 C1
Woodley RG5 . . . . . . . . . . . . .60 C1
Ryecroft Gdns GU17 . . . . .150 C2
Ryehurst La RG42 . . . . . . . .90 C3
Ryeish Green Comp Sch
RG7 . . . . . . . . . . . . . . . . . .113 B2
Ryeish La RG7 . . . . . . . . . .113 B2
Ryemead La RG42, SL4 . . . .92 B3
Ryhill Way RG6 . . . . . . . . .113 C4
Ryland Cl TW13 . . . . . . . . . .98 C2
Rylstone Cl SL6 . . . . . . . . . .39 B2
Rylstone Rd RG30 . . . . . . . .85 B4
Ryvers Ave GU46 . . . . . . . .149 A3
Ryvers End SL3 . . . . . . . . . .43 C2
Ryvers Rd SL3 . . . . . . . . . . .43 C2
Ryvers Sch SL3 . . . . . . . . . .43 B2

## S

Sabah Ct TW15 . . . . . . . . . .98 A2
Sackville St RG1 . . . . . . . . .86 A4
Sacred Heart Coll SL5 . . .121 B2
Sacred Heart
RC Prim Sch The RG9 . . . .15 B1
Saddleback Rd GU15 . . . .151 C4
Saddlebrook Pk TW16 . . . .98 C1
Saddler Cnr GU47 . . . . . . .150 A4
Saddlewood GU15 . . . . . . .151 B2
Sadlers Ct RG41 . . . . . . . . .88 B1
Sadlers End RG41 . . . . . . .115 B4
Sadlers La RG41 . . . . . . . .115 B4
Sadlers Mews SL6 . . . . . . . .40 A4
Sadlers Rd RG17 . . . . . . . .127 A3
Saffron Cl Datchet SL3 . . . .68 A3
Earley RG6 . . . . . . . . . . . . . .87 B2
Newbury RG14 . . . . . . . . . .104 C2
Saffron Ct TW14 . . . . . . . . .98 B4
Saffron Rd RG12 . . . . . . . .118 A3
Sage Cl RG6 . . . . . . . . . . . . .87 A1
Sage Rd RG31 . . . . . . . . . . .57 B2
Sage Wlk RG42 . . . . . . . . . .91 B1
Sagecroft Rd RG18 . . . . . .106 B3
Sailing Club Rd SL8 . . . . . . .3 A2
Sainsbury Ctr The KT16 . .124 A1
St Adrian's Cl SL6 . . . . . . . .39 A2
St Agnes Mews RG2 . . . . . .86 B1
St Agnes Terr RG17 . . . . . . .25 A1
St Alban's St SL4 . . . . . . . .67 B3
St Albans Cl 16 SL4 . . . . . .67 B3
St Andrew's Ave SL4 . . . . . .66 C3
St Andrew's Cl
Old Windsor SL4 . . . . . . . . . .68 A1
Upper Halliford TW17 . . . . .125 B3
Wraysbury TW19 . . . . . . . . .68 C1
St Andrew's Cres SL4 . . . .66 C3
St Andrew's Sch RG8 . . . . .55 B1
St Andrew's Way SL1 . . . . .41 B3
St Andrews RG12 . . . . . . .117 C2
St Andrews Cl
Bradfield RG7 . . . . . . . . . . . .82 B3
Crowthorne RG45 . . . . . . . .142 C3
St Andrews Cotts 1 SL4 . . .67 A3
St Andrews Ct Ascot SL5 . .120 B2
Colnbrook SL3 . . . . . . . . . . .69 B4
35 Reading RG1 . . . . . . . . . .86 B4
23 Slough SL1 . . . . . . . . . . .42 C2
St Andrews Rd
Caversham RG4 . . . . . . . . . . .58 C2
Henley-on-T RG9 . . . . . . . . . .35 B4
St Ann's Cl KT16 . . . . . . . .123 C2
St Ann's Heath
Cty Mid Sch GU25 . . . . . .122 C2
St Ann's Hill Rd KT16 . . . .123 B2
St Ann's Rd KT16 . . . . . . . .123 C2
St Anne's Ave TW19 . . . . . .97 B4
St Anne's Cl RG9 . . . . . . . . .15 B1
St Anne's Prim Sch TW19 .97 C4
St Anne's RC Prim Sch
Caversham RG4 . . . . . . . . . . .59 A1
Chertsey KT16 . . . . . . . . . .124 A1
St Annes Glade GU19 . . . .145 B2
St Annes Rd RG4 . . . . . . . . .59 A1
St Anthony's RC Prim Sch
SL2 . . . . . . . . . . . . . . . . . . .22 B1
St Anthony's Way TW14 . . .71 C2
St Anthonys Cl RG42 . . . .118 A4
St Augustine's
RC Prim Sch GU16 . . . . . .151 C1
St Barnabas Rd
Caversham RG4 . . . . . . . . . . .59 A3
Earley RG2 . . . . . . . . . . . . . .86 C1
St Bartholemew's Sch
RG14 . . . . . . . . . . . . . . . . .104 C1
St Bartholomews Rd RG1 .86 C4
St Bernard's Convent Sch
SL3 . . . . . . . . . . . . . . . . . . .43 B2
St Bernard's Prep Sch
SL1 . . . . . . . . . . . . . . . . . . .43 A2
St Bernards Rd SL3 . . . . . . .43 B2
St Birinus Rd RG31 . . . . . . .84 B3
St Catherine's Sch GU15 .151 B2
St Catherines Cl RG41 . . . .88 A1
St Catherines Ct
Staines TW18 . . . . . . . . . . . .97 A2
3 Windsor SL4 . . . . . . . . . . .67 A3
St Catherines Hill RG7 . . .136 C3
St Catherines Rd GU16 . . .152 A1
St Cecelia Ct RG2 . . . . . . . .86 B2
St Chad's Rd SL6 . . . . . . . . .39 A2
St Christophers Gdns
SL5 . . . . . . . . . . . . . . . . . .119 B4
St Clements Cl RG6 . . . . . . .87 B1
St Columba's Cl SL6 . . . . . .39 A2
St Crispin's Comp Sch
RG40 . . . . . . . . . . . . . . . . .116 C3
St Cuthbert's Cl TW20 . . . .95 B1
St Cuthbert's RC Prim Sch
TW20 . . . . . . . . . . . . . . . . . .95 B1
St David's Cl SL6 . . . . . . . . .39 A2
St David's Jun Sch TW15 . .97 C3
St David's Rd RG14 . . . . . .104 C1
St Davids Cl RG4 . . . . . . . . .58 C3
St Davids Dr TW20 . . . . . . . .95 B1
St Dominic Savio
RC Prim Sch RG5 . . . . . . . .87 B4
St Donats Pl RG14 . . . . . . .105 A1
St Dunstan's Rd TW13 . . . . .98 C3
St Edmund Campion
RC Prim Sch SL6 . . . . . . . .39 A3
St Edward's RC Sch
Reading RG30 . . . . . . . . . . . .85 B4
Windsor SL4 . . . . . . . . . . . . .67 A3
St Edward's Royal Free
Ecumenical Mid Sch
Reading RG30 . . . . . . . . . . . .85 B4
Windsor SL4 . . . . . . . . . . . . .67 A3
St Edwards Rd RG6 . . . . . . .87 A3
St Elizabeth Cl RG2 . . . . .113 A4
St Elmo Cl SL2 . . . . . . . . . . .22 B1
St Elmo Cres SL2 . . . . . . . . .22 B1
St Ethelbert's RC Sch SL2 .43 A4
St Finian's RC Prim Sch
RG18 . . . . . . . . . . . . . . . . .106 B4
St Francis RC Sch SL5 . . .120 A2
St Gabrial's Sch RG20 . . . .131 A3
St George's Ave RG14 . . .104 C1
St George's Cl SL4 . . . . . . .66 C3
St George's Cres SL1 . . . . .41 B3
St George's La SL5 . . . . . .120 A3
St George's Rd GU15 . . . .151 B3
St George's Sch
Ascot SL5 . . . . . . . . . . . . . .120 A3
Windsor SL4 . . . . . . . . . . . . .67 B4
St Georges Ct GU47 . . . . .143 C1
St Georges Ind Est GU15 .151 A2
St Georges Rd RG30 . . . . . .85 B4
St Georges Terr RG30 . . . . .85 A4
St Giles Cl RG1 . . . . . . . . . .86 A3
St Giles Ct 14 RG1 . . . . . . .86 A3
St Helens Cres GU47 . . . .150 A4
St Helier Cl RG41 . . . . . . .116 A2
St Hilda's Ave TW15 . . . . . .97 C2
St Ives Cl RG7 . . . . . . . . . . .83 B1
St Ives Rd SL6 . . . . . . . . . . .40 A4
St James Cl
Pangbourne RG8 . . . . . . . . . .56 B3
Twyford RG10 . . . . . . . . . . . .61 C3
St James Ctyd 4 SL7 . . . . . .1 C1
St James Pl SL1 . . . . . . . . . .41 B4
St James Rd RG40 . . . . . .141 C4
St James Wlk SL0 . . . . . . . .44 C2
St John the Evangelist
CE Sch RG14 . . . . . . . . . .104 C1
St John's Beamont
Prep Sch SL4 . . . . . . . . . . .95 A3
St John's CE Prim Sch
RG1 . . . . . . . . . . . . . . . . . . .86 B4
St John's Gdns RG14 . . . .104 C1
St John's Rd
North Ascot SL5 . . . . . . . . . .92 C1
Sandhurst GU47 . . . . . . . . .150 B4
St Johns Cl RG5 . . . . . . . . . .87 C4
St Johns Ct TW20 . . . . . . . . .96 A2
St Johns Dr SL4 . . . . . . . . . .67 A3
St Johns Hill RG1 . . . . . . . . .86 B4
St Johns Inf Sch RG7 . . . .137 A3
St Johns Rd
Caversham RG4 . . . . . . . . . . .59 B1
Mortimer RG7 . . . . . . . . . . .137 A3
Newbury RG14 . . . . . . . . . .105 A1
Reading RG1 . . . . . . . . . . . . .86 B4
Slough SL2 . . . . . . . . . . . . . .43 A3
Thatcham RG19 . . . . . . . . .106 B2
Windsor SL4 . . . . . . . . . . . . .67 A3
St Johns St
Crowthorne RG45 . . . . . . . .143 A2
Reading RG1 . . . . . . . . . . . . .86 B4
St Johns Way KT16 . . . . . .124 A1
St Joseph's Convent Sch
RG1 . . . . . . . . . . . . . . . . . . .86 C3
St Joseph's Convent Sch
Prep Sch RG1 . . . . . . . . . . .86 C3
St Joseph's Ct 7 RG14 . .105 A2
St Joseph's RC Prim Sch
Bracknell RG12 . . . . . . . . .118 B4
Newbury RG14 . . . . . . . . . .105 A2
St Joseph's RC Sec Sch
SL2 . . . . . . . . . . . . . . . . . . .43 A4
St Jude's CE Sch TW20 . . . .95 B1
St Jude's Cl TW20 . . . . . . . .95 B2
St Jude's Cotts TW20 . . . . .95 B2
St Jude's Rd TW20 . . . . . . .95 B2
St Katherines Rd RG9 . . . . .35 B4
St Laurence Way SL1 . . . . .43 A2
St Lawrence Sq RG17 . . . .100 B3
St Leger Ct RG14 . . . . . . .104 C2
St Leonard's Ave 29 SL4 . . .67 B3
St Leonard's Rd
Windsor SL4 . . . . . . . . . . . . .67 B2
Windsor, Clewer Green SL4 . .66 B1
St Leonards Hill SL4 . . . . . .66 C2
St Leonards Wlk SL0 . . . . . .44 C2
St Luke's CE Prim Sch
SL6 . . . . . . . . . . . . . . . . . . .39 C4
St Luke's Rd
Maidenhead SL6 . . . . . . . . . .39 C4
Old Windsor SL4 . . . . . . . . . .68 A1
St Lukes Ct RG4 . . . . . . . . . .59 A2
St Lukes Way RG4 . . . . . . . .59 A3
St Margaret Clitherow
RC Prim Sch RG12 . . . . . .117 C1
St Margaret's Rd SL6 . . . . .39 A4
St Margarets Ave TW15 . . .98 A2
St Mark's Cl RG7 . . . . . . . . .83 A3
St Mark's Cres SL6 . . . . . . .39 A4
St Mark's Hospl SL6 . . . . . .39 B4
St Mark's Pl SL4 . . . . . . . . . .67 B3
St Mark's Rd
Binfield RG42 . . . . . . . . . . .117 B4
Henley-on-T RG9 . . . . . . . . . .15 C1
Maidenhead SL6 . . . . . . . . . .39 B4
Windsor SL4 . . . . . . . . . . . . .67 B3
St Marks Cl RG19 . . . . . . . .106 B2
St Marks Rd Binfield RG42 . .90 B1
Henley-on-T RG9 . . . . . . . . . .35 B4
St Martin's Ct TW15 . . . . . .97 B2
St Martins Cl 3 RG6 . . . . . .87 B1
St Martins RC Prim Sch
RG4 . . . . . . . . . . . . . . . . . . .59 C3
St Mary's All Saints
CE Prim Sch RG1 . . . . . . . .85 C3
St Mary's Ave TW19 . . . . . .97 B4
St Mary's CE Comb Sch
SL3 . . . . . . . . . . . . . . . . . . .68 A3
St Mary's CE Jun Sch
RG18 . . . . . . . . . . . . . . . . .106 B2
St Mary's CE Prim Sch
Kintbury RG17 . . . . . . . . . .102 A1
Slough SL1 . . . . . . . . . . . . . .43 A2
Winkfield RG42 . . . . . . . . . .92 A2
St Mary's CE Sch TW19 . . .97 C4
St Mary's Cl
Maidenhead SL6 . . . . . . . . . .40 A4
Stanwell TW19 . . . . . . . . . . .97 B4
St Mary's Cres TW19 . . . . .97 B4
St Mary's Ct 6 RG14 . . . .105 A2
St Mary's Dr TW14 . . . . . . . .98 B4
St Mary's Gdns GU19 . . . .145 C2
St Mary's Hill SL5 . . . . . . .120 B2
St Mary's Jun Sch RG7 . . .137 B3

St Mary's Pl 14 RG14 ....105 A2
St Mary's RC Prim Sch
SL6 ....19 C1
St Mary's Rd Ascot SL5 ...120 A2
Camberley GU15 ....151 B3
Slough SL3 ....43 C2
St Mary's Sch SL5 ....120 A1
St Mary's Wlk SL6 ....39 C4
St Marys Ave RG8 ....57 B3
St Marys Butts RG1 ....86 A4
St Marys Cl
Henley-on-T RG9 ....35 A4
Sandhurst GU47 ....150 B4
St Marys La SL4 ....92 B3
St Marys Rd
Mortimer RG7 ....137 A3
Newbury RG14 ....105 A2
Wokingham RG41 ....88 A1
St Marys Way RG7 ....111 A2
St Matthew's Ct TW15 ....98 A2
St Michael's CE Prim Sch
RG12 ....118 A2
St Michael's Ct SL2 ....21 B1
St Michael's RC Prim Sch
TW15 ....98 A2
St Michael's Rd
Newbury RG14 ....104 C1
Reading RG30 ....84 B4
St Michaels CE Prim Sch
GU47 ....149 C4
St Michaels Cl RG17 ....25 A1
St Michaels Cotts RG40 ..143 B4
St Michaels Ct RG10 ....61 C3
St Michaels Rd
Ashford TW15 ....98 A2
Camberley GU15 ....151 A3
Sandhurst GU47 ....149 C4
St Micheal's CE Sch SL5 .120 B2
St Nazaire Cl TW20 ....96 B2
St Nicholas CE Comb Sch
SL6 ....20 C1
St Nicholas CE Prim Sch
Hurst RG10 ....88 C4
Shepperton TW17 ....125 A2
St Nicholas Dr TW17 ....125 A1
St Nicholas' Rd RG14 ....104 C1
St Nicolas CE Jun Sch
RG14 ....105 A1
St Olave's Cl TW18 ....96 C1
St Patrick's Ave RG10 ....61 A3
St Patrick's Cl SL6 ....39 A2
St Paul's CE Comb Sch
HP10 ....3 B2
St Paul's CE Jun Sch
RG41 ....116 A3
St Paul's Cl TW15 ....98 B2
St Paul's Ct SL6 ....39 C3
St Paul's Gate RG41 ....116 A3
St Paul's RC Prim Sch
RG31 ....84 B4
St Paul's Rd TW18 ....96 B1
St Pauls Ave SL2 ....43 A3
St Pauls Ct RG1 ....86 A3
St Peter St SL7 ....1 C1
St Peter's CE Comb Sch
SL1 ....21 A1
St Peter's CE Mid Sch
SL4 ....67 C1
St Peter's CE Prim Sch
RG6 ....87 A3
St Peter's Cl Burnham SL1 ..21 A1
Old Windsor SL4 ....68 A1
Staines TW18 ....96 C1
St Peter's RC Comb Sch
SL7 ....1 B2
St Peter's Rd SL6 ....19 B1
St Peters Ave RG4 ....58 C2
St Peters Gdns GU46 ....149 B3
St Peters Hill RG4 ....58 C2
St Peters Rd RG6 ....87 A3
St Pinnock Ave TW18 ....124 A4
St Pirans Ind Day Sch
SL6 ....19 C1
St Richards Rd RG14 ....105 A2
St Ronans Rd RG30 ....85 A4
St Saviour's Terr 9 RG1 ....86 A3
St Saviours Rd RG1 ....85 C3
St Sebastian Cl RG40 ....142 C4
St Stephens Cl RG4 ....59 A1
St Swithins Cl RG20 ....75 B2
St Swithuns Ct RG10 ....61 B2
St Theresa's RC Prim Sch
RG40 ....116 B3
St Theresa's Rd TW14 ....71 C2
St Thomas Ct RG18 ....106 C2
St Thomas Wlk SL3 ....69 B4
St-Cloud Way SL6 ....40 A4
Salamanca RG45 ....142 C3
Salcombe Dr RG6 ....87 A2
Salcombe Rd
Ashford TW15 ....97 C3
Newbury RG14 ....104 C1
Reading RG2 ....86 B2
Sale Garden Cotts RG40 ..116 B3
Saleby Cl RG6 ....87 C1
Salesian Gdns KT16 ....124 A1
Salesian Sch KT16 ....124 A1
Salford Cl RG2 ....113 B4
Salisbury Ave SL2 ....42 B4
Salisbury Cl RG41 ....116 A1
Salisbury Ct SL6 ....39 C3
Salisbury Mews SL2 ....22 B1
Salisbury Rd
Blackwater GU17 ....150 B3
Harlington TW6 ....71 B1
Salisbury Rd *continued*
Hungerford RG17 ....100 B2
Reading RG30 ....85 C4
Salmon Cl RG7 ....113 A1
Salmond Rd RG2 ....113 B3
Salt Hill Ave SL1 ....42 B3
Salt Hill Dr SL1 ....42 B3
Salt Hill Mans SL1 ....42 B3
Salt Hill Way SL1 ....42 B3
Salters Cl SL6 ....40 A4
Salters Rd SL6 ....40 A4
Saltersgate Cl RG6 ....87 B1
Saltire Gdns 2 RG42 ....118 A4
Salva Ct 6 RG1 ....86 B3
Salwey Cl RG12 ....118 A2
Samarkand Cl GU15 ....152 A2
Samian Pl RG42 ....90 C1
Sampage Cl RG2 ....113 B3
Sampson Bsns Pk GU15 .151 A2
Sampson Ct TW17 ....125 B2
Sampson Pk RG42 ....117 B4
Sampsons Gn SL2 ....21 C1
Sanctuary Cl RG30 ....84 C4
Sanctuary Rd TW19, TW6 ..71 A1
Sandcroft Rd RG4 ....58 C3
Sanden Cl RG17 ....100 B3
Sandford Down RG12 ....118 C2
Sandford Dr RG5 ....60 C1
Sandford La RG5, RG10 ....88 B3
Sandgate Ave RG30 ....57 C1
Sandhills Ct GU25 ....122 C2
Sandhills La GU25, TW20 .122 C2
Sandhills Mdw TW17 ....125 B1
Sandhills Way RG31 ....84 C2
Sandhurst La GU17 ....150 A3
Sandhurst Rd
Crowthorne RG45 ....143 A2
Wokingham RG40 ....142 A4
Yateley GU46 ....149 C4
Sandhurst Sch GU47 ....150 B4
Sandhurst Sta GU47 ....150 A4
Sandisplatt Rd SL6 ....39 A3
Sandleford Cl RG2 ....113 B3
Sandleford Hospl RG14 ..131 A4
Sandleford Rise RG14 ..131 A4
Sandlers End SL2 ....22 A1
Sandown Ave RG31 ....84 A2
Sandown Cl GU17 ....150 B3
Sandown Dr GU16 ....151 C1
Sandown Rd SL2 ....41 C4
Sandown Way RG14 ....105 B1
Sandpit Hill RG14,RG20 ..130 B2
Sandpit La RG7 ....140 A3
Sandringham Ct SL1 ....41 B4
Sandringham Dr TW15 ....97 B2
Sandringham Rd
Maidenhead SL6 ....19 C1
Stanwell TW19, TW6 ....70 C1
Sandringham Way RG31 ..84 A2
Sands Farm Dr SL1 ....21 B1
Sandstone Cl RG41 ....88 B1
Sandy Cl RG18 ....79 A2
Sandy Dr TW14 ....98 C4
Sandy La Bracknell RG12 ..118 B4
Camberley GU15 ....151 C3
Hermitage RG18 ....78 C2
North Ascot SL5 ....119 B4
Sandhurst GU47 ....143 A1
Sunningdale SL5 ....121 A2
Virginia Water GU25 ....122 C3
Wokingham RG41 ....115 B2
Sandy Lane Inf Sch RG42 ..91 B1
Sandy Lane Jun Sch RG42 .91 B1
Sandy Mead SL6 ....40 B1
Sandy Ride SL5 ....120 C3
Sandy Way KT12 ....125 C1
Sandygate Cl SL7 ....1 B2
Sandygate Rd SL7 ....1 B2
Sapgood Cl RG19 ....106 C1
Sapphire Cl RG41 ....115 C4
Sarsby Dr TW19 ....96 A3
Sarum RG12 ....117 C1
Sarum Cres RG40 ....116 B4
Sarum Ct 1 RG30 ....85 B3
Sarum Rd RG26 ....135 A1
Sarum Way RG17 ....100 B2
Satis Ho SL3 ....68 B4
Saturn Cl RG41 ....115 C3
Saturn Croft RG42 ....92 A1
Saunders Cl RG10 ....61 C2
Saunders Ct RG8 ....57 A3
Saunton Ave UB3 ....71 C4
Savernake Cl RG30 ....84 C4
Savernake Way RG12 ....118 C2
Savill Gardens The TW20 ..94 C1
Savill Way SL7 ....1 C1
Saville Cres TW15 ....98 B1
Saville Gdns GU15 ....152 A3
Savory Wlk RG42 ....90 B1
Savoy Gr GU17 ....150 B2
Sawmill Rd RG18 ....79 A2
Sawpit Rd RG10 ....88 C4
Sawtry Cl RG6 ....87 C1
Sawyer's Cl SL4 ....66 C4
Sawyers Cl SL6 ....39 A1
Sawyers Cres SL6 ....39 A1
Saxby Cl RG7 ....111 A2
Saxon Cl SL3 ....43 C2
Saxon Ct 22 Reading RG1 ..86 B4
Stanwell TW19 ....70 A1
Thatcham RG19 ....106 A2
Saxon Cty Jun Sch
TW17 ....125 A2
Saxon Dr RG42 ....118 C4
Saxon Gdns SL6 ....20 B1
Saxon Rd TW15 ....98 B1
Saxon Way
Harmondsworth UB7 ....70 B4
Saxon Way *continued*
Old Windsor SL4 ....68 A1
Saxons Acre RG20 ....28 B2
Sayers Cl RG14 ....131 A4
Scafell Cl RG31 ....57 A1
Scafell Rd SL2 ....41 C4
Scampton Rd TW6 ....70 C1
Scania Wlk RG42 ....92 A1
Scarborough Rd TW6 ....71 B1
Scarborough Way SL1 ....42 A2
Scarlet Oaks GU15 ....151 C2
Scarletts La RG10 ....37 B1
Sch of Electronic
Engineering RG2 ....114 C1
Scholars Cl Caversham RG4 .58 C2
Great Shefford RG17 ....48 A2
School Cl GU24 ....153 C2
School Hill
Crowthorne RG45 ....143 B2
Sandhurst GU47 ....143 A1
Wargrave RG10 ....36 B1
Woolhampton RG7 ....107 C2
School Ho TW19 ....70 B1
School La Bagshot GU19 ..145 C1
Boxford RG20 ....76 C2
Burghfield Common RG7 ...111 A1
Caversham RG4 ....59 A1
Caversham, Emmer
Green RG4 ....59 A3
Cookham SL6 ....20 A4
Cookham, Cookham
Dean SL6 ....19 A4
East Garston RG17 ....47 B3
Egham TW20 ....96 A2
Froxfield SN8 ....99 A1
Little Marlow SL7 ....2 B3
Littlewick Green SL6 ....38 A2
Lower Halliford TW17 ....125 A1
Maidenhead SL6 ....19 C1
Medmenham SL7 ....17 A3
Silchester RG7 ....136 A1
Stoke Poges SL2 ....23 A2
Swallowfield RG7 ....139 C2
Wargrave RG10 ....36 B1
Windlesham GU20 ....146 B2
Yateley GU46 ....149 A3
School of Military Survey
RG18 ....78 C4
School Rd Arborfield RG2 .114 C1
Ascot SL5 ....120 B2
Ashford TW15 ....98 A1
Burghfield Common RG30 ..111 B3
Chieveley RG20 ....78 A4
Compton RG20 ....31 C2
Harmondsworth UB7 ....70 B4
Hurst RG10 ....88 C4
Padworth RG7 ....109 C1
Reading RG31 ....84 B4
Swallowfield RG7 ....139 C2
Waltham St Lawrence RG10 .62 C2
Windlesham GU20 ....146 A3
Wokingham RG40 ....116 B3
Wooburn Green HP10 ....3 C4
School Terr RG1 ....86 C4
Schroder Ct TW20 ....95 A2
Scotland Hill GU47 ....150 A4
Scotlands Dr SL2 ....22 A3
Scots Cl TW19 ....97 B4
Scots Dr RG41 ....115 C4
Scott Cl Caversham RG4 ....59 A3
Farnham Common SL2 ....22 B4
Woodley RG5 ....88 A4
Scott Terr RG12 ....118 C4
Scott's Ave TW16 ....98 C1
Scott's Way TW16 ....98 C1
Scottalls La RG18 ....52 C3
Scours La RG30 ....58 A1
Scratchface La RG7 ....81 C3
Scrivens Mead RG19 ....106 C2
Scylla Cres TW6&TW14 ....98 A4
Scylla Rd TW14, TW6 ....71 A1
Seacourt Rd SL3 ....44 A1
Seafield Ct 26 RG1 ....85 C4
Seaford Gdns RG5 ....87 C3
Seaford Rd
Stanwell TW19, TW6 ....70 B1
Wokingham RG40 ....116 B3
Sealand Rd TW6 ....71 A1
Searing Way RG26 ....135 A1
Searles Farm La RG30 ....85 A1
Seaton Dr TW15 ....97 C3
Seaton Gdns RG2 ....86 B1
Seaton Rd GU15 ....151 A3
Second Ave RG7 ....135 B1
Second Cres SL1 ....42 B4
Second St E RG19 ....132 A3
Second St W RG19 ....131 C2
Seddon Hill RG42 ....91 A1
Sedge Gr RG18 ....106 C2
Sedgefield Rd RG14 ....131 B4
Sedgmoor Cl HP10 ....3 A4
Sedgmoor Gdns HP10 ....3 A4
Sedgmoor La HP10 ....3 A4
Sedgmoor Rd HP10 ....3 A4
Seebys Oak GU47 ....150 C3
Sefton Cl Stoke Poges SL2 ..22 C2
West End GU24 ....153 C3
Sefton Paddock SL2 ....23 A3
Sefton Park Cotts SL2 ....23 A2
Segsbury Gr RG12 ....118 C3
Selborne Cl GU17 ....150 B3
Selborne Ct 2 RG1 ....86 B4
Selborne Gdns RG30 ....58 A1
Selby Rd TW15 ....98 B1
Selcourt Cl RG5 ....87 B4
Sellafield Way RG6 ....87 B1
Selsdon Ave RG5 ....87 C4
Selsey Way RG6 ....114 A4
Selwood Cl TW19 ....70 B1
Selwood Gdns TW19 ....70 B1
Selwyn Cl SL4 ....66 C3
Selwyn Dr GU46 ....149 A3
Selwyn Pl 2 SL1 ....41 C3
Sen Cl RG42 ....91 B1
Send Rd RG4 ....59 B1
Servite Ho SL6 ....40 A4
Setley Way RG12 ....118 C3
Seton Dr RG31 ....84 C3
Sett The GU46 ....149 A3
Sevenoaks Dr RG7 ....113 A2
Sevenoaks Rd RG6 ....87 A2
Seventh St RG19 ....131 C3
Severalls The SN8 ....126 B2
Severn Cl Sandhurst GU47 .150 B4
Thatcham RG18 ....106 A3
Severn Cres SL3 ....69 A4
Severn Way RG30 ....84 C3
Sewell Ave RG41 ....116 A4
Sewell Cl RG18 ....79 A1
Seymour Ave RG2 ....113 C3
Seymour Cl SL6 ....39 A2
Seymour Court La SL7 ....1 A3
Seymour Court Rd SL7 ....1 B2
Seymour Dr GU15 ....152 A4
Seymour Ho SL3 ....43 C2
Seymour Park Rd SL7 ....1 B2
Seymour Plain SL7 ....1 B3
Seymour Rd SL1 ....42 B2
Seymour Way TW16 ....98 C1
Shackleton Ct 6 TW19 ....70 C1
Shackleton Rd SL1 ....42 C3
Shackleton Way RG5 ....88 A4
Shafer Ct RG14 ....105 A1
Shaftesbury Cl RG12 ....118 B2
Shaftesbury Cres TW18 ....97 B1
Shaftesbury Ct
Maidenhead SL6 ....39 C3
6 Slough SL1 ....42 C2
Wokingham RG40 ....116 B4
Shaftesbury Mount
GU17 ....150 B2
Shaftesbury Rd
Bisley GU24 ....153 C2
Reading RG30 ....85 A4
Shaggy Calf La SL2 ....43 A3
Shakespeare Cl RG4 ....59 B3
Shakespeare Rd RG18 ....106 B2
Shakespeare Way RG42 ..118 C4
Shalbourne Cl RG17 ....100 A3
Shalbourne Rise GU15 ....151 B3
Sharney Ave SL3 ....44 A2
Sharnwood Dr RG31 ....84 C3
Sharonelle Ct RG40 ....116 A3
Sharpethorpe Cl 2 RG6 ....87 A1
Shaw Ct SL4 ....68 A1
Shaw Farm Rd RG14 ....105 A3
Shaw Hill RG14 ....105 A3
Shaw Mill RG14 ....105 A3
Shaw Pk RG45 ....143 A2
Shaw Rd Newbury RG14 ...105 A2
Reading RG1 ....85 C3
Shaw The SL6 ....19 C3
Shaw-Cum-Donnington
Parochial Prim Sch
RG14 ....105 A3
Shears Ct TW16 ....98 C1
Sheehy Way SL2 ....43 A3
Sheep Fair Way RG17 ....25 A1
Sheep Leaze La RG20 ....29 B1
Sheep Wlk RG4 ....59 A2
Sheepcote La
Bourne End SL1 ....3 C1
Holyport SL6 ....64 B2
Sheepcote Rd Eton SL4 ....42 A1
Windsor SL4 ....66 C3
Sheepdrove Rd RG17 ....25 B2
Sheephouse Rd SL6 ....20 A1
Sheephouse Way RG20 ....49 A3
Sheepridge La SL7,HP10 ....2 C4
Sheeps Ditch Cl TW18 ....97 A1
Sheepwalk Littleton TW17 .125 A2
Shepperton TW17 ....124 C2
Sheepwash RG20 ....131 A1
Sheepways La RG4 ....58 A4
Sheerlands Rd RG2 ....140 C4
Sheet St SL4 ....67 B3
Sheet Street Rd SL4 ....94 A4
Sheffield Rd
Harlington TW14, TW6 ....71 B1
Slough SL1 ....42 B4
Sheffield Way TW14, TW6 ..71 B1
Shefford CE Sch RG17 ....48 A2
Shefford Cres RG40 ....116 B4
Shefford Lodge 5 RG14 .105 A1
Sheldon Gdns RG2 ....86 B1
Shelgate Wlk RG5 ....87 B4
Shelley Ave RG12 ....118 C4
Shelley Cl Medmenham SL7 .17 B4
Slough SL3 ....43 C1
Wooburn Green HP10 ....3 C4
Woodley RG5 ....87 C2
Shelley Ct
Camberley GU15 ....151 B3
28 Reading RG1 ....86 B4
Shelley Rd 12 Marlow SL7 ....1 C2
Thatcham RG18 ....106 B2
Shelley Walk GU46 ....149 A3
Shelson Ave TW13 ....98 C2
Shelton Ct SL3 ....43 B2
Shenstone Cl RG40 ....142 A4
Shenstone Dr SL1 ....21 B1
Shenstone Pk SL5 ....120 C3
Shenstone Rd RG2 ....86 A2
Shephards La RG42 ....91 A1
Shepherd's Hill RG20 ....76 C2
Shepherds Ave RG6 ....87 A4
Shepherds Chase GU19 ..145 C1
Shepherds Cl Hurley SL6 ..17 C2
Shepperton TW17 ....125 A2
Shepherds Ct SL4 ....66 C3
Shepherds Hill
Bracknell RG12 ....118 B4
Compton RG20 ....31 C2
Earley RG6 ....87 B4
Woodley RG5 ....60 B1
Shepherds House La RG6 .87 A4
Shepherds La
Caversham RG4 ....58 B3
Hurley SL6 ....17 C2
Shepherds Mount RG20 ...31 C2
Shepherds Rise RG20 ....31 C2
Shepherds Way RG45 ....142 C2
Shepherds Wlk RG6 ....87 B4
Shepley Dr Reading RG30 ...85 B2
Wentworth SL5 ....121 B2
Shepley End SL5 ....121 B2
Shepperton Bsns Pk
TW17 ....125 B2
Shepperton Court Dr
TW17 ....125 A2
Shepperton Ct TW17 ....125 A2
Shepperton Rd
TW17, TW18 ....124 B3
Shepperton Sta TW17 ...125 B2
Shepperton Studios
TW17 ....124 C3
Sheraton Cl GU17 ....150 C2
Sheraton Dr RG31 ....57 A1
Sherborne Cl SL3 ....69 C3
Sherborne Ct SL6 ....39 C3
Sherborne Rd TW14 ....98 B4
Sherbourne Dr
Maidenhead SL6 ....39 B2
Wentworth SL5 ....121 B2
Windsor SL4 ....66 C2
Woodley RG5 ....87 C4
Sherbourne Gdns TW17 .125 C1
Sherbourne Wlk SL2 ....22 B4
Sherfield Cl RG2 ....86 B2
Sherfield Dr RG2 ....86 B2
Shergold Way SL6 ....19 C3
Sheridan Ave RG4 ....59 A2
Sheridan Cres RG26 ....134 C1
Sheridan Ct
Maidenhead SL6 ....40 A4
Newbury RG14 ....105 B2
1 Slough SL1 ....41 C3
Sheridan Way RG41 ....115 C3
Sheringham Ct 9 RG1 ....86 B3
Sherman Rd Reading RG1 ..86 A3
Slough SL1 ....42 C4
Sherrardmead RG14 ....105 A3
Sherring Cl RG42 ....91 B1
Sherwood Cl
Bracknell RG12 ....119 A4
Slough SL3 ....43 C2
Sherwood Ct
Colnbrook SL3 ....69 B4
Slough SL3 ....43 C1
Sherwood Dr SL6 ....39 A3
Sherwood Gdns RG9 ....35 B4
Sherwood Ho 11 RG1 ....85 C3
Sherwood Pl RG8 ....57 A2
Sherwood Rd RG41 ....88 B1
Sherwood Rise RG8 ....57 A3
Sherwood St RG30 ....85 B4
Shield Rd TW15 ....98 B2
Shifford Cres SL6 ....19 C2
Shildon Cl GU15 ....152 B2
Shilling Cl RG30 ....85 A3
Shinfield CE Jun Sch
RG2 ....113 C2
Shinfield Cty Inf Sch
RG2 ....113 C2
Shinfield Rd RG2 ....86 C2
Shinfield Rise RG2 ....86 C1
Shiplake Coll RG9 ....35 C1
Shiplake Ho Bourne End SL8 .3 A2
Bracknell RG12 ....118 C3
Shiplake Sta RG9 ....36 A2
Shipley Cl RG5 ....61 A1
Shipton Cl RG31 ....57 B1
Shire Cl GU19 ....145 C1
Shire's Head Cl RG30 ....85 B3
Shires The RG41 ....115 B2
Shires Way GU46 ....149 B4
Shirley Ave Reading RG2 ..113 B4
Windsor SL4 ....66 C3
Shirley Rd SL6 ....39 B3
Shoesmiths Ct 4 RG1 ....86 A4
Sholto Rd TW6 ....71 A1
Shooters Hill RG8 ....56 B3
Shooters Way RG2 ....112 C4
Shop La
Leckhampstead RG20 ....49 C3
Newbury RG14 ....104 C3
Shoppenhanger's Rd SL6 .39 C2
Shoreham Rd (E) TW6 ....70 C1
Shoreham Rd (W) TW6 ....70 C1
Shoreham Rise SL2 ....21 B1
Shorland Oaks RG42 ....91 B1
Short La TW15, TW19 ....97 C4
Short Rd TW19 ....70 C1
Short St Caversham RG4 ....59 A1
Pangbourne RG8 ....56 B3
Reading RG1 ....86 A3
Short The RG8 ....57 B3
Shortfern SL2 ....43 B4
Shortheath La RG7 ....110 C2
Shortlands UB3 ....71 B4
Shortlands Hill OX10 ....13 B2
Shortwood Ave TW18 ....97 A3
Shortwood Cty Inf Sch
TW18 ....97 A3

Shrewsbury Terr RG14 ....104 C1
Shrewsbury Rd
TW14, TW6 ....71 B1
Shrivenham Cl 3 GU47 ..150 B4
Shropshire Gdns RG42 ....91 C1
Shrubbs Hill La SL5 ....121 B2
Shrubland Dr RG30 ....85 A2
Shrublands Dr GU18 ....153 A4
Shute End RG40, 41 ....116 A3
Shyshack La RG26 ....134 C1
Sibley Park Rd RG6 ....87 A1
Sibson RG6 ....87 B1
Sidbury Cl SL5 ....121 A2
Sidestrand Rd RG14 ....130 C4
Sidings The TW18 ....97 A2
Sidmouth Ct 5 RG1 ....86 B4
Sidmouth Grange Cl RG6 .87 A4
Sidmouth Grange Rd RG6 .87 A4
Sidmouth St RG1 ....86 B4
Sidney Rd Staines TW18 ....97 A2
Windsor SL4 ....66 B2
Silbury Cl RG31 ....84 A2
Silchester CE Prim Sch
RG7 ....136 A1
Silchester Ct TW15 ....97 C3
Silchester Ho SL6 ....40 A4
Silchester House Sch SL6 .40 B4
Silchester Rd
Reading RG30 ....85 B2
Tadley RG26 ....135 B1
Silco Dr SL6 ....39 C3
Silk La RG10 ....61 B2
Silver Birches RG41 ....115 B2
Silver Cl SL6 ....39 A3
Silver Dr GU16 ....152 B2
Silver Fox Cres RG5 ....87 B3
Silver Hill GU47 ....150 C4
Silver La RG7 ....136 A4
Silver St RG1 ....86 A3
Silver Street Flats 23 RG1 .86 A3
Silverdale Rd Earley RG6 ....87 B2
Tadley RG26 ....135 A1
Wargrave RG10 ....36 C1
Silverglades GU46 ....149 B2
Silverthorne Dr RG4 ....58 C3
Silvertrees Dr SL6 ....39 A3
Silverwood Dr GU15 ....152 A4
Silwood RG12 ....117 C1
Silwood Cl SL5 ....120 B4
Silwood Pk
(Imperial Coll) SL5 ....120 C3
Silwood Rd SL5 ....120 C3
Simkins Cl RG42 ....92 A1
Simmonds Cl RG42 ....117 C4
Simmonds St RG1 ....86 A4
Simmons Cl SL3 ....44 A1
Simmons Field RG18 ....106 C2
Simmons Fields RG10 ....61 A2
Simmons Pl TW18 ....96 C2
Simmons Rd RG9 ....15 B2
Simms Farm La RG7 ....136 C2
Simod Ct RG30 ....85 B4
Simons Cl RG31 ....57 B2
Simons La RG41 ....115 B4
Simons Wlk TW20 ....95 B1
Simpson Cl SL6 ....40 A4
Sindle Cl RG41 ....88 A1
Sindlesham Rd RG2 ....114 C2
Sindlesham Specl Sch
RG41 ....114 C4
Singer La RG9 ....15 C1
Singers Cl RG9 ....35 C4
Singers La RG9 ....35 C4
Sinhurst Rd GU15 ....151 A2
Sipson Cl UB7 ....71 A4
Sipson La UB3, UB7 ....71 A4
Sipson Rd UB7 ....71 A4
Sipson Way UB7 ....71 A4
Sir Sydney Camm Ho SL4 .67 A3
Sir William Borlase's
Gram Sch SL7 ....1 B1
Sir William Perkin's Ind
Sch for Girls KT16 ....123 C1
Sirius Cl RG41 ....115 C3
Sirl Cotts SL5 ....120 B3
Six Acre La RG17 ....126 A3
Sixth St RG19 ....131 C3
Skarries View RG4 ....58 B4
Skeffling Cl RG6 ....87 C1
Skelmerdale Way RG6 ....87 C2
Skelton Fields RG42 ....91 B1
Skerries Ct SL3 ....44 A1
Skerrit Way RG8 ....57 B2
Skillman Dr RG19 ....106 C2
Skilton Rd RG31 ....57 B2
Skimpedhill La RG12 ....118 A4
Skinners Green La RG14 .130 A4
Skippons Cl RG14 ....130 B3
Sky Bsns Pk TW20 ....123 B4
Skydmore Path SL2 ....21 C1
Skye Cl RG31 ....84 C2
Skyes Dr TW18 ....97 A2
Skylings RG14 ....105 B2
Skyport Dr UB7 ....70 B4
Skyway 14 Trad Est SL3 ....69 C2
Slade Hill Gdns RG20 ....129 C1
Slaidburn Gn RG12 ....118 C1
Slanting Hill RG18 ....79 A2
Sledmere Ct TW14 ....98 C4
Slim Rd GU15 ....151 B4
Sloan Cl RG8 ....34 B3
Slopes The RG4 ....59 B1
Slough & Eton CE Sec Sch
SL1 ....42 B2
Slough Gram Sch SL3 ....43 A2
Slough Mus SL1 ....43 A2
Slough Rd Datchet SL3 ....68 A4
Eton SL4 ....42 C1
Slough Sta SL1 ....42 C3
Slough Trad Est SL1 ....42 A4
Smallmead Rd
Burghfield Common RG2 ....85 B1
Reading RG2 ....86 A1
Smallridge RG14 ....130 B2
Smith Hospl RG9 ....15 A3
Smith Sq RG12 ....118 B4
Smith's La SL4 ....66 C3
Smitham Bridge Rd
RG17 ....100 B3
Smithfield Cl SL6 ....38 C2
Smithfield Rd SL6 ....39 A2
Smiths Hill OX12 ....6 C3
Smithy's Gn GU20 ....146 B2
Snake La RG20 ....104 A4
Snape Spur SL1 ....42 C4
Snelsmore Common
Ctry Pk RG18 ....77 C1
Snipe La RG20 ....131 C1
Snowball Hill
Maidenhead SL6 ....39 A1
White Waltham SL6 ....64 A4
Snowberry Cl RG41 ....115 C3
Snowden Cl SL4 ....66 B2
Snowden Dr RG31 ....84 A3
Snowdon Cl RG19 ....106 B1
Snowdon Rd TW6 ....71 B1
Snowdrop Copse RG18 ....106 C2
Snowdrop Gr RG41 ....88 B2
Snows Paddock GU20 ....146 A4
Snows Ride GU20 ....146 A3
Soane End RG4 ....59 A4
Soham Cl RG6 ....114 B4
Soho Cres HP10 ....3 B2
Soho Mills Ind Est HP10 ....3 B2
Soke Rd RG7 ....135 C2
Soldiers Rise RG40 ....142 B4
Solent Ct 15 RG1 ....86 A3
Solent Rd TW6 ....70 C1
Somerford Cl SL6 ....40 A4
Somersby Cres SL6 ....39 C2
Somerset Cl
Hungerford RG17 ....100 B3
Wokingham RG41 ....115 B3
Somerset Gr RG42 ....91 C1
Somerset Hospital SN8 ....99 A3
Somerset Lodge 3 SL6 ....39 C3
Somerset Way SL0 ....44 C2
Somerset Wlk RG31 ....84 A3
Somerton Gdns RG6 ....87 A1
Somerton Gr RG19 ....106 B1
Somerville Cres GU46 ....149 C3
Somerville Gr RG41 ....115 B2
Somerville Rd SL4 ....42 B1
Sonning CE Prim Sch
RG4 ....60 B2
Sonning La RG4 ....60 B1
Sonning Mdws RG4 ....60 B1
Sonninge Cl GU47 ....150 B4
Sopwith Cl RG5 ....88 A4
Sorrel Cl
Burghfield Common RG7 ....111 A2
Newbury RG14 ....105 B3
Wokingham RG40 ....116 C4
Sorrel Dr GU18 ....152 C4
Sospel Ct SL2 ....22 B2
South Ave Egham TW20 ....96 B1
Henley-on-T RG9 ....35 C4
South Bank RG8 ....14 B2
South Cl Burnham SL1 ....41 B3
Medmenham SL7 ....17 B4
Wokingham RG40 ....116 B2
South Dr Reading RG2 ....86 C1
Sonning RG4 ....60 B1
Sulhamstead RG7 ....110 B4
Wentworth GU25 ....122 A1
Wokingham RG40 ....116 B3
South End Rd RG7 ....82 A1
South Farm La GU19 ....146 A1
South Field Cl SL4 ....41 B2
South Gate Ave TW13 ....98 B2
South Gn SL1 ....42 C3
South Gr KT16 ....123 C2
South Groves RG17 ....73 A1
South Hill Pk RG12 ....118 B1
South Hill Rd RG12 ....118 A2
South Lake Cres RG5 ....87 C3
South Lake Inf Sch RG5 ....87 C3
South Lake Jun Sch RG5 ....87 B3
South Lynn Cres RG12 ....118 A2
South Mdw RG45 ....143 B2
South Meadow La SL4 ....67 B4
South Oak Way RG2,RG7 .112 C4
South Path SL4 ....67 B3
South Pl Marlow SL7 ....1 C1
Wokingham RG40 ....116 B3
South Rd Bisley GU24 ....153 C2
Bracknell RG40, RG12 ....117 C1
Crowthorne RG45 ....143 C2
Englefield Green TW20 ....95 B1
Maidenhead SL6 ....39 C3
South Row Chilton OX11 ....10 B4
Fulmer SL3 ....23 C4
South St Blewbury OX11 ....12 A4
Caversham RG4 ....59 A1
Reading RG1 ....86 B4
Staines TW18 ....96 C2
South Stoke Cty Prim Sch
RG8 ....14 A2
South View Cookham SL6 ....19 C4
Hungerford RG17 ....100 B3
Wooburn Green HP10 ....3 C4
South View Ave RG4 ....59 B1
South View Gdns 9
RG14 ....105 A2
South View Pk RG4 ....59 B1
Southampton Cl GU17 ....150 B3
Southampton Rd
TW19, TW6 ....70 C1
Southampton St RG1 ....86 A3
Southbank Gdns RG17 ....25 B1
Southbourne Dr SL8 ....3 A2
Southbury La RG10 ....61 C3
Southcote Dr GU15 ....152 A3
Southcote Farm La RG30 .85 B2
Southcote La RG30 ....85 B2
Southcote Lodge RG30 ....85 A2
Southcote Prim Sch RG30 .85 B2
Southcote Rd RG30 ....85 B3
Southcroft
Englefield Green TW20 ....95 A2
Slough SL2 ....22 A1
Southdown Rd
Caversham RG4 ....59 A3
Tadley RG26 ....135 A1
Thatcham RG19 ....105 C2
Southend RG18 ....106 B3
Southern Cotts TW19 ....70 A1
Southern Ct 10 RG1 ....86 A4
Southern Hill RG1 ....86 B3
Southern Ind Area RG12 .117 C3
Southern Perimeter Rd
East Bedfont TW6 ....71 A1
Hatton TW14, TW6 ....71 B1
Stanwell TW19, TW6 ....70 B1
Southern Rd GU15 ....151 B3
Southerndene Cl RG31 ....57 B1
Southfield Gdns SL1 ....41 A4
Southfields Boxford RG20 ....76 B2
Chieveley RG20 ....78 A4
Southfields Ave TW15 ....98 A1
Southfields Sch RG40 ....116 B3
Southgate Ho SL6 ....39 C4
Southglade RG2 ....113 B4
Southlake Ct RG5 ....87 B3
Southlands Cl RG40 ....116 B3
Southlands Rd RG40 ....116 B2
Southlea Rd SL3 ....68 A3
Southview Cl RG10 ....61 C3
Southview Rd SL7 ....1 C2
Southville Cl TW14 ....98 C4
Southville Cres TW14 ....98 C4
Southville Jun & Inf Schs
TW14 ....98 C4
Southville Rd TW14 ....98 C4
Southwark Cl GU46 ....149 B3
Southway GU15 ....151 A2
Southwell Park Rd GU15 .151 B3
Southwick GU19 ....145 C1
Southwick Ct RG12 ....118 C2
Southwold RG12 ....117 C1
Southwold Cl RG6 ....87 B1
Southwold Spur SL3 ....44 B2
Southwood RG40 ....116 B2
Southwood Gdns
Burghfield Common RG7 ....111 A2
Cookham SL6 ....19 C3
Southwood Rd SL6 ....19 C3
Sovereign Dr GU15 ....152 A4
Sovereign Ho TW15 ....97 C2
Sovereign Way RG31 ....84 B3
Sowbury Bank RG20 ....78 A4
Spackman Cl RG19 ....106 B1
Spackmans Way SL1 ....42 B2
Spade Oak Mdw SL8 ....2 C2
Span Hill RG4 ....60 A4
Sparrow Cl RG41 ....115 C3
Sparrowbill RG20 ....28 C1
Sparvell Way GU15 ....151 B3
Speedbird Way UB7 ....70 B4
Speedwell Way RG18 ....106 C2
Speen Hill Cl RG14 ....104 C2
Speen La RG14 ....104 B2
Speen Lodge Ct RG14 ....104 C2
Speen Pl RG14 ....104 C2
Speenhamland Ct 5
RG14 ....105 A2
Speenhamland Prim Sch
RG14 ....104 C2
Spelthorne Coll TW15 ....97 C2
Spelthorne Cty Inf Sch
TW15 ....98 C1
Spelthorne Gr TW16 ....98 C1
Spelthorne La
TW15, TW17 ....125 B4
Spelthorne Mus TW18 ....96 C2
Spelthorne Sports Club
TW15 ....98 B1
Spencer Cl
Silchester RG26 ....135 C1
Wokingham RG41 ....115 B3
Spencer Gdns TW20 ....95 B2
Spencer Rd
Bracknell RG42 ....117 C4
Newbury RG14 ....130 B3
Reading RG2 ....113 A4
Slough SL3 ....43 C2
Spencers Cl SL6 ....39 B4
Spencers La SL6 ....19 C3
Spencers Rd SL6 ....39 B4
Spenwood Cl RG7 ....113 A1
Sperling Rd SL6 ....19 C1
Spey Rd RG30 ....85 A4
Spinfield Cty Comb Sch
SL7 ....1 A1
Spinfield La W SL7 ....1 B1
Spinfield Mount SL7 ....1 A1
Spinfield Pk SL7 ....1 B1
Spinis RG12 ....117 C1
Spinner Gn RG12 ....118 A2
Spinners Wlk Marlow SL7 ....1 B1
Windsor SL4 ....67 B3
Spinney SL1 ....42 A3
Spinney Cl RG4 ....59 A4
Spinney Dr TW14 ....98 B4
Spinney La SL4 ....93 A4
Spinney The Ascot SL5 ....120 C2
Frimley GU15 ....152 B3
Reading RG31 ....84 C2
Wokingham RG40 ....141 C4
Yateley GU46 ....149 B4
Spinningwheel La RG42 ....90 B4
Spitfire Way RG5 ....88 A4
Spittal St SL7 ....1 B1
Splash The RG42 ....91 A1
Spode Cl RG30 ....84 C4
Spout La TW19 ....70 A2
Spout La N TW19 ....70 A2
Spray La RG20 ....28 B1
Spray Rd Ham SN8 ....126 C2
Inkpen RG17 ....127 A2
Spriggs Cl RG19 ....106 B1
Spring Ave TW20 ....95 C1
Spring Cl Maidenhead SL6 ....19 C1
Pangbourne RG8 ....55 B3
Spring Cnr TW13 ....98 C3
Spring Gdns Ascot SL5 ....120 A3
Bourne End SL8 ....3 A2
Frimley GU15 ....152 A3
Marlow SL7 ....1 C2
Shinfield RG7 ....113 A1
Wooburn Green HP10 ....3 C4
Spring Gr RG1 ....86 A3
Spring Hill SL6 ....39 C2
Spring Ho SL7 ....1 C2
Spring La
Aldermaston RG7 ....135 B4
Aston Tirrold OX11 ....12 C4
Caversham RG4 ....60 A3
Cold Ash RG18 ....106 B4
Cookham SL6 ....19 B3
Farnham Common SL2 ....22 B3
Mortimer RG7 ....137 A3
Slough SL1 ....41 C3
Swallowfield RG7 ....139 A2
Spring Mdw RG12 ....118 B4
Spring Mdws RG17 ....48 A2
Spring Rd TW13 ....98 C3
Spring Rise TW20 ....95 C1
Spring Terr 29 RG1 ....86 A3
Spring Wlk RG10 ....36 B1
Spring Wood La RG7 ....111 A1
Spring Woods
Sandhurst GU47 ....143 B1
Virginia Water GU25 ....122 A3
Springate Field SL3 ....43 C2
Springcross Ave GU17 ....150 B2
Springdale Earley RG6 ....87 A1
Wokingham RG40 ....141 C4
Springfield
Lightwater GU18 ....153 B4
Slough SL1 ....43 A2
Springfield Cl SL4 ....67 A3
Springfield Ct SL6 ....40 A4
Springfield Cty Prim Schs
TW16 ....125 C4
Springfield End RG8 ....34 B4
Springfield La Marlow SL7 ....1 A1
Newbury RG14 ....131 A4
Springfield Mews RG4 ....59 A2
Springfield Pk
Maidenhead SL6 ....40 B1
Twyford RG10 ....61 C2
Springfield Prim Sch
RG31 ....84 A4
Springfield Rd
Ashford TW15 ....97 C2
Bracknell RG12 ....117 B4
Brands Hill SL3 ....69 A4
Frimley GU15 ....152 A3
Silchester RG26 ....135 C1
Windsor SL4 ....67 A3
Springfields Cl KT16 ....124 A1
Springhill Ct RG12 ....118 A3
Springhill Rd RG8 ....34 B4
Springmead Ct GU47 ....143 C1
Spruce Ct 26 SL1 ....42 C2
Spruce Dr GU18 ....153 A4
Spruce Rd RG5 ....88 A3
Spur The Slough SL1 ....41 B4
Wargrave RG10 ....36 C2
Spurcroft Prim Sch
RG19 ....106 B1
Spurcroft Rd RG19 ....106 B1
Square The Bagshot GU19 .145 C2
Bracknell RG12 ....118 C3
Earley RG6 ....114 A4
Harmondsworth TW6 ....70 A3
Lightwater GU18 ....146 B1
Pangbourne RG8 ....56 B3
Shinfield RG7 ....113 A1
Squire's Bridge Rd
TW17 ....125 A3
Squire's Rd TW17 ....125 A3
Squires Bridge Rd KT17 .124 C3
Squires Ct
Camberley GU15 ....151 B2
Chertsey KT16 ....124 A1
Squires Wlk TW15 ....98 B1
Squirrel Cl GU47 ....150 A4
Squirrel Dr SL4 ....93 A4
Squirrel Rise SL7 ....1 B3
Squirrels Drey RG45 ....142 C3
Squirrels Way RG6 ....87 A1
Stable Cl RG7 ....111 A2
Stable Cotts SL7 ....18 B3
Stable Croft GU19 ....145 B1
Stable Ct RG14 ....105 A3
Stable View GU46 ....149 B4
Stables Ct SL7 ....1 A1
Stacey's Ind Est RG26 ....135 B1
Staddlestone Cl RG31 ....57 B1
Stadium Way RG30 ....58 A1
Staff Coll GU15 ....151 B4
Staff College Rd GU15 ....151 A3
Stafferton Way SL6 ....40 A3
Stafford Ave SL2 ....22 B1
Stafford Cl Burnham SL6 ....41 A4
Woodley RG5 ....87 C4
Stafford Lake GU21,GU24 .153 C1
Staffordshire Cl RG30 ....84 C4
Staffordshire Croft RG42 ....91 C1
Stag Hill RG17 ....73 A1
Stainash Cres TW18 ....97 A2
Stainash Par TW18 ....97 A2
Staines By-Pass
TW15, TW18 ....97 B2
Staines Central Trad Est
W18 ....96 C2
Staines La KT16 ....124 A2
Staines Lane Cl KT16 ....123 C2
Staines Prep Sch The
TW18 ....97 A2
Staines Rd Chertsey KT16 .124 A3
East Bedfont TW14 ....98 B4
Laleham TW18 ....124 A4
Wraysbury TW19 ....95 C4
Staines Rd W TW15,TW16 ....98 B1
Staines Sta TW18 ....97 A2
Stainford Cl TW15 ....98 B2
Stamford Ave GU16 ....151 C1
Stamford Rd SL6 ....39 B3
Stanbrook Cl RG7 ....82 A1
Stanbury Gate RG7 ....113 A2
Stanfield RG26 ....135 A1
Stanford Dingley
Circular Wlks RG18 ....80 C4
Stanham Rd RG30 ....84 C4
Stanhope Heath TW19 ....70 B1
Stanhope Rd
Camberley GU15 ....150 C2
Reading RG2 ....86 B2
Slough SL1 ....41 B4
Stanhope Way TW19 ....70 B1
Stanlake La RG10 ....61 C2
Stanley Cl SL7 ....1 C2
Stanley Cotts SL2 ....42 C3
Stanley Gn E SL3 ....43 C1
Stanley Gn W SL3 ....43 C1
Stanley Gr 5 RG1 ....85 C4
Stanley Ho SL4 ....68 A1
Stanley Rd Ashford TW15 ....97 C2
Newbury RG14 ....105 A1
Wokingham RG40 ....116 C3
Stanley St RG1 ....85 C4
Stanmore Cl SL5 ....120 A3
Stanmore Gdns RG7 ....136 C3
Stanmore Rd Beedon RG20 .30 B1
East Isley RG20 ....30 C3
Stanshawe Rd RG1 ....86 A4
Stansted Rd TW6 ....70 C1
Stanton Cl RG6 ....87 B2
Stanton Way SL3 ....43 C1
Stanway Cotts
7 Chertsey KT16 ....124 A1
Reading RG1 ....86 C3
Stanwell Cl TW19 ....70 B1
Stanwell Gdns TW19 ....70 B1
Stanwell Moor Rd
TW19, TW6, UB7 ....70 A2
Stanwell New Rd
TW18, TW19 ....97 A3
Stanwell Rd Ashford TW15 .97 C2
East Bedfont TW14,
TW19, TW6 ....98 A4
Horton SL3, TW19 ....69 B2
Stapleford Rd RG30 ....85 B2
Staplehurst RG12 ....117 C1
Stapleton Cl Marlow SL7 ....1 C2
Newbury RG14 ....130 B3
Star La Knowl Hill RG10 ....37 C2
Reading RG1 ....86 A4
Star Post Rd GU15 ....151 C4
Star Rd RG4 ....59 B1
Starling Cl RG41 ....115 C3
Starlings Dr RG31 ....84 A3
Starmead Dr RG40 ....116 C3
Starting Gates RG14 ....105 B1
Startins La SL6 ....19 B4
Starwood Ct SL3 ....43 B2
Statham Ct RG42 ....117 C4
Station App Ashford TW15 ....97 C2
Maidenhead SL6 ....39 C3
Marlow SL7 ....1 C1
Reading RG1 ....86 A4
Shepperton TW17 ....125 B2
Staines TW18 ....97 A2
Virginia Water GU25 ....122 B3
Station Cres TW15 ....97 C2
Station Flats SL5 ....121 A1
Station Hill Ascot SL5 ....120 A3
Cookham SL6 ....19 C4
Hampstead Norreys RG18 ....52 C3
Reading RG1 ....86 A4
Station Ind Est RG40 ....116 A3
Station Par Ashford TW15 ....97 C2
Cookham SL6 ....19 C3
Sunningdale SL5 ....121 A1
Virginia Water GU25 ....122 C2
Station Path TW18 ....96 C2
Station Rd Ashford TW15 ....97 C2
Bagshot GU19 ....145 C2
Ball Hill RG20 ....130 A2
Bourne End SL8 ....3 A2
Bracknell RG12 ....118 A4
Chertsey KT16 ....124 A1
Cookham SL6 ....19 C4
Earley RG6 ....87 B2

**Station Rd** *continued*
East Garston RG17 .47 B3
Egham TW20 .96 A2
Frimley GU16 .151 B1
Goring RG8 .34 B3
Great Shefford RG17 .48 A2
Henley-on-T RG9 .15 C1
Hungerford RG17 .100 B3
Kintbury RG17 .102 A1
Marlow SL7 .1 C1
Newbury, City RG14 .105 A1
Newbury, Speen RG14 .104 B3
Pangbourne RG8 .56 B3
Reading RG1 .86 A4
Shepperton TW17 .125 B2
Shiplake RG9 .36 A2
Slough SL1 .41 C4
Slough, Langley SL3 .44 A2
Sunningdale SL5 .121 A2
Taplow SL6 .40 C4
Thatcham RG19 .106 C1
Theale RG7 .83 C2
Twyford RG10 .61 B2
Wargrave RG10 .36 B1
Wokingham RG40 .116 A3
Woolhampton RG7 .108 B1
Wraysbury TW19 .69 A1
**Station Rd N** 5 TW20 .96 A2
**Station Rise** SL7 .1 C1
Station Road Ind Est RG19 .106 C1
Station Yard Ind Est RG17 .100 C3
**Staunton Rd** SL2 .42 B4
**Staveley Rd** TW15 .98 B1
**Staverton Cl**
Bracknell RG42 .91 A1
Wokingham RG40 .116 C3
**Staverton Rd** RG2 .86 B2
**Stayne End** GU25 .122 A3
**Steam Farm La** TW14 .71 C2
**Steeple Wlk** RG6 .113 C4
**Steerforth Copse** GU47 .143 C1
**Steggles Cl** RG5 .87 B4
**Stepgates** KT16 .124 A1
**Stepgates Cl** KT16 .124 A1
Stepgates Prim Sch KT16 .124 A1
**Stephanie Chase Ct** RG40 .116 B4
**Stephen Cl** Egham TW20 .96 B1
Twyford RG10 .61 C2
**Stephen's Rd** RG7 .136 C3
**Stephens Cl** RG7 .136 C3
**Stephens Firs** RG7 .136 C3
**Stephenson Cl** RG18 .106 B2
**Stephenson Ct** 21 SL1 .42 C2
**Stephenson Dr** SL4 .67 A4
**Stephenson Rd** RG2 .141 A4
**Sterling Ave** TW17 .125 C3
**Sterling Ctr The** RG12 .118 B3
**Sterling Est** RG14 .105 A1
**Sterling Gdns** GU47 .150 C4
**Sterling Way** RG30 .58 A1
**Stevens Hill** GU46 .149 C3
**Stevenson Dr** RG42 .90 B2
**Stewart Ave**
Littleton TW17 .125 A3
Slough SL1 .42 C4
**Stewart Cl** SL6 .65 B3
**Stewarts Dr** SL2 .22 A4
**Stewarts Way** SL7 .1 B4
**Stile Rd** SL3 .43 B2
**Stilton Cl** RG6 .87 C1
**Stilwell Cl** GU46 .149 C3
**Stirling Cl** Caversham RG4 .59 B3
Frimley GU16 .151 C1
Windsor SL4 .66 B3
**Stirling Rd** Slough SL1 .42 A4
Stanwell TW19, TW6 .70 C1
**Stirling Way** RG18 .106 B2
**Stirrup Cl** RG14 .131 A4
**Stockbridge Way** GU46 .149 B2
**Stockbury Cl** RG6 .87 A1
Stockcross CE Prim Sch RG20 .103 C3
**Stockdales Rd** SL4 .41 C1
**Stockton Rd** RG2 .86 B1
**Stockwells** SL6 .20 B1
**Stockwood Rise** GU15 .151 C3
**Stoke Common Rd** SL3 .23 A4
**Stoke Court Dr** SL2 .22 C2
**Stoke Gdns** SL1 .42 C3
**Stoke Gn** SL2 .23 A1
**Stoke Park Ave** SL2 .22 B1
**Stoke Poges La** SL1, SL2 .42 C4
Stoke Poges Sch SL2 .23 A3
Stoke Poges Sch The SL2 .22 C3
**Stoke Rd** SL2 .42 C4
**Stoke View** SL1 .42 C3
**Stoke Wood** SL2 .22 C4
**Stokeford Cl** 5 RG12 .118 C2
**Stokes La** RG26 .134 B1
**Stokes View** RG8 .56 B3
**Stokesay** SL2 .42 C3
**Stokesley Rise** HP10 .3 C4
**Stomp Rd** SL1 .41 B4
**Stompits Rd** Holyport SL6 .65 B4
Maidenhead SL6 .40 B1
**Stone Copse** RG14 .105 C4
**Stone Cres** TW14 .98 C4
**Stone House La** SL6 .2 B1
**Stone St** RG30 .58 A1
**Stonea Cl** RG6 .114 B4
**Stonebridge Field** SL4 .42 A1
**Stonecroft Ave** SL0 .44 C4
**Stonefield Pk** SL6 .39 B4
**Stonegate** GU15 .152 B3
**Stoneham Cl** RG30 .85 A3
**Stonehaven Dr** RG5 .88 A3
**Stonehill Rd** GU18 .146 A1
**Stonehouse Rise** GU16 .151 C1
**Stoneleigh Ct** GU16 .151 C1
**Stoney Cl** GU46 .149 B2
**Stoney La** Burnham SL2 .22 A2
Newbury RG14, RG18 .105 B3
Thatcham RG19 .106 C2
**Stoney Meade** SL1 .42 A3
**Stoney Rd** RG42 .118 A4
**Stoney Ware** SL7 .18 C4
**Stoney Ware Cl** SL7 .18 B4
**Stoneyfield** RG7 .109 A3
**Stoneyland Ct** 5 TW20 .95 C2
**Stoneylands Rd** TW20 .95 C2
**Stookes Way** GU46 .149 A2
**Stornaway Rd** SL3 .44 B1
**Stour Cl** Reading RG30 .85 A4
Slough SL1 .42 A2
**Stovell Rd** SL4 .67 A4
**Stow Rd** RG9 .35 C4
**Stowe Rd** SL1 .41 C3
**Strachey Cl** RG8 .56 B1
**Straight Bit** HP10 .3 A4
**Straight La** RG17 .46 C2
**Straight Mile The**
Hurst RG10 & RG40 .89 B3
Waltham St Lawrence RG10 .62 C1
**Straight Rd** SL4 .68 A1
**Strand La** SL6 .19 C3
**Strand View Wlk** SL6 .19 C3
**Strand Way** RG6 .87 B1
**Stranraer Gdns** SL1 .42 C3
**Stranraer Way** 1 TW6 .70 C1
**Stratfield** RG12 .117 C1
**Stratfield Ct** SL6 .40 A4
**Stratfield Rd** SL1 .43 A2
**Stratford Cl** SL2 .21 B1
**Stratford Dr** HP10 .3 B2
**Stratford Gdns** SL6 .39 B2
**Stratford Rd** TW6 .71 B1
**Stratford Way** RG31 .84 A3
**Strathcona Cl** HP10 .3 B4
**Strathcona Way** HP10 .3 B4
**Strathearn Ave** UB3 .71 C4
**Stratheden Pl** 9 RG1 .85 C4
**Strathmore Ct** GU15 .151 B3
**Strathmore Dr** RG10 .61 A2
**Strathy Cl** RG30 .85 A4
**Stratton Gdns** RG2 .86 B1
**Stratton Rd** TW16 .125 C4
**Strawberry Hill**
Newbury RG14 .104 C2
Newell Green RG42 .91 C1
**Streamside** SL1 .41 C3
Streatley CE Sch RG8 .33 C3
Streatley & Goring Bridge RG8 .34 A3
**Streatley Hill** RG8 .33 C3
**Street The**
Aldermaston RG7 .135 A4
Bradfield RG7 .83 A3
Mortimer RG7 .137 B3
Moulsford OX10 .14 A3
South Stoke RG8 .14 A2
Swallowfield RG7 .139 B4
Tidmarsh RG8 .56 B1
Waltham St Lawrence RG10 .63 A3
**Streets Heath** GU24 .153 C4
**Stretton Cl** RG7 .82 A1
**Strode St** TW20 .96 A2
Strode's Coll TW20 .95 C2
**Strode's Cres** TW18 .97 B2
**Strodes College La** TW20 .95 C2
**Stroller Cl** RG19 .105 C2
**Stroma Ct** SL1 .41 B3
**Strongrove Hill** RG17 .100 B3
**Strood La** SL5 .93 B1
**Stroud Cl** SL4 .66 B2
**Stroud Farm Rd** SL6 .65 A4
**Stroud Way** TW15 .98 A1
**Stroude Rd** Egham TW20 .96 A1
Virginia Water GU25, TW20 .122 C3
**Strouds Mdw** RG18 .106 B4
**Strouds The** RG7 .108 C3
**Stuart Cl** Caversham RG4 .59 A3
Windsor SL4 .66 C3
**Stuart Ho** RG42 .117 C4
**Stuart Rd** RG14 .130 B3
**Stuart Way** Staines TW18 .97 A1
Virginia Water GU25 .122 A3
Windsor SL4 .66 C3
Stubbington House Sch SL5 .120 A1
**Stubbles La** SL6 .19 A3
**Stubbs Folly** GU47 .150 B4
**Studios Rd** TW17 .124 C3
**Studland Cl** RG2 .113 B4
Studland Ind Est RG20 .129 A2
**Sturbridge Cl** RG6 .87 B1
**Sturdee Cl** GU16 .151 C1
**Sturges Rd** RG40 .116 B3
**Sturt Gn** SL6 .64 C4
**Styventon Pl** KT16 .123 C1
**Sucks La** RG8 .54 B2
**Suffolk Cl** Bagshot GU19 .145 C1
Slough SL1 .41 C4
Wokingham RG41 .115 B3
**Suffolk Combe** RG42 .91 C1
**Suffolk Ct** SL6 .39 C4
**Suffolk Rd** Maidenhead SL6 .39 B2
Reading RG30 .85 B4
**Sulham La** RG8 .56 C2
**Sulham Wlk** RG30 .85 A2
**Sulhamstead Hill** RG7 .110 B3
**Sulhamstead La** RG7 .110 B2
**Sulhamstead Rd** RG7, RG30 .111 A3
Sulhamstead & Ufton Nervet Prim Sch RG7 .110 B2
**Sullivan Rd** GU15 .151 A3
**Sumburgh Way** SL1 .42 C4
**Summer Gdns** GU15 .152 B3
**Summerfield Cl** RG41 .88 C1
**Summerfield Rise** RG8 .34 B4
**Summerhouse La** UB7 .70 B4
**Summerlea** SL1 .42 A3
**Summerleaze Rd** SL6 .20 A1
**Summers Rd** SL1 .21 B1
**Summit Cl** RG40 .141 C4
Summit Ctr UB7 .70 B4
**Sun Cl** SL4 .67 B4
**Sun Gdns** RG7 .111 A1
**Sun La** Maidenhead SL6 .39 C4
Swallowfield RG7 .139 A1
**Sun Pas** SL4 .67 B3
**Sun Ray Est** GU47 .150 A4
**Sun St** RG1 .86 B4
**Sunbury Cres** TW13 .98 C2
**Sunbury Cross Ctr** 14 TW16 .98 C1
**Sunbury Ct** SL4 .67 B4
Sunbury Int Bsns Ctr TW16 .125 C4
Sunbury Manor Sch TW16 .125 C4
**Sunbury Rd** Eton SL4 .67 B4
Feltham TW13 .98 C2
**Sunderland Cl** RG5 .88 A4
**Sunderland Ct** 11 TW19 .70 C1
**Sunderland Pl** RG18 .106 B2
**Sunderland Rd** SL6 .39 A4
**Sundew Cl**
Lightwater GU18 .153 B4
Wokingham RG40 .116 C4
**Sundial Cl** RG30 .85 A3
**Sundon Cres** GU25 .122 B2
**Sundown Rd** TW15 .98 B2
**Sunley Cl** RG14 .130 B3
**Sunning Ave** SL5 .120 C1
**Sunning Ho** Ascot SL5 .120 B3
Windlesham SL5 .146 C4
Sunningdale Pk (Civil Service Coll) SL5 .120 C2
Sunningdale Sch SL5 .120 C2
Sunningdale Sta SL5 .121 A1
**Sunninghill Cl** SL5 .120 B3
**Sunninghill Ct** SL5 .120 B3
**Sunninghill Lodge** SL5 .120 B4
**Sunninghill Rd** Ascot SL5 .120 B3
Windlesham GU20 .146 A4
Winkfield SL4, SL5 .93 C1
**Sunnybank** Ascot SL5 .120 A3
Marlow SL7 .1 B2
Sunnymeads Sta TW19 .68 C2
**Sunnymede Cotts** SL6 .20 A1
**Sunnyside** RG14 .104 C3
**Surbiton Rd** GU15 .145 A1
**Surley Row** RG4 .59 A3
**Surly Hall Wlk** SL4 .66 C3
**Surrey Ave**
Camberley GU15 .151 A2
Slough SL2 .22 B1
**Surrey Ct** RG42 .91 C1
Surrey Heath Mus GU15 .151 B3
**Surrey Rd** RG2 .86 A2
**Surridge Ct** GU19 .145 C1
**Sussex Cl** SL1 .43 A2
**Sussex Gdns** RG5 .87 C4
**Sussex Ho** SL2 .22 B3
**Sussex Keep** SL1 .43 A2
**Sussex La** RG7 .113 B1
**Sussex Lodge** 7 SL6 .39 C3
**Sussex Pl** SL1, SL3 .43 A2
**Sutcliffe Ave** RG6 .87 B2
**Sutherland Ave** TW16 .125 C4
**Sutherland Chase** SL5 .119 C4
**Sutherland Gdns** TW16 .125 C4
**Sutherland Gr** RG31 .84 C2
**Sutherland Grange** SL4 .66 B4
**Sutherlands** RG14 .130 C4
**Sutherlands Ave** RG1 .86 B3
**Sutton Ave** SL3 .43 B2
**Sutton Cl** Cookham SL6 .20 A4
Maidenhead SL6 .39 B3
**Sutton La** Brands Hill SL3 .69 A4
Slough SL3 .44 B1
**Sutton Pl** SL3 .69 A4
**Sutton Rd**
Camberley GU15 .145 A1
Cookham SL6 .20 A3
Newbury RG14 .104 B3
**Sutton Wlk** RG1 .86 B3
**Suttons Park Ave** RG6 .86 C4
**Swabey Rd** SL3 .44 A1
**Swainstone Rd** RG2 .86 A3
**Swaledale** RG12 .118 A2
**Swallow Cl** Reading RG31 .84 B3
Staines TW18 .96 C2
Yateley GU46 .149 A3
**Swallow Ho** SL7 .2 A1
**Swallow St** SL0 .44 B4
**Swallow Way** RG41 .115 C3
**Swallowfield** TW20 .95 A1
**Swallowfield Dr** RG2 .113 B3
**Swallowfield Gdns** RG7 .83 C2
Swallowfield Pk RG7 .139 C4
**Swallowfield Rd** RG2 .114 B1
**Swan Ct** RG14 .104 C2
**Swan Dr** RG7 .109 A2
**Swan Ho** GU47 .150 A4
**Swan La** GU47 .150 A4
**Swan Pl** 10 RG1 .86 A4
**Swan Rd** SL0 .44 C4
**Swan Wlk** TW17 .125 C1
**Swancote Gn** RG12 .118 A2
**Swandrift** TW18 .96 C1
**Swangate** RG17 .100 B4
**Swanholm Gdns** RG31 .84 C2
**Swanmore Cl** RG6 .87 C1
**Swanscourt** RG10 .61 C2
**Swansdown Wlk** RG19 .106 A2
**Swansea Rd**
Harlington TW14, TW6 .71 B1
Reading RG1 .59 A1
**Swansea Terr** RG31 .57 B1
**Swanston La** RG8 .56 B4
**Sweeps Ditch Cl** TW18 .97 A1
**Sweeps La** TW20 .95 C2
**Sweet Briar Dr** RG31 .84 B2
**Sweetbriar** RG45 .143 A4
**Sweetzer's Piece** RG7 .136 C3
**Swepstone Cl** RG6 .87 B1
**Swift Cl** RG41 .115 C3
**Swift Ho** SL7 .2 A1
**Swift La** GU19 .145 C2
**Swinbrook Cl** RG31 .57 B2
**Swindon Rd** TW6 .71 B1
Swinley County Prim Sch SL5 .120 A2
Swinley Forest Golf Club SL5 .119 C1
**Swinley Rd** SL5 .119 B2
**Swiss Cottage Cl** RG31 .84 B4
**Switchback Cl** SL6 .19 B1
**Switchback Rd N** SL6 .19 C2
**Switchback Rd S** SL6 .19 B1
**Switchback The** SL6 .19 B1
**Swithin Chase** RG42 .91 C1
**Sycamore Cl** 13
Bourne End SL8 .3 A2
Burghfield Common RG30 .111 A2
Frimley GU16 .151 C1
Maidenhead SL6 .39 B2
Sandhurst GU47 .150 A4
Woodley RG5 .87 B3
**Sycamore Ct** SL4 .67 B2
**Sycamore Dr**
Frimley GU16 .151 C1
Marlow Bottom SL7 .1 B3
Twyford RG10 .61 B3
**Sycamore Lo** 11 TW16 .98 C1
**Sycamore Rd** RG2 .86 C1
**Sycamore Rise**
Bracknell RG12 .118 B3
Newbury RG14 .105 B3
**Sycamore Wlk**
Englefield Green TW20 .95 A1
Slough SL3 .43 C4
**Sycamores The** GU17 .150 A3
**Sydings The** RG14 .104 B3
**Sydney Cl**
Crowthorne RG45 .143 B4
Thatcham RG19 .106 C2
**Sydney Cres** TW15 .98 A1
**Sydney Gr** SL1 .42 B4
**Sydney Lodge** RG19 .106 C2
**Syke Cluan** SL0 .44 C2
**Syke Ings** SL0 .44 C2
**Sykes Cotts** RG12 .118 C1
**Sykes Rd** SL1 .42 A4
**Sylvan Ridge** GU47 .143 A1
**Sylvan Wlk** RG30 .85 B2
**Sylvanus** RG12 .117 C1
**Sylverns Ct** RG42 .91 B1
**Sylvester Cl**
Newbury RG14 .104 C3
Winnersh RG41 .88 B2
**Sylvester Rd** SL6 .19 C1
**Symondson Mews** RG42 .90 B2
**Sympson Rd** RG26 .135 B1

## T

**Tachbrook Rd** TW14 .98 C4
**Tadcroft Wlk** RG31 .84 C2
**Tadham Pl** RG19 .106 B1
**Tadley Common Rd** RG26 .135 B1
**Tadmor Cl** TW16 .125 C3
**Taff Way** RG30 .85 A4
**Tag La** RG10 .37 A1
**Talbot Ave** SL3 .43 C2
**Talbot Cl** Caversham RG4 .59 B1
Newbury RG14 .104 C3
**Talbot Ct** 7 Reading RG1 .86 A4
Windsor SL4 .67 A2
**Talbot Pl** Bagshot GU19 .145 C2
Datchet SL3 .68 B3
**Talbot Rd** TW15 .97 C2
**Talbot Way** RG31 .57 B2
**Talbots Dr** SL6 .39 A3
**Talfourd Ave** RG6 .87 A3
**Talisman Cl** RG45 .142 B3
**Tall Trees** SL3 .69 C3
**Tallis La** RG30 .85 B2
**Tamar Ct** RG30 .85 B3
**Tamar Gdns** RG2 .86 B2
**Tamar Way** Slough SL3 .44 A1
Wokingham RG41 .115 C4
**Tamarind Ct** 3 TW20 .95 C2
**Tamarind Way** RG6 .86 C1
**Tamarisk Ave** RG2 .86 C1
**Tamarisk Rise** RG40 .116 B4
**Tamarisk Way** SL1 .42 A2
**Tamerisk Ct** RG18 .106 C2
**Tamesa Ho** TW17 .125 A1
**Tamesis Pl** RG4 .59 A1
**Tamworth** RG12 .118 B1
**Tamworth Cl** 2 RG6 .87 B1
**Tangier Ct** SL4 .67 B4
**Tangier La** SL4 .67 B4
**Tanglewood** RG40 .142 A4
**Tanglewood Ride** GU24 .153 B4
**Tangley Dr** RG41 .116 A2
**Tanglyn Ave** TW17 .125 A2
**Tanhouse La** RG41 .116 A3
**Tank Rd** GU15 .150 C3
**Tanner Ct** RG14 .105 A2
**Tanners Cl** RG7 .110 C1
**Tanners La** RG4 .58 C4
**Tanners Yd** GU19 .145 C2
**Tape La** RG10 .88 C4
**Tapestries The** SL4 .68 A1
**Taplow Common Rd** SL1 .21 A2
**Taplow Rd** SL6 .41 A4
Taplow Sta SL6 .40 C4
**Tarbat Ct** 6 GU47 .150 B4
**Tarbay La** SL4 .66 A3
**Target Cl** TW14 .71 C1
**Target Hill** RG42 .91 B1
**Targett Ct** RG41 .88 A1
**Tarlton Ct** RG30 .84 C3
**Tarmac Way** UB7 .70 A4
**Tarn Howes Cl** RG19 .106 A2
**Tarn La** RG14 .130 C4
**Tarnbrook Way** RG12 .118 C1
**Tarragon Cl** Earley RG6 .86 C1
Newell Green RG42 .91 B1
**Tarragon Way** RG7 .111 A2
**Tarrant Gn** RG42 .91 B1
**Tarrants Hill** RG17 .100 B3
**Tasker Cl** UB3 .71 B4
**Tasman Ct** 1 TW16 .98 C1
**Tatchbrook Cl** SL6 .40 A4
**Tattersall Cl** RG40 .116 C3
**Tavistock Cl**
Maidenhead SL6 .39 A4
Staines TW18 .97 B1
**Tavistock Rd** RG2 .86 A2
**Tawfield** RG12 .117 C1
**Tay Rd** RG30 .85 A4
**Taylor Ct** 13 RG1 .85 C4
**Taylor's Cl** SL7 .1 C1
**Taylors Ct** SL6 .39 A4
**Taynton Wlk** 32 RG1 .86 A3
**Tazewell Ct** RG1 .85 C3
**Tebbit Cl** RG12 .118 B4
**Teesdale Rd** SL2 .41 C4
Teikyo Sch (UK) SL3 .23 B3
**Tekels Ave** GU15 .151 B2
**Tekels Ct** GU15 .151 C2
**Tekels Way** GU15 .151 C2
**Telford Ave** RG45 .143 B4
**Telford Cres** RG5 .60 C1
**Telford Dr** SL1 .42 A2
**Telston Cl** SL8 .3 A3
**Tempest Rd** TW20 .96 B1
**Templar Cl** GU47 .150 A4
**Templars Pl** 9 SL7 .1 C1
**Temple Gdns** TW18 .123 C4
**Temple La** SL7 .18 B3
**Temple Mews** RG5 .87 C4
**Temple Mill Cotts** SL7 .18 B3
**Temple Mill Island** SL7 .18 B3
**Temple Pk** SL6 .17 C2
**Temple Pl** RG1 .86 A3
**Temple Rd** SL4 .67 B3
**Temple Way** Binfield RG42 .90 C1
Farnham Common SL2 .22 B4
**Templecroft** TW15 .98 B1
**Templedene Ave** TW18 .97 B1
**Templeton Gdns** RG2 .86 B1
**Templewood La** SL2 .22 B4
**Ten Acre La** TW20 .123 B4
**Tenaplas Dr** RG8 .54 C3
**Tenby Ave** RG4 .59 B3
**Tenby Dr** SL5 .120 B2
**Tennyson Rd**
Ashford TW15 .97 C2
Thatcham RG18 .106 B2
Woodley RG5 .87 C2
**Tennyson Way** SL2 .21 C1
**Tensing Ct** TW19 .97 C4
**Teresa Vale** RG42 .91 C1
**Tern Cl** RG30 .85 A3
**Terrace Rd N** RG42 .90 B2
**Terrace Rd S** RG42 .90 B1
**Terrace The** Ascot SL5 .120 B2
Camberley GU15 .151 A3
Crowthorne RG45 .143 B3
Maidenhead SL6 .40 B2
Wokingham RG40 .116 A3
**Terrent Ct** SL4 .67 A3
**Terrington Hill** SL7 .1 A1
**Terry's La** SL6 .19 C4
**Tesimond Dr** GU46 .149 A3
**Tessa Rd** RG1 .58 C1
**Test Cl** RG30 .85 A4
**Testwood Rd** SL4 .66 B3
**Tetbury Ct** 14 RG1 .85 C4
**Teviot Rd** RG30 .84 C4
**Thackery Lodge** TW14 .71 B1
**Thakerays The** RG19 .106 B1
**Thames Ave**
Chertsey KT16 .124 A3
Pangbourne RG8 .56 B3
Reading RG1 .59 A1
Windsor SL4 .67 B4
**Thames Cl** Bourne End SL8 .3 A2
Chertsey KT16 .124 B1
**Thames Cres** SL6 .20 A1
**Thames Dr** RG10 .60 C4
Thames Ind Est SL7 .1 C1
**Thames Mdw** KT12, TW17 .125 C1

Thames Mead SL4 66 C3
Thames Rd Goring RG8 34 A3
Slough SL3 44 A2
Thatcham RG18 106 A3
Thames Reach
Medmenham SL7 17 B3
Purley on T RG8 57 B3
Thames Side
Henley-on-T RG9 15 C1
Laleham KT16, TW18 124 B2
Reading RG1 59 A1
Staines TW18 96 C1
Windsor SL4 67 B4
Thames Side Prom RG1 59 A1
Thames St Sonning RG4 60 B2
Staines TW18 96 C2
Walton-on-T KT12 125 C1
Windsor SL4 67 B4
Thames Valley Bsns Pk RG6 60 A1
Thames Valley Univ SL1 42 C3
Thamesbourne Mews SL8 3 A2
Thamesfield Ct TW17 125 B1
Thamesfield Gdns SL7 1 C1
Thamesgate TW18 124 A4
Thameside Prim Sch RG4 59 A1
Thamesmead Sch TW17 125 B2
Thanington Way RG6 87 A1
Thatcham Nature Discovery Ctr RG19 106 A1
Thatcham Sta RG19 106 C1
Thatchers Dr SL6 39 A3
Theal Cl GU47 150 B4
Theale CE Prim Sch RG7 83 B2
Theale Green Com Sch RG7 83 B2
Theale Rd RG30 111 B3
Theale Sta RG7 83 C1
Theobald Dr RG31 57 B2
Theobalds Way GU16 152 B2
Thetford Ho 10 RG1 85 C3
Thetford Mews RG4 59 B3
Thetford Rd TW15 97 C3
Thibet Rd GU47 150 B4
Thicket Gr SL6 38 C4
Thicket Rd RG30 84 C4
Thickthorne La TW18 97 B1
Third Ave Marlow SL7 1 C1
Tadley RG7 135 B1
Third Cres SL1 42 B4
Third St Greenham RG19 131 C3
Newtown RG19 132 A3
Thirkleby Cl SL1 42 B3
Thirlmere Ave
Burnham SL1 41 B4
Reading RG30 57 C1
Thirlmere Cl TW20 96 A1
Thirlmere Wlk GU15 152 B2
Thirtover RG18 79 A1
Thistledown RG31 57 B1
Thistleton Way RG6 87 C1
Thomas Dr RG42 91 C1
Thomas La RG40 141 C4
Thomas Rd HP10 3 B2
Thompkins La SL2 22 A3
Thompson Cl
Hermitage RG18 78 C3
Slough SL3 44 A1
Thompson Dr RG19 106 C1
Thomson Wlk RG31 84 C2
Thorburn Chase GU47 150 C3
Thorn Cl RG41 115 B2
Thorn Dr SL3 43 C4
Thorn La 12 RG1 86 A4
Thorn St RG1 86 A4
Thornaby Pl HP10 3 C4
Thornbank Cl TW19 70 A1
Thornbers Way RG10 61 A3
Thornbridge Rd RG2 113 A4
Thornbury Cl RG45 143 A3
Thornbury Gn RG10 61 B3
Thorncroft TW20 95 B1
Thorndike SL2 42 A4
Thorndown La GU20 146 B2
Thorne Cl
Crowthorne RG45 143 A4
Littleton TW15 98 B1
Thorney Cl RG6 87 C1
Thorney La N SL0 44 C3
Thorney La S SL0 44 C3
Thornfield RG19 132 B2
Thornfield Gn GU17 150 C2
Thornford Rd RG19 132 C2
Thornhill RG12 118 C3
Thornhill Way TW17 125 A2
Thorningdown OX11 10 B4
Thornton Mews RG30 85 B4
Thornton Rd RG30 85 B4
Thorp Cl RG42 90 B2
Thorpe By-Pass TW20 123 A3
Thorpe CE Fst Sch TW20 123 A3
Thorpe Cl RG41 116 A2
Thorpe Ho 7 RG30 85 A4
Thorpe Ind Est TW20 123 B4
Thorpe Ind Pk TW20 123 B4
Thorpe Lea Prim Sch TW20 96 B1
Thorpe Lea Rd TW20 96 B1
Thorpe Pk TW20 123 C3
Thorpe Rd Chertsey KT16 123 B2
Egham TW18, TW20 96 B2
Thorpeside Cl TW18 123 C4
Thrale Mews RG30 85 A4
Three Acre Rd RG14 130 C4
Three Firs Way RG7 110 C1
Three Gables La RG8 34 A4
Three Post La RG17 25 A1
Threshfield RG12 118 A2
Thrift La Holyport SL6 64 B4
Maidenhead SL6 39 B1
Throat Handpost Cnr The RG40 116 A1
Throgmorton Rd GU46 149 A3
Thrush Cl RG7 111 A2
Thurlby Way SL6 39 B2
Thurlestone Cl TW17 125 B2
Thurlestone Gdns RG2 86 B1
Thurlestone Par TW17 125 B2
Thurleys Cotts SL3 23 A2
Thurnscoe Cl RG6 113 C4
Thurso Cl RG30 85 A4
Thurston Rd SL1 42 C4
Thyme Cl RG6 87 A1
Tichborne Cl GU17 150 B3
Tichbourne Cl GU16 151 C2
Tickenor Dr RG40 141 C4
Tickhill Cl RG6 113 C4
Tickleback Row RG42 91 A4
Tidmarsh La RG8 56 A1
Tidmarsh Rd RG8 56 B2
Tidmarsh St 1 RG30 85 A4
Tidwells Lea RG12 118 C4
Tierney Ct 10 SL7 1 C1
Tiffany Cl RG41 115 B3
Tiger Cl RG5 88 A4
Tigerseye Cl RG41 115 B4
Tilbury Cl RG4 59 B2
Tilbury Wlk SL3 44 A2
Tile Barn Row RG20 129 C1
Tilebarn Cl RG9 15 B1
Tilecotes Cl SL7 1 B1
Tilehurst La RG42 90 B2
Tilehurst Rd RG1 & RG30 85 B4
Tilehurst Sta RG31 57 C2
Tilling Cl RG31 57 A1
Tilly's La TW18 96 C2
Tilney Way RG6 113 C4
Tilstone Ave SL4 41 C1
Tilstone Cl SL4 41 C1
Timbers Wlk SL6 39 A3
Timline Gn RG12 118 C4
Timsway TW18 96 C2
Tindal Cl GU46 149 B3
Tinkers La SL4 66 B3
Tinsey Cl TW20 96 A2
Tinsley Cl RG6 113 C4
Tintagel Dr GU16 151 C1
Tintagel Ho SL1 42 B3
Tintagel Rd RG40 142 A4
Tintern Cl SL1 42 B2
Tintern Cres RG1 85 C3
Tinwell Cl RG6 87 C1
Tippett Rise RG2 86 A3
Tippings La RG5 88 A4
Tippits Mead RG42 117 B4
Tiptree Cl RG6 113 C4
Tiree Ho SL2 42 A4
Titcombe Way RG17 102 A1
Tite Hill TW20 95 B2
Tithe Barn Dr SL6 40 C1
Tithe Cl Maidenhead SL6 40 B1
Wentworth GU25 122 B2
Tithe Ct Slough SL3 44 A1
Wokingham RG40 116 B4
Tithe La TW19 69 A1
Tithe Mdws GU25 122 B2
Tithebarn Gr RG31 84 C2
Titlarks Hill Rd SL5 121 A1
Tiverton Cl RG5 60 C1
Tiverton Way GU16 151 C1
Toad La GU17 150 C2
Tocker Gdns RG42 91 A1
Tockley Way SL1 21 A1
Tofrek Terr RG30 85 B4
Tokers Green Rd RG4 58 C4
Tokersgreen La RG4 58 B3
Toll Gdns RG12 118 C3
Tollgate SL6 39 A3
Tolpuddle Way GU46 149 C3
Tomlin Cl RG19 106 C1
Tomlin Rd SL2 21 C1
Tomlins Ave GU16 151 C1
Tomlinscote Sch GU16 152 A1
Tomlinscote Way GU16 152 A1
Tomlinson Dr RG40 142 A4
Toogood Pl RG42 91 B2
Top Common RG42 91 B1
Topaz Cl Slough SL1 42 A3
Wokingham RG41 115 C4
Tope Cres RG2 140 C4
Tope Rd RG2 140 C4
Torcross Gr RG31 84 A2
Torin Ct TW20 95 B2
Torquay Spur SL2 22 A1
Torridge Rd SL3 69 A4
Torrington Rd RG2 86 B1
Toseland Way RG6 87 C2
Totale Rise RG42 91 A1
Totnes Rd RG2 86 B1
Tottenham Wlk GU47 143 B1
Totterdown RG7 110 C1
Toulouse Cl GU15 152 A4
Toutley Cl RG41 88 C1
Toutley Rd RG41 89 A1
Toutly Works RG41 89 A1
Tower Cl Caversham RG4 59 B4
Flackwell Heath HP10 3 B4
Tower Hill RG20 49 A4
Tower Ho Iver SL0 44 C4
4 Slough SL1 42 C2
Towers Dr RG45 143 A2
Town Farm Cty Prim Sch TW19 97 B4
Town Farm Way TW19 97 B4
Town La Stanwell TW19 97 B4
Town La *continued*
Wooburn Green HP10 3 B2
Town Mills 23 RG14 105 A2
Town Quay TW18 124 B3
Town Sq Bracknell RG12 118 B4
Camberley GU15 151 B3
17 Slough SL1 42 C2
Town Tree Rd TW15 98 A2
Townlands Hospl RG9 15 B1
Townsend Cl RG12 118 C2
Townsend Rd
Aldworth RG8 32 C2
Ashford TW15 97 C2
Streatley RG8 33 A4
Townside Pl GU15 151 B3
Towpath TW17 124 C1
Tozer Wlk SL4 66 B2
Trafalgar Cl RG41 115 C3
Trafalgar Ct RG1 85 C3
Trafalgar Way GU15 150 C2
Trafford Rd RG1 58 C1
Transport & Road Research Laboratory RG45 143 B4
Travic Rd SL2 21 C1
Travis Ct SL2 22 A1
Travis La GU47 150 B4
Treble Ho Terr OX11 12 A4
Tredegar Rd RG4 59 A3
Tree Cl RG30 84 B4
Tree Tops Ave GU15 152 A4
Trees Rd SL8 3 A2
Treesmill Dr SL6 39 B2
Treeton Cl RG6 113 C4
Trefoil Cl RG40 116 C4
Trefoil Dro RG18 106 C2
Treforgan RG4 58 C3
Trelawney Ave SL3 43 C2
Trelawney Dr RG31 57 A1
Trelleck Rd RG1 85 C3
Tremayne Wlk GU15 152 B2
Trenchard Rd SL6 65 A4
Trenches La SL0, SL3 44 A3
Trent Cl RG41 115 C4
Trent Cres RG18 106 A3
Trent Rd SL3 69 A4
Trent Villas Est SL3 68 A3
Trenthams Cl RG8 57 A3
Trenton Cl GU16 152 A1
Tresham Cres GU46 149 A3
Tressel The SL6 39 B3
Trevelyan RG12 117 C1
Trevelyan Mid Sch SL4 67 A3
Trevithick Cl TW14 98 C4
Trevor Ct TW19 70 A1
Trevor Ho 5 RG30 85 A4
Trevose Ho SL2 22 A1
Treyarnon Ct RG1 86 B3
Triangle The
Greenham RG14 131 A4
Reading RG30 84 B4
Trident Ind Est SL3 69 C2
Trilakes Ctry Pk GU46,GU47 149 C4
Trindledown RG42 91 A1
Tring Rd RG31 57 B1
Trinity GU47 143 C1
Trinity Ave SL7 1 B2
Trinity Cl TW19 70 B1
Trinity Cres SL5 121 A2
Trinity Ct RG7 83 B2
Trinity Ho SL6 19 C3
Trinity Pl Reading RG1 85 C4
Windsor SL4 67 B3
Trinity Rd SL7 1 B1
Trinity Sch RG14 105 A3
Trinity St Stephens CE Fst Sch SL4 67 A3
Triumph Cl Harlington UB7 71 B3
Woodley RG5 87 C3
Troon Ct Ascot SL5 120 B2
33 Reading RG1 86 B4
Troston Ct TW18 96 C2
Trotsworth Ave GU25 122 C3
Trotsworth Ct GU25 122 B3
Trotwood Cl GU47 143 C1
Trout Cl Earley RG6 87 A4
Marlow SL7 18 B4
Trout Wlk RG14 105 B2
Troutbeck Cl Slough SL2 43 A3
Twyford RG10 61 B3
Troutbeck Wlk GU15 152 B2
Trowes La Beech Hill RG7 138 B2
Swallowfield RG7 139 B3
Trumbull Rd RG42 91 A1
Trumper Way SL1 41 C3
Trumps Green Cl GU25 122 C2
Trumps Green Cty Fst Sch GU25 122 B2
Trumps Mill La GU25 122 C2
Trumpsgreen Ave GU25 122 B2
Trumpsgreen Rd GU25 122 B2
Truro Cl SL6 39 A4
Truss Hill Rd SL5 120 B2
Trust Cnr RG9 35 C4
Trusthorpe Cl RG6 87 C1
Tubbs Farm Cl RG17 25 A1
Tubwell Rd SL2 23 A2
Tudor Ave RG20 51 B2
Tudor Cl Ashford TW15 97 C2
Wokingham RG40 116 C3
Tudor Ct Maidenhead SL6 20 B1
3 Stanwell TW19 70 C1
Tudor Dr
Wooburn Green HP10 3 B4
Yateley GU46 149 B2
Tudor Gdns SL1 41 B4
Tudor Ho RG12 118 A2
Tudor La SL4 95 B4
Tudor Mill HP10 3 C3
Tudor Rd Ashford TW15 98 B1
Newbury RG14 105 A1
Reading RG1 86 A4
Tudor Way SL4 66 C3
Tull Way RG14 105 C3
Tunnel Link Rd TW6 71 A1
Tunnel Rd E TW6 71 A3
Tunnel Rd W TW6 71 A3
Tuns Hill Cotts RG6 87 A3
Tuns La Henley-on-T RG9 15 C1
Slough SL1 42 B2
Tupsley Rd RG1 85 C3
Turbary Gdns RG26 135 A1
Turf Hill Rd GU15 151 C4
Turks Head Ct SL4 67 B4
Turks La RG7 137 A2
Turmeric Cl RG6 86 C1
Turnberry RG12 117 C1
Turnberry Ct 30 RG1 86 B4
Turnbridge Cl RG6 114 A4
Turner Pl GU47 150 B3
Turner Rd SL3 43 B2
Turners Cl TW18 97 A2
Turners Dr RG19 106 C1
Turnery The RG19 106 B2
Turnfields RG19 106 B2
Turnoak Pk SL4 66 C2
Turnpike Comp Sch RG14 105 B2
Turnpike Ind Est RG14 105 B3
Turnpike Rd
Bracknell RG42 117 B4
Newbury RG14, RG19 105 C2
Turnstone Cl RG41 88 A2
Turnstone End GU46 149 A3
Turnville Cl GU18 146 A1
Turpin Rd TW14 71 C1
Turpins Gn SL6 39 A3
Turpins Rise GU20 146 A3
Turton Way SL1 42 B2
Tuscam Way GU15 150 C2
Tuscan Cl RG30 57 C1
Tuxford Mews RG30 85 A4
Tweed Ct RG30 85 A4
Tweed Rd SL3 69 A4
Twin Oaks RG4 59 A3
Twinches La SL1 42 A3
Twinwoods RG20 49 A2
Two Mile Dr SL1 41 C2
Two Rivers Sh Ctr TW18 96 C2
Two Rivers Way RG14 105 B2
Two Tree Hill RG9 35 A4
Twycross Rd RG40 116 C4
Twyford Rd
Binfield RG10 & RG42 90 B4
Waltham St Lawrence RG10 62 C3
Wokingham RG40 89 A1
Twyford Sta RG10 61 C2
Twynersh Ave KT16 123 C2
Twynham Rd SL6 39 A4
Tyberton Pl RG1 85 C3
Tydehams RG14 130 C4
Tyle Pl SL4 68 A1
Tyle Rd RG30 84 B4
Tyler Cl RG4 58 C3
Tyler Dr RG2 140 C4
Tylers La RG7 80 A1
Tylers Pl RG30 84 C4
Tylorstown RG4 58 C3
Tyne Way RG18 106 A3
Tyrell Gdns SL4 66 C2
Tyrrel Ct 8 RG1 86 B4
Tytherton RG12 118 B4

## U

Uffington Cl RG31 84 B4
Uffington Dr RG12 118 C3
Uffoott Cl RG6 113 C4
Ufton Court Yd SL8 3 A2
Ufton Ct SL8 3 A2
Ullswater RG12 117 C1
Ullswater Cl Burnham SL1 41 B4
Lightwater GU18 146 A1
Thatcham RG19 106 A2
Ullswater Dr RG31 57 B2
Ullswater Rd GU18 146 A1
Ulster Cl RG4 59 B3
Umberville Way SL2 21 C1
Underhill OX10 14 A2
Underhill Cl SL6 39 C3
Underwood RG12 117 C2
Underwood Ct RG42 90 B1
Underwood Rd RG30 85 A2
Union Cl GU47 143 C1
Union Rd RG7 82 B2
Union St RG1 86 A4
Unity Cl RG4 59 A3
Unity Ct RG4 59 A3
Univ of Reading
Earley RG6 87 A3
Reading RG1 86 B3
Reading, Whiteknights RG6 86 C2
Unwin Ave TW14 71 B1
Upavon Dr RG1 85 C3
Upavon Gdns RG12 118 C2
Upcroft SL4 67 A2
Upcroft Prim Sch RG30 84 C4
Updown Hill GU20 146 B2
Upland Rd GU15 151 B4
Uplands Hungerford RG17 100 B3
Marlow Bottom SL7 1 B3
Uplands Cl GU47 150 A4
Uplands Cty Prim Sch GU47 150 A4
Uplands Rd RG4 58 C3
Upper Bray Rd SL6 40 B2
Upper Broadmoor Rd RG45 143 B3
Upper Charles St GU15 151 B3
Upper Chobham Rd GU15 152 A2
Upper College Ride GU15 151 C4
Upper Crown St RG1 86 A3
Upper Eddington RG17 100 C4
Upper End RG20 49 A4
Upper Gordon Rd GU15 151 B3
Upper Halliford Rd TW17 125 C3
Upper Halliford Sta TW16 125 C4
Upper Lambourn Rd RG17 25 A2
Upper Lees Rd SL2 22 A1
Upper Meadow Rd RG2 86 B1
Upper Nursery SL5 121 A2
Upper Park Rd GU15 151 C3
Upper Red Cross Rd RG8 34 B4
Upper Redlands Rd RG1 86 C3
Upper Ventnor Cotts SL6 19 B4
Upper Verran Rd GU15 151 B2
Upper Village Rd SL5 120 B2
Upper Warren Ave RG4 58 B2
Upper Wlk GU25 122 C3
Upper Woodcote Rd RG4 58 B3
Uppingham Dr RG5 60 C1
Uppingham Gdns RG4 59 B3
Upshire Gdns RG12 118 C3
Upton Cl Henley-on-T RG9 15 C1
Slough SL1 42 C2
Upton Court Rd SL3 43 A1
Upton Hospl SL1 42 C2
Upton House Sch SL4 67 B3
Upton Lea Par SL2 43 A3
Upton Pk SL1 42 C2
Upton Rd Reading RG30 85 A4
Slough SL1 43 A2
Urquhart Rd RG19 106 C1
Usk Rd RG30 84 C3
Uxbridge Rd SL1, SL2, SL3 43 B3

## V

Vachel Rd RG1 86 A4
Vale Cres RG30 57 C1
Vale Gr SL1 42 C2
Vale Rd Camberley GU15 151 A2
Windsor SL4 66 C3
Vale View RG10 61 A2
Valentia Cl RG30 85 B4
Valentia Rd RG30 85 B4
Valentine Cl RG6 86 C1
Valentine Cres RG4 59 B2
Valentine Wood Ind Est RG7 135 C2
Valeview Dr RG7 138 B3
Valley Cl Caversham RG4 59 A2
Goring RG8 34 B3
Valley Cres RG41 116 A4
Valley End SL3 23 B1
Valley Gdns TW20,GU25 121 C4
Valley Rd
Burghfield Common RG7 111 A2
Frimley GU16 152 B1
Henley-on-T RG9 35 A4
Newbury RG14 130 C4
Valley Road Prim Sch RG9 35 B4
Valley View GU47 150 A4
Valley Way RG26 135 C1
Valon Rd RG2 140 C4
Valpy St RG1 86 A4
Valroy Cl GU15 151 B3
Vanbrugh Ct RG1 86 B4
Vandyke RG12 117 C2
Vanguard Ho 5 TW19 70 C1
Vanlore Way RG31 84 B3
Vanners La RG20 129 B3
Vansittart Est SL4 67 B3
Vansittart Rd Bisham SL7 18 C4
Windsor SL4 67 A3
Vantage Rd SL1 42 A3
Vanwall Bsns Pk SL6 39 B3
Vanwall Rd SL6 39 B2
Vastern Rd RG1 59 A1
Vaughan Almshouses TW15 98 A2
Vaughan Copse SL4 42 B1
Vaughan Gdns SL4 41 C1
Vaughan Way SL2 21 C1
Vauxhall Dr RG5 88 A3
Vegal Cres TW20 95 B2
Venetia Cl RG4 59 B4
Venning Rd RG2 140 C4
Ventnor Rd RG31 57 B1
Venus Cl RG41 115 C3
Verbena Cl RG41 88 A2
Verdon Ct SL2 22 A1
Verey Cl RG10 61 C2
Vermont Rd SL2 21 C1
Vermont Woods RG40 141 C4
Verney Cl SL7 1 B1
Verney Mews RG30 85 B4
Verney Rd SL3 44 A1
Vernon Cres RG2 113 A4
Vernon Dr SL5 119 C4
Vernon Rd TW13 98 C3
Verran Rd GU15 151 B2

Viburnum Ct GU24 153 C3
Vicarage Ave TW20 96 A2
Vicarage Cl Cookham SL6 20 A4
Wokingham RG40 141 C3
Vicarage Cres TW20 96 A2
Vicarage Ct
East Bedfont TW14 98 B4
Egham TW20 96 A1
Vicarage Dr SL6 40 B2
Vicarage Flats SL4 67 B4
Vicarage Gdns Ascot SL5 120 A2
White Waltham SL6 63 C4
Vicarage La
Cold Ash RG18 106 B4
Laleham TW18 124 B3
Wraysbury TW19 95 C4
Yateley GU46 149 B4
Vicarage Rd Ashford TW16 98 C1
Bagshot GU19 145 B2
Blackwater GU17 150 C2
Egham TW20 96 A2
Henley-on-T RG9 35 C4
Maidenhead SL6 39 C4
Reading RG2 86 B3
Staines TW18 96 C3
Yateley GU46 149 B4
Vicarage Way SL3 69 B4
Vicarage Wlk SL6 40 B2
Vicarage Wood Way
RG31 57 A1
Vickers Cl Shinfield RG2 113 C2
Woodley RG5 88 A4
Vickers Ct 9 TW19 70 C1
Victor Cl SL6 39 A4
Victor Rd Thatcham RG19 106 C2
Windsor SL4 67 B2
Victor Way RG5 88 A4
Victoria Ave GU15 151 A3
Victoria Ct Bagshot GU19 145 C1
Henley-on-T RG9 15 C1
2 Marlow SL7 1 C1
Slough SL1 42 C3
Victoria Dr GU17 150 B2
Victoria Gdns RG14 105 A2
Victoria Ho SL4 68 A1
Victoria La UB3 71 B4
Victoria Mews RG30 85 B4
Victoria Rd Ascot SL5 120 A2
Caversham RG4 59 A2
Eton SL4 41 C1
Farnham Common SL2 22 B3
Marlow SL7 1 C1
Mortimer RG7 136 C3
Reading RG31 84 B4
Sandhurst GU47 143 C1
Slough SL2 43 A3
Staines TW18 96 C3
Wargrave RG10 36 C1
Victoria St
Englefield Green TW20 95 B1
Reading RG1 86 B4
18 Slough SL1 42 C2
Windsor SL4 67 B3
Victoria Way 16 RG1 86 B4
Victory Rd KT16 124 A1
Vigo La GU46 149 B2
Viking RG12 117 C2
Villa Mews RG1 86 C4
Village Cl RG2 113 A3
Village Ct SL5 120 B2
Village Gate TW17 125 A2
Village Rd Dorney SL4 41 A2
Thorpe TW20 123 B3
Village Sh Ctr The 18 SL1 42 C2
Village The
Finchampstead RG40 141 C2
Old Windsor SL4 94 A3
Village Way Ashford TW15 98 A2
Yateley GU46 149 B4
Villiers Ct SL4 67 A4
Villiers Mead RG41 116 A3
Villiers Rd SL2 42 B4
Villiers Way RG14 130 B3
Villiers Wlk RG14 130 B3
Vincent Cl Chertsey KT16 123 C1
Harmondsworth UB7 71 A4
Woodley RG5 87 C3
Vincent Dr TW17 125 C3
Vincent Ho 10 RG1 85 C4
Vincent Rd Chertsey KT16 123 C1
Thatcham RG18 106 C2
Vincent Rise RG12 118 C3
Vine Cl TW19 70 A1
Vine Cres RG30 85 A2
Vine Ct Newbury RG14 105 A1
Stoke Poges SL2 23 A3
Vine Rd SL2 22 C3
Vineries Cl UB7 71 A4
Vinery The RG10 36 B1
Vines The RG41 115 B2
Vineyard Dr SL8 3 A3
Vinter Ct TW17 125 A2
Viola Ave TW19 97 C4
Viola Croft RG42 118 C4
Violet Gr RG18 106 C3
Virginia Ave GU25 122 B2
Virginia Beeches GU25 122 B3
Virginia Cl TW18 124 B3
Virginia Ct Ashford TW15 97 C2
Virginia Water GU25 122 B3
Virginia Dr GU25 122 B3
Virginia Water SL5 121 C3
Virginia Water Prep Sch
GU25 122 B3
Virginia Water Sta GU25 122 C2
Virginia Way RG30 85 A3
Viscount Ct 37 SL4 67 B3
Viscount Ind Est SL3 69 C2
Viscount Rd TW19 97 C4
Viscount Way Hatton TW6 71 C2
Woodley RG5 88 A4
Vivien Cl SL6 19 C3
Vivienne Ho TW18 97 A2
Vo-Tec Ctr RG14 105 C1
Voller Dr RG31 84 B3
Volunteer Rd RG7 83 B1
Vulcan Cl Sandhurst GU47 150 A4
Woodley RG5 61 A1
Vulcan Way GU47 150 A4

## W

Waborne Rd SL8 3 A2
Wade Dr SL1 42 A3
Wadham GU47 143 C1
Wadham Cl TW17 125 B1
Wagbullock Rise RG12 118 B2
Waggoners Hollow
GU19 145 C1
Wagner Cl SL6 38 C2
Wagtail Cl RG10 61 C2
Waingel's Copse Sch
RG10 61 A1
Waingels Rd RG5, RG10 61 A1
Wainscot SL5 120 C2
Wakefield Cres SL2 22 C3
Wakeford Cl RG26 135 C1
Wakeford Ct RG26 135 C1
Wakelins End SL6 19 C4
Wakeman Rd SL8 3 A2
Wakemans RG8 55 B2
Walbury RG12 118 C3
Waldeck Rd SL6 40 A4
Waldeck St RG1 86 A3
Waldegrave Pl RG14 105 A2
Walden Ave RG2 114 B2
Waldens Cl SL8 3 A2
Waldorf Hts GU17 150 B2
Waldron Hill RG12 118 C4
Waldrons The RG17 47 B3
Waleys Pl 7 RG4 59 B1
Walgrove Gdns SL6 63 C4
Walk The Ashford TW16 98 C1
Eton SL4 42 A1
Walker Cl TW14 98 C4
Walker Rd SL6 40 A2
Walker's Ridge GU15 151 C3
Walkers La RG17 25 A2
Walkers Pl RG30 85 B4
Wall La RG7 136 B1
Wallace Cl Marlow SL7 1 C2
Upper Halliford TW17 125 B3
Woodley RG5 87 B3
Wallace Wlk SL4 42 C1
Wallcroft Cl RG42 90 C1
Walled Gdn The RG10 36 B1
Waller Ct RG4 59 A1
Waller Dr RG14 105 C3
Wallingford Cl RG12 118 C3
Wallingford Rd
Compton RG20 31 C3
Goring RG8 34 B4
South Stoke RG8 & OX10 14 B3
Wallington Rd GU15 145 A1
Wallington's Rd RG17 101 C1
Wallis Ct SL1 43 A2
Wallner Way RG40 116 C3
Walmer Cl
Crowthorne RG45 143 B3
Reading RG30 85 A3
Walmer Rd RG5 60 C1
Walnut Cl
Wokingham RG41 115 C3
Yateley GU46 149 B2
Walnut Tree Cl
Bourne End SL8 3 A1
Twyford RG10 61 C3
Walnut Tree Ct RG8 34 B3
Walnut Tree Ho TW20 95 C2
Walnut Tree Rd TW17 125 B4
Walnut Way Bourne End SL8 3 A1
Reading RG30 84 B4
Walpole Rd
Old Windsor SL4 95 A4
Slough SL1 41 B4
Walrus Cl RG5 88 A4
Walsh Ave RG42 91 C1
Walter Inf Sch RG41 116 A3
Walter Rd RG41 115 C4
Walters Cl RG18 106 B4
Waltham Cl
Maidenhead SL6 38 C1
Sandhurst GU47 143 B1
Waltham Rd
Twyford RG10 62 A3
White Waltham SL6 38 C1
Waltham St Lawrence
Cty Prim Sch RG10 62 C2
Walton Ave RG9 35 C4
Walton Bridge Rd
KT12, TW17 125 C1
Walton Cl RG5 87 B4
Walton Dr SL5 119 C4
Walton Gdns TW13 98 C2
Walton La Burnham SL2 21 C2
Lower Halliford KT13,TW17 125 B1
Walton-on-T TW17 125 C1
Walton Way RG14 105 B2
Wandhope Way RG31 57 B1
Wansey Gdns RG14 105 B3
Wanstraw Gr RG12 118 C1
Wantage Cl RG12 118 C2
Wantage Rd
Great Shefford RG17 48 B3
Lambourn RG17 25 B3
Reading RG30 85 B4
Sandhurst GU47 150 B4
Streatley RG8 33 C4
Wapshott Rd TW18 96 C2
War Memorial Pl RG9 35 C4
Waram Cl RG17 100 C4
Warbler Cl RG31 84 A3
Warbler Dr RG6 87 A1
Warborough Ave RG31 84 A4
Warborough Rd OX12 7 A4
Warbreck Dr RG31 57 A2
Warbrook La RG27 141 A1
Ward Cl Iver SL0 44 C4
Wokingham RG40 116 B4
Ward Gdns SL1 41 C3
Ward Royal 6 SL4 67 B3
Ward Royal Par 3 SL4 67 B3
Wardle Ave RG31 57 B1
Wardle Cl GU19 145 C2
Wards Pl TW20 96 B1
Wards Stone Pk RG12 118 C1
Wareham Rd RG12 118 C2
Warehouse Rd RG19 131 C3
Warfield CE Prim Sch
RG42 91 C1
Warfield Rd
Bracknell RG12 & RG42 91 B1
East Bedfont TW14 98 C4
Warfield St RG42 91 B2
Wargrave Hill RG10 36 B1
Wargrave Rd
Remenham Hill RG9 15 C1
Twyford RG10 61 B3
Wargrave Sta RG10 36 B1
Wargrove Dr GU47 150 B4
Waring Cl RG6 114 B4
Warings The RG7 109 A4
Warley Rise RG31 57 B2
Warner Cl Harlington UB3 71 B4
Slough SL1 41 C3
Warners Hill SL6 19 B4
Warnford Rd RG30 84 C4
Warnsham Cl 1 RG6 87 A1
Warren Cl
Burghfield Common RG7 111 A2
Sandhurst GU47 150 A4
Slough SL3 43 C2
Warren Ct 7 SL2 22 B4
Warren Down RG42 117 C4
Warren House Rd RG40 116 B4
Warren La RG40 141 C3
Warren Rd Ashford TW15 98 C1
Newbury RG14 130 B3
Woodley RG4,RG5 60 B1
Warren Rise GU16 151 C2
Warren Row SL5 119 B4
Warren Row Rd RG10 37 B3
Warren The RG4 58 B2
Warrington Ave SL1 42 B4
Warrington Spur SL4 95 A4
Warwick RG12 118 C2
Warwick Ave Slough SL2 22 B1
Staines TW18 97 B1
Thorpe Lea TW20 123 B4
Warwick Cl Frimley GU15 152 A2
Maidenhead SL6 39 A2
Warwick Ct 34 SL4 67 B3
Warwick Dr RG14 105 A1
Warwick Ho RG2 86 B2
Warwick Rd Ashford TW15 97 C2
Reading RG2 86 B2
Warwick Villas TW20 123 B4
Wasdale Cl GU47 143 B1
Wash Hill HP10 3 C2
Wash Hill Lea HP10 3 C2
Wash Water RG20 130 A2
Washbury Ho RG14 130 C4
Washington Ct SL7 2 A2
Washington Dr Slough SL1 41 B3
Windsor SL4 66 C2
Washington Gdns RG40 142 A4
Washington Rd RG4 59 A1
Wasing La RG7 134 B3
Watchetts Cty Jun Sch
The GU15 151 A1
Watchetts Dr GU15 151 B1
Watchetts Lake Cl GU15 151 B2
Watchetts Rd GU15 151 A2
Watchmoor Pk GU15 151 A2
Watchmoor Rd GU15 151 A2
Watchmoor Trade Ctr
GU15 151 A2
Water La RG19 131 B4
Water Rd RG30 85 A4
Water Splash La SL5 120 C4
Water St RG18 52 C3
Waterbeach Cl SL1 42 B4
Waterbeach Rd SL1 42 B4
Waterfall Cl GU25 122 A3
Waterford Way RG40 116 B3
Waterham Rd RG12 118 A2
Waterhouse Mead
GU47 150 B4
Waterloo Cl
Camberley GU15 152 A4
East Bedfont TW14 98 C4
Moulsford OX10 14 A4
Waterloo Cres RG40 116 C2
Waterloo Rd
Crowthorne RG45 143 A2
Reading RG2 86 A3
Wokingham RG40 116 C3
Waterloo Rise RG2 86 A2
Waterman Ct 5 SL1 41 C3
Waterman Pl RG1 59 A1
Watermans Bsns Pk The
TW18 96 C2
Watermans Rd RG9 35 C4
Watermans Way RG10 36 B1
Watermead TW14 98 C4
Watermeadows The
RG14 105 A2
Watermill Ct RG7 108 B1
Waters Dr TW18 96 C2
Watersfield Cl 4 RG6 87 A1
Waterside HP10 3 C4
Waterside Ct RG14 105 B2
Waterside Dr
Purley on T RG8 57 B3
Slough SL3 44 A2
Theale RG7 83 C2
Waterside Gdns 9 RG1 86 A4
Watersplash La RG42 91 A1
Watersplash Rd TW17 125 A3
Watery La Kintbury RG20 128 C3
Wooburn Green HP10 3 C4
Watkins Cl RG40 141 C4
Watlington St RG1 86 B4
Watmore La RG41 88 B1
Watson Cl RG40 115 C1
Watts La OX11 12 A4
Wavell Cl RG2 86 C1
Wavell Gdns SL2 21 C1
Wavell Rd SL6 39 A3
Wavendene Ave TW20 96 B1
Waverley RG12 117 C2
Waverley Cl GU15 151 C2
Waverley Ct 18 RG30 85 B3
Waverley Dr
Camberley GU15 151 C3
Virginia Water GU25 122 A3
Waverley Rd
Bagshot GU19 145 C2
Reading RG30 85 B4
Slough SL1 42 B4
Waverley Sch RG40 115 C1
Waverley Way RG40 115 C1
Waverleys The RG18 106 B2
Waybrook Cres RG1 86 C3
Wayland Cl RG12 118 C3
Waylands TW19 68 C1
Waylands Cl RG7 82 B2
Waylen St RG1 85 C4
Ways End GU15 151 C2
Wayside Mews SL6 39 C4
WC Lee's Resthouses
GU20 146 B2
Weald Rise RG30 57 C1
Wealden Way RG30 84 C4
Weardale Cl RG2 86 B2
Weaver Moss GU47 150 A4
Weavers Ct 37 RG1 86 B4
Weavers La RG17 127 B3
Weavers Way RG10 61 B2
Weavers Wlk 20 RG14 105 A2
Webb Cl Bagshot GU19 145 C1
Binfield RG42 90 C1
Slough SL3 43 B1
Webb Ct RG40 116 C4
Webb's Cl RG1 85 C3
Webbs Acre RG19 106 C1
Webbs La RG7 109 A4
Webster Cl SL6 39 A3
Wedderburn Cl RG41 88 B1
Wedgewood Way RG30 57 C1
Weekes Dr SL1 42 A2
Weighbridge Row RG1 58 C1
Weir Cl RG31 84 C2
Weir Pl TW18 123 C4
Weir Rd KT16 124 A1
Weirside Ct 13 RG1 86 B4
Welbeck RG12 117 C2
Welbeck Rd SL6 39 B3
Welby Cl SL6 39 A2
Welby Cres RG41 88 A1
Weldale St RG1 85 C4
Welden SL2 43 B4
Welford Pk RG20 75 C4
Welford Rd RG5 88 A4
Welford & Wickham
CE Prim Sch RG20 75 B2
Well Cl GU15 151 A2
Well House La RG27 140 A2
Well Mdw RG14 105 A3
Welland Cl Brands Hill SL3 69 A4
Reading RG31 57 B1
Wellbank SL6 20 C1
Wellburn Cl GU47 150 A4
Wellcroft Rd SL1 42 A3
Weller Dr Barkham RG40 141 A3
Camberley GU15 151 B2
Wellers La RG42 91 B4
Wellesley Ave SL0 44 C2
Wellesley Cl GU19 145 B2
Wellesley Ct SL0 44 C2
Wellesley Dr RG45 142 C3
Wellesley Path SL1 43 A2
Wellesley Rd SL1 43 A2
Welley Ave TW19 68 C2
Welley Rd TW19 68 C1
Wellfield Cl RG31 84 B4
Wellhill Rd OX12 27 B3
Wellhouse La RG18 79 C3
Wellhouse Rd SL6 19 C1
Wellington Ave
Reading RG2 86 B2
Virginia Water GU25 122 A2
Wellington Bsns Pk
RG45 142 C2
Wellington Cl
Newbury RG14 105 B3
Sandhurst GU47 150 B4
Walton-on-T KT12 125 C1
Wellington Coll RG45 143 A2
Wellington Cotts
Ball Hill RG20 129 A1
Knowl Hill RG10 37 B3
Wellington Cres RG26 134 B1
Wellington Ct
Ashford TW15 97 C2
Shinfield RG7 113 A2
Stanwell TW19 97 C4
Wellington Ctry Pk RG7 139 B1
Wellington Dr RG12 118 C2
Wellington Gdns RG7 82 A1
Wellington Rd
Ashford TW15 97 C2
Crowthorne RG45 143 B2
Hatton TW14 71 C1
Maidenhead SL6 39 B4
Sandhurst GU47 150 B4
Wokingham RG40 116 A3
Wellington St SL1 43 A2
Wellington Terr GU47 150 B4
Wellingtonia Ave
RG45,RG40 142 B2
Wells Cl SL4 67 A4
Wells La SL5 120 A3
Welsh La RG7, RG7 139 A1
Welshmans Rd RG7 136 A3
Welwick Cl RG6 87 C1
Welwyn Ave TW14 71 C1
Wendan Rd RG14 130 C4
Wendover Ct TW18 96 B2
Wendover Dr GU16 152 B2
Wendover Pl TW18 96 B2
Wendover Rd
Bourne End SL8 3 A3
Burnham SL1 41 A4
Egham TW18, TW20 96 B2
Wendover Way RG30 84 B4
Wenlock Edge RG10 61 A2
Wenlock Way RG19 106 B1
Wensley Cl RG10 61 B3
Wensley Rd RG1 85 C3
Wensleydale Dr GU15 152 B3
Wentworth Ave
North Ascot SL5 119 B4
Reading RG2 113 B4
Slough SL2 22 A1
Wentworth Cl
Ashford TW15 98 A2
Crowthorne RG45 142 C3
Yateley GU46 149 B3
Wentworth Club GU25 122 A2
Wentworth Cres SL6 39 B3
Wentworth Ct RG14 105 A1
Wentworth Dr GU25 121 C3
Wentworth Way SL5 119 B4
Wescott Inf Sch RG40 116 B3
Wescott Rd RG40 116 B3
Wesley Dr TW20 96 A1
Wesley Pl SL4 93 A3
Wessex Cl RG17 100 B3
Wessex Ct 4 TW19 70 C1
Wessex Gdns RG10 61 C2
Wessex Inf Sch SL6 39 A2
Wessex Jun Sch SL6 39 A2
Wessex Rd Bourne End SL8 3 A1
Harmondsworth TW19, TW6 70 C2
Wessex Road Ind Est
SL8 3 A1
Wessex Way SL6 39 A2
Wessons Hill SL6 19 B4
West Cl Ashford TW15 97 C2
Medmenham SL7 17 B4
West Cres SL4 66 C3
West Ct RG4 60 C1
West Dean SL6 39 C4
West Dr Reading RG31 84 C3
Sonning RG4 60 B1
Wentworth GU25 121 C1
West End Ct SL2 22 C2
West End La
Harlington UB3 71 B4
Newell Green RG42 91 A2
Stoke Poges SL2 22 C2
West End Rd RG7 136 C3
West Fryerne GU46 149 B4
West Gn GU46 149 A4
West Green Ct RG1 85 C3
West Hill RG1 86 A3
West Ilsley Ho RG20 10 A1
West La RG9 15 B1
West Mead SL6 19 C1
West Mead Sch RG40 116 C3
West Mills RG14 104 C2
West Mills Yd RG14 104 C2
West Point SL1 41 B3
West Ramp TW6 71 A3
West Rd Bracknell RG40 117 B1
Camberley GU15 151 B3
East Bedfont TW14 98 B4
Maidenhead SL6 39 C4
West Ridge SL8 3 A2
West Sq SL0 44 C4
West St Henley-on-T RG9 15 B1
Maidenhead SL6 39 C4
Marlow SL7 1 B1
Newbury RG14 104 C2
Reading RG1 86 A4
West Surrey Est TW15 125 B4
West View
East Bedfont TW14 98 B4
Peasemore RG20 50 B4
West View Cotts RG18 52 C3
West Way TW17 125 B2
Westacott Bsns Ctr SL6 38 C1
Westacott Way SL6 38 B2
Westborough Ct SL6 39 B3
Westborough Rd SL6 39 B3

**Westbourne Rd**
Feltham TW13 98 C3
Sandhurst GU47 150 C4
Staines TW18 97 A1
**Westbourne Terr**
3 Newbury RG14 105 A2
Reading RG30 85 B4
**Westbrook** SL6 40 C1
**Westbrook Cl** RG17 100 B3
**Westbrook Gdns** RG12 118 B4
**Westbrook Gn** OX11 11 C4
**Westbrook Rd**
Reading RG30 58 B1
Staines TW18 96 C2
**Westbrook St** OX11 11 C4
**Westbury Cl**
Crowthorne RG45 143 A3
Shepperton TW17 125 A2
**Westbury La** RG8 57 A3
**Westcombe Cl** RG12 118 C1
**Westcote Rd** RG30 85 B3
**Westcotts Gn** RG42 91 B1
**Westcroft** SL2 22 A1
**Westdene Cres** RG4 58 C2
**Westende** RG40 116 B3
Westende Jun Sch RG40 116 B3
**Westerdale** RG19 106 B2
**Westerdale Dr** GU16 152 A2
**Westerham Wlk** 33 RG1 86 A3
**Western Ave**
Chertsey KT16 124 A3
Henley-on-T RG9 35 C4
Newbury RG14 104 C2
Thorpe TW20 123 A3
Woodley RG5 60 C1
**Western Cl** KT16 124 A3
Western Ctr The RG12 117 C4
**Western Dr**
Shepperton TW17 125 B2
Wooburn Green HP10 3 C3
**Western Elms Ave** RG30 85 C4
**Western End** RG14 104 C1
Western House Inf Sch
SL1 41 C3
**Western Ind Area** RG12 117 C4
**Western Oaks** RG31 57 C1
**Western Perimeter Rd**
TW19, TW6, UB7 70 A3
**Western Perimeter Rd**
**Rdbt** TW19 70 B1
**Western Rd**
Bracknell RG12 117 C4
Henley-on-T RG9 35 C4
Reading RG1 85 C3
**Westfield Bglws** SL7 16 C3
**Westfield Cotts** SL7 16 C3
**Westfield Cres**
Shiplake RG9 36 A2
Thatcham RG18 106 A2
Westfield Inf Sch SL8 3 A2
**Westfield Rd**
Camberley GU15 151 A1
Caversham RG4 59 A1
Cholsey OX10 13 B3
Maidenhead SL6 39 A4
Slough SL2 22 A1
Thatcham RG18 106 A3
Winnersh RG41 88 A1
**Westfield Way** RG14 104 C1
**Westfields** RG20 31 B2
Westfields Inf Sch GU46 149 A3
**Westgate Cres** SL1 41 C3
**Westgate Ct** RG14 104 C1
Westgate Cty Sec Sch
SL1 42 A3
**Westgate Rd** RG14 104 C1
**Westhatch Cnr** RG42 91 B3
**Westhatch La** RG42 91 B3
**Westhead Dr** RG14 131 A4
**Westhorpe Rd** SL7 1 C2
**Westland** RG18 106 A2
**Westland Cl** TW19 70 C1
**Westlands Ave** Earley RG2 86 C1
Slough SL1 41 B4
**Westlands Cl** SL1 41 B4
**Westlands Rd** RG14 131 A4
**Westley Mill** Binfield RG42 90 C4
Holyport RG42 63 C1
**Westlyn Rd** RG26 135 C1
**Westmacott Dr** TW14 98 C4
**Westmead** SL4 67 A2
**Westmead Dr** RG14 130 C4
**Westminster Way** RG6 87 B1
**Westmorland Cl** RG41 115 B3
**Westmorland Dr**
Bracknell RG42 91 C1
Frimley GU15 152 A2
**Westmorland Rd** SL6 39 B3
**Weston Gr** GU19 145 C1
**Weston Rd** SL1 41 C4
**Westonbirt Dr** RG4 58 C2
**Westons** RG20 51 B4
**Westridge Ave** RG8 57 B3
**Westview Dr** RG10 61 C3
**Westward Rd** RG41 115 C4
**Westwates Cl** RG12 118 B4
**Westway** RG8 34 B4
Westwood Farm Jun
& Inf Schs RG31 57 B2
**Westwood Glen** RG31 57 B1
**Westwood Gn** SL6 19 C3
**Westwood Rd** Marlow SL7 1 B1
Newbury RG14 105 B1
Reading RG31 57 B1
Windlesham GU20 146 C3
**Westwood Row** RG31 57 B1
**Wetherby Cl** RG4 59 B3
**Wetherby Ho** GU15 151 B4
**Wethered Dr** SL1 41 A4
**Wethered Pk** SL7 1 B1
**Wethered Rd** SL7 1 B1
**Wetton Pl** TW20 95 C2
**Wexford Ct** SL6 40 A4
Wexham Court Comb Sch
SL2 43 B4
Wexham Cty Sec Sch SL2 43 B4
Wexham Park Hospl SL3 23 B1
**Wexham Park La** SL3 23 B1
**Wexham Pl** SL2 23 B3
**Wexham Rd** SL1, SL2 43 A3
**Wexham St** SL3 23 A2
**Wexham Woods** SL3 43 B4
**Wey Ave** KT16 124 A3
**Wey Cl** GU15 151 A3
**Weybridge Mead** GU46 149 C4
**Weycrofts** RG42 90 C1
**Weymead Cl** KT16 124 B1
**Whaley Rd** RG40 116 B4
**Wharf La** Bourne End SL8 3 A2
Henley-on-T RG9 15 C1
**Wharf Rd** Newbury RG14 105 A2
Wraysbury TW19 95 B4
**Wharf St** RG14 105 A2
**Wharf The** Newbury RG14 105 A2
Taplow SL6 40 B4
**Wharfedale Rd** RG41 88 A2
**Wharfside** RG7 109 B2
**Whatley Gn** RG12 118 A2
**Whatmore Cl** TW19 70 A1
**Wheatash Rd** KT15 124 A1
**Wheatbutts The** SL4 41 C1
**Wheatfield Cl** SL6 39 A2
**Wheatfields Rd** RG2 113 C3
**Wheatlands Cl** RG31 84 C2
**Wheatlands La** RG14 130 A3
**Wheatlands Rd** SL3 43 B2
**Wheatley** RG12 117 C2
**Wheatley Cl** RG2 86 C1
**Wheatsheaf La**
Newbury RG14 105 A2
Staines TW18 96 C1
**Wheatsheaf Par** SL4 68 A1
**Wheble Dr** RG5 87 B4
**Wheeler Cl**
Burghfield Common RG7 111 A2
Wokingham RG41 115 C3
**Wheeler Ct** RG31 57 C1
**Wheelers Green Way**
RG19 106 C1
**Wheelton Cl** RG6 87 C2
**Wheelwrights Pl** SL3 69 B4
**Whins Cl** GU15 151 A2
**Whins Dr** GU15 151 A2
**Whinshill Ct** SL5 121 A1
**Whistler Gr** GU47 150 B3
**Whistlers La** RG7 136 A1
**Whistley Cl** RG12 118 C3
**Whitakers Cl** RG18 106 A2
**Whitamore Row** RG9 35 C4
**Whitby Ct** RG4 59 B3
**Whitby Dr** 7 RG1 86 B3
**Whitby Gn** RG4 59 B3
**Whitby Rd** SL1 42 B3
**Whitchurch Cl** SL6 19 C2
Whitchurch Prim Sch
RG8 56 C4
**Whitchurch Rd** RG8 56 B3
**White Bridge Cl** TW14 71 C1
**White City** RG45 143 B3
**White Cl** Hermitage RG18 78 C3
Slough SL1 42 B3
**White Gates** RG20 75 B3
White Hart Ind Est GU17 150 C2
**White Hart Rd**
2 Maidenhead SL6 39 C4
Slough SL1 42 B2
**White Hart Row** 3 KT16 124 A1
**White Hill**
Remenham Hill RG9 16 A1
Shiplake RG9 35 A3
Windlesham GU20 146 A3
Wooburn Moor HP9 3 C4
**White Horse La** RG40 141 B3
**White Horse Rd** SL4 66 B3
**White House Gdns** GU46 149 B4
White House Prep Sch
RG41 116 A2
**White House Rd** OX10 14 C4
**White Lilies Island** SL4 67 A4
**White Lion Way** GU46 149 B4
**White Lodge Cl**
Marlow Bottom SL7 1 B3
Purley on T RG31 57 A2
**White Paddock** SL6 39 A1
**White Rd** Chilton OX11 10 B4
Sandhurst GU15 150 C3
**White Rock** SL6 20 A1
**White Shoot** OX11 12 A3
White Waltham
CE Prim Sch SL6 63 B4
**Whiteacres Dr** SL6 40 A1
**Whitebeam Cl** RG41 115 B2
**Whiteford Rd** SL2 42 C4
**Whitegates La** RG6 87 A4
Whitegrove Prim Sch
RG42 91 C1
**Whitehall** SL6 20 A1
**Whitehall Dr** RG2 140 C4
**Whitehall Farm La** GU25 122 C3
**Whitehall La** Egham TW20 95 C1
Horton TW19 69 A1
**Whitehaven** SL1 42 C3
**Whitehill Cl** GU15 151 B4
**Whitehill Pl** GU25 122 C2
**Whitehills Cl** SL7 1 B3
**Whitehills Gn** RG8 34 B3
**Whitehouse Way** SL3 43 B2
Whiteknights Prim Sch
RG6 86 C1
**Whiteknights Rd** RG6 86 C3
**Whitelands Dr** SL5 119 B4
Whitelands Park Prim Sch
RG18 106 B3
**Whitelands Rd** RG18 106 B2
**Whiteley** SL4 66 C4
Whitelocke Inf Sch
RG40 116 B4
**Whitelocks Piece** RG17 73 A1
**Whitemoor La**
Lower Basildon RG8 34 B1
Upper Basildon RG8 54 C3
**Whitepit La** HP10 3 B4
**Whites Hill** RG7 110 B3
**Whites La** Beenham RG7 109 A4
Datchet SL3 68 A4
**Whitestone Cl** RG6 87 C2
**Whitewalls Cl** RG20 31 C3
**Whiteways Ct** TW18 97 A1
**Whitewell Cl** RG2 114 C1
**Whitley Cl** TW19 70 C1
Whitley Park Inf Sch RG2 86 A1
Whitley Park Jun Sch
RG2 86 A1
**Whitley Park La** RG2 86 B2
**Whitley Rd** GU46 149 B2
**Whitley St** RG2 86 A3
**Whitley Wood La** RG2 113 B4
**Whitley Wood Rd** RG2 113 B4
**Whitmoor Rd** GU19 145 C1
**Whitmore Cl** GU47 143 B1
**Whitmore La** SL5 121 A3
**Whitstone Gdns** RG2 86 B1
**Whittaker Rd** SL2 21 C1
**Whittenham Cl** SL2 43 A3
**Whittle Cl**
Sandhurst GU47 143 A1
Wokingham RG40 141 C4
**Whittle Parkway** SL1 41 B4
**Whitton Cl** 6 RG6 87 B1
**Whitton Rd** RG12 118 C3
**Whitworth Rd** RG2 141 A4
**Whurley Way** SL6 19 C1
**Whynstones Rd** SL5 120 A2
**Whyteladyes La** SL6 19 C3
**Wick Hill La** RG40 142 A3
**Wick La** TW20 94 C2
**Wick Rd** TW20 95 A1
**Wickets The**
Ashford TW15 97 C2
Maidenhead SL6 39 B4
**Wickford Way** RG6 113 C4
**Wickham La** TW20 96 A1
**Wickham Rd**
Camberley GU15 151 C4
Earley RG6 87 C1
**Wickham Vale** RG12 117 C2
**Wickhurst Cotts** SL6 38 A3
**Wicks Gn** RG42 90 A2
**Widbrook Rd** SL6 20 A2
**Widecroft Rd** SL0 44 C4
**Widmere La** SL7 1 A3
**Wield Ct** RG6 87 C1
**Wiggett Gr** RG42 90 B1
**Wigmore La** Reading RG30 58 A1
Reading RG30 58 B1
Theale RG7 83 B1
**Wigmore Rd** RG26 134 C1
**Wilberforce Mews** SL6 39 C4
**Wilberforce Way** RG12 118 B2
**Wilcox Gdns** TW17 124 C3
**Wild Briar** RG40 141 C4
**Wild Cl** RG6 114 B4
**Wildcroft Dr** RG40 116 A1
Wilde Theatre RG12 118 B1
**Wilder Ave** RG8 56 C3
**Wilderness Ct** RG6 87 A2
**Wilderness Rd** Earley RG6 87 A2
Frimley GU16 151 C1
**Wilders Cl** Bracknell RG42 91 A1
Frimley GU16 151 C2
**Wildgreen N** SL3 44 A1
**Wildgreen S** SL3 44 A1
Wildridings Cty Prim Sch
RG12 118 A3
**Wildridings Rd** RG12 118 A3
**Wildridings Sq** RG12 118 A3
**Wildwood Dr** RG26 134 B1
**Wildwood Gdns** GU46 149 B2
**Wilford Rd** SL3 43 C1
**Wilfred Way** RG19 107 A2
**Wilfrids Wood Cl** HP10 3 A3
**Willats Cl** KT16 124 A2
William Byrd Sch UB3 71 B4
**William Cl** RG19 106 B1
**William Ellis Cl** SL4 68 A1
William Gray Cty Inf Sch
The RG5 87 B4
William Gray Cty Jun Sch
The RG5 87 B3
William Penn Comb Sch
SL2 22 B1
**William Sim Wood** RG42 92 A1
**William St** Reading RG1 85 C4
Slough SL1 42 C3
Windsor SL4 67 B3
**Williant Cl** SL6 38 C1
**Willington Cl** GU15 151 A3
Willink Sch The RG7 110 C1
**Willis Cl** RG18 79 A2
**Willoners** SL2 42 A4
**Willoughby Rd**
Bracknell RG12 117 C3
Slough SL3 44 A2
**Willow Bank** SL7 1 B3
Willow Bank Jun & Inf Schs
RG5 60 C1
**Willow Cl**
Burghfield Common RG30 111 A3
Colnbrook SL3 69 B4
Flackwell Heath HP10 3 C3
Newbury RG14 104 C1
**Willow Cotts** OX10 13 C3
**Willow Court La** OX10 13 C3
**Willow Ct** 2 Charlton TW16 98 C1
Frimley GU16 151 B1
Wokingham RG41 116 A3
**Willow Dr** Bracknell RG12 118 B4
Maidenhead SL6 40 A1
Twyford RG10 61 B3
**Willow Gdns**
Purley on T RG31 57 A1
Reading RG2 86 C1
**Willow Gn** GU24 153 C3
**Willow Gr** SL4 67 A2
**Willow La**
Blackwater GU17 150 B2
Wargrave RG10 36 B2
**Willow Lo** 10 TW16 98 C1
**Willow Par** SL3 44 A2
**Willow Pk** SL2 23 A3
**Willow Pl** SL4 67 B4
**Willow Rd** Newtown RG20 131 C1
Poyle SL3 69 C3
**Willow St** 3 RG1 86 A3
**Willow Tree Glade** RG31 84 B2
**Willow Way** GU47 142 C1
**Willow Wlk**
Chertsey KT16 124 A1
Englefield Green TW20 95 B2
**Willow Wood Cl** SL1 21 A2
**Willowbrook** SL4 42 B1
**Willowbrook Rd** TW19 97 C3
**Willowdale** RG40 141 C4
**Willowford** GU46 149 B3
**Willowherb Cl** RG40 116 C4
**Willowmead** TW18 124 A4
**Willowmead Cl** 10
Marlow SL7 1 C2
Newbury RG14 130 B3
**Willowmead Gdns** SL7 1 C2
**Willowmead Rd** 8 SL7 1 C2
**Willowmead Sq** 9 SL7 1 C2
**Willows Ct** RG8 56 B3
**Willows End** GU47 150 A4
**Willows Rd** SL8 3 A2
**Willows The**
14 Bourne End SL8 3 A2
9 Bracknell RG12 118 C3
Caversham RG4 59 A1
Lightwater GU18 146 B1
Windsor SL4 66 B4
**Willowside** RG5 60 C1
**Willson Rd** TW20 95 A2
**Wilmington Cl** RG5 87 C4
**Wilmot Cl** RG42 90 B1
**Wilmot Rd** SL1 21 A1
**Wilmot Way** GU15 151 C2
**Wilmot Wlk** RG14 130 B3
**Wilsford Cl** RG6 113 C4
**Wilson Ave** RG9 35 C4
**Wilson Cl** RG20 31 C2
**Wilson Ct** RG41 88 A1
Wilson Prim Sch RG30 85 B4
**Wilson Rd** RG30 85 B4
**Wilson Valkenburg Ct**
RG14 104 C2
**Wilstrode Ave** RG42 90 C1
**Wilton Cl** UB7 70 B4
**Wilton Cres** SL4 66 B2
**Wilton Rd**
Camberley GU15 151 A2
Reading RG30 85 B4
**Wiltshire Ave**
Crowthorne RG45 143 A3
Slough SL2 22 B1
**Wiltshire Cl** RG17 100 B3
**Wiltshire Dr** RG40 116 B4
**Wiltshire Gr** RG42 91 C1
**Wiltshire Lodge** 2 SL6 39 C3
**Wiltshire Rd** Marlow SL7 2 A2
Wokingham RG40 116 B4
**Wiltshire Wlk** RG31 84 A3
**Wilwood Rd** RG42 117 C4
**Wilwyne Cl** RG4 59 B2
**Wimbledon Cl** GU15 144 C1
**Wimbledon Rd** GU15 144 C1
**Wimblington Dr** RG6 114 B4
**Wimbourne Gdns** RG30 58 A1
**Wimbushes** RG40 141 B3
**Winbury Ct** SL6 39 C4
Winbury Sch SL6 40 A2
**Wincanton Rd** RG2 113 B4
**Winch Cl** RG42 90 B2
**Winchbottom La** SL7 ,HP10 2 A4
Winchcombe Cty
Jun & Inf Schs RG14 105 A2
**Winchcombe Rd**
Newbury RG14 105 A1
Twyford RG10 61 C2
**Winchester Cl** SL3 69 C3
**Winchester Dr** SL6 39 A2
**Winchester Ho** 12 RG14 105 A1
**Winchester Rd**
Harlington UB3 71 C4
Reading RG2 86 A2
**Winchester Way** GU17 150 B3
**Winchgrove Rd** RG42 91 A1
**Winchstone Cl** TW17 124 C3
**Wincroft Rd** RG4 58 C3
**Windermere Cl**
East Bedfont TW14 98 C4
Stanwell TW19 97 B3
**Windermere Cl** *continued*
Thorpe Lea TW20 96 A1
Winnersh RG41 88 B2
**Windermere Rd**
Lightwater GU18 146 A1
Reading RG2 86 B2
**Windermere Way**
Slough SL1 41 B4
Thatcham RG19 106 A2
**Windermere Wlk** GU15 152 B3
**Winding Wood Dr** GU15 152 A2
**Windle Cl** GU20 146 B2
**Windlebrook Gn** 3 RG42 118 A4
Windlemere Golf Ctr
GU24 153 C4
**Windlesham Ct** GU20 146 B3
**Windlesham Rd**
Bracknell RG42 117 C4
West End GU24 153 C4
Windlesham Village
Cty Inf Sch GU20 146 A3
**Windmill Ave** RG41 115 C4
Windmill Bsns Village
TW16 125 C4
**Windmill Cl** Charlton TW16 98 C1
Windsor SL4 67 A3
Wokingham RG41 115 C4
**Windmill Cnr** RG7 137 A3
**Windmill Ct** RG7 137 A3
**Windmill Field** GU20 146 B2
**Windmill La** RG7 108 A3
**Windmill Lodge** TW16 125 C4
**Windmill Rd**
Bracknell RG42 118 A4
Charlton TW16 125 C4
Cookham SL6 19 C3
Fulmer SL3 23 B4
Mortimer RG7 137 A3
Slough SL1 42 B3
**Windmill Rd W** TW16 125 C4
**Windmill Terr** TW17 125 C1
Windmill Trad Est TW16 125 C4
**Windrush Ave** SL3 44 A2
**Windrush Ct** 8 RG30 85 A4
**Windrush Ho** SL8 3 A2
**Windrush Hts** GU47 150 A4
**Windrush Way**
Maidenhead SL6 39 C4
Reading RG30 85 A4
Windsor Boys Sch SL4 67 A3
Windsor Bsns Ctr The
SL4 67 B4
Windsor Castle SL4 67 C4
**Windsor Cl** SL1 21 B1
**Windsor Ct** 16 RG1 85 C4
**Windsor Dr** TW15 97 B2
Windsor & Eton
Central Sta SL4 67 B3
Windsor & Eton
Riverside Sta SL4 67 B4
**Windsor Forest Ct** SL5 119 B4
Windsor Girls Sch SL4 67 A2
Windsor Great Pk SL4 94 B2
**Windsor Hill** HP10 3 C3
**Windsor Ho** RG9 35 C4
Windsor L Ctr SL4 67 A4
**Windsor La** SL1 21 B1
**Windsor Park Rd** UB3 71 C4
**Windsor Pl** KT16 124 A2
**Windsor Rd** Datchet SL3 68 A4
Englefield Green
TW19, TW20 95 C3
Fulmer SL2 23 A4
Holyport SL6 40 B1
North Ascot SL5 120 A4
Slough SL1 42 C2
Wraysbury TW19 68 C1
**Windsor Ride**
Bracknell SL5 119 B2
Sandhurst GU15 151 A4
Wokingham RG40 142 A4
**Windsor Rise** RG14 131 B4
**Windsor Sq** 24 RG1 86 A3
**Windsor St** KT16 124 A2
**Windsor Way** RG31 84 A2
Windsor Youth Hostel
SL4 67 A4
**Wing Cl** SL7 1 B1
**Wingate Rd** RG5 87 C3
**Wingfield Gdns** GU16 152 B2
**Wingrove Rd** RG30 85 B3
**Winkfield Cl** RG41 116 A2
**Winkfield La**
Oakley Green SL4 66 A1
Winkfield SL4 92 B4
**Winkfield Rd** Ascot SL5 120 A4
Windsor SL4 66 C1
**Winkfield Row** RG42 92 A2
**Winkfield St** SL4 92 B3
**Winkworth La** RG7 135 B1
**Winnersh Gate** RG41 88 B1
**Winnersh Gr** RG41 88 B1
Winnersh Prim Sch RG41 88 B2
Winnersh Sta RG41 88 B1
Winnersh Triangle Ind Est
RG41 88 A2
Winnersh Triangle Sta
RG41 88 A2
**Winscombe** RG12 117 C2
**Winser Dr** RG30 85 B3
**Winston Cl** RG7 113 B1
**Winston Way**
Purley on T RG8 57 A3
Thatcham RG19 105 C2
**Winter Hill** SL6 2 B1

Winter Hill Rd SL6 . . . . . . . .19 A2
Winterberry Way RG4 . . . . .58 C3
Winterbourne Ct RG12 . . .118 B4
Winterbourne Rd RG20 . . .76 C2
Winterton Dr RG14 . . . . . .104 B3
Winton Cres GU46 . . . . . . .149 B3
Winton Rd RG2 . . . . . . . . . .113 B4
Wintoun Path SL2 . . . . . . . .21 C1
Wintringham Way RG8 . . . .57 B3
Winvale SL1 . . . . . . . . . . . . .42 C2
Winwood Slough SL2 . . . . . .43 B4
Windsor SL4 . . . . . . . . . . . .66 C3
Wisdom Ct 14 RG30 . . . . . . .85 B3
Wises Firs RG7 . . . . . . . . . .110 B2
Wishmoor Cl GU15 . . . . . .151 C4
Wishmoor Rd GU15 . . . . .151 C4
Wispington Cl RG6 . . . . . . .87 B1
Wistaria La GU46 . . . . . . . .149 B3
Wisteria Cl RG41 . . . . . . . .115 C3
Wiston Terr RG1 . . . . . . . . . .86 A4
Witcham Cl RG6 . . . . . . . . .114 B4
Withey Cl SL4 . . . . . . . . . . . .66 C3
Witheygate Ave TW18 . . . . .97 A1
Withy Cl Lightwater GU18 . .146 B1
Reading RG31 . . . . . . . . . . . .84 B3
Withybed La RG17 . . . . . . .101 C2
Withybed Way RG18 . . . . .106 C3
Withycroft SL3 . . . . . . . . . . .43 C4
Withys The RG18 . . . . . . . . .53 C1
Wittenham Ave RG31 . . . . .84 A4
Wittenham Rd RG12 . . . . .118 C4
Wittington Cotts SL7 . . . . . .17 B3
Woburn Cl Caversham RG4 .58 C2
Frimley GU16 . . . . . . . . . . .152 A1
Wokefield Row RG7 . . . . .137 B4
Wokingham Hospl
RG41 . . . . . . . . . . . . . . . . .116 A3
Wokingham Rd
Bracknell RG42 . . . . . . . . . .117 C4
Earley RG6 . . . . . . . . . . . . . .87 B2
Hurst RG10 . . . . . . . . . . . . . .88 C4
Sandhurst RG45,GU47 . . . . .142 C1
Wokingham Sta RG40 . . .116 A3
Wokingham Theatre
RG40 . . . . . . . . . . . . . . . . .116 A4
Wolf La SL4 . . . . . . . . . . . . . .66 C2
Wolseley St RG1 . . . . . . . . . .86 A3
Wolsey Rd Ashford TW15 . . .97 C2
Ashford, Felthamhill TW16 . . .98 C1
Caversham RG4 . . . . . . . . . . .59 A1
Wolsingham Way RG19 . .106 B1
Wondesford Dale RG42 . . .90 B2
Wooburn Grange HP10 . . . . .3 B2
Wooburn Manor Pk HP10 . .3 C3
Wooburn Mews HP10 . . . . . .3 C3
Wood Cl SL4 . . . . . . . . . . . . .67 B2
Wood End RG45 . . . . . . . . .142 C2
Wood Gn RG2 . . . . . . . . . . .113 B4
Wood Green Cl RG30 . . . . .85 C4
Wood La Arborfield RG41 . .114 C2
Beech Hill RG7 . . . . . . . . . .138 C3
Binfield RG42 . . . . . . . . . . . .90 B1
Iver SL0 . . . . . . . . . . . . . . . . .44 B4
Slough SL1 . . . . . . . . . . . . . .42 A2
Wood Moor RG40 . . . . . . .141 C1
Wood Rd Camberley GU15 .151 A1
Littleton TW17 . . . . . . . . . . .125 A3
Wood Ridge RG14 . . . . . . .130 C4
Woodberry Cl RG4 . . . . . . . .59 A3
Woodbine Cl Earley RG6 . . .87 B1
Sandhurst GU47 . . . . . . . . .150 B4
Woodbine Cotts TW20 . . . .95 C1
Woodbine La RG20 . . . . . .130 C1
Woodbourne Cl GU46 . . . .149 B3
Woodbridge Dr GU15 . . . .151 B4
Woodbridge Rd
Blackwater GU17 . . . . . . . .150 A3
Reading RG31 . . . . . . . . . . . .84 A3
Woodbury RG17 . . . . . . . . . .25 B1
Woodbury Cl SL8 . . . . . . . . . .3 B2
Woodby Dr SL5 . . . . . . . . .120 C1
Woodcock Ct RG7 . . . . . . .113 A2
Woodcote SL6 . . . . . . . . . . . .39 B3
Woodcote House Sch
GU20 . . . . . . . . . . . . . . . . .146 A3
Woodcote Pl SL5 . . . . . . . .119 C4
Woodcote Rd
Caversham RG4 . . . . . . . . . . .58 C2
South Stoke RG8 . . . . . . . . . .14 C2
Woodcote Way RG4 . . . . . . .58 B3
Woodend Cl SL5 . . . . . . . .119 C4
Woodend Dr SL5 . . . . . . . .120 A2
Woodenhill RG12 . . . . . . . .117 C1
Woodenhill Cty Prim Sch
RG12 . . . . . . . . . . . . . . . . .117 C1
Woodfield Dr SL6 . . . . . . . .39 A3
Woodfield Way RG7 . . . . . .83 C2
Woodford Cl RG4 . . . . . . . . .58 C2
Woodford Gn RG12 . . . . . .118 C3
Woodford Way SL2 . . . . . . .22 A1
Woodhall La SL5 . . . . . . . .146 C4
Woodhaw TW20 . . . . . . . . . .96 A2
Woodhouse La RG19 . . . .133 C1
Woodhouse St RG42 . . . . . .90 C1
Woodhurst La RG41 . . . . .115 C4
Woodhurst Rd SL6 . . . . . . .20 A1
Woodhurst South SL6 . . . . .20 B1
Woodies Cl RG42 . . . . . . . . .90 B1
Woodland Ave Slough SL1 . .42 B3
Windsor SL4 . . . . . . . . . . . . .66 C2
Woodland Cl SL7 . . . . . . . . . .1 C2
Woodland Cres RG42 . . . . .91 B1
Woodland Dr RG30 . . . . . . .84 B4
Woodland Way SL7 . . . . . . . .1 C2
Woodlands GU46 . . . . . . . .149 B2
Woodlands Ave
Burghfield Common RG7 . . .111 A2
Wokingham RG41 . . . . . . . .115 C4
Woodley RG5 . . . . . . . . . . . . .87 B4
Woodlands Bsns Pk SL6 . .39 A1
Woodlands Cl Ascot SL5 . .119 C2
Farnborough (Hants) GU17 .150 C1
Hermitage RG18 . . . . . . . . . .78 C3
Woodlands Cotts 4 SL2 . . .22 B4
Woodlands Ct GU47 . . . . .143 C1
Woodlands Gr RG4 . . . . . . .59 C2
Woodlands La
GU20,GU24 . . . . . . . . . . . . .146 C2
Woodlands Par TW15 . . . . .98 B1
Woodlands Park Ave
SL6 . . . . . . . . . . . . . . . . . . .39 A1
Woodlands Park Prim Sch
SL6 . . . . . . . . . . . . . . . . . . .39 A1
Woodlands Park Rd SL6 . .39 A2
Woodlands Rd
Camberley GU15 . . . . . . . . .151 A3
Shiplake RG9 . . . . . . . . . . . . .35 C2
Tadley RG26 . . . . . . . . . . . .134 B1
Virginia Water GU25 . . . . . .122 B3
Woodlands Rd E GU25 . . .122 B3
Woodlands Rd W GU25 . .122 B3
Woodlands Ride SL5 . . . .120 A2
Woodlands The RG41 . . . .115 B2
Woodlands Wlk GU17 . . . .150 C1
Woodlee Cl GU25 . . . . . . . .122 B4
Woodley CE Prim Sch
RG5 . . . . . . . . . . . . . . . . . . .88 A4
Woodley Gn RG5 . . . . . . . . .87 C4
Woodley Park Est RG5 . . . .87 B4
Woodman Cl RG2 . . . . . . . .113 B3
Woodmancott Cl RG12 . . .118 C2
Woodmans La RG7 . . . . . .110 C2
Woodmere RG12 . . . . . . . .118 C3
Woodmere Cl RG6 . . . . . . . .87 A1
Woodmoor End SL6 . . . . . .20 A4
Woodpecker Cl RG10 . . . . .61 C2
Woodpeckers RG12 . . . . . .118 A3
Woodridge Cl RG12 . . . . . .118 B3
Woodrow Dr RG40 . . . . . .116 C3
Woods Rd RG4 . . . . . . . . . . .59 C2
Woodsend Cl RG6 . . . . . . .113 C4
Woodshore Cl GU25 . . . . .122 A2
Woodside
Blackwater GU17 . . . . . . . .150 B2
Cold Ash RG18 . . . . . . . . . . . .79 B1
Flackwell Heath HP10 . . . . . . .3 B3
Newbury RG14 . . . . . . . . . .130 B4
andhurst GU15 . . . . . . . . . .150 C4
Woodside Ave HP10 . . . . . . . .3 B4
Woodside Bsns Pk RG2 . .113 A4
Woodside Cl
Bucklebury RG7 . . . . . . . . . .107 B3
Mortimer RG7 . . . . . . . . . . .137 A3
Wokingham RG40 . . . . . . . .141 C4
Woodside Dr RG18 . . . . . . .79 A3
Woodside La SL4, SL5 . . . . .93 B2
Woodside Rd SL5 . . . . . . . .93 A1
Woodside Way
Reading RG2 . . . . . . . . . . . .113 B4
Virginia Water GU25 . . . . . .122 A3
Woodstock RG40 . . . . . . . .116 B3
Woodstock Ave SL3 . . . . . . .43 B1
Woodstock Cl SL6 . . . . . . . .19 C1
Woodstock St RG1 . . . . . . .86 C4
Woodthorpe Rd TW15 . . . .97 B2
Woodview Rd RG8 . . . . . . . .56 B3
Woodville Cl GU17 . . . . . .150 A3
Woodward Cl RG41 . . . . . . .88 B1
Woodway GU15 . . . . . . . . .151 A3
Woodway Rd OX11 . . . . . . .12 A4
Woodwaye RG5 . . . . . . . . . .87 B4
Woodyer Cl RG5 . . . . . . . . .87 C3
Woolacombe Dr RG6 . . . . .86 C1
Woolf Dr RG40 . . . . . . . . . .116 A4
Woolford Cl RG42 . . . . . . . .92 B1
Woolhampton
CE Prim Sch RG7 . . . . . . .108 B2
Woolhampton Hill RG7 . .108 B2
Woolhampton Way
RG12 . . . . . . . . . . . . . . . . . .118 B2
Woolton Lodge Gdns
RG20 . . . . . . . . . . . . . . . . .129 C1
Woosehill RG41 . . . . . . . . .115 C3
Woosehill Ct RG41 . . . . . .115 C4
Woosehill La RG41 . . . . . .115 C3
Wootton Cl RG31 . . . . . . . . .84 B4
Wootton Dr HP10 . . . . . . . . . .3 C4
Wootton Rd RG9 . . . . . . . . .35 B4
Wootton Way SL6 . . . . . . . .39 B3
Worcester Cl
Maidenhead SL6 . . . . . . . . . .39 B2
Reading RG30 . . . . . . . . . . . .85 A3
Worcester Ct
Ashford TW15 . . . . . . . . . . . .98 A2
Staines TW18 . . . . . . . . . . . .97 A2
Worcester Dr TW15 . . . . . . .98 A2
Worcester Gdns SL1 . . . . . .42 B2
Worcestershire Lea RG42 .91 C1
Wordsworth RG12 . . . . . . .117 C2
Wordsworth Ave GU46 . . .149 A2
Wordsworth Ct RG4 . . . . . .59 B4
Wordsworth Rd
Slough SL2 . . . . . . . . . . . . . .21 B1
Thatcham RG18 . . . . . . . . . .106 B2
Worlds End Hill RG12 . . . .118 C2
Wormersley Rd RG19 . . . .131 B4
Worple Ave TW18 . . . . . . . .97 A1
Worple Rd TW18 . . . . . . . . .97 A1
Worple The TW19 . . . . . . . .68 C1
Worrall Way RG6 . . . . . . . .113 C4
Worsley Pl RG7 . . . . . . . . . .83 C2
Worster Rd SL6 . . . . . . . . . .19 C3
Worton Dr RG2 . . . . . . . . .113 A4
Worton Grange Ind Est
RG2 . . . . . . . . . . . . . . . . . . .113 A4
Wrabness Way TW18 . . . .124 A4
Wraysbury Cty Comb Sch
TW19 . . . . . . . . . . . . . . . . . .68 C1
Wraysbury Rd TW18, TW19 .96 B3
Wraysbury Sta TW19 . . . . .69 A1
Wren Cl
Burghfield Common RG7 . . .111 A2
Wokingham RG41 . . . . . . . .115 C3
Yateley GU46 . . . . . . . . . . .149 A3
Wren Ct Egham TW20 . . . . . .96 A2
Slough SL3 . . . . . . . . . . . . . .44 A2
Wrenfield Dr RG4 . . . . . . . .58 C3
Wrens Ave TW15 . . . . . . . . .98 B2
Wrensfield SL7 . . . . . . . . . . . .1 B1
Wrenswood Cl RG2 . . . . . .113 A4
Wright SL4 . . . . . . . . . . . . . . .66 B2
Wright Cl RG5 . . . . . . . . . . .88 A4
Wright Gdns TW17 . . . . . .125 A2
Wright Sq SL4 . . . . . . . . . . . .66 B2
Wright Way SL4 . . . . . . . . . .66 B2
Wroxham RG12 . . . . . . . . .117 C2
Wroxham Rd RG5 . . . . . . . . .87 B4
Wyatt Rd Staines TW18 . . . . .97 A2
Windsor SL4 . . . . . . . . . . . . .66 B2
Wychcotes RG4 . . . . . . . . . .58 C2
Wychelm Rd
Lightwater GU18 . . . . . . . . .153 B4
Shinfield RG2 . . . . . . . . . . .113 C3
Wychwood Ave RG12 . . . .118 C3
Wychwood Cl RG6 . . . . . . . .86 C1
Wychwood Cres RG6 . . . . . .86 C2
Wycombe La HP10 . . . . . . . . .3 C4
Wycombe Rd SL7 . . . . . . . . . .1 C2
Wye Cl Ashford TW15 . . . . . .98 A2
Reading RG30 . . . . . . . . . . . .84 C3
Wye Rd HP10 . . . . . . . . . . . . .3 B4
Wye Valley Sch SL8 . . . . . . . .3 A2
Wykeham Cl UB7 . . . . . . . . .71 A4
Wykeham Rd RG6 . . . . . . . .87 A3
Wylam RG12 . . . . . . . . . . . .117 C2
Wylands Rd SL3 . . . . . . . . . .44 A1
Wyld Court Hill RG18 . . . . .53 A3
Wyld Court Rainforest
RG18 . . . . . . . . . . . . . . . . . . .53 B3
Wymers Cl SL1 . . . . . . . . . . .21 A2
Wymers Wood Rd SL1 . . . .21 A2
Wyncote Cl RG2 . . . . . . . . . .86 C1
Wyndale Cl RG9 . . . . . . . . . .15 C1
Wyndham Cl GU46 . . . . . .149 B4
Wyndham Cres
Burnham SL1 . . . . . . . . . . . . .21 A2
Woodley RG5 . . . . . . . . . . . . .60 B1
Wyndham Rd RG14 . . . . . .105 B3
Wynford Cl RG30 . . . . . . . . .85 B2
Wynnstay Gdns SL7 . . . . . . . .1 C3
Wynsham Way GU20 . . . . .146 A3
Wyre Ct RG31 . . . . . . . . . . .57 B2
Wyresdale RG12 . . . . . . . . .118 C1
Wythe Mead RG42 . . . . . . . .90 A1
Wythegate TW18 . . . . . . . . .96 C1
Wyvern Cl RG12 . . . . . . . . .118 A3
Wyvern Ct TW15 . . . . . . . . .97 C3

## Y

Yale Cl GU47 . . . . . . . . . . . .143 C1
Yard Mead TW20 . . . . . . . . .96 A3
Yardley RG12 . . . . . . . . . . . .117 C2
Yarmouth Rd SL1 . . . . . . . . .42 B3
Yarnold Cl RG40 . . . . . . . . .116 C4
Yarnton Cl RG4 . . . . . . . . . . .59 B3
Yateley Common Ctry Pk
GU17,GU46 . . . . . . . . . . . . .149 C2
Yateley Inf Sch GU46 . . . .149 B3
Yateley Manor Prep Sch
GU46 . . . . . . . . . . . . . . . . . .149 B3
Yateley Rd GU47 . . . . . . . .149 C4
Yateley Sch GU46 . . . . . . . .149 B3
Yates Copse RG14 . . . . . . .105 C3
Yattendon CE Prim Sch
RG18 . . . . . . . . . . . . . . . . . . .53 C1
Yattendon Ct RG18 . . . . . . .53 C1
Yattendon La RG8,RG18 . . . .54 B1
Yattendon Rd RG18 . . . . . . .79 B4
Yaverland Dr GU19 . . . . . .145 B1
Ye Meads SL6 . . . . . . . . . . . .40 C3
Yelverton Rd RG2 . . . . . . . . .86 B2
Yeomans La RG20 . . . . . . .131 A1
Yeomans Way GU15 . . . . .151 C3
Yeosfield RG7 . . . . . . . . . . .139 B2
Yeoveney Cl TW19 . . . . . . . .96 B3
Yeovil Ent Ctr SL1 . . . . . . . .41 C4
Yeovil Rd Sandhurst GU47 .143 C1
Slough SL1 . . . . . . . . . . . . . .41 C4
Yew Cl RG41 . . . . . . . . . . . .115 C3
Yew Gate RG14 . . . . . . . . . .104 C3
Yew La RG1 . . . . . . . . . . . . . .85 C3
Yew Tree Cl SL6 . . . . . . . . . .39 C4
Yew Tree Ct RG8 . . . . . . . . . .34 B3
Yew Tree Rd SL1 . . . . . . . . .43 A2
Yew Tree Rise RG31 . . . . . . .84 B3
Yew Tree Stables RG20 . . . .31 C2
Yew Tree Wlk GU16 . . . . . .151 C1
Yew Trees TW17 . . . . . . . . .124 C3
Yewhurst Cl RG10 . . . . . . . .61 B3
Yews The TW15 . . . . . . . . . .98 A2
Yewtrees TW20 . . . . . . . . . .123 B3
Yield Hall La 11 RG1 . . . . . .86 A4
Yield Hall Pl RG1 . . . . . . . . .86 A4
Yockley Cl GU15 . . . . . . . .152 B2
Yoreham Cl RG6 . . . . . . . . . .87 C1
York Ave Slough SL1 . . . . . .42 B4
Windsor SL4 . . . . . . . . . . . . .67 A3
York Cl RG14 . . . . . . . . . . . .105 A1
York Ho RG42 . . . . . . . . . . .117 C4
York Rd Binfield RG42 . . . . . .90 B2
Camberley GU15 . . . . . . . . .151 B4
Henley-on-T RG9 . . . . . . . . . .15 B1
Hungerford RG17 . . . . . . . .100 B2
Maidenhead SL6 . . . . . . . . . .40 A4
Marlow SL7 . . . . . . . . . . . . . . .1 B1
Newbury RG14 . . . . . . . . . .105 A1
Reading RG1 . . . . . . . . . . . . .59 A1
Windsor SL4 . . . . . . . . . . . . .67 A3
York Town Ind Est GU15 . .151 A3
York Way GU47 . . . . . . . . .150 A4
Yorkshire Pl RG42 . . . . . . . .91 C1
Yorktown Rd
Sandhurst GU47 . . . . . . . . .150 A4
Sandhurst GU47 . . . . . . . . .150 C4
Youlden Cl GU15 . . . . . . . .152 A3
Youlden Dr GU15 . . . . . . .152 A3
Young Cres RG19 . . . . . . .131 B4
Young's Ind Est RG7 . . . . .134 C2

## Z

Zealand Ave UB7 . . . . . . . . .70 C4
Zenith Ct GU47 . . . . . . . . . .143 B1
Zetland Ct SL6 . . . . . . . . . . .40 A4
Zinnia Cl RG41 . . . . . . . . . .115 B4
Zinzan St RG1 . . . . . . . . . . . .85 C4